EYEWITNESSES TO MASSACRE

EYEWITNESSES TO MASSACRE

AMERICAN MISSIONARIES BEAR WITNESS TO JAPANESE ATROCITIES IN NANJING

ZHANG KAIYUAN

EDITOR

Foreword by Donald MacInnis

Published with the assistance of
Martha Lund Smalley,
Yale Divinity School Library

AN EAST GATE BOOK

M.E. Sharpe

Armonk, New York
London, England

An East Gate Book

Library of Congress Cataloging-in-Publication Data

Eyewitnesses to massacre : American missionaries bear witness to Japanese atrocities in Nanjing / edited by Zhang Kaiyuan ; foreword by Donald MacInnis.
    p. cm.
    Letters from M. Searle Bates, George A. Fitch, Ernest H. Foster, John G. Magee, James H. McCallum, W. Plumer Mills, Lewis S.C. Smythe, Albert N. Stewart, Minnie Vautrin, and R.O. Wilson located at the Yale Divinity School Library.
    "An East gate book."
    Includes index.
    ISBN 0-7656-0684-4 (alk. paper)—ISBN 0-7656-0685-2 (pbk. : alk. paper)
    1. Nanking Massacre, Nanjing, Jiangsu Sheng, China, 1937—Personal narratives, American. 2. Missionaries—China—Jiangsu Sheng. 3. Nanjing (Jiansu, China) 4. Sino-Japanese Conflict, 1937-1945—Atrocities. I. Chang, K´ai-yuan.

DS796.N2 E93 2000
940.53—dc21
                                          00-059528

Printed in the United States of America

The paper used in this publication meets the minimum requirements of American National Standard for Information Sciences Permanence of Paper for Printed Library Materials, ANSI Z 39.48-1984.

BM (c)   10   9   8   7   6   5   4   3   2   1
BM (p)   10   9   8   7   6   5   4   3   2   1

Contents

Foreword

In the summer of 1940 I spent six weeks as a delegate to the seventh Japan–America Student Conference. I was one of 60 American and 120 Japanese college students who met for two weeks in scholarly discussion groups at Tsuda College near Tokyo, then traveled together in Japan, Korea, and Manchuria. We made many friends in Japan that summer and saw little evidence of the massive military buildup then in full swing.

Rather than return home for my senior year at UCLA, I traveled third class on a small Japanese ship to Shanghai, where I secured a job teaching English to high school boys in a Methodist-sponsored secondary school in south China.

The Sino-Japanese War of Resistance was in its fourth year when I arrived at the school in its wartime location, a village deep in the interior of Fujian province. The following summer I returned to Shanghai and worked my way home on the crew of *The City of Dalhart*, an American merchant vessel, which delivered its cargo of Philippine sugar and shredded coconut at New York harbor one month before the attack on Pearl Harbor.

In Shanghai I had seen the ruins of Chapei—the densely populated Chinese district adjoining the International Settlement. It had been indiscriminately bombed and shelled by Japanese planes and ships in the battle for the city in 1937; thousands of its residents had been killed.[1] During my year of teaching, a sister school located in Chungan, an undefended town not far from us, was bombed by a flight of Japanese planes from Formosa, then a Japanese colony. Fifty bombs were dropped, killing five students, three staff persons, and a small child, as well as a number of townspeople. The bombing of Chungan and other upriver towns served no military purpose except providing target practice for the air crews. There were no antiaircraft guns in the province and few anywhere else in China then.

Of these and other atrocities, by far the worst was the rape of Nanking, where a conquering Japanese army was turned loose by its officers to loot, rape, torture, and burn at will in a savage rampage that lasted seven weeks. Thousands of disarmed Chinese soldiers were shot or bayoneted. Estimates of soldiers and noncombatants killed range from 260,000 to 350,000—more than the combined death toll of both the atomic bombs dropped on Japan (140,000 and 70,000).

An estimated 20,000 to 80,000 Chinese women were raped, and many of them were killed.

While most foreign journalists, businessmen, diplomats, and missionaries had evacuated the city, a few foreigners remained, including fourteen missionaries who lived in the Nanking International Safety Zone established by an International Committee under the leadership of John Rabe, a German businessman. One of those missionaries was George A. Fitch, a YMCA secretary, whose diary was the basis for a widely read article, "The Sack of Nanking," that appeared in the July 1938 *Reader's Digest.* (I remember the shock and horror of reading it.) His diary and letters and the diaries and letters of nine other missionaries who lived through those terrible events make up this book.

Of the missionaries who remained in Nanking throughout this catastrophic period, six were core members of the International Committee. All of them took part in relief work—procuring rice for the refugees, protecting the women, caring for the wounded, and rescuing the dying. The campuses of two mission institutions inside the International Safety Zone—the University of Nanking and Ginling Women's College—provided space for thousands of refugees. All told, a quarter of a million Chinese took refuge inside the Safety Zone.

Three of the missionaries testified at the International Military Tribunal for the Far East held in Tokyo after the war. One of them, John Magee, took twelve rolls of 16–millimeter movie film, which were used as evidence of the war crimes committed in Nanking. During the crisis itself, missionaries on the International Committee wrote countless letters reporting atrocities to the Japanese embassy and the Japanese High Command. One of them, Lewis S.C. Smythe, an American missionary who taught at the University of Nanking and served as secretary of the International Committee for the Nanking Safety Zone, wrote sixty-nine such letters to the Japanese embassy from December 14, 1937, to February 19, 1938. A sociologist, he later organized systematic regional surveys to assess the human losses and property and crop damage. His letters to his family, many of them in this book, are painfully detailed reports of what he saw and heard.

Until Iris Chang's book, *The Rape of Nanking: The Forgotten Holocaust of World War II,* became a best-seller in the years following its publication in 1997, few people born outside of China after 1940 had heard of this orgy of unrestrained violence. When Zhang Kaiyuan, a historian and coeditor of this volume, discovered these diaries and letters in the China Records Collection at Yale Divinity School, he determined to use them to tell the terrible story for today's generation of readers. Other recent books deal with these and other atrocities committed by the Japanese military,[2] but none more graphically than these first-hand accounts written in the midst of the bloody terror that raged in China's national capital for seven weeks.

Notes

1. A famous *Life* magazine photograph showed an abandoned infant crying in the ruins.

2. James Yin and Shi Young, *Rape of Nanking: An Undeniable History in Photographs* (Chicago: Innovative Publishing Group, 1996); George L. Hicks, *The Comfort Women: Japan's Brutal Regime of Enforced Prostitution in the Second World War* (New York: W.W. Norton, 1997); Toshiyuki Tanaka et al., *Hidden Horrors: Japan's War Crimes in World War II* (Boulder: Westview, 1997); John Rabe et al., *The Good Man of Nanking: The Diaries of John Rabe* (New York: Alfred A. Knopf, 1998); Sheldon H. Harris, *Factories of Death: Japanese Biological Warfare, 1932–1945 and the American Cover-up* (New York: Routledge, 1995); Hal Gold, *Unit 731 Testimony* (Boston: C.E. Tuttle, 1995); Honda Katsuichi, *The Nanjing Massacre: A Japanese Reporter Confronts Japan's Shame* (Armonk, NY: M.E. Sharpe, 1999).

Donald MacInnis
Brunswick, Maine

Preface

The Nanking Massacre, the brutal crime committed by the Japanese invading army against the Chinese people in the winter of 1937–38, took place over sixty years ago. Yet, this horrid event, like a nightmare, cannot perish as long as it remains in people's memory.

China and Japan are close neighbors separated only by a strip of water. The two countries had been good friends for over one thousand years. According to some Japanese scholars, the early development of Japanese culture had absorbed rich nourishment to the full from Chinese culture. In Kyoto, in Nara, we can still feel the breath of Tang civilization.

After the Meiji reform, a few generations of Chinese with advanced ideas considered Japan as a model of power achieved through political reform. Even at present, some scholars still view Japan as a successful example of modernization for Asian countries. Unfortunately, these scholars often neglect the other side of the coin. As the historical facts show, modernized Japan constantly brought disaster to her Asian neighbors, among which Korea and China bore the brunt of her aggression. In less than fifty years after 1894, Japan launched three large-scale invasions into China. She first swallowed up Taiwan, then annexed three provinces of northeast China. And last, she was obsessed with the ambition to extinguish China by intruding from north China into the east and south, then into central and southwest China.

The Chinese of my generation had long suffered as a result of Japan's invasion. The first song we learned was "September eighteenth, at that miserable moment. . . ."[1] The first composition our teacher asked us to write was "A Letter of Salutation to the Soldiers on the North China Front Line." Our young hearts were persistently bothered by the evil shadow of the Japanese invaders.

In the autumn of 1937, just as I entered junior high school, the flames of war drove my family to join the refugee tide moving to the west of China. Forced to leave our beloved hometown for faraway Sichuan Province, we started eight years of a vagrant and destitute life. It can be said that the golden dream of my childhood was shattered by Japan's invasion of China. Such "splendid" slogans as "Mutual Existence and Prosperity," "Mutual Aid," even "Great Eastern Asia Mutual Prosperity Circle," which were repeatedly shouted by Japanese militarists at that time—and by their few successors even at present—can only call up agonized memories.

Before the end of the war in 1945, I had known nothing about the Nanking Massacre, for I had been living in the out-of-the-way, destitute village of Sichuan for a long time. Without any newspaper or radio, we were almost completely cut off from the outside world. It was not until 1946, when I returned home and entered the University of Nanking, that I began to hear about this event in the history of Nanking. At that time, the Kuomintang administration had been corrupted to the extreme. Inflation and soaring prices had brought the national economy to the brink of collapse. We university students threw ourselves enthusiastically into democratic movements and did not think of exploring more about the atrocities committed by the Japanese.

China and the world have undergone so much change since 1949 that after the defeat of Japan and the signing of the peace treaty, the wretched past event, the Nanking Massacre, has actually faded from people's memory. The world knows that China, as a victim of that disastrous war, has been lenient with Japan, which initiated and failed to complete the invasion. For many years, some Japanese have not drawn lessons from their defeat. They would not take the defeat lying down. What is more, they have never given up their wishful thinking of reviving an old dream of ruling the roost of Asia and contending for hegemony of the world. It is this handful of Japanese who are refusing by every possible means to take responsibility for the aggression, beautifying the evil acts of the militarists, touching the historical sore spot time and again, and persistently provoking international conflicts. Harsh reality has taught us that history should not be ignored, nor should it be distorted. As for historians, we should do our best to defend the truth and dignity of history.

Of course, those Japanese mentioned above are in the minority, but they are a very active minority. As far as I am concerned, most of the Japanese people are against the revival of militarism, of which they also are the victims. I have many Japanese friends in academic circles. Some of them were forced to join the invading army during the war when they were still innocent young students. As mere "cannon fodder" who survived the war, they should not have to shoulder the responsibility for the war, yet their sense of social duty as scholars urges them to feel guilty. And the guilt is like a nightmare that will harass them for the rest of their lives. I also know some Japanese historians who were born after the war. Although they do not have any personal experiences of the war, they step forward bravely, just as their former generations did. In order to resist the misleading history textbooks promulgated by the Japanese Ministry of Education and to expose the various atrocities committed by the invading army, they are fighting against the right-wingers fearlessly and unremittingly, even though some have been threatened by letters enclosing bullets.

It is because of these negative and positive influences that I went to Columbia University in New York in May of 1988 and participated in the initiation of the Chinese Alliance of Memorial and Justice. During my three years' stay in the United States, I took part in a series of academic activities organized by the Alliance in order to protect the historical truth of the Sino-Japanese War. I joined the assembly held in New York on December 12, 1991 by the Alliance in Memory of the Victims of the Nanking Massacre. At the assembly I introduced for the first time the documents about the Nanking Massacre in the "Bates's Papers" kept in the Divinity School library at Yale University. I solemnly declared that "[w]hen we mourn with our deep grief for those victims of the Massacre, we should remember one name—Miner Searle Bates."

Bates was my teacher when I studied in the history department at the University of Nanking from 1946 to 1948. During the Nanking Massacre, he enthusiastically took part in the relief work organized by the International Committee for the Nanking Safety Zone and was the last chairman of that committee. Thus he was able to keep a large collection of the archives of the Committee and took it to America in 1950. As far as I can remember, during my two years' study at the university, Bates never mentioned the miserable past to us either in or out of the classroom, though he had appeared as an eyewitness at the International Military Tribunal for the Far East in Tokyo and the Chinese Military Tribunal in Nanking for the Nanking Massacre war crimes trial. What I remember is his solemn and grave expression, as if he were enduring a heavy burden deep in his mind. I believe that the mind of any person of good conscience who experienced that terrible holocaust will be etched with painful and unforgettable memories.

The first time I found these documents was in June of 1988. I just browsed through them roughly and recognized their precious historical value. In July of 1991, I again went to Yale University and worked in the Special Collection in the Divinity School library for eight months. My main work was reviewing those 1,162 rolls of "Bates's Papers," sorting out some original archives concerning the International Committee for the Nanking Safety Zone letters and diaries written by some Committee members. I made copies of some materials and also took some notes. After I returned to China in 1994, to commemorate the fiftieth anniversary of China's victory over Japan, I wrote two books based on those precious documents. They are *An Eyewitness' Historical Records of the Nanking Massacre* (Hubei People's Press, 1995) and *Nanking: November, 1937–May 1938* (Hong Kong Sanlian Bookshop, 1995). Since it was the first time the original archives of the International Committee for the Nanking Safety Zone had been used systematically, the books quickly aroused the interest of the mass media at home and abroad. The publications also caught the attention of Bates's former students at the University of Nanking, Guo Junhe and

Wu Tianwei. Guo is in charge of Taipei Jinhe Press and Wu is a professor in the history department of Southern Illinois University. They both thought highly of the publication of these documents. They consulted with me and decided to publish some of them in facsimile form so as to enable the world to know their original appearance. The fruit of their collaboration, *American Missionary Eyewitnesses to the Nanking Massacre, 1937–1938*, edited by Martha Lund Smalley, New Haven, 1997, was published as the Yale Divinity School Library, Occasional Publication, No. 9. The range of that book was expanded from Bates' papers to those also of George A. Fitch, Ernest H. Forster, John G. Magee, James H. McCallum, W. Plumer Mills, Lewis S. C. Smythe, Minnie Vautrin, Robert O. Wilson, and others. There are also a number of photo-offset copies of representative original archives. Thus it holds many accounts from people who were present during the Nanking Massacre. Owing to the limited space, however, the quantity of the compiled papers is not large, and it is hard to show fully the whole picture of the Massacre. In addition, the book separated the letters and diaries and rearranged them according to date, which makes it even more difficult for the reader to recognize the original spontaneity of the papers. Hence, I decided to go to Yale again to edit a more complete and persuasive collection of Nanking Massacre archives.

My wife, Huang Huaiyu, and I went to Yale Divinity School in May 1998 and worked there for a month and a half. We first reread the relevant files in "Bates's Papers," then added some omitted valuable materials. Then we reviewed the China Records Project Miscellaneous Personal Papers Collection and Archives of the United Board for Christian Higher Education in Asia. We made copies of the records made by George A. Fitch, Ernest H. Forster, James H. McCallum, John G. Magee, W. Plumer Mills, Lewis S. C. Smythe, Minnie Vautrin, and Robert O. Wilson. At the same time we discovered some large files, the "Albert and Celia Steward Papers," from which we selected many valuable materials. During this time, Martha Smalley, who is in charge of the Special Collection, kindly offered to help us. Nancy Chapman, director of the Yale–China Association, arranged our daily life attentively. We are deeply impressed by and very grateful for their concern and friendship.

Introduced by Shao Tziping and Wu Changchuan of the Alliance in Memory of Victims of the Nanking Massacre, we had a pleasant talk with David Magee, son of John Magee, and Douglas Merwin, an editor at M.E. Sharpe Publishing Company, in Shao's house located in beautiful Rye, New York. As a result of this meeting, we planned to select some documents related to the Nanking Massacre in the Special Collection of the Yale Divinity School library and to edit a more nearly complete authentic collection so as to reveal to the people of North America and the rest of the world the historical truth of the Nanking Massacre of over sixty years ago.

After our return in the autumn of 1998, my wife and I, with the help of our two young colleagues, Liu Jiafeng and Wang Weijia, worked together on selecting, classifying, and editing these documents. We attentively checked and proofread. At last we finished the job and added some necessary explanations and annotations for readers in America and other Western countries.

We dedicate this book to all those of good conscience who can make their own judgment about the tragedy in Nanking according to these truly original materials recorded day by day.

More than fifty years have gone by since the end of World War II, the Cold War has come to an end. Peace and development are the common wish shared by most nations and peoples. The causes of war still exist, and various wars are continuing in many parts of the world. Human beings are still killing each other and the rapid development of high technology has made wars more cruel in extent and scope. Therefore, we should educate people by means of historical lessons and wake up millions to oppose aggressive war and to distinguish its source. This is the mission we should shoulder today.

On November 29, 1938, Bates wrote in a letter to a friend, "The first necessity of work for peace or for any other improvement, is to face the facts honestly." What we have done is just to follow Bates's instructions and continue his unfinished work. At the same time, we are appealing to the peace-loving people of the whole world: Please listen to Dr. Bates's call from the bottom of his heart in those tragic days, "Peace on Earth, good will to men."

Note

1. By 1931 Japanese militarists were ready to take a more active role on the Chinese mainland. As a first step they provoked an incident that ended in the death of the Chinese warlord in Manchuria and led to the establishment of the state of Manchukuo there, presided over by the former Chinese emperor, the puppet Puyi.

Zhang Kaiyuan

* * *

Publisher's note: While we have spelled Nanjing in the title of this book according to its contemporary pinyin rendering, we have retained its pre-pinyin historical spelling as "Nanking" throughout the text.

Appendix: Archives' Distribution Based on the Book *American Missionary Eyewitnesses to the Nanking Massacre, 1937–1938*

Name	Number	Content
Bates, M.S.	RG10: B1, F7–11	Family letters to wife and son
	RG10: B4	Letters between Bates and Japanese Embassy, Association of University of Nanking founders, and H.J. Timperley
	RG10: B86, B87, B90 RG10: B102, F861–871 RG10: B103, F872–873 RG10: B126, F1132, F1137	Articles written by Bates, materials on Nanking during the Anti-Japanese War, materials on Chinese politics and religious conditions, on biographies, copy of Bates's testimony to the International Military Tribunal for the Far East
Fitch, G.	RG11: B9, F202	Letters
Foster, E.	RG8: B263–265	Letters, collected documents, and pictures
McCallum, J.	RG8: B119, B22x	Account of the Japanese atrocities at Nanking during the winter of 1937–38
Magee, G.	RG8: B263	Letters collected in Forster's papers and film
Mills, W. P.	RG8: B114	Letters to wife
Smythe, L.S.C.	RG10: B102, F864–869 RG10: B4, F67 RG11: B225, F3815	Letters, War Damage in the Nanking Area, December 1937–March 1938
Vautrin, M.	RG8: B206 RG11: B134, F2698–2700 RG11: B145, F2870–2881	Diaries, letters, and reports
Wilson, R.O.	RG11: B145, F3874–3876	Letters and reports
Steward, Albert and Celia	RG20: B10, F220	

Source: American Missionary Eyewitnesses to the Nanking Massacre, 1937–1938, New Haven: Yale Divinity School Library, 1997.

Introduction

Historical Background

Zhang Kaiyuan

On August 13, 1937, the Japanese invading army spread the flames of war from North China to Shanghai, Kunshan, Jiading, Tacang, and other places. After the fall of Shanghai, the Japanese army moved westward. From November 8, they marched toward Nanking from two routes: One tailed behind the left wing of the Chinese troops pushing along the Huning Line (Shanghai to Nanking); the other concentrated their forces on the route to Huzhou along the south bank of Taihu Lake with the aim of blocking the route of retreat of the Chinese troops.

The Chinese government decided to defend the city of Nanking tenaciously and prevent the western movement of the Japanese. Unfortunately, they kept on losing battles. The Japanese army occupied Guangde and encircled Nanking from southeast to southwest at the end of November. Then they attacked the fortress of Jiangyin on December 1; thus the first line of defense in Nanking was completely exposed to the enemy.

By that time, the national government had moved to Wuhan. Though the rear troops were fighting bravely, they suffered heavy casualties. These troops, entrenched in a besieged city, were without any aid, and Nanking was in imminent danger. Ignoring their governments' urgent notice to retreat and heedless of their own safety, more than twenty foreigners who lived in Nanking volunteered to organize the International Committee for the Nanking Safety Zone, in order to prevent more harm to the city's civilians.

In his old age Hang Liwu, who was then the chairman of the Board of Trustees of the University of Nanking, wrote about the organization's work in his memoirs:

> In the winter of 1937, after fighting against the Japanese army for three months, the National Army retreated to the vicinity of Nanking. The government had already moved to west China. Three-quarters of the civilians within the city and most of the foreign residents had left or were about to leave. Then large groups of soldiers withdrawing from the front line poured in and made the disordered city worse off. The capital of Nationalist China was on the verge of collapse. Just before this, I read in the newspaper that in Shanghai, Father Jacquinot[1] had established a refugee zone and helped many women and children. At the time, I was the secretary of the Chinese–British Culture Foundation as well as the chairman of the Board of Trustees of the University of

Nanking. In consideration of the dangerous situation, I invited the Americans who were serving at various Christian universities and a few British and German businessmen (about twenty of them) to discuss emergency measures. We decided to follow the example of the Shanghai refugee zone and set up an international relief organization, which would be called the International Committee for the Nanking Safety Zone. We delimited a boundary line from the University of Nanking, the Ginling Women's College, Drum Tower [Hospital], Shanxi Lu Residence to Xin Jiekong as the Safety Zone in which we took in homeless refugees. The Safety Zone was also called the Refugee Zone. After the designation of the area, we entrusted Father Jacquinot in Shanghai to ask for permission from the commander in chief of the Japanese army. Later Father Jacquinot told me that the commander in chief accepted the map and said, "We've already known this." These maps with the Zone marked out were found on the soldiers who entered the city of Nanking.

The members of the Nanking Safety Zone included Lewis S.C. Smythe, John Magee, J.V. Pickering, M.S. Bates, W.P. Mills, C.S. Trimmer, and Charles Riggs from America; P.H. Munro Faure, P.R. Shields, Ivor Mackay, and D.J. Lean from Britain; John H.D. Rabe, G. Schultze Pantin, and Edward Sperling from Germany; and J. M. Hanson from Denmark. All together there were fifteen people. John H. D. Rabe was selected as the chair of the Committee, and Lewis Smythe, the secretary. George Fitch and I were deputy director and director respectively. Later I was asked to escort the historical relics from the Palace Museum to Chongqing, so Fitch acted as the director. At the time, General Tang Shengzhi, the garrison commander, had promised to move the military institutions from the Safety Zone and to dismantle the antiaircraft gun position so as to guarantee the neutrality of the Zone. Before mayor Ma Chaojun left Nanking, he turned over the municipal government and its resources as well as 450 policeman in the Safety Zone. Zhang Qun provided his personal residence for me to use as the Committee's office. On December 10, refugees began to surge into the Zone and soon all places were occupied. We could requisition only the Supreme Court and the Overseas Chinese Committee buildings.[2]

In the autumn of 1986, I happened to meet Hang Liwu at the annual meeting of the Asian Scholars Association in Singapore, and we had a very delightful conversation. He also mentioned the above action to me. Though he was over eighty years old, his mind and memory did not show any trace of decline, and his remarks were concise and well organized. According to Appendix I of the existing number one document of the International Committee of the Nanking Safety Zone, that is, the official letter to the Japanese military authorities, we can see Hang's memory is accurate.

The table following is a list of the personnel of the International Committee.

Name	Nationality	Organization
1. John H.D. Rabe	Germany	Siemens Company
2. Lewis S.C. Smythe	U.S.	University of Nanking
3. P.H. Munro-Faure	Britain	Asiatic Petroleum Company
4. John Magee	U.S.	American Church Mission
5. P.R. Shields	Britain	International Export Company
6. J.M. Hanson	Denmark	Texas Oil Company
7. G. Schultze-Pantin	Germany	Hsinmin Trading Company
8. Ivor Mackay	Britain	Butterfield and Swire
9. J.V. Pickering	U.S.	Standard Vacuum Oil Company
10. M.S. Bates	U.S.	University of Nanking
11. W.P. Mills	U.S.	North Presbyterian Mission
12. Edward Sperling	Germany	Shanghai Insurance Company
13. D.J. Lean	Britain	Asiatic Petroleum Company
14. C.S. Trimmer	U.S.	Drum Tower Hospital
15. Charles H. Riggs	U.S.	University of Nanking

As Hang Liwu soon left for Chongqing, he did not know that seven of the above members withdrew from Nanking by order of their respective companies by early December 1937. These men therefore participated only in the organizing work but not the actual operation of the International Committee. According to Appendix II of number one document of the International Committee about the change of the personnel, they were P.H. Munro-Faure, J.M. Hanson, G. Schultze-Pantin, Ivor Mackay, D.J. Lean, P.R. Shields, and J.V. Pickering. Those who remained in Nanking and participated in the relief work were John H.D. Rabe, Lewis S.C. Smythe, John Magee, Edward Sperling, M.S. Bates, W.P. Mills, C.S. Trimmer, Charles Riggs, James H. McCallum (American, from United Christian Missionary Society), Hubert Sone (American, from Nanking Theological Seminary), Ernest H. Forster (American, American Church Mission), Albert N. Steward (American, University of Nanking), C.Y. Xu (Chinese, University Hospital), F.C. Gale (American, Methodist Mission), James F. Kearney (American, Society of Jesus), and S. Yasumura (Japanese, Japan Baptist Church).

From the above sources, we can see that six of them were core members of the International Committee: M.S. Bates (vice president of University of Nanking, professor of history), Lewis S.C. Smythe (professor of sociology), Charles Riggs (professor of agronomy), James H. McCallum (administrative director of Drum Tower Hospital), C.S. Trimmer (administrative director of Drum Tower Hospital), and C.Y. Xu (clerk of University Hospital). They had been working industriously for a very long time. Another two names should be mentioned here—Robert O. Wilson (physician of Drum Tower Hospital) and Minnie Vautrin (vice president of Ginling Women's College, professor of education). They did not belong to the International Committee, but they were members of the Nanking International Red Cross Committee and worked indefatigably day and night. They made a great contribution to healing the wounded and rescuing the dying as well as protecting the refugees.

The faculties of the University of Nanking and Ginling Women's College had endeavored to help 250,000 Nanking refugees within the Safety Zone. The two campuses had provided dwelling places for tens of thousands of refugees. This is the Light of Ginling, as well as the Light of the University of Nanking as Ginling's successor. We should bear in mind this heroic and moving history forever: Harsh as it is, it is the embodiment of dedication and fearless courage.

In order to let readers better understand the documents collected in this book, it is necessary to make a skeleton examination of the principal and subsidiary causes of these events in the history of Nanking and of this small foreign group who left behind them so many precious diaries and letters.

According to the account by W.P. Mills, the earliest Protestant missionary who entered Nanking was George Duncan (Scotch, Inland Mission). He arrived at Nanking three years after the failure of the Taiping Movement (1860s). At that time, the city had not yet fully recovered from the ravages of the Taiping rebellion. A stranger in a strange land, he could live only in a boat at the very beginning. Later he was permitted to live in the Drum Tower and even later to carry out his missionary work. In October 1868, Duncan married a Miss Brown and settled down in Nanking. This couple and their colleagues increased their influence among the civilians day by day. Tragically, Duncan fell ill in 1872, so the family went back to England. Soon Duncan died of acute tuberculosis. Fortunately, in his last three years in China, he had already trained capable successors who expanded their missionary work to Anqing.[3]

There is no full and accurate account of the early life of American residents in Nanking. I found in the "Steward Papers" some inscriptions on tombstones that perhaps were copied from the Nanking Foreign Cemetery before the outbreak of anti-Japanese war. There were 108 headstones, but only eighty-nine of them were legible and recorded. According to the description of the professions of the deceased, most of them were missionaries, and a few were businessmen. Some of their offspring had also died. Few died in old age, most people died in the prime of life or even in childhood. The causes of death were mainly tuberculosis, typhoid, and other infectious diseases. So it can be seen that the medical conditions at that time were very poor.

Among the tombstones, two were obviously relevant to the University of Nanking. One is the tombstone of Paul Dewitt Twinem, pastor of the university. He was born on March 5, 1894, and died on September 23, 1923. His wife was buried in the tomb next to his. Another is that of Dr. John E. William, vice president of the university, who died accidentally in the chaos of war. His tombstone was erected by Wang Zhengting, a high-ranking official of the National Government. All these tombstones concisely recorded the long or short lives of over one hundred foreign residents in Nanking, together with their joys and sorrows, partings and reunions. Not a few of them considered themselves as "lifelong friends of China."[4] They should be viewed as the forerunners of the members of the International Committee for the Nanking Safety Zone.

After World War I, more foreign missionaries came to China. There was an obvious change in their cultural quality. One of the reasons is the rise of the Student Volunteer Movement. People called the new generation of missionaries "missionary educators." They were different from their predecessors in that they had received a better higher education before they arrived in China, but they were also born into Christian families, educated in Christian schools, and had the same spirit of dedication as earlier missionaries. They had professional specialties, so they belonged to the group of scholar-type missionaries. Regarding their wide vision and rich knowledge, they were far better qualified than those earlier missionaries and their wives from midwestern America.

The authors of these journals and letters belonged to this new generation of missionaries.

Minnie Vautrin: In 1912, Vautrin graduated from the University of Illinois with a major in education. Then she was commissioned by the United Christian Missionary Society as a missionary to China. Vautrin became chairman of the education department of Ginling College when it was founded in 1916, and she once served as acting president of Ginling College.

Miner Searle Bates: Bates won a Rhodes Scholarship to study history at Oxford University and earned his M.A. in 1920. The United Christian Missionary Society then commissioned him as a missionary to teach at the University of Nanking. He was a professor in the departments of politics and history and once served as the vice president of the university.

Albert Steward: After he graduated from Oregon Agricultural College in 1921, Steward was stationed in Nanking as an educational missionary under the Methodist Board of Missions. He established the department of botany at the University of Nanking and was a professor in the department.

Robert O. Wilson: Born in Nanking in 1906, Wilson was the son of a Methodist missionary family. Wilson graduated from Princeton University and received his M.D. from Harvard Medical School in 1929. Appointed to the staff of the University of Nanking hospital in 1935, he arrived there in 1936.

Lewis S. C. Smythe: Smythe received his Ph.D. in sociology from the University of Chicago and was appointed to teach at the University of Nanking by the United Christian Missionary Society in 1934. He was a professor in the department of sociology.

Several other people, though they were not full-time staff at the University of Nanking, were closely connected with it.

James H. McCallum: McCallum graduated from the University of Oregon in 1917 and earned his B.D. from Yale Divinity School in 1921; later he earned a master's degree at Chicago Divinity School and did doctoral work at the Union Theological Seminary while on furlough. He moved to China in 1921, and engaged in evangelical and community center work for the United Christian Missionary Society. In the winter of 1937, he volunteered to remain in Nanking as administrator of the University of Nanking hospital.

John G. Magee: Magee graduated from Yale in 1906 and received a B.D. from the Episcopal Theological School in Cambridge, Massachusetts, in 1911. He was ordained as a minister in the Episcopal Church and set off for China in 1912. He served as chairman of the Nanking Branch of the International Red Cross after the capture of Nanking. Together with M.S. Bates, he was engaged in relief work for the refugees.

George A. Fitch: Born in Suzhou, China, in 1883, Fitch was the son of a Presbyterian missionary family. He graduated from Wooster College in 1906, then attended Union Theological Seminary in New York. He was ordained in 1909 and returned to China to work with the Young Men's Christian Association (YMCA) in Shanghai. He served as director of the Safety Zone after the fall of Nanking.

W. Plumer Mills: Mills graduated from Davidson College in 1903 and received a B.A. from Oxford University in 1910 and a B.D. from Columbia Theological Seminary in 1912. Mills served under the YMCA in China from 1912 to 1931 and then under the Presbyterian Foreign Mission Board in Nanking from 1933 to 1949. He is one of the important leaders of the relief work during the fall of Nanking.

Ernest H. Forster: Forster graduated from Princeton University in 1917. In 1919, Forster went to China as an Episcopal missionary and taught at Mahan School in Yangzhou. He and his family were transferred from Yangzhou to Nanking to serve at St. Paul's Episcopal Church only about one month before the capture of Nanking. Forster, with John Magee, another Episcopal minister, remained in Nanking throughout the critical months of the Nanking Massacre and helped in the relief work.

Most of these Americans lived in Nanking or its surrounding areas for many years. They were married there and started their careers there, and some of them had even been born in Nanking. They learned the Chinese language and understood Chinese history and culture. They were familiar with the local conditions and customs of the Nanking area and became attached to the Nanking inhabitants with whom they had been closely associated. They ardently introduced Nanking's history, scenic spots, and relevant touring information to the people outside China. There was a copy of *Sketches of Nanking* in the "Steward Papers," which was edited and published by the Foreign Residents Nanking Women's Club, Literature Branch. The first edition was published in 1923 and the second, in 1933. Most of the authors and the members of the Literature Branch were the wives of professors at the University of Nanking and their relatives. The chair of the branch was Mrs. Samuel J. Mills. The content of the book includes Nanking's history, anecdotes of Ginling, scenic spots and historical sites, temples in Nanking, and so on. The cover bears an inscription *Kai Men Jian Shan,* which is a Chinese idiom whose literal meaning is "Open the door and see the mountain." On the title page is a picture of a section of the winding, ancient city wall against the background of the lofty Purple Mountain. The preface says, "It is the hope of those presenting this volume, that it will, in spite of its many deficiencies, help those who pursue it to a better understanding and deeper interest in the city and that it will stimulate some to a search for more relics of the glory that was Nanking's in ages past, and that we trust will again be hers."

We long ago noticed that Bates and his missionary colleagues, whether they were in Nanking or came back to the States, often called one another "old citizens of Nanking" or "we Chinese." Now we also found that these people even called themselves the "Nanking gang." In the "Steward Papers," there was a group of letters to Mrs. W.P. Mills, whose husband was the second chair of the International Committee. All the writers were their American colleagues and friends who had lived in Nanking (especially at the University of Nanking and Ginling College). The letters are dated from December 1942 to March 1943. At that time the Millses had already left Nanking and were back in the States. Most of the letter writers had moved to Chengtu and still worked at the University of Nanking and Ginling College, which had also moved to Chengtu. The initiators and organizers of the group correspondence were Grace Riggs and Lucile Jones. The former was working at the dean's office in the agricultural college, and the latter was a professor in the department of philosophical education at the University of Nanking.

In her letter dated November 24, 1942, Grace Riggs wrote, "A few days ago Lucile Jones and I invited the 'Nanking gang' for tea, and to have a visit with as many of you as had written lately. All recent letters were brought and shared among us, and the enclosed expresses the thoughts of some of us. It was a pleasant get-together, and not once was mentioned the high cost of living. We lived mostly in the past for those couple hours, with now and then a hopeful peep into the future." A letter written by Mrs. Smythe, who had worked at the president's office, dated March 12, 1943, also said, "Today a group of us have gotten together here to talk over old times in Nanking." Other letters either sighed, "We do miss Nanking," or showed their sentiments, "so far from our old Nanking," or "absence and distance surely make the heart grow fonder in relation to you all, and the Nanking bond somehow seems different from any other." The last of these affectionate letters is from Mrs. Margaret Roy, whose children had all grown up on the campus of the University of Nanking. One of them was Stapelton Roy, who became the American ambassador to China. In the letter, she mentioned her other son, David, whom I met at a cocktail party at the University of Chicago in the autumn of 1979. At that time, David was already a distinguished professor of Chinese classical literature at this university, and had made a profound study and translation of *Jin Ping Mei*, a famous Chinese classic. We talked glowingly of the past in Nanking, proposing toasts and clinking glasses time and again. Occasionally, we imitated the Nanking local dialect, which aroused laughter that rocked the whole room. David's generation, I think, may have inherited some "Nanking gang" gene from their old generation.

Though this group of American residents, represented by Bates and Smythe, did not blend into the mainstream of Nanking society, they never considered themselves foreigners. On the contrary, they identified themselves as citizens of Nanking from the bottom of their hearts. It was Nanking that had provided them with stable and advantageous professions and the environment in which to start their careers and bring up their children. What's more, the long history and the charming ambience of this city had attracted them deeply. The Qinhuai River bathed in the moonlight, Xuanwu Lake at the dawn of spring, the Rain of Flowers Terrace with its colorful pebbles, and Qixia Mountain covered with maple leaves—all these had become cherished memories and would follow them for the rest of their lives. Of course, they had been most emotionally attached to the unsophisticated and industrious people of Nanking, as well as their colleagues and students with whom they had been together day and night. We can see from the "Steward Papers" that those Americans not only studied earnestly Mandarin Chinese, but also learned the Nanking dialect. They worked out forms with English, Mandarin, and Nanking dialect in them. It reflected their strong desire to become part of the Nanking people. It is no wonder that they called Nanking "one of the most beautiful cities in the world" and called Ginling College "a college set up in the capital of a country." They felt quite proud of themselves for being citizens of Nanking.

Unfortunately, the invasion of the Japanese army on December 13, 1937, thoroughly destroyed the peaceful and quiet life of this beautiful city. The great city wall, the symbol of the ancient capital, had been breached by a bomb. The prosperous city proper became a sea of flames. The honest and kind citizens became the victims of killing and raping. Nanking instantly turned into a hell on earth. The disaster came so suddenly, everybody had to face it. Under these harsh conditions, everyone had to make a serious choice. Bates and his American colleagues and friends had every reason to leave the city, and the American embassy had repeatedly urged them to withdraw. It even sent a warship to meet them. Yet they could not tear themselves away from the helpless 200,000 refugees who were deserted by the municipal government. They preferred to share all this suffering with the city and its people, and they did their best to help them with the status of a third party's nationality. In those days of sanguinary slaughter, they relied upon petition, argument, and even their own flesh and blood to carry out the relief work for the victims of the Japanese bayonets. Together with their Chinese colleagues, they gathered the refugees into their shelters and provided them with board and lodging. They worked valiantly day and night, sending their protests and appeals to the Japanese military and diplomatic authorities and keeping a record of Japanese atrocities day by day. They could not receive any information about their family members whom they were so eagerly yearning to see. Husbands or wives did not know whether their better halves were still alive or had been imprisoned. This small group of foreign residents was almost completely isolated from the outside world. Yet they chose to stay. Just as Bates said, the Christian who tries to do his duty need not fear for his life, but only for his own shortcomings before great challenges.

The following is what we dedicate to the readers: the record of the Nanking Massacre, the brutal crime committed by the Japanese invading army, written with the hearts, blood, and tears of this small group of foreign residents.

Notes

1. R.P. Jacquinot, Catholic priest, chair of the China International Famine Relief Committee, vice president of the Shanghai Red Cross Association, and chair of the Supervisory Committee of the Nanking Refugee Zone.

2. Hang Liwu, *Hang Liwu Xiansheng Fangwen Jilu,* pp. 23–24. Taipei: Modern History Institute, Sinica Academy, 1991.

3. W.P. Mills, "Early Days in Nanking," from "The Story of Eighty Years of Protestant Missions in Nanking, China, 1867–1947," RG20, B10, F3–10.

4. From "Information on Stones in Foreign Cemetery, Nanking, China," (RG20, B20, F224).

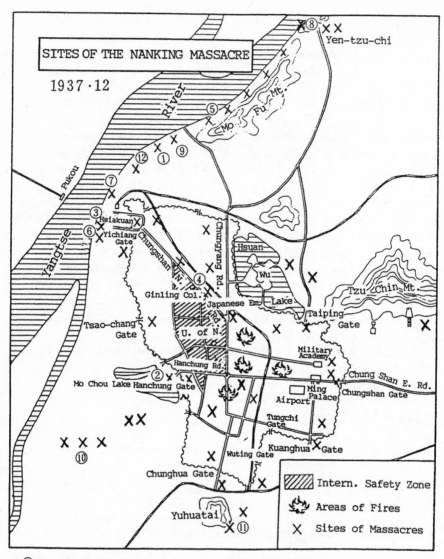

SITES OF THE NANKING MASSACRE

1937·12

① Yu-lei-ying
② Outside of Han-chung Gate
③ Chung-shan Pier
④ Ta-fang-hsiang Square
⑤ Tsao-hsieh-chia
⑥ Hsia-kuan
⑦ Lung-chiang-kou
⑧ Yen-tzu-chi
⑨ Pao-ta-chiao
  and the vicinity of Yu-lei-ying
⑩ Shang-hsin-ho
⑪ Hua-shen Temple outside
  the Chung-hua Gate
⑫ Mei-tan Port

EYEWITNESSES TO MASSACRE

Miner Searle Bates

Miner Searle Bates was born May 28, 1897, in Newark, Ohio. His father was a minister who became president of Hiram College. Bates received his B.A. from Hiram College in 1916 and won a Rhodes Scholarship to study at Oxford University. With the United States entering World War I, he joined the YMCA and served in Mesopotamia until the end of the war. He returned to Oxford to finish his B.A. and did some graduate work in 1920. In the summer of that year, the United Christian Missionary Society commissioned him as a missionary to teach at the University of Nanking. In 1923, he married Lilliath Robbins, a Canadian teaching at Ginling College. In 1934–35, Bates was Rockefeller Foundation Fellow studying Japanese and Russian at Harvard University. He received a Ph.D. in Chinese history from Yale University in 1935.

When the Nanking Massacre occurred, Bates was alone in Nanking as his wife and two children were staying in Japan. He plunged himself into the work of the International Committee for the Nanking Safety Zone, protecting many Chinese from being murdered and raped by the Japanese army and saving thousands of them from starvation. To enhance his power to deal with the Japanese, the directors of the University of Nanking appointed him vice president of the university on January 13, 1938. Only two days after the fall of Nanking, Bates lodged his first protest against Japanese atrocities with the Japanese embassy, followed by his famous letter of protest of January 10, 1938, a copy of which reached free China.

Bates was a major moving spirit behind H.J. Timperley's book, Japanese Terror in China *(New York: Modern Age Books, June 1938). Except for seven brief trips to Japan and one to India to attend conferences, Bates remained in Nanking from 1937 to 1941, fearlessly challenging the Japanese authorities about their activities, especially narcotics trafficking. On behalf of the Nanking International Relief Committee, he wrote two pamphlets: one titled "Crop Investigation in Nanking Area" and the other "The Nanking Population," both of which are crucial to our understanding of the Nanking Massacre. After the war he was summoned as a witness at the Tokyo Trial and subsequent Chinese trials of war criminals.*

Some Pictures from Nanking (Dec. 15, 1937)[1]

At Nanking the Japanese Army has lost much of its reputation, and has thrown away a remarkable opportunity to gain the respect of the Chinese inhabitants and of foreign opinion. The disgraceful collapse of Chinese authority and the break-up of the Chinese armies in this region left vast numbers of persons ready to respond to the order and organization of which Japan boasts. Many local people freely expressed their relief when the entry of Japanese troops apparently brought an end to the strains of war conditions and the immediate perils of bombardment. At least they were rid of their fears of disorderly Chinese troops, who indeed passed out without doing severe damage to most parts of the city.

But in two days the whole outlook has been ruined by frequent murder, wholesale and semi-regular looting and uncontrolled disturbance of private homes including offenses against the security of women. Foreigners who have traveled over the city report many civilians' bodies lying in the streets. In the central portion of Nanking they were counted yesterday as about one to the city block. A considerable percentage of the dead civilians were the victims of shooting or bayoneting in the afternoon and evening of the 13th, which was the time of Japanese entry into the city. Any person who ran in fear or excitement, and any one who was caught in streets or alleys after dusk by roving patrols was likely to be killed on the spot. Most of this severity was beyond even theoretical excuse. It proceeded in the Safety Zone as well as elsewhere, and many cases are plainly witnessed by foreigners and by reputable Chinese. Some bayonet wounds were barbarously cruel.

Squads of men picked out by Japanese troops as former Chinese soldiers have been tied together and shot. These soldiers had discarded their arms, and in some cases their military clothing. Thus far we have found no trace of prisoners in Japanese hands other than such squads actually or apparently on the way to execution, save for men picked up anywhere to serve as temporary carriers of loot and equipment. From one building in the refugee zone, four hundred men were selected by the local police under compulsion from Japanese soldiers, and were marched off tied in batches of fifty between lines of riflemen and machine-gunners. The explanation given to observers left no doubt as to their fate.

On the main streets the petty looting of the Chinese soldiers, mostly of food shops and of unprotected windows, was turned into systematic destruction of shop-front after shop-front under the eyes of officers of rank. Japanese soldiers require private carriers to help them struggle along under great loads. Food was apparently in first demand, but everything else useful or valuable had its turn. Thousands upon thousands of private houses all through the city, occupied and unoccupied, large and small, Chinese and foreign, have been impartially plundered. Peculiarly disgraceful cases of robbery by soldiers include the following: scores of refugees in camps and shelters had money and valuables removed from their slight possessions during mass searches; the staff of the University Hospital were stripped of cash and watches from their persons, and of other possessions from the nurses' dormitory (their buildings are American, and like a number of others that were plundered, were flying foreign flags and carrying official proclamations from their respective Embassies); the seizure of motor cars and other property after tearing down the flags upon them.

There are reported many cases of rape and insult to women, which we have not yet had time to investigate. But cases like the following are sufficient to show the situation. From a house close to one of our foreign friends, four girls were yesterday abducted by soldiers. Foreigners saw in the quarters of a newly arrived officer, in a part of the city practically deserted by ordinary people, eight young women.

Under these conditions the terror is indescribable, and lectures by suave officers on the "sole purpose of making war on the oppressive Chinese Government for the sake of the Chinese people," leave an impression that nauseates.

Surely this horrible exhibition in Nanking does not represent the best achievement of the Japanese Empire, and there must be responsible Japanese statesmen, military and civilian, who for their own national interests will promptly and adequately remedy the harm that these days have done to Japanese standing in China. There are individual soldiers and officers who conduct themselves as gentlemen worthy of their profession and worthy of their Empire. But the total action has been a sad blow.

Excerpts of Letters to the Japanese Embassy (Dec. 14–27, 1937)[2]

December 14:

[Japanese] Soldiers tore down the American flag and official notice of the American Embassy upon the gate of our [University of Nanking] Agricultural Economics Department (Hsiao T'ao Yuan), robbed several teachers and assistants living there, and broke several doors without waiting for keys.

December 15:

In our new Library Building, where we are taking care of 1,500 common people, four women were raped on the property; two were carried off and released after being raped; three were carried off and not returned; one was carried off but released by your Military Police near the Embassy. These acts of soldiers have brought great pain and fear to these families, to their neighbors and to all Chinese in this part of the city. More than a hundred similar cases in other parts of the Safety Zone have been reported to me this morning. They are not my business now, but I mention them to show that this University problem next door to you is only a sample of the great misery of robbery and rape carried on by soldiers among the people.

We earnestly hope that discipline may be restored among the troops. Now the fear is so great that people are afraid even to get food, and normal life and work are impossible. We respectfully urge that your authorities may arrange for their proper inspections to be carried out systematically under the immediate direction of officers than by stray bands of soldiers who enter the same place as many as ten times in one day and steal all food and money from the people. And secondly, we urge that for the reputation of the Japanese Army and the Japanese Empire, for the sake of good relations between the Japanese authorities and the common people of China, for your own thought of your wives, sisters and daughters, that the families of Nanking receive protection from the violence of soldiers.

The disorder and failure of the Chinese army gave a good chance for the Japanese troops to secure the confidence of the people, and it is unfortunate for all concerned if that chance is lost by delay or indifference to ordinary human welfare and morality.

December 17:

The reign of terror and brutality continues in the plain view of your buildings and among your own neighbors.

1. Last night soldiers repeatedly came to our Library building with its great crowd of refugees, demanding money, watches, and women at the point of the bayonet. When persons had no watches or money, usually because they had been looted several times in the two preceding days, the soldiers broke windows near them and roughly pushed them about. One of our own staff members was wounded by a bayonet in this manner.
2. At the Library building, as in many other places throughout this part of the city last night, soldiers raped several women.

3. Soldiers beat our own unarmed watchmen, because the watchmen did not have girls ready for the use of the soldiers.
4. Last night several of our American-owned residences, with flags and Embassy proclamations on them, were entered irregularly by roving groups of soldiers, some of them several times. These residences included houses in which three American members of our staff are living.

We respectfully ask you to compare these acts, which are small samples of what is happening to large numbers of residents of Nanking, with your Government's official statements of its concern for the welfare of the people of China, likewise of its protection of foreign property.

We do not wish to emphasize personal matters, and refer to two other incidents merely to indicate the degree of wild license among uncontrolled soldiers. Yesterday one American member of our staff was struck by an officer upon entirely false charges which the officer did not investigate, and also by soldiers. During the night another American and myself were pulled out of bed by a drunken soldier with a rifle.

This letter is not written to ask for special protection on behalf of the University, but to emphasize, by reason of the nearness of the University to yourselves, the urgency of peril to all peaceable people.

We believe that the Japanese Army has the power and the efficiency to maintain respectable conduct, and to give conquered people a chance to work and live under good order. We are unable to understand why it does not do so, and do it before further damage is done to local people, to Japan's reputation.

December 18:

Misery and terror continues everywhere because of the violence and robbery of the soldiers. More than 17,000 poor persons, many of them women and children, are now in our buildings hoping for safety. They are still crowding in, because conditions elsewhere are worse than here. Yet I must give you the past twenty-four hours in this *relatively good* position.

1. University Middle School, Kan Ho Yen. One frightened child killed by a bayonet; another critically wounded and about to die. Eight women raped. Several of our own staff, who are trying to feed and care for these wretched people, were struck by soldiers for no reason whatever. Soldiers climb over the walls many times day and night. Many persons could not sleep for three days, and there is hysterical fear. If this fear and despair result in resistance against the attack of soldiers upon women, there will be disastrous slaughter for which your authorities

will be responsible. American flag scornfully torn down by soldiers.

2. Sericulture Building, Chin Ying Chieh. Two women raped.
3. Agricultural Implements Shop, 11 Hu Chia Ts'ai Yuen, two women raped.
4. Faculty residence, 11 Hankow Road, inhabited by our own staff. Two women raped.
5. Faculty residence, 23 Hankow Road, inhibited by American member of our staff. One woman raped.
6. Agricultural Economics Department (Hsiao T'ao Yuan). This place has received terrible treatment so many times that all women have fled. This morning while visiting there, I was approached by six soldiers, one of whom repeatedly pointed a pistol at me with his finger on the trigger, although I did nothing except ask a courteous question as to whether he found any difficulty there.

These plain facts do not tell the misery of ordinary people visited as many as ten times in one day and six times in one night by wandering groups of soldiers looking for women and loot. They do indicate the urgent need for control *at once*.

Certain of your representatives declared that there would be military police at the gates of several of these buildings last night (as at certain other points where large bodies of refugees are gathered). But not one guard was seen. Since soldiers are everywhere climbing over walls, a few guards will not do much good, anyhow, unless there is a genuine restoration of general discipline.

The presence of the Akiyama Department Headquarters in the residence formerly belonging to Ho Yin-ni'in, constitutes a special peril to this neighborhood until your soldiers are controlled. It could be made a means of security if the generals so desired.

Here and all through the city, people are becoming desperate with hunger, since soldiers have taken their food and money; also many are cold and sick because soldiers have taken their clothing and bedding. How do the Japanese authorities plan to deal with this problem?

It is said on every street with tears and distress that where the Japanese Army is, no person and no house can be safe. Surely this is not what the statesmen of Japan wish to do, and all residents of Nanking expect better things from Japan.

I believe that if you have an opportunity, it would be well for one of you to go with me through some of the places where this terror and suffering continues, so close to your own walls. The writing of this letter has been interrupted in order to deal with seven soldiers engaged in their usual business called "inspection," which means looking for women whom they will return to seize at night.

I slept in these buildings last night, and will continue to do so in the hope of giving a little aid to helpless women and children. Other foreign friends and myself in doing such humanitarian work have repeatedly been threatened by your soldiers. If in the course of these efforts we are killed or wounded by drunken and disorderly soldiers, the responsibility will be entirely clear.

This letter is written in a courteous and friendly spirit, but it reflects something of the unhappy despair in which we have lived since the Japanese Army entered the city five days ago. Immediate remedy is greatly needed.

December 21:

In accordance with your request this morning, I submit the following facts, most of which have been observed by myself since I saw you, and the remainder I have carefully investigated after they were told me by reliable people.

1. This afternoon seven persons were taken from our Library Building by soldiers. These included members of our own staff. There was no accusation or fact of their being soldiers (Chinese), but they were simply seized for forced labor without regard to your proclamation.
2. At No. 4 T'ou T'iao Hsiang, near the entrance to your Embassy, a woman was raped this afternoon by two soldiers. Does this suggest that a few gendarmes are restoring order?
3. While I was with you in the Embassy today, my own house was looted for the fourth time. Seven other University houses have been looted today, and many have been entered several times.
4. Fires systematically laid by large bodies of soldiers working under the direction of officers, are rendering thousands of people homeless and without hope of return to normal life and work. They are going ahead all day just the same as before.
5. The Shuang Lung Hsiang gate of the University Hospital was broken in today, although it carried your proclamation. In another part of the Hospital, an American just saved the ambulance, which soldiers were stealing.
6. I have seen myself five cases of soldiers taking this afternoon food and bedding from poor people, usually requiring the people then to go with the loot as carriers.
7. In An Lot Li next to our Middle School, I answered a call for help from a Red Cross Dressing Station that was caring for three persons wounded in the night by soldiers demanding women and money. One woman was raped upstairs in that house last night. Two soldiers were thoroughly robbing the house when I went in. The very good man doing the medical work said that in his own house at 58 Kao Chia Chiu Khan, two women were raped last night.

8. I returned through several hundred straw huts of very poor people south of Wu T'ai Shan; some people said that conditions were better last night. Others said they were worse, for soldiers were still seizing girls in their homes, looting from the poorest people, and taking the rickshas of men who have no other means of living.
9. Yesterday, for the second time, the American flag was torn down from the American Primary School (Wu T'ai Shan) and trampled by soldiers. Soldiers threatened to kill any servant or other person who should put it up again.

I feel sure that not so many people were raped or wounded last night as the night before. But the robbery, illegal entry, and terrible burning continues as bad or worse than before. Two members of the International Committee who have driven several miles in a car have not yet seen a gendarme. They are not effective.

If the generals intend to destroy the people's homes and take away their last food and clothing, it is better to say so honestly than to deceive them and us with false hopes of order. . . .

December 25:

I have tried for a couple of days to refrain from troubling you further. However, many difficulties occur every day, and today they are worse than usual. New parties of stray soldiers without discipline or officers are going everywhere stealing, raping and taking away women.

Some cases follow:

1. Just now soldiers forcibly entered the University and towed away a truck used to supply rice to refugees.
2. In our Sericulture Building alone there are on the average of more than ten cases per day of rape or of abducting women.
3. Our residences continue to be entered day and night by soldiers who injure women and steal everything they wish. This applies to residences in which Americans are now living, just the same as to the others.
4. Soldiers frequently tear down the proclamations put up by your military police.
5. This morning an American member of our staff was struck by an officer who suddenly approached him and angrily tried to tear off the arm band supplied by your Embassy.
6. Other buildings not mentioned above are daily entered several times each by soldiers who utterly disregard your proclamations, looking for women and for loot.

7. Despite this disorder caused entirely by soldiers, we have no guard whatever and no military police have been sent near us.

December 27:

Beginning more than a week ago, we were promised by you that within a few days order would be restored by replacement of troops, resumption of regular discipline, increase of military police, and so forth. Yet shameful disorder continues, and we see no serious effort to stop it. Let me give a few examples from University property close to you, without covering all portions of the University.

1. Yesterday afternoon a soldier cut the rope and took away the American flag from our Rural Leaders' Training School at Yin Yang Ying and Shanghai Roads.
2. Last night between eleven and twelve o'clock, a motor car with three Japanese military men came to the main University gate, claiming that they were sent by headquarters to inspect. They forcibly prevented our watchman from giving an alarm, and kept him with them while they found and raped three girls, one of whom is only eleven years old. One of the girls they took away with them.
3. Stray soldiers continue to seize men to work for them, causing much fear and unnecessary inconvenience. For example, a soldier insisted on taking a worker from the Hospital yesterday; and several of our own servants and watchmen have been taken.
4. Several of our residences are entered daily by soldiers looking for women, food, and other articles. Two houses within one hour this morning.
5. Example 5 is from the Bible Teachers' Training School for Women, Chien Ying Hsiang, a place which has suffered terribly from your soldiers for a long time, and which I believe you once promised to protect especially—but where no military policeman has appeared. Yesterday seven different times there came groups of three or four soldiers, taking clothes, food and money from those who have some left after previous looting of the same type. They raped seven women, including a girl of twelve. In the night larger groups of twelve or fourteen soldiers came four times and raped twenty women.

The life of the whole people is filled with suffering and fear—all caused by soldiers. Your officers have promised them protection, but the soldiers every day injure hundreds of persons most seriously. A few policemen help certain places, and we are grateful for them. But that does not bring peace and order.

Often it merely shifts the bad acts of the soldiers to nearby buildings where there are no policemen.

Does not the Japanese Army care for its reputation? Do not Japanese officers wish to keep their public promises that they do not injure the common people?

While I have been writing this letter, a soldier has forcibly taken a woman from one of our teachers' houses, and with his revolver refused to let an American enter. Is this order?

Many people now want to return to their homes, but they dare not because of rape, robbery, and seizure of men continuing every day and night. Only serious efforts to enforce orders, using many police and real punishments will be of any use. In several places the situation is a little better, but it is still disgraceful after two weeks of army terrorism. More than promises is now needed.

Note on Aftermath of Registration at the University (Dec. 26, 1937)[3]

Registration was begun in the main compound. To the relatively small number of men there, the authorities added more than two thousand from the new Library. Out of the total of about three thousand massed together on the tennis courts below Swazey Hall, between two hundred and three hundred stepped out in answer to a half-hour of haranguing to this effect; "All who have been soldiers or who have performed compulsory labor (Fu Juh) pass to the rear. Your lives will be spared and you will be given work if you thus voluntarily come forth. If you do not, and upon inspection you are discovered, you will be shot." The speeches were repeated by Chinese under the instruction of Japanese officers; they were Chinese who wished to save as many of their people as possible from the fate that others had met as former soldiers or men accused wrongfully of being former soldiers. The speeches were clearly and thoroughly heard by Mr. Fukuda, Mr. Tanaka and myself, as well as by many members of the University staff. It was thought by some Chinese that certain men who stepped out were influenced by fear or misunderstanding of the term for compulsory labor, and certainly that a number of them had never been soldiers.

Toward five o'clock in the afternoon, the two or three hundred men were taken away in two groups by military police. Next morning there came to the University Hospital a man with five bayonet wounds. This man twice reported with fair clarity that he had been a refugee in the Library building, but was not present at the tennis courts. He was picked up on the street and added to a group that did come from the courts. That evening (vaguely west or near Kuling Ssu) about 130 Japanese soldiers killed most of 500 similar captives with bayonet thrusts. The victim recovered himself to find the Japanese gone, and managed to crawl back during the night.

Also on the morning of the 27th there was brought to me a man who said that he was one of 30–40 out of the 200–300 taken away the previous evening who had escaped the death. Since the man desired help for himself and one or more companions in the registration then continuing and since I was surrounded by military police at the moment, I had to tell him the plain fact that registration was for that time and place limited to women, and that it was best not to speak further at the moment. When I endeavoured three times later to get in touch with this man or his associate, I got no response. There were other rumors that the men taken away had been killed, but they did not seem to be specific. Later I talked with one who had escaped. Confirmed.

In the course of the same day and the next (27th and 28th) I heard and checked indirect but apparently careful and circumstantial reports that part of the men taken away were bound in groups of five and ten, to be passed successively from a first room in a large house into a second room or court where there was a big fire. As each group went forward, groans and cries could be heard by the remainder, but no shots. Some twenty remaining from an original sixty broke in desperation through a back wall and made their escape by an adjoining house. Part of the detachment brought from the University were said to have been saved by the pleas of priests living in the neighborhood ([from] Wu T'ai Shan, clearly specified in all this group of reports). A similar story had been heard by M.R. early in the evening of the 26th, too soon to come from the same incident. This confusion or complexity of reports was discouraging, and several attempts at further inquiry met with little result while other duties and problems pressed upon each day.

Today (31st) two men living nearby have given a request for aid, with their story, to a trusted assistant who offers to bring them to me for confirmation if desired. One admits that he was formerly a soldier, a frankness which creates some presumption in favor of his truthfulness. The two men say that the 200–500 from the University was split up into various groups. They themselves were taken first to Wu T'ai Shan, then to the bank of the canal outside Han Hsi Men, where a machine gun was turned upon them. They fell, one of them wounded, among the dead men and smeared themselves with their blood. Thoroughly confirmed in my own interview later.

These notes are prepared in the first place for criticism and suggestion by several persons who know or may be able to find out something concerning these circumstances. It seems that the men taken from the University were taken away variously, and were probably mixed with men from other places that same evening. It should be remembered that this incident is only one of a series that had been going on for nearly two weeks, with changes on the main theme of mass murder of men accused rightly or wrongfully of being ex-soldiers. Other incidents involved more men. My special interest in this is two-fold; first because of the close connection of our property, personnel and protégés (refugees) with the unfortunate outcome; second, because of the gross treachery of terms by which the men were selected. As a general finding, I am convinced that a large majority of the men thus deceived were murdered the same night.

31 December, 1937
Not yet fully revised.

Letter to Friends (Jan. 10, 1938)[4]
Nanking, January 10, 1938*

Dear Friends:—A few hasty jottings amid rape and bayonet stabs and reckless shooting, to be sent on the first foreign boat available since the situation developed after the Japanese entry—a U.S. Navy tug engaged in salvage work on the *Panay.* Friends in Shanghai will pick this up from the Consulate-General, and will get away somehow on a foreign boat without censorship.

Things have eased a good deal since New Year within the crowded Safety Zone, largely through the departure of the main hordes of soldiers. "Restoration of discipline" is very scrappy indeed, and even the military police have raped and robbed and ignored their duties. A new turn may come at any moment, through fresh arrivals or vacillations in action. There is no policy visible. At last foreign diplomats have been allowed to re-enter (this week) which seems to indicate a desire for stabilization.

More than ten thousand unarmed persons have been killed in cold blood. Most of my trusted friends would put the figure much higher. These were Chinese soldiers who threw down their arms or surrendered after being trapped; and civilians recklessly shot and bayoneted, often without even the pretext that they were soldiers, including not a few women and children. Able German colleagues put the cases of rape at 20,000. I should say not less than 8,000 and it might be anywhere above that. On University property alone, including some of our staff families and the houses of Americans now occupied by Americans, I have details of more than 100 cases and assurance of some 300. You can scarcely imagine the anguish and terror. Girls as young as 11 and women as old as 53 have been raped on University property alone. On the Seminary compound 17 soldiers raped one woman successively in broad daylight. In fact, about one-third of the cases are in the daytime.

Practically every building in the city has been robbed repeatedly by soldiers,

---

*Preceded by notation "NOT FOR PUBLICATION:
Will try to write articles soon."

including the American, British, and German Embassies or Ambassadors' residences, and a high percentage of all foreign property. Vehicles of all sorts, food, clothing, bedding, money, watches, some rugs and pictures, miscellaneous valuables, are the main things sought. This still goes on, especially outside the Zone. There is not a store in Nanking, save the International Committee's rice shop, and a military store. Most of the shops after free-for-all breaking and pilfering were systematically stripped by gangs of soldiers working with trucks, often under the observed direction of officers, and then burned. We still have several fires a day. Many sections of houses have also been burned deliberately. We have several samples of the chemical strips used by the soldiers for this purpose, and have inspected all phases of the process.

Most of the refugees were robbed of their money and at least part of their scanty clothing and bedding and food. That was an utterly heartless performance, resulting in despair on every face for the first week or ten days. You can imagine the outlook for work and life in this city with shops and tools gone, no banks or communications as yet, some important blocks of houses burned out, everything else plundered and now open, to cold and starving people. Some 250,000 are here, almost all in the Safety Zone and fully 100,000 entirely dependent on the International Committee for food and shelter. Others are scraping along on tiny holdovers of rice and the proceeds of direct or indirect looting. Japanese supply departments are beginning to let out for monetary and political reasons a little of the rice confiscated from considerable Chinese government supplies, though the soldiers burned no small reserves. But what next? When I asked Japanese officials about post and telegraph services they said, "There is no plan." And that seems to be the case with everything economic and most things political.

The International Committee has been a great help, with a story little short of miraculous. Three Germans have done splendidly, and I'd almost wear a Nazi badge to keep fellowship with them. A Dane and three Englishmen aided a good deal in the preliminary stages, but were pulled out by their companies and governments before the Chinese retired from Nanking. So the bulk of the work has come on American missionaries, only nine of whom have been outside the confining strain of the Hospital filled with bullet and bayonet cases; and of course some of us have had varying duties and conceptions of duty. Naturally there has been considerable Chinese aid and cooperation from the beginning, and most of the detail has had to be done by and through Chinese. Yet at some stages nothing could move, not even one truck of rice, without the actual presence of a foreigner willing to stand up to a gun when necessary. We have taken some big risks and some heavy wallops (literally as well as figuratively), but have been allowed to get away with far more than the situation seems to permit. We have blocked many robberies, persuaded or bluffed many contingents into releasing groups marked for death, and pulled scores of soldiers away from rape and intended rape, besides all the general work of feeding, sheltering, negotiation, protecting, and protesting after sticking our eyes and noses into everything that has gone on. It is no wonder that a Japanese Embassy officer told us the generals were angry at having to complete their occupation under the eyes of neutral observers, claiming (ignorantly, of course) that never in the history of the world had that been true before.

Sometimes we have failed cold, but the percentage of success is still big enough to justify considerable effort. We must recognize that although in some points the relationship is far from satisfactory, we have gained a good deal by the effort of the Japanese Embassy to put cushions between the Army and foreign interests, the relative decency of their Consular Police (few and not altogether angelic), and by the fact that the main figures of the enterprise have been Germans of the Anti-Comintern Pact and Americans to be appeased after the barbarous attacks on American ships. The Japanese refused twice to send out for us a mild request for the return of American officials because of the great number of property cases and flag problems; and even with this week's improvement we are still in practical isolation even from the countryside and river front, except for the opportunities of American naval wireless through the Embassy for a limited scope of messages.

No mail since December 1, and that most tardy. Electric light in our house last night by special arrangement (seven Americans, among whom were personal links to the staff of the power plant). Japanese shot 43 of the 54 technical men on the staff, falsely accusing them of being government employees. Bombing, shelling and fires on top of that and you can imagine that utilities are slow in resumption. But insecurity of workers and their families was the main stumbling block, at that. Water depends on electric pumps, but we are beginning to get a trickle at low levels of the city. No dreams of telephone or bus or even rickshas. The Zone is about two square miles in area, not all built up. In this concentration we have had no accidental fire of notice, and practically no crime or violence except that of soldiers, until this present week's turning to looting outside the area in open buildings—especially for fuel. (No armed police.)

The University has 30,000 refugees on various parts of its property. Problems of administration are fearful, even on the low scale of living that can be maintained. We have very few indeed of regular University staff and servants, most of whom have done splendid work. There are many volunteer helpers hastily got together by the International Committee, who have come with considerable adulteration of motives. Now we must add delation and the intimidation and purchase of agents by the Japanese. I'm in three hot spots right now over this sort of business, and begin to wonder whether they are out to get me or the University into a corner. For instance, the two occurring in the past three days involve a contradiction of my report of losses for the University Middle School (thus putting me down for lying and cheating to the Japanese, and striking between me and a key man in that tremendous refugee camp); and a severe shove through the gate of a terrible military police officer when I tried to inquire about a good-spirited interpreter whom they carried off bound as for death (after he had refused to leave the Middle School camp to accept their offers or submit to their threats). Incidentally, police from that office last night took a woman from a University house and raped her thoroughly, after putting a bayonet against our man Riggs when he happened along at the wrong time. So you get a little of the flavor of our daily diet while struggling to do something for these wretched but remarkably durable and cheerful people.

The real military police numbered 17 at the time that over 50,000 soldiers were turned loose on Nanking, and for days we never saw one. Eventually, soldiers were given special armbands and called police, which means that they have special preserves for their own misdeeds, and keep out *some* of the ordinary run. We have seen men scolded for being caught by officers in the act of rape, and let go without a tie [?]; others made to salute an officer following robbery. One motorized raid on the University at the night was actually conducted by officers themselves, who pinned our watchman to the wall and raped three women refugees before carrying off one of them (another was a girl twelve years old).

Lilliath had every reason to think that I was finished or wounded on the *Panay,* for my messages about remaining in Nanking had not got through to her and the papers in Tokyo implied that all foreigners were taken on the boats. But after 48 hours of distress she read in a Japanese paper an interview that a couple of dumb-bells got out of me shortly after the Japanese entry. The paper responsed to the thanks of her friends by rushing out reporters and a photographer on the 17th, (entry on 13th, *Panay* sinking on the 12th, reported slowly). One of their men brought me a picture and a letter on New Year's Day, the latter of course dutifully read in the Japanese Embassy. Thus we were saved a good deal of prolonged concern. I have no other word since November 8th save that letter, although she wrote and wired many times by all sorts of routes and agencies. On December 17th she expected to come to Shanghai the first week of January, but I have heard nothing more. Perhaps a recent radio through the newly arrived gunboat will get some information from Shanghai.

However, I am not allowed to pass through a Nanking gate, and she would not be allowed to start west of Shanghai even if means of communication were open to her. How long this state will continue we do not know. Chinese have been greatly afraid lest Americans or all foreigners would be expelled from Nanking, but *they* seem more afraid to have us go than to have us stay—so far. Meanwhile I try to keep on friendly terms with Embassy staff and a few Japanese in semiofficial posts, and even with a few of the less violent and treacherous of the police and soldiers. But it's hard going. Four weeks today! The shells and bombs were almost comfortable, if we had only known it. And what's ahead?

If you can supply faith for battering, do so.

(Signed) Miner Searle Bates

***

Excerpts of Letters to Mr. Allison of the American Embassy (Jan. 14–June 16, 1938)[5]

American Embassy, Nanking
14 January, 1938

Dear Mr. Allison:
Last night four Japanese came into a classroom of the Middle School. Full details of their conduct there are not available, because of the serious intimidation of responsible watchers. However, they carried off one girl. The Japanese were military policeman, at least part of them from the guard assigned to the Middle School gate. They made use of Chinese cloth shoes and in part of Chinese clothes.

This situation is most serious and disgraceful, and calls for fundamental remedy. If American property is to be entered daily by Japanese military for criminal purposes, regardless of law and protests, we have come to an end of decent relations. This would be called intolerable except that we have undergone it so long!

At the very least there should be action concerning the existing police, who obviously do not give protection. We have many reasons to distrust the district office at 32 Hsiao Fen Ch'iao, so close to the Middle School, and from which the guards are assigned.

Mrs. Liu Wen-pin has information that her husband was shot in 21 Shansi Road. I just now received this report, and am unable to say more as yet. Intimidation at the Middle School, and fear of vengeful retaliation, is now so great that it is difficult to get the full facts and for people to do their ordinary work.

The writing of this letter has been interrupted by half an hour taken to expel a military policeman (soldier with *hsien ping* armband from the Special Service Organ) from 19 Hankow Road, an American house flying the American flag and with American and Japanese proclamations upon the gate. The policeman entered over the wall, and had been there about one hour pawing over the ransacked personal property of University teachers and of Dr. Brady of the University Hospital. The house is about 250 yards from the district office mentioned above.

This morning we have secured an indirect report that the Kiangtangchieh Church was burned on the night of the 15th/16th; and the direct testimony of a servant of an American missionary who returned there on the morning of the 17th, that she saw some timbers still smoking and that part of an adjoining or supplementary roof fell in before her eyes. The servant worked for Miss Brethorst, who had lived on the property until summer. The first report was given to us by an old woman employee of the church, who left it intact on the morning of the 15th, after Japanese soldiers had entered the building several times. Two of them slept in it the night of the 14th, and two others began robbery and intimidation on the morning of the 15th.

Respectfully submitted,
M. S. Bates

***

American Embassy, Nanking
15 January, 1938

Dear Mr. Allison:
Yesterday afternoon at 4:45 three Japanese military with yellow tabs on the collar insisted upon entrance to our group residence at 3 P'ing Ts'ang Hsiang, entered two motor cars, and asked for assistance or means to drive them away. Fortunately Mr. Riggs was nearby, and when summoned by servants he was gradually able to get rid of the soldiers. As usual, the soldiers showed no sign of respect for the American flag, the American proclamation, or the Japanese proclamation, all plainly visible at or on the main gate by which they entered.

Last night at six o'clock the guards from the main gate of the university were withdrawn and have not been replaced. I have no explanation or understanding of the procedure.

As yet I have no word of how the Middle School or other units fared last night.

I will appreciate a word through any of our group concerning the matters taken up yesterday and the fate of Liu Wen-pin.

Enclosed is Mr. McCallum's statement regarding the burning of the State Theatre. It is possible that we can still get something further from our friends.

Yours truly,

***

American Embassy, Nanking
24 January, 1938

Dear Mr. Allison:
It is my duty to report that during the night of the 22nd–23rd January, a Japanese soldier climbed over the high main gate of our Hsiao T'ao Yuan Compound, and got a woman whom he returned last night with a promise that he would be back again for her with rewards for another trip in prospect. The gate bears Japanese and American proclamations, and has the American flag above it. Also, the gate is diagonally opposite the office of the military police at 32 Hsiao Fen Ch'iao, about which we continually complain.

Yesterday a soldier went through the main University gate in company with a Chinese assistant, and found three women who were willing to go with them. This was a long trip to dormitories.

Other problems of approach for laborers and women we will need to discuss in detail. Likewise the results of intimidation.

***

25 January, 1938

Before there is time for a more thorough report from the University for the happenings of yesterday and 1st night, I must send you information of a visit made at eleven p.m. to our Agricultural Implements Shop at 11 Hu Chia Ts'ai Yuen, by Japanese soldiers wearing light armbands.

They threatened the storekeeper with a gun and searched him. They took away a woman, raped her, and released her two hours later. She believes that she can identify the place to which she was taken, and we will attempt to secure that information as well as any other details that may be available.

This case involves forcible and irregular entry, intimidation by military weapons, abduction, rape. It was done presumably by military police (the only other possibility, judging by the armbands, would be the less likely Special Service men).

We do not have order, security, respect for American property as marked by proclamations and flag, or respect for Japanese proclamations and Japanese orders.

P.S. After this letter was finished. I was reliably informed that the soldiers tore down the Japanese proclamation from the door.

***

25 January, 1938

Dear Mr. Allison:

Entirely aside from rape and robbery, which seem officially to be frowned upon, there are many problems arising from the frequent entry of soldiers and police-men upon American property for purposes which they seem to consider legiti-mate. I refer particularly to search, intimidation, more or less forcible removal of persons from the premises, the securing of laborers, and questionable efforts to get women.

We have tried to take a fair and reasonable attitude in these matters, and wish to act in right relations with the Japanese authorities and with yourselves, while doing what we should for the people on our property and working in our insti-tutions and our homes:

1. We do not oppose orderly and properly authorized search, if the proce-dure is satisfactory to you.
2. We do not try to protect any one from the consequences of wrongful acts, nor to interfere with the proper political and military control of the population.
3. We object to irregular, unauthorized, or forcible entry of our property, and point out that the entry of armed or uniformed men is under present conditions essentially a forcible entry.
4. We object to arbitrary interference with our employees and with legiti-mate enterprises undertaken by us on American property, including intimidation and abduction of Chinese assistants.
5. We favor and encourage *bone fide* solicitation of workers from among refugees on our property, male or female. But the experiences of the past six weeks have been so severe that the procedure must guard care-fully against intimidation, veiled as well as open. Our staff people will be glad to assist in this matter, but they must be protected against the continued abuse of military who demand that they supply a certain number of men or women with certain specifications. They can only pass on the request, and bring out any refugees who are willing to go. The presence of Japanese under existing conditions constitutes pres-sure, and they should therefore remain outside the gates. If they wish to send in their own Chinese agent, that is all right providing he goes with the understanding of a responsible staff person.
6. If abuses continue, we shall need to ask for the writing of a list with names and time of departure and return for all persons solicited from our premises. But we hope that will not be necessary.
7. We suggest that a clear and uniform agreement on these points should

be followed on all American properties after requisite consultation with the Japanese authorities; that the latter take responsibility for notifying all their military and police offices with strict instructions in this matter; that they or you supply every considerable American property with a notice in Japanese that adequately reminds and instructs those who need such provision.

8. We suggest that police inquiries be carried out either by notice to you or by the visit of a consular policeman, the latter in the familiar uniform unless he is a man well known to us, and thereby able to take responsibility for his acts upon our property or in relation to our staff. We do not see any need for removing a person from the premises for the sake of inquiry, unless it be a very serious case taken up with you in advance.

Respectfully presented,

***

25 January, 1938

In continuation of this morning's letter, I should add that Mr. Riggs and myself cautiously took the woman who was the victim of last night's abduction from 11 Hu Chia Ts'si Yuen, and gave her an unprejudiced opportunity to trace her route of the forced journey. She made a fully clear identification of the building in which she was raped three times. Also, she returned from one wrong road because it did not have districtive signs which were found readily on the right road. The total number of checks was five, and mistake seems impossible. The building was the familiar office of the military police for this district, at 38 Hsiao Fen Chi'ao.

Continual report of the doings of these enemies of decent people has brought no relief. It seems that it is high time for a clean sweep of the whole outfit, officers and men alike. Certainly it has been completely proved that this area will have no security so long as they are in it, likewise that the Japanese Embassy people have been able to do nothing by any means that may hypothetically have been employed to date.

This noon I was called to give friendly help against soldiers in No. 8 Chin Ying Chieh, a house in the same fenced area as our Sericulture Building, though not our property. Yesterday soldiers came through our property to that house and committed rape. The women were sent last night to the University for refuge. Today soldiers came again, and finding no women, angrily robbed the men and smashed windows. This case illustrates the dependence of our American welfare upon decent discipline in the city as a whole, rather than upon occasional attention of the Japanese authorities to American property as such. This particular house has been entered by soldiers five times within the past week, coming on more than one occasion through our Sericulture Compound. Only today, when their experiences seemed increasingly severe, did the occupants venture to call upon the only source of aid they have seen to exist in this part of this city.

***

20 March, 1938
American Embassy
Nanking

Dear Mr. Allison:
Yesterday between 3:30 and 4:00 p.m. a Japanese soldier committed rape upon a refugee, a nineteen-year-old girl, in our Hsiao Tao Yuan compound at 3 Hsiao Fen Ch'iao. The soldier came and went on a bicycle with yellow markings.

I arrived there about 4:05. As I approached the soldier, he brandished his bayonet and insolently said: "Want girls." The situation was uncomfortable for several minutes, but finally the soldier decided to withdraw. There was no indication of drunkenness.

Each day there are made known to us through direct personal contacts three or four cases of murder, wounding, or rape by soldiers. Many more must occur unknown to us, since regularly there are some which bring themselves to our attention. We have made no formal reports, since these cases seldom occur on our property. But they greatly concern our proper relief work, and they indicate a lack of order and discipline that has possibilities of more serious trouble. On March 11 Mr. Sone and I observed the completion to the raping of a woman by two soldiers in a hut just adjoining the wall of our own residence.

New military units have recently come into the city. Will not the Japanese authorities, for the sake of their Army's reputation, if not for humanitarian reasons, put a stop to these crimes continuing more than three months? If strict orders are not made plain to the soldiers, it is clear that the generals do not care about such crimes. If orders are made plain, it is clear that the soldiers show contempt for the generals. In any case innocent persons suffer and there is insecurity.

Respectfully yours,

***

American Embassy
Nanking
May 6, 1938

Dear Mr. Allison:
On Sunday, May 1, I was walking with Dr. Smythe in the southern part of the city, where I took some pictures of street scenes and canals. At about 4:15 we turned into Chung Hwa Lu and walked northward. I took a picture across the street, and remained carrying my small camera in my hand. There were no soldiers in sight, and neither then nor at any other time did I take a picture of anything military.

Suddenly there came from behind and passed us, several trucks with soldiers, drawing good-sized guns on mounts behind them. I did not wish to have any difficulties, and slipped my camera into my pocket. The trucks went far on to the north, and all was quiet. I took another picture across the street, perhaps three of four minutes later, a group of soldiers came running southward and blocked our way. They were followed by an officer in a car.

The officer asked me in English if I took pictures, and I said that I did, pulling out my camera to show to him, while stating that I had snapped buildings and scenes. The officer said, apparently following the statement of a soldier who pointed to me while speaking in Japanese, that I had photographed the Japanese army. I replied that I had not done so at all. The officer was very courteous, and seemed puzzled to know what to do next. I offered to give him my film so that they could see I had taken nothing military. He encouraged the idea, and I took out the film with some difficulty and loss, since the roll of 36 exposures had been only partly used and I was not accustomed to the process of removing a film before complete exposure (my camera requires complete use of the roll, then reverse winding for removal). The officer asked me for my name and address, which I gave with a card as well. He said that the pictures would be returned in about three days.

Dr. Smythe was close at hand during the whole affair, and can answer questions if need be.

This account will serve as a record for the brief conversation with you late Sunday afternoon.

Yours truly,

***

American Embassy
Nanking
May 6, 1938

Dear Mr. Allison:
Here is a written report of the interview reported orally to you this morning.

On Thursday, May 5, I went to the Japanese Consulate-General to report to Mr. Kasuya, as previously requested through a call by Mr. Takatama during my absence from home. Mr. Kasuya said that the Consulate-General wished to speak to me about "the incident of May 1." He remained in the room with Mr. Hanawa while the latter carried on the conversation.

"The military are very indignant at your taking picture. Tell us what occurred." I then gave my account, substantially as reported to you.

"That is very different from what the military have given us to understand. According to their letter, we got the idea that you were stopped by the solders while taking military pictures." This I denied as a question of face. Mr. Hanawa then said: "Well, then you were about the take a picture." I explained how the soldiers had passed well beyond us and later returned, drawing a diagram, and emphasizing that this was all apart from the actual taking of a picture. I suggested reference to the courteous officer who was on the spot, as well as to Smythe, for evidence on this point. Mr. Hanawa then looked at the letter from the military, and said it was not very specific in its suggestion that I was stopped in the process of photographing.

Mr. Hanawa remarked that I ought not to take pictures under present conditions. I said that if it was considered an offence to photograph a scene on a main street, when nothing military was involved, it would be better to give notice in advance. Certainly no foreigners realized that such was an offence, since several Japanese shops sell photographic equipment, and since Japanese are freely taking pictures everywhere.

Mr. Hanawa said: "But the military consider that foreigners in Nanking are really supporting the Hankow Government." He and Mr. Kasuya looked at each other and laughed heartily. I replied that American residents, whom I knew well, were not engaged in any sort of political or military activity, and were attending to their proper business. Such an attitude as that of the military was unfounded and irrelevant.

At one stage I was asked, with apparent sincerity, whether I had yet received back my film. It seemed that the turning over of the film and the volumary pledge to return it, were not clearly known to them.

Mr. Hanawa thanked me for my report, and said he would talk again with the military. I asked whether he wished the statement written out, and received an affirmative answer. I then wrote down the essence of what I had said, and asked Mr. Kasuya to check it over for clarity.

The entire conversation was friendly in manner. I gathered the impression that the military letter was a vague explosion, and that the Consul-General was really trying to ease things if my account gave him a basis for doing so.

The question of proper procedure, and the right of a Japanese official to summon an American for a presumed offence, I leave of course to your discretion. I wish to make a few comments only:

1. On the unfounded suspicion of a soldier, I was accused of an anti-Japanese act of military bearing, disregarding the testimony of myself, of Dr. Smythe, and of the film.
2. What I did was done publicly on a main street, where there were no sentries or other indications of restriction. I made no effort to avoid the issue, and at some little loss and inconvenience to myself I offered my film for investigation. No report has been made from the film on the central point of whether I did or did not take a military picture. My "sincerity" was met only with suspicion.
3. There was an active background of general hostility toward foreigners, expressed in unjustifiable terms, and apparently brought to bear upon this case without regard to specific evidence.
4. Not only did Mr. Takatama of the Consular Police come here to summon me, but he has declared to at least one foreigner upon his own initiative, that I was in trouble because of taking military photographs.

I resent any implication of guilt, and believe the Japanese authorities should clear it entirely with the military, for the sake of the organizations and interests with which I am connected, and for the welfare of other foreigners in the future. Commutative suspicions may result in serious trouble hereafter.

Yours respectfully,

*** *

Mr. John M. Allison
American Embassy
Nanking
June 16, 1938

Dear Mr. Allison:
We have again been receiving frequent visits from Japanese soldiers in the University Gardens at No. 1 Hankow Road, they refuse to pay any attention to the proclamations in Japanese, and bother the workmen considerably. However, they have usually been satisfied with a few flowers, and we have made no

complaint. But last night between seven and eight o'clock three soldiers gave the workmen a long, hard time, demanding valuable trees and shrubs, and under threat of the bayonet ordering them to cut down trees. At least two were partly drunk. They were seen to go into the former Ministry of Justice Building at the corner of Chung Shan and Hankow Roads.

The guard placed at the back of the same building has been searching passers-by at his own will, and removing cash from them. This practice has caused our own staff people to take a roundabout route in the course of their ordinary movements.

We are not in a position to identify individual soldiers and bring charges against them; and, indeed, that is perhaps not what the situation calls for. We do ask that soldiers in this general area, and particularly those in the building mentioned, be given sufficiently strict instructions and supervision to protect us from these abuses.

Yours respectfully,

***

Letters to Wife (Feb. 1, 13, 1938)[6]

1 Feb. 1938

Dearest:

Have not discovered milk for Mills or for two or three of us. There was a shipment of Nestle's for Lewis in unwanted substitution for the Anchor Brand he ordered months ago. But that lot seems to be a unit, and not in the form mentioned by you. Don't especially need milk, I think.

Found your old coverlet on third floor, as I hoped—but didn't dare give any encouragement without search. Don't think there can be any possibility of mistaken identity.

Don't know at all in what form you need to make plans for summer in Japan, but will approve your taking some risks financial and otherwise if you desire. I probably could not go for very long, and the outlook is very precarious for us in general as well for a particular time and place. But we have to work on possibilities (there are no probabilities worth mentioning on the positive side of human affairs in this part of the world), and it will be better for you and the boys to be out of Shanghai if you can.)

This week's struggle is mostly on the order that with seven days' notice people are to leave the large camps for their homes not later than the 4th. Also, makeshift shops in the Zone are to be torn down by force, and hints are given about others returning from private houses to their homes elsewhere in the city. For instance, a Japanese with subordinate policemen came to University to say to refugees that on the 4th gates would be sealed after eviction by soldiers, and no one would be allowed to take out bedding or other property.

Naturally we don't take this lying down, yet we cannot directly oppose their police order from military authorities. All sorts of appeals and indirections, which probably will culminate in strong requests to foreign governments to appeal to Tokyo over the heads of local officers (that's what really caused Allison incident and the risks to Riggs and me, for it makes these fellows terribly resentful), and in direct press releases much more bold than anything we have done before.

Literally thousands of women have knelt down in large groups to various ones of us, many of them swearing that they will die where they now are rather than go home to be raped and killed as so many have been raped (and some literally killed) this week in their efforts to stay in their scattered homes. I have been trying this morning to find the bodies of two young girls killed yesterday after refusing soldiers' importunities; the mother took them out from our Camp in fear that the Japanese would drive them out without bedding. Scores of other cases, usually straight rape, are flowing into our reports.

We have the possibilities of a massacre on Friday, and I don't see myself staying out of sight while soldiers use their bayonets on women and children who have trusted us. Understanding with embassies that any acts of brutality will be adequately witnessed and promptly reported. Meanwhile Japs distribute free food to those who go home, while shutting down elsewhere. Enclosed is a poster supplied to outside Zone, which we have in our living room with additions of place burned next door to posters, and so on.

13 Feb. 1938

Dearest:

Last night got your last letter (undated) with appreciated valentine, and a little other mail. Your No. 9 of 6 Dec., also clippings posted on a French boat which have gone Via Hong Kong and Hankow and back.

Here are blanks and so forth requested by Claude. His "advisors' blanks" is ambiguous, so I have tried to cover the full ground. Don't see any chance for permits for him or others at present. A possibility on the one doctor normally resident here—that's the net result of many, many efforts by us and by the diplomats. Kearney is here as a French agent for three days only, and they very soundly slapped him (in words) when they found he was American.*

---

*Handwritten note in margin: Matsumoto [?] probably slept next door. But I did not know he came to Nanking till J. diplomats answered inquiries by saying that he was here less than 2 days and was very busy. Official insulation considerable, I think. S.

Please tell Timperley, Mrs. Millican, and yourself, that the statements by the official spokesmen denying program of forceful expulsion from Safety Zone are absolutely contrary to elaborate declarations by a high officer to our camp leaders, which were then emphasized by individual visits to camps and by violent posters including details of tearing to pieces all makeshift shops on the new marts of Shanghai and Ninghai Road. However, through a combination of influences they decided not to carry out the threats for the time being. Meanwhile we had terror and great misery among large numbers of people who went home under very difficult conditions. Fully two hundred women have come back after being raped, and many others return grimly without saying anything.*

Now the long-foreseen problem appears. A woman has brought her daughter to the University today, asking for abortion to relieve the engaged girl from continuing a pregnancy resulting from Japanese rape.

Here is a program of an army band concert used as the excuse for elaborate newsreel pictures to exhibit us among Japanese officers and geisha—friendly international relations in Nanking. The music was good. Military Officers' School band brought here for Matsui's two-day visit.

Kearney has come for lunch, but I have had to spend so much time unexpectedly on Intern. Com. budget problems that I'm weak for the Lincoln service this afternoon, and can't do much apart from last licks on my utilization of reading already completed.

Received papers with satisfaction, and will hope to read them tomorrow.

Army authorities will not let us land the beans which the Navy permitted to be shipped from Shanghai, and there is much rushing about in a desperate effort to save the day. Shanghai army people suggested that they should be turned over to the Self-Government Committee instead of being consigned to foreigners. Actually we are in cahoots with some of the Self-Government men, and are arranging that they will receive the beans, give us warehouse receipts, and release them to our order only—if the J's will accept that. But they may refuse to let the beans come into the Zone in any way whatsoever, if they carry out former regulations which we have beaten only by stealth in small quantities. Meanwhile the big scrap over supplies continued.

A note from Aunt Eunice Nov. 29.**

With much love and thought,

Searle

***

---

*Handwritten note in margin: They and we are contradicting orders there.

**Handwritten note: Thanks a lot for all your efforts on the typed materials and other jobs.

Letter from Timperley (Feb. 17, 1938)[7]

c/o American Club
Shanghai, February 17th, 1938

Dear Bates,

Thank you for your letter of February 11th confirming your message to Boynton, encouraging my book project and signifying your willingness to agree to George Fitch's visit to America. In the latter connection I am enclosing a copy of a letter I have written to Hornbeck.

Yesterday I went over to Boynton's office and looked through his files of material from Nanking and elsewhere. There is so much on Nanking alone that I rather think of limiting the book to this subject and making it a kind of history under the title of "The Ordeal of Nanking" or something like that.

Subject to further study, I should like to publish the whole of the documents relating to the Nanking Safety Zone as a sort of appendix to the letters from Fitch, yourself and others. Do you think that it would be alright for me to do this or are there some of the documents which you feel it would be inadvisable to publish? If you can get more eye-witness stories they would be very useful for the first part of the book. It would assist me a great deal if you would give me a definite indication as to which of the documents, or what portions thereof, should be excluded.

I hope to arrange to provide Mrs. Bates with some stenographic assistance so as to facilitate the copying of material in Boynton's office and the collection of other material for general publicity purposes.

I am afraid I have not much in the way of general news to give you this time except perhaps the following excerpt from a letter which reached me yesterday from Wen Yuan-ning in HongKong:

"A British intelligence man in HongKong has just come back from Hankow, we had lunch together last Saturday. He tells me that the Central Government is still not cooperating with the 8th Route Army whole-heartedly. There is still a good deal of fear of the former Reds. For instance, although the Soviets have offered to give free of charge, eighty planes and some other equipment to the Red Army, the Central Government has refused the offer. And then also he tells me that the Soviet planes at Hankow are not doing much flying. But he says the spirit at Hankow is good, and although he thinks that in a military sense China is still very weak as compared with Japan, in other ways, financial and political, China is much stronger."

With best wishes,
Yours sincerely,

***

Letter to Timperley (Mar. 3, 1938)[8]

University of Nanking
Nanking, China
March 3, 1938

Dear Timperley:
Mail closes today for the "Oahu."

You surely received the radio message through Mrs. Bates, indicating our preference for your earlier proposal over that contained in your letter of February 17th. We note that this was made just after you looked over Boynton's Nanking files, and was "subject to further study." That was the result of the *first careful conference* I could arrange with Smythe and Mills. It is extraordinarily difficult to get thorough consideration for anything beyond what was to be done *today,* since the demands upon these men are so manifold.

Here are some of our thoughts. For purpose of impressing a distant public with the brutality of warfare waged as this one has been waged, it seems much more effective to have a base wider than that of one city. It is so easy for any one at a distance to feel that after all Nanking was exceptional—political hatred centered on that name, accidents of time and personnel, and so on. But if similar stories come over a period of months from Shanghai, Sungkiang, Soochow, Wusih, Huchow, Hangchow, the total effect is far more massive and convincing.

Moreover anxiety about personal or institutional retaliation is multiplied if you come to down to one city, with accounts based rather largely on our documents. That means pretty much Smythe as Secretary, Mills as Vice-Chairman (now really Chairman since Rabe has gone), and myself as the most strenuous reporter from the University. I wonder if you realize the venom with which the Japanese officers and even the diplomats now regard the Committee. They continually press the Self-Government to demand that they shall not in any way let us be connected with this or that enterprise (an interesting set-off to their ridiculous formula of "cooperation" which they publicly require from us; actually we do cooperate just as much the Self-Government Committee dares to risk under subterfuges and downright lying to the Japanese). The chief officer of the Embassy formally referred to me as "anti-Japanese"; and previously asked others if I were "nervous"—much to their amusement. The latter term came after I argued with him one afternoon in refusing to accept his patient formula; the military are doing all in their power to remedy the situation, and therefore there is no grounds for complaint. He thought I was excited or afraid, because I insisted on the facts of disorder and danger. Some of the foreign group here have continually besought me (and to a lesser extent Smythe and Mills)—Fitch also when he was here—to cease the thorough reporting and protesting and indirect publicity, lest all missionaries be excluded from Nanking. This is put in here merely to suggest that for a while there is some reason to be cautious. Fitch and I were formally cited to the Ambassador, who defended us at least in a code radio to Allison (all this to be kept under your hat, for I really do not know its significance). There has been a steady stream of lying charges against the University in the Sin Shun Pao, the propagandist organ widely distributed in Shanghai and East China generally. I want to stand to my guns, and yet not damage the future of the University and of mission interests generally by any error of judgment or method. I've spoken for myself simply because my case in more "personalized" than that of others. But there is not a day passing without some dig at the International Committee by some Japanese. I enclose a translation of a Domei item that illustrates fairly their whole attitude, not stated extremely in this particular instance. Please note carefully the implication of exclusiveness which marks everything they do here, with little regard to truth in concrete matters, as you are well aware.

Also, our group here is inclined to think that the story of Japanese methods and the story of the International Committee are two different things, not necessarily benefited by combination. The former would seem to be by far the more important for the present. No doubt you can arrange now some contacts for the Soochow-Hanghow regions which will get you stories from there. Smythe's full "case-list" now reaches 460 items, and will shortly be available in complete form for you in Shanghai. We can make some supplements to it, and elaborate some stories if you wish. Also, Wuhu information should be available through Dr. Brown, Mr. Gale, and others. Yangchow likewise, I believe, and possibly Chinkiang.

As for the Safety Zone, Mills has the idea of a small book, say a hundred pages. But neither he nor others of us would feel that the document could be fully published in the near future without imperilling necessary relief work in this region and endangering the possibilities of foreign service in say Hankow. I also have thought of an article for International Conciliation (or some other medium if you suggest) which might encourage minds in the west to think of the whole problem of civilian survival in the coming wars. This experience cannot be transferred, but it might encourage others to look for possibilities in their particular situations. These are not mentioned to inhibit you, but to seek your counsel.

Indeed, the main set is favourable for you to employ any facts you want from our material, trusting your purpose and methods and experience, and greatly interested in how you do it.

Probably others have called to your attention the small error in your interesting and useful letter to Hornbeck of February 16th. Magee is an American. Unfortunately there was no Britisher in the city until your rather cautious and subdued diplomats arrived. We are, however, appreciative of Prideaux-Brune's and Jeffrey's good qualities and their aid in several matters. Williams is now a passable aid to Jeffrey, while P.B. has left for Home.

I enclose some economic notes requested by Allison for the Ambassador. They assume knowledge of the general destruction and stoppage. Also plans of two inquiries which are being launched this week under fearsome cover of the Self-Government Committee. Smythe set up the agricultural one with our Chinese, and I am starting the city show with plenty of consultation. We want a sound basis for our relief policy and will try to boost the Self-Government Committee at the same time—a feeble and corrupt lot, but approachable and with some elements of good intentions. Probably can send you soon a memo of information desired by Allison on them and their work.

With hearty good wishes,
Searle Bates

P.S.—These messages all go to and from Hankow, Nanking, Shanghai, Peiping, Washington, Tokyo. So I don't know the origin or primary destination of the citation and of Johnson's response.

***

Letter to Friends (Apr. 12, 1938)[9]

Shanghai
April 12, 1938

Dear Friends:
This note is written from Shanghai. After long effort I was able to secure military passes for a visit of ten days on behalf of the International Relief Committee and other organizational enterprises as well as for family reasons.

Without wishing to frighten you I desire to give you information in advance that will prepare you for possible shocks in the summer. It may be that the problem here presented will not result in serious consequences, but we have had to face that possibility.

There is in active preparation for publication in England and America a book by Mr. H. J. Timperley, experienced correspondent of the *Manchester Guardian,* which will probably be entitled "The Japanese Terror in China." Mr. Timperley is a journalist of the highest character who has been in close touch with Christian leaders in Peiping and in Shanghai over a long period of years. He has secured from the relief groups here a large body of documents and letters which indicate the actual character of the warfare carried on in China. That material is presented in a fair and essentially constructive way.

Although not legally responsible for this enterprise I have been connected with it from the first, have checked over the plan and various phases of its development, and have also examined a final draft of the complete manuscript. Moreover, the book uses a statement which I prepared on the 15th of December to be utilized by the various correspondents living Nanking on that date. It also includes my letter of January 10th describing in general terms the terror of the preceding weeks in Nanking. The appendices contain many letters to the Japanese Embassy during December. Although my name is not used it will be perfectly obvious to the Japanese officials in Nanking and Shanghai, if not in Tokyo, that these documents are from my hands. Dr. Smythe will be less critically involved through his signature upon various documents and case reports coming from the office of the Secretary of the International Committee.

The book is not geographically limited in scope and contains a fair amount of material from other cities and regions in China. However, the Nanking items have the most bite in them because of the concentrated cruelty in our city. It is therefore probable that the Japanese authorities will be acutely resentful toward the small group of missionaries in Nanking, and perhaps toward me in particular. Mr. George Fitch will also be seriously involved because of the use of his diary, and Mr. John Magee because of the employment of some of his pictures.

We originally gave our approval to the production of a book along these lines with the expectation that our material would be drawn upon for facts, but would not appear in recognizable units. However, Mr. Timperley and his consultants in Shanghai found themselves drawn more and more toward the use of entire documents or considerable selections from them. They desired the directness and authenticity of first hand materials, and likewise they were critically pushed for time by their friends in London and in New York who were their agents in approaching publishers. No one of us would have done the whole thing in exactly the way that has actually been adopted. However, all the missionaries concerned in the Nanking material and a considerable group of mission leaders in Shanghai have carefully considered the whole problem and are convinced that it is right and desirable to go ahead with publication.

We feel that there is a certain moral necessity to make known the terrible facts in a constructive way. Only ourselves or people working with us can do that. Others are gaining access to the materials more and more freely by indirect means and are bringing them out in semi-commercial form. On the one hand this will perhaps lessen the intensity of the Japanese attacks upon us while at the same time it impels us to seek a comprehensive and good-spirited account of the experiences of the Chinese people. I need not discuss all the general principles and issues involved which you can imagine or think out for yourselves.

It is possible that there may be retaliatory restriction upon individuals or upon groups of missionaries. We do not believe however that such action is a certainty. Perhaps it is not even a probability. Most of the fears of the past year have never become realities in the form that we anticipated. On the positive side we hope definitely to exercise some deterrent restraint upon the management of the Japanese forces in other parts of China during the remainder of the struggle. Moreover, the people of the rest of China, of the Orient, and of the other parts of the world have a right to know this significant chapter in the experience of our times. The book will be translated into several languages, and after that translation has been paid for all profits will go into the International Relief Fund.

I am sorry to inflict such a lengthy statement upon you, but it may be of value to you in considering other problems of publicity than the present one. Moreover if serious difficulties do arise for some of us you will understand the background and the consideration that we have given to the issues. I do not feel that timidity as such has accomplished anything whatsoever in the world that we confront. Let us do what we consider to be our duty. Do it in a good spirit and accept the consequences likewise.

Sincerely yours,

MSB: EOH

P.S. It is expected that the book will be published in London by Gollancz in June, and somewhat later in America by a publisher not yet known to me.

***

Letter to Japanese Consulate-General (May 11, 1938)[10]

Mr. Y. Hanawa
Japanese Consulate-General, Nanking

Dear Mr. Hanawa:
Your friendly attitude the other day in the question of taking pictures was much appreciated. I have therefore wished to allow time for the matter to be adjusted. But now ten days have gone by since the original problem arose, and six since your talk with me. It is highly unsatisfactory to leave things as they are.

In the first place, the officer who spoke to me in English accepted my offer to let him take the film for evidence, and he voluntarily promised to return it to me in three days. In western countries there is a tradition that "an officer's word is as good as his bond." I believe this Japanese officer was also sincere and honorable in his promise. Who then has prevented the return of the film?

Secondly, I was wrongly accused of photographing the Japanese army. Actually, neither on that occasion nor on any other have I photographed anything of military significance. The evidence of myself, of Dr. Smythe, and of my film seems to be disregarded, and the unfounded suspicion of a soldier was accepted as the basis of charge against me. This position ought to be fairly and honorably cleared up.

Moreover, you informed me that the military consider the foreigners in Nanking to be supporters of the Hankow Government, suggesting that this view had some bearing upon the suspicion of military photography. I assure you that neither I nor my foreign friends are engaged in military or political activity. From long residence in Nanking I know thoroughly the faults as well as the good points of the Kuomintang rule, and actually I had many difficulties with the Chinese military and civil authorities in December while helping to organize the Safety Zone and to protect American property in various places.

On the other side, difficulties with the Japanese army have been only those forced upon me by cases of disorder, which we have long hoped are coming to an end. Indeed, I encouraged many friends, Chinese and others, to remain in Nanking for useful work of all kinds, saying that from the past record and reputation of the Japanese army we should expect stern order and discipline from the time of its entry. The attitude of other foreigners has been similar to mine. We object equally to wrongful and injurious acts by any soldiers or officials or civilians, whether Chinese or Japanese or American or German. We respect good work by men of any nationality. We have not taken a position of supporters of one government against another. It is therefore unjust for the military to act toward me or toward other neutrals as if we were agents of the Hankow Government or persons generally hostile to Japan. I will be hostile to Japan only if the military make me so.

You as a diplomatic officer have the opportunity to reduce friction between Japanese and foreign interests by assisting the military to understand the real position of foreigners in Nanking. I have therefore written in a frank and friendly spirit, responding to the commendable attitude which you showed in the recent conversation in your office.

Your respectfully,
M. S. B.

***

Open Letter on the Narcotic Problem in Nanking (Nov. 22, 1938)[11]

(Sent to certain Japanese Friends and published in *China Press,* and *Shanghai Evening Post* and *Mercury.* Omitting concrete details of the retailing system and taxes.)

To Japanese and Chinese who care for the welfare of the people of the Nanking Area:

As an old resident of Nanking long observant of the progress and well-being of its people, I am interested to learn this week of a movement in the "Legislative Yuan of the Reformed Government" looking toward a revision of policy in the supply of narcotics. Permit me to use this opportunity to make an appeal for recognition of the great evil now in process, and for the prompt efforts of men of high character to secure not merely some small adjustment, but a significant reversal of system.

At various times during the past few months, I have mentioned to Japanese friends, and to other visitors from outside Nanking, that the narcotic problem was becoming serious. Several of them said they had not heard of it, and asked for information.

I began to observe more closely, and in the rapid developments of the current month become convinced that the attention of public spirited persons ought to be drawn to the matter at once, if the people of this city and surrounding districts are to be saved from irreparable harm.

The information here presented comes from these sources:

a. The direct observation of myself and reliable friends.
b. Regulations of the Tupan's Office (governing the Nanking Area) Establishing the Opium Suppression Bureau; and By-Laws of the Opium Supply Establishments and for Retail Stores; "Provisional Regulations for Special Licenses and Sales in Smoking Dens"; Application Blanks for the Registration of Domestic Smokers (covering daily issue of opium with taxes.)
c. Statements from dealers and officials secured of course through personal connections.

Report on the Narcotic Trade in Nanking

1. Sharp Reversal of Conditions

The present generation has not known large supply and consumption of opium in Nanking, nor open sale in a way to attract the poor and ignorant.

Particularly during the last five years has the use of opium been slight, due to fairly consistent and cumulative government pressure against the trade, plus the result of educational effort during the past thirty years. Heroin was practically unknown.

But the changes of the year 1938 have brought an evil revolution. Today opium and heroin are abundantly supplied by the public authorities or by those who enjoy their favor and protection. Tens of thousands of persons have become addicts, including children and numerous young people of both sexes. Thousands are engaged in the business. A new generation is beginning with the weight of ruling authority thrown in favor of narcotics. Some officials are notorious and open consumers. Public revenues are being built upon the ruin of human bodies and spirits.

Licensed dens in the public system advertise upon the streets that their products increase the health and vigor of those who use them; and the one newspaper in Nanking, official in character, invites citizens to places of doom.

2. The Nature of the Trade

A. Opium

1. The Public System.
For administrative purposes in general Nanking City (including Hsiakwan) is divided into five districts. Each district is supposed to have one Opium Supply Establishment (T'u Kao Hang) authorized to sell up to 750 ounces per day. Actually the Opium Suppression Bureau is issuing opium directly to the subordinate sale agencies now to be described.

Each district may have five retail stores (T'u Kao Tien) say the basic Regulations. They are taxed in three grades presumably according to the amount of business they do, at $4,200, $2,840, or $1,420 per quarter. Each district was supposed to have ten Smoking Dens (Shou Hsi So), of which forty odd were doing business as of November 15.

They are taxed according to the number of lamps employed; nine lamps at $150, six lamps $100 and three lamps at $50. But while this report is being written the official Regulations have been changed to permit in each of the five municipal districts ten Retail Stores and thirty Smoking Dens. I observed several opening for the first time on November 19. One friend has secured at my request the names and addresses of 52 stores and Dens which he found in one day in the southern half of the Walled City, only.

2. Observations on the Public System.
The Opium Suppression Bureau is under the Municipal Finance Office of the

Tupan's Administration. Recently there has been some police pressure, associated with interests in fines, upon users of narcotics other than opium. The Bureau's Regulations and By-Laws are concerned mainly with bringing all private trade and consumption into the revenue net.

There is vague and kindly mention of a possible institution for breaking the narcotic habit; but more specific are the measures to control expected crookedness within the system, and to ensure requisite secrecy in this "public" enterprise. The broad social view of the Opium Suppression bureau is indicated by the arrangements for supplying hotels and brothels with special licenses and even by the private licenses (for a seven-day limit, which is surely generous) to cover marriages, funerals and social entertaining.

3. Private Trade, Sources of Opium Supply, Price, Volume of Business.
From examining the official scheme, one might think that only 75 (now 200) establishments would be dealing in opium in Nanking. But one must recall the large number of hotels and brothels of all sizes and names, plus the fact that a host of domestic lamps, licensed and unlicensed are doing more than domestic duty. One very small neighborhood, near my home, and not in a thickly populated portion of the city, is found to have fourteen obvious centers of distribution and consumption.

Within the past few days, one organization of Japanese and Korean "hostesses" and ronin brought in 80 cases of opium. An important dealer in the public system says that Japanese agents a fortnight ago delivered here over 400 cases of Iran opium; but this shipment seems to have had some relation to the Opium Suppression Bureau, and therefore should not be criticized. However, there is abundant testimony that the major opium supplies come from Dairen through Shanghai.

The daily sales under the hands of the proper officials are in principle limited to 6,000 ounces. Not a few of the sales go out to the surrounding country. Actual totals must be much greater than the legal limitations. But 6,000 ounces alone represent $66,000 per day wholesale, or $2,000,000 per month.

B. Heroin

Destructive and alarming as is the trade in opium, it is overshadowed in viciousness, perhaps roughly equalled in monetary volume, and probably surpassed in number of persons affected by the totally new development of heroin.

Heroin is more convenient to take and a very small quantity is effective. It is commonly said that at the present prices a moderate addict's daily use on a low plane costs fifty cents to one dollar in opium but only thirty or forty cents in heroin. (Portions of opium or lamp privileges in the official Smoking Dens run from 20 cents to $5, according to quantity, quality and the style of the establishment.)

A sensible private estimate is that 50,000 persons, one-eighth of the Nanking population, are now users of heroin. Others put it higher. The trade in heroin is private, widely scattered in retail peddling and conducted through agents who work under a hierarchy of intimates. One friend knows of 72 places of sale.

It is commonly reported that the Special Service Department of the Japanese Army has close and protective relations with the semi-organized trade in heroin. An agent of considerable standing says that the Special Service Department has recorded monthly sales above $3,000,000 in the area of which Nanking is a center.

There is general testimony that a good deal of the wholesale trade is carried on by Japanese firms which outwardly deal in tinned goods or medicines, but handle heroin through rooms in the rear.

C. Conclusion

One cannot imagine a shorter sight and narrower greed than that which exploits the war-time ruin of a relatively decent society to draw the hungry and sick and hopeless down the false road that leads only to destruction. In most cases the first use of narcotics is through deception or lack of comprehension of the real nature of the step taken.

To make cheap supplies universally available, and to increase their use by advertising and the building up of a vast public and private financial interest in the extension of sales, is a policy based either upon stupidity or upon inhuman greed. Do either Chinese or Japanese interests require for the future a drugged people, short-lived and infecund, physically indolent and morally irresponsible? That is the kind of people who are being developed in the Nanking Area today by the Opium suppression Bureau and by the heroin merchants of all types.

Here is a flat test of the statesmanship and the character of the Reformed Government and its sponsors. No Chinese of real worth will trust or assist an administration which ruins society before his eyes. And conversely, if the new administration wants the support of the better elements of the population, the first step to secure it is an instant and resolute stoppage of the flood of narcotics.

These words are written not as supercilious advice to officials who presumably understand what they are doing, but to emphasize the original appeal to Japanese and Chinese friends who are not yet aware of the urgency of the problem in the hope that they may exert constructive influence at once.

All educated persons and even some who are illiterate can distinguish between deceptive words and the reality of a policy. The present hypocrisy only increases the contempt of decent persons for the trade.

While scores of newly licensed dens are openly advertising all sorts of benefits for twenty cents and forty cents, the very Regulations that provide for getting extra revenue, even from the domestic smoker, piously drone: "All users of opium who because of sickness or of age cannot break the habit must register."

The official reason for the provision of public dens is that of compassion for the hardships of poor laborers, expressed more than once in the documents. Another justification for the easy and cheap supply is to protect the public from exploitation by private trade (which does not pay assessments to the right office). Then there is the humane desire to save the people from "the powerful poisons with a life-long clutch from which no escape is possible," meaning, of course, the heroin now being distributed in every street even among children (but the heroin profits go to another gang).

Finally, what do legitimate economic interests, Chinese and Japanese, think of a policy that takes away from the impoverished population of this region a minimum of $5,000,000 monthly, reducing their buying power for decent goods and their ability to do productive labor of any kind?

Surely there are men who will reverse the present judgment that the first and greatest achievement of Sino-Japanese co-operation in this important region is the poisoning of the common people. Is "lasting peace in the Far East" the deadly dream of an opium den?

If I, as a foreign guest and friend, have spoken badly, let Chinese and Japanese come forward to speak more effectively for the welfare of the plain persons who do most of the productive work. But let none waste breath or ink in declaring that the purpose of the Opium Suppression Bureau is misunderstood.

M. S. Bates
Nanking, November 22, 1938

***

Letter to Friends (Nov. 29, 1938)[12]

Lloyd Triestino SS *Conte Verde*
Nearing Hong Kong en route to Madras
November 29, 1938

Dear Friends:
Most of you received our letters of just a year ago and of January 10, but nothing since. This report will go by China Clipper to San Francisco, while I continue toward the International Missionary Conference, which meets December

13–30. After two additional weeks in India, I will return to Shanghai, arriving about January 19; and will go to Nanking immediately if I get the requisite military pass.

The criminal misery of Nanking has at last become general knowledge, though there are few who grasp its despairing total. Timperley's book, *What War Means: The Japanese Terror in China,* is straight stuff. Unfortunately there are some people who shrink from confronting the evil of the present world, by refusing to believe what they term "atrocity stories." The first necessity of work for peace or for any other improvement, is to face the facts honestly. Then the interpretation of the facts, the formulation of program, and the going forth to action, are further steps—all subject to modification as new facts require. Certain friends take a position, and then dismiss or arrange facts in defense of the position, which puts them in illusory ether.

Our final estimate of the number of civilians killed in Nanking was 12,000, nine-tenths of them apart from military operations, and including many women, children, and aged men. That figure is in the ratio of one to every four families then in the city. We have specific reports from resident families, given with some reluctance and concealment because retaliation was feared, of one member in every five families killed, injured, or taken away not to return. More than 30,000 military prisoners who had abandoned their arms, were mercilessly butchered, most of them tied in long lines and machine-gunned on the river-bank. Many thousands of women were raped (8,000 was a careful figure set early in the process, and the most conservative given by any observer).

Immediately outside the wall, there was extensive burning by the Chinese army in preparing its poor defense. Within the wall, the buildings and their contents were practically intact at the time of transfer; but during a period of six weeks, beginning one week after entry, the Japanese military burned several thousand buildings (over 4,000 street numbers). These all belonged to the ordinary citizens whom they have come to "liberate," and none to the Government or Party whom they execrate. For the whole city, 24 per cent of the buildings were burned. An additional 63 per cent suffered serious looting, primarily by soldiers, which stripped almost all the people of their unburned tools, stocks, clothing, even food. The foregoing figures are from the Nanking International Relief Committee's survey (printed as "War Damage in the Nanking Area,") which inspected every one of the 40,000 house numbers in the city and investigated in detail every tenth one. The losses were the more shameful because less than two per cent were incurred by actual military operations.

Nor was the fearful injury limited to Nanking. The investigations directed by our trained sociologist, Dr. Lewis Smythe, to estimate the remaining resources and the relative needs for various types of relief, found that in a wide area of country 40 per cent of farm buildings had been burned, nearly half the implements and animals lost, and one resident in every seven families killed. The brutal destruction of villages still continues spasmodically but on a considerable scale, often because infuriated farmers have attacked a small patrol that seized their women, or because local people have been caught between the conflicting demands of guerillas and Japanese for supplies and labor.

Can you think what life was like among defenseless people in long periods of such terror and danger, when the appearance of a soldier in the street, or a rap at the door, or a false report by disreputable police hirelings, meant immediate risk to person and almost certain loss of humble possessions? Three weeks were intensely bad, and not until June did gradual easing off end in reasonable security of life and limb. There is still confiscation of land and buildings at will: more than 20 per cent of the real property in Nanking has been taken by the military, by their Chinese servants of varying titles, and by the 3,000 Japanese civilians and 302 Japanese shops now set up in the city in the best buildings that escaped burning. I do not know of one case of free commercial transfer; and among scores of instances with which I am familiar, the only actual compensation was $5 per family given to some thousands of persons in a large area seized entire. That is "economic cooperation," about which diplomats make after-dinner speeches. One side provides the property and labor; the other, gun in hand, takes control and profits with only nominal investment aside from the gun. In our experience it works just the same from electric power plant to corner store and private residence. Attila was a simple greenhorn.

Politics as such are not our business, but we are deeply concerned with the life and welfare of the people of our city. A year's work on relief enterprises, with especial attention since June to investigation and observation of economic conditions (losses and injuries, crops, village situations, fuel, clothing and bedding, employment), gives me a large body of chill facts and a continual flush of indignation that plain folks should have to suffer so deeply to no good purpose. In the winter and through May, I did my part in the International Committee's general work, but was required to give a good deal of attention to problems of personnel and property in the University's extensive plant, which received 30,000 refugees at one time and kept an average of over 15,000 till late spring.

This autumn we (University) are trying out the needs and the possibilities of educational service by running on various sites a good-sized primary school, a training course for young farmers, a few classes in languages and mathematics for stranded boys of junior middle school grade, and a little work for illiterates. So far we have only visits from military police, but no interference. Limitations of staff and funds, with the expectation that by spring the "Reformed Government" will have to show to their masters some results of "the new education," require us to be cautious about enlargement (though the nerveless municipal system and the total of Christian schools provide for only a fraction of the children and young people who should be receiving some training).

But I have wandered from relief, in the mixed duties common to most days. The International Committee in December of last year provided 250,000 people with housing (in highly relative security), including 70,000 in 25 refugee camps. It was necessary to supply food for many of the latter, even until May, though numbers had gradually dwindled with partial restoration of order. $345,000 in Chinese currency has been expended to date, mainly in food (exchange was $3.40 to the American dollar until spring but now is more than six to one). Cash relief, conduct of the camps, work relief projects, clothing, sanitary and health work, and small loans for starting trade or production, have been the other chief forms of aid.

Nearly $185,000 is now in hand in cash and food for the winter's work, which confronts a people with absolutely no reserves, private or public. That sounds like a lot of money. But even in terms of the low-valued Chinese currency, it is about one dollar per person for the abject poor in Nanking City alone. It will feed that group for about two weeks on cereal alone; or buy them each one of the cheapest winter garments of cotton. The larger part of the Committee's resources came from rice and money turned over by the old Municipal Government, and from a grant by the National Government's Relief Committee in May, there have also been useful contributions from various American organizations, from a British relief fund, and from a group of Chinese bankers and other old residents of Nanking now in Shanghai. The Committee has maintained high standards of investigation of applicants for relief, and has passed its accounts through well-known auditors in Shanghai.

This bare account gives some idea of the scale and difficulty of the International Committee's responsibilities. The romance of the local struggle to carry on relief, which has literally cost life and blood and imprisonment and tears; the story of the cooperation of German Nazis and British businessmen with us American missionaries who have had to do more than our national share; the part of Mohammedans, Buddhists, and Catholics in our inner groups; the remarkable qualities shown by many of our hastily gathered Chinese staff; the actual achievement in the face of guns and of a still potent distrust expressed in repeated "dissolutions" and orders to Chinese to have nothing to do with us: All these require more space and skill than are now at your service.

Nanking's population has now come up to practically 400,000 (as compared with 250,000 in the Safety Zone period and just 1,000,000 before the war). Recent additions are largely refugees from the country, some of whom went there from the city in search of safety, but have now used or been deprived of all their money (and often of their clothes) in the precarious hinterland of guerillas and punitive raids. There has been a remarkable effort by farmers, small merchants, and some makers of household necessities, to reestablish themselves.

Yet even now we can scarcely tell how half the people keep alive, and are undertaking a specific investigation of occupation and income in order to find out.

There is a good deal of common labor in the military supply and transport services, and a socially unhealthy provision for soldiers' requirements of all sorts. But I am long past blaming a coolie for serving his country's enemy in order to feed his crying children, or a girl from doing anything to avoid starvation, if they don't bring too much direct injury to others (such as joining in armed extortion rackets, or spreading heroin and opium). For a good deal of comfortable morality can hardly stand against the basic needs of life itself, and the war has already brought down scores of millions of us in economic and social ruin. Incidentally, we now have large open brothels, advertising in the official newspaper; and an entire new class of brazen girls as waitresses in restaurants, a complete revolution in manners for Nanking.

One of the grim features of life for an American pacifist in Nanking is the experience of seeing squadrons of bombing planes through hundreds of successive days, some with American equipment and almost all fed with American gasoline. In the river an extensive navy propelled with American oil; on the roads hundreds of military trucks from General Motors and other American markers. Plus the realization that many of his pacifist friends in America are condemning the weaker nations of the world to destruction by resolutely opposing international cooperation in the first weak steps toward world government, and by opposing withdrawal from economic partnership with aggressors, lest Al-Capone nations should be displeased. Does good will have any practical meaning toward other than Great Powers? The "haves" should make economic adjustments for the benefit of all rather than toss their weaker neighbors to armed greed.

This is not much of a personal or Christmas letter. But we've been thoroughly lost in the struggle around us, family life included. Lilliath was able to get back from Japan with Bobby in late January, and remained in the Shanghai American School till June, when she returned to Lake Nojiri to make a decent summer for the boys. I got down to Shanghai on a military boat for ten days of relief business in April, and was with the family off and on during August, utilizing many opportunities in the visit to Japan for exchange of information with old friends, Japanese and foreign alike. Lilliath and Bobby came to Shanghai and Nanking at the end of September, and we have fared well enough in our own house, for our losses were not crippling. Fortunately another one of Nanking's six foreign children, David McCallum, is also a boy and ten years old and in the fifth grade. So he and Bobby conduct the "MacBay Academy," employing two mothers, one Chinese teacher, two pups, and a pair of strawberry finches from Singapore (just the size of humming-birds) with an occasional hour from stern fathers.

Meanwhile Morton had such important advantages in the Canadian Academy at Kobe (sufficient address for him), that despite all misgivings we left him there a second year to finish the seventh-eighth grade combination. At the times of the Russian war scare in August and the Czechoslovakian crisis in September there were heavy strains on our faith and judgment. But Shanghai or Nanking might easily be worse than Kobe, we could always think in consolation. I will use this opportunity of writing a second Christmas letter alone, to state my appreciation of Lilliath's cheerful cooperation in the many undomestic situations that the war has brought. She has played the game finely, which is a big help. Last spring she did lots of running and office work for the University and the Nanking Relief Committee in the improvised Shanghai establishment.

There are a hundred more things pressing to be said. But this dose is heavy enough, and I am tempted to add a recent summary of the war situation in China as a whole, with cuttings from an Open Letter containing a report on narcotics in Nanking. The past year and a half don't leave to an analytical mind much remainder from certain conventional beliefs in a benign providence, and I can see little indication of God in the tremendous wave of cruelty and greed that has engulfed a big piece of our world. Yet the worth of human character, and the need of men for the life and vision that Jesus gave, have never loomed so great. The invigoration of fighting unarmed for the lives of persons in pressing danger, and the thrill of standing for truth and humanity when you know that any moment you may be wiped out by unregarding force—maybe that's life eternal, if we lose our slavery to time. There is a new sense of freedom to go ahead according to the light that's given, take whatever comes. If life stopped now, it still would have been worth while, and the investment of others in nurture and opportunity, which used to weigh heavily, would not have been lost. So far an open procedure in the immediate struggle, and an attempt to keep clear of narrow partisanship, have been rewarded by continuance. But one vindictive military policeman, one narrow reader of suspicious clippings, can radically tear out a lifetime's work.

"Peace on Earth, good will to men." But can the peace before us be a peace of good will? Every spiritual concept seems drawn irresistibly to the test in this awful situation, though I know it shouldn't be misplaced or twisted. "Be not overcome of evil," is a call right to the heart. "Overcome evil with good," requires a more powerful "good" than is visible to most eyes, but there's no doubt of its being the right way to work. So that will have to do for faith this Christmas. There is not much hope in the ordinary sense, but there's a good deal of love, some of it found in unexpectedly rough and desperate places.

Searle Bates

***

Letter to Friends Abroad (Nov. 28, 1939)[13]

University of Nanking, Nanking
(or, 21 Kankow Road)
November 28, 1939

Dear Friends abroad:

"Have you had any dangerous thoughts during the past year?" With this question a gendarme greeted a missionary traveling from one part of the Japanese Empire to another. How should we answer the gendarme's question under the conditions that have actually come upon us? That, in little, is the problem of our lives today.

Our last letter was written as Searle was on his way to the International Missionary Conference at Madras. He was a member of the China Delegation, and worked particularly in the section on The Church and International Order, as well as on various problems connected with the Far East. He was strongly moved by the Christian advance represented in the splendid delegation from Africa; by the qualities shown in the contributions of individuals like Bishop Azarian of India, Professor Kraemer of Leiden, Dr. Laubach of the Philippines, Secretary Visser t' Hooft (Netherlands) of the nascent World Council of Churches; by the frequent divergence in outlook between the "eschatological Christianity" so earnestly maintained among many German or other continental Christians, and the "striving toward the Kingdom" so important to Americans, Chinese, and others.

The meaning of the Conference was enhanced by the weeks of close association in travel with the excellent Chinese delegates, who impressed all (including their Japanese brethren) with their steadiness of spirit as they came from a struggling, grievously damaged country. Brief stops in Hongkong, Singapore, and Colombo were instructive in their contacts with well-informed friends or in their glimpses of Christian groups working within unfamiliar societies. India renewed the interests of twenty-two years ago through observed change and comparison, and enlarged them during two crowded weeks in fresh territory: Delhi, Agra, Allahabad (with a day in Nehru's home) and Benares; stations of the United Christian Missionary Society in the Central Provinces; and the historic-religious centers of the South, Trichinopoly and Madura, Indians were intensely interested in China, and sympathetic with Chinese sufferings.

Now let's jump a few months in this mixture of personal and outer worlds. Lilliath again took Bobby to Japan in order to pick up Morton in Kobe when his dormitory closed, and to get the benefit of a Lake Nojiri summer. Searle was not able to leave Nanking for long, but once more appreciated the opportunity for association with old friends at Tokyo and other points. He still maintains cordial relations with many Japanese, though it's hard to combine a calm and concilliatory manner with truthful facing of the tremendous evil of the war.

The peculiar problems brought by the semi-political extension of Japanese religious activity to China have called for special study and conference. Japanese Christians sent here must of course have the approval or even the backing of the Army; and as individuals the range all the way from cautiously contrite humanitarians to bald agents of military conquest. The authorities push Japanese religionists to persuade Chinese of the benevolent program of their country, and to rival or to divert to their benefit the cordial spirit now existing between the Chinese and western missionaries. How should missionaries and Chinese pastors meet the overtures made to them in the name of peace and cooperation? These questions must be answered before God, and also in the hearing of the military police. It is not easy to serve two masters.

We did not have Morton venture upon high school work in Kobe, even though the immediate environment and relationships were excellent, for transfer from the Canadian program should be made now if at all; and it is hardly to be conceived that we should be able and willing to have him remain there for three or four more years. Morton has made the necessary social adjustments in the Shanghai American School (10, Avenue Petain), and is already a First-Class Scout and a Patrol Leader, if not on top in classes or in physical skills. Bobby is now doing six-grade work at home, and is getting along without American playmates of his own age, by making the most of Chinese acquaintances, parents, birds, and neighbors' dogs. Next year he will be twelve and eligible for boarding in Shanghai if he gains physically. The old folks are in satisfactory general health, though Lilliath has picked up unpleasant bacteria at times. She is doing some teaching and helping with various activities aside from home and Bobby.

The University is somewhat dispersed in Szechuan, though the main group are at Chengtu. They have to meet serious problems of crowding and of cooperation as one among several institutions generously received by the West China Union University; but they are carrying on many services of public value. At Nanking remain Searle and Dr. Steward (botanist), with three Chinese of high rank and a hundred assistants and laborers. Maintenance and emergency services are the twin *motifs*. Four main sets of buildings within the city, besides many extras and residences; six farms outside the city; gardens, nurseries, and forest plots. Three subordinate schools are conducted; a large primary school, a small middle school for boys (though you must not use the name); and a one-year practical school for farm boys. The responsible group have enjoyed excellent comradeship in facing many difficult problems.

Searle and Dr. Steward are officers of the International Relief Committee, which used the University Chapel for storing hundreds of tons of rice, and the Girls' Dormitory as distribution office. The Committee in the course of last winter and spring gave a little boost to over 130,000 persons. This year's work faces equal needs, but with somewhat smaller funds and at greatly increased prices. So far the Japanese authorities have failed to give the committee the necessary permit for purchasing rice in outlying districts (which are overrun by privileged Japanese buyers, who have the further exclusive right to transport for sale in Tientsin, Shanghai, and Japan, at three times their investment). It has not yet been possible to exchange more than fraction of our money for grain, even at the doubled Nanking prices maintained by an extortionate monopoly. We are about to lodge formal protests through the diplomatic services of the three western nations represented in the committee (American, British, and German). Most of our present funds come from American givers, and we should use that leverage in Tokyo for any possible pressure on the greedy interests that exploit the occupied area.

The situation is shameful beyond description, and this report only illustrates the processes of confiscation, bayonet-profiteering, and economic subjugation which are continuing the ruin of scores of millions of people. Reconstruction? Development? Cooperation? They are cheat-words in the mouths of professional spokesmen, disconnected from fact.

During last winter and spring we had a good deal of trouble from Japanese military elements hostile to Christian and to foreign groups. There were a number of long detentions, and an abortive deportation of the members of the International Relief Committee. But for some months there has been practically no interference with us in Nanking, and relatively little with our comrades in nearby areas. Did relief come from the failure of the military police cases to manufacture an "anti-Japanese movement," or from an improvement in the type of Japanese officers in charge, or from the desire to placate American opinion for reasons of high policy? Presumably the last, for the hideous treatment of churches and hospitals connected with British missions and the increasing supervision of Chinese pastors in the North suggest that our security is precarious, particularly if American economic support for Japan is to be reduced. Even in this province, a short time ago a Japanese sentry killed one Canadian Catholic, wounded a second, and imprisoned a third.

Meanwhile, Nanking's twenty churches flourish in service, and some 6,000 young people are in Christian schools which are closely watched but are not forced to work according to a political program. A draft set of new textbooks was printed, of a type and quality very difficult, perhaps impossible, for Christian schools to accept. But they have not been definitively published, possibly because the critical changes in Japan's international relations have soured some of the pabulum prepared for little tots. How can one write a primer when alliances and enmities are not yet redetermined by an all-powerful (but badly fooled and perplexed) government?

Searle's program has been compounded of administrative work for the University unit in Nanking, relief work, investigations for the International Relief Committee and other organizations, and services to churches and schools. This term he has been going to Shanghai once a month for a week of classes, to introduce for the Nanking Theological Seminary a course in the History of Western Civilization. This requires use of the Chinese language, which Searle has not previously had to employ in teaching history; and gives opportunity for conferences with national Christian Council people and with old friends who are students of public affairs. A new issue has just been raised by a request from the International Missionary Council to serve them for a year in collaboration with a colleague from Japan, working on some of the eastern questions brought forward at Madras. It is very difficult to measure this special opportunity against present responsibilities in Nanking, particularly when one cannot tell what new crises may arise in coming months.

How is the war going? When will it end? What kind of settlement will there be? These questions torture every Chinese mind; the second, often the first and third also, are painful to the Japanese. This year has seen remarkably little change in military positions, and neither side can safely rejoice in achievements or in hopes. Secondary Japanese attempts to advance west and south of Hankow, and to move westward from their Shansi bases, have been successfully checked. On the other hand, the Japanese have easily seized a number of ports on the southern coast and thus have tightened the blockade.

Guerrilla accomplishments are generally disappointing to the Chinese; as also are puppet enterprises to the Japanese. Neither party has found a way to break the deadlock without yielding what it will not yield until it is under much greater strain than it has yet experienced. Compromise is peculiarly difficult, since the determined aim of one side is to force the other to give up its national independence; and to commit the power to choose its leaders, its foreign relations, and its economic and cultural future, into the hands of military conquerors. Japan has gained great and ruinous successes. But her aims are so excessive that realization is almost impossible.

"Free China" deserves great praise for maintaining the morale and the cooperation to build new armies, to advance painfully with new transport lines, and to struggle with the appalling industrial problem. Currency and finance have been rather well managed. Yet the effective military power is much short of the task set for it, and can soundly expect only to be one factor in the desired recovery of unity and freedom. Japan has thus far stood rather easily the costs of war, which now are tending to decrease somewhat. But needs outrun supplies in metals, oil, cotton, fuel; normal industry and consumers alike are beginning to suffer from the relentless demands of the armed forces. If the situation on the continent is a little easier, on the other hand Japan has lost her hope of present success with the Axis, and at last is anxious about American economic policy; while no real settlement in China can be expected in any near future.

The European War has greatly increased Japan's dependence upon the United States for the supplies with which to complete her subjugation of China. Uncle Sam can continue to be prime partner in the whole evil business, or by withholding essential materials he can require reconsideration now and reduce the risks of later conflict.

It is difficult to consider coolly the condition of the people of this region, even when the price of coal has flown from $25 to $145 a ton. It is true that things are improved by comparison with the first months of occupation. Wholesale rape and murder by soldiers are succeeded by the denunciations and brutalities of the military police, and by the slow, mass ruin of poisonous drugs. Burning and looting have given way to more orderly plunder in the working of Japanese monopolies and confiscations. But employment and wages lag behind the partial recovery of population and the leaps of prices. Nanking has 550,000 Chinese residents as compared with 1,000,000 before the war; 7,500 Japanese civilians as against 100; 100 Westerners as compared with 500. Government and all public services are wretched. Schools are few and inferior. Culture is department of propaganda. Public and private morals have greatly deteriorated. On a thousand walls, the somewhat abstract but certainly creditable virtues of the New Life Movement have given way to the Japanese patent medicine advertisements which grace the New Order in East Asia. Of drugs you may judge for yourself from the enclosure.

What is Christian duty in this situation? *How* is love to triumph over contempt and over hatred, truth to surmount political instruction and defiled "news," justice to supplant exploitation? We must be ready to recognize the individual worth of men, regardless of nationality; and to aid any enterprise that brings men together on a high plane. In those ways we can and do meet usefully some scores of Japanese. But the great problems that are millstones about the necks of millions. Are they to remain untouched? Or can they be met by conciliation alone? The gentleness of Jesus, his concern for the meek and the poor, were intimately bound to the terrible "Woe's" and to the condemnation of smug power!

But the writing of this letter must not run on till Christmas. For we want it to reach you then with cordial greetings of the season. And now it's time to have another try for military permission to be charitable!

Lilliath Robbins Bates
Miner Searle Bates

P.S. If you'd like to hear from us again, a card would help. Real letters from old friends are most welcome. Remember that suspicious eyes may see them, and don't make them involve us in matters of public welfare as much as this communication does. Opium is a necessary exception to our usual restraint. On that subject, publish without quarter.

***

Lecture in New York (June 25, 1941)[14]

Foreign Mission Conference of N. A.
156 Fifth Avenue, New York, N.Y.

COMMITTEE ON EAST ASIA *Strictly Confidential*

July 10, 1941 *Not for Publication*

To Secretaries of Mission Boards having work in China

Dear friends:
The following statement by Dr. M. Searle Bates was made to a group in New York City on June 25, 1941. Please note that it is marked *Strictly Confidential* and *Not for Publication*. A reading of the document will indicate clearly why the material should not be published and why Dr. Bates should not be quoted. Dr. Bates is one of the most competent missionary observers in China. He was in Nanking in December 1937, when the Japanese captured the city, and has resided there until May of this year. In the interim he made several trips to Japan, and at least one trip into West China. He is a missionary of the United Christian Missionary Society and a member of the faculty of the University of Nanking.

Very sincerely yours,
John H. Reisner, Acting Secretary[15]
COMMITTEE ON EAST ASIA

***

THE SETTING FOR THE CHRISTIAN TASK IN PENETRATED CHINA

1. The Economic Situation
Transportation is completely monopolized by the Japanese, and also transportation is used to maintain control over the movement and sale of commodities. Practically all wholesale business has been taken into Japanese hands. All pub-

lic utilities are Japanese monopolies, as also are building materials, cotton, yarn, wool and machinery.

The distress among the common people is very great. There is not merely lack of food, but lack of economic exchange of all kinds. By military operations and by the rival economic blockades, the whole nation is cut into jigsaw sections. City is cut from country, factory from farm.

The situation is aggravated by the currency eccentricities. There are three kinds of money now in circulation in Nanking:

1. Regular Chinese currency.
2. Notes of the Central Reserve Bank (official bank of the puppet regime).
3. Japanese military yen (used for all transportation and utility charges and all wholesale transactions).

Separate currencies are maintained by the local puppet orders in North China, and again in Inner Mongolia. South China has its own peculiarities.

The price index for Nanking and much of the Yangtze Valley at the end of March was about 825 as compared with 100 in the first six months of 1937. Rice was well over 1,000.

The wages of unskilled laborers are about 240 as against 100 in 1937. An able-bodied man makes just about enough to feed himself without anything for his family. If he does not eat he will not be strong enough to work tomorrow; if he does eat his wife and children will not eat. What is he to do? What would you do? The fight the people are putting up is beyond all praise—men, women, and children.

2. The Wang Ching-wei Puppet Regime

Among the representatives of the puppet regime, we are unable to discern any considerable character or intelligence. They are a poor lot. Many of them have come from Nanking or from coastal ports, seeking work. Not a few of these people held out for two or three years against having anything to do with the puppet regime, but when there was nothing else to do they sought this work merely to make a living. They are apologetic, but they don't see any way out. They salve their consciences by the feeling that they are in a position for sabotage when the right time comes. This work draws a large number of men whose morals and outlook are not of a high type. The present Minister of Social Welfare is probably the most outstanding assassin in China. His friends told me they knew of 138 political murders to his credit. They have a bureau for the registration of specialists, which is an office for selling jobs with the Japanese or with the puppet government. Their own morale politically is very low.

In December last the puppet Minister of Education conceived the idea of helping to re-start the University of Nanking in Nanking, which means, being interpreted, a plan to confiscate and use our buildings for his own government university. He asked me to come to his residence to discuss the matter, and there were two dinner parties in the official club, then a return dinner at my house, where I had to feed two of the Wang Ching-wei gunmen. We put him off by playing on his hobby, the study of ancient philosophy, and his greed for news of international affairs, which he could get through us. He was not willing to cut off that source of news by pressing too hard on the university problem. In my house the Minister delivered a lecture of two hours and forty-five minutes, during all of which he was apologizing for the puppet regime in Nanking, and he concluded with this statement: "We in Nanking have no hope whatsoever and the fellows in Chungking have very little hope. The one chance for the Chinese people is that the British with American help will beat down the Germans and then the Japanese will have to back out of China."

Wang Ching-wei himself does not get away from Nanking; in fact the current trip to Tokyo was his first journey in a year. There is a great amount of feeling that acceptance of jobs in the puppet regime is something temporary. Very few Chinese think of them as anything that is going to last very long. Recently a number of these persons employed by the puppet government arranged to have their pictures taken with a group of us. The purpose was to prove to the free Chinese regime, upon its return, their relationship with American social service. Some of these included men whose reputations are worthy of investigation. Two came to my home privately by night and wanted very detailed information as to just when I was going to get back, and who would stand sponsor for them if the Chungking army came before I returned.

3. Missionary work

By and large, the Japanese and the puppet regime have not interfered with missionary work in all its phases so much as we had feared. We have had much better chances than we could have reasonably expected. There is a certain looseness about the Japanese procedures which we can often out-wait and often out-guess.

Also, in Central and Southern China the Japanese are not very confident about remaining, and they are not putting in much money. Many things are being done with a temporizing spirit, and they do not carry things through to the natural Japanese conclusion. That gives us advantages.

Most of us have not had to introduce textbooks prepared or passed on by the puppet regime in our Primary Schools. We have feared it, but have been able to hold it off.

Of course, you have heard about the very serious case of the Brethren Mission in Shansi Province where late in autumn or early in the winter thirteen Christians, including some leading workers, were killed by the Japanese in an effort to intimidate Christians into breaking all connections with the missionaries. That brought moral compulsion upon the missionaries to withdraw. It is an extreme case and stands almost alone. There have been some other cases which have been pretty bad, but they are seldom followed up or carried out over a large area.

How is missionary work carrying on, and what are missions able to do in comparison with former times? The answer, of course, would vary according to the region and the personnel in the different localities. However, the story is that hospitals are going ahead with an accomplishment as great as usual in numbers of patients treated and greater than ever in the quality of the response, because there is so very little else of that kind available to the people and because the people appreciate so deeply the contribution made by the doctors and nurses under the conditions of difficulty which surround them. Most of the hospitals have lost the larger part of their Chinese doctors and trained nurses and are very short of staff. There is some supplementing by German-Jewish doctors and other refugee doctors, most of whom have been a real help. In spite of all the hospitals have suffered from loss of buildings, personnel and equipment, they have been able to keep their services going in a most unusual way. We are fearing that the difficulty in getting drugs from now on will become critical, because the Japanese are getting tighter and tighter on that subject. Shipments from America also have more restrictions.

4. Schools

Schools present a somewhat mixed picture. The situation in the colleges and universities is familiar to you. Christian Middle Schools are now about the same in number for China as a whole as before the war, some 250. Many of them are down in quality because they have lost some of their best teachers and because they have lost heavily in buildings and equipment, and most of them are unable to pay their teachers a decent living wage at this time. Nevertheless the quality of their service is appreciated all the more because the government-supported schools are at an extremely low ebb, and they are still worse in quality than the lowest of the Christian schools. The spirit and tenor of the non-Christian schools is far from what the parents desire.

As to the Primary Schools, no adequate information can be supplied. In general there is a tendency for missions to re-establish work among young children, but often the work is connected with religious services or with a program resembling that of a daily vacation Bible School; and not so much trying to meet government standards. Yet there are also some useful Primary Schools of regular type.

5. Emergency Work

The emergency services carried on in penetrated areas are magnificent. Most of the missionaries are connected with the work of relief in one form or another. They are also working in certain schools with an effort to get a little more of the vocational emphasis and direction than before. They are working in connection with the feeding enterprises for children under the national Child Welfare Commission. Money for these is administered through the National Christian Council. There are also many forms of direct relief. The missionaries and foreign pastors are considerably burdened by this work, but with few exceptions they feel it is a necessary burden. You cannot simply say to a whole group of hungry people "Be ye warmed and fed." When you go into a church where two-thirds of the people have on garments that are patches upon patches, you cannot be comfortable about it unless you are doing everything you can to meet that need. The problems of relief have been heavy, but they have not been overpowering. The churches are reporting that they are being spiritually benefited by their efforts in relief, more frequently than they complain of the old burden of rice-Christians.

6. Conclusion

My final word is simply this: The missionaries in the penetrated areas are determined that so long as the way is open to them, they should meet the great human needs that are there. The response spiritually and otherwise is very remarkable, and we feel that while there is a strong case for transferring persons and enterprises to the free areas wherever there are specific needs and ways of getting started immediately on useful jobs, at the same time it is wrong to abandon entirely the large numbers of worthy and interested people who have risen to the emergency in a way much better than could have been expected. The church will not die in those areas even if the missionaries should be taken out tomorrow. It would, however, be set back severely in its growth. At the best, the story of the church will be one of hardship. We expect that. [W]e expect that the transfer of regime will bring with it an era of destruction and violence. The going out of the Japanese is not pleasant to contemplate. The regime which will continue on the borderlines is not pleasant to contemplate, and no one knows who will take over these areas. There is plenty of trouble ahead even if the Japanese go out.

However, we are especially happy to see the comeback the Christians and the churches have made to the severe blows dealt them in the early periods of the war and since then.

***

Question: In the relief work, are we strengthening the puppet regime?
Answer: The consensus is that the contribution to the Japanese is very slight; that the contribution to Chinese morale and character much more than over-balances anything we are doing for the Japanese. The Japanese do not look with favor upon our work, and put many rocks in our way.

In Chungking I found that a large part of the leading people look with very distinct favor upon the work of the missions in the occupied areas at this time. They do not find that political considerations overbalance the obvious human good that is being done. They are sympathetic with their own relatives and friends, cut off temporarily in the penetrated areas. General Chiang Kai-shek sent for me when he heard I was in the city and his purpose was to express his appreciation of what the Christian missionaries are doing in the lower Yangtze Valley, as he has frequently done through various channels. He asked two questions:

1. What is the condition of the common people?
2. What about opium?

Question: How do you get hospital supplies?
Answer: There is no commercial transport of medical supplies into the interior, but we are able to get them moved as our own property.

Question: How long do you count upon the continuance of present conditions?
Answer: You are dealing with irrational persons in an unaccountable situation. While we dare to go ahead, no one can make any adequate predictions of the future.

Question: What is the opium situation?
Answer: The major tendency is a revival of the growing of opium throughout the occupied areas, even on the outskirts of cities.

Question: Are the Japanese beginning to use the drug?
Answer: Japanese use is not great, but it is an ever-present problem to them. They have very close restrictions, and they inspect carefully. They require owners of opium dens to report any Japanese that enter their places.

In Korea the officials have recently required some farmers to start the growing of opium.

Question: What is the extent of Chinese losses?
Answer: The more or less standard figure is 3,000,000 dead and seriously

wounded, as against 1,000,000 for the Japanese. It is the kind of war in which a million casualties may never be recorded.

Question: Is there a change in the attitude of the Japanese?

Answer: The change in the Japanese attitude is indicated in the declining morale about the Chinese enterprise. They are pretty blue about it. I found firsthand evidence of that in the efforts to get Mr. Mills and myself to use our influence to push on American mediation. We had remarkable interviews with one of the Japanese generals. In my relations with certain independent Japanese I got a fairly full story of the peace negotiations, or attempts at peace from last August to the present time. They have been going on intermittently during that period. What it amounts to is that the Japanese are prepared to offer what might sound like tremendously generous terms, if the words mean the same to them as they do to us. And that is the heart of the problem. They are saying latterly that they would be willing to withdraw troops from China. However, at the same time the military leaders expect to maintain garrisons in North China and Mongolia. They said, "We expect it will be understood that legally the Japanese troops have been removed, but in the meantime agreements will have been reached with the Chinese to the effect that we remain as protection against the Soviet." They have not gotten beyond the stage of holding these two incompatibles side by side. However, they have recently said things which they would have killed each other for a year ago. It is the beginning of the education of the Japanese generals, at the terrific price already referred to.

Question: What is the effect on Japan of the present Russian situation?

Answer: The Russo-Japanese agreement had no meaning at all, as was long since clear in statements by Japanese generals. I think the immediate effect of the present situation will be that the Japanese military "remain poised for an emergency"; which means getting higher up on the wall before they decide which way to jump. One important faction will press for attack upon Siberia as the Germans advance.

Question: What about the efforts of Japan to move Southward?

Answer: Efforts in the direction of the South Seas are discouraged. In Tokyo the cabinet has long been balanced on the question of whether to go in as an ally with Germany, or to try to slip in without a clash.

Question: What is the number of Germans in Japan and Japanese-controlled China?

Answer: Not many in China. In Japan it has reached approximately 10,000. They hold all kinds of good offices there, and are in many journalistic and economic positions. They are pushing hard and their argument is very appealing. They say, "If you wait and the British win, you will get nothing; if we destroy the British and you don't help us now, you will get nothing." Such opportunism meets positive response in the Japanese phrase: This is the time of ten thousand generations.

Question: Is there friction between the Germans and the Japanese?
Answer: Yes, in the case of the liberal type of Japanese. It is not observed among the Japanese who might decide for violent moves.

Question: Have there been places in penetrated China where the presence of the missionaries has made it more difficult for the Chinese?
Answer: Yes, but they are very few, and with the one exception that I named to you they have not been lasting. The answer is rather overwhelmingly the other way, that so long as the U.S. and Japan are not at war, the presence of the missionaries, even in a nearby locality, is of great assistance in many ways to the local Chinese.

Question: If the Japanese take over, will American citizens be taken into custody and American property confiscated?
Answer: We expect that all the foreigners, including missionaries, would be put into custody, and a good deal of property known to be American and associated with Americans would be taken over by the Japanese or the puppet regime. I should not expect very much direct interference with churches as such, but hospitals and schools probably would suffer a good deal. On the other hand, China is China. There are elaborate relationships formed in various ways between Chinese Christians and Chinese in the puppet regime. Conditions in many localities because of these relationships would be mitigated, to say the least. What would happen on any large scale, I cannot say. The set-up would be bad for institutional properties are much desired by Japanese and puppets alike, in cities where semi-public buildings have suffered destruction, looting and neglect. I know place after place in which puppets and occasionally Japanese in important posts have said, "You don't need to fear confiscation as long as you go ahead and do what you are doing now and have nothing to do with politics." It is an indication of the attitude in certain quarters, though too tenuous to count upon.

***

Court Record of the International Military Tribunal for the Far East, July 29, 1946[16]

Miner Searle Bates, called as a witness on behalf of the prosecution, being first duly sworn, testified as follows:

DIRECT EXAMINATION BY MR. SUTTON:

Q: Dr. Bates, will you please state your full name?

A: Miner Searle Bates.

Q: When and where were you born?

A: At Newark, Ohio; May 28, 1897.

Q: Where did you receive your education?

A: At Hiram College, Hiram, Ohio; at Oxford University in England; and in later years graduate work in history at Yale and Harvard universities.

Q: Where is your residence?

A: At Nanking, China.

Q: How long have you been a resident of China?

A: Since 1920.

Q: What is your business in China?

A: Professor of history in the University of Nanking.

Q: Were you connected with any of the committees which were organized in the late fall of 1937 at Nanking?

A: Yes. I was a member, a founding member, of the International Committee for Safety Zone in Nanking.

Q: Will you please tell when this committee was formed, and its function?

A: This committee was set up in the last days of November, 1937, anticipating the attack of the Japanese Army upon Nanking.

Following the example of the international committee organized by Father Jacquinot, a French priest in Shanghai, which was of considerable help to a large body of Chinese civilians there, we attempted in Nanking to do something similar in our very different conditions.

This committee was organized at first with a Danish chairman, with German, British, and American members. But because foreign governments withdrew almost all of their nationals from the city, there were at the time of the Japanese attack only Germans and Americans remaining upon it.

The chairman was a distinguished German merchant, Mr. John Rabe. This committee was assisted to get into touch with the Chinese and Japanese commanding officers through the communications and good officers of the American, German, and British embassies. The purpose was to provide a refuge in a small, noncombatant zone where civilians might escape the dangers of the fighting and actual attack.

Q: Who was the secretary of this committee?

A: Professor Lewis Smythe, professor of sociology in the University of Nanking.

Q: Did this committee make reports from time to time?

A: The committee expected that its chief duties would be to provide housing and if necessary some food during a period of a few days or possibly of a few weeks when the city was under siege and when Chinese civilian authority might have disappeared but Japanese military authority would not yet have been established.

The actual event was very different, because the Japanese attack and seizure of the city was swift. But then the troubles began. The treatment of civilians was so bad that the chairman and secretary of the committee went regularly to any Japanese officials who could be reached and soon began to prepare daily reports of the serious injuries to civilians that occurred within the safety zone. Over a period of several weeks a total of several hundred cases, many of them compound cases, involving groups and large numbers of individuals, were thus reported in writing and orally to Japanese officials. They were later published under the editorship of Professor Shu-hsi Hsu, of Nanking University, by the British firm of Kelly and Walsh, in Shanghai, in the year 1939 or 1940.

Q: By whom were most of these reports in writing that were made—change the question. Just disregard the question. I will change it, please.

Whose signature appeared to most of these reports that were made in writing by the International Committee for the Nanking Safety Zone to the Japanese authorities?

A: Most of them were signed by Professor Smythe, as secretary, though part of them were also signed by Mr. Rabe, as Chairman.

Q: Was there any resistance on the part of the Chinese troops or any resistance on the part of the Chinese people against the Japanese forces in the city of Nanking after December 13, 1937?

A: Greatly to the disappointment of the Chinese population, and to the surprise of the small group of foreign residents, there was no resistance of any kind within the city. In the many conferences which Mr. Rabe, Professor Smythe, and I had with Japanese officials on the matter of atrocities, we found that the Japanese officials never in any way alleged that there was resistance or gave any such excuse for the attacks upon civilians. One case only, about ten days after the entrance in the city, involved a single sailor at the river.

Q: Did you conclude your answer?

A: The answer to that question?

Mr. McMANUS: Mr. President, members of the Tribunal, may I point out at this time that, in lieu of an objection to this testimony, that—to call the Court's attention that no conspiracy has been established as yet. Not one of these accused has been tied in any way to a conspiracy charge so far. So, in view of that, if your Honor pleases, how do these atrocity stories affect the accused? I ask your Honors, and I think that such testimony as this should not be permitted until the time that one of these men—or at least a semblance of a prima-facie case is established.

THE PRESIDENT: We are all of the opinion that the link can be established at any stage of the trial. Of course, if it isn't established, why, there is no case in conspiracy. But the order of evidence isn't that you must give evidence of a conspiracy first.

We have already given a decision on this point, if my recollection serves me rightly.

Mr. McMANUS: Thank you, your Honor.

THE PRESIDENT: The objection is overruled.

Q: What was the conduct of the Japanese soldiers toward the civilians after the Japanese were in control of the city of Nanking?

A: The question is so big, I don't know where to begin. I can only say that I, myself, observed a whole series of shootings of individual civilians without any provocation or apparent reason whatsoever; that one Chinese was taken from my own house and killed. From my next door neighbor's house two men, who rose up in anxiety when soldiers seized and raped their wives, were taken, shot at the edge of the pond by my house, and thrown into it. The bodies of civilians lay on the streets and alleys in the vicinity of my own house for many days after the Japanese entry. The total spread of this killing was so extensive that no one can give a complete picture of it. We can only say that we did our best to find out, in checking up carefully upon the safety zone and adjoining areas.

Professor Smythe and I concluded, as a result of our investigations and observations and checking of burials, that twelve thousand civilians, men, women and children, were killed inside the walls within our own sure knowledge. There were many others killed within the city outside our knowledge whose numbers we have no way of checking, and also there were large numbers killed immediately outside the city, of civilians. This is quite apart from the killing of tens of thousands of men who were Chinese soldiers or had been Chinese soldiers.

Q: What were the circumstances under which the former soldiers or alleged soldiers were killed?

A: Large parties of Chinese soldiers laid down their arms, surrendered, immediately outside the walls of the city and there, within the first seventy two hours, were cut down by machine gun fire, mostly upon the bank of the Yangtze River.

We of the International Committee hired laborers to carry out the burials of more than thirty thousand of these soldiers. That was done as a work relief project inspected and directed by us. The number of bodies carried away in the river, and the number of bodies buried in other ways, we cannot count.

Within the Safety Zone a very serious problem was caused by the fact that the Japanese officers expected to find within the city a very large number of Chinese soldiers. When they did not discover the soldiers, they insisted that they were in hiding within the zone and that we were responsible for concealing them. On that theory, Japanese military officers and non-commissioned officers were sent among the refugees in the safety zone day after day for about three weeks attempting to discover and seize former soldiers. It was their common practice to require all able-bodied men in a certain section of the zone, or in a certain refugee camp, to line up for inspection and then to be seized if they had callouses upon their hands or the marks of wearing a hat showing on the skin of the forehead.

I was present throughout several of these inspections and watched the whole process. It was undoubtedly true that there were some soldiers—former soldiers among these refugees, men who had thrown away their arms and uniforms and secured civilian clothes. It was also clearly true that the majority of the men so accused or seized—and seized were ordinary carriers and laborers who had plenty of good reasons for callouses on their hands. The men so accused of having been soldiers were seized, taken away, and, in most cases, shot immediately in large groups at the edges of the city.

In some cases a peculiar form of treachery was practiced to persuade men to admit that they had been soldiers. Using the proclamation issued by General MATSUI before the Japanese Army took Nanking, and distributed widely by airplane, the proclamation which declared that the Japanese Army had only good will for peaceful citizens of China and would do no harm to those who did not resist the Imperial Army, Japanese officers tried to persuade many Chinese to come forward as voluntary workers for military labor corps. In some cases these Japanese officers urged Chinese men to come forward, saying, "If you have previously been a Chinese soldiers, or if you have ever worked as a carrier or laborer in the Chinese Army, that will all now be forgotten and forgiven if you will join this labor corps." In that way, in one afternoon, two hundred men were secured from the premises of the University of Nanking and were promptly marched away and executed that evening along with other bodies of men secured from other parts of the safety one.

Q: What was the conduct of the Japanese soldiers toward the women in the city of Nanking?

A: That was one of the roughest and saddest parts of the whole picture. Again, in the homes of my three nearest neighbors, women were raped, including wives of University teachers. On five different occasions, which I can detail for you if desired, I, myself, came upon soldiers in the act of rape and pulled them away from the women.

The safety zone case reports, to which we have previously referred, and my own records of what occurred among the thirty thousand refugees on the various grounds and in the building of the University of Nanking, hold a total of many hundreds of cases of rape about which exact details were furnished to the Japanese authorities at the time. One month after the occupation, Mr. Rabe, the Chairman of the International Committee, reported to the German authorities that he and his colleagues believed that not less than twenty thousand cases of rape had occurred. A little earlier I estimated, very much more cautiously and on the basis of the safety zone reports alone, some eight thousand cases.

Every day and every night there were large numbers of different gangs of soldiers, usually fifteen or twenty in a group, who went about through the city, chiefly in the safety zone because that's where almost all the people were, and went into the houses seeking women. In two cases, which I remember all too clearly because I nearly lost my life in each of them, officers participated in this seizing and raping of women on the University property. The raping was frequent daytime as well as night and occurred along the roadside in many cases.

On the grounds of the Nanking Theological Seminary, under the eyes of one of my own friends, a Chinese woman was raped in rapid succession by seventeen Japanese soldiers. I do not care to repeat the occasional cases of sadistic and abnormal behavior in connection with the raping, but I do want to mention that on the grounds of the University alone a little girl of nine and a grandmother of seventy-six were raped.

Q: What was the conduct of the Japanese soldiers with regard to the personal property of Chinese civilians in the City of Nanking?

A: From the very hour of entry, the soldiers took anything, at any time, from any place.

THE PRESIDENT: The witness must not hold back anything because he thinks it is too horrible to tell us.

THE WITNESS: I hardly know how to respond to that invitation; but, unless I am questioned, I believe I will let it go because my own personal knowledge does not include a great number of the sadistic cases.

In the first days of the occupation the soldiers, whom we roughly guessed to be about fifty thousand in number, took a great deal of bedding, cooking utensils and food from the refugees. Practically every building in the city was entered many, many times by these roving gangs of soldiers throughout the first six or seven weeks of the occupation. In some cases the looting was well organized and systematic, using fleets of army trucks under the direction of officers. The vaults in the banks, including the personal safe deposit boxes of German officials and residents, were cut open with acetylene torches. On one occasion I observed a supply column, two-thirds of a mile long, loaded with high-grade redwood and blackwood furniture.

After some months a few foreign residents were given the opportunity to recover pianos taken from their own houses, and they were led to a place where more than two hundred pianos were in one storage hall.

The foreign embassies were broken into and suffered robbery, including the German Embassy and the personal property of the Ambassador. Practically all commercial property of any noticeable value was taken.

Q: What was the conduct of the Japanese soldiers toward the real estate, the buildings in the City of Nanking after they were in complete control of that city?

A: On the very night of the entry the Japanese forces placed adequate and effective guards upon the Sun Yat-sen tomb and upon the government and party buildings. With the exception of one or two minor fires, apparently started by drunken soldiers, there was no burning until the Japanese troops had been in the city five or six days. Beginning, I believe, on the 19th or 20th of December, burning was carried on regularly for six weeks. In some cases the burning followed the looting of a line of stores, but in most instances we could not see any reason or pattern in it. At no time was there a general conflagration, but the definite firing of certain groups of buildings each day. Sometimes gasoline was used, but more commonly chemical strips, of which I secured samples.

The other major problem in regard to real property was the seizure of private property in order to supply incoming Japanese residents. I leave aside the taking of buildings for military purposes and offices, and refer only to the fact that during 1938 and part of 1939 any Japanese merchant coming to Nanking would receive a commercial and a residential property taken from the Chinese by the gendarmerie or the special service. I have again and again seen in the street outside their house a Chinese family put out on twelve hour's notice. These included some dozens of my own friends of many years.

Q: Were the buildings of the Russian Embassy burned by Japanese soldiers?

A: Yes, they were burned at the beginning of 1938. Also, just to illustrate the range of burning, the Y. M. C. A. Building, two important church buildings, the two chief German commercial properties with the Swastika flying upon them, were among those burned.

Q: Did you personally make to the Japanese authorities reports as to the conduct of the soldiers in the city of Nanking?

A: Yes. On four or five occasions I accompanied Mr. Rabe and Dr. Smythe in their interviews with the officials in the Japanese Embassy, who were sent there by the Gaimusho in an effort to provide cushions between this little group of foreign residents and the Japanese military. Furthermore, because the University of Nanking was immediately adjoining the Japanese Embassy, and because it was a very large and important test case of American property with the American flag, and this large number of refugees, it was agreed between Mr. Rabe and myself that I should make supplementary reports on behalf of the

University. Almost daily for the first three weeks I went to the Embassy with a typed report or letter covering the preceding day, and frequently had also a conversation with the officials regarding it. These officials were Mr. T. FUKUI, who had the rank of consul, a certain Mr. TANAKA, vice-consul, Mr. Toyoyasu FUKUDA. The latter is now secretary to the premier YOSHIDA. These men were honestly trying to do what little they could in a very bad situation, but they themselves were terrified by the military and they could do nothing except forward these communications through Shanghai to Tokyo.

THE PRESIDENT: We recess now for fifteen minutes.

(Whereupon, at 10:45, a recess was taken until 11:12, after which the proceedings were resumed as follows:)

MARSHAL OF THE COURT: The Tribunal is now resumed.
THE PRESIDENT: Mr. Sutton.

BY MR. SUTTON (Continued):
Q: I believe you had not completed your answer to the last question.
A: I should like to read a few sentences from these daily typewritten reports given to the officers in the Japanese Embassy. I will do this from my own notes made last month from the carbon copies of the originals. These copies are on file in the American Embassy at Nanking. The originals are in my own baggage which I believe to be on board ship between the United States and China at this time.

MR. McMANUS: Mr. President, I think the witness is capable of testifying himself without offering any notes, particularly copies. He said he has the originals, are not here, and he is very capable of testifying himself. I don't see why any notes should be offered to the Court.

THE PRESIDENT: Well, if the strict rules of evidence applied, he would have to refresh his memory if he needed to do so, from notes made at the time. But they don't apply, and substantially your position is not affected. There is no reason why, if he needs to refresh his memory, he should not use these copied notes that he made from the original. The objection is overruled.

Mr. McMANUS: Mr. President, if the witness uses these notes, may we examine them?

THE PRESIDENT: The Tribunal will allow you to peruse the notes if you have any doubt about them.

THE WITNESS: If the Court pleases, my purpose is only to state with a little more accuracy exactly what I reported to the Japanese officers in the Japanese Embassy.

A: (Continuing): In the letter of December 16th I complained of many cases of abduction of women from the University's propeties and of the rape of thirty women in one University building the previous night.

In the letter of December 17th, besides detailing the specific cases by rote, the reign of terror and brutality continues in the plain view of your buildings and among your own neighbors.

In the letter of December 18th I reported that on the previous night rape had occurred in six different buildings of the University of Nanking. For three days and three nights many of the thousands of women on our property had not been able to sleep and, in the hysterical fear that was developing, violent incidents might occur. I reported the saying common among the Chinese that where the Japanese Army is, no house or person is safe.

In a letter of December 21st, I complained that many hundreds of refugees had been taken away for forced labor. My own house had just been looted for the fourth time by Japanese soldiers and, indeed, every University house was being regularly entered. I also reported that for the second time the American flag had been torn down from the American school and trampled by Japanese soldiers who issued a threat of death to anyone who would put up the flag again.

I may say in passing, this was not in this particular letter, that the American flag was torn down six times from the University of Nanking and six times we put it up again.

THE PRESIDENT: That is not evidence of any war crime.

A: (Continuing): On Christmas Day I reported that in one building of the University about ten cases per day of rape and abduction were continually occurring.

On the 27th of December, after a long list of individual cases, I wrote: "Shameful disorder continues and we see no serious efforts to stop it. The soldiers every day injure hundreds of persons most seriously. Does not the Japanese Army care for its reputation."

THE PRESIDENT: He is not refreshing his memory from his notes. He is just reading them.

THE WITNESS: These are sufficient to show the nature of the reports and the way in which they were clearly or even strongly stated.

THE PRESIDENT: This sort of thing is only provoking the defense which I am saving time by anticipating it.

Q: How long did the conduct on the part of the Japanese soldiers which you have detailed continue following the fall of the City of Nanking on December 13th, 1937?

A: The terror was intense for two and one-half to three weeks. It was serious to a total of six to seven weeks.

Q: What measures did the Japanese military authorities take to control the troops?

A: We were assured by the civil officials in the Embassy that on several occasions strong orders were sent from Tokyo to restore order in Nanking. We saw no significant results of such orders until the coming of some kind of high military deputation about the fifth or sixth of February. At that time, as slightly indicated in the newspapers and more fully by foreign diplomats and by a Japanese friend who accompanied the deputation, I learned that a high military officer called together a large body of lower officers and non-commissioned officers, telling them very severely that they must better their conduct for the sake of the name of the Army.

Prior to that time we saw and heard of no instance of effective discipline or penalty inflicted upon soldiers who were seen by high officers in the very act of murder and rape. On three or four occasions, Mr. Rabe and other members of the committee were in the presence of high officers when they saw the shooting or bayoneting of a civilian or an act of rape. In each case the soldier was required to give an extra salute to the officer and an oral reprimand was administered but the name of the soldier was not taken nor was there any other indication of discipline. It was impossible for us neutral observers to report the names of individual criminals because there was no name or number worn upon the outside of the uniform and, during the first weeks of the occupation, there was not even an indication of the unit to which a soldier belonged.

The several officers in the Embassy declared that one great reason for difficulty was the small number of military police or gendarmes available which, at the moment of occupation, they declared to be seventeen in number. After, three days after the entry, the civil officials secured from high officers of the gendarmerie certain small posters or proclamations to be put up at the entrance to foreign property ordering all soldiers to keep away. Not only did the soldiers daily disregard these proclamations from the gendarmerie headquarters but they also frequently tore them down. I took several of these torn proclamations to the Japanese Embassy for transmission to the gendarmerie. After February sixth or seventh there was a noticeable improvement in the situation and, although many serious cases occurred between then and summer, they were no longer of a mass and wholesale character.

Q: Who was the commanding general of the Japanese forces at the time of the capture of the City of Nanking during the remainder of December, 1937, and January, 1938?

A: We were not aware of any one local commander at Nanking, since each detachment or butai seemed to be independent. However, the official proclamations and the general statements of the newspapers, including the Japanese newspapers, indicated that General Iwane MATSUI was in command for the Shanghai–Nanking region.

Q: Were the Chinese allowed to conduct private business following the occupation of the City of Nanking by the Japanese soldiers?

A: There was no general prohibition of Chinese private business, although as a matter of fact so many of the business men lost their commercial property by looting and burning and lost their store buildings by confiscation for the use of Japanese merchants that there were dealt very heavy blows at the beginning. Then monopolies and exclusive controls were set up which reserved transportation, banking, the wholesale trade in rice, cotton, metals, and building materials for Japanese concerns.

Mr. McMANUS: Mr. President, may I enter an objection at this time as to the relevancy of this particular type of testimony, and also an objection on the ground that the testimony now is becoming repetitious, and I am requesting the Court to permit me to make that objection.

THE PRESIDENT: I take the evidence to be directed to the provisions of The Hague Convention, requiring belligerents to respect property rights. It rests with the prosecution, of course, to establish the connection between the accused and this conduct which is testified to. I fail to notice any repetitious evidence here. The objections are overruled.

THE WITNESS: A further difficulty was caused by the pressure put upon many Chinese business men to accept Japanese partners. In many cases this was done by the direct instruction of the gendarmerie or the special service. In other cases it was done by the threat that the Chinese business man could not receive permits, or carry on his business freely unless there was a Japanese whose name could be used to secure such permission. Among my friends were many such business men who were required to admit Japanese partners, men who invested no capital but were given influence of control and a share of the profits in return for that power to get permits from the controlling military authorities. The controls were employed in a way desperately injurious, not only to Chinese business men but also to producers and consumers as well. For example, on behalf of the International Relief Committee, I tried during a period of three months to purchase rice outside of the City of Nanking for the use of that committee. At that time the price of rice within the city was held by the monopoly at 18 to 22 dollars per picul. In producing areas 40 miles west on the Yangtze River the price was held by the monopoly to 8 and 9 dollars per picul. At the same time the monopoly was transferring rice to Shanghai to be sold at 35 dollars per picul and to Chinan in Shangteng to be sold at 45 dollars per picul. Our committee applied to the food control office of the municipal government for permission to make these purchases in the producing area and so save half the cost of rice to be distributed in relief work. We met with the standard reply of those years, "this matter can be done only through the colonel of the special service," and then we tried to approach him through the Japanese Embassy. The civil authorities approved our efforts and tried to assist this relief enterprise, but they could not persuade the military monopoly to give up its profits even for that purpose. I have given this case merely because it shows from my own experience the typical situation of the working of the controls.

Q: Did you have occasion to report these facts to the Japanese authorities?

A: I reported them in full in the course of three months of conversations and letters over this effort to secure permits to buy rice outside the city. The other more general facts regarding the monopolies in the list of commodities and enterprises which I previously named were reported in an economic survey that I undertook on behalf of the International Relief Committee. I sent that report to the Japanese Consul General and later published it within the occupied areas.

Q: Have you had occasion, Dr. Bates, to make special studies in connection with the opium and narcotic problem in the occupied area?

A: Yes. My attention was drawn to the startling developments in the use of opium and heroin while carrying on relief work in the summer and autumn of 1938. We found that many poor refugees were being approached by peddlers who urged the use of opium, saying, "if you take this your stomach won't hurt you any more." Slightly later but similarly heroin was peddled with the statement, "If you take a little of this you won't be so tired and you will feel as if you could jump over mountains." In a short time the rapidly expanding trade in narcotics became a public enterprise, set up outwardly by the puppet government. When public stores, that is, government stores, were opened and when advertisements of opium dens began to appear in the one newspaper of Nanking, the official newspaper, I then decided the matter must be investigated.

Q: Were your investigations made on your own behalf or on behalf of the United States Government?

A: The United States Government had no connection with them in any way and did not know about them until after the reports were published.

Q: What was the situation in Nanking with regard to the sale of opium and narcotics prior to the Japanese occupation in December, 1937?

A: There was no open and notorious sale or use of opium for some ten years before the Incident of 1937. Opium was used in back rooms, chiefly by older men of the gentry and merchant types, but there was no open parading of it before young people, and indeed, in my residence there from 1920 to 1937 I never saw opium or learned to recognize its odor or appearance.

THE PRESIDENT: We will adjourn now until half past one.

(Whereupon, at 1200, a recess was taken.)

AFTERNOON SESSION

DEPUTY MARSHAL OF THE COURT: The International Military Tribunal for the Far East is now resumed.

MINER SEARLE BATES, called as a witness on behalf of the prosecution, resumed the stand and testified as follows:

DIRECT EXAMINATION (Continued)

THE PRESIDENT: Captain Brooks.

MR. BROOKS: If the Tribunal please, I believe that this questioning he is developing on the opium is only—the evidence that the witness is giving is only cumulative and could be objected to on that ground. And I think that it would be quite possible to eliminate a lot of this matter on the opium situation if, and I feel that the Tribunal could take judicial notice that opium is an old and great evil in China, and that the Chinese people are inclined to fall into the habit of using it more than any other important group.

THE PRESIDENT: Well, you do not suggest that we could take judicial notice that the Japanese have greatly increased the sale of opium and have sold opium quite openly? I am not saying that is the fact but it is the evidence.

MR. BROOKS: I believe that the Court could go further and say that the potential demand there is enormous for the sale of opium, and in the past hundreds of years various private and official elements, Chinese and foreign, have at times supplied and developed the narcotic trade. If the Tribunal can take such notice, and since previous witnesses have testified along these lines, I think that any further testimony is objectionable as only being cumulative.

THE PRESIDENT: The evidence only becomes cumulative in that sense when quite a number of witnesses will necessarily testify to the same thing. The objection is overruled.

BY MR. SUTTON:

Q: Dr. Bates, you may continue your answer.

A: Investigation of the narcotic business was not easy because it was done—although it was done by open sale yet the information as to their management and finances were kept well behind the scenes, and naturally there were no clear or honest official reports.

In the autumn of 1938, in November of 1938, I, with the help of several old friends under my direction, visited several of the opium stores and a considerable number of the opium dens. We also secured copies of the regulations which the official monopoly made for the use of dealers under it, and tax slips and tax reports which they made to the monopoly. At that time the regular system provided for 175 licensed smoking dens and for 30 stores which distributed to and through those dens. The official sales were set at 6,000 ounces per day, which figure the dealers reported to be exceeded because the demand from the country districts outside Nanking was so great. The sales price was eleven Chinese dollars per ounce which worked out then, in the 6,000 ounces per day, at almost exactly two million dollars per month.

A Chinese agent in Special Service reported to us that the sales of Heroin under the direction of the Special Service reached three million dollars per month at that same period. Although the figures of the narcotic section of the municipal police were much higher, my investigation concluded conservatively that fifty thousand persons were using Heroin, one-eighth of the population at that time. The increase of robbery by hundreds upon hundreds of Heroin addicts became a serious matter for everyone, including the University of Nanking.

The officials connected with the opium monopoly attempted to pull the Heroin users to the use of opium by arresting and prosecuting them in the courts.

I transmitted the completed report to the Japanese Consul General, asking for any comments or corrections in matters of fact; and then some ten days later I published it in Shanghai without any objection protest from the authorities then or at a later time.

By the following autumn the system had become well developed and established. We inquired again. This time we were able to see for a brief time, brief period, the book of the chief inspector of the 175 licensed dens, and we were also able to get the statement of the girl who sliced in portions the 3,000 ounces per day sold at that time within the city walls of Nanking. The figures of the consumption and revenue secured in this way agreed very closely with the figures in a report of the Ministry of Finance of the puppet government then called the Reformed Government. The unpublished mimeographed financial statement of that government showed in the autumn of 1939 a monthly income of three million dollars, made up of a so-called tax of three dollars on each of one million ounces of opium. The financial officers complained continually that there were many sales outside the official system. These one million ounces were used in the portions of three provinces which were controlled by the Reformed Government at that time.

In the summer of 1939, I visited Tokyo and was taken by friends to talk with the opium expert of the Gaimusho. This man, Mr. Haga, had just returned from a two months' inspection tour in Central China. He told me that he was greatly distressed at the terrible addiction that he saw in Hankow and other cities of the Yangtze Valley. When I asked him if there was any hope for improvement, he shook his head sadly and said, "No, the generals told me that so long as the war continues, there is no hope of anything better because no other good source of revenue has been found for the puppet governments."

In the report made to the Japanese officials and subsequently published I wrote, "The revenue of three million dollars from opium is the main support of the Reformed Government and is declared by Japanese and Chinese officials to be indispensable for the maintenance of any government in this area under present supervision and circumstances." The retail price at that time for opium was twenty-two dollars per ounce, which covered eight dollars paid for the basic supply at Dairen, two dollars to other Japanese interests for transportation, the so-called three-dollar tax, and left nine dollars' margin for profit, in which the Special Service and the gendarmerie shared.

The gendarmerie complained of this accusation and tried to get me to withdraw it, and at the same time to give the names of those from whom I got the information. When I replied that I would gladly make and publish any demonstrated correction of fact but could not make any other changes, they dropped the matter.

Over a period of many decades missionaries in China had been active in educational and even when necessary in political work against opium. In the ten years preceding the Japanese War these efforts had become much less necessary and less important. But in the summer of 1940 the great deterioration of the situation caused the editors of the China *Christian Yearbook,* which is the publication of the National Christian Council of China, to ask me to prepare a report on the narcotic problem in China as a whole. I sent to some forty friends in various parts of China copies of the reports that I prepared in Nanking and a set of questions which I hoped they would attempt to answer by investigations in their own localities regarding narcotics. Despite the censorship and accompanying anxieties more than half of these persons replied with considerable care.

For example, Professor Sailer, head of the Sociology Department of Yenshing University, reported that in Peking there were, in the spring of 1940, more than 600 licensed opium shops and that there were even more people using Heroin than opium. Bishop Gilman of Hankow found in that city that there were 340 licensed dens and 120 hotels licensed to supply opium for a population of only 400,000.

MR. BROOKS: I want to object on the basis that the witness is reading testimony—been sitting there continuously looking down, reading this testimony. He is not refreshing his mind; he is just reading into the record phrases. We don't know whether it was prepared for him or how he got it. But, if he wants to testify in answer to the question, he should answer the question directly; and, if he has to refresh his memory, he should refresh his memory and then testify.

THE PRESIDENT: There is no objection to him reading from his notes to a limited extent so far as his notes contain statements of fact. This morning he was reading things which were not statements of fact, such things as questions to himself.

The objection is overruled.

A: (Continuing) To make the fact clear, I'd simply like to say that I am not reading from any prepared text, that I have notes of these figures which I will gladly show to the Court in demonstration. If that is objectionable, I, of course, accept the Court's ruling.

Bishop Gilman very strongly emphasized the terrible contrast between the pre-war days of severe suppression of opium sales and consumption with the wide-open, well-advertised, well published trade of 1940. I will not trouble you with similar figures from several provincial capitals and other important cities but will mention simply Canton where in the city proper, which at that time had only 500,000 people, there were 852 registered dens beside some 300, unregistered as found by Dr. Thompson, Superintendent of the Canton Hospital.

The situation throughout the occupied areas was one of open sale of opium in government shops or licensed shops and the aggressive peddling of Heroin. In some cases there was attractive advertising of opium. In some cases Japanese soldiers used opium as payment for prostitutes and for labor engaged on military supply dumps. The general testimony of dealers and of officials was that the opium came almost entirely from Dairen although in the year 1939 there were some large shipments brought from Iran.

Heroin dealers reported that their supplies came largely from Tientsin and secondarily from Dairen. Throughout the occupied areas there was no real effort at suppression. The only apparent restriction or control was the effort to force irregular buying into the channels that would produce revenue.

This 1940 general report was published in the *China Christian Yearbook, 1938–39*. It was also reprinted in the monthly magazine, the *Chinese Recorder,* published in Shanghai.

Q: When did you leave China following the occupation of Nanking by the Japanese troops?

A: I left in May, 1941.

Q: And when did you return to China?

A: I returned to Nanking in October, 1945, after going earlier to Chengtu in West China where the University of Nanking was carrying on.

MR. SUTTON: The defense may cross-examine the witness.

CROSS-EXAMINATION

BY MR. LOGAN:

Q: Mr. Bates, you testified this morning in substance that you submitted reports and complaints to three officers of the Japanese Consul at Nanking, but they were terrified, and they were not able to do anything about them except to send them to Tokyo. Now, will you state, in answer to this question, yes or no, if possible: Do you know of your own knowledge that they were sent to Tokyo by the Japanese Consulate's office?

A: Yes.

Q: Who in the Japanese Consulate's office in Nanking sent these messages?

A: I do not know which one of these three men I named took the actual responsibility for sending messages. MR. FUKUI was the Consul in charge.

Q: Did you see the messages?

A: I did not see the messages. If you want to know my reasons –

Q: No, I don't.

A: All right.

MR. SUTTON: If it please the Court, I respectfully submit that the witness has a right to complete his answer. And the fact that counsel for the defense does not wish to hear it does not deny that right.

MR. LOGAN: I am sure, if the Tribunal please, if anything is left unanswered, it can be drawn out in redirect by the prosecution if they see fit.

THE PRESIDENT: We agree with you, Mr. Logan. Proceed.

Q: So, Mr. Bates, not having seen the messages, I assume you do not know of your own knowledge to whom they were sent in Tokyo, is that right?

A: I have seen telegrams sent by Mr. Grew, the Ambassador in Tokyo, to the American Embassy in Nanking, which referred to these reports in great detail and referred to conversations in which they had been discussed between Mr. Grew and officials of the Gaimusho, including Mr. HIROTA.

MR. LOGAN: I ask that the answer be stricken and that the reporter be directed to read my question.

THE WITNESS: I should be glad to give you some more evidence from Japanese sources on that.

MR. LOGAN: If your Honor please, I ask this witness be directed not to give—to volunteer statements.

THE PRESIDENT: His answer will stand. He must, of course, confine his answer to the question. But he may add any explanation.

MR. LOGAN: I ask that the previous question be answered. I don't think he has answered it, your Honor. He has given another explanation to it.

THE PRESIDENT: We will get it to save time.

(Whereupon, the last question was read by the official court reporter as follows:)

Q: So, Mr. Bates, not having seen the messages, I assume you do not know of your own knowledge to whom they were sent in Tokyo, is that right?

A: I know they were sent to the Gaimusho in Tokyo; I do not know to what individual other than the statement I gave you from Mr. Grew. I have other evidence that they were sent to the Gaimusho.

Q: Let me see if I understand you, Mr. Bates. Not having seen these messages, the testimony that you have with regard to them is hearsay, comes from somebody else, isn't that so?

A: Yes.

MR. LOGAN: That is all.

CROSS-EXAMINATION (Continued)

BY CAPTAIN KLETMAN:

Q: Doctor, on these reports that you say you saw: wherein you refer to Mr. Grew, was the Privy Council ever mentioned?

A: The messages I saw, which were strictly limited to the question of what was happening in Nanking in January and February of 1938, referred to the conversations of Mr. Grew with Mr. HIROTA and, I believe, Mr. YOSHIZAWA at the Gaimusho. I do not recall that other persons were mentioned.

Q: Doctor, did you hear my question?

A: I thought so.

THE PRESIDENT: How would he know whether the Privy Council was consulted?

Q: How long have you been in China, Doctor?

A: How long have I been in China? With the exception of furloughs—normal furloughs in the United States; I was there from 1920 to 1941 and from 1945 until a few weeks ago.

Q: And at the University in China, did you teach history?

A: I did.

Q: And are you acquainted with political divisions of Japanese Government, Doctor?

THE PRESIDENT: You must confine your cross-examination to matters arising in chief. The mere statement that he was a historian doesn't introduce any matter of the kind to which you refer.

CAPTAIN KLEIMAN: If it please the Tribunal, I am asking preliminary questions to show the unwillingness of this witness to present the entire truth. We want all those facts out. Whether it hurts or not, we want all the facts out.

THE PRESIDENT: Do not argue with me that way. I said that he has not testified really as to any Japanese political divisions. He is a professor of history. I called him a historian. Perhaps that's a wrong term. But the questions you ask don't arise out of the examination in chief.

CAPTAIN KLEIMAN: Mr. President, I wonder if it's possible to take up that question again with respect to confining ourselves to testimony in chief. This witness, I understand, has been here for a time awaiting time to testify. Now, he may have some information which might be of aid to the defense. In order for me to secure this witness, I would have to go to China, bring him here at great expense, and then—

THE PRESIDENT: You interpret that. Translate that, please.

I told you what the Tribunal's decision was, and I showed how you are infringing it, and you have not shown that you did not infringe it in your question.

You must accept the Tribunal's decision. We are not going to alter that to meet this particular case.

CAPTAIN KLEIMAN: We will abide by the Tribunal's decision. The only request I made was, your Honor, so that we can save time when the defense is to put in its testimony. Two questions now may lead to two answers which may save us two or three days when the defense puts in its testimony.

THE PRESIDENT: I have told you what the decision is. I have told you that it excludes those questions, and why. You have given me no answer that suggested the Tribunal is wrong in excluding the questions. You must obey the Tribunal's decision.

CAPTAIN KLEIMAN: Is it the Tribunal's decision that we may not ask questions, aside from what was brought out by examination in chief, for the purpose of attacking credibility of the witness? I'm not saying that I attempted to do that with this witness; I just want to know the ruling so that we can abide by that ruling in the future, may it please the Court.

THE PRESIDENT: You appear to be the only counsel who misunderstands the Tribunal's decision. That decision does prevent you from examining outside the scope of the examination in chief in order to test credibility.

CAPTAIN KLEIMAN: I'm sorry, your Honor. This practice is so different from the practice that we have in the United States, I've had difficulty in understanding the ruling. I'm sorry, sir.

THE PRESIDENT: It so happens that it is the practice of the United States and the practice of its highest courts.

CAPTAIN KLEIMAN: If it please the Tribunal, we are, in the States, permitted to ask a witness questions not brought out on direct examination, but we are bound by his answers; he becomes our witness. We can not impeach him. This is what I wanted to do with this witness.

THE PRESIDENT: There is a limit to this Tribunal's patience, Captain Kleiman.

CAPTAIN KLEIMAN: All right. No further questions.

MR. SAMMONJI: I am Shohei SAMMONJI, counsel for the defendant, KOISO. With your kind permission, I wish to put a few questions.

CROSS-EXAMINATON (Continued)

BY MR. SAMMONJI:

Q: The witness seems to be greatly familiar with the economic situation in China. Do you know the—how prices were during the period 1930 to 1939?

A: I am sorry I didn't get that word. Do I know what?

Q: This is my question: Which was higher, prices in Nanking before December, 1937, or prices in Nanking after 1937, during the years 1938 and 1939?

A: I would not know how to answer that. I do not claim to be an economic expert. I reported the conditions which I found affecting the life of the people, as I was doing the work of the International Relief Committee in Nanking from 1937 to 1941.

Q: If you have been investigating the standard of living—living conditions of the general public—I should think you ought to have a great deal of interest in the question of prices.

A: What is the question?

THE PRESIDENT: There is no question; there is a statement.

Q: You seem to be an expert on opium. Have you ever investigated the areas where opium is produced in the world?

A: I am sorry I haven't had such wide privileges of travel. I have done some general reading on the subject.

THE PRESIDENT: That question is beyond the scope of the examination in chief.

Q: Have you ever investigated which was greater: the consumption of opium and Heroin before December, 1937, and that in Nanking, and after December, 1937?

A: Before 1937 there was no consumption that could readily be measured or investigated. There was very little, and as I said, confined to back rooms without open, public sale.

Q: Then, have you ever investigated the complete—the total of opium and Heroin smoked by Chinese in all parts of China before—for the whole of China—before December, 1937, and the prices thereof?

A: No, I have not; because there was no local problem which loomed up as conspicuous; my attention was not brought to opium in any grievous manner until the spring and summer of 1938.

Q: But in your testimony you have stated that opium was imported from Dairen and from Tientsin, and that before December, 1937, opium was secretly smoked; so that you seem to have carried on your investigations quite extensively. Then do you know—if you know where this opium came from—do you not know also where it was produced?

A: That question is not clear to me.

THE PRESIDENT: He said where it came from.

THE WITNESS: Before 1937 or after 1937?

Q: What I want to ask is that in 1937 and after 1937 where did this opium come from, and where was it produced?

A: As for after 1937, I have already given that in direct testimony; that my investigation—the reports from dealers—regularly brought the statement that the opium came from Dairen with the exception of fairly important shipments which came in 1939 from Iran. Before 1937 I do not have such detailed knowledge, because I did not go into investigation. I only know what were the general statements at that time—that there was opium imported from various sources, that there was also opium produced in China, particularly in the far western provinces near the Tibetan frontier. From missionary friends in various parts of East China I learned that areas formerly producing opium had ceased to do so, it should be added that under the Japanese occupation in various provinces, such as northern Anhui, Honan, and Shanghai provinces, that opium growing was begun locally once more where it had been stamped out over a period of many years. This locally grown opium was usually sold outside the official system.

Q: Are you aware that China is the country where opium—with the greatest consumption of opium and Heroin in the world?

A: I think probably that is true, but I should like to see it specified with dates, and I myself do not have much comparative knowledge.

Q: Since the Opium War to the present day.

A: From the Opium War to the present day?

Q: Yes.

A: Yes, I think that is probably true.

Q: Well, there is much opium—as you have said, there is much opium consumed in all China. Do you know—there is much opium growing in China, but as to opium that comes from foreign sources, do you know from what country was the greatest source of—what country is the greatest source of opium, from what country opium is imported, what country produces opium, and what country imported opium the most?

A: At what time?

Q: Since the Opium War to the present date?

A: That would have to be broken up into several different periods, and would be a subject only for a great expert. I can give general statements, but they are not of specific knowledge.

THE PRESIDENT: We will recess now for fifteen minutes.

(Whereupon, at 1445, a recess was taken until 1506, after which the proceedings were resumed as follows:)

MARSHAL OF THE COURT: The International Military Tribunal for the Far East is now resumed.

Q: Mr. Witness, in regard to the last question, I request that you would answer even in general terms.

THE WITNESS: Mr. President, I wonder just where this gets us. I have not testified in regard to conditions in varying countries around the world nor on conditions since the Opium War. I am willing to start on what little I know on this, but I have in no way posed as an historian of opium on a world-wide scale.

THE PRESIDENT: The witness merely testified as to conditions in and about Nanking. That does not authorize cross-examination as to conditions in other parts of the world relating to opium nor do I think it justifies questions dealing with the opium trade right back to the Opium War.

MR. SAMMONJI: Then I will go into another question.

Q: Mr. Witness, you said earlier that after the Japanese Army entered Nanking in 1937 the Japanese sold opium officially. Was not this selling of opium officially to supervise the illicit trade in opium and also to treat opium patients?

THE MONITOR: Correction: Instead of "Japanese sold opium," it should read: "Opium was sold in open market." "Japanese" should be deleted.

A: There was no remedial action of any kind in hospitals or treatment of addicts which I ever saw on the part of the public system in Nanking after the entry of the Japanese. Not only in the general situation of the few years before 1937, but in the first few weeks and months after the Japanese came in, there was no apparent trade and no widespread consumption of opium. Then within a period of a few months the large system of public supply and sales, which I described, was built up.

Q: Mr. Witness, as far as the illicit buying of opium is concerned and also the selling of opium on open market, do you not think that the selling, buying of opium illicitly proves far more fascinating to these opium addicts?

A: I don't know how to answer that question. I think it was very largely a matter of price and that if opium could be secured illicitly below the price of the official system, people, addicts were very glad to get it that way. So far as I can interpret the situation, so far as I saw the situation, the public sale was greater than the illicit sale, but illicit sale never disappeared. The enormous scale of the official trade as reported did not leave room for a very big illicit trade.

Q: Do you not know that in all Chinese families above the middle class they have medical dispensary for opium drinking? Do you not know that in all Chinese families above the middle class they have a room which is suitable for drinking opium—smoking opium?

THE MONITOR: "Provided for smoking opium."

A: I do not know that. It is quite contrary to my experience and acquaintance of twenty-five years in Naking.

Q: Then I shall ask another question. Do you not know that when a person first smokes opium, he does not become an immediate addict and it takes some time before he becomes an addict to the opium, for a time, say, around one year? At first when a person first smokes opium, he encounters physiological discomfort.

A: Well, that is an interesting observation. What is the question?

THE PRESIDENT: That type of cross-examination is useless.

MR. BROOKS: No further questioning.

THE PRESIDENT: That will do, Professor. Unless you wish to re-examine, do you, Mr. Sutton?

MR. SUTTON: The prosecution has asked to call as its next witness, Mr. Peter J. Lawless.

MARSHAL OF THE COURT: Mr. President, the witness is in court and will now be sworn.

Notes

1. RG10, B102.
2. RG10, B102, F865.
3. RG10, B4, F67.
4. RG10, B4, F52. This important letter had appeared in H.J. Timperley *What War Means, The Japanese Terror in China*, London, New York, 1938.
5. RG10, B4, F67.
6. RG10, B1, F5–11.
7. RG10, B4, F65.
8. RG10, B4, F65.
9. RG10, B4, F52.
10. RG1, B4, F59.
11. RG10, B4, F52. This open letter was an attachment of the letter dated Nov. 29, 1938 for Bates' friends.
12. RG10, B4, F52.
13. RG10, B1, F7–11.
14. RG10, B98, F800.
15. J.H. Reisner, had been the professor and president in the College of Agriculture and Forest, University of Nanking.
16. RG10, B126, F1137.

George Ashmore Fitch

George Ashmore Fitch was born in Soochow, China, in 1883, the son of Presbyterian missionaries George F. and Mary McLellan Fitch. After receiving his B.A. from Wooster College in 1906, Fitch attended Union Theological Seminary in New York. He was ordained in 1909 and returned to China to work with the YMCA in Shanghai.

When the Nanking Massacre occurred, Fitch was the head of the YMCA at Nanking. He quickly became active in assisting the International Committee for the Nanking Safety Zone. Fitch's diary of events in Nanking was carried to Shanghai by the first person able to leave Nanking after its occupation by the Japanese on December 13, 1937. As Fitch has written, "My story created a sensation in Shanghai, for it was the first news of what had happened in the capital since its evacuation, and it was copied and mimeographed and widely distributed there."

In 1938 Fitch traveled throughout the United States giving talks about the Nanking Massacre and showing films to document it. He returned to China to serve with the YMCA and the United Nations Relief and Rehabilitation Agency, then went on to serve the YMCA in Korea and Taiwan until his retirement in 1961.

Diary[1]

What I am about to relate is anything but a pleasant story; in fact it is so very unpleasant that I cannot recommend anyone without a strong stomach to read it. For it is a story of such crime and horror as to be almost unbelievable, the story of depredations of a horde of degraded criminals of incredible bestiality, who have been, and now are, working their will, unrestrained, on a peaceful, kindly, law-abiding people. Yet it is a story which I feel must be told, even if it is seen by only a few. I cannot rest until I have told it, and unfortunately, or perhaps fortunately, I am one of a very few who are in a position to tell it. It is not complete for it is only a small part of the whole; and God alone knows when it will be finished. I pray it may be soon—but I am afraid it is going to go on for many months to come, not just here but in other parts of China. I believe it has no parallel in modern history.

It is now Christmas Eve. I shall start with say December 10th. In these two short weeks we here in Nanking have been through a siege; the Chinese army has left, defeated, and the Japanese [Army] has come in. On that day Nanking was still the beautiful city we were so proud of, with law and order still prevailing; today it is a city laid waste, ravaged, completely looted, much of it burned. Complete anarchy has reigned for ten days—it has been a hell on earth. Not that my life has been in serious danger at any time; though turning lust-mad, sometimes drunken soldiers out of houses where they were raping the women, is not altogether a safe occupation; nor does one feel, perhaps, too sure of himself when he finds a bayonet at his chest or a revolver at his head and knows it is handled by someone who heartily wishes him out of the way. For the Japanese [Army] is anything but pleased at our being here after having advised all foreigners to get out. They wanted no observers. But to have to stand by while even the very poor are having their last possessions taken from them—their last coin, their last bit of bedding (and it is freezing weather), the poor ricksha man his ricksha; while thousands of disarmed soldiers who had sought sanctuary with you, together with many hundreds of innocent civilians are taken out before your eyes to be shot, or used for bayonet practice, and you have to listen to the sound of the guns that are killing them; over a thousand women kneel before you crying hysterically, begging you to save them from the beasts who are preying on them; to stand by and do nothing while your flag is taken down and insulted, not once but a dozen times, and your own home is being looted; and then to watch the city you have come to love and the institutions to which you had planned to devote your best years deliberately and systematically burned by fire—this is a hell I had never before envisaged.

We keep asking ourselves "How long can this last?" Day by day we are assured by the officials that things will be better *soon*, that "we will do our best"—but each day has been worse than the day before. And now we are told that a new division of 20,000 men are arriving. Will they have to have their toll of flesh and loot, of murder and rape? There will be little left to rob, for the city has been well nigh stripped clean. For the past week the soldiers have been busy loading their trucks with what they wanted from the stores and then setting fire to the buildings. And then there is the harrowing realization that we have only enough rice and flour for the 200,000 refugees for another three weeks and coal for ten days. Do you wonder that one awakes in the night in a cold sweat of fear and sleep for the rest of the night is gone? Even if we had food enough for three months, how are they going to be fed after that? And with their homes burned, where are they going to live? They cannot continue much longer in their present terribly crowded condition; disease and pestilence must soon follow if they do.

Every day we call at the Japanese Embassy and present our protests, our appeals, our lists of authenticated reports of violence and crime. We are met with suave Japanese courtesy, but actually the officials there are powerless. The victorious army must have its rewards—and those rewards are to plunder, murder, rape at will, to commit acts of unbelievable brutality and savagery on the very people whom they have come to protect and befriend, as they have so loudly proclaimed to the world. In all modern history surely there is no page that will stand so black as that of the rape of Nanking.

To tell the whole story of these past ten days would take too long. The tragic thing is that by the time the truth gets out to the rest of the world it will be cold—it will no longer be "news." Anyway, the Japanese have undoubtedly been proclaiming abroad that they have established law and order in a city that had already been looted and burned, and that the downtrodden population had welcomed their benevolent army with open arms and a great flag-waving welcome. However, I am going to record some of the more important events of this period as I have jotted them down in my little diary, for they will at least be of interest to some of my friends and I shall have the satisfaction of having a permanent record of these unhappy days. It will probably extend beyond the date of this letter, for I do not anticipate being able to get this off for some considerable time. The Japanese censorship will see to that! Our own Embassy officials and those of other countries together with some of the business men who went aboard the ill-fated *Panay* and the Standard Oil boats and other ships just before the capture of Nanking, confidently expecting to return within a week when they left, are still cooling their heels (those who haven't been killed or wounded by Japanese bombs and machine guns) out on the river or perhaps in one of the ports. We think it will be another fortnight before any of them is permitted to return, and longer than that before any of us is permitted to leave Nanking. We are virtually prisoners here.

Two weeks before the fall of the city our International Committee for Nanking Safety Zone had been negotiating with both the Chinese and Japanese for the recognition of a certain area in the city which would be kept free of soldiers and all military offices and which would not be bombed or shelled, a place where the remaining two hundred thousand of Nanking's population of one million could take refuge when things became too hot, for it had become quite obvious that the splendid resistance which the Chinese had put up for so long at Shanghai was now broken and their morale largely gone. The terrific punishment which they had taken from the superior artillery, tanks, and air force could not be endured forever and the successful landing of Japanese troops on Hangchow Bay attacking their flank and rear was the crowning event in their undoing. It seemed inevitable that Nanking must soon fall.

On December 1st Mayor Ma virtually turned over to us the administrative responsibilities for the Zone together with a police force of 450 men, 30,000 piculs (2,000 tons) of rice, 10,000 bags of flour, and some salt, also a promise of a hundred thousand dollars in cash—80,000 of which was subsequently received. Gen. Tang, recently executed we have been told, charged with the defense of the city, cooperated splendidly on the whole in the very difficult task of clearing the Zone of the military and anti-aircraft, and a most commendable degree of order was preserved right up to the very last moment when the Japanese began, on Sunday the 12th, to enter the walls.

There was no looting save in a small way by soldiers who were in need of provisions, and foreign property throughout the city was respected. We had city water until the 10th, electricity until the following day, and telephone service actually up to the date the Japanese entered the city. At no time did we feel any serious sense of danger, for the Japanese seemed to be avoiding the Zone with their air bombs and shells, and Nanking was a heaven of order and safety as compared with the hell it has been ever since the Japanese came. It is true we had some difficulty with our trucking—the rice was stored outside the city and some of our drivers did not relish going out where the shells were falling. One lost an eye with a splinter of shrapnel, and two of our trucks were seized by the military, but that was nothing compared with the difficulties we have since faced.

On December 10, the refugees were streaming into the Zone. We had already filled most of the institutional buildings—Ginling College, the Law College and other schools, and now had to requisition the Supreme Court, the Law College and the Overseas buildings, forcing doors where they were locked and appointing our own caretakers. Two Japanese blimps were visible just beyond Purple Mountain, probably to direct artillery fire. Heavy guns were pounding the south gate, and shells were dropping into the city. Several shells landed just within the Zone to the south the following morning, killing about forty near the Bible Teachers' Training School and the Foo Chong Hotel. Mr. Sperling, our inspector, a German, was slightly injured at the latter place where he was living. The U.S.S. *Panay* moved upriver, but before it left I had a phone call (the last city gate had been closed and we had forfeited our right to go aboard the gunboat) from Paxton of our Embassy giving me the last two navy radiograms to reach Nanking. He was phoning from outside the city, of course. The messages were from Wilbur and Boynton.

We were now a community of twenty-seven—eighteen Americans, five Germans, one Englishman, one Austrian and two Russians. Out on the river was the *Panay* with the two remaining Embassy men, Atcheson and Paxton, and half a dozen others; the Standard Oil and Asiatic Petroleum motor ship with many more, a hulk which had been fitted out as a sort of floating hotel and towed upstream with some twenty foreigners including Dr. Rosen of the German Embassy and some four hundred Chinese, and other craft. All were looking forward to an early return to the city. How many of them have met their fate we do not know, but it will be a long time before any of them get back now. And what a Nanking they will see!

On Sunday the 12th I was busy at my desk in the Safety Zone all day long. We were using the former residence of Gen. Chang Chun, recently Minister of Foreign Affairs, as headquarters, so were very comfortably fixed, and incidentally had one of the best bomb-proof dugouts in all Nanking. Airplanes had been over us almost constantly for the past two days, but no one heeded them now, and the shellfire had been terrific. The wall had been breached and the damage in the southern part of the city was tremendous. No one will ever know what the Chinese casualties were, but they must have been enormous. The Japanese say they themselves lost forty thousand men taking Nanking. The general rout must have started early that afternoon. Soldiers streamed through the city from the south, many of them passing through the Zone, but they were well-behaved and orderly. Gen. Tang asked our assistance in arranging a truce with the Japanese and Mr. Sperling agreed to take a flag and message—but it was already too late. He [Tang] fled that evening, and as soon as news got out disorganization became general. There was panic as they made for the gate to Hsiakwan and the river. The road for miles was strewn with the equipment they cast away—rifles, ammunition, belts, uniforms, cars, trucks—everything in the way of army impedimenta.

Trucks and cars jammed, were overturned, caught fire; at the gate more cars jammed and were burned—a terrible holocaust—and the dead lay feet deep. The gate blocked, terror mad soldiers scaled the wall and let themselves down on the other side with ropes, putties and belts tied together, clothing torn in strips. Many fell and were killed. But at the river was perhaps the most appalling scene of all. A fleet of junks was there. It was totally inadequate for the horde that was now in a frenzy to cross to the north side. The overcrowded junks capsized, they sank, thousands drowned. Other thousands tried to make rafts of the lumber on the river front, only to suffer the same fate. Other thousands must have succeeded in getting away, but many of these were probably bombed by Japanese planes a day or two later.

One small detail of three companies rallied under their officers, crossed the San Chia Ho three miles up the river and tried to attack the Japanese forces that were coming in from that direction, but were out numbered and practically decimated. Only one seems to have succeeded in getting back. He happened to be the brother of a friend of mine and appeared in my office the next morning to report the story. A fellow officer had drowned while the two of them were trying to swim the small tributary to the Yangtze which they had crossed before on rafts, and before daylight he had managed to scale the wall and slip in unobserved.

So ended the happy, peaceful, well-ordered, progressive regime which we had been enjoying here in Nanking and on which we had built our hopes for still better days. For the Japanese were already in the city and with them came terror and destruction and death. They were first reported in the Zone at eleven o'clock that morning, the 13th. I drove down with two of our committee members to meet them, just a small detachment at the southern entrance to the Zone. They showed no hostility, though a few moments later they killed twenty refugees who were frightened by their presence and ran from them. For it seems to be the rule here, as it was in Shanghai in 1932, that any who run must be shot or bayoneted.

Meanwhile we were busy at headquarters disarming soldiers who had been unable to escape and had come into the Zone for protection. We assured them that if they gave up their equipment their lives would be spared by the Japanese. But it was a vain promise. All would have preferred to die fighting, to being taken out and shot or sabred or used for bayonet practice, as they all were later on.

There was still some shell fire that day, but very little that landed in the Zone. We discovered some fragments of shrapnel in our yard that evening; Dr. Wilson had a narrow escape from shrapnel bits that came through the window of his operating room while he was operating; and a shell passed through one of the new University dormitories; but there were no casualties. The Communications building, the most beautiful in all Nanking, with its superb ceremonial hall, was in flames, but whether from shell-fire or started by the retreating Chinese, we do not know.

On Tuesday the 14th the Japanese were pouring into the city—tanks, artillery, infantry, trucks. The reign of terror commenced, and it was to increase in severity and horror with each of the succeeding ten days. They were the conquerors of China's Capital, the seat of the hated Chiang Kai-shek government, they were given free reign to do as they pleased. The proclamation on the handbills which airplanes scattered over the city, saying that the Japanese were the only real friends of the Chinese and would protect the good, of course, meant no more than most of their statements. And to show their "sincerity" they raped, looted and killed at will. Men were taken from our refugee camps in droves, as we supposed at the time, for labor—but they have never been heard from again, nor will they be. A colonel and his staff called at my office and spent an hour trying to learn where the "six thousand disarmed soldiers" were. Four times that day Japanese soldiers came and tried to take our cars away. Others in the mean time succeeded in stealing three of our cars that were elsewhere. On Sone's they tore off the American flag and threw it on the ground, broke a window and managed to get away all within the five minutes he had gone into Prof. C. Smith's house. They tried to steal our trucks—did succeed in getting two—so ever since it has been necessary for two Americans to spend most of their time riding trucks as they delivered rice and coal. Their experience in dealing daily with these Japanese car thieves would make an interesting story in itself. And at the University Hospital they took the watches and fountain pens from the nurses.

Durdin, of the *New York Times*, started for Shanghai by motor that day, though none of us had much faith he would get through, I hurriedly wrote a letter for him to take, but he was turned back at Kuyung. Steele of the *Chicago Daily News*, managed to get out to the river and reported that a number of Japanese destroyers had just arrived. A lieutenant gave him the news of the sinking of the *Panay* but had no details, nor did he mention the other ships that were sunk. After all their efforts to have us go aboard, finally leaving us with a couple of lengths of rope, by which we could get down over the wall and to the river—it was ironical indeed that the *Panay* should be bombed and we still safe.

Mr. Rabe, our Chairman, Nanking head of Siemens China Company, and Smythe, our secretary, called at military headquarters in the hope of seeing the commanding officer and stopping the intolerable disorder, but had to wait until the next day as he had not yet entered the city. Their calls were quite useless anyway.

On Wednesday I drove around to my house, which is just outside the Zone, to see if everything was all right. Yesterday the gates were intact, but today the side gate was broken in, and the south door open, in spite of the American and Japanese proclamations with which they were sealed. My two American flags had been torn down and destroyed. I had no time to investigate, but asked a friendly looking major who had just moved in across the street to keep an eye on the place, which he promised to do. A staff officer from the Japanese Navy was waiting for me. He expressed his deep concern over the loss of the *Panay,* but he too could give no details. The Navy would be glad to send a destroyer to Shanghai with any of the members of the American community who wished to go, also to send radio messages of purely a personal nature. He seemed somewhat disappointed in the brevity of the message I wrote out: "Wilbur, National Committee YMCA, Shanghai: All foreigners Nanking safe and well. Please inform interested parties"; also when I told him that with the exception of a couple of newspapermen the rest of us wished to stay in Nanking.

I offered to drive him back to his ship—he had been obliged to walk the four miles in—but half way we were stopped by an army major who told us that no civilians were allowed further north as they were still rounding up some Chinese soldiers and it was unsafe. We happened to be beside the Ministry of War at the time and it was all too evident that an execution was going on, hundreds of poor disarmed soldiers with many innocent civilians among them—the real reason for his not wanting me to go further. So Mr. Sekiguchi of H.I.J.M.S. Seta had to walk the rest of the way. But that afternoon I stole a march on the surly major: I went to Hsiakwan by back roads. At the gate I was stopped, but I had Smith of Reuters and Steele with me who were leaving on that destroyer, so we were finally allowed to pass. I have already described the conditions at that gate—we actually had to drive over masses of dead bodies 2 to 3 feet deep, and 90 feet in length, to get through. But the scene beggars description. I shall never forget that ride.

At the jetty we found Durdin of the *Times* and Art Mencken of Paramount Films, with whom I had just made the trip to the Northwest, to Shansi and Sian, already there, for they were going too, and I had promised to drive Durdin's car back to the American Embassy for him. Mr. Okamura of the Japanese Embassy just arrived from Shanghai, was also there and gave us the names of the killed and wounded on the *Panay* and the Standard Oil boats, so I offered him a lift back to the city. But at the gate we were stopped again and this time the guard positively refused to let me enter. No foreigners were allowed to enter Nanking and the fact that I had just come from there made no difference. Even Mr. Okamura's appeals were in vain—the Embassy cuts no ice with the army in Japan. The only thing to do was to wait while Okamura took one of the cars to military headquarters and sent back a special pass. It took an hour and a half; but I had the November *Reader's Digest,* the last piece of mail to reach me from the outside, with me, so the time passed quickly. The stench at the gate was awful—and here and there the dogs were gnawing at the corpses.

At our staff conference that evening word came that soldiers were taking all 1,300 men in one of our camps near headquarters to shoot them. We knew there were a number of ex-soldiers among them, but Rabe had been promised by an officer that very afternoon that their lives would be spared. It was now all too obvious what they were going to do. The men were lined up and roped together, in groups of about a hundred, by soldiers with bayonets fixed; those who had hats had them roughly torn off and thrown on the ground—and then by the light of our headlights we watched them marched away to their doom. Not a whimper came from the entire throng. Our own hearts were lead. Were those four lads from Canton who had trudged all the way up from the south and yesterday had reluctantly given me their arms among them, I wondered; or that tall, strapping sergeant from the north whose disillusioned eyes, as he made the fatal decision, still haunt me? How foolish I had been to tell them the Japanese would spare their lives! We had confidently expected that they would live up to their promises, at least in some degree, and that order would be established with their arrival. Little did we dream that we should see such brutality and savagery as has probably not been equalled in modern times. For worse days were yet to come.

The problem of transportation became acute on the 16th, with the Japanese still stealing our trucks and cars. I went over to the American Embassy where the Chinese staff were still standing by, and borrowed Mr. Atcheson's car for Mills to deliver coal. For our big concentrations of refugees and our three big rice kitchens had to have fuel as well as rice. We now had twenty-five camps, ranging from two hundred to twelve thousand, and in Ginling College, which was reserved for women and children, the three thousand were rapidly increased to over nine thousand. In the latter place even the covered passageways between buildings were crowded, while within, every foot of space was taken. We had figured on sixteen square feet to a person, but actually they were crowded in much closer than that. For a while no place was safe, we did manage to preserve a fair degree of safety at Ginling, to a lesser degree in the University. Miss Vautrin, Mrs. Twinem and Mrs. Chen were heroic in their care and protection of the women.

That morning the cases of rape began to be reported. Over a hundred women, that we knew of were taken away by soldiers, seven of them from the University library; but there must have been many times that number who were raped in their homes. Hundreds were on the streets trying to find a place of safety. At tiffin time Riggs, who was associate commissioner of housing, came in crying. The Japanese had emptied the Law College and Supreme Court and taken away practically all the men to a fate we could only guess. Fifty of our policemen had been taken with them. Riggs had protested, only to be roughly handled by the soldiers and twice struck by an officer. Refugees were searched for money and anything they had on them was taken away, often to their last bit of bedding. At our staff conference at four we could hear the shots of the execution squad near by. It was a day of unspeakable terror for the poor refugees and horror for us.

On Wednesday I dashed over to my house for a few minutes on the way to tiffin at Prof. Buck's where I was living with six others. The two American flags were still flying and the proclamations by the Embassy still on the gates, and front doors; but the side gate had been smashed and the door broken open. Within was confusion. Every drawer and closet and trunk had been opened, locks smashed. The attic was littered ankle deep. I could not stop to see what was taken but most of the bedding was gone and some clothing and food-stuffs. A carved teak screen had been stripped of its embroidered panels, a gift of Dr. C.T. Wang, and a heavy oak buffet battered in.

Yates McDaniel of the Associated Press, the last of our newspapermen, left in the afternoon by another destroyer for Shanghai. With him I sent another short letter which I hope got through.

Friday, December 17. Robbery, murder, rape continue unabated. A rough estimate would be at least a thousand women raped last night and during the day. One poor woman was raped thirty-seven times. Another had her five months infant deliberately smothered by the brute to stop its crying while he raped her. Resistance means the bayonet. The hospital is rapidly filling up with the victims of Japanese cruelty and barbarity. Bob Wilson, our only surgeon, has his hands more than full and has to work into the night. Rickshas, cattle, pigs, donkeys, often the sole means of livelihood of the people, are taken from them. Our rice kitchens and rice shops are interfered with. We have had to close the latter.

After dinner I took Bates to the University and McCallum to the hospital where they will spend the night, then Mills and Smythe to Ginling, for one of our group has been sleeping there each night. At the gate of the latter place we were stopped by what seemed to be a searching party. We were roughly pulled from the car at the point of the bayonet, my car keys taken from me, lined up and frisked for arms, our hats jerked off, electric torches held to our faces, our passports and purpose in coming demanded. Opposite us were Miss Vautrin, Mrs. Twinem and Mrs. Chen, with a score of refugee women kneeling on the ground. The sergeant, who spoke a little French (about as much as I do), insisted there were soldiers concealed there. I maintained that, aside from about fifty domestics and other members of their staff, there were no men on the place. This he said he did not believe and said he would shoot all he found beyond that number. He then demanded that we all leave, including the ladies, and when Miss Vautrin refused she was roughly hustled to the car. Then he changed his mind: The ladies were told to stay and we to go. We tried to insist that one of us should stay too, but this he would not permit. Altogether we were kept standing there for over an hour before we were released. The next day we learned that this gang had abducted twelve girls from the school.

Saturday, December 18. At breakfast Riggs, who lives in the Safety Zone a block away, but has his meals with us, reported that two women, one a cousin of Wang Ding, our Y.M.C.A. secretary, were raped in his house while he was having dinner with us. Wilson reported a boy of five years of age brought to the hospital after having been stabbed with a bayonet five times, once through his abdomen; a man with eighteen bayonet wounds, a woman with seventeen cuts on her face and several on her legs. Between four and five hundred terrorized women poured into our headquarters compound in the afternoon, and spent the night in the open.

Sunday, December 19. A day of complete anarchy. Several big fires raging today, started by the soldiers, and more are promised. The American flag was torn down in the number of places. At the American School it was trampled on and the caretaker told he would be killed if he put it up again. The proclamations placed on all American and other foreign properties by the Japanese Embassy are flouted by their soldiers, sometimes deliberately torn off. Some houses are entered from five to ten times in one day and the poor people looted and robbed and the women raped. Several were killed in cold blood, for no apparent reason whatever. Six out of seven of our sanitation squads in one district were slaughtered; the seventh escaped, wounded, to tell the tale. Toward evening today two of us rushed to Dr. Brady's house (he is away) and chased four would-be rapers out and took all women there to the University. Sperling is busy at this game all day. I also went to the house of Douglas Jenkins, of our Embassy. The flag was still there; but in the garage his house boy lay dead. Another servant, dead, was under a bed, both brutally killed. The house was in utter confusion. There are still many corpses on the streets, all of them civilians as far as we can see. The Red Swastika Society would bury them, but their truck has been stolen, their coffins used for bonfires, and several of their workers bearing their insignia have been marched away.

Smythe and I called again at the Japanese Embassy with a list of fifty-five additional cases of violence, all authenticated, and told Messrs. Tanaka and Fukui that today was the worst so far. We were assured that they would "do their best" and hoped that things would be better "soon," but it is quite obvious that they have little or no influence with the military whatever, and the military have no control over the soldiers. We were also told that seventeen military police had recently arrived who would help in restoring order. Seventeen for an army of perhaps fifty thousand! Yet we rather like the three men of the Embassy. They are probably doing their best. But I had to smile when they asked my help in getting cars and a mechanic for them after so many of ours had been taken. I felt like referring them to their own military, but instead I took them around to the American Embassy and borrowed our Ambassador's and two others for them and later sent them our Russian repair man.

Monday, December 20. Vandalism and violence continue absolutely unchecked. Whole sections of the city are being systematically burned. At 5 p.m. Smythe and I went for a drive. All Taiping Road, the most important shopping street in the city, was in flames. We drove through showers of sparks and over burning embers. Further south we could see the soldiers inside the shops setting fire to them, and still further they were loading the loot into army trucks. Next, to the YMCA—and it was in flames—evidently fired only an hour or so ago. The surrounding buildings were as yet untouched. I hadn't the heart to watch it, so we hurried on. That night I counted fourteen fires from my window, some of them covering considerable areas.

Our group here at the house drafted a message to the American Consulate-General in Shanghai asking that diplomatic representatives be sent here immediately as the situation was urgent, then asked the Japanese Embassy to send it via navy radio. Needless to say it was never sent.

Tuesday, December 21. Fourteen of us called on Tanaka at 2:30 and presented a letter signed by all twenty-two foreigners protesting the burning of the city and continued disorders. More promises! Rabe fears for his house, for buildings are burning across the street from him. He has over four hundred refugees living in mat sheds in his garden. The problem of feeding is becoming serious —some refugees, hungry, started rioting in the University. Our coal will soon be finished, but Riggs is scouting for more. The Japanese have sealed all supplies of coal and rice. Soldiers came into our place today, over the wall, and tried to take our cars while we were all out, and at another time they nearly got Sone's truck from him. Rabe had a letter today from Dr. Rosen of the German Embassy, through Mr. Tananka, saying he was on the H.M.S. *Bee* at Hsiakwan; replied that he was glad to be able to inform him that two houses were not looted, the Ambassador's and his own, and that two cars were still left! (There are over fifty German residences in Nanking.)

Wednesday, December 22. Firing squad at work very near us at 5 a.m. today. Counted over a hundred shots. The University was entered twice during the night, the policeman at the gate held up at the point of a bayonet, and a door broken down. The Japanese military police recently appointed to duty there were asleep. Representatives of the new Japanese police force called and promised order by January 1. They also asked for the loan of motor cars and trucks. Went with Sperling to see fifty corpses in some ponds a quarter of a mile east of headquarters. All obviously civilians, hands bound behind backs, one with the top half of his head cut completely off. Were they used for sabre practice? On the way home for tiffin stopped to help the father of our Y.M.C.A. writer who was being threatened by a drunken soldier with his bayonet, the poor mother frantic with fear, and before sitting down had to run over with two of our fellows to chase soldiers out of Gee's and Daniel's houses, where they were just about to rape the women. We had to laugh to see those brave soldiers trying to get over a barbed wire fence as we chased them!

Bates and Riggs had to leave before they were through tiffin to chase soldiers out of the sericulture building—several drunks. And on my arrival at the office there was an SOS call, which Rabe and I answered, from Sperling and

Kroeger who were seriously threatened by a drunk with a bayonet. By fortunate chance, Tanaka of the Embassy, together with some general arrived at the same moment. The soldier had his face soundly slapped a couple of times by the general but I don't suppose he got any more than that. We have heard of no cases of discipline so far. If a soldier is caught by an officer or MP he is very politely told that he shouldn't do that again. In the evening I walked home with Riggs after dinner—a woman of fifty-four had been raped in his house just before our arrival. It's cruel to leave the women to their fate, but of course it is impossible for us to spend all our time just protecting them. Mr. Wu, engineer in the power plant which is located in Hsiakwan, brought us the amazing news that forty-three of the fifty-four employees who had so heroically kept the plant going to the very last day, and had finally been obliged to seek refuge in the International Export Company, a British factory on the river front, had been taken out and shot on the grounds that the power company was a government concern—which it is not. Japanese officials have been at my office daily trying to get hold of these very men so they could start the turbines and have electricity. It was small comfort to be able to tell them that their own military had murdered most of them.

Thursday, December 23. Sone was the one to get manhandled today. At Stanley Smith's house he found an officer and soldier who had just removed the American flag, also the Japanese proclamation, forced the refugees living there out, and said they must use the place as a registration center. He must have had a pretty uncomfortable time of it, for he was finally forced to sign a paper giving them the right to use the place for two weeks. And Sone is not a man to take things lying down! A protest to the Embassy finally got the soldiers out of the place. Seventy were taken from our camp at the Rural Leaders Training School and shot. No system—soldiers seize anyone they suspect. Callouses on hands are proof that the man was a soldier, a sure death warrant. Ricksha coolies, carpenters and other laborers are frequently taken. At noon a man was led to headquarters with head burned cinder black—eyes and ears gone, nose partly, a ghastly sight. I took him to the hospital in my car where he died a few hours later. His story was that he was one of a gang of some hundred who had been tied together, then gasoline thrown over them and set afire. He happened to be on the outer edge so got the gas only over his head. Later another similar case was brought to the hospital with more extensive burns. He died also. It seems probable that they were first machine-gunned but not all killed. The first man had no wounds but the second did. Still later I saw a third, with similar head-and-arm burns, lying dead at the corner of the road to my house, opposite the Drum Tower. Evidently he had managed to struggle that far before dying. Incredible brutality!

Friday, December 24. Mr. Tang of the U.S. Embassy reports that the Chinese staff and their relatives living in the Embassy, were all robbed last night by an officer and his men; Paxton's office door was bayonetted, three cars stolen from the compound and two more this morning. Later I had the pleasure of telling Tanaka that Mencken's car, which I had promised him the use of yesterday, was among those stolen. Registration of Chinese started today. The military say there are still twenty thousand soldiers in the Zone and that they must get rid of these "monsters." I question if there are a hundred left. Anyway, many more innocent must suffer and all are fearful and nervous. The Chinese Self-Government Committee, formed day before yesterday at the invitation of Tanaka, may be helpful in this; but there are spies already at work. We caught one here. I just saved him from a bad beating, so locked him up in our basement and later turned him over to the Chinese police. What will they do to him? Strangle him I suppose—but I have told them to be careful! Constant interference from the Japanese today; more of our sanitary squad taken, also the policeman at the University gate, and they are constantly trying to get our trucks. They also sealed up one of our coal depots but Riggs finally managed to talk them out of that.

Christmas Eve. Kroeger, Sperling and Dr. Trimmer in for dinner with us—a good dinner, too, with roast beef and sweet potatoes. Rabe did not dare to leave his house, as Japanese soldiers come over his wall many times a day. He always makes them leave by the same way they come instead of by the gate, and when any of them objects he thrusts his Nazi armband in their faces and points to his Nazi decoration, the highest in the country, and asks them if they know what that means. It always works! He joined us later in the evening and gave each of us a beautiful leather-bound Siemens diary. We sang Christmas songs with Wilson at the piano.

Christmas Day. A perfect day too, as far as weather is concerned. And conditions also seem slightly better. There were crowds on the streets with quite a number of stalls selling things. But at tiffin time, while we were sitting at roast goose, with Miss Vautrin, Miss Bauer, Miss Blanche Wu, and Miss Pearl Bromley Wu as our guests, we had to answer three calls for help and then turn soldiers out of Fenn's and the Chinese faculty houses and the sericulture building. That day, too, the American flag was taken from the Rural Leaders Training School. Seven soldiers spent the night and the night before in the Bible Teachers' Training School and raped the women, a girl of twelve was raped by three soldiers almost next door to us and another of thirteen, before we could send relief. There were also more bayonet cases; Wilson reports that of the 240 cases in the hospital three-quarters are due to Japanese violence since the occupation. At the University, registration commenced. The people were told that if any ex-soldiers were there and would step out, they would be used in the labor corps and their lives would be saved; about 240 stepped out. They were herded together and taken away. Two or three lived to tell the tale and, by feigning death after they were wounded, escaped and came to the hospital. One group was machine-gunned, another was surrounded by soldiers and used for bayonet practice. We have had quite a number of cases where men have faced the execution squad, escaped with only a wound or two, perhaps lying all day and into the night covered by the corpses of their comrades to escape detection, and then getting to the hospital or to friends. A rash bit of carelessness on the part of the Japanese!

Monday, December 27. The third week of Japanese occupation begins and is celebrated with the arrival of a Nisshin Kisen Kaisha ship from Shanghai. Four representatives of the company called at my office and promised that a regular service will soon be established on the river. A number of ladies are in the party and are taken on a sight-seeing trip of the city. They distribute a few sweets to some children and seem tremendously pleased with themselves, also with Japan's wonderful victory, but of course they hear nothing of the real truth, nor does the rest of the world, I suppose. The soldiers are still completely out of control, and there is no co-operation between the army and the Embassy. The army even refuses to recognize the new Self-Government Committee which was called into being by the Embassy, and its members are deliberately slighted. They are told that they are a conquered people and should expect no favors. Our list of disorder and cruelty keeps mounting and those we never hear of must be many, many times what are reported or observed. A few of today's: a boy of thirteen, taken by the Japanese nearly two weeks ago, beaten with an iron rod and then bayoneted because he didn't do his work satisfactorily. A car with an officer and two soldiers came to the University last night, raped three women on the premises and took away one with them. The Bible Teachers' Training School was entered many times; people were robbed and twenty women raped. The hospital night superintendent was taken by soldiers in spite of Miss Bauer's protests. The burning of the city continues and today two of the Christian Mission School buildings in the south part of the city were fired, also Kiessling and Bader's (German restaurant). But Takatami, chief of the Embassy police, calls and now promises protection for all foreign buildings and starts out with Sperling to inspect German properties. Personally, I think he is promising far more than he can deliver. What a list of claims Japan will have presented to her and it all seems so utterly useless, for there are hundreds of foreign properties in Nanking and almost all of them have been looted by her soldiers. And the cars that they have stolen. I think I forgot to mention that yesterday Symthe and I called at the

British Embassy which is in the far north western part of the city, out of the Zone. All the cars, eleven of them, had been taken by soldiers, also a couple of trucks, but fortunately the servants had fared fairly well. Every block or so one now sees abandoned cars—batteries and anything else useful taken—left where they are, usually overturned.

There was one bright spot today, though, and that was the arrival by the NYK boat, through the Japanese Embassy, of a letter to me from Dr. Fong Sec—the first and only letter to come to any of us in all these past three or four weeks. He wanted to know if we might not be in need of funds for our relief work and offered to hold some of the money that was coming in in response to our appeal through Rotary International. That's Fong, all over. And we'll need additional funds all right—many, many thousands. I have a nightmare every time I think of what we'll soon be needing; where are we going to get it?

Tuesday, December 28. What we had feared—bad weather. A steady drizzle and then snow. The poor refugees living in huts, many no longer than a pup tent, will have a miserable time of it, for most of these huts are not rain proof. And then there is the sticky mud. But we have certainly been fortunate in having had ideal weather up to this. I inspected some of the camps today. The crowding in most of them is terrible and of course it is impossible to keep them clean. Our camp managers and their assistants, all volunteer workers, are doing a splendid job on the whole in maintaining discipline, feeding the people and keeping things fairly sanitary. But how long must we maintain these camps? When are the people going to be permitted to return to their homes—those who have any homes left? When will order ever be established?

I went over to our Y.M.C.A. school today for the first time. It is located not far beyond my residence. Everything had been turned upside down, and many of the instruments of the physics laboratory deliberately smashed. On the athletic field was a dead cow, half eaten by the dogs. The Embassy proclamation had been torn from the gate.

Wednesday December 29. Weather better today, fortunately. Registration continues, most inefficiently, and the people are given no information as to where and when to appear. More taken as ex-soldiers. Women and old men come kneeling and crying, begging our help in getting back their husbands and sons. In a few cases we have been successful, but the military resents any interference from us. Word comes through from Hsiakwan by a representative of the Chinese Red Cross Society that there are approximately twenty thousand refugees along the river front. The supply of rice we let them have before the Japanese arrived is nearly exhausted and there is great suffering. They ask to come into the Safety Zone, but we are already too crowded. Anyway, the Japanese wouldn't permit it nor will they permit us to go out there and render help. For the time being they will have to get along as best they can.

Guards are at last posted at the various foreign embassies. But why wasn't it done two weeks ago? Our homes are still left unprotected; and the few guards posted at some of our camps are often more of a nuisance than a help. They demand fire and food, beds and often other things of the people.

Thursday, December 30. I called in the servants at the Y.M.C.A. today, eighteen of them, paid them up to the 15th of the month and told them that they have been with us for many years and are fine, faithful fellows. Wong and I hope it may be possible to start something in a small way in the old school buildings, if and when we get order established, but few of our members are left and it will be a difficult matter to build up a new constituency from the material that is now in Nanking. Wong Ding has done a splendid job as assistant housing commissioner, and so has Y.S. Chang as one of the camp superintendents, while our servants have all been doing their bit in one way or another.

When I called at the Japanese Embassy this afternoon they were busy giving instructions to about 60 Chinese, most of them our camp managers, on how the New Year's was to be celebrated. The old five-barred flag is to replace the Nationalist flag, and they were told to make a thousand of these and also a thousand Japanese flags for that event Camps of over a thousand must have twenty representatives present, smaller camps ten. At one o'clock New Year's day the five-barred flag is to be raised above the Drum Tower, there will be "suitable" speeches and "music" (according to the program)—and of course, moving pictures will be taken of the happy people waving flags, and welcoming the new regime. In the meantime the burning of the city continues, three cases of girls of twelve and thirteen years of age being raped or abducted are reported; Sperling has a busy time chasing sliders out of houses in the immediate vicinity of headquarters; the sericulture building (a part of the University of Nanking—American property) has a cordon thrown around it while soldiers engage in a man hunt, etc., etc.

Friday, December 31. A comparatively quiet day. For the first time no cases of violence were reported for the night. The Japanese are busy with their New Year's preparations. Two days of holiday are announced. We dread them, for it means more drunken soldiers. Refugees are advised to stay indoors. Rabe invited our household to his house after dinner and lighted his Christmas tree for us, and each of us received a New Year's card with our Zone emblem—a circle with a cross within it in red—signed by all twenty-two of the foreign community in Nanking. He also entertained us with stories of some of his experiences in South Africa. On his walls hang some magnificent trophies of his hunts.

New Year's Day! Thoughts of home and loved ones come crowding in. What wouldn't one give for a letter from "home"! Evidently we are going to have to exercise patience a while longer, for the Japanese Embassy tells us that it will still be weeks before the postal services are re-established here. They also tell us that it will be a month at least before any of us is allowed to leave the city on a visit to Shanghai. We are virtually prisoners here!

There is perhaps no purpose to be served by going further with this story, and telling of acts of horror that have been committed since. It is now the 11th of January, and while conditions are vastly improved there has not been a day that has not had its atrocities, some of them of a most revolting nature. With the arrival on the 6th of three representatives of the American Embassy, and on the 9th of three of both the British and German Embassies, we feel a little more assurance that conditions will still further improve. But only last night I drove past four new fires that had just been started and saw soldiers within a shop just starting a fifth. There has not been a day since December 19th that fires have not been started by the Japanese soldiers. And Kroeger, who managed to slip out of the East Gate the other day, tells us that all the villages as far as he went, some twenty miles, are burned and that not a living Chinese or farm animal is to be seen.

We are at last in touch with the outside world through the radio, and that is a great blessing; for last Sunday I got our house connected up and we now have electricity. At our committee headquarters we had current a few days earlier. Only the Japanese are supposed to have electricity, though, so we are not advertising the fact. Then we have seen a couple of issues of a Shanghai Japanese paper and two of the Tokyo *Nichi Nichi*. These tell us that even as early as December 28th the stores were rapidly opening up and business returning to normal, that the Japanese were co-operating with us in feeding the poor refugees, that the city had been cleared of *Chinese* looters, and that peace and order now reigned! We'd be tempted to laugh, if it all wasn't so tragic.

I have written this account in no spirit of vindictiveness. War is brutalizing, especially war of conquest, and it would seem to me from my experiences in this, as also in the Shanghai "war" of 1932, that the Japanese army, with no background of Christian idealism, has today become a brutal, destructive force that not only menaces the East but also may some day menace the West, and that the world should know the truth about what is happening. How this situation should be dealt with I shall leave to abler minds than mine to consider.

There is a bright side of this story, of course, and that is the wonderful spirit of service that has been shown by our Chinese and foreign friends alike and the intimate fellowship we have enjoyed in our common cause. Our hearts have been frequently warmed, too, by the innumerable times the refugees have expressed appreciation for what we have tried to do; and our own losses and inconveniences seem so trivial when compared with what they have suffered. Then our three German friends on the committee have won both our admiration and affection. They have been a tower of strength—without them I don't see how we would have got through.

Consular officials—American, British, German—returned, but were treated with scorn by the Japanese military and were powerless to control them. John Allison, American consul, had his face slapped for seeking to "interfere"—a humiliating experience. But it was the food situation that caused us the greatest concern. Our stores of salt cabbage were exhausted. Our stores of rice were still holding out, but rapidly dwindling. The surrounding area for miles around had been completely laid waste, and nothing was allowed to be brought into the city except for the Japanese. Cases of beri-beri were appearing and it seemed imperative to bring in a shipload of supplies to prevent disaster.

After lengthy negotiations with the Japanese, I finally secured permission to go to Shanghai by the H.M.S. *Bee* which had just landed the British consul and some of his staff. I do not recall the exact date I boarded the British gunboat but it must have been in late January. My first lunch in Shanghai was with the late highly esteemed Admiral Harry Yarnell on board his flagship. He was anxious, as were many others, to get the latest news about Nanking. I had to speak a number of times and also give interviews, but in the meantime I arranged the purchase of a shipload of soy beans, rice, wheat flour and a few other commodities for early delivery at Nanking. I was also asked by a group of Americans to fly to Washington at the earliest possible date and report the Nanking situation to our Government. I had promised the Japanese authorities, however, that I would return—permission to leave the city was dependent on that—and of course I also wanted to ensure the safe delivery of my cargo of foodstuffs. I promised my friends, however, that as soon as I got back I would start negotiating for another permit to leave.

The voyage up the Yangtze was made on the U.S.S. *Oahu*, as arranged by Admiral Yarnell, and was uneventful. On my arrival I learned to my dismay that the Japanese military had gone back on their word and now refused permission to land the cargo. The ship proceeded on to Wuhu to await negotiations. Fortunately a second permission was finally obtained, our ship returned and we took delivery of its cargo without interference. This may have been because of the posters which the Japanese were putting up all over the city saying that they were now looking after the welfare of the people. One poster showed a smiling Chinese woman and child kneeling before a soldier who was giving them a loaf of bread. The star poster, though, was captioned "Japanese Troops gently soothe the Refugees. The harmonious atmosphere of Nanking City develops enjoyable," and then went on with utterly fantastic lies about how people, oppressed by the anti-Japanese armies, had suffered and could get no food or medical help, but "fortunately the Imperial Army entered the city, put their bayonets into their sheaths, and stretched forth merciful hands . . . diffusing grace and favor to the excellent true citizens. . . . Many thousands of herded refugees cast off their former absurd attitude of opposing Japan and clasped their hands in congratulation for receiving assurance of life." And so on ad nauseam for several paragraphs, winding up with a picture of "Soldiers and Chinese children happy together, playing joyfully in the parks. Nanking is now the best place for all countries to watch, for here one breathes the atmosphere of peaceful residence and happy work." This translation was made by a member of my staff, and I can vouch for its authenticity, incredible as it may seem.

It was now two months since the occupation of Nanking began and yet the atrocities continue daily. On January 18, two men came to us, both shot through their arms because they could not satisfy soldiers who demanded money of them; another was brought to the hospital who had been shot through his jaw and neck because he hadn't the strength to carry a heavy load; and yet another who had a serious bayonet wound on his head. Were they wearying of their inhumanities, or was, perhaps, the army trying to show signs of control and discipline? I don't know. Anyway, I was soon to leave. A wire (by pre-arrangement) from Hollis Wilbur in Shanghai said, "Be in Shanghai before 23rd." Armed with this I finally got my permit to leave again, and the following morning at 6:40 took the Japanese military train to Shanghai. I was crowded in with about as unsavory a crowd of soldiers as one could imagine in a third class coach, a bit nervous because sewed into the lining of my camel's-hair great-coat were eight reels of 16 mm. negative movie film of atrocity cases, most of which were taken in the University Hospital. My baggage would undoubtedly be carefully examined by the military when we got to Shanghai. What might happen if they discovered these films? Fortunately they weren't discovered, and as soon as I could after my arrival I took them to the Kodak office for processing. Most of the exposures were made by John Magee, of the American Episcopal Mission, later Dean of St. John's Episcopal Church in Washington. They were so terrible that they had to be seen to be believed. The Kodak representative rushed through four sets for me and of course I was asked to show the film at the American Community Church and one or two other places.

Miss Murial Lester of the Fellowship of Reconciliation (British) happened to see one of the showings and expressed the thought that if some of the Christian and political leaders in Japan could see the film they would work for an immediate cessation of hostilities. She offered to go to Japan and show it there to selected groups if we would supply her with a copy. I didn't have much faith in the success of her plan but nevertheless gave her one of the copies which I then had. Some weeks later she reported that she had shown it before a small group of leading Christians in Tokyo, but that they felt only harm could come from an effort to show it further so she finally abandoned her plan.

Many people came to see me about Nanking affairs; and I finally got out to Hungchiao Road to see our house. This was outside the Settlement area and I confess I ventured there with some trepidation for Japanese soldiers were all around. In the corner of the garden there was a charred area about ten feet in diameter where my library (except the books taken to Nanking and destroyed there), including all my diaries dating back to 1902 (a total of over 1,500 volumes), had been burned. Nearby was a bathtub which had been torn out from the third floor bathroom, evidently with the idea of taking it somewhere, while within the house there was general chaos. I hurried away.

What of the future? The immediate future is anything but bright, but the Chinese have an unsurpassed capacity for suffering and endurance, besides their many other qualities, and right must triumph in the end. Anyway, I shall always be glad that I threw in my lot with them.

A Letter to Dear ——— (January 6, 1938)[2]

Nanking, Jan 6, 1938

Dear ———,

Our consular representatives are here at last—the first to come of any consuls: Allison, Espy and McFadyen. And were we glad to see them! They arrived at 11 and had tiffin with us and brought us a lot of news from the outside world. We gave them an earful too! The British and German officials will come on the 10th, but we have no information as to when any of the rest of our community are to come. Many of course will never return. There is so little left to bring them back. For Nanking has been systematically looted and burned until it is only a skeleton of its former self. Most of the foreign properties are still standing, though almost without exception they have been looted, and so are most of the government buildings, but most of the shops and many of the homes of the Chinese have been burned out—after the victors had taken everything from them that they wanted.

The Y.M.C.A. went with the rest, deliberately fired. I got there just an hour or so after it had been started. I wonder if that brief note of mine in which I mentioned that it had "gone up in smoke" ever reached you? We have had no letters for weeks . . .

At present we are virtually prisoners here. We cannot even [go] outside the walls to Hsiakwan. That can't last forever, though. . . . On the whole we have fared pretty well—our foreign group of 22, I may . . . as far as food and material comforts go.* But Nanking has been a hell on earth if there ever was one. I never

---

*Edge of original copy is obscured.

dreamt anything could be quite so hellish in this modern age. I am glad I stayed, of course, for aside from escaping the bombing of the *Panay* our group here has been able to perform a service that the city, the people, would have been worse off without. Though we sometimes wonder if anything could possibly be worse. Nor is it all over yet. Only this noon, while Allison and the rest were still here and Okasaki, the consul-general from Shanghai had just come in for a brief call, three of us had to hurry off to chase soldiers out of Brady's house; and from there to the office where we were stopped to oust soldiers in the Rural Leaders' Training School; who were demanding women both places within the Zone where soldiers are now supposed to be prohibited, and both places flying the American flag and showing posters from the Japanese embassy. And yesterday soldiers held up our gateman at the point of the bayonet and made him open the house so they could loot, both morning and evening; and they were there the day before too. But these are mere trivialities. Things are incomparably better than they were—and that is something to be thankful for.

Yes, my house has been looted. I wish you could see the mess it is in. But practically every foreign house has been looted, even some of the embassy houses. I was fortunate in that I brought over a number of trucks to Buck's house, where I've been staying for the past month, so I really haven't lost such a frightful lot. Some places have suffered much worse, even those houses in the Zone—mine is outside. And the Russian Embassy was burned to the ground just the other day. I started writing my story of the rape of Nanking the other day. . . . It won't be pleasant reading! I've not exaggerated—simply told a few of the things that have happened here, that have come to my personal attention.

A Letter to Peter Shih (February 14, 1938)[3]

Nanking, Feb. 14, 1938

Dear Peter,
I have long wanted to write to you—I have thought of you daily ever since we said goodbye to each other, now nearly three months ago. For a long time it was impossible to write, of course; and then I got so busy in this relief work that there was no time for writing any but the most necessary letters. My hands are still very full, but I feel that I mustn't delay longer in getting word to you about the situation here.

You have heard, I suppose, that the YMCA building was burned on the 20th of December. It was practically a total loss, though somehow the restaurant in the rear escaped and also the shower and the bathroom and your little southwest corner room on the ground floor of the main building. The safe was broken open before we could get to it ourselves, but fortunately most of the papers were [not] discovered. Such money as may have been there was gone, of course; and I am afraid all the records have been destroyed. S.Y. Chang, Liu Hwa and Chen-rei are all staying down there now and salvaging such things as may still be worth anything. The school escaped the burning but was pretty badly looted. It was first occupied by Chinese troops and then by Japanese for a while. After conference with S.C. Lung and Wilbur in Shanghai last week, it was decided to give up the school buildings, move such furniture as may still be worth salvaging to 22 Chung Hwa Road, and return the lease to the Christian Advent Mission. I had hoped we might use the school as a place where we could start up some sort of a program in time and also run a hostel there. I am afraid, though, that judging from the way things are going now there is little if any chance of our doing anything useful as an Association for some considerable time to time. The question of finance, of course, presents a most serious difficulty —there seems to be no constituency here from which we could secure support and the National Committee needs what little funds it has for war and emergency work. It was with the greatest reluctance that I finally consented to the temporary closing of our work here. The matter of a Board of Directors is another difficulty—at present there isn't a single member of our Board in Nanking, and I'm afraid it will be a long time before any of them return here.

As for staff—Wong Ding and S.Y. Chang are the only ones here, besides some 17 servants. Wong Ding and I have arranged to be taken on by our Safety Zone Committee for the being; the National Committee will pay Chang's and the two servants' wages to look after the property. The other servants I have released, paying them up to the middle of January, though two of them, Siao Hu and Lao Li, I have working here at our Committee Headquarters. I put three into the school compound to clean that place up, but they will be released at the end of this month. We have had no word from any of the rest of our staff except Chow, who is living at the Y in Chungking. I have written him suggesting that he find work in Szechuan if he can. I am worried, though, about Chow and Esieh and Hu; do you suppose they will be able to find something to do? It's odd that I haven't heard from them. Also Kao. Kao promised to be back before the end of November, but either he got cold feet or something happened to delay him. Shaw also promised to be back after taking his family to Luho. If you have any word from any of these man, I wish you'd let me know. Address me at the National Committee YMCA, 131 Museum Road, Shanghai, for the postal services are not yet re-established here. The National Committee sends me mail by every available gunboat coming up the river. There is also a chance that I shall be going to Shanghai again next week. I went the time before, leaving Jan. 29, by a British gunboat, the *Bee*, and returned the 10th by the U.S.S. *Oahu*. It was only with the greatest difficulty that I get permission from the Japanese authorities to go and return.

You will be greatly distressed to see Nanking as it is today. About 80% of the stores have been burned down and nearly 50% of the homes. Wong Ding's home was burned just about three weeks ago and he lost everything. I haven't any idea of what the condition of your home is, for we are not allowed to go outside the city gates. Fortunately things have taken a turn for the better now and the people are leaving the Zone for their homes—those that have any homes left. Our camp population has gone down from 70,000 to just about half that figure. For two months, however, there has been terror and violence, unrestrained— the suffering of the poor people has been appalling. It would have been much worse, however, if it had not been for the Zone and the work of our Committee; so I shall always be grateful that I remained here through it all. Perhaps some day I shall have an opportunity to tell you something of our experiences.

I wish I could write at greater length, must not do so now. Please let me hear from you at your very earliest convenience, and let me have any suggestions and information that might be helpful in the situation here. Please give my most cordial greetings, too, to your colleagues in the W.A.S.C.—to J. L., Sam May (tell him I saw his wife last week—sat by her at a tiffin in my honor at the YW), Singfee, Teddy, Jack Young, Doc Lee, Stean and the rest of the good fellows. By the way, if you type your letter, send a carbon to me c/o Y.M.C.A., Kowloon for there is some probability that I will be down there between the 28th of this month and the 2nd of next—but that's not for publication!

Ever with the best of wishes.
Most sincerely yours,
George A. Fitch

P.S.—About the future: I hope it may be possible for you and me to continue to work together again once this wretched war is over. Where we are going to get another building from is a question, of course; but may be we can find friends in America who will help us. We'll see if we can get clearance for an appeal, anyway.

G. A. F.

Notes

The edited version presented in this chapter is based on Fitch's book, *My Eighty Years in China* (rev. ed.), chap. 10, "Naking Doomed 1937–1938." Taibei: Mei Ya Publications, 1974.

1. RG11, B9, F202. Fitch's diary had appeared in H. J. Timperley book, *What War Means, The Japanese Terror in China*, Modern Age Books Inc. London, New York, 1938, and in Hsu Shu-hsi ed. *Documents of Nanking Safety Zone*, Shanghai, British Kelly and Walsh Firm, 1939–1940. The diary was first used as the basis for an article in *Ken* magazine (no longer published) entitled *"The sack of Nanking, as told to John Maloney by an American, with 20 years experience in China, who remained in Nanking after its fall."* It was also reproduced in full in the July 1938 issue of *Reader's Digest*.

2. RG8, B263–4.

3. RG8, B103.

Ernest H. Forster

Ernest H. Forster was born in 1895 in Philadelphia and graduated from Princeton University in 1917. After serving as assistant headmaster at St. Paul's School, Baltimore for two years, Forster went to China as an Episcopal missionary and taught at Mahan School in Yangchow. In 1936, he married Clarissa Townsend, daughter of prominent lawyer Irving U. Townsend, in Boston. The Forsters returned to China and were stationed at Yangchow. They were transferred from Yangchow to Nanking to serve at St. Paul's Episcopal Church only about one month before the capture of Nanking by the Japanese. Clarissa Forster was evacuated from Nanking to Hankow in late November 1937 and by the middle of January 1938 arrived at Shanghai via Hong Kong. Forster, with John Magee, another Episcopal minister, remained in Nanking throughout the critical months of the Nanking Massacre.

Letters, reports, and photographs in the Ernest and Clarissa Forster Papers held at the Yale Divinity School Library provide thorough and graphic documentation of the Nanking Massacre.

Mrs. Forster's Accounts[1]

Nanking

On Nov. 2nd we left Shanghai on the river steamer en route to Nanking, together with Mr. Green who was trying to get back to Yangchow. Arriving at Tunchow the following noon we had to wait the rest of that day and until late afternoon of the following day before we could make arrangements to go further. With three other foreigners and some Chinese customs officials, we hired a private launch, which took us by inland canal directly to Yangchow in 23½ hours. Mr. Forster and I decided to stay in Yangchow long enough to pack up and remove our belongings to Nanking whenever we could get them through. We chartered part of a junk and sent the cook with some furniture, bedding and all our food supplies to Nanking where we were to keep house for John Magee. The rest of our belongings we locked in two downstairs rooms of the Yangchow house. There were only about two air raids in Yangchow during our stay there.

After one week in Yangchow we started for Nanking. At first we thought of going by boat but the weather was not good and we did not want to risk a small motor boat going up the Yangtse without a tug. Mr. Fairfield decided to go along with us in order to go over with Mr. Forster the Yangchow accounts and to take the books back to Yangchow. The books had previously been taken to Nanking by Mr. Forster. We left early Friday morning, Nov. 12th, but getting to Chinkiang found that no trains were running until night so that we spent the day at the C.I.M. Home. Troops pouring in from upriver being rushed to the front in Soochow jammed the railway stations and made us stop many times on the way, so that it took us four hours to get from Chinkiang to Nanking. We arrived at the Hsiakwan compound about 11 o'clock that night, having learned that Mr. McNulty had just left that noon, returning to Soochow, and that our compound in Wusih had been bombed.

Mr. Magee was head over heels in plans for the relief of wounded soldiers who were pouring into the railroad station with inadequate facilities for their care. Our plan was to live with Mr. Magee in Hsiakwan for the winter to save on fuel and food and to co-operate in the work. Mr. Forster immediately set to work at the Mission accounts as he was handling most of these in the station west of Shanghai during the emergency and Mr. Archie Tsen, who had been helping out during his absence, had only recently come from Hankow and was leaving at once for Shanghai. Mr. Forster also went over to St. Paul's Church to get acquainted with the staff and start with the work there. Personal interviews with the ceaseless stream of visitors, government officials, Red Cross people, soldiers, newspaper reporters, students and parishioners, from early morning till late at night was no small part of the day's work.

On Monday, Nov. 15th, after one week on the way, our cook and the furniture and supplies arrived at the back door of the compound, while the five refugees from Wusih, Dr. Lee, Dr. Roberts, Mr. Dyer, Miss Lenhard, and Miss Selzer, drove up to the front door in Dr. Lee's car, having left Wusih at five o'clock that morning. Until Thursday we ran a dormitory and mess in the house for ten people, Miss Rolf Suess who is doing publicity work for the government joining us for one day. Mr. Fairfield left for Yangchow on Tuesday, Nov. 16th, and on Nov. 18th the Wusih people got off for Shanghai by boat.

At times soldiers had tried to come into the city compound and even the Hsiakwan compound, then it was reported to us that soldiers were occupying the compound of the C.T.S. transportation by bus or taxi being impossible to obtain I drove Dr. Lee's car which he had left with us for mission and emergency use, to the C.T.S. on Sunday, Nov. 21st, while Mr. Forster and Dean Tong interviewed the officer in charge, requesting them to move elsewhere. They were very polite about it and said they thought, because of its name, that it belonged to the Central University and would move at once.

After our foreign guests left, we turned our attention to the immediate problem of the wounded soldiers at the railroad station. We found the entire space there, platforms, waiting rooms, and ticket office floors, covered with wounded soldiers who had been dumped there, most of whom had no straw or bedding, scanty clothing and no food. There were two coolies for a short time during the evening, to do a little sweeping, but the whole place was a dreadful mess and the conditions vile. John and Mrs. Twinum went off to get some bedding which we doled out to the worst cases and Mr. Forster and I turned our attention to carrying to those who wanted it, teapots of hot water and bowls of rice gruel, to discovering the most severe cases, and trying to find the one doctor in charge to care for them. Also we tried to get the worst cases into the two ambulances for the University Hospital. Many soldiers died while we were there and we could get no one to take the responsibility of moving the bodies, so that they lay right next to the wounded. This visiting the station went on night after night, but as the wounded kept pouring in as the fighting drew nearer, and the numbers increased, the organizations became less and less able to cope with the situation. Also many refugees from the trains wandered in to the crowd of the dead and dying soldiers and tried to get the food meant for the soldiers. Col. Hwang donated a handsome sum of money and provided bedding for the use of the soldiers, while Dr. J. Hueng Liu, the Govt. Medical officer, promised his assistance and a corps of workers, who, as it happened, were most intermittent in their work. I planned to keep hot coffee always on hand in our house for various people who might be brought in at any hour of the night. While I was there, two wounded army officers spent the night enjoying for the first time a real bed and some good food.

With the orders to move all Govt. Officers up-river, Nanking was thrown into a panic. Refugees were fleeing to the city, others were rushing out of the city, and there were no means of conveyance in either direction, so that the household and office equipment just lined the streets and sidewalks. The Foreign Embassies were also moving and many of our Christian families were also leaving. Mr. Hall Paxton of the U.S. Embassy urged all foreign women to leave town. As I knew no Chinese and the other foreign and Chinese women were leaving, it seemed most sensible for me to go as it would leave the men freer to carry on the work. For two days we tried to reach Yangchow by phone to try to find out what conditions were and to urge Miss Bremer to leave and join me. We could get no word through as the wires were down. Later we learned that they were already in Chinkiang at that time. Last Sunday night I learned that there was an opportunity to get on the boat chartered by the German Govt. which was leaving for Hankow at 11 o'clock the next morning. The only other possibility was to get on the U.S.S. *Panay.* (Starting at seven in the morning there had been air raids all day in Nanking, so that my boat, which did not sail until midnight on the 21st, kept moving up and down the river to avoid the planes. A good many bombs were dropped.) The boat stopped at Wuhu where I saw Sister Constance, Mr. Craighill and Dr. Anderson. They and Mr. Lanphear were not planning to leave.

I picked up the baggage of Miss Mary Parke whom Mr. Craighill had wired to get on the gunboat at Nanking and proceed to Kuling via Kiukiang. As the German boat was making no regular stops, I had to put her baggage in the care of 9 refugee Red Cross nurses, who got off at Kiukiang in a tiny sampan in the dark and promised to get the baggage to the China Travel Service. One of our Sheng Kung Hui Chinese doctors was also a refugee on the boat and had helped to get these nurses on their way. I gave them the address of our Rev. Ralph Chiang in Kiukiang. I arrived in Hankow at noon on Thanksgiving Day and staid with Miss Elise Dexter. I attended Language School there in Hankow until a radiogram from Bishop Roberts, two weeks later, was received, saying, "Kiang ladies return Shanghai via Hong Kong." I left with the others on the International Train for Hong Kong. Although it was only a few days before Nanking fell mail from there had been coming through fairly regularly and twice I had had telephone communication, so that I knew all was well up to that time. Before I left Hankow the Rev. and Mrs. Kuo and family from St. Paul's, Nanking, had arrived and were staying with Dss. Stewart. Mr. Hsia, the catechist from St. Paul's, also came to Hankow. I met several Mahan School students on the street who were refugeeing with their families, and who came to see me before leaving.

The following extracts from letters of Mr. Forster's will give later news of Nanking:

Letters to Wife[2]

Nov. 23rd. Urgent signal has just been given for air raid. Conditions at the railroad station more frightful and disorganized today than ever before. There were 250 wounded at the station when I arrived, and 750 more came before the night was over. Some Boy Scouts were on the job, but, due to rain and cold and lack of transportation, no other volunteers showed up. Most of the men were serious wound cases—*John Magee is still trying to get plans for more volunteer help through the Ministry of Health and also more ambulances.—Mr. Paxton of the Embassy transmitted the following wire today: 'Wusih groups arrived. Wire Yangchow close institutions and come to Shanghai. Magee and Forster when evacuating come Shanghai if possible. Roberts.'—

Nov. 24th. I rode into town to see Miss Mary Chen, sister of the president of Nanking University, who turned over to [me] money for refugees, relief, etc. Also showed me supplies available for soldiers and refugees. Ceaseless round of the telephone, callers, and committee meetings.—Miss Shao and Miss Chiang arrived from Yangchow last night and I have just been talking with them. They reported that Mr. Green, Mr. Fairfield and Miss Bremer had left.—Prospects are favorable for the establishment of a neutral zone. Chinese authorities have consented and Gen Matsui, Japanese commander-in-chief in Shanghai, is reported to be regarding it favorably, in view of the success of a similar plan in Nantao. The area designated will include Nanking and Ginling Colleges.—The gateman just rushed in to say that soldiers are coming into the compound on horses but I managed to persuade them to leave. I rushed off in the car to Nanking Univ. to consult about places for ourselves and Chinese workers to live if the neutral plan goes through. Also took proclamations to put on the compound walls in the city to the effect that it is American property.—Air raid today. For the first time since Sept. 25th they dropped bombs in the city, the beginning of the turn for the worst.—Forty persons are reported killed or injured.—

Nov. 22nd.[3] A card written on the 22nd from Mr. Ma of Chinkiang says that he is on his way home in Anhui and that Althea, Steve and Leslie are with him. (This explains his misconception that the Yangchow people had gone up river instead of down to Shanghai.)—Had an express letter from Mr. Ko of Yangchow that the Prov. Govt. wants to 'borrow' some of our Mahan building for offices —Yesterday afternoon we went to Thanksgiving Service and Tea at the Embassy. It was a very nice service. Dr. Bates of the Nanking U. gave a perfectly splendid Thanksgiving address. Some nice officers from the American gunboats, the Captain, the doctor and the young ensign from Sheboygan, Wis., who said that he was an Episcopalian, were among the number that came to the service. He and the other officers were just as nice as they could be and were very sympathetic with missionaries and their work.—Conditions are better at the r.r. station. Col. Hwang has given a big sum of money to get a dressing

---

*Dashes appeared in the original and are being reproduced here.

station started.*** †The Generalissimo himself went to the station yesterday to see conditions.—

Nov. 27th. "Yesterday we had some interesting callers. A group of 15 boys and girls offered their services for the wounded. They are from Soochow and banded together in August to work together behind the lines. The girls have had first aid training and help with the dressings. The boys acted as stretcher-bearers. They had two trucks, one of which was taken by the military. They have retreated northward as the line has fallen back and now want to serve in Nanking. The larger part of them are Christian and they are showing a splendid spirit, roughing it along with the soldiers, two meals a day, eating and sleeping in the open, etc., what an experience of life they have had! China seemed to jump from one extreme to another! It is good to see this spirit of willing sacrifice where one also sees so much callousness and selfishness.—

Nov. 28th. I got up early and went to St. Paul's in the city where I celebrated Holy Communion and helped in the Morning Prayer Service. Not many people were there. So many more have left and are still leaving since the departure of the various Govt. Departments. I guess that is all to the good for the fewer people around to worry about, the better.——Mr. Kuo is very much worried about his family whom he can't move from Wuhu. We have advised him to join them and I believe he will as soon as he can find a way to go to Wuhu.——I have sent Mr. Ko (of Yangchow) a letter to take to the magistrate refusing the use of the buildings of Mahan School. I'd like to go to Yangchow to see how they all are but there is too much to do here and travelling conditions are so uncertain that a trip might involve several days and things are happening so rapidly that we just live from hour to hour.——The two women workers from Yangchow, Miss Shao and Miss Chiang, are doing valiant work in the University Hospital, making dressings and rolling bandages. They are showing a lovely spirit.——The Japanese have not given their reply about the neutral zone. The foreigners are going on the assumption that the scheme will go through. The manager of the Texas Oil Co., Mr. Hanson, has invited John and me and all our Chinese friends to their company residences which are well located in the proposed neutral zone. We went there to look the place over yesterday. It is grand and also has a good dugout.——Our group of Christian boys and girls are still with us. They are going to stick and are showing a splendid spirit. I wish there were more like them.——I got things out of the safe this morning. *** The next thing is to know what to do with them. We have got to make provision for about

---

†Asterisks appeared in the original and are reproduced here.

fifteen youngsters who have gotten separated from their families during the fighting and have trekked to Nanking. We are certainly running a seven ringed circus these days.

Nov. 30th. Mr. Paxton came to see us yesterday to tell us that the last chance of getting to Hankow by steamer was today. He did not insist on our going but indicated that we would be taken on the gunboat if it became necessary and we wanted to go. Some say the city will be defended and can hold out a long time. Others that the Chinese will not attempt to make a stand here. **** I think the Univ. of Nanking is moving today. That will take several women away and some men. We have more or less decided that if the Japs begin bombing and shelling the city, we'll move into the Hanson's. Otherwise we will remain where we are and try to carry on the best we can. It almost tears my heart out to see the need all around us and so few on hand to do anything about it. It is a terrible feeling to stand by and be unable to do anything when one knows in the right circumstances so much might be done.***

Dec. 2nd. I spent the night in the rr station where conditions were pretty bad since more organizations which had been helping have closed up shop and moved away, and those who should be taking responsibility are indifferent. The whole thing is practically on our shoulders now. Some of the British Embassy staff came down to look over the situation. The suffering of the soldiers and the failure of responsible organizations to do their duty by them is hard to see and bear. Such conditions as we are dealing with make one realize how necessary it is for us to present the Gospel as death unto self and life unto God. Everybody is concerned for himself and if you happen to be helpless, wounded and desti-tute, it is too bad for you. One seems to find more faithfulness and charity among the humble than among others.—Yangchow is still quiet apparently.

Dec. 3rd. Today John Magee and I attended the Press Conference at the British Sino * Cultural Association. The Mayor of Nanking and the spokesman from the officer in charge of the defense of Nanking were present. It is good to see so many foreigners still here. Reply had been received from the Japanese about the proposed neutral zone. It was purposely couched in indefinite terms but seems to be sufficiently assuring that the plan will be allowed to be tried. Com-mittees on housing, feeding, etc., are already busy at work. A great deal of rice and flour have been contributed by the City Government to be sold in the Zone at a fixed price to prevent profiteering. The great difficulty is in getting them transported because trucks etc. are at a premium. Yesterday we moved some of our things to Mr. Hanson's house in the neutral zone. Every time the truck goes into town we try to send some things along. We can't take furniture but I packed some clothing and bedding for John and myself. There is another group of about ten or fifteen from Tsingtao who are helping Miss Shao and Miss Chiang make dressings and rolling bandages. The neutral zone is to have a German for mayor and George Fitch for one of the secretaries. The Embassy issued a final warning about Americans leaving Nanking and asked us to indicate which of the three decisions we would follow: (1) To make arrangements to leave the city independently of the Embassy; (2) To accept accomodations of the U.S. *Panay*; (3) To remain in the city. John and I have decided on the latter, since we feel it will require the co-operation of as many foreigners as possible to insure the success of the neutral zone plan which is the only way left now to provide for our workers and Christians. Also, we have been using our decision to stay to encourage nurses and dressers to be faithful to their duty. We cannot go back on that, and it has helped to keep some here who are rendering much assistance in the very desperate situation. Mr. Paxton has just phoned to say that Althea, Steve, and Leslie arrived in Shanghai on Nov. 28th. That is a relief.

Dec. 5th. Since yesterday, John and I are living with a Mr. Kola in Mr. Schultze's house in the city, in the reserved area. With the Japanese drawing nearer, so many persons to be responsible for, we thought it best to leave Hsiakwan and bring the Chinese workers in. Yesterday was a busy day with packing and moving. Servants came in the afternoon to get the kitchen ready. We had coolies bring in all the food boxes so we shall have those to live on for a while. We brought in the Victrola and records. We are bringing in two beds because we shall probably have to take in more people. We are not staying at Mr. Hanson's of the Oil Co. because some of his people who were supposed to leave came back and are occupying some of the houses we were to have had. However, we have taken in quite a group over there and they are sleeping on the floor in dormitory fashion.—I went to the Buck residence for the English Service which Mrs. Twinum asked me to take, it was very simple and I spoke briefly on the purpose of the Bible, this being Bible Sunday—Just as I was about to start for the service at St. Paul's this morning an air-raid alarm sounded. The chauffeur said we could travel if I wasn't afraid since the police were no longer stopping people on the streets. I was anxious to get there since it was the First Sunday in the month and we were having late Communion. When we got about half way there, three big bombers flew over, the anti-aircraft started firing and we had to leave the car and take shelter before going on. We had a nice service; not many were present but more than I had dared to expect. Most of them, strange to say, were women—Work with the wounded and soldiers has slackened this last week, fewer have come to the station, they have been moved away faster, and at last we have had dressers on the job most of the 24 hours of the day. I am glad we finally got that much accomplished. As the fighting line draws nearer to Nanking, they must find other ways than the railway to bring in the wounded. In fact, 50 or 60 arrived on foot from Tanyang and were all in when they got here. They said that not a few had had to drop out en route and that some had died.—John had service over at Hanson's house this morning in the big room down stairs where they have set up an altar for daily use. John said the service was quite impressive. I think a number of non-Christians were present too. It will be an excellent opportunity to apply Christianity in a concrete way.— Things are getting tighter and tighter here as the fighting line draws nearer the city. The Chinese have been advised not to try to defend the place but they insist that they are going to do so. How long they can hold out is the question, since the troops they will have to use are not fresh and most of the crack troops have been wiped out. We hope for the sake of all concerned that it will not be a long struggle. All we can do is to pray and bear a Christian witness of fidelity to our charge. We are helpless but God isn't.—A letter from Rev. Mr. Ko stated that Yangchow is still peaceful, tho many people have fled from the city. Our Mahan buildings are still intact and have not been occupied so far.

Dec. 7th. The Japanese have not broken through so far.—Opinion varies as to how soon they will get here. Post Office no longer delivers mail.—We heard that two of the British river steamers were bombed at Wuhu yesterday.

Dec. 8th. The Chinese are burning down a lot of straw huts outside of the city in order to remove obstruction to their view when the enemy finally gets here. It is hard on the poor folk that live in them. We hear that they are also cutting down a lot of beautiful trees in the Sun Yat Sen Mausoleum Park in Spirit Valley. That too is a great pity. What a wasteful thing war is! Some people report hearing firing not far from the city. *** It looks as though the army would get to Nanking before the fleet, in which case we may be in for less trouble. However, we will not worry. We are in God's hands and He is mindful of His own. There is not much news here in the city. It was a very deserted looking place yesterday afternoon and yet in the section where the Rev. J.L. Chen has one of his chapels, life is going on pretty much as usual. They are mostly straw hut people in a section of the city which is largely country.—

Dec. 9th. Starting at six o'clock in the morning I tried to call you on the telephone today but by the time I got connected through, you had gone out, but I had a talk with Frances Roots and knew that all was well. By the way, our phone number is Nanking 31678, and the house address is 10 Sze Tiao Hsiang, Kulow,—It is just noon and the Japanese planes have been over to drop bombs on strategic points. They have apparently started some fires as I can see some from out the window. We have been busy getting refugees housed in this area. I think most of the people for whom we are responsible are accounted for, but there are always new ones turning up. For instance, a scout leader came yesterday to ask us to find a place for himself, his group of associates and a group of Christians whom they had helped get inside the city. He is a member of All Saints' Church, Shanghai. I wish you could see the people pouring into this area from other parts of the city. All the roads leading here are dotted with groups moving whatever possessions they can and with whatever they can,—tireless rickshaws, some even drawn by students, wheel-barrows, trucks, baby carriages, anything with wheels on it, and of course people carrying as much as they can in their hands. The people from the model village which the Chinese burned down in order to clear the view are accommodated next door to us. It is remarkable to see how well the Rev. J.L. Chen has them organized and how they are depending upon him and upon the "vestry" to care for them. He has certainly made a place for himself and the Church among them.—We have had no word from Shanghai for a long time. According to the last reports from Yangchow the two Chinese clergy and both catechists were still there.—I hear canonading in the far distance, so it will not be long before the army arrives. God has been wonderfully good to us and put His peace in our hearts, so that we do not feel afraid.—The planes are back again and the anti-aircraft guns are firing. It is marvelous how calm the people are, they are dropping bombs as they did in Chapei and we can hear the sounds of explosions in the distance.—

Dec. 12th. The city gates are practically closed except to the military. The Japanese are still outside the city. We hear that once or twice a detachment broke through but were driven back. The firing has been intermittent, but today it has seemed nearer. You never saw such disorganization as exists. Everybody seems to be everywhere except where they should be. I should think the best thing the Chinese could do would be to withdraw as quickly as possible and let the Japanese take over quietly. The day before yesterday some shells dropped on Chung Shan Road near Hsin Chieh K'ou. Fifteen persons were killed. Yesterday nine of the corpses were still lying on the pavement. An old women with a young girl with their market baskets, a middle aged man who made his living carrying a travelling kitchen, a soldier, a young boy about fourteen and a young man of thirty, etc. Fortunately death must have been immediate as the wounds were horrible. Yesterday Kola and I rode our bicycles to the Ku Low Hospital to see if we could be of any help. We found a wounded soldier on the street and tried to get an ambulance for him. An air raid was on and we would see the planes operating in the southern section of the city. Fires were burning in several parts too. When things quieted down a bit, we decided to ride down to St. Paul's to see how things were there. We discovered that a Chinese hotel just opposite our residence compound on Peh Hsia Lu had been knocked into a cocked hat by a bomb or shell, fragments of which had bounded across the street, struck our pavement, and had driven two holes through our compound gate. The holes are thru the tin which covered the gate, but the iron rods had been dented and twisted by the impact, too. We found several fragments of shell, one of which was still warm, and I am keeping them for you to see. As we were investigating, a window in the China hotel next to the one that had been hit opened and two scared men called to us. They said the place had been hit only a little while before. We urged them to come over to the safety zone. By and by a woman came along, We urged her to leave too but she merely smiled and assented and after we had turned our backs picked up some of the splintered wood from the hotel door, and carried it off to her home to cook supper, I suppose. All along the Tao Ping Road we met soldiers rifling the shops of soda water, fruit juices, other edibles and such articles as they could carry and as they found convenient to use. There were few soldiers around but many of the shops had been forced open. There seems to be no order or discipline, as soldiers whole and wounded seemed to be wandering around at random. We met a man, his wife, and little child, hurrying down Peh Hsia Lu to a rather dangerous spot. We urged them not to go but they insisted they had to go back and fetch rice as they had not had anything to eat for the two days they had been living in the safety zone. I suggested that he go alone, but he replied that his wife and child would not remain behind and that if he went alone he would be impressed by the soldiers for carrying and hauling. If he was killed they all wanted to die together. The larger part of Hsiakwan has been burned down by order of the military authorities. Archie Tsen's residence is only a charred ruin now. The last we knew our buildings were still intact.—Thousands and thousands of people have lost everything except what they could carry. Many haven't even that much. About 1,500 are still on the river bank, without shelter, hoping for a chance to get across the river. The International Committee gave them a month's supply of rice, but that is about all we can do for them. Until their attention was called to the plight of the Hsiakwan people the Govt. and military authorities hadn't apparently given them a thought. They finally agreed to transport them across the river after the wounded soldiers had been taken over. The wounded soldiers are in a sad plight, too, as unit after unit detailed for dressing and caring for them vanish in thin air, and the men are left to die of cold and hunger, in their misery. The Kulow Univ. Hos. is in a terrible plight as only three doctors are left, Wilson, Trimmer, and a Chinese. Only Wilson is a surgeon and he is working night and day. There are so many civilian casualties that they can no longer treat the wounded soldiers, although last night forty to fifty forced their way into the hospital for treatment.—The Safety Zone is packed full of people and there is practically no way to control them.—The water supply has ceased so we are reduced to drawing water from wells and ponds, and the likelihood is that the electricity will also cease to function very soon.— This morning I took the service over at Hanson's house where most of our Church people are located. I had most of Morning Prayer since there were a good number of non-Christians present, too, and then ended with the Communion Service. John took the service in our house for the people from the Model Village.—

Dec. 14th. The city has fallen. We are all safe and are busy looking after the wounded and destitute. We have organized a committee of the International Red Cross. Don't worry! Am sending this by Mr. Durdin of the New York Times.

Dec. 15th. Mr. Durdin of the N.Y. Times could not get thru to Shanghai yesterday. The Japanese soldiers began coming into the city on Sunday and there was a precipitate retreat. There was a good deal of bombing and shelling on Sat. and Sun,—We heard that there were wounded in three buildings, the Ministry of Foreign Affairs, of War, and of Railways. At the first there were lots of wounded with not a doctor or a nurse and no food or water. As I was in the gate someone called me by name, it was a ricksha coolie from Yangchow who lives on the Er Lung Miao. He was impressed for carrying and was wounded. I brought him to our house and then took him to the Kulow Hosp., where he will have to have one foot amputated. While John was trying to get things in order at the Ministry of War office, Mr. Lowe, a Chinese, and I in the Ministry of Railways. I wish you could have seen the condition of Chung Shan Road. At one place there was a congestion of artillery trucks, horses and mules loaded with anti-aircraft shells, etc. A truck had burned up and some of the embers were still alive. The horses loaded with munitions standing there were tied or tangled with wheels and bicycles. We released one poor animal who was unharmed but another was already burned to a crisp and others we could not help. I have never in my life seen such confusion and mess. The beautiful Ministry of Communications Building is a ruin. It was bombed probably with incendiary bombs on Sunday. Many fires were burning that day and night, including the woods on top and side of Purple Mountain. Yesterday I was busy all day. Three of us foreigners and a Chinese interpreter tried to find the highest Japanese officer in the city in order to let him know about the Safety Zone and the Red Cross Committee. He was living in a hotel near St. Paul's Church so we rode around there to see what its condition was. The Church is intact. Some windows are broken and the door under the tower, but a shell hit the front gate of the compound and the roof of the parish house at the end where the main reception room is. The timbers are still there but I did not go inside. Fortunately it did not burn. We found two Japanese soldiers in the Roberts' house, one carrying a hatchet, the other in the act of bringing down one of the children's bicycles from the third floor. When they saw me they disappeared. Drawers have been ransacked but the safe untouched. We have the Roberts' silver and papers from the safe with us. The compound and the house are open. I will try to put someone on the place as soon as it is safe to do so. We expect headquarters to be established today so that we may hope for a restoration of order fairly soon.—The Jap. soldiers are impressing men to carry and work for them. Some of our own people, those we know, have been taken, 7 yesterday, but 3 came back soon afterwards. The Safety Zone, while not ideal, has certainly saved the lives of countless thousands. It was the southern section of the city that got the worst of the bombing and shelling. But yesterday we saw less than 25 corpses on the road we traversed. The population of the Safety Zone increased tremendously on Sat., Sun., and Mon. There must be at least 100,000 people in the area. We decided to concentrate on the Ministry of Foreign Affairs as a Red Cross Hosp. for the wounded, but yesterday the Japanese took it over and will let none in or out. We can only pray for the fate of those inside. They do not like us foreigners to be around as our presence does curb some of their activities. We have no information about the Hsiakwan buildings as the gate has been closed and there has been sporadic fighting in that section, the last day or so. We haven't much hope of their being still intact. We may be thankful that the things have gone as well thus far for the plans made for the protection of the people. God has been a very present Help in time of trouble. I am sure that our Christians and many others realize that in a way they will never forget.—

Dec. 19th. It has not been possible for me to write you since my last letter which was sent to you by Mr. Durdin of the N. Y. Times. We have been through an even worse hell since he and the other correspondents left. It is impossible to write all that has happened, but I never dreamed that such human beasts existed as we have had to deal with. They have not loved us foreigners since we insisted on staying here when they did not want us to be here to see all their fiendishness. On the 15th and 16th they searched for soldiers and took off men in droves regardless of whether they had ever shouldered guns or not. They murdered most of them in cold blood. We heard that they took a group of two to three hundred to a pond, shot them one by one and let them fall into the water. Another big group was forced into a mat shed, surrounded with machine guns and burned alive. Fourteen men from Mr. Chen's congregation at the Model Village were carried off several days ago and have not yet returned. Among them was Mr. Chen's oldest boy about 16 years. He had not yet returned either. Then the soldiers have been looting and raping to their hearts' content. John and I usually spend the day taking women and wounded civilians to the hospital and in guarding the two residences where most of our Christians and many others, particularly girls, are taking refuge. Our presence there helps to keep soldiers out. We also sleep there.

Kola and his Tartar friend stay on guard here. We have about 100 people in our house including Buddhist nuns. The number increased when the raping assumed such large proportions. It was quite evident that the soldiers were out of hand. Today seemed better in some ways, as some officers seemed to be patrolling this afternoon. But this a.m. it was one continuous succession of soldiers going into houses to get whatever they wanted. Many civilians have been killed. John was in Hsiakuan with one of the secretaries of the J. Embassy yesterday a.m. The only buildings left standing are ours, which have been looted, the Yangtse Hotel and Socony Installation. He said the streets were littered with hundreds of corpses. The J. Embassy people have been decent, but have lost face over their inability to accomplish anything with the military. All property, foreign and Chinese, has been looted and tumbled upside down. We are hoping that things will get a little better. I had a long talk this p.m. with a J. soldier who is a merchant from Yokohama on Benton Dori. He said their soldiers were very short of food upon their arrival, since their service of supplies could not get things to them as they neared Nanking. So for several days their soldiers were desperate for food. Now that the River is open and the motor road being repaired, they are getting supplies again. He was very decent and told me lots of interesting things. We hope that foreigners will soon be able to get back to Nanking to help us as the job is getting impossible for the few of us to handle. Over three thousand women and girls are herded into Ginling, some have been carried off by the soldiers, women and children have been raped in the Univ. of Nanking library building, and other Univ. buildings which are crowded with refugees. Last night several soldiers got into the nurses quarters in the Univ. Hosp. and frightened a number of girls almost out of their wits. Yesterday p.m. they raped one of the Model Village women. Last night they raped some Buddhist nuns who had crossed the street from our house to get supper and then were afraid to come back because of soldiers in the street.

We are cut off from all news here, so do not know what is happening. None of the foreign embassy people have returned, and we suspect the J. do not want them back for a while.

This is now the 20th. We have had a quiet uneventful night and I have just returned to the house where I am standing guard. It is a great life if one doesn't weaken. The J. are trying to get Kola to get the electric light company running again. He is certainly a very interesting clever youngster, and has been grand in adapting himself to the situation and helping in every way.

Dec. 26th. We have just had Morning Prayer in No. 25, at which I preached on St. Stephen and baptized two infants for Rev. Mr. Chen. John is staying at our house (Mr. Schultze-Pantine) for the service for the Christians in the Model Village. He baptized seven persons yesterday. Last night he did not spend at 25 as he had gone home for supper and on his way back slipped and sat down too hard on the end of his spine. So I was responsible for guarding No. 17 and 25. Two soldiers climbed over the gate at No. 25, bent on mischief, but I was called in time and drove them out. I did not know that they had stolen a watch from one of the men, or I would have demanded it from them. They had their eyes on a girl or two, but fortunately my arrival on the scene prevented that. When they saw and heard me, they walked out rather sheepishly. John is o.k. this morning but the fall shook him up somewhat. The soldier who is carrying a letter to you left this a.m. I think, so I hope you will have news from me soon.

Yesterday I heard that five J. soldiers who are apparently Christians joined in the service the Methodist pastor had at the woman's Bible School and contributed $5 to the offering. Mr. Negamni is not a Christian but I gave him a N. T. in Chinese to take along. Also two boxes of sardines, a cake of soap and two dollars for the journey. He was very decent and very grateful, anxious as anything to get back to his family in Japan. I am afraid they have found Nanking poor pickings, as we have been cut off from supplies for so long, and they cannot get fruit or fish and the things they are accustomed to eating. With our water supply dependent upon wells or ponds, they have not found the water very appetizing either. Our presence is a help to the people here in their distress and a tremendous witness for the Gospel.

Christmas day. I am wondering where and how you are celebrating Christmas. It is a beautiful day here and we have just had a service at No. 25, Mr. Hansen's. Rev. Mr. Chiang and Dr. Tong took the service because I feel that the Chinese Christians should interpret the great days of the Church Year themselves. Besides I am still doing police duty, keeping unauthorized soldiers out of the house, etc. I had to go into action during the service as three came in for a look-see. One of them spoke some English. He lingered while the other two disappeared. Apparently they had been to the house before when neither John nor I were on hand, had had some coffee and relieved some of the people of their bedding, etc. They asked for coffee this a.m. but Mr. Hanson's cook could not supply any, so the one who lingered had to be satisfied with tea and sugar.

Conditions seem to be improving from day to day, and I think before long the people will be able to move back to such homes as they can find. Practically the whole southern part of the city has been burned down. Our buildings on Tai Ping Road and Pei Hsia Lu are about the only ones standing with the exception of a few that in some unaccountable way escaped the flames. I went down to our place on Thursday to see if our buildings are still intact and discovered one of the Christian women who had refused to leave with the others before the soldiers came and then found her escape cut off. I had tried to find her the week before, but unsuccessfully, so we assumed that she had either gone to some other place or had been killed. She was in the Church Tower for ten days during the shelling and bombing, burning and looting and she escaped unscathed. She is the widow of a former catechist at St. Paul's. Since she is also a trained nurse, we hope that she can be of service in the Univ. Hosp. which is filled to overflowing with sick and wounded persons. We had rain on Thursday which made it hard for the refugees who have to sleep outdoors and semi-outdoors as at Ginling college where there innumerable women and children.

Miss Vautrin and Mrs. Twinum are living at Ginling to look after the refugees. Military police have been on duty there for several days, so conditions are better. Today a man returned who was carried off by the soldiers about ten days ago. He brought word that one of the Christians from All Sts. Church, Shanghai, who was also carried off at the same time, is still being held by the soldiers outside the city where he is cooking and working for them, but he has been promised his freedom in another two weeks. His name is Tsu An-sheng, and he is nephew of a former or present catechist at All Saints'. He was living with us here, having refugeed from Shanghai when he was taken by the soldiers. You might communicate this to Mr. Wei of All Saints. The fact that some men have returned gives us hope that the others of our acquaintance may still be alive and will also return. All the foreigners here are well. We have no news of the outside world and we hope very much that other foreigners will try to get back as soon as possible as they can be of tremendous service to us in all sorts of ways. Whether they will be permitted to come is another question. We assume that the Newspaper correspondents got through all right. Much has happened since they left. No diplomatic officials have been able to get back yet excepting the Japanese. The latter are doing their best but seem to be having their own difficulties with the military. . . . I had to interrupt this letter in order to see about two soldiers who paid a visit to one of our houses. They turned out to be two who were here this morning during the service. One is a policeman in Osaka. They have just left.

This has been a quiet uneventful Christmas, but God has given us the Lord, Christ, so we need not ask for more.

Dec. 27th. Just a few minutes ago the J. sargeant [*sic*] brought back Tsu An-sheng, the young boy whom they carried off a week ago. They have released him to our great joy, and apparently treated him quite decently. We wish that many others whom they carried off had had as good a fate . . . Yesterday p.m. I drove down to St. Paul's with Miss Chang to try to get a few more of her things. We moved the parish hall piano into Mr. Kuo's house. It had been taken out on the lawn and Mr. Kuo's piano was carried away. The shell which struck the parish house did so at an angle. It penetrated the roof and went diagonally across the room and out through the front wall which will have to be rebuilt. The floor is not damaged, though much plaster is fallen. Another shell fell and exploded on the concrete driveway inside the main gate of the Church compound. The wall is badly nicked by shrapnel but it is standing. The wooden gates are all down, so that the compound is quite open. We are not yet able to do anything about it since life has not yet returned to normal. Miss Chang has been taken on as a nurse in the Univ. Hosp. I spent several hours yesterday afternoon helping Mrs. Twinum salvage some things from her house which has been looted. She is living at Ginling. We hear various rumors about what is going on in the outside world but nothing very certain. One thing is that the railway is functioning after a fashion, but I doubt that very much. If it were, I am sure some foreign men would be returning. We are still only a small group as before.

Dec. 28th. I have been doing police duty at 17 and 25 again, but have not had any troubles to deal with, thank the Lord. Last few days, I have had a chance to get in a little reading. John spent the night at 25 and I was here at 17. Then I went home to breakfast and John went later. He does not usually get up until about eight and by that time I am eating breakfast. He has not returned to relieve me here, so I may decide to eat Chinese supper and not go back to our house. The two servants are well. Yu-fok seems to have recovered, but has gotten quite thin and white. They are both functioning under difficulties as the house is so full of refugees they can scarcely move. Things seem to be better in general, as a great many troops seem to have left town, and the people feel freer about walking on sts. They are still scared as stray soldiers are still looting and raping, and men suspected of having been soldiers are still being executed. But it is still much better in many respects than it has been and we are no end thankful. If only more foreigners would come back and help out it would be a great relief to the congested conditions now obtaining. At Ginling college alone there must be over ten thousand women and children. We do not know when people will be allowed to move in and out of the city freely. The problem of finding food for so many is getting very acute. We hear that the farmers outside the city are destitute, too, since their grain, farm animals and implements are largely gone. Fires are still being set in some sections of the city, so that the southern part is mostly ruin. No plea on the ground of humanity seems to be of any avail. Don't worry about us. We are o.k.

Dec. 29th. Every morning we people have prayers together. I picked out some hymns and practiced for New Years Day and Sunday. We are planning to have a service on New Year's Eve which will probably take the form of a litany and Penitential Office with meditations and suitable hymns. You will be glad to know that there are five groups of people preparing for the catechumenate, etc., which consist of persons who have been refugeeing with us. There is also a

Bible class for Christians and many people are helping to make padded garments, which are much needed, since many of the people have been robbed of their warm clothes and bedding by the soldiers. The situation in that respect has improved a great deal by the withdrawal of troops to other places. All men in the city are required to register with the military authorities which are combing out all soldier suspects. Machine guns were working again yesterday. We do not know whether it was regular drill, or Chinese ammunition being destroyed, or men being executed. Countless people, civil and military, have been done to death. God grant that it may soon end. God has been wonderfully good and we have entrusted ourselves to Him entirely.

Dec. 30th. This has been another quiet day so far. All of our people went off to be registered early this a.m. and found that only the men are required to be. The J. are still "mopping" up which would be more accurately described by another name, as they are systematically combing out all soldier suspects. The report is that no men between the ages of 18 and forty will be allowed to leave the city. That will not be so bad if they do not molest them while they are in the city. We have heard that they are trying to force them to be soldiers against their own compatriots. I have spent a greater part of the morning preparing a form of service for New Year's Eve, and now at No. 17 I am reading Morton's "In the Steps of the Master."

Dec. 31st. John has just been in to say that the International Committee wants me to help inspect some rice kitchens that are being run for the refugees.

I have some sad news. When I woke up this a.m. I found a note from Mr. Lu and his purse. (He has been acting as catechist in Tangshan and Tungliu). He has become very morose over the situation and in his note indicated that he was planning to commit suicide by drowning. He was to have registered today. He had nothing to fear in that respect as he is over forty, and went off early this morning alone. I looked at some nearby ponds but could not discover his body so I hope he has changed his mind. I had heard that he had been entertaining such thoughts lately and last night before retiring tried to encourage him to live for China, as long as God wanted him to do so. He was a very quiet gentle person but I am afraid not one to be easily diverted from his purpose when once he had made up his mind.

Mr. Rabe, the Nanking representative of Siemans Co. and chairman of the International Committee, has had three letters from his wife in Shanghai via the J. Consul, from which we gather that you know nothing of what has been happening in Nanking since the J. occupation.

We hear some American Consular people are on their way here. Their presence will not be especially welcome here since ours is not particularly acceptable. Things on the whole, however, seem better. It is now nearly one o'clock and we have only inspected one place where about 3,000 people are being cared for. It was some sight but on the whole the people seem to be making the most of a hard situation. Our servants have come back from being registered. That is a big relief to us and to them. I am enclosing a copy of the form of service for this evening. We hope we can hold it without interruption. Do you remember that we were in Nagasaki last New Year's Day? We are hoping that the soldiers will not overstep bounds in their celebrations here. We can only warn people to stay indoors as much as possible. We wish that regular transportation were re-established between here and Shanghai so that news and people could go back and forth but I am afraid it will be some time before things are regular again. Some J. merchants I hear have been bringing up some supplies by truck and cars so that may be a possibility of getting supplies. We are living largely on the groceries we brought from Yangchow, but will soon be out of a few staples like milk and sugar. Eggs have been and still are very hard to get. Yu-foh bought three before Christmas and with two made a Chocolate cake, but we cannot complain when we realize how little other people have. May God grant you a very blessed New Year full of joy and many happy surprises.

P.S. please be circumspect about retailing news about conditions here, since the J. are anxious to keep as much undercover as possible.

Jan. 2nd: Just to let you know John and I are both well. We haven't much contact with the outside world so we have to depend upon occasional opportunities to send a message by someone who is going to Shanghai. This time it happens to be some merchants who are doing a little freighting and who are bringing supplies to the Japanese army. I am glad that the weather so far has not been too severe. Otherwise the suffering of people would be much greater. John and I spend most of our time doing police duty. The last few days I have been helping to inspect the refugee centers to see that the people have been getting enough food. Yesterday was a general holiday with lots of flags and fire crackers. I do not know where the latter appeared from, but for many people they broke the tension of the past two weeks. Conditions are gradually being brought under control.

(Brought down by Japanese messenger)

Jan. 3rd: Our Committee went out this morning and inspected two refugee centers. Several mass meetings were held for the inauguration of a self-government society for the city. It is significant that the old five barred Chinese flag was used with the J. flag, and that no flags of the central govt were in evidence. In fact at the mass meeting which was poorly attended, all the sins of the latter were exposed by the orators, and the blessings the people might expect from the new regime were proclaimed. John and I had been invited to a New Year's dinner at the Univ. of Nanking, but we decided that I was to go and John was to stay on guard. John was persuaded by George Fitch to attend the dinner anyway, so he went. But we had just finished eating when Catechist Fan and Paul Tong came running to say that some J. soldiers had entered No. 17 and were raping the women there. We rushed over immediately in Geo. Fitch's car but the men had left about three minutes before. We tried to trace them but unsuccessfully. As I got the story, what happened was this: Two soldiers came into Chiang's room, the Chinese priest from Puchen, and stole his sweater and a pair of gloves. They saw Mrs. Chiang and decided to come back for her. She managed to escape, however, by a bathroom door. Then one of the soldiers went to the 3rd floor and started to rape an unmarried girl there. She resisted and succeeded in tripping up the soldier and thus escaping. Then the soldiers attacked two young married women on the second floor. We took them to the hospital for treatment. A soldier beat one of them and Mrs. Chou who was trying to protect her with a bayonet. Mr. Lu, the Chinese helper at Tungshan and Tunglieu has apparently carried out his threat of suicide. He was not returned since early morning of Dec. 31st. Neighbors told us that they saw a body in a pond nearby which they think is his, but we have not yet received permission from the authorities to drag for the body. It is very sad. He seems to have entertained this idea for some time and his determination has increased by the sufferings of the people, since the occupation of the city. Yesterday I preached at the service for the Model Village Christians. We had a good service and the people listened well. After lunch I went over to No. 17 to relieve John who had worshipped with the Christians from Hsiakuan and St. Paul's. I spent the afternoon typing our report of the inspection we have made so far. John came back to house 25 to spend the night and reported two incidents that had happened. About 4:30 a Jap. soldier tried to rape the mother of five children. Her husband was at home and struggled with the soldier so that his wife could escape. The soldier left in anger, returned with his rifle and shot the man dead. John went to report the matter and found that Mr. Fitch was already on his way to Mr. Rabe's house to report the case. While they were conferring, neighbors rushed in to say that a J. soldier was trying to rape a woman in a nearby hut. John and George rushed out and drove the fellow off. . . . So it goes.

At the Woman's Bible School the soldiers have been doing a good deal of raping and looting. After much protesting a group of military police was stationed there. The other night one of them went in and raped a woman. Yesterday afternoon several men came in to report happenings at the Texico [*sic*] Installation outside the Han Hsi Men. The place was looted by J. soldiers who took down two Am. Flags, stating that since America and Japan were enemies, the flags could not be flown. They made the servants at the point of guns sign and fingerprint a statement to the effect that they had sold the loot to the soldiers for a sum of money, and then forced one man and his 63 yr. old father to push the motor cars and trucks which belonged to the Texas Oil co. to another place. The men had one meal in three days. They killed a number of people in and around the Installation. In one family of nine, only a woman and child escaped. The soldiers fired on them and then set fire to the dugout. The woman escaped by covering herself and the baby with a heavy quilt and then running through the flames. These are just samples of what has been happening here.

Things are somewhat better though it is quite evident that neither the military nor civil J. officials have the soldiers in hand. What has happened here has been repeated I fear all along the line of march. Yesterday we had a visit from the Chinese planes who dropped some bombs at Hsiakuan [*sic*] and outside the south gate in the airdrome. There was anti-aircraft firing for a few minutes. Then all was quiet again. There are rumours that Yangchow is now in J. hands as well as Taichow, I-ling, Tai-hsien, etc. so I guess we may expect the worst. Today for the first time in many weeks we have electric lights again which means also that we can get radio news. Unfortunately, John's is not functioning. . . .

I have just had lunch and taken a woman to the hospital for treatment. Ru-yuan went along to see his ricksha coolie friend who had to have his leg amputated below the knee. He is getting along all right. I have taken him on as a servant for various reasons as I think he can be more useful and he certainly can't pull richshas [*sic*] any more for a living. He is very grateful for all we have done for him.

I surely would like to have some news from you. Maybe I shall for we hear that somebody from the German and American Diplomatic staff is returning. For Christmas Mr. Rabe gave each of us a nice leather-bound diary with the compliments of the Siemens co. and for New Years he had special greeting cards made with the Safety Zone emblem on the front and the signatures of all the foreigners in Nanking on the back. It will be a very nice souvenir of this experience. I wonder whether you have yet received the note I sent by Mr. Negani. I sent another by some J. merchants just to let you know that we are O.K. and that you are not to worry.

Jan. 7th: Yesterday I was most happy to receive letters from Bishop Roberts, Althea, Leslie, Steve and K. P. through some American officials who have come to the Embassy. The letters were all old, Dec. 12–20th, but from them I learned that you had reached Hongkong safely and I certainly was glad for the news. Things are better in certain respects. There is hope that communications will be restored to a more normal state. So far we have been completely isolated. I do not know therefore what is happening at Yangchow or anywhere else. The Embassy people reported our Wuhu property as O.K. and Lanphear and Sister

Constance safe and well. I am sending you letters I have written and accumulated. You must use your own judgment about letting the contents be known as it may have an unfavorable reaction upon us here. We have been a thorn in the flesh of the J. military as it is. And if any letters or statements were published at present, it might make difficulties for us here and the people here still need us very much. I am sure you will understand.

Jan. 10th: This is to let you know that I am all right and there is no reason to worry. I sent you a whole batch of letters the other day that I have been waiting an opportunity to send. They will tell you all about things here. This a.m. I took various persons to the hospital and also rode down to our Church and residence compound. Things there are much the same as before. A part of the old Kongkuan burned but not very much. Everything has been looted, but many things are still left, all topsy turvy. I chased a J. soldier out of Miss Sims' house this a.m. Was he scared! Then I called at the Embassy since I had not had a chance to meet the officials who came. Had a nice talk with Mr. Allison who was formerly consul in Tsinan. We do not think our places will be spared further looting unless somebody, a foreigner, lives there. That isn't easy since there are too few of us to go around, but people are more important than things. Officials of the British and German Embassies have returned too, which ought to make things better. Yesterday I was on duty at 17 and 25 all day. We had Morning Prayer in 25 at which Rev. Chiang of Puchen preached. There was a large attendance, including many non-Christians. John preached at the service in the University yesterday in the a.m. and at the English service in the Union Church in the afternoon. I could not leave to go. We have recovered Mr. Lu's body from a nearby pond in which he committed suicide on Dec. 31st. It is very sad, but I think he would have carried out his intentions even if we could have stopped him this time. Allison said somebody had inquired through the Secretary of State about John's and my welfare. I guess it was Father or Dr. Wood. We are both o.k.

Jan. 11th: What a grand Christmas present I had yesterday afternoon [w]hen John brought me your letters of Dec. 16th, 26th and Jan. 5th, together with those from Father, Betty and Sophie. I was just in the midst of writing to Althea, K.P. etc., when he brought me the pack, and was I ever glad to get mail! I am so happy that you have reached Shanghai safely and that you made the trip from Hankow safely. You probably know I called you by long distance the morning before you left Hankow and Frances Roots took the message. Life goes on pretty much the same from day today. We had an uneventful night. John and I came back to Mr. Shultze house for breakfast and then I took the car to the Univ. Hosp. taking with me a nurse who has had her training at St. Andrew's, Wusih. She did not graduate as her grandmother got sick and died before she could take her N.A.C. exams. But she has had about four years' training and the hospital is going to give her a chance since they are so short-handed. From there we drove to the Presb. Girls' school with Miss Lucy Chen to get some clothes that had been contributed for refugees, and from there I went to the Embassy to leave some letters and to tell them at their request about the Texas Oil co. property in which we have been living. It doesn't sound as though I had accomplished much in the a.m. but we had to wait in each place. John and I were both grateful for all the mission news. We were sorry to hear about so many having been sick, but were most interested to hear about what you and everyone is doing. Please give them our regards. . . . Do not worry about our food. We still have some supplies and expect to get more soon. The Embassy has offered to get some for us so we are putting in an order thru George Fitch who will buy through the Commissary Dept. in Shanghai.

The servants are both well. They do not venture out much alone since men are still being impressed for coolie work by the soldiers. Our servants have escaped so far. I saw the richsha man in the hospital yesterday. He was very cheerful and is getting along well. His wound is almost healed. He is so grateful to have had his life saved. John and I still do guard duty, though I think it may soon become unnecessary. It is usually when one is off one's guard that trouble happens. John and I are both well. Yesterday I sent cables to the family (Newton and Phila.) to the effect that we were well and that you were expected in Shanghai. That was before I knew that you had actually arrived there. Today we are trying to send one to Dr. Wood. By now you know how we spent our Christmas, they had made some festive decorations for the big reception room in 25 and everything was very nice. It was a gloriously mild day. I was on guard the whole day.

John baptized some people from the Rev. Mr. Chen's congregation on Christmas. I baptized two infants the day after Christmas. I know how you would love to be here, but conditions are too uncertain to warrant your coming provided you could get permission to come. Now I must hurry off to leave this at the Embassy for delivery to the boat.

Jan. 12th: I am waiting for the barber to cut my hair which hasn't had the shears since the first of November. In the first place it is hard to find a person to do it and in the 2nd place it is hard to find time and a suitable place to have it done. John and I have just had breakfast. At 9 o'clock I am to attend a meeting to consider plans for rehabilitation. The Committee which investigated various refugee centers made its report and recommendation and was asked to consider itself a rehabilitation committee, and formulate plans for enabling people to get back to their homes and work. I was busy yesterday p.m. taking medical supplies to the Univ. hospital. The municipal health dept. had turned over a lot of them to us to use at Hsiakuan. When we came into the city we brought them along and decided to turn them over to the hosp. since we no longer had use for them. We had no other transport but the small car, so I had to make several trips. I also took Miss Chen along to get old clothing for refugees which had been stored in the Presbyterian Girl's School. The women are planning to make some of them over so that it can be used when needed.

Things were quiet enough for both John and me to come back to Mr. Schultze's house for supper, the first time we have been able to do so in many weeks. I think the presence of the officials in the American, German and British Embassies are responsible for the difference. The J. have no face at all over the looting of foreign property (even the embassy) by their troops, and they cannot put the blame on the shoulders of the Chinese for very often when the foreign officials go around to examine the state of the foreign property they find J. soldiers on the premises in the act of looting. They stole all motor cars they could get, even took out cars that were put in the American Embassy for safekeeping. Now the J. Embassy is trying to collect all they can get back from the military as a face-saving gesture. But I don't think it is setting very well with the foreign officials. If things like this have been going on here, one does not need much imagination to know what has gone on in Yangchow and other places. Of course we have no news here of Yangchow or Chinkiang. I am anxiously waiting to hear whether you have received the letters I have sent on various occasions once by a J. soldier and another by a J. merchant, etc. An old lady, aunt of one of the Model Village Christians, died this morning early in the hospital. She was 69 years old and was ill with I don't know what, exactly. John and I sent a long cablegram to Dr. Wood yesterday through the kindness of the Embassy in reply to his cable about us. We hear that the J. want the people to leave the refugee zone and return to their own homes. That is easier said than done since so many persons have nothing but ruins to go back to. Also there is utter lack of transportation facilities, since all were taken by the soldiers. What richshas there are all tyre-less or out of commission. Bicycles have shared the same fate or have been carried off. Motor cars the same way. Fortunately I have saved your bicycle and mine so far. I think I brought all of our things from Hsiakuan except the two over-stuffed armchairs. Whether they are still left I do not know. Will you please send me some two cent stamps as we cannot buy any here. We have electricity in Mr. Schultze's house again, but no running water yet.

Jan. 13th. John took the letter to be left at the Embassy yesterday, but failed to do so, so I'll just add a line this a.m. to let you know that we are well. I slept at home (Mr. Schultze's house) last night as we think it no longer necessary for two people to be on guard during the night at No. 17 and 25.

It is cloudy today and is trying to snow. I am going out in a few minutes to help investigate another refugee center. Then I shall take a sick woman to the hospital and leave the letters at the Embassy.

I hope all is well with you. Please tell Gilmore I shall send him a statement very soon. It is simply a case of checking up his statements of deposits and typing out my accounts for him. We can't work at night because we have no electricity at #17 and #25 and the days are occupied with many activities.

I am eagerly awaiting the next mail from you. Perhaps I'll find some at the Embassy when I call there.

Jan. 14th. It is my turn to sleep at home tonight, so I am in the dining room—the only place we have a stove—and am writing letters. . . . John went to the hospital to take some patients there and also to take some pictures. I staid on guard and spent the time writing a letter for the family which I am enclosing. There are two extra copies which you can send to whomever you think best. This afternoon after John came to relieve me I went over to Ginling College to see Mrs. Twinem and Miss Vautrin whom I hadn't called on for some time. Mrs. Twinem was home alone. . . . She gave me two pots of mincemeat which she had salvaged from her home. It had been looted by soldiers who also stole her motor car. They were going to burnt it down, having already taken out their magnesium matches to do so when the servant had presence of mind to show them her visiting card, indicating that she was a foreigner, even though she has taken out Chinese citizenship. The soldiers left the house but did not take the matches along. We have samples of them.

Tonight we're having some lovely radio music. John's radio was broken in transit from Hsiakuan, but we have retrieved a fine one from the Sino-British Cultural Association which we will keep till some responsible person comes back to take it over. Just now they are playing Paderewski's lovely record La Campanella and the Nocturne in F by Chopin. There has also been some grand opera.

It has been a quiet day. I heard that the night before last a J. soldier climbed over the wall of the University Middle School and abducted a girl. When resistance was offered he fired twice and hit a blackboard in one of the classrooms full of refugees. He got the girl over the wall, but before he could get himself over, she ran away and climbed back over the wall in another place, so he was foiled. Last night, however, another girl was taken. Unfortunately she did not escape so successfully. Dr. Bates was called over to Dr. Brady's house yesterday and found two J. (a soldier and a military police) looking over the place. It is constant occurrences like these which make the people afraid to go back to their homes.

John went over to the Central Theological School with Dr. Tong this afternoon, and found things there in an awful mess—everything topsy-turvy and

many things looted. The houses everywhere are in the same condition. . . . I feel
ten pounds lighter and ten years younger. Guess why? I had my hair cut this
morning! We had tried to get the University barber several times, but that gentleman seemed to find 8 a.m. too early to ply his trade, so in desperation I called in
a barber who lives across the street. He did a pretty good job and I feel much
better. It's funny what a difference such little things make. Oh, for a chance at a
good hot tub bath or shower, and a dry cleaner for some of my clothes. . . .

Jan. 15th. Before I go over to #17 to spend the night I want to send you a little
note with my love. I just heard that a British boat is leaving tomorrow so I want
to get this mail off by it. I think the contents will explain themselves.

I was busy this a.m. with the car, first going to Ginling to arrange about our
workers helping with evangelistic work among the refugees there. We have
agreed to go five afternoons every week—two of us each day—to preach at 2
p.m. to different groups of women. Then I had to take a number of sick people
to the hospital clinic. By the time they had been seen and we got back to the
house it was already noon. John was out all afternoon and is now at the J.
Embassy for Sukiyaki supper to which he and a number of others were invited.
I am to celebrate Holy Communion tomorrow morning for the Model Village
Christians and to take the Union English service tomorrow afternoon. This afternoon I read and wrote and then played with some of the children at #17. We
just kicked a tennit [*sic*] ball around but they enjoyed it immensely and we all
got some good exercise.

Jan. 24th: Just have time to write a little before the broadcast comes, of which
we type notes and send them around to our friends who have no other chance to
get news. Mr. Kroeger should have reached Shanghai last night. He left here
yesterday at 7:30 a.m. the best accommodations offered were on an open box
car. At least his view was not obstructed and he probably got two eyes full
along the way—Yesterday I went out with the Chinese manager of the Metropolitan Hotel who is a member of our rehabilitation Committee to deliver
questionaire forms at five of the refugee centers. On getting back we had a
service at 10:30 at #25. We heard at the Old Language School which serves as
a refugee center that a woman had been taken from there by J. soldiers during
the night. Our service was well attended. We had shortened Morning Prayer
which I took which was followed by Holy Communion which Dr. Tong took.
He also preached. After service a group of us were invited to a Chinese dinner
given by Mr. Lowe (Liu) the manager of the Hotel. It was his wife's birthday
and also George Fitch's. Mrs. Lowe is in Shanghai but we had a bang up feast
lasting from 12:30 to 3:30. Then John and I went to the English service led by
Mr. Mills.

Today had another full day. I had to be at the Embassy at 10:00 to meet some Jap. military police who had come on Sunday afternoon when I was out, to have me look at a piano, thinking it might be the one taken from our parish hall. Since I was not home yesterday they made an appointment for me this morning. Mr. Espy of the Consulate also had an appointment to visit the Texeco [sic] Installation from which a lot of gasoline and other things had been taken. So he went off first and I went to Ginling to deliver the news sheet and have a chat with Miss Vautrin and Mrs. Twinem. They told of a man who was carried off by the soldiers on Dec. 18th and who returned a day or so ago. He was taken to Changshing in Chekiang and made [to] work for an officer for eight days; while he was very severe, he did not mistreat the man who was told he might return to Nanking. On the way he was taken at I-shing near Wusih by another group of men and again made to work for an officer who was very kind to him and treated him very well. They exchanged addresses and after 18 days of service they gave him some money and sent him home. He made his way back by small country paths and reached Nanking after 8 days travel. The country people treated him very kindly when they heard his story and helped him along the way. He said that over in Anhui the Big Sword Society is very active in protecting the countryside against J. and Chinese soldiers and against brigands so that the people there are prosperous and the food plentiful and cheap. That is very interesting. He had passed through many places; Huchow is deserted and ninety percent destroyed; Changshing, Kuangteh, I-shing, Lishui, Liyang, Chuyoung are also deserted and mere heaps of ashes and ruin.

The piano we looked at was not ours and so we came back. We had just finished lunch when neighbors ran in to say that a soldier had tried to get a woman and had threatened her with a bayonet. The three of us, John, Kola and I, rushed out. The man took fright and ran away, but Kola and I caught sight of him and gave chase. I yelled and Kola yelled and we both ran, and the soldier beat it off as fast as his legs would carry him. But he left behind his bayonet which we are turning over to the Am. Consul to be presented at the Jap. Embassy with an account of the incident. The soldier came back the second time to get his bayonet which had been brought to us. We gave chase again through the mud and over ditches but he ran away. When the excitement died down I went to No. 17 and then to make an appointment with the Univ. architect to build our parish house to have him give me an estimate of the damages to our property at St. Paul's. I also have to lead a Bible class tomorrow afternoon at the University. Incidents are still happening. That is, on Sat. night, just after our Consular people had finished dinner, a servant came to report that some J. soldiers were in one of the Embassy garages. He found two playing majong with some Chinese. He asked them to leave promptly which they did. But then as he was wondering whether he ought to have put them out, another servant came to say that a Jap. soldier had taken off his older daughter. While the two had gone into garage No. 3 to play majong this fellow had gone into No. 5 and insisted on taking the older girl along. So Allison and some of the others rushed out on the street to find her. They met her returning and she said that just as her abductor was trying to force her into a motor car, his two cronies who had been chased off the premises came along and told him that since they had been trespassing on the Am. Embassy property, that he had better send the girl back or there would be the devil to pay. There have been cases which did not end so happily, however. We have heard of two very sad ones which seem to be authentic. A young woman was raped by a J. soldier who forced an empty beer bottle into her and then shot her. The other case was seen by a member of the British Embassy staff. A woman was raped and a golf stick rammed into her. She was found dead in that condition. It hardly seems possible that such human devils were in existence. But instance after instance can be mentioned. A young boy was brought into the hospital with a bullet in his jaw the other morning. A Jap. soldier had told him to catch a pig and when he was unable to do so shot him in the jaw. We know of another instance of a boy who was unable to produce a pig for a soldier was disemboweled and thrown into a pond. Another instance in the same neighborhood was that of a man who had been carried off to Wuhu by the soldiers. He succeeded in making his way back to find his home gone and his womenfolk in hiding. Tired and hungry he had just prepared a bowl of cabbage when a J. soldier came along, demanding money and women. When the man could produce neither, the soldier urinated into the bowl of cabbage and went off. Allison and the British and German Consuls are not standing for any nonsense. When their protests, etc. are tabled by the J. Embassy officials, they get into direct communication with Tokyo through Washington, London and Berlin. This has made the J. awfully mad here, as you may imagine, and they are being told that our Govt's do not consider a small and unimportant matter to have the property of their nationals looted and people living on those premises for protection carried off by troops whom their officers will not control. One of the J. Consular police is very angry because Allison reported to Washington that he came to the Univ. of Nanking to get women to wash clothing, but when he refused those who offered to go and demanded others who were young and beautiful, he placed his motives under grave suspicion. He came to our house the other day also, and asked Kola to supply him with Chinese girls. Kola asked him what the hundred Jap. and Korean girls they brought here were for. He replied that he did not want them, but Chinese girls from good families. Now he is trying to find out what Chinese reported his visit to the Nanking Univ. to the authorities, and today they seized a pastor in charge of the Univ. Middle School refugee camp to try to get information from him. So we live from day to day, never knowing what a new day is going to bring forth. Since Allison communicated directly with Tokyo through Washington the local J. officials here have been more tractible, though still not all they should be. Guess they would like to kill us, one and all. We are looking forward to mail perhaps tomorrow or the day afterward by the H.M.S. Aphis. Please ask Bp. Roberts and Bessie Sims to send me as soon as possible an inventory of the things which they left in their houses so that I can check the things that have been taken. Also get a list from Miss VanVoast. The Consul wants us to file preliminary claims as soon as possible. Our Embassy now has a wireless sending set with an operator from the Navy. The J. refused at first, but Allison won out. More power to him! He is awfully nice as are Espy and MacFadgeon, the two vice-consuls. Tell Dyer that the wife of one of the Wusih Christians named Li died in the hospital yesterday of blood-poisoning, I suspect. They refugeed with us at Hsiakuan and here. They have one little girl. The woman had been ill for some time with dysentery. If possible get from Mr. Kuo the number of his piano and that in the parish hall for identification purposes.

Jan. 25th. After supper I am going over to #17 to spend the night. I began the day with a bath, not in a tub but standing in the bathroom to the tune of two oil stoves. As John said afterwards, I looked quite respectable again. I certainly feel that way. He was tempted to take one, too, but couldn't bring himself to it, even though he needed it more than I. After breakfast went to the Committee Headquarters of the leaders of the various refugee centers. It was a typical meeting, much time being spent over the question, and realizing at the end that the question had no concern with us. The meeting lasted till after 12, when I came back for lunch and prepared for the meeting at the Univ. of Nanking. There was really an evangelistic meeting rather than a Bible class, even though we used Mt. XIX as a basis, since most of the people who came were non-Christians. One of the Professors of the Univ., a Hsiakuan Christian, told me he counted more than four hundred people in the audience and that it was the biggest attendance they had had. The Meeting was held in the science lecture room which was certainly packed, and the people listened very attentively. So you see God has not lessened our opportunities. I believe there will still be a rich harvest over this trouble and sorrow. As I walked back I passed an open field where many coffins were placed awaiting burial. I saw a man weeping by the side of a child's coffin that had apparently just been placed there. Immediately the thought came to me that I ought to try and comfort him and ask him to turn to the Lord Jesus for comfort. I walked on a little way but soon turned back and spoke to the man. He said that the child was his little girl who had just died. He told me that he had heard the Gospel in various preaching halls from time to time and he seemed to take some comfort as his tears stopped flowing. But suddenly as he saw a group of people, including a policeman coming along the nearby street, he left me very abruptly and hurried away. But I am glad I followed my impulse and spoke to him. On the way another man offered me a part of a Russian tea brick. He said he had bought it which may be true, but I politely declined to accept it, as I thought he would appreciate it more than I. The people certainly seem grateful for what the Committee has been trying to do to help them. As I mentioned in a previous letter, a new set of troops has come, so women are again having a pretty hard time of it. I was glad to learn of the protest which Ambassador Grew had made to the foreign office in Tokyo, and we all hope it will bear fruit. We heard that a J. soldier got into the Ministry of Foreign Affairs which we tried to organize into an International Red Cross Hosp. for wounded soldiers, of whom a number had been left there before the J. entered the city. John had installed some doctors and dressers in there to look after these men, but when the J. took over the building, we foreigners were no longer permitted to go in. Nor can we get permission even now. We get word occasionally from people inside about conditions there. This J. soldier went in last night and murdered one of the coolies with his bayonet when he refused to take him to where the girl nurses were sleeping. Then he threatened another coolie who finally led him to a room in which five girls were. They realizing what was threatening dressed quickly and when the door was opened, three of them rushed out and escaped. The other two led the soldiers through a series of rooms to where a Chinese doctor was staying and by playing for time managed to foil the soldier's plan. He was very angry of course, but, having murdered one person, he had accomplished enough mischief for one night. The wind is blowing strong from the north so it will be a very cold night, and I am to sleep at No. 17.

Jan. 26th. It has been very cold today as a result of the strong wind, but the sun has been shining most of the time and moderated the cold. I am glad for the people as the cold is so hard on them with so few means of keeping warm. I could spend some time this morning making notes from Headlan's Christian Theology, an excellent book with much material useful for preaching to non-Christians, especially the educated class. Then I conducted a preliminary burial service for Mrs. Li, the wife of one of the Wusih Christians who died in the hospital on Sunday. We placed the coffin in a bamboo grove, near No. 17 alongside of that of Evangelist Lu. I used practically the same service. I lunched at the Buck house where most of the American men are living, because they wanted to use the occasion to discuss some plans for our rehabilitation committee. This lasted until after two, when I came back to No. 17 to investigate the shooting of a fourteen year old girl yesterday afternoon very near our house. She and her mother and brother are in Wusih and are living in one of the refugee centers. The girl and her brother had gone to a nearby field for some turnips when a J. soldier appeared. He tried to get the girl but she became frightened and ran away, whereupon the soldier fired his gun and shot her through the head, killing her almost immediately. We have been plying the J. Embassy with case after case of outrages which the soldiers are committing. They are making a pretense of investigating them, but so far as we can find out, none of the guilty persons are punished as they deserve, and as they would be in any western army. I'll tell you something that happened today. Mr. Allison, our consul was slapped in the face by a J. soldier, and Mr. Riggs of the Univ. manhandled. A girl had been taken by soldiers from one of the Univ. buildings and raped. On her return, the case was reported to the consul and he and Riggs accompanied the girl to the place where she had been taken. It was no less a place than the military police headquarters. Some Military police, Japanese, had accompanied the Consul as they do when he goes out. The girl was asked to enter the building, perhaps to identify her assailant but Allison and Riggs were not permitted to go along in. They stood about two feet inside the gate. A soldier tried to push them out, and when an officer came along foaming with rage and shouted that they were Americans, a soldier reached over from behind and slapped Allison's face. When one of the Military Police who had accompanied Allison said to the others that he was the American Consul, another soldier grabbed Riggs and shook him by the overcoat collar until he tore it. They waited, however, until the girl was delivered back in their hands. Allison does not know yet whether to report the incident as he is afraid it may have serious results, as far as the relations between the two countries are concerned. Technically he was wrong in being inside the gate of the military police headquarters, but that does not excuse the conduct of the soldiers and the officer. The latter was the same who slapped Riggs' face once before, and they think it is he also who pushed Dr. Bates down stairs when he had gone to intercede for a middle school graduate whom the J. had forced to act as an interpreter. The boy sent back a note to his wife that he was going to be executed, and he probably has been since he has not returned.

This morning they fished out the dead bodies of a big group of men who were machine-gunned soon after the J. entered the city and their bodies thrown into a pond just at the end of the street where we are living. They are mostly civilians but were all taken and executed on suspicion of being ex-soldiers. John went today to a house in which fourteen occupants were killed by the soldiers soon after their entry into the city. Eleven were women all of whom had been raped and then killed. The bodies are still there. John has adequate evidence of that. A woman came into the hospital this a.m. who had been carried off to the southern part of the city more than a month ago. Her husband was carried off at the same time and has not yet returned and probably never will. They had been married four years and had had no children. J. soldiers raped her from seven to nine times every day and finally released her when she could no longer be used. She has three forms of venereal disease in their worse state as a result of her experience, but of course the J. army never does such things and it is we foreigners that invent these lies to encourage the Chinese! So you see we are not exactly popular. But you can imagine what is in store for the Chinese if Japan has her way. After I had investigated the case of the girl who had been shot yesterday, I attended another meeting of our rehabilitation committee which lasted until five.

Jan. 28th. It was a great treat to receive the mail and packages which came by the *Aphis* this morning and to know how you were all faring. I have not yet seen the socks, letter and $30 which you say you sent I presume by Japanese. The last consignment coming through Domei arrived O.K. as you know by now. I wonder whether you sent the other things by that J. merchant. He was to have come back in 2 wks time with a fresh load of supplies but has not yet appeared. Kola ordered milk and a radio tube by him and another person entrusted him with $50 to be delivered in Shanghai. We wonder whether he has absconded, has not had a chance to return or was hindered on the way. I have found my pipe very useful and comforting these days while doing police duty. I find it very useful to have cigarettes to give J. soldiers on occasions. We do not need cash sent to us as we can get it from the International Committee and John has a considerable cash supply on hand. Yesterday I did not get a chance to write as I was busy preparing for Sunday's services at which I am to preach. Then I was invited to a Chinese dinner. One of the men at #17 celebrated his 30th birthday and as it is so near the Chinese New Year, they prepared a special meal for the occasion. In the p.m. I and Cola, one of the Chinese teachers and the Chinese architect of Nanking Univ. (he built the St. Paul's parish house) rode down to St. Paul's to look over the damage. When we got there we found that nearly all of the remaining portions of the Kung Kuan had been burned down. Some of the timbers were still smoldering on the ground, and the bricks and tiles were hot. It happened on Wednesday a.m. since one of our servants spent Tuesday and Tuesday night in our day school building on the Roberts compound, and the Kung Kuan was burning fiercely at about seven o'clock on Wednesday morning. Allison had visited the compound on Tuesday and the building was still intact. We went through all the houses, though nothing much seems to have been touched in them since my previous visit. Soldiers had started a fire in the Church sacristy as there were evidences of the red festival scrolls having been burned and the door and other parts of the wardrobe in which they had been stored were charred and scorched. Fortunately the fire did not gain headway but it indicates that soldiers still wander through the buildings at will. We are trying to get passports for some of our servants to go there to live. It is still a risk without such a passport, as they might be impressed and carried off. Their money and clothing and bedding might be stolen or they might be injured if they are asked to provide women and cannot do so. It's hard to know what to do but we will try to think of a good plan. With soldiers irresponsibly starting fires in buildings there is a chance for anything to happen. Bessie Sims sewing machine is gone, that is the machinery. I retrieved a small box full of extra fittings for it. Her piano, if she had one, is also no more. The Roberts piano was still there yesterday but their victrola is gone and the records strewn over the floor in fragments. Their rug and camphor chest (emptied of contents) are still on hand. I'd like to gather up everything and bring them here, but we can't get transportation, and if we could, I do not know where we could store the things safely. If we can get some servants down there we may be able to get everything into one house and nail it shut. There is no use to do that now, that is without someone staying on the premises. In a few minutes I've got to go to the Univ. to lead the meeting. We shall study St. Mt. XX today. I hear the *Aphis* is going back tomorrow a.m. so all mail must be at the Embassy by nine tonight. John and I are both well. So is Kola though the latter has been laid up with grippe for a few days. I was pleased over the surprise party for Gilmore. He has certainly done valiant service. The news about Yangchow isn't happy, but we'll be patient and see. Things do not matter so much. To be acceptable to Him we have to be content with much or little. . . . Had a good meeting at the Univ. today. John is ready to start for the Embassy now with the letters. We understand there will be another chance to send on Tuesday.

Jan. 28th. John took the letters to the Embassy this evening but came back with a whole carload of mail which I have been reading until now and it is nearly 11 o'clock. He also said we could have as late as 9 o'clock tomorrow to get mail all in. The mail we got this evening has been stacked up in Nanking somewhere and has just been retrieved by the J. It includes your letters from Hankow and from the family at home. I also had letters from K.P. Steve, and a letter from you written last Sunday. I do not understand why the J. are so insistent about not letting anybody come to Nanking, if they are letting them go to other places. Geo. Fitch is desperate to get down to Shanghai as all his teeth and filling are falling out. But while he can get permission to go down, he can't get permission to get back, so he is trying to be patient. I hope Steve can get back to Yangchow. A Britisher from the Int. Import and Export Lumber Co. Hsiakuan, has been back for several days but Kola reported this evening that he had received an ultimatum to clear out by tomorrow a.m. The Britisher said that would be impossible since his car was out of order, so they told him to get it fixed and go. According to the radio broadcast at 1 today the J. have issued statements about the slapping of Allison. The meeting at the Univ. was very good this afternoon and the people listened attentively. Prof. Chen told me that every evening he has a group of young men and girls studying the Bible for two hours, and he hopes that John and I may eventually baptize them. I had an amusing experience this afternoon. Just as I was about to turn in at the Univ. gate a youngster spied me and said in approved Yangchow fashion "Foreign devil, Oh, I mean Mr. Foreigner!" We certainly are glad to get supplies from time to time. We are enjoying the candy ever so much, and the two tins of tobacco will keep me well supplied for the old pipes have been a great comfort in these tumultuous days.

Jan. 30th. Yesterday I also didn't get a chance to write. The mail which came on Friday was such a treat that I went through it all over again yesterday. In the a.m. I took one of the servants to the Hospital, the old gateman whom Mr. Schultze had left on the place to look after things. As I had to wait for the doctor to examine him to find out what was wrong, I went to the Hospital office where Miss Bower was holding an indignation meeting. Thinking she would give the nurses an extra treat on account of China New Year, she sent the cook out to buy some pork, which he did, 9 lbs of it for which he paid $4.50. On his way back he was accosted by J. soldiers who demanded the meat. He protested that he had bought it for the hospital and was responsible for it, so they took the meat and gave him about sixty cents for it. Such things are happening all the time, so you can understand why people are afraid to go outside the refugee zone, albeit this happened in the safety zone itself, which the J. are trying to force the civilians to leave. In fact they have issued an ultimatum through the "self-Gov't society" that they must leave the refugee centers by Feb. 4th or they will be driven out by force. While I am on the subject I'll tell of another incident that happened. The wife, or widow? of that Univ. Middle School student who was taken by the J. to interpret for them, and was put through the third degree by one of the Consular police and, we believe executed for he was not yet returned, the woman was going to buy some things at a district outside the refugee zone which has been designated by the Japanese as safe for civilians to live in. She and about 19 other young women were taken into a truck by passing J. soldiers and brought to a building used by officers. A Chinese man who had been impressed to work for the officers whispered to her that her only chance to escape was to force herself to vomit several times, which she did. She was thus released from a fate which would have been worse than death. You can easily understand why the people do not feel encouraged to go back. Yesterday a girl was forced into a straw hut opposite #17 by three passing soldiers who defamed her for over an hour. Imagine what is in store for the J. women when their men come back having contracted every sort of disease. Yesterday a.m. I rode down to St. Paul's with Mr. McCallum. Everything seemed much as it had been when I was down there the previous time. There are rumors that this will be in the special area reserved for soldiers, so we may not be able to go back. On our way back we passed the Kiangsu bank in which Kola and Mr. Sangreen lived and had their office. A truck was being loaded with furniture from the building. I told Kola and he went down in the p.m. to look-see. He found that many of the offices and rooms had been stripped bare of furniture and that two over-stuffed chairs of theirs had been taken too. Second-hand shops in Hongkew and Chapei must be doing a thriving and profitable business! We had a heavy snow-fall all day yesterday. I spent a comfortable night at #17 coming back at seven for breakfast and to change my clothes. I preached at No. 25 and took Morning Prayer while the Rev. Mr. Chiang celebrated the Communion. We had a good attendance. After lunch I went back again to No. 25 to be present at the Sunday School which we have started for the smaller children. About 16 came. Miss Shao told them the story of the infant Moses, Paul Tong conducted the worship and taught them several children's songs. The other day I retrieved in St. Paul's parish hall the hymns written on cloth that had been used for the children previously. Also the wooden standard for hanging the hymns. And from the dayschool building we rescued some more hymns and some picture charts. So we feel quite well equipped. John and I were invited to a New Years' supper along with the refugees from #25 and #17 who get their food from our common kitchen. (There are a good many who cook their own.) The food was placed in circles on the floor of #25 and we sat around on kneeling cushions to eat it. In order to save rice and money, the people have been taking only two meals a day and they are chiefly vegetarians with thick rice congee. The managing committee asked for permission to serve dry cooked rice and an extra bowl of food. John readily agreed. In addition I contributed $5 as from you and me and John contributed $5 as from himself and Faith, so they were all able to have two extra dishes of meat. It was a grand party, about fifty people and everybody ate to his heart's content for once. Fortunately we have not had any very serious illness so far among the people. The fifteen refugee boys from Tsingpoo look well and have rosy cheeks, reminding me of Daniel and his three friends preferring the beans and pulse to the wine and rich viands from the King's palace. But we must not let the young people become undernourished. That will be one of the great dangers unless a larger and more varied food supply can be procured for the people. Everything that they are accustomed to is scarce and the price very high. One egg when procurable costs eight cents and meat, varying much in quality, around fifty cents a pound, Fish around 70 cents, chickens and ducks around $1.50 depending on the size; besides these things are all scarce. Gradually however, some of the people outside the city are managing to bring more in, but if they carry in or buy much, it is very apt to be taken by J. soldiers. Each day brings its incidents, but God has been wonderful in caring for his people, and we are deeply grateful for His many mercies. . . . Tell the family they can use any of the news bits provided they are careful about using my name in connection with anything that the J. might find unpalatable reading. Not that I am afraid to back up anything I have written, but I should hate to have my usefulness here endangered by such publication. I have typed some of the extracts from Father's letters about the reaction of the people and press toward the Nanking situation. Bates suggested this as he said some of the foreigners needed some encouragement under the strain of life here. Geo. Fitch left on Saturday for Shanghai by the H.M.S. *Bee*. He has been having tooth trouble, and as somebody else remarked, needs a change of scenery for a while. He hopes to come back on the *Oahu* next week. He did not get a military pass, as the J. civil authorities felt he had more chance of getting back by going to and from the boat with the Am. Consul when he takes the mail, etc. down to Hsiakuan. John hopes to go down to Hsiakuan tomorrow in this way. The news does not look too good for Japan, does it? They are finding Chinese gorilla [*sic*] warfare and the activities of the Yellow Spears and Big Sword Society not only decimating for their troops, many of whom have been killed and wounded in such encounters, but also hard on the morale of their troops who, I have heard on good authority, are scared to death of these outlaws whom they regard with superstition, since they claim to make themselves invulnerable by a magic formula, and who in reality work themselves into a frenzy in which they fear neither God, man nor the devil. Also this continual harrassing makes it necessary to deploy many troop units and thus delay and make impossible many times a concerted action against a definite objective. It also allows the Chinese troops to reform their lines and consolidate their position. It is very excellent strategy and may prove the undoing of J. arrogance. I wonder what experience Lee will have at Wusih and Steve at Yangchow if he is permitted to go there. I take it that Lee has recovered from his recent operation and I hope he is strong enough to rough it for a month.

John and I contributed a similar amount to the refugees from the Model Village. They have no common kitchen, however, so I do not know how they used the money for all.

Feb. 1st. Just heard that the mail must be in the Embassy by four o'clock this afternoon. My cold, fortunately was much better and it was not necessary for me to stay in bed yesterday. About eleven a J. Consular policeman and a Military Police came to ask me to look over some pianos they have collected to see whether the two from St. Paul's were among them. They weren't which apparently did not please some of the military police who said among themselves that I was trying to hold out for new pianos. Kola went with me and understood their conversation. They wanted me to select two pianos and call it quits, but I refused to accept what obviously did not belong to me. When they started on their piano search after I had reported our loss, they were most insistent that I should know the exact number of the piano, their make, etc. They are certainly a double-tongued gang of thieves. John was able to get down to Hsiakuan yesterday with Mr. Bishopric (an American from the China Imp. and Exp. Lumber Co. who got permission to return to Nanking) to look over the mission premises there. He found them in pretty good condition. There has been some looting, but not as much as he feared. Some of the rooms and closets have not yet been broken open, as has happened everywhere else. Our two arm chairs were still there. Also the corpses of two Chinese soldiers in the trunk room of John's house, and another corpse on the compound. Since it was Chinese New Year, some of the J. soldiers apparently decided to celebrate, too. They came to #17 and #25 in the morning while John was there and were "too happy" to be trusted very far. It was much milder yesterday, so I went over, but no soldiers came in, fortunately. Last night I slept at #10 and am feeling fine today. This morning there was a meeting of the managers of the refugee centers which I attended. At present there are about 58,000 people being cared for in these centers by the International Committee. These centers are all located in the Refugee Zone. It is interesting to see how they are distributed. 36,271 or 62% in American property; 601, or 1% in German property; 17,900 or 31% in Chinese government property; 3,139 or 6% in private property, Chinese. The Japanese are insisting that the people must move out of these centers by Feb. 4th or they will be driven out by force. Notices to this effect have been posted in all the centers and some people have begun to move back into the areas designated as safe by the J. authorities. But at the meeting this a.m. practically every camp manager has reported incidents which have caused people to come back into the refugee centers. Women suffered from raping and men from robbery by the soldiers. Ginling college alone has more than forty authenticated cases which have happened since Jan. 28th when the people started moving back. Other certers [sic] also had many cases to report. All these will be presented to the J. as an indication that they are not carrying out their promises to protect the people if they go back to their homes. Just 5 min. ago John and I were called to a neighboring house where two drunk J. soldiers had locked a girl into a room and raped her. We broke down the door and drove them out, turning one of them over to some J. soldiers on guard in a nearby street crossing. We hear that the high military official dispatched from Tokyo to investigate conditions in Nanking arrived today. He will be here about two days but representatives of the three Embassies are hoping to confront him with all the evidence that has been accumulating of their outrages and atrocities. We were interested to hear over the radio that J. has already expressed regrets over the slapping of Consul Allison, which means that they were confronted as in the case of the *Panay* incident with irrefutable evidence. Perhaps they will believe some day that their army isn't quite so nice in the opinion of the world as it is in their own . . . Now John wants me to type some notes for him about the atrocity cases which came to the Univ. Hosp. and of which he took movies. I will send a copy along with this letter.

Feb. 3rd. This is just a short note before I go over to #17, which I hope can go down by Mr. Bishopric tomorrow. I have quite a letter ready to go but think it safer to find some other way, as Mr. B. is driving down in his car and there is no telling what might happen on the way. I just wanted to send something to let you know that we are safe and well. Many of the people are returning to their homes in pursuance of orders that have been issued from above but we are not breaking up our group yet since it is still uncertain whether we shall be able to live either at Hsiakuan or in the southern part of the city, the one being in the outside of the city and the other in the section set aside for the military. I was down at St. Paul's this afternoon to take four men servants for whom I received a passport from the American Embassy to the effect that they are servants sent to watch our premises. We had to make two trips down, since there wasn't enough room in the car for the men and their bedding too. When we reached the Church compound, I found a lot of military trucks lining the sides of the street for a whole block or so, and in our compound a group of from twelve to fifteen soldiers eating their food. They had built two fires on the lawn outside the parish hall and had dragged out one of the heavy teak clergy stalls to hold the iron bar upon which they had suspended their rice buckets. The chair has a piece hacked out of the back of one end and has also been whittled on one side in front. Some of the other soldiers were sitting around the fire which they had built on the floor inside the room or passageway which leads into the Kungkuan meeting room. There is only a small section of the Kungkuan still standing and it was in this that they had built the fire. Another soldier on my second trip was cooking his food over a fire in the room used by the gateman, the fire having been made on the floor also. I drove the soldiers all out and made them carry water to extinguish the fire which they did. But I have enough evidence to convince me how the rest of the building was burned last week. I reported the matter to Mr. Allison and he expected to bring it up at the J. Embassy this p.m. where he was going for dinner. I am also giving him a written report. While I was remonstrating with the soldiers around the fire, another came from behind the parish house with an armful of good chairs which I suppose were either to be carried off or to supply fuel for the fires. We have four servants there now, two on the Church compound and two on the residence compound. I found a J. soldier who had had a few drinks amusing himself on the Roberts piano. I escorted him to the door, too. I have told the servants to do what they can to block up the entrances into the compound, to gather up all loose things on the floors of the houses, and to store all the furniture into one or two rooms so that it will be easier to look after. It has been a gray raw day. And this afternoon it began to snow very hard and the snow was very wet. I spent the morning taking women to the hospital for treatment and also called at Ginling and the Am. Embassy. I have heard that the new garrison commander is quite a different type from those who have preceded him. He was in charge of the district around Chinkiang and when the news of his transfer was announced the Chinese petitioned that he might be retained. Also Mr. Hidaka, who has come to replace the recently returned Ambassador Kawagoe, is also well-thought of by the Chinese. So let us hope that this will make a change for the better in the general situation. The socks, money and letters you sent last month have not yet put in an appearance, so I am afraid we must kiss them goodbye. The radio broadcast spoke of fighting at Yangchow on the Grand Canal. I wonder what that means. I asked Allison what the chances were of my getting permission to visit Chinkiang and Yangchow. He didn't give me much encouragement. My cold is much better so it is just a case of getting some exercise and working it off. I suppose you have had a chance to see Geo. Fitch and perhaps Kroeger. We heard that a business man recently returned to Shanghai from Nanking had told a small group of conditions here. Were you in that group? We understand that the next mail will not come until about the 14th. That seems a long time off, but is better than not being able to hear at all.

Feb. 4th. This is just a chance for a p.s. as Mr. Bishopric did not leave today, which has been another wet snowy day. The morning started by taking a woman to the hospital, then coming back for another at #25 and stopping at the Am. Embassy en route to get certificates for the servants we are sending to Hsiakuan and the C.T.S. to guard the places against looting. While the people were being treated at the Hosp. I drove down to St. Paul's to find that the servants I had left there yesterday had had a good night and were unmolested. For noon today John and I were invited to a Chinese feast by one of the members of St. Paul's living at #17 which was not really a feast but a nice meal consisting mostly of a certain kind of patty popular at this time of the year. Some were filled with chopped meat, some with vegetables, some with sugar and chopped nuts. Some were fried, others were cooked. This was the day by which the people from the refugee centers were to have moved back to the other parts of the city. It was said that force would be used upon those who did not return voluntarily, but I am glad to say that there were no instances of it. We went around to the various centers to observe in case any was used, but everything was quiet.

Feb. 12th. John has gone to a meeting of the International Committee, so while I wait for him to come home for supper, I have a little chance to write. . . . Yesterday John and I were both busy all day, trying to get mail ready for Mr. Bos to take. We had been told that it should be at the Embassy by four, but John asked me to take a letter to Mr. Bos personally authorizing him to get a copy of John's films in Shanghai. John himself had to speak at a Bible class at the Univ. Mr. Bos was staying with Dr. Rosen of the German Embassy. When I got there they were entertaining Count [?] the French Military attache who recently came to Nanking for a look-see. Mr. Bos said he would be glad to deliver the letters in person, as he lives on Yu Yuen Road, not far from your compound. I was awfully glad as it would give you a chance to meet him. We did not stamp any of the letters, as I thought you might want to add to some, and in any case read them. The letters for persons in Shanghai you can probably deliver personally. John came back from the meeting which Geo. Fitch attended. The *Oahu* got in about three o'clock, I think. All it brought me was a letter from Betty; since you did not read it, I wonder if there was some other mail which you did not receive. In your last letter you said you were sending by the *Oahu*. John was disappointed not to have any letter from Faith either in this batch or the one which came by H.M.S. *Bee*. We are having a chance to send mail tomorrow by Father Kearney who is going back to Shanghai on a French boat. He came only yesterday, I believe. We are mighty glad for every chance to send or receive mail. I have at last located the lists I made of our furniture, etc. which we left in Yangchow, and I am sending the black note-book herewith. The contents of the trunks are not listed, so I guess you will have to do that from memory. I have not had a chance to check up on Miss Sims' or the Roberts' things but hope to do that soon. Last night I spent at #17. This a.m. John and I have had a meeting with some of our Chinese staff to discuss the question of moving back. They did not seem awfully keen to do so, but I fear we will never succeed in getting other people to return to their homes unless we do so ourselves. The thought has been constantly in my mind lately that I should be willing to move back to St. Paul's with any who may be willing to go with me. Hsiakuan being outside the gate presents complications. The question in my mind is whether if I move back I can be of as much service as by staying here. I suppose there is no answer except to try it out. I asked Mr. Mills today about it and he felt I could be of great use by keeping an eye on things at that end of the city. Our rehabilitation committee will set up its first relief office in the Christian Mission building on Chung Hua Road which is not so far from our place. So I can probably be helpful there. Another problem will be that of transportation. I have my bicycle which will be o.k. in good weather, but for many reasons I think the experiment is worth trying. I hate to have the door of every church closed in the districts to which the people are returning. My going will certainly create confidence among the people who have gone back. What I think I shall do is to stay down there at night but still take my meals, or most of them with John at No. 10. That will give me a chance to size up the situation and see if it is worth while. I hope it will be possible for you and Bessie Sims to come back soon. Won't that be a grand day!

This afternoon we had a meeting of our Rehabilitation Committee at which we discussed a possible budget. We hope to have about $100,000 for this work.

It will be used for helping people to repair their homes, to go back to their native places, and for grants-in-aid for widows, orphans and other destitute persons. We'll need all we can get. It was wonderful to hear that Geo. Fitch had been able to get a fine sum in Shanghai for relief here. Have not had a chance to see him but hope to tomorrow. Did you see him in Shanghai? John is awfully pleased that his pictures turned out so well. A number of Embassy people want copies. Dr. Rosen is ordering a set to send to Hitler to see. Am sending down a roll of films which contains, I believe, pictures which Steve took of our house in Yanghcow. If I can remember to bring my camera over from #17 I may send another roll which contains pictures of men who were killed in the Temple precincts across from No. 17. Would you please send me some rolls of films because I can probably get some interesting snapshots. I am also sending down a few other personal things which I came across in suit cases. It is awful to have things tucked around in suitcases and drawers and then not remember where. I hope things will get straightened out some day. . . . Kola and Sindberg came in from Chi Hsiashan this morning and stayed for lunch and then went off again. Sindberg knows Sangreen and Mr. Suhr. It seems a long time since we made that trip, doesn't it? (Nov. 2nd from Shanghai to Yangchow) This afternoon Chinese planes paid us a visit. The J. fired off a lot of anti-aircraft and made a lot of noise but widely missed their mark and did no damage. Spring will soon be here and I am wondering if it will not be wise to have some vegetable seeds to start a garden at St. Paul's. It may be useless to do so, and also it may be a very wise move. Will you get some seeds and send them. I don't think that we can get them from the Univ. here. I have just typed out the news from tonight's broadcast. Those to whom I give it are crazy to receive it and almost mob me when I appear. Tomorrow I am to preach for Mr. Chen's Christians next door so I must be getting to bed.

Feb. 13th. Just a postscript which will have to be sent out in less than an hour. We had a good service this morning with fine attendance despite the rain, and with reverent attention all through. I preached to them on the Epistle, running the race that is set before them, etc. I talked over with John again the question of moving back to St. Paul's, and he thinks it a very good idea. We shall still take most of our meals together. He will stay on at Mr. Schultze's house until the Hsiakuan situation becomes clearer. So I expect to move this week, which reminds me that you might send me several tins of cigarettes which I can hand around to the soldiers who might chance to drop in. They do not have to be the most expensive brand. John and I are both well and busy. I'd like to drop in for a Yangchow Old Home Week. Give my best to all the folks.

***

Letter to Family[4]

#10 Sze T'ao Hsiang
Kulou, Nanking
December 7, 1937

Dear family:

I fell down last week about writing to you, so I will try to make amends this week. Please excuse me. We had a rather busy week which ended with our moving from Hsiakwan to the above address which is the residence of the German gentleman who invited Crisso to go to Hankow aboard the ship which the German Embassy had chartered for its nationals. A young Russian whom we call Kola since his real name is very difficult to pronounce is taking care of the house for Mr. Schultze-Pantin. You see our Hsiakwan compound is just outside the main gate of Nanking city from the north. We are really only a stone's throw from the gate and as the situation has grown tighter with the approach of the J. upon Nanking we decided it would be better for us and our Chinese workers and Christians to move inside the city lest the city gate be suddenly closed without warning and we be left outside with no place to go to. Mr. Hansen, the manager of the Texas Oil Co. very kindly invited us to use his company residences for ourselves and our people. These are within the area which the International Committee has been trying to reserve for a safety zone in order to save the civilians who cannot leave Nanking. We had quite a large group of workers and Christians to provide for so we decided it would be best to move them in and get them settled. John Magee and I decided to come to this house since the other place was quite crowded and we had to be a little freer to carry on our work. So here we are. We have been busy moving in as many of our things as possible for if the Chinese really defend the city, our residences on the Hsiakwan compound are in for a lot of shelling, etc. It has been a hectic time trying to make all arrangements, and I think that when I can no longer qualify as a missionary I'll hire myself out as a mover and packer! From the news we are receiving it looks as the J. would be here very soon. Everybody is wondering how much of a fight the C. will put up. They are certainly making preparations to put up some resistance but it is uncertain how long they can hold out. Their casualties were very great around Shanghai and included some of the very best troops. Those who will defend Nanking will be either fresh troops of uncertain fighting calibre or else men who have already had a pretty heavy dose of fighting. We are realising more and more that only God can help, and we feel sure that He will accomplish His purpose. He has called us here, has given us work to do from day to day, and we are trusting Him implicitly to see it thru to the end. It is a great comfort to our Chinese believers, many of whom cannot go to other places and some of whom have come here from places that have been bombed and annihilated, to have us here. There is no complaining. In the house where many of them are living they have set up an altar and they have prayers there in the morning and evening. John Magee celebrated the Communion there while I did the same at St. Paul's. We did not have many at the latter place but even so it was thrilling to have as many as we did. On my way to the church we got caught in an air raid and had to leave the motor car to take shelter. The car was left here by the Wusih group when they went to Shanghai. We have found it invaluable, as Nanking is a city of tremendous distances, and for nearly three weeks practically all bus and rickshaw traffic has stopped and cars are not to be hired. The next week ought to decide the fate of the city. We hope it will be over quickly so that life can settle down normally. I rode my bicycle to St. Paul's this afternoon. The city was like a deserted place with only an occasional person to be seen here and there.

Our work for the wounded soldiers has borne some fruit. Conditions at the railway station where the men arrived were simply terrible. People who were being paid to do the work simply did not turn up and the wounded were left sometimes for days without any one to dress their wounds and feed them. We went down ourselves to help and made such a to-do about things that those high in authority became interested and did something. Now there are doctors and dressers on hand twenty-four hours a day and the men are moved rapidly to hospitals. Not a great many are coming in that way now since the fighting line has come so close that it is practically impossible to use the railway. John met an American who has been connected with the Chinese air force for four years. He had just returned from Shanghai from which place it had taken him two weeks to get here. He came by small boat, and reported Yangchow to be full of Chinese soldiers who retreated across the Yangtse from Chinkiang. That may mean that our buildings there have been occupied by them. Mr. Ko, our Chinese priest, wrote me that the Yangchow magistrate had tried twice to get our Mahan buildings for the use of the Kiangsu Provincial Government. We refused, of course, since our consent would involve our government. We have been allowing our buildings to be used for refugees and for the wounded, but not for military or official purposes. If they take them by force we have no recourse. The last word I had from Mr. Ko was that the buildings had not been taken. Mail is no longer being delivered in Nanking, so we have been cut off from communications for quite a time. Mail is still being sent out. I write to Crisso every day and send it air-mail to Hankow. I have had only one letter from her telling of her safe arrival there at noon on Thanksgiving Day. I have received no other letters from her. Last week she succeeded in calling me up by long distance telephone. She said she was well and that she had been getting my letters. I am glad of that. She is also going to language school in the mornings. From her experience in Nanking she realized how necessary it is for her to have a speaking knowledge of Chinese. I am glad she is able to study with others as it is easier and more regular than having to do it alone. She is staying with Miss Dexter. The Embassy called me up the other day to report that they had had an inquiry from the State Department as to Clarissa's plans at Hankow, so I take it that you have received my cable, sent thru the embassy, telling of her departure for Hankow. I think she will be all right there, and if she has to leave she will do so in the company of some of the other Mission folk there whenever they deem it wise to leave. She can either go to Hongkong and then to Shanghai or else go further west into Szechuen Province whither the Central government has moved. In any case I do not think there is any cause to worry about her safety.

There are a number of foreigners remaining in Nanking, most of them having responsibility for various activities or people. The committee is working very hard to have a "neutral" zone respected by both sides in case fighting takes place. The Nanking University Hospital is carrying on valiantly with a small staff of two foreign doctors, one Chinese doctor, and two foreign and several Chinese nurses. They are about worn to a frazzle thru pressure of work and lack of personnel, since the Chinese superintendent and about 49 other doctors and nurses connected with the hospital deserted and went to Hankow for safety. That has been one of the heart-breaking things we have had to endure—so many of the professional classes whose services are direly needed here have run away. On the other hand we have also seen some very encouraging exhibitions of loyalty to duty in the midst of great danger. We are realising the truth of Christ's parable of the hirelings and the good shepherd, and of the meaning of trying to save one's life and losing it.

We hope you are all fine. Our dearest love and best wishes for Christmas and the new year.

***

Letter to Friend[5]

Nanking, January 14, 1938.

Dear

Another week has slipped by since I wrote my last letter to some of you. This is just to assure you that I am still well and that I appreciate all your letters and inquiries. Thru the kindness of the American Embassy I cabled you a few days ago. I had just sent the message I had been able to get from her since she left Hankow and it was a big relief to know that she was well and safe among our

Mission people in Shanghai. She has been very brave thru all the troubles we have been forced to undergo and witness. She wrote me that various letters had arrived from you but that she was holding them in Shanghai for the present until she is sure they will get thru to me in Nanking without difficulty. She did send Father's letter of Oct. 12 and Betty's and Sophie's letters which had arrived for my birthday. Thank you all very much. I think the poems Father wrote are very fine. She also sent me the cablegrams you sent for Christmas. So you see I had quite a grand Christmas present when all these arrived in one batch of mail.

We are still confined to the city limits of Nanking. The river is open to shipping to a very limited extent; we hear the railway is running after a fashion for the military; the J. are using the motor road and also aeroplanes; but one cannot move anywhere without military permission and this is not readily forthcoming. Last week representatives of the American, British, and German Embassies were permitted to come to Nanking. We were certainly glad to see them for now there is somebody official here to deal with. The J. authorities have lost and are losing a great deal of face because of the looting and burning by their soldiers. Despite official notices from the J. and the foreign embassies posted on the doors of foreign residences and property in the city the soldiers still go in to loot etc. Very often they are actually found on the premises when embassy officials are making their inspection of the places, so they cannot claim, as they have tried to do, that the looting and burning has been done by Chinese soldiers and civilians! On the whole, however, the general situation has improved since many of the troops have been removed to other places. But we still do not feel that it is safe for the people to return to their homes, supposing the latter are still left, or to leave our people whom we have been looking after in several residences belonging to the Texas Oil Co. and others. One of us is still on guard during the day, and one of us sleeps in one of the residences at night. Large sections of the city have been burned, fires still being a daily occurrence.

I have had no news as to the fate of Yangchow, except that there was fighting there and the city was supposed to be in Japanese hands. Whether they have treated the civilians there as they have treated them here I do not know. I fear they have had a hard time of it too. Mr. Green, Mr. Fairfield, and Miss Bremer were ordered to proceed to Shanghai by the Bishop and they got thru safely toward the end of November. So far as we know only two foreigners were left there, Mr. Stamps and Miss Demarest of the Southern Baptist Mission. They refused to leave.

We have had a fairly moderate winter so far. It was very cold for several days around the 8th, that being, according to the Chinese calendar, the time for the "Little Cold" spell. The "Big Cold" is due around the 20th. It is amazing how accurate these calculations often turn out to be. After the "Big Cold" we may expect a gradual diminution of the cold weather and the approach of Spring. We are glad that the weather, on the whole, has been comparatively dry also; for otherwise the plight of the thousands and thousands of refugees here would be even greater. We shall be facing a very big problem this winter and spring until normal conditions can be restored to some extent, as so many persons have nothing but what they could carry away with them; their houses, places of business, their possessions are all gone, and so far there has been very little opportunity for them to do any work or to go back to their old locations and try to get started in business again. There is also a large group of persons who depended on income from rents, etc. to keep them alive. They have had no rents for months and in ever so many cases the houses they had let to others have been destroyed by fire. I have been asked to serve on a Rehabilitation Committee whose object will be to investigate cases of need and so far as is possible supply the people with something to enable them to get started earning a livelihood again. Thousands of men were taken by the soldiers and executed—often in a most barbaric manner—on the suspicion of being ex-soldiers. But since the judge and the jury were the same persons, and they often not more than a corporal or a sergeant, you can imagine that countless innocent people were done to death. There is less of this now than there was when the city fell, but it was terrible while it lasted. Any private seems to have complete authority to determine the life or death of any persons he wants to deal with.

Yesterday I held a preliminary burial service for our Evangelist, Mr. Lu, of Tangshan—one of the country stations of St. Paul's Church. He became very morbid and depressed over what was happening in Nanking and China, and on December 31 he committed suicide by drowning in a nearby pond. We had tried to dissuade him but to no avail. We were able to recover the body a few days ago and later to secure a coffin. It was very sad, and adds one more to the many tragedies we have been called on to witness.

I suppose Clarissa will add to this letter as I intend to send it to her to be mailed from Shanghai. The post office is not functioning here so that is the only way I can get mail to you. She is in good hands in Shanghai, so please do not worry about her or about me. We wish very much that we could be together. I could possibly get down to Shanghai from here, but would not be allowed to return. At present I feel that I am too much needed here to leave. But I am sure that in God's own time we shall get together again. A great deal of relief work is going on in Shanghai also with which she will undoubtedly help. In certain ways our people in Shanghai are as confined as we are here since they are not allowed to venture outside Shanghai into the interior.

I hope this will find you all well. You are all in my thoughts almost constantly. Please do not worry unduly. My best love and lots of it to you all.

***

Letter to Family[6]

Nanking, January 21, 1938

Dear

This is just a little note to let you know that I am still well. There is a chance for mail to go down to Shanghai in the next day or two so I am sending this along with the request that Crisso forward it to you. It was good to have your cablegram yesterday afternoon thru the State Dept. From it I saw that you had received my cablegram of the 10th and I gathered that you are all well. I am glad of that. I hope that Grandma and Aunt Gertrude are as well as can be expected and that they are not suffering too much.

There is not much news here lately. Things go on pretty much as usual; i.e. as they have been going since the occupation of the city. Efforts are being made by the authorities to get the people to go back to their homes(!) but without much success as so many people have no homes to go back to and there is still considerable risk in doing so. As one group of soldiers is transferred elsewhere a new group is sent to replace them; and so the old difficulties crop up anew. But conditions on the whole are much better than they have been, in general at least. There is a great deal of suffering among the people many of whom have used up the little reserves of food and money they brought into the Refugee Zone with them. With transportation and business at a virtual standstill it is impossible for them to recoup themselves. We have also had rain, and snow all day yesterday, with the consequent cold raw weather which we expect at this time of the year. On the whole, however, the weather this winter has been quite moderate, for which we are thankful.

It was good to hear of the amendment which Rep. Hamilton Fish is making in Congress to the Naval Appropriation Bill for the calling of an international conference on naval limitation. It is rather late in the day to be proposing such a step but it is best to be optimistic of the possibilities of such a proposal. It can do no harm and may even yet be the guide-rope to keep this old world from sliding over the abyss of chaos.

I need not write about the military situation as you are probably much better posted by radio and newspaper than we are. Needless to say I have received none of the letters which you, Father, have been writing so faithfully each week and adressing to Nanking. They are probably held up in Shanghai and it is very possible that Crisso has received them. We hear there is possibility of mail coming to us by a British ship next Tuesday. It will be wonderful to know what is transpiring elsewhere and how you all are.

I have had no further word from Crisso since the letters that came on Jan. 10th but I assume that she is o.k. else I should have had a telegraphic message thru the Embassy. It will be a grand and glorious day when we can all get together again and talk to our hearts' content. Let us hope that that day is not too far distant.

With much love to you all,

***

Letter to Family[7]

Nanking, February 10, 1938

Dear

The letters which I wrote last week did not get off as I had hoped, so I will add further news this week and send both off tomorrow afternoon. Yesterday was a grand day for we got a shipment of mail from Shanghai in which were letters from Clarissa and also some from you all. Mother's airmail letter to Crisso of Jan. 11; Father's letters #52, #55, #61, together with copies of Father's letters #51, #60, and #61. The latter having been written in the early part of January got through fairly quickly, you see. We were happy to have all the news about your various activities and to know that you had a blessed Christmas and celebrated in the usual way. We were also happy to have Betty's letter of December 29th. Crisso wrote that she had received more letters and would send them to me by the next boat which ought to arrive fairly soon. So if I have not acknowledged the receipt of other letters you will know that they have not yet reached me.

You ask, Father, what psalms I read during the air raid. I cannot remember them all exactly, but the 46, the 27, and the 71 were among those I used, so you guessed some correctly. I am sending you a copy of two addresses made by Professor Bates of the Nanking University which I think you will find interesting. He has a very keen mind and has done no end of good for the civilians in the city during their troubles. He is fearless, as you could gather from the spirit he shows in the two addresses.

It was interesting to hear that you had seen the newsreel containing my picture. I should really not have been in the picture as I am not a member of the Executive Committee of the International Committee for the Refugee Zone, but only on one of its subcommittees. But Mr. Menken insisted that all the foreigners who were present that morning should be in the picture. John Magee did not happen to be there so he was not in the picture. We are also interested to receive reports about now public feeling in America is changing. I hope the U.S.A. will not become involved in a war. Nothing has happened here as yet that should made such a step necessary; but our feeling has been all along that if England

and America had adopted other measures—economic or political pressure, for instance, Japan would never have dared to go as far as she has. The time for such action, however, should have been in 1931 when Japan was permitted to begin her career of madness that is causing such havoc now. The saying that "Whom the gods would destroy they first make mad" certainly seems to be fulfilling itself in this instance. Had the Foreign Powers taken a firm stand, and the League of Nations Investigating Commission in Manchuria declared unequivocally that Japan was in the wrong, the history of the past seven years out here might have been very different. But neither nations nor individuals can hang on to their selfishness and expect the principles of the Kingdom of God to be effective in their relations with others.

Bishop Roberts sent me a nice letter in this mail too. He has asked me to serve on his Council of Advice for 1938, though I do not think I shall be able to attend many meetings unless we can get permission to move back and forth between Nanking and Shanghai freely. That does not seem likely with the present attitude of the military authorities. They have lost a great deal of face over the publicity their misdeeds here have received at our hands, and they are not exactly pleased. The Japanese, even less than the Chinese, are [un]able to stand criticism. The other day, for instance, the new commanding general here invited the various foreign diplomatic representatives to a tea at the Japanese Embassy. He read them a long speech in Japanese which was then read in translation by one of the Embassy secretaries. In it he spoke of the fine reputation Japanese soldiers have throughout the world for discipline, etc. and that there had been no untoward incidents or outrages in North China. The only reason such things had happened in Nanking (he had to admit that they did happen!) was that the people here had resisted at the instigation of the nationals of a certain foreign power (meaning us). His speech was meant to be a rebuke and unwittingly gave his whole case away. Afterwards the diplomatic representatives asked for a copy of his speech and were refused on the ground that it had been extempore (when both the original and the translation were read!) Last Monday there was a memorial service for the Japanese dead here. It is said to be one of the most solemn services in the J. army so that any speech made on the occasion is considered of great significance. General Matsui, head of the Japanese forces in this area, made the speech in which he stressed the absolute necessity of Japanese troops maintaining the strictest discipline and order in the areas under their control. We thus had another confirmation from the very highest quarters that such discipline and order has not been observed by the troops hitherto.

Such brazen lying on the part of Japanese of high standing, especially when the truth comes back at them in an irrefutable and embarrassing manner, as in the case of the shooting of the British Ambassador, the killing of Catholic missionaries in North China, the *Panay* Incident, the Chapei and Nanking outrages and atrocities, etc., makes one entertain doubts as to the intelligence of the Japanese, and wonder at their utter lack of understanding of foreign psychology, due no doubt to their extreme insularity and their arrogant pride.

In pursuance of orders from the military authorities many of the refugees have moved out of the zone to other city districts designated as safe by the military. These who have gone back have had experiences of various sorts, and they have not been able to develop much confidence in the promises of protection that have been made. Our Christian groups have not yet dispersed, but it is possible that we may do so soon. We now have servants living on the various compounds of the Mission to keep what is left from being burned by soldiers or looted by civilians who are trying to re-establish themselves. Our servants have not been molested so far, I am glad to say. I think J. realizes that she has gone as far as she dare go in antagonising other nations as she is finding herself increasingly playing a lone role. But she has done enough mischief already and it is time that a halt were called.

I hope this will find all of you well. John Magee and I are both fine, and are breathing deeper now that the days are growing longer and the sun is shining brighter and warmer. Bp. Roberts is asking John and me to stay on here as long as we possibly can, since the small foreign group in Nanking is the only means by which many missions can hang on to the Christian enterprise outside Shanghai at present. Our furlough plans are in abeyance therefore for the time being until we see how the situation develops further. Some of our people are going home to help raise the Emergency Fund for relief work in China among our people.

With love and best wishes to you all,
Affectionately,
Ernest

***

Nanking, February 10, 1938

Dear Bishop:
It was good to have your letter yesterday with all the news about our various Diocesan workers and their families. I have given your note to Paul Tong who was very much relieved to have some definite word about his sister and his fiancée. I have also given your note to the blind man Tsai. We have taken care of him so far from general funds, so he is not lacking for the wherewithal to live. It has not been easy for him to be deprived of definite employment and I hope it will soon be possible for him to become re-established in something to help him while away the time.

I intend to check over your inventory lists as soon as I can get a chance to do so. Two servants are living on the residence compound and two on the Church compound. I try to visit them nearly every day to see how they are getting along. So far they have had no trouble. Their first job was to find some temporary way of stopping up the various entrances to the compounds. At the Church compound, all three wooden gates were blown out by the explosion of shells, and the main gateway and wall were damaged as well from the same cause. J. soldiers broke an opening through the wall on the south side of the Church so that they could get to our well more easily from the Chinese hotel in which they had made their residence. Later on most of the rest of the wall on that side fell down too, so that will have to be rebuilt. The difficulty is not only to get workmen to do this but materials as well. A section of the wall between your compound and the hotel immediately in front of your house fell down shortly before the troops entered the city. It was impossible at that time to make repairs. We have now stopped it up temporarily with bamboo fencing, etc. which will be all right for the present since the hotel is not occupied. A good deal of your furniture, and all your books, I think, are still left. I should be glad to send them down to you if there were any way to do so. It is possible that our St. Paul's group may move back to the compounds there soon. The military want the people to go back to their homes. We think it is a wise step too for with the unsanitary conditions in the city—there are still many only-partially buried corpses around, and no way to have night-soil taken out of the city—and the approach of warmer weather, we shall probably be faced with epidemics of one sort or another. It would be fatal to have the people crowded together as they have been in the various refugee centers. Their scattering to their own homes will be a preventative of sorts, but it also increases the difficulty of investigating and helping relief cases. Our Rehabilitation Committee is already at work on this and we have established an office in each of the districts to which people have returned in any considerable numbers. The Christian Mission building on Chung Hwa Road is being used for one such office, and the Presbyterian building at Shuang Tang for the other. We are not yet sure that John can move back to Hsiakwan even though that has been designated as one of the districts to which people may return. The soldiers at the gate can make and have made lots of trouble for people. Our two compounds in the city are just within the area designated for the use of the J. soldiers. In it the Self-government Society has no jurisdiction, but I understand that people may live there if they care to and are willing to take their chances. So we are still more or less between the devil and the sea. John and I cannot yet decide whether the right time has come yet for us to split forces—he going to Hsiakwan and I to St. Paul's. He has already written you of some of the opportunities for Christian work that have come to us, so you will know there is a plenty to keep us busy. The car has been indispensable, and would be all the more so if we dispersed since there are no means of transportation of any kind in the city. And you know what the distances are!

I think Clarissa has already told you that we are willing to forego furlough this year if it is for the best interests of the Mission for us to do so. John and I are both willing and anxious to hold on here as long as it is possible to do so. I am wondering whether it might not be a good thing for Mr. Kuo to get in his year of study in America now. Knowing his family to be in comparative safety in Shanghai, he could leave them with a quiet heart, and they would also be relieved of anxiety for his safety. It might be too late for him to have any theological study this term, but I understood that his intention was to spend some time in observation and practical work, anyway. He could get that now and be ready for a term's study in the fall, and then return to Nanking in time to allow us to go on furlough. I am simply putting this out as a suggestion. There may be practical difficulties in the way that I do not know about.

It is impossible to make any definite plans for the future of the work in Nanking. The Kung Kwan is a total loss except for the bricks and one small section in which the gateman lived. How much of our old constituency will ever return to Nanking is problematical since nobody can foretell what part the city is going to play again in Chinese political life. We shall have to start pretty much from the bottom again, I am afraid. Circumstances must also decide what direction our work shall take. I have no doubt that we shall be faced for a long time with the care of widows and orphans, and other destitute persons. There is a tremendous opportunity before us, however, and we can be confident that God will grant us wisdom to know how to deal with it.

With all good wishes and kindest regards, I am, Yours sincerely,

Thank you for the honor of appointing me on your Council of Advice. So far I seem to have graced it with my absence! If for any reason you prefer to have someone who can grace it with his presence, please feel free to appoint such a person in my place.

***

Letter to American Embassy[8]

Nanking, March 10, 1938
The American Embassy
Nanking, China

Gentlemen:
I should like to make the following statements about damage done to and looting of property belonging to the American Church Mission and situated at #209 Peh

Hsia Lu and #—Tai Ping Lu, the former address being a residence compound and the latter a church and residence compound. It is my belief that the damage and the looting were due to Japanese military operations and Japanese soldiers.

On Saturday, December 11, 1937, at about 2 p.m., Mr. Cola Podshivaloff and I rode on our bicycles to the property mentioned above. On our way we stopped at the University Hospital where we heard the sound of heavy artillery fire and bombing in the direction of the southern part of the city. We also saw the smoke of burning buildings that had apparently been struck. When we passed our Church compound on Tai Ping Lu it was still intact; but when we reached the residence compound we found that the iron gate of the compound had been struck by a shell which damaged the concrete gate post and broke and twisted a part of the iron gate. We found fragments of the exploded shell lying about, and they were still warm. A Chinese hotel across the street was completely demolished at the same time, and two Chinese who were living in another hotel, adjacent to the one which was demolished, told us that it had happened a few moments before our arrival.

On Tuesday, December 14, 1937, in the company of Messrs. John H. D. Rabe and Lewis Smythe and a Chinese gentleman named Sun, I paid a hasty visit to our two compounds. On our way we saw no Chinese civilians or soldiers, but Japanese soldiers were entering and looting shops and houses along Tai Ping Lu. At our church compound we found that a shell had hit and demolished the main gate, and that the doors on two smaller gates were also gone. The parish hall had been hit by a shell and badly damaged, windows and doors in St. Paul's Church had been shattered and the roof tiles damaged. There were numerous holes in the compound wall and the concrete sidewalks caused by fragments of exploding shells. A large Chinese-style residence on the compound had also been hit and badly damaged, the roof having been caused to fall in several places. Upon entering our residence compound on Peh Hsia Lu I found that the residences had been entered and looted despite the fact that an official notice from the American Embassy was posted on the gate of the compound and an American flag was flying in the compound. I met two Japanese soldiers in the residence formerly occupied by Mr. Roberts. They were equipped with hatchets, and one of them was in the act of stealing a boy's bicycle from the house. When I appeared one of the soldiers hastily withdrew; the other, left the bicycle and also withdrew. This bicycle, as well as several others, were later stolen from the residences.

I also found a photograph album and some clothing lying on the compound, indicating that looting had been going on.

On December 17, 1937, I again visited the compounds and found Japanese soldiers on the premises and drove them off. They were armed with hatchets, and I found that the doors of the residences had been battered in and boxes and trunks pried open and the contents scattered over the floors.

Japanese soldiers were living in a Chinese hotel adjacent to St. Paul's Church. They had broken a hole through the wall separating the two compounds. They were using the well beside the church for washing vegetables, etc. One soldier was polishing his bayonet behind the church, and ran back into the hotel through the wall when I indicated that he had no right to be on our premises. I found another soldier looting the residence of our Chinese clergyman, this residence being American property and situated on the Church compound.

On December 23, 1937 I visited the Church compound and found Mrs. Ch'en, the widow of one of our Church workers and herself a nurse. She had taken refuge in the Church tower and saw the soldiers coming and going with loot they had taken from our property. She witnessed the theft of a piano from the residence of our Chinese clergyman.

On December 26, 1937 I again visited the Church compound with Mrs. Ch'en who wished to return to see if she could retrieve a few of her things which she had left behind. We found that the piano had been removed from our Parish Hall and placed out on the lawn near the residence of our Chinese clergyman.

On January 10, 1938 I visited our compounds in the company of the Rev. James McCallum of the Christian Mission who had been occupying a house on our Peh Hsia Lu compound. We found that the northeastern section of our big Chinese-style residence on the church compound had been burned down. The Parish Hall piano which I had removed from the lawn into the residence of our Chinese clergyman—it having suffered considerably from exposure to the weather and from careless handling by soldiers—was still present. I found a Japanese soldier looting in Miss Sims' residence on our Peh Hsia Lu compound and compelled him to leave. The porcelain bath-tub, several beds, and all mattresses had been looted from Mr. Roberts' residence, and all mattresses from Miss Sims' residence.

On January 15, 1938 I visited our compounds and found a Japanese soldier playing the piano in Mr. Roberts' residence.

On January 17, 1938 I visited our compounds in the company of Mrs. Paul Twinem. The Parish Hall piano, which I had placed in the residence of the Chinese clergyman on our church compound, was gone.

Between January 17 and January 26 I made several other visits to our compound, and on several occasions found soldiers in them and more and more articles taken from the residences.

On January 26, 1938 the greater part of the Chinese-style residence on our Church compound was burned down together with the contents.

On January 27, 1938 I visited our compounds in company with Mr. Ch'i, architect of the University of Nanking. We found the ruins of the Chinese-style residence still smouldering.

On February 2, 1938 I again visited the compounds.

On February 3, 1938 I found a Japanese truck transport unit parked in the street before our Church compound. They had taken some of the furniture from our premises and were using it on the street. Inside the compound I found a group of Japanese soldiers seated around a fire on the lawn. They were using a finely carved teakwood Clergy chair from the church to support the iron rod by which they hung their rice buckets over the fire to cook. The chair had been whittled in front and a piece hacked out of the back. In the remains of the fire I found burned pieces of furniture and the remains of a door lock.

Inside a small room of the Chinese-style residence I found another group of Japanese soldiers around a fire which they had built on the floor of the building. They were sitting on furniture which they had taken out of our premises. One soldier was in the act of carrying chairs out of our buildings presumably for fuel. I required the soldiers to leave and to pour water over the fires before leaving.

On a later visit shortly afterwards a Japanese soldier had re-entered the Chinese-style residence and built a fire on the floor to cook his food. I required him to leave after extinguishing the fire.

Soldiers had also built a fire in the Sacristy of the church. They burned festival silk hangings, a window frame, and partly burned a wardrobe for hanging vestments.

About February 10 I placed two servants on each of our two compounds to watch the premises. Since February 17, I have been living on our residence compound on Peh Hsia Lu. We have not been annoyed by soldiers since that time.

As I have stated above, it is my firm conviction that the damage to our buildings and the looting was done by Japanese and not by Chinese, since on none of my frequent visits to our compounds did I find any Chinese on the premises in the act of looting or destroying the property.

This misuse of our property took place despite the fact that there were official notices from the American Embassy at the gates of both compounds, American flags flying in each, and notices from the Japanese Embassy, in Japanese, certifying it to be American property and therefore not to be molested by Japanese troops.

Yours respectfully,
Ernest H. Forster

***

Letter to Friends[9]

March 16, 1938

Dear Friends:

Our letter No. 2 was written to you from the River Steamer as we were returning to our new work in Nanking, little dreaming then what proportions the
"China Incident" was going to assume, and that we would shortly be separated
for another indefinite period (now four months). The week in Yangchow and
the ten days in Nanking were extremely busy and tiring, as in the first we were
dismantling our house and leaving things packed to be sent later to Nanking,
while in the latter we were running a six-ring circus.

It took the first few days in Nanking to get the Magee's house adjusted to a
new routine, and to get used to the constant coming and going of many people.
Simultaneously Ernest was balancing Mission accounts to give to Leslie Fairfield,
who had come up to Nanking with us, was giving examinations to a candidate
for Holy Orders, interviewing people helping John Magee in his plans for relief
work among the wounded soldiers, and getting started in his new parish work.
In the midst of this our cook, having been on the way from Yangchow by junk
for a week, arrived at the back door with some of our furniture and all of our
food supply, while our five Wusih missionaries, having been bombed out of
their station and the Christians scattered to the country, arrived by motor at the
front door. Our "refugees" were with us for five days of fine comradeship and
exchange of experiences until they proceeded to Shanghai by boat, leaving the
car for our use. Thousands of wounded soldiers were pouring into the railroad
station and all help possible was needed for their care. Then suddenly all the
Government Departments and the foreign embassies began moving "up River,"
and Nanking was thrown into a panic. Mr. Hall Paxton, of our Embassy, tried to
get all Americans out, but we "stubbornly" refused to go, and were then offered
the *Panay* as a place of safety in an emergency. Clarissa, not knowing the language and not having medical training, was finally persuaded to go to Hankow
via the boat chartered by the German Government for its nationals. Ernest and
John Magee stayed at Nanking and shortly moved inside the city wall to the so-
called Safety Zone, which had been agreed upon by all parties concerned. They
faced together with the other foreigners and Chinese the horrors of the succeeding months, which it is useless at this time to dwell on, as many incidents have
already reached the outside world. Many bombing incidents, including the *Panay*,
happened in rapid succession. We might easily have been on the *Panay*, but that
was one incident that we were spared.

Clarissa, receiving a cable from Bishop Roberts, proceeded (after two weeks
in Hankow living with Elise Dexter of Massachusetts, and studying the lan-

guage) to Shanghai via the constantly bombed railroad to Canton and Hong Kong. She left Hankow on December 10 when things were so critical in Nanking. She was, for those terrible days, outside of all communication with Nanking, living in uncertainty as to the fate of Ernest and John, learning of the *Panay* incident and not knowing whether or not they were on the boat. She was in Hong Kong two weeks awaiting a passage and having no word from Ernest, but receiving on Christmas two cables, one from Mother and Father and the other from brother Irving. With these happy messages, a beautiful midnight Mass, an impressive Christmas morning service, and two festival dinners, Clarissa and Bessie Sims boarded late Christmas night the Italian SS *Verde* for Shanghai, where they arrived on December 28 (Mother and Father's wedding anniversary) to be given a warm welcome by the Shanghai mission family. Clarissa received a batch of mail from Ernest which was brought down from Nanking by Mr. Durdin of the New York Times. Since that time there has been fairly regular communication with Nanking (every ten days and sometimes oftener) via the United States and British gunboats. By this method Clarissa is able to send supplies, etc. to Ernest and John. It seems very strange that in such a short distance (180 miles) it is still impossible to get back and forth to see each other. Ernest will probably get down to Shanghai now in a short time for a visit.

In the meantime, Yangchow was entered and our Mahan School and Church compound completely looted of all belongings, and the buildings taken over by the Japanese and used as their barracks. The other two compounds in the city were not treated so badly. Our Christians had gone en masse to the country and were having worship together. Our Chinese priests returned at intervals to the city and have finally been able to move back. Many Christians have made their way with difficulty to Shanghai bringing recent news of conditions, which is not too good. The foreign Yangchow staff here in Shanghai has made repeated attempts to return, but the Japanese command will not allow them to return.

In Nanking, Ernest writes that conditions have eased somewhat, and that he is starting in regular parish services since he has moved from the Safety Zone to our residence compound not far from St. Paul's Church. Many Christians are beginning to return and are glad to find the Church open after three months of enforced closure. Quite a little damage from bombing, looting and fire occurred on the church compound and to a lesser degree on the residence compound.

Sunday, February 20, was a day of great rejoicing, as on that day Ernest was able to hold services in St. Paul's Church again, having had it cleaned and set in order. It had miraculously escaped the shells which struck the parish house twenty feet away, but many window panes had been broken by the explosion of the shells, and Japanese soldiers had entered the church building and used it. They had started a fire on the concrete floor of the Sacristy, burned up all festival hangings, and the wardrobe for vestments in part. Ernest had succeeded in saving all the communion silver and altar ornaments. Thus the material damage to the church was not very great. That first congregation consisted of sixteen persons, including a Japanese soldier who was a baptized Christian. The service consisted of Morning Prayer, the baptism of an infant, and ending with the Holy Communion. Paul Tong helped with the service, and after it was over Ernest took movies and photographs of that memorable occasion. The next Sunday there was a congregation of thirty, and on March 13 there were about fifty in the congregation including children.

Nanking is a city of depression with buildings burned for blocks on end, with dead bodies unburied and sickness becoming more prevalent with the approach of spring and the fear of atrocities not yet over. The problem of relief and rehabilitation everywhere is demanding the greatest ingenuity and planning.

Throughout all of these experiences in China, reports from all quarters are unanimous that the opportunities for Christian witness and service have never been greater than today. By hundreds and thousands people are asking for the strength and courage which they have seen the Church profess. Chinese have exhibited wonderful courage, faith, and forgiveness under very trying circumstances.

Regular classes and services are held daily at Ginling University where Ernest has spoken to large groups of women and girls, and at Nanking University. On March 14, there was a workers' meeting to decide about lending further help to Ginling University, which now has over one thousand women and girls enrolled in twenty-two classes, studying the life of Christ as recorded by St. Mark. They are very short of teachers, so they have appealed to Ernest and John Magee to help, in addition to their taking the preaching every afternoon. This will give you some idea of the opportunities before us for the spread of the Gospel.

Special classes for inquirers, for those wanting baptism, etc. are demanding not a little time. Childrens' services with instruction, as well as some special classes for young people, are under way. Because of limited space, the number at women's meetings is limited to four hundred. We also understand that tickets are issued so that those desiring to attend will not always miss out. Truly the fields are ripe unto the harvest. Shanghai is overcrowded with thousands of refugees and tremendous camps are in full swing. One of the large ones (over 17,000) was forced to start moving its people to other places because the Japanese came along and demanded the buildings. So, even in greater Shanghai, each day brings new problems to which we have to adjust ourselves.

As this letter goes to you the Lenten season is half over and Easter will soon be here. In our St. Paul's rectory garden at Peh Hsia Lu, violets have been in bloom for some time, with bachelor buttons, daffodils and hyacinths.

In listening to the daily radio broadcasts we can scarcely hope that this Eastertide will be a time of peace and joy for most people in the world. But those of us who do believe in the Risen Lord and in His Message to go forward in His Name must constantly turn to Him to renew our courage, hope and faith. Arms and ammunitions will not usher in the Kingdom of God, but only a fearless witness of the God of Love, in the midst of this fast rising tide of selfishness and hate.

With sincerest wishes for a beautiful Eastertide and that the coming summer months may bring you joy and relaxation.

Sincerely,
Ernest and Clarissa Forster

Temporary Address
Mrs. Ernest H. Forster
American Church Mission
99C Jessfield Road
Shanghai, China

Regular Address
Rev. Ernest H. Forster
American Church Mission
Nanking, China

Notes

1. RG8, B263–4.
2. RG8, B263–4.
3. Should be 25th or 26th.
4. RG8, B263–2.
5. RG8, B263–4.
6. RG8, B263–5.
7. RG8, B263–6.
8. RG8, B263–6.
9. RG8, B263–6.

John G. Magee

The Rev. John Gillespie Magee
was born October 10, 1884, in
Pittsburgh, Pennsylvania. After
finishing high school in Connecti-
cut, he received a B.A. from Yale
in 1906 and a B.D. from the Episcopal Theological School in Cambridge, Massachusetts, in 1911.
He was ordained as a minister of
the Episcopal Church and set off
for China in 1912. In China he met
Faith E. Backhouse, an English
missionary from the China Inland
Mission, whom he married in July
1921. They had four sons.

John Magee played a role in saving thousands of Chinese from being murdered by the Japanese, setting up a refugee hospital to take care of wounded
soldiers and refugees, and serving as chairman of the Nanking Branch of the
International Red Cross and member of the International Committee for the
Nanking Safety Zone. Films taken by Magee in Nanking and sent to the West
were among the first available visual documentation of the Nanking Massacre.
After the war, Magee was a witness at the Tokyo Trial. Jiro Takidani's Witness
to the Nanking Incident (Tokyo, 1993) documents Magee's work during the
Nanking Massacre.

When Magee first returned to American in the summer of 1938, after 28
years of service in China, he made an extensive tour to speak about the Nanking
Massacre. Magee died on September 9, 1953, in Pittsburgh.

Letters to Wife (December 12, 1937–February 5, 1938)[1]

No. 25 Lo Chia Rd, Nanking
Dec. 12, 1937

Darling:

The last few days have been terrible ones for the poor people of this city. The Japanese, according to what we have heard, broke into the Shwei Si Men this afternoon and the Chinese soldiers are in retreat along the Chungshan Road and by other roads. As I write there is the sound of heavy guns inside the city as well as rifle and machine gun fire. Some troops are evidently holding up the retreat while the main body of troops are going to Hsiakwan in the endeavor to get across the river. I suppose. There are fires in many parts of the city, either the work of the Chinese soldiers or of Japanese shells, I do know which. A shell hit just across the street from the house almost next to us here where some of our people and the Christians from St. Paul's Church are and frightened them all very much.

I shall now go back for a few days and tell you a little of what I have been doing beginning with Wednesday. I wish I had written a little each day in the form of a diary as there have been so many things doing that it has been hard to keep track of the days. I'm not sure just which day I wrote my air mail letter to you but think it went off on Wednesday, the last day the P.O. accepted any mail. I was busy at our place trying to get some things into the city. We did succeed in getting our piano and Louise Hammond's in but had no time to get Archie Tsen's in—I only succeeded in getting ours in by the skin of my teeth as I had to get a special permit from the commanding general's headquarters. Then there were a great many people from Hsiakwan that the military would not let in—a sentry did not even want to let me in but I walked past him and talked to an officer at the gate.

While I was there quite a number of our Ssu So Ts'uen Christians came up. I would not have known them but Chen Ru Ling had given them each a slip of cloth stamped with "Sheng Kung Hwei" so I could recognize them and vouch for them. What the officer told me they were afraid of was spies. Many others tried to come in with them but I could not vouch for them.

The next day (Thursday—Dec. 9th) I heard that there were some wounded civilians at the station so I went down in the car. I forgot to mention that the day before I had found a poor old woman from Wusih or somewhere near there, whose hands had been handly torn by a bomb. I was able to get her and her daughter to the Drum Tower Hospital where she had to have a finger amputated. The daughter is living with our Wusih refugees or possibly with our Ssu So Ts'uen Christians.

On Thursday I went to the station with J.L. Ch'en, after making sure that the officer at the gate would let us in again. There were no wounded there but we filled the ambulance from the Drum Tower Hospital with medicines and quilts that we had been using for wounded soldiers at the station, and then J.L. Ch'en and I went in the Ford to Ssu So Ts'uen to get a girl who had been wounded in the leg several weeks before and who could not walk. A little child had also been wounded in the head. This family were not Christians but had occasionally attended Church. The place was pretty largely deserted but some people were still about. This girl did not want to move and it was only by considerable urging that we could get them to move. We told them that Ssu So Ts'uen would be burned no doubt. This happened the next day which I could see when I was in Hsiakwan.

On Thursday while I was in Hsiakwan the soldiers were burning the buildings outside the Hsing Chung Men—whether the Bridge Hotel has been burned by now I do not know. The buildings in Chiang Chia Yuan back of Archie Tsen's house were in flames and I could see soldiers running about Archie Tsen's house and it was set ablaze just after I left as George Fitch came by there later and saw it burning. The next day only the walls were standing. While I was there Kwoh Tz-Shuang, the man who refused to sell us the land near our front gate, was there on the road with such things as he could tie up. He was weeping and pointing to some of his houses which were burning and said they would not let him into the city. I told him to come with me to the gate and I would do what I could but the sentry did not even want to let me in. Kwoh went back in despair—if he had waited till I could find the officer I could have got him in. It seems so utterly senseless as well as heartless to burn the houses of the people. If it would enable them to hold the city for a month later it might have been reasonable but this could not be the case.

I took some wounded soldiers down to the river bank as they were being evacuated by train from Pukow as rapidly as possible and tried to find some wounded civilians who I heard were there. There were many hundreds of people there on the wharves some of whom had been waiting for days to go across and many of them had had nothing to eat for several days. The day before G. Fitch and I had proposed to the acting Chief of Police that they find some way of sending these people across the river that they might escape and I was glad to see that the ferries were taking them after the wounded soldiers were provided for, but I heard yesterday that there were about 1500 still waiting.

Then yesterday (Saturday, Dec. 11th) I took some wounded soldiers in the Drum Tower ambulance to a dressing station for wounded soldiers in the Capitol Theatre. Just before I arrived a large shell had fallen in the street and killed about 11 people. Two motor cars were burning immediately opposite the Capitol Theatre in front of the Fu Chang Hotel. I got rid of my wounded soldiers just as the Japanese bombers came overhead and when the anti-aircraft guns near at hand were firing very hard. We got out of that place as soon as possible and went back to the hospital. Soon some people came saying a number of people had been wounded inside the neutral zone. We took the ambulance and this time went down a back street also taking the Ford. After passing the University

Middle School and before we arrived at Hua Chung Road we saw a number of dead bodies lying in the road. A house had been hit by a shell and close to 20 people killed, 7 or 8 of them being hurled into the street. A poor old couple were simply frantic as their son, aged 33, was lying dead with a huge hole in the front of his face. They were simply beside themselves with grief. Great crowds were standing around out of curiosity and I told them to leave immediately and get behind something. The masses in China are certainly unintelligent about such things. There was danger that another shell might arrive at any moment.

This morning Ernest took the service for the Christians from Taosheng and St. Paul's Parishes who are living over in two houses from where I am now writing (Hansen's house) while I took a service on the ground floor of Schultz-Pantin's house where E. and I have been living. I preached on the Advent hope and again God gave me freedom of expression and a message—not the same as the previous Sunday, even though I had had no previous preparation. Just as I was in the midst of my sermon the telephone rang and I answered it as it was near me (a new experience while preaching!) and I was told I was wanted immediately over at the Neutral Zone Committee's headquarters. After the creed I asked J. L. Ch'en to carry on and I hurried over to enter into a discussion about a new plan concerning the Zone.

In the afternoon I went to the U. Hospital to try to be of help and while there or perhaps before leaving headquarters, heard that the Japanese had broken into the city. The Chinese were preparing to defend that corner and had stationed guns in the park near the Drum Tower, which they should not have done as it was in the Neutral Zone. Many of us got busy hurriedly moving the drugs from the drug room as it was near the corner of the building where the soldiers were preparing to make a stand and we feared it would be bombed or shelled and all the hospital drugs destroyed. After working at this for some time I walked across to Schultz-Pantin's house where I had supper and then walked over here. As there is still electric light in this section I've been able to write this letter. While writing the firing has much lessened and I suppose the Chinese positions have been occupied or their guns captured. What the morrow will bring forth I do not know. There is still a little rifle fire.

Dec. 15, 8:50 a.m.

The night before last when I finished writing I thought the fighting was over but later there was heavy firing from artillery quite close to us and also much machine gun and rifle fire—heavier than before.

Yesterday turned out to [be] a most unpleasant day—that is putting it mildly. On Sunday afternoon when the Chinese soldiers began to retreat I went to the Ministry of Foreign Affairs where I found many wounded soldiers but no medical officers or nurses. Later Ernest and I went to the Ministry of War at San Pai Lou where we found many more wounded soldiers and about ten or twenty army nurses and doctors but none of them were doing anything at all but planning to leave. I told them that the International Red Cross Committee would take them over if they would stay and work for the wounded soldiers there. We had organized the day before with a number of people who had been interested in helping the wounded—Germans, British (Munro-Faure who, however, like all the British had been ordered out of Nanking and was living on a boat in the river), Chinese, young Cola, our Russian friend, but mostly Americans. I was made chairman and Ernest secretary of our Committee.

Some members of our Safety Zone Committee had got into touch with some Japanese officers and they said the hospitals would be respected so long as they did not harbor armed men and that the soldiers would not be harmed if they did not resist. Then many of us got busy in various parts of the city passing on the word to the Chinese soldiers, all of us taking their arms and throwing them away. The street in front of the Ministry of War was in the wildest confusion—small and heavier artillery, mules, horses, shells, hand grenades and every kind of war material. We stopped to set free a mule. It made one feel very uncomfortable to pass hand grenades and artillery shells lying near the fire. Once a bullet blew out just near our feet. When I got back to the Ministry of War the nurses and doctors that I had asked to wait there had left and the poor wounded soldiers were left with no one to attend them.

By evening the hospital for wounded soldiers began to take on some semblance of order as the hundred or so dressers had begun to get to work.

The next morning I took an ambulance full of wounded soldiers to the Ministry of Foreign Affairs. When we had just succeeded in helping up the steps those who were able to walk (some had to be taken on stretchers) along came a squad of Japanese soldiers some of whom were like wild beasts. I was helping a poor fellow who was coming along most painfully but a soldier grabbed him from me and began to jerk his wounded arms terribly and tied his hands together and also the hands of another wounded man. Fortunately I found a Japanese medical officer who came about that time and pointed to the bloody clothes of these men. He spoke in German and I said in poor German that this was a hospital for wounded soldiers and he made the soldiers release them. A little while before a Japanese newspaper reporter told me in good English that some of the Japanese soldiers were very bad. I then found a decent Colonel who spoke English and told him I wanted go to headquarters to get permission to tend to the wounded soldiers and he sent me and the young Russian to headquarters in our ambulance (borrowed from the Red Swastika Society). We went to the Central Hotel west of the officers Moral Endeavor and saw a small man with a pointed head and heavy beard. I said through Cola that there were many wounded soldiers in the Ministry of War and I wanted permission to move them to the Ministry of F. A. He went back into an inner room where the highest officer in the city was located and then said that I must wait several days. I said they have not been tended to for days and did not even have anyone to bring them water and he said we must wait. We went away in disappointment. I returned to the headquarters of our Neutral Zone Committee and there found a number of wounded soldiers and took two loads of them to the Wounded Soldiers' Hospital at the Ministry of Foreign Affairs. Each time I had difficulty with the soldiers. Some high staff officers we met in a car were afraid I was carrying wounded soldiers away but I told him we wanted to bring them in, not take them away. They gave us permission to bring one more load. After the second trip we met an officer at the gate as we were trying to go back who seemed beside himself with rage. I never saw such a person before. His talk sounded like the barking of a dog and the looks he gave me would have burned me up if I were inflammable. He told Cola not to let this American (myself) come around there again—the Americans were very bad. Cola said, "We had permission to take another trip," and he said, "I am the commanding officer in the city." With much difficulty we succeeded in getting back our ambulance.

Sunday—Dec. 19

The horror of the last week is beyond anything I have ever experienced. I never dreamed that the Japanese soldiers were such savages. It has been a week of murder and rape, worse, I imagine, than has happened for a very long time unless the massacre of the Armenians by the Turks was comparable. They not only killed every prisoner they could find but also a vast number of ordinary citizens of all ages. Many of them were shot down like the hunting of rabbits in the streets. There are dead bodies all over the city from the south city to Hsiakwan. Just day before yesterday we saw a poor wretch killed very near the house where we are living. So many of the Chinese are timid and when challenged foolishly start to run. This is what happened to that man. The actual killing we did not see as it took place just around the corner of a bamboo fence from where we could see. Cola went there later and said the man had been shot twice in the head. These two Jap. soldiers were no more concerned than if they had been killing a rat and never stopped smoking their cigarettes and talking and laughing. J.L. Ch'en's oldest boy, Ch'en Chang, 16 years (Chinese count) was carried off with a great body of possibly 500 from right around where we live two days ago and I think there is very little chance that he is alive. In this group were also 11 other Ssu So Ts'uen Christians. We have been able to get no trace of them since, although I gave the names of our people to the newly arrived Consul-General Tanaka yesterday.

Our school cook's boy who was rinsing rice at a pond about five days ago was carried off with more than 100 others to Ssu So Ts'uen on that same day, all with their wrists tied with rope. Near Ssu So Ts'uen they were shot one by one. Fortunately for him and a shop keeper from Kulou they were at the end of the line and their wrists were tied in front of them and not behind as I've seen in many cases. They began gnawing on the knots with their teeth and succeeded in undoing the knots. Without being seen they were able to hide in a drain or culvert where they stayed for two nights and a day and a half. Then they came out and met with a Japanese soldier who was unable to carry away a cask of wine which he had looted. He made them carry it for him, which they were very glad to do as this rendered them safe and enabled them to enter the city whence the boy was able eventually to reach the house (Hansen's) where our Hsiakwan people are housed. My chauffeur's two younger brothers were carried off in the same group with Ch'en Chang. As this crowd was being gathered quite near the house where Ernest and I have been living. I went out with the chauffeur's wife as he was afraid to go (and with good reason). She finally saw her two younger brothers-in-law and walked up to a party officer, probably a sergeant and raising two fingers said in English "Two men—not soldiers." This man was looking at me with supreme hate as I approached and said in great rage something which I took to mean "go" and I turned to the woman and said "It is hopeless" and we returned. If I had known Ch'en Ch'ang was in that group I would have tried to reach a high officer to save him. I think it was the day before yesterday that Mr. T'ung's son (they are San Pai Lou Christians) was shot in the street near here. About Tuesday night (Dec. 14th) I met with two groups of men being forced along the street, all tied together four by four. One man had no trousers on. A great many of them (it was just dusk when I met the first group so I could distinguish them)—there must have been between 5,000 and 6,000 of them. For several days we could hear the route of machine guns as these men (not only these 6,000 in different parts of the city were being murdered. There is no way of finding out how many have been butchered but my guess is 20,000 including those killed in the streets. There may have been more or may have been less.

The Japanese were furious in not catching more prisoners, as great numbers of soldiers must have escaped on Sunday night.

Yesterday I went to Hsiakwan with the new Japanese Consul-General Tanaka as he wanted to paste up notices on foreign property that this was American or British property, etc. as the case might be. The only building standing at Hsiakwan, about, are our place, Standard Oil, China Import & Export Co. and the Yangtsze Hotel. Our front door was smashed and the house was in the greatest confusion with all drawers dumped in the middle of the floor. On the third floor all remaining boxes were smashed open. I had fortunately left the smaller of my tin-lined boxes open and had taken the locks off the cupboards. There was considerable blood on the floor and on a bed in the 3rd floor and at least one gun with a broken barrel so I'm thinking some Chinese soldier or soldiers may have been cornered there, or at the least taken refuge there. The Chinese probably broke open the boxes looking for clothing into which to change from their soldier uniforms. Other valuable things seem to have been left untouched. I am happy that the house was not burned down as I feared would be the case. The sight of Hsiakwan is appalling with almost all familiar sights gone. The Bridge House is no more and I am exceedingly sorry for Mrs. Sims. To try to begin again at her age is pretty discouraging. Hsiakwan was undoubtedly burned by Chinese as they did not want to leave it for the Japanese and it also probably helped to cover the Chinese retreat to the bank. On the bank there were three great piles of charred bodies—partially burned. I imagine a great many of the fires that have been started by Japanese during the last four or five days have been for the purpose of burning up the dead that they have slaughtered. As I write two fires are burning—one towards Hsiakwan and one towards the south.

The Japanese have been looting Nanking of everything they can lay hands on during this whole week. They even took a motor car from the German Embassy and have entered the American Embassy a number of times to be kicked out each time. Even officers are looting. Yesterday they came to the house (Hansen's) where I am and attempted to take out a remaining motor car (two others had already been taken from here.) With this group were two Ronin (Japanese civilian rescals). I pointed at the sign put up by the Japanese Consul General and also the U.S. Embassy sign and tried to close one side of the big gate. A Japanese pushed me back and they went into the garage but this remaining car was broken so they left it. One of the Ronin asked me in good English for my passport which I showed and he said "Thank you." The looting has continued for days and they keep taking the scanty food of the people and then bedding and every kind of article they can lay hands on. One cannot leave a motor car for a second or it will be gone.

But the most horrible thing now is the raping of the women which has been going on in the most shameless way that I have ever known. The streets are full of men searching for women. Ernest and I, one or the other of us, have to stay and keep our eyes on these houses where our Christians from Hsiakwan and St. Paul's as well as many other refugees we have taken in, are located and Schultz-Pantin's house where we keep our clothing and take such meals as we can. Cola stays at the house as does another man, a Turco-Tartar who is a mechanic. The Ssu So Ts'uen and San Pai Lou Christians are housed next door to us and Jap. soldiers keep going in there and robbing these people of the little that they have. It is a regular nightmare to deal with these reverted groups of men. The house where we keep our things is loaded with women and some even sleep in our dining room. They sit in the house all day in dreadful fear. Several days ago a Buddhist priest from a little temple across the street came in and said he had heard that Japanese had carried off two Buddhist nuns and begged me to take some nuns in which I have done. The house is really packed like Sardines. They sleep in the halls upstairs and down and for a while we had a mother and daughter in our bathroom. Quite a number of girls are in the Kulou Hospital where they are helping as nurses even though the real nurses are best. Last night a soldier went in there in the women's quarters and got into bed with three different girls—each of them screamed which frightened the man so he got out and never accomplished his evil purpose before Bob Wilson arrived and kicked him out. He pulled a gun on Bob and the latter thought he was going to use it. About 4,000 women are in Ginling College and I understand 12 of them were carried off last night. Several nights ago while Ernest and I were walking over here a woman came weeping and running after us just as a soldier had called to her. We took her with us and kept her with the women in this house (Hansen's) on the second floor. The next morning I heard her story direct from her. Four men came about 6 p.m. and dragged her off from her 28 year old husband and 3 months old baby and put her in a motor car. They took her three or four miles where three men raped her. Then they tried to give her some food they had stolen and sent her part of the way back in the car and turned her loose near to where she met us. It was dark and she did not know how to get home and it was a mercy that we happened along, as otherwise she would probably have been abused all night. I took her to the hospital the next morning where Dr. Wilson tended to her. Yesterday afternoon a German, Mr. Sperling, and I went to some houses where soldiers were in most every house raping women. We went into one house where one woman was sitting weeping on the ground floor and they told us she had been raped. They said there is still a soldier up stairs so I went to a room on the third floor, which the Chinese pointed out, and pounded furiously on the door. The Japanese inside made some response and I shouted in both German and English "Open the door." Then Sberling came and shouted and pounded too. The man finally came out and I said to him as he went down the stairs "Chuh seng" (beast). A soldier that I had seen below and who knew some Chinese was coming up the stairs and heard me and did not like it at all. Such horrible things are happening all over the city. When we were telling a Japanese Consul General who had hurried from America some of these tales, he said "It was inevitable" and today when I was telling a newspaper man from the Asahi-Shimbun, he said "It was inevitable." What a judgment upon the Japanese character, all the more forceful since so spontaneous without realizing the impression it made on me.

The Japanese have spoken contemptuously so often about the undisciplined Chinese soldiers but they have been as bad or worse than the worst bandits I have ever seen here. Consul General Tanaka said the high command had already issued two orders about this unruliness but it has gone on today worse than ever.

Recent nights I have been sleeping on the floor at Hansen's house. I should say that the last two nights I have slept on a couch and been quite comfortable. But most I need a bath. I did get one more than a week ago at Buck's house where a number of American men are living together.

I have really only told you a little of what I have been doing. Yesterday morning when I took that woman to the hospital I said I must hurry to bring a woman to the hospital who had been bayoneted in the neck by a soldier who had tried to take her quilt from her bed. They said at the hospital, "She was brought in the morning." I then went to the bed where she was and found out she lived in a different place so I knew this was another case, so hurried off to bring this terrified and half-witted woman 41 years old and her old mother. Miss Hynds told me today of an 8 year old boy who had been stabbed in the stomach in four or five places by a Japanese soldier. Of course we only hear of a small fraction of the cases that actually occur but I think I have said enough to let you know what a hell the people of this city have been through. It is like a horrible dream and when I wake up at night or in the morning it is horrible to find out that it is not a dream. Yesterday I heard that there were a number of girls in the rear of the Quaker Church so I took the hospital ambulance and went down there. Three of them had already been carried off and the others were in perfect terror and could not talk straight and piled pell mell into the truck—about 18, I think—and I took them to the Drum Tower Hospital. It was into their room that a soldier went last night.

Dec. 20, 8 p.m.

I have been spending the last four evenings after most of the others have gone to bed to write to you.

Yesterday—4th Advent—neither I or Ernest took part in the services as we each had to be on duty any moment to keep these wretched thieves from stealing our people's goods or from raping the women. Our people from Ssu So Ts'uen and San Pai Lou came into Schultz-Pantin's garden for service as it was a nice day. J.L. Ch'en took the service (Morning Prayer) and preached and also played the little organ which was set on the lawn. I took moving pictures while he was preaching.

Just as we had finished the service there was a knock on the door and in came two Japanese newspaper correspondents who proved to be very decent. I invited them in and said that they could take a picture if they wanted to, so they took a picture of Ch'en Ru-ling playing the organ with cassock and surplice on and the people sitting on the grass. I then had a good talk with one man who spoke English, Mr. Mariyama (or something similar) who was the correspondent of the Asahi Shimbun. I told him of the terrible things that had happened, of the carrying off of 14 of our people, not 12 as I at first thought, of the probable death of the clergyman's son who had just preached, of the Buddhist priest across the way who had begged me to take in his nuns, and of many other stories. He said, "You must not think that all Japanese people are like these soldiers" and I said I of course knew this and spoke of my various trips to Japan. I then told him of the wounded soldier problem, the slaughter of innocent people and a little of my life in China. He seemed very interested and only left when it was time to go to lunch, and said he would like to come again and I said I should be glad to help him in any way that I could.

As usual I was busy as were all the foreigners with various things, mostly in protecting women from these brutes, so have only seen him on the street.

Today has been very full. This morning Ernest went over to Schultz-Pantin's house early and I stayed here till his return. When I am here I eat with the Fan family. When I got over to our place I was busy immediately in driving out Jap. soldiers from our two houses almost next door where the Ssu So Ts'uen and San Pai Lou Christians are housed. One of our Christian women (or inquirers, I'm not sure which) was raped this a.m. before I could get over. I then took her with another girl, who had been raped, for treatment to the hospital. Before I had left came back one of the 14 who had marvelously escaped from about 1000 men who were carried off at the same time. He rejoiced us all by saying that Ch'en Ch'ang had been released before the Japanese began to mow them down with a machine gun on the river bank at Hsiakwan. It was no doubt his youth that saved him, although we know of a number as young or younger who have been killed. This man, Su Kuan-wai, says he had seen Ch'en Ch'ang in the electric light Co. so I am going to try to find him tomorrow. J.L. Ch'en told me tonight he thinks he is dead for it has been so long since he was seen. But to go back to Su's story. He was standing at the rear of the crowd with one foot almost touching the river water. When they began to fall after the firing he fell too, although he had not been hit. He quickly covered himself with three dead bodies and lay quite still for some time till he thought it was safe to move. He then was able to reach the bank without being seen and walked away. Soon a Jap. soldier got him and made him work which he did for two days cooking food for a group and they released him giving him a note which enabled him to get into the city.

This afternoon while standing on the street between the two or three places where we have our people, some women came begging us to save them. Ernest was there too. I later took them to the U. of Nanking in a bunch as that is now being guarded by Military Police. While we were standing talking some people came from the very next house begging me to go there as a girl of 12, Chinese count, or 10 or 11 in our reckoning, had been raped by a soldier. I got there in time to keep three soldiers from going in. The family had taken the girl to the Police Station, controlled by our Refugee Zone Committee, for safety. She soon came with her guardian, as her father was a Szechuanese officer who had left Nanking earlier but had not been able to take his daughter along. I took this girl to the hospital for treatment and then brought the smaller car back to Schultz-Pantin's house to pick up several loads of younger women or girls from our house which was so crowded that you could hardly get up stairs. They were standing close together in the lower hall and sitting on the steps. Our boy has to sleep on the floor in our bedroom, all the space on the lower floor is packed and an empty bedroom on the second floor. Girls are even sleeping in our dining room. While I was going with some girls next door to stand there while they packed their roll of bedding, someone came running from the house immediately south in the same alley saying soldiers were there after women so I ran there and found three on the second floor landing and I told them in no uncertain tones to beat it pointing to the stairs. The Chinese beckoned to a room on that same floor where they said a soldier was. I gave the door a great bang and it flew open to disclose the beast in the very act. I yelled to him "Chu-ba" which they seem to understand. I went in and he got out immediately and soon left the room, I following him till he had left the alley altogether.

I forgot to mention that while at our place in the morning Chang Wen Ming of Ssu So Ts'uen came running telling me that a man was after his wife's younger sister. I ran as fast as I could go to the house and got there in time. He was in the room with several girls and I pointed to the door and told him to go.

Just after lunch someone came running to tell me a soldier had beaten old Mr. T'ung of San Pai Lou. I ran and found that they had been having a Bible reading group after lunch when a Japanese soldier walked into their midst. They all rose and old T'ung opened his Bible to show him what they were reading. He picked up one of those long Chinese smoking pipes with a brass bowl and hit him a terrific blow on the head. When I went there I found quantities of blood on the floor and his face covered with blood, and his head bound up with a towel to stop the blood. I took him to the Emergency Hospital which I have opened just to the rear of the University Hospital with the funds in my hands.

These are some of the things I have done today. If you will understand that many of the foreigners in town are having the same experiences daily and then remember that the same thing is happening in a hundred places where there are no foreigners to see, you can imagine the horror of these days. While I was in the hospital today two men were registering, both of whom had been bayonetted by Japanese; one showed me a vicious wound in his neck. In the dispensary dressing room was a woman who was having the cuts in her face dressed. Her face was literally a mass of cuts, cheeks and forehead. I suppose she had resisted some brute. She told me it was a Japanese soldier who had done it and I did not ask for details to embarrass her in the presence of several men nurses. "How long, oh Lord, how long!"

Dec. 21

I am glad to say that this day has not been so eventful. I had hoped as soon as I could get away to go with someone from the Japanese Consulate to Hsiakwan in the hope of seeing Ch'en Ch'ang. After leaving here about 9 a.m. I had my shave, interrupted several times by various things, requests from some of the women living in our place—you can hardly move without bumping into them— and going next door as a Japanese soldier had come demanding that our people repair some rickshas. When I did get to the Consulate I had a long delay before I could see Consul General Tanaka. Then it was almost 12 and too late to attempt going to Hsiakwan so I arranged to come after lunch. But then during lunch Lewis Smythe came and got me and Cola to sign a petition from the foreigners asking them in the name of humanity to stop the burning of houses which is taking place all day long all over the city. He asked me to join a group of foreigners who would present the petition in person at 2 p.m. After that was over Mr. Tanaka sent along with me a Consular policeman who was rude and who had no intention of helping me find Ch'en Ch'ang. We got down as far as Jehol Road (leading to the station) and then he said we could go no further in the direction of the river. I said "But the boy was seen there near the electric power plant." By considerable talk I got as far as the Yangtse Villa and he refused to go further motioning that the soldier would bayonet me if I went further. Then we started up the road that leads past the former Infectious Disease Hospital and after going a few rods came to a dead body and he stopped the car and said we must turn back. Then we started up Jehol Road (leading to the station) but soon came to more dead bodies and he said, "There are no Chinese at Hsiakwan" and stopped the car again. The real fact is that he did not want me to see all the evil they had done, not knowing that I had been to the bank a few days before and had seen the large number of dead bodies on the bank—probably three to four hundred.

There has been some improvement in the situation today, although raping has continued. The looting has been mostly of bedding, food and various kinds of things that the soldiers wanted to use but the sad thing is that most of it has been taken from the poor who had so little to lose.

Ernest has had several talks with a Japanese soldier who has a position in a shop at Yokohama and who speaks English. He knows Mrs. Relfsnider and others in our Mission and has had much to do with tourists. He says the Japanese have lost 20% of their effectives in the campaign and lost a considerable number in taking Nanking. He says the war will not last much longer as Japan cannot afford to continue since she has lost so much already. He seemed very decent and it is good to know that there are nice people among them. The Consul told me that the 9th Division which is in Nanking, is being changed for a better Division, the 16th, and he says that they will get better every day and thinks that by the 24th the city will be settled. I hope so for it would be nice to have a peaceful Christmas.

Dec. 22

Today the soldiers have been leading away men again. I have heard the machine guns and slow regular rifle fire again a number of times which means more slaughter. About 45 minutes ago I saw about 60 or 70 men led off. Several days ago Japanese officials with an engineering officer came to our Committee asking us to find them workmen familiar with the electric light works, so Mr. Rabe and others did find 54 men. These men began working in the electric light works and living at the International Export Co. I think it was yesterday that soldiers shot forty-three of the fifty-four workmen. The only reason why they did not kill the remaining 11 was that the Sikh watchman at the Export Co. recognized them and said they formerly worked there. Their excuse for killing the others was that the electric light Co. was a government concern and therefore these men were government employees and should be killed! As a matter of fact the company was not wholly owned by the government but that makes not the slightest difference.

Such sights as I have seen in the Drum Tower Hospital today! The dead body of a little boy, aged 7, who had been stabbed by a bayonet in the abdomen four or five times and whom they were not able to save. Again a woman 19 years old who was with child (the first time) 6 months along and who resisted rape. She was jabbed in about 7 places on her face and almost 8 places on her legs, as well as a deep stab of about two inches in the abdomen. It was this that caused her to lose her baby. They will save her. I saw a little girl of 10 who was standing with her mother and father near a dugout in our Refugee Zone watching the Jap. soldiers enter. They killed the parents and gave this girl a horrible stab in the elbow which will cripple her for life. Another woman, employed at the International Export Co. was in a house at Hsiakwan when the soldiers entered. They killed all the others for no reason and gave her a horrible bayonet stab in the neck which they probably though would kill her. The marvel is that she is still living, although Dr. Wilson says she will never use one leg and one arm. (She died later.) Another, a farmer, was marched out with many others and mowed down with machine guns as so many thousands of civilians have been, but was not killed. The doctor said yesterday, however, that he would die.

Dec 23, 12 noon

Yesterday while I was at the house almost next door from Schultz-Pantin's place, a woman from the same group of houses came running and weeping saying that a soldier had just taken $80 from her but I could do nothing about it. Another soldier came into the house where our Christians were who could speak a few words of Chinese. He was evidently of the new division that has been placed in the Refugee Zone. He and the officer who later came in were again looking for soldiers. I told them both that these people were all Sheng Kung Hui and gave the officer my card. They were civil and left.

The great thing this a.m. has been that I've had a bath! It is about 2 weeks since I had a bath at Buck's house where a number of foreign university teachers are living. The weather is not very cold today so I stood and had a thorough bath with two big basins of hot water and have changed my clothes so feel decent again. I also gave Chang Sao-ts (Louise Hammond's fat amah) some clothing to wash. Ernest and I do not dare to leave Hansen's and Stimes' house at the same time as the soldiers keep coming. Then at night we have been sleeping here, I at Hansen's and he at Stimes' house a few doors away where some Christians from St. Paul's Church are living and also the C.T. Chiangs from Puchen in addition to a number of people we have taken in. The women sleep upstairs mostly and the men down stairs, although there are exceptions. Recently I had to bring over a number of the younger Christian women from J.L. Ch'en's congregation as some of his people had been raped and we could not protect them. For a while I slept on the floor, although the first day here (Dec. 12) when the Chinese were retreating I had a fine bed up stairs. We were not so crowded then. The last four nights I have been sleeping on an upholstered settee and so have been reasonably comfortable. Ernest has slept on the floor at No. 17 (Stimes' house) from the beginning. To give you some idea of how crowded we are, in the large down stairs room of the Hansen house with an enclosed porch adjoining, fifty or more people, including children, sleep. One end of the room has been enclosed off by upholstered chairs for J.L. Ch'en's younger women. In the day time bedding is rolled up and put along the sides and it is this room also that is used as a Church for the St. Paul's and Tao Sheng Christians. As I write the people are having their very slim midday meal. While here I've been eating with the Fans. Every day we eat "Hsi Fan" or soft rice as this will make the rice go longer. A great problem is vegetables and meat which are very scarce. The Japanese have stolen almost everything available. Last night we had a treat as a decent Japanese soldier 38 years old from Yokohama who works in a silk shop there frequented by tourists and who knows Mrs. Reifsnider, gave Ernest a piece of beef. We also had a dish of some salt pork which the Fans had brought with them from Hsiakwan when we moved into town, and in addition some cabbage. Over at Schultz-Pantin's when we have a meal (we never eat there together) we fare much better as Ernest's excellent cook is there and also all of our stores (mostly his). The Forsters had a great deal of stuff as their cook put up many jars of fruit and beans last summer. I have had more meals at the other house than has Ernest. The cracked wheat I brought from Tsinan is still holding out and is like the widow's curse.

The Japanese will not allow any foreigners to enter the city so we are shut off from the outside world. We have heard about the sinking of the *Panay*, however, and that Pres. Roosevelt has refused to accept the Japanese apology, demanding a personal apology from the Emperor. We have also heard of the attempted bombing of the British gunboat and possibly of the B. &. S. hulk where Mrs. Sims and so many other foreigners have been living. The news was brought to us through a Dane who lives at Tsih Hsia Shan (just near to Shih Pu Ch'iao) who walked in from the other side of Nanking where the Japs. were evidently not expecting any foreigners and who had therefore given no orders regarding foreigners entering the city from that direction. I hope some more foreigners will learn that method of returning. We need a great many more foreigners as we cannot do all that is required of us in the protecting of the people.

Mary Twinem's house was looted today. She has been for several days helping Minnie Vautrin at Ginling as they have thousands of women over there occupying all their buildings. They are even sleeping on the covered walks between the buildings but it has drizzled today most of the day and I do not know what the people there will do tonight. Ernest who has been going about helping today, tells me that they want to open Hwei Wen to relieve the congestion but cannot do so unless there is a foreigner to stay there on guard and there does not seem anyone available for that.

I've had all three of my meals here with the Fans today. This evening we had with our soft rice, peanuts, salt cabbage, cooked cabbage and another cake of don-fu-lu, or fermented bean curd. Its all right for me to have an occasional foreign meal but hard on the Chinese here who have been here for three weeks on a faulty slim diet. But we are thankful to have what we have.

If the Japanese would only allow some ships to come here with food the situation would be relieved. I think our Refugee Zone Committee only have food for about another week. The Japanese do not want any more foreign eyes to see the result of their cruelty in the many dead bodies still lying about.

Dec. 30

Many days have passed since I last wrote. Things are better than they were but life is still uncertain for the people. Everybody, or rather all men, must register with the government, giving name, age and occupation. There have been immense crowds endeavoring to register but the crowds are so great that all have not been able to do so—even though they rise at 3 a.m. Today they announced that all who have not registered by two tomorrow will be shot! (This proved to be a bluff but it frightened the people.)

Still we have been kept in complete isolation from the rest of the world. I heard that they are giving out that it is still dangerous for foreigners to come here as there are still Chinese soldiers about! The real danger from the Japanese standpoint is that they do not want more foreign eyes to see the dreadful things we have seen. Things are much better now as there is much less raping and robbery although this still continues. The worst division has been taken away from the city but I pity the poor people where it goes as there will be no foreigners to help them.

A few days ago Japanese soldiers went to the U. of Nanking where there were about 4000 men refugees and announced to the people that if the soldiers among them gave themselves up they would give them work but spare their lives. They gave them twenty minutes to think it over and then asked the soldiers to step forward. 200 came forward and they marched them off. On the road they picked up some others who were not soldiers but who they claimed to be such. They were marched off near the Ku Ling An Temple between Hsiakwan and Ginling College and there bayoneted. Can you imagine such perfidy!

All the past ten days fires have been lit all over the city by the Japanese who have been gradually burning down the city, with the exception of the best foreign establishments in Hsiakwan, the P. O. and Customs—when I was last there everything had been burned down. It is only fair to say of Hsiakwan, however, that a good part of it has been burned down by the Chinese. Practically the whole of Taiping Road with the exception of our Church and residences has been burned. Part of the Kungkuan on our property—that part which was used as a preaching hall was burned as well. (Later, on Jan 26th, it was totally burned.) There have been four fires inside the Refugee Zone but unfortunately this part, especially the Shansi Road district, is sparsely populated. Just what the future has in store for Nanking it is hard to say but it certainly will be many years before the city recovers and I think it is possible that it will not again be the capital, at least until China is safe from all molestation from the outside.

Dec. 31

Several days ago someone came to J.L. Ch'en's place while he was away to say that he had seen Ch'en Ch'ang going along with some Japanese soldiers in the direction of the south gate. The family had just about given him up but this has revived hope again. Many of the soldiers have Chinese boys working for them so we are hoping that someday he will return. A few days ago while at the University Hospital I saw a boy 13 or 14 years old who had been brought in covered with blood. The Japanese soldiers had taken him from Ch'angchow and brought him along to work for them. He had been with them for three weeks but said that one day before he was brought to the hospital he complained to them that he had not eaten for two days and wanted to go home. Upon that a soldier beat him with an iron rod and then I think ran a bayonet through his ear.

Such terrible cases continue to be brought to the hospital although most of the injuries were received a week or sometimes two or more weeks ago. The other day I saw an old woman—she looked about seventy but she may have only been in her sixties—who had been shot in the shoulder, the bullet coming out through her back, and again in the neck. She was very lucky as both wounds were clean and were healing up. She was shot for no reason at all, so far as I can find out, except terrorism when the troops entered. The most awful cases are those of men bayoneted or shot who were then set on fire with gasolene. One was of the owner of a small boat at Hsiakwan. His body was scorched black. (This man later died in the hospital.) I think I have said enough of these horrible cases—there are hundreds of thousands of them. Seeing so many of them finally makes the mind dulled so that you almost cease to be shocked any more. I did not imagine that such cruel people existed in the modern world.

Today we are all feeling very sad as we think that Evangelist Lu Hsiao T'ing, who works at Tanshan and Tunglin, has drowned himself. He has been taking a most pessimistic attitude towards the situation since before the Japanese came here and from his conversation with Ernest yesterday and what he has written he has been influenced by the example of some Chinese in history who killed himself in protest against intolerable conditions. It is a decidedly oriental point of view—Ernest told him yesterday that the Christian idea was to live and not to die. He went off very early this morning, long before daylight, leaving a note for Ernest and also a little poem as well as his purse. Ernest had been sleeping in the same house with him. It is very sad indeed as he has shown a very fine spirit and has been so unselfish and helpful during these trying days. Ernest and I have both been impressed by him and I had come to the idea that we ought to recommend him to go to the Theological School. In his letter he said that he did not believe God would hold this act as a sin.

We observed Christmas, first, with a carol service on Christmas Eve—very informal—with prayer, reading of Scripture over here in Hansen's house. About 250 were present, many of them non-Christians. The next day we had Holy Communion and a service here. Dean Tong preaching while I baptized 7 persons at the service at Ta Fang Hsiang for Rev. J.L. Ch'en's Christians. On New Year's Eve we had a very nice service led by Ernest and Dean Tong which Ernest had arranged. The next morning at both places we had Holy Communion for the Christians.

Jan. 3

In both places now we are busy with Bible classes, classes for the preparation of Catechism, etc. Many people in these houses are not Christians and they are very often new to the Gospel.

Jan. 4

I have only recorded in these notes a small number of the terrible things that I have seen and heard. The night before last I left Hansen's house a little before 5 p.m. and went over to a house near here on some business en route to the other house (Schultz-Pantin's) where I was going to have supper. While I was in the street talking to Mr. Sone, a policeman came running to say that a man had been killed. I went with him a short distance to a Chinese house where I found a number of people weeping. It seems that about 4.30 a Japanese soldier had come there and tried to drag a woman into a room to violate her. Her husband helped her so she was able to run through the room and out a back door into an alley to escape. The soldier left and came back within about twenty minutes armed and killed the husband. The woman has five small children and they kept a little noodle shop somewhere in the South City and were simply taking refuge in the Refugee Zone like everybody else. After getting the facts I went back to our Neutral Zone headquarters where I had left my (St. Andrews Hospital) car as one never dares to leave a car outside as Jap. soldiers would steal it. Before I could get into the car a police again came running to say that more soldiers had come back. I ran to the house and found three soldiers there and told them to "Chu-pa" and they went, I following them through the alley to the avenue. Then I took the car and went to the home of Herr Rabe, our Chairman, as I wanted to go to the Japanese Consulate to report this case as they had promised that soldiers would be kept out of the Neutral Zone (at least not to live there) and that things would be better. While waiting at Herr Rabe's gate for the gateman to come neighbors came running saying that a Japanese soldier was threatening them with as sword. It was now dark but George Fitch (who was in a car outside the gate) went in his car and I ran to the place and drove out a lone soldier.

On New Year's Day, Ernest and I were invited to the Buck house where most of the men are living for New Year's dinner. I decided not to accept as I feared to have both of us away from those three houses which we are constantly guarding also I had had Christmas dinner—consisting of a goose in our house and Ernest had not insisted on his going, although he tried to make me go. (He always tries to give me the best of everything.) Later Geo. Fitch persuaded me to go as things were much better and he said he would come for me in a car and later take me back so as to save time. I then decided to go and did. We had a dinner that tasted very good indeed to Ernest and me as we had not had so many delicacies in a long time. Just as we were finishing up Mr. Fan and Paul Tong came hurrying to tell us that two soldiers were in No. 17 after our girls. It took them 20 minutes to come but we shot back in George's car and were just too late to catch the men although we could only have had a look them. One soldier had gone to the 3rd floor but a girl there was very clever and tripped him up and escaped. I think it was she who ran out on a porch and half fell, half slid down a bamboo pole that me [?] in the garden put up for her. Two of our girls were raped. (So they told the nurse at the hospital where I took them.) Mrs. Chen of the Orphanage knelt before a soldier trying to save one girl but was beaten over the head with a bayonet. I do not know how many girls I've taken to the hospital for treatment after such experiences. The vast number never get to the hospital at all. We just took in another young woman today who fled here and knelt outside the gate in the street begging me to save her. The girl was violated last night at 8 p.m. All of us foreigners hear of these cases constantly. Think of the number of cases among the 200,000 or more people in this Zone that we never know about!

Yesterday morning I had a talk with two Chinese from the Texas Oil Co. warehouse (or Installation, I think they call it) outside the Hansimen. They said that there were a great many dead bodies of men, women, and children. Mr. Sindbery, a Dane, said that the same was true outside the Chungshan gate. I myself saw hundreds of dead bodies in Hsiakwan. These men told me of a man whose house had been burned near them by the Japanese so he put his family which contained ten people, in a dugout. He stayed outside himself as he wanted to see when the Japanese were coming so as to warn the children not to cry or speak. The soldiers did come and killed the man and then looked inside. When they saw only women and children they stuffed the mouth full of rice straw and then set it on fire. One woman was clever and wrapped herself and child up in a quilt and rushed through the flames and both were saved. These Texas Oil Co. men said a little girl of ten (Chinese) or nine the way we count, was raped by a soldier there. I said, "Did you hear this, or do you actually know it?" they said they knew it as it happened just near them. Dean Tong, who works in the office of our Neutral Zone Committee and translates many of these reports which are handed in, said he knew of a case of a girl of 12 who was raped by three soldiers. It seems perfectly awful to repeat these ghastly tales but I think a record ought to be kept so that the unvarnished truth will be known.

Jan. 5

Today we started off very early—or at least about 8 a.m. with a great group of girls and women from Hansen's and Stimes' house and also the 2nd Texas Oil Co. residence and picked up quite a crowd here at Schultz-Pantin's house which is filled with women we are protecting. Everybody has to register with the government, the men having practically all done so already. We had a procession of 304 people and went to the University of Nanking to register as we heard that the soldiers were much more decent there than at the other registration place Ginling College. A Mr. Liu, who formerly taught in Tao Sheng School and who is connected in some way with the self-government Committee of Chinese here established by the Japanese, helped to put us through more promptly so we were finished up by about 1 p.m. and got back to the houses at about 2 p.m. I walked along with them and stayed with them the entire time. We called the roll before and after and arranged the women in lines of four asking each one to note that all of her line came back safely. We did this to make sure that all the girls came back as we heard of some nice looking girls being kept behind on a previous day at Ginling, although I have not verified this. The soldiers were for the most part civil but as we came out of the gate near the chapel a petty officer of some kind was coming in. He was a most insolent looking person and for no reason at all that I could see, other than the possible fact that they were coming out when he was going in, roughly slapped the heads or faces of two old women. Then he came to me as I was at the head of our column and said something in a surly way to me which I took to mean, "What are you doing" and I said in Chinese I was escorting these people. Many of the Japanese understand a little Chinese.

For the first time since the Japanese have entered the city I saw Ch'en Tsung-ih at the University today, although I had heard a number of times about him. He said that it would have been impossible to believe that the Japanese could have done such things as have happened unless we had seen them with our own eyes. I agreed. This is the common opinion of us all. I had heard a few things beforehand from Chinese who were frightened and were running away from Nanking before the Japanese came, but I thought they were mere rumours. Now the reality proves to be worse than the rumours.

I heard from Searle Bates today that the army are provoked very much that we foreigners are here and say that no conquering army ever allows neutral observers. This of course is not true, as there were plenty of neutral observers in Belgium during the German occupation. It shows, however, what we have believed from the beginning, that they did not want any of us here and tried to get us all out through our Embassies saying that it was too dangerous. It is amazing that not even Embassy or Consular officials have been allowed to enter the city yet, although the Japanese entered on Dec. 12th. We hear that they have announced that it was dangerous as mopping up of Chinese troops was continuing. As a matter of fact I do not think there has been any resistance since Dec. 12th unless it was in some isolated place. They might well have said that murdering of disarmed soldiers and thousands of innocent civilians has continued ever since they entered. The machine gun at its deadly work is still heard, at least I heard it the day before yesterday (I think it was). We know that in many cases they did not bother to shoot the victims but bayoneted them one by one. A number of people who had been bayoneted and left for dead have returned to report this. I talked to a policeman in the hospital the other day who had been forced by a soldier to go along the street with a woman who was not his wife as the soldier wanted to use her for his purposes but did not dare to drag her along the street and tried to made it appear that she was the wife of the policeman. As it got dark the policeman tried to escape and did escape from that man only to be caught by others who bayoneted him from the rear in 22 places by actual count. It is a marvel that he escaped as he said in two places the bayonet came out the front. They left him for dead. He was finally able to free his hands from the rope that tied them. By slow stages and also by sleeping overnight in a bed in some house on the way he was able to reach the hospital.

I also talked to a Buddhist nun, who lives back of a temple in the south city. When the soldiers came there they killed about 25 people in the immediate environs of this house according to a tailor who brought the nun to the hospital. She told me they killed the "mother superior" aged 65 and a little apprentice nun, aged ten (Chinese). An old nun of seventy was crushed under the weight of bodies on top of her (presumably in the city where this nun took refuge.). She herself was shot in the hip and her little apprentice, aged twelve (Chinese) was bayoneted in the back. They got into a pit where they stayed five days without food or drink, feigning death and lying among a number of dead bodies. Then the nun heard a soldier say in Chinese "How pitiable!" and she opened her eyes and looked at him, asking him to save her. He pulled her out and got some Chinese to carry her to an army dressing station where she was tended to and was brought to the hospital some days later. When I heard about the little apprentice who had been stabbed in the back Mr. McCallum went down in the hospital ambulance and brought the child as there was no one to look after her. Dr. Wilson says he doubts if the nun will recover but if she does she will never use that leg. The child's wound is not very bad. It turned that she had to stay several weeks and is now in our house.

Jan. 11

Yesterday morning Hotz, a Hugarian, who is one of our small group of foreigners in the city (in all we had 20 before the diplomatic people arrived) saw two Japanese push a Chinese whose hands were tied into a pond just off Shansi Road. While standing with the water almost up to his waist they shot him dead. Any last corporal or common soldier seems to be able to determine the fate of the poor Chinese!

The night before last a fine young Chinese who is a student in the Nanking University Middle School and whose father is a merchant in Japan was bound and carried off and we fear for his fate. As the boy can talk Japanese they have been trying to get him to help them. Searle Bates said that they were able to make up some kind of excuse for him (or he made the excuses, I'm not sure which) and they finally came and took him. He later was able to send word to his wife that he was to be shot. His wife was kidnapped on Jan. 29 and carried off in a truck with 20 others and taken to a house in the south city for the use of officers but escaped by making herself vomit.

Yesterday in the hospital I saw a woman who had been stabbed in a number of places and her head almost severed. She had been taken with four other women from the University of Nanking by Japanese who said they needed to have some women wash for them and serve them. According to this woman's story, the younger and prettier of them had been raped about forty times at night after washing clothes in the day time. She herself and the others had worked in the day and then were raped ten or twenty times at night. One day two soldiers told her to follow them and they took her to an empty house and there tried to cut off her head. She has a perfectly horrible cut in her neck and the marvel is that she is alive. Fortunately no vital part was cut. She said some of the men were officers.

Some of the American Embassy staff arrived some days ago and now the Germans and British are here. It means a great deal to us all to have them here as they have brought letters to us and taken letters and messages for us. They have all of them been fired upon in the river but only the USS *Panay* was hit.

I have by no means written down all the terrible things I have seen and heard and have only put down some of the things I have heard at first hand or that I was convinced were true. I do not want to paint a picture of unmitigated blackness as it only fair to say that some kind deeds have been done by Japanese soldiers. For instance, I saw a woman yesterday who had been hit by Japanese machine guns from the air outside the city before the fall of Nanking and had one eye knocked cut and wounded in various places. She had a number of children but had to leave a three months old baby outside the city to save the others. When some Japanese soldiers found her they helped her. Also some soldiers who had taken our gardener for labor a few days ago had paid him 50 cents for a day's work and also gave him good food to eat. The people in the Japanese Embassy with the exception of one of the Consular Police who has proved a most disagreeable person, have tried to be of service and are ashamed of the terrible things the soldiers have done and have tried to protect foreign property. I do not believe they know how many terrible things have been done as we came to the conclusion that we had told them enough and that continuing to make reports and complaints would hinder rather than help.

The military hate us foreigners in the extreme, although there are no doubt exceptions. They are trying to put our International Refugee Zone Committee out of business and get control of the food, oil and funds in our hands. We are glad to give over into the hands of the Chinese Self-Government Committee such official functions as we have assumed at the request at Mayor Ma. But we have flatly refused to give up our supplies of food, money, etc. as we say that these were given to us to administer and we propose to continue as help will be needed for a long time to come. The whole life of the city has been disarranged and a great many of the people will have to be helped until industries and business begin again even on a much reduced scale.

I have heard from doctors and nurses in the International Red Cross Hospital for wounded soldiers at the Ministry of Foreign affairs that they have been protected, both men and women, although none of us foreigners have been allowed to enter since Dec 14th when I took three truck loads of wounded soldiers there.

It was at the entrance as I was attempting to come out that I met the commanding officer in the city up to that time who was so extremely angry with me. I do not remember ever to have had anyone in my life-time so angry with me. I thought at the time that the reason was that he thought I had disobeyed his orders after going to his headquarters but later I have thought that it may have been because a foreigner had been to these hospitals and had claimed that they were being run under the auspices of the International Red Cross which made it impossible, or at least difficult for him to do other than protect them. There is no question what the type of soldiers that first came in would have done if they had had a chance, although I met a very civil colonel who spoke English when I first went there and it was through him that I was able to go to the headquarters. I think that it is probable that our efforts saved the lives of some hundreds of wounded men as well as many of the doctors and nurses there. The women have not been molested which is remarkable and shows that the Japanese army people can control their men when they want to. (Later a soldier did try to get into the women's rooms but was frustrated by a ruse.) In the issue of the Japanese paper published in Shanghai it was said (I think on Dec. 17 although it might have been later) that the Chinese soldiers there were so grateful to the Japanese for their merciful care that when one soldier was asked whether he wanted to be a soldier again he replied. "If I should be a soldier again I must fight for the Japanese!" (Later we learned that a Chinese soldier had been killed by bayonet, the favorite method—for losing his temper on having his rice spilled.) I think an exemplary treatment of these wounded is deliberately planned for propaganda purposes in order to offset the unspeakable cruelty that has been the general rule. The doctors and nurses there have not realized what terrible things were happening outside. The Japanese have sent some rice although most of this has been supplied by funds in our hands. We have a committee of about ten persons of various nationalities for the International Red Cross here of which I am Chairman. We have not been able to do much actually, except to use funds that have been put in our hands but I think that our organization has been of very great use because of the protection that we have been able to give. Whatever the motives the Japanese have had for protecting these wounded soldiers and doctors, etc. I am glad that it has been actually done and thank God.

Jan. 30th

This evening Ernest and I had a China New Year's dinner with our people at Hansen's house at 4.30 p.m., they having invited us to eat with them. They have two meals per day, 9 a.m. and 4 p.m. Today in addition to "dry" rice they had six bowls of "Tsai" which was a big treat for them as they get pretty slim food. Ernest preached there and I preached for J.L. Ch'en's Christians almost next door. Also I attended a little service at 2 p.m. J. L. Ch'en had arranged for the refugees living with us in Schultz-Pantin's house. Some nuns and a young apprentice monk attended also. Then at 4 p.m. he had Evening Prayer for his own people. He announced an Evangelistic Meeting on Wednesday for the refugees. There are many such meetings being held at Ginling College also at the University of Nanking as well as at our houses and at the Bible Teachers Training School where Pastor Shen of the Central Methodist Church holds services. Our staff has had a considerable share in this work, not only for our people and the refugees in our houses but also for Ginling and the U. of Nanking.

This past week I saw the most terrible sight and heard the most awful story, the truth of which there can be no doubt in its main features as I got it direct from the neighbors and from a little eight year old girl who was in the house when these things happened. Japanese soldiers came to a house in the south eastern part of the city when they first entered the city. They killed all the people in the house, thirteen in all, except two children aged eight and three or four respectively, the eight year old with whom I checked the story of her uncle and an old woman neighbor. This little girl was bayonetted in the back and side but was not killed. The dead included an old man 76 and old woman 74, a mother and three daughters, aged 16,14 and 1. Both girls were raped about three times each and then they were all killed in the most horrible fashion, although the younger was only stabbed with a bayonet and not treated like the other two in an unspeakable way. I have heard of four such horrible cases happening in Nanking, the secretary of the German Embassy telling of one woman having had a golf stick rammed into her body. He said, "It is the Japanese technique." I took a picture of the dead bodies, the mother lying with her one year old child. The little girl said one of the landlord's children, aged one (not the one mentioned as with her mother) had his head split in two by a Japanese sword. The eight year old girl after being wounded crawled to the body of her mother in another room and stayed there with her little sister for fourteen days living on puffed rice and the rice crust left in the cooking pan the Chinese call "Go-ba" and water from the well. Everybody had fled from this area to the safety zone established by the foreigners but they were rescued by an old woman neighbor when she came back fourteen days later. Japanese soldiers kept coming in and then the children hid under some old sheets.

We had a meeting of our Safety Zone Committee yesterday to deal with a new crisis. The Japanese have notified the German Embassy (they ignore us now but our chairman, Rabe, is a German) that the people must be all moved back to their homes by Feb. 4th or they would be compelled to do so. This in spite of the fact that so large a part of the city has been burned and consequently the homes of thousands are no more. They say that for such they will establish camp. This in spite of the fact that we have 25 camps where there are 58,000 people in addition to all the houses in the Safety Zone being occupied. Their real object is to get these people away from foreign property and away from us who have been their protection during these terrible weeks. It will mean constant raping for the women and probably many murders, so we are going to do our best to fight against this. Just today (or possibly yesterday) the young widow of a student at the Middle School who would not help the Japanese and who was carried off and murdered, went down near the Ming Teh School (outside the Safety Zone) to do a little buying of something thinking that things were safer now. A truck stopped and carried her off with twenty other women to the south city where she was taken to a house where are Japanese officers—to be used by them, of course, for their own foul purposes. A Chinese man who had been taken there to act as a servant said the only way for her to escape was for her to make herself vomit and mess up the place so that they would think she was dirty and kick her out. She succeeded in doing this and they did drive her out and she was able to get back to tell the tale. You can imagine how this makes us feel when they say the people are to be driven out. We shall certainly stand up to them if they try to take women off foreign property but they may retaliate by allowing no food to come in. The Japanese seem to be a people without sexual morality. A country where it is looked upon as filial piety when a girl will be become a prostitute for several years for the sake of helping her parents financially and who can then marry, certainly has a special code of its own. These people that we have to deal with don't see the enormity of rape at all. A Japanese Consular police whose duty seems to be to spy on us foreigners and who comes into our houses all the time went out a week ago to the University Middle School and said he wanted five women to wash clothes. The people there picked out five older women and he said, "These won't do; they must be young and pretty" and they said, "But the older women are more experienced in washing." Later when Mr. Allison reported this to the Japanese Embassy, he denied it and demanded to know the name of the Chinese who reported this. Of course we do not report our informants as they would either be killed or beaten. This same man came (on that same day, I think) to the house where we live while we were at lunch and began to talk with Cola in Japanese as Cola understands it. He knew we had a lot of women and wanted to know if he could get any girls!

Feb. 1

Ernest has just come in (now 12:25) to say that some Japanese Military Police had just taken a Chinese girl, who was walking with her sister on Ninghai Road, into the military post at the foot of Shansi Road presumably for the usual reason. It is just a few doors from our Neutral Zone Headquarters so Lewis Smythe went in there (later, Cola went to translate) and the girl could not be found in the Police Station and her sister said she did not know into which house she had been taken. It was unfortunate from our standpoint since we had called people from the Japanese Embassy and then could not find the girl in the house where they thought she was. The girl was taken but her sister did not know into which house they had taken her. When the party went into the Post they found a number of drunken soldiers.

Only yesterday I was able to keep the drunken soldiers from our two houses (Hansen's and Herr Stimes'). They were civil enough and readily went away but came back to Herr Stimes' house after I had left and made motions to the gateman that they wanted girls. I kept one of them from going up stairs to the women's quarters and very shortly afterwards drove out two other soldiers from No. 21 Loh Chia Road next door to one of the houses we are protecting. One soldier had gone up to the third story but readily left when I began pounding and shouting on a door on the second floor where I thought he was.

About nine days ago Ernest went to see the corpse of a girl who had been shot dead by a Japanese soldier near Herr Stimes' house. She was picking turnip or some vegetable in a field when the soldier called to her. She ran, as most Chinese women in Nanking would have done, and he shot her.

February 2

For some reason we have again had a great many cases of complaints about rape—it is not the complaints that are strange, but the increased number of cases. Perhaps we have had a worse lot of soldiers come in than we had had, although there is not much to choose among them. Just yesterday after lunch when Ernest and I were hurrying to get off letters to go down on the U.S.S. *Oahu*, a young boy came running to tell us that soldiers had come to his house for girls. It was little more than a stone's throw away and we ran there and were let in by the occupants, who pointed to a bedroom, and we knocked on this door shouting "Open the door" and when there was no response we broke in the door and found two soldiers on a bed with young girl of fifteen years (as we later learned). They had finished their foul business unfortunately but we shouted in great anger for them to get out. They both jumped. One was quite drunk and was slow about getting away but the other one grabbed for his revolver and belt (the other was not armed) and for a moment I wondered whether he would use it on us, but he made off at top speed. The other one staggered out and we pushed him through a hole in the wooden partition as neither one was willing to go through the front door which was very public. We were pretty rough, Ernest pushing his shoulders and I grabbing his feet, and dumped him head foremost through the hole. Afterwards I thought that we did not do the best thing to be so rough as the man was so drunk. He tried to shake hands with us but we would have none of this, Ernest running ahead to find a Military Police while I followed the man, pushing him forward when he tried to turn back. When he got out to where the Chinese were looking on he began to show fight but was too drunk to do anything. It was good that he was, as he was a powerfully built man. We delivered him to a sentry and I tried to indicate to the sentry by writing Chinese characters with my hand that this man had taken a woman. The father told us today that his young daughter had been raped five times, the first by two men on January 14th, the next by one man on about January 22nd, and then again by these two yesterday. It was only the day before I prevented a drunken soldier from going up the stairs to the women's quarters in the house where our Hsiakwan Christians are living. This man was drunk also but easily handled.

Ernest learned today from a member of the Self-Government Committee (the body set up by the Japanese to attempt to govern the city) that today in the morning a truck–load of armed soldiers came to their Headquarters and demanded at least 13 girls or as many more as they could find. The Chinese tried to stall them off but they surrounded the place and were still there this afternoon. The Committee did succeeded in finding two prostitutes but these were not enough. What the eventual result was I do not know.

The Japanese authorities have announced that the Chinese must leave the Safety Zone by February 4th and go back to their houses in spite of the fact that a large part of the city has been burnt. Those who have no homes they propose to put in camps but why not let them remain in the centers that we have arranged? We are greatly troubled at the prospect for it will mean constant molestation, rape and robbery and possibly murder. We are asking for time through the German embassy. The real reason, or at least one reason they want them to leave, is that we foreigners constantly hear of the complaints and have been able to protect them here.

The root trouble so far as rape is concerned is that the Japanese do not look with any horror upon it. The army commanders have made no real effort to stamp it out. If they had shot a few soldiers the thing would have possibly stopped—I really do not believe so, as it is evident that the army as a whole does not look upon this as a crime, or it is a heinous thing at most. I thought yesterday after we had been so rough with the drunken soldier, we cannot blame him as we might an American soldier in the same situation. The chief crime about rape in their eyes, so far as I can see, is to be found out and to have the news get out to foreign papers.

There is no doubt but that they hate us Americans thoroughly. Today Cola and Ziall, a Tatar mechanic who also lives with us, were walking on Taiping Road and when some Japanese soldiers were passing one of them looked at them and said with a scowl, "Americans?" and Cola who speaks Japanese, replied, "No, Russians" and they walked on with some comment.

February 5

Yesterday and the day before I examined about thirty people men, women and children, for being admitted Catechumens. Some of them had not wanted to enter the church, e.g. Mrs. T'ung whose husband is a communicant and whose son was killed in December by the Japanese, shot down near the house when he went to try to find some fuel. The dangers of the present situation and the reality of the work of the Church and the faith of Christians have moved many. I admitted these people today as Catechumens while Rev. J.L. Ch'en preached. In the congregation was one of the Buddhist nuns who have been taking refuge in this house where Ernest Forster and I are living. Every Sunday afternoon J.L. Ch'en has two services of Evening Prayer, one for these non-Christian women, including three Buddhist nuns and others from the temple across the street included among them, and the next service for our own people. The downstairs room which they use for the services is so small that all these people would not be able to worship at the same time. We have certainly had an opportunity to witness to the spirit of Christianity—by we, meaning all the missionaries and some of the business people who had remained. Several weeks ago a Mr. Ma who is one of the Volunteer secretaries working for our International Refugee Zone Committee, and who is a Mohammedan, told a number of people at a dinner given by Mr. Lowe (Chinese) the manager of the Metropolitan Hotel, that in spite of his grandfather being the chief Ahung of the Mohammedan in Shanghai, he thought that Christianity was the religion best suited to modern times. He had been impressed by what we had all been trying to do.

Many of the people who had attempted to go home are now coming back because the rape, robbery and outrage continue. A woman and her daughter and her daughter's husband came here today and begged Ernest and me on their knees to allow the girl to stay there as they had gone home and a soldier tried to get the girl last night and threatened to stab her husband. They escaped in the night, I think. There have been more than a hundred complaints during the past few days. Just today as I was taking a Mrs. Hwang, a refugee at Hansen's house, to the hospital, people stopped me on the street and told me of two soldiers getting in over the wall on the next street last night and robbing the people in one house of about $27.30 and a ring, while a family next door was robbed of $5.00. If such things happen in our Safety Zone where there are a few foreigners to help, what will be the result if they go far off from the Zone?

Today Herr Rosen, secretary of the German Embassy, said that the General who had been sent here to create order gave a dinner last night to the American, British and German Embassy secretaries. He made a speech which he read and which was translated by Mr. Fukuda, secretary of the Embassy, from a manuscript also. The speech was to the effect that the Japanese army[2]

John Magee

***

Report of a Trip to Tsih Hsia Shan (February 16–17, 1938)[3]

Refugees

At present there are 10,000 refugees in the camps inside the grounds of the Tsih Hsia Shan Cement works under the supervision of Dr. Gunter and Mr. Simberg. The numbers there are increasing at the present time and new huts were being built as I walked through the camp. Most of the huts are built of rice straw while there were a few larger mat sheds. The camp is managed by a number of head men working under the foreigners.

A priest at the temple, which has also been housing refugees, told me that at one time they had 20,000 refugees there but that now they only had something over 10,000. Apparently some of those in the temple had moved to Cement Works camp as the number at the camp there was increasing in size while that at the temple was decreasing.

On the evening of February 16th, I met with the head men of the Cement Works camp, possibly 25 in all, when I had the opportunity of hearing them talk and also of asking them questions. I will give here a report of this conference as well as what I saw myself in the dispensary and also on my drives with Mr. Simberg through the countryside.

Outrages

One representative said that in a square of between 10 and 20 *li* each way he calculated that from 700 to 800 of the civilian population had been killed. This estimate seemed to be agreed to by the others. Let us call this, then, five miles square or 25 square miles. They said the cases of rape of women between 30 and 40 years old were too numerous to give an estimate while cases were known of girls about ten years old being raped.

These outrages are still happening. They said that soldiers had come to Shih Pu Ch'iao, a town less than a mile from the railway station at Tsih Hsia Shan, on Feb. 15th and demanded some girls from some old people who had returned. When this couple said there were none the soldiers burnt down their house. When I asked the head men when they would be returning to their homes they said they were afraid to do so since the Japanese would come and demand either girls or food (especially the former) and when these were not forthcoming their homes would be destroyed or they would suffer some other injury.

Another man reported that at his village, Hwa Shu Ts'uen, about five miles from the camp, soldiers had come on Feb. 15th and killed 7 people and wounded another. These villagers had recently been vaccinated and the soldiers avowed that the marks were bullet wounds and that therefore they were soldiers.

In the dispensary on Feb. 17th I saw a farmer who had been shot in the hand on Feb. 15th by two soldiers who had demanded that he produce some girls. It was a most painful wound.

A child was brought to the dispensary while I was there who had been horribly burnt when Japanese soldiers set fire to the house in which it was living. As the father had fled at their approach the soldiers asked this child of three where its "ma-ma" was and when he made no satisfactory answer they set fire to the house. A neighbor rescued him. The mother was already living in the camp.

I also talked to a young farmer in the dispensary who had been badly burnt in the upper part of his body when soldiers threw kerosene oil on him and set him afire. They had demanded money from him but he had told them that he was a poor farmer and had no money. This happened in the outskirts of Nanking on Feb. 9th.

Cases are also being brought into the dispensary in which the injury has been caused by bandits. While I was there a woman of 49 years was carried in who had been injured on February 14th. Bandits had come in the night demanding money. When she and her husband said they had none they battered her head and breast with a stool and burnt her feet until she disclosed their saving of between four and five dollars.

Burning of homes

These head men estimated that along the main highway from Taiping Gate to Lungtan, a distance of between ten and twelve miles, about 80% of the houses had been burnt down while they thought that about 40–50% of the houses on the small roads away from the main highways had been destroyed. From my own trips about the country I should say that these estimates were about right.

Food

They thought that the comparatively few more well-to-do families living in the camp had food to last for four months more but that the great majority had food only for one month. Dr. Gunter told me that up to the present the refugees had been providing their own food.

Buffaloes

They said that only about 10% of the water buffaloes were left in the area running from Taiping Gate to Lungtan—T'angshan—Nanking. One place hidden away in the hills had pretty well escaped. I myself noticed a few buffalo in the camp, and I also saw three at a village near to Tsih Hsia Shan that had, I think, been kept at the camp and had only recently been taken home.

In reply to my question as to what crop they might be able to produce without oxen and with human labor alone they said they would only be able to produce 1/3 of a normal yield.

They estimated that in an area from Taiping Gate to Lungtan to Chi-Ling Men and back to Nanking they would need 3,000 oxen to bring about normal conditions. In reply to my question they said that if the banks could advance money to establish cooperatives for buying oxen they could repay the loan in three years.

Seed

They reported very little seed on hand and went on to say that even if they had seed the farmers would not dare to go back to their farms in any large numbers in present circumstances.

In my drives with Mr. Simberg over the countryside as well as on the road between Tsih Hsia Shan and Nanking I saw a few people on the roads apparently going back to their farms. They seemed to be particularly noticeable near to Tsih Hsia Shan the camp at night. One woman casting manure on her fields as though nothing had happened stands out in my memory as women were so rare. In one village I saw three men, two women and some children starting to rebuild their home, the substantial stone walls of which were still standing.

Medical work

Dr. Gunter and Mr. Simberg have opened a small hospital and dispensary in one of the buildings belonging to the Cement Works, helped by several gifts of medicines, bandages, etc. from the University Hospital. Six or more in-patients were being cared for while there were 24 dispensary cases the morning I was there. Some lives have been saved in spite of the total lack of trained medical staff at the beginning. At present there is one graduate nurse with two women and one man dresser who have had very little training. Cases were there needing an operation and it is unquestionably true that more lives would be saved if they had a more adequate staff. While I was at Tsih Hsia Shan the foreigners had a conference with three old-fashioned Chinese doctors who agreed to start work in the camp tending to cases needing internal medicine. Dr. Gunter's idea was that the farmers would probably prefer Chinese medicine and there was also the fact they had no doctor at the dispensary to attend to internal diseases. These Chinese doctors were going to make up a list of the medicines they would need. The plan is to have them start work in another part of the camp so as not to interfere with the work at the dispensary.

There can be no question of the need in this place. If a doctor could attend, even once a week, a great deal of suffering could be relieved and many lives would be saved. In the substantial buildings belonging to the Cement Works an operating room could be easily set up. Once there were proper facilities for medical and surgical work the news would spread over the countryside and the numbers of patients would greatly increase.

A letter to J. C. Mckim[4]

As from 99 D. Jessfield Road
Shanghai
April 2nd, 1938

The Rev. J. C. McKim
c/o Dr. John W. Wood
281 Fourth Avenue
New York City

Dear Mr. McKim:
It has been brought to my attention that you have been writing letters to the *Times* saying that the stories of Japanese atrocities in Nanking were false. Perhaps by this time you will have learned that they were too true. If I had not seen with my own eyes the things that I have seen I could not have believed that such

things could have happened in the modern world. It reminded one of an ancient Assyrian rape. We were not expecting such horrors and it was a terrible shock to us all when they began to happen.

The head of the Chinese Benevolent Association that has done the major part of the burying told me that between January 23rd, when they began work, to March 19th, they had burned 32104 bodies and that they estimated that a similar number remained yet to be buried. Some other organizations did some burying as well, while many were buried by friends and relatives. For instance, the caretaker of our Church Cemetery about a mile outside one of the gates, told me that between 2000 and 3000 people had been killed outside that gate and that they had been buried by the local people. (I might say that his own wife had been shot out there only a few weeks ago by a Japanese soldier. The bullet has now been extracted and she has left the hospital.) It will be a long time before we know how many of our own people, including catechumens and inquirers, have been killed, as so many fled to the country and the more well-to-do moved further into the interior. On December 16th 14 men were taken from a place in the Refugee Zone where we were caring for two poor congregations. The group carried off at that time included at least two boys, one of whom was the son of the Chinese priest, a boy of 16 (Chinese reckoning or 14–15 years old). One of this group escaped miraculously when the rest were being mowed down by machine guns on the bank of the river. He fell over with the others, feigning death although not hurt, and covered himself with the bodies of those about him. In the darkness he was able to escape and came back to tell us of what had happened. Later on I saw hundreds of bodies piled up on the river bank. Another member of that congregation volunteered to try to get some fuel and was shot in the streets not far away. His father was one of a group in a Bible class which the priest was holding several weeks later when a Japanese soldier came in. The whole group arose and this Mr. T'ung opened his Bible to show him what they were studying. The soldier picked up a long heavy brass pipe lying near at hand and hit this Mr. T'ung a vicious blow on the head. Some one ran to me as I was [with] a refugee in a German friend's house near at hand. When I arrived I found T'ung with his face covered with blood and blood on the floor and took him to the hospital. I went another time to a house where 11 people had been killed, all of them women and children except three men, one of whom was a 76 year old man. Of the children I remember that one was less than a year old. Only one person was spared, a child of five (Chinese count) while a girl of nine was bayoneted in the back and side but recovered. This child's mother was raped and then had a bottle rammed up her vagina. Two daughters of this woman, aged 14 and 16, were stripped, raped several times apiece and then killed, the older girl having a stick rammed up into [her] in the same barbarous manner as the mother had been treated. Before they were killed their grandparents, aged 76 and 74, who had tried to protect them, had been shot dead. If this awful tragedy had been an isolated event one might say that it was the work of sadists but there have been many authentic stories of such horrors, although this was the worst tragedy that I have personally been brought into contact with. I took another little girl of fifteen years to the hospital who told me her story. Her older brother, brother's wife, older sister and father and mother were all killed with the bayonet before her face and then she was carried off to some barracks where there were some 200 to 300 soldiers. She was kept in a room and her clothes taken away and there raped a number of times daily for about a month and a half when she took sick and they were afraid to use her. She told me that there were a number of other girls held there in the same way as herself. I have talked to an old lady of 76 who was raped twice. Her daughter, a widow was rapped between 18 and 19 times, she is not sure which. This is the oldest case I personally know about but a Bible woman told me of a woman of 81 with whom she was living and who was told to open her clothes. She said she was too old and the man shot her dead. I have taken carload after carload of women in our Mission Ford to the hospital to be treated after rape, the youngest being a girl of ten or eleven years. Mr. Forster, my fellow-priest here, and myself spent much of our time guarding two houses, in fact more than that, where our people were living. In the daytime during the worst period one or the other of us stood in the street where we could watch several houses and we would then run to one house or the other when soldiers were attempting to get in. On New Years Day when things seemed to be a little quieter we thought we would both accept an invitation to dinner and left for a brief period. We had just finished dinner when two of our men came running to say that Japanese soldiers were after our girls, so we hurried back in a car only to find that two girls had been raped. Another girl had escaped by a ruse, and an elderly woman who had knelt and begged that the girl might be spared had been beaten over the head by a bayonet. I could go on for many pages telling you of such things as these but I think I have written enough to let you know that the stories of atrocities were not exaggerated. Things have greatly improved but murder and rape still continue, only on a smaller scale here in Nanking.

When you said, I understand you wrote to the *Times*, that these outrages were not perpetrated by Japanese but by Chinese soldiers, you were misinformed so far as Nanking was concerned. There was a small amount of looting of some shops by Chinese just before the Japanese entered. It is true that the homes of many people immediately outside the city walls were burnt down by the soldiers for defensive purposes, and this was certainly an outrage, but it was done with the mistaken idea that it would help in the defense of the city which did not prove to be the case. It is true that Chang Hsueh Liang's troops which showed up so miserably in the fighting looted between here and Shanghai but they were executed by the hundreds. It is certainly unjust to have publicly accused the Chinese of such horrible things that happened here. I think I have written enough to let you know what horrors have happened. If you want to know further you could ask Dr. John W. Wood to let you see a copy of a kind of diary letter that I wrote to my wife.

The only reason why I am writing this letter is that I believe that all friends of Japan should know the truth. It is the part of real friendship for the Japanese to let them know what is actually happening in China. I believe that a great many people in Japan would be horrified if they knew what was happening over wide areas of this land, just as we who have seen it have been, and their horror might be used to break the power of the military in Japan which has been the real cause of this conflict.

I hope you will in the cause of justice and truth correct any misinformation you may unknowingly given to the papers. I would ask you also to be careful about using my name in any publicity. I do not fear the personal consequences but rather that I might be run out of the city or that the relief work that we foreigners here have been carrying on for the benefit of the people of the city might be further curtailed than it has been. If we had not been here and established the Safety Zone and all of us been busy trying to protect the people the tragedy would have been worse as every Chinese in the city knows.

I have visited Japan a number of times and once had the pleasure of living with my family alongside of your sister at Mayabashi. It is a beautiful country and I thought the people charming. How to reconcile the Japan that I have seen and the savagery that I have seen here is a problem that I have not solved yet.

Sincerely yours,

***

Introduction of Magee's Film[5]

The pictures shown herewith give but a fragmentary glimpse of the unspeakable things that happened following the Japanese occupation of Nanking on December 13, 1937. If the photographer had had more film and more time, he could have taken a great many more scenes. He, like many others, was kept busy from morning till night trying to protect and help the people of the city in various ways. And it was only occasionally that he had time for picture-taking. Moreover, great care had to be exercised not to be seen so as not to have his camera smashed or confiscated. It was for this reason that he could not take pictures of people being killed or of the vast numbers of dead lying about in many parts of the city. If he had been able to stay in the Mission Hospital Dispensary and to take all the cases of outrage and injury brought there for treatment, the film would have been much longer. He remembers especially an old woman of 70 who had been shot through the shoulder, the bullet coming out through the back. By good fortune it had not touched a vital spot, and was a clean wound healing readily. One must remember also that of the thousands injured only a small percentage got to the hospital or was heard about. Thousands and tens of thousands in the countryside and small towns and cities were outraged and done to death where there were no foreign eyes to see, but of which occasionally authentic word was received.

It seemed to be the attitude of the Japanese officers and men that it was all right to do anything to the Chinese as they were enemies. Rape was lightly looked upon by army authorities, and seemed to be wrong only because of the impression it made on foreign public opinion or because of pressure from above.

It is fair to say that many Japanese admitted that their soldiers, in part, were very bad. Two newspaper correspondents acknowledged this to the photographer, one of them saying that it was "inevitable," that such things should have happened. A Consul-General who acknowledged the lack of discipline, used the same word. What a comment on the Japanese Army!

War brings out the worst in people of every land, and it is of course true that all countries have the criminal and the sadist who has a chance to exercise his worst instincts in war. Perhaps the widespread cruelty and the bloodthirstiness manifested by the Japanese soldiers was the inevitable result in a country which approves of such a horrible custom as hari-kiri and which gives its children such blood-thirsty stories as most Japanese children read.

These pictures have been taken with no thought of stirring up a spirit of revenge against the Japanese, but with a desire to make all people, Japanese included, realize how horrible this war has been and to determine that every legitimate means should be used to stop this conflict manufactured by the Japanese military.

The photographer has often been to Japan and knows how beautiful that country is, and that many noble people are to be found there. If the people of Japan could really know how the war was made, and how it has been conducted, a vast number of them would be horrified.

Film 1

This consists mostly of Japanese air-raids on Nanking during September and October 1937. Either the end of this film or the beginning of Film 2 shows Chinese Christians at an open air service in one of the places where they are taking refuge, December 19, 1937.

Film 2

1. Japanese bombers flying over Nanking several days after the occupation of the city by Japanese troops.
2. December 16, 1937. Chinese women on Shanghai Road, Nanking, kneeling and begging Japanese soldiers for the lives of their sons and husbands when these were collected at random on the suspicion of being ex-soldiers. Thousands of civilians were taken in this way, bound with ropes, carried to the river bank in Hsiakwan, to the edges of ponds, and to vacant spaces where they were done to death by machine-guns, bayonets, rifles, and even hand grenades.
3. This man, Liu, Kwang-wei, an Inquirer in the Chinese Episcopal Church at Ssu Shou Ts'un, the model village at Hsiakwan, came into the Refugee Zone with fellow-Christians before the occupation of the city by the Japanese. On Dec. 16, he was carried off by Japanese soldiers with thirteen others of this Christian group. They were joined to another group of 1000 men (according to his estimate), taken to the river bank at Hsiakwan, arranged in orderly lines near the Japanese wharf and mowed down with machine-guns. It was dusk but there was no chance to escape, as the river was behind them and they were surrounded on three sides by machine guns. This man was in the back immediately next to the water. When the lines of men began to fall he fell with them although uninjured. He dropped into shallow water and covered himself with the corpses of those about him. There he staid for three hours, and was so cold when he came out that he could hardly walk. But he was able to make his way to a deserted hut where he found some bedding. Here he took off his wet clothing and drapped himself in the bedding, staying there for three days without food. He finally became so hungry that he left the hut to find something to eat, putting on his clothing which was still damp. He went to the China Import and Export Lumber Company, a British concern in which he had been employed, but found nobody there. Just then he met three Japanese soldiers who struck him with their fists, led him off to Paohsing Street Hsiakwan where they made him cook for them. After several days he was released, being given a note signed with the seal of two of the Japanese soldiers. This enabled him to get through the city gate and back to his family in the Refugee Zone.
4. This nineteen year old woman was a refugee at the American School in the Refugee Zone. She was six and one-half months pregnant with her first child. She resisted rape and was therefore stabbed many times by a Japanese soldier. She has nineteen cuts on her face, eight on her legs,

and a cut two inches deep in her abdomen. This caused a miscarriage the day after her entrance into the University Hospital. She recovered from her wounds.

5. All the other members of the immediate family of this young woman except her husband, who was fortunately absent, were killed when Japanese soldiers entered her house at Hsiakwan. She was employed in the International Export Co., a British packing plant. She herself had this horrible wound from a bayonet which affected her spinal column and caused her death through Meningitis. No resistance had been offered to the soldiers.

6. This girl, of about 11 years of age, was standing with her parents near a dug-out in the refugee Zone as the Japanese entered. The soldiers killed her father with a bayonet, her mother with a rifle-shot, and gave the girl this horrible slash in the elbow with a bayonet. She will recover but will always have a crippled arm.

7. This is the corpse of a boy about seven years old who died three days after his admission into the University Hospital (a Mission institution). He had received five bayonet wounds in the abdomen, one of them perforating the stomach.

8. This man had been employed in a Chinese hotel. He is the sole survivor, so far as he knows, of a group of eighty men who were taken from houses in the Refugee Zone and led to hills west of the Zone where they were shot down with rifles. He himself received wounds in the neck, cheek, and arm, but will recover. He escaped by feigning death, and eventually made his way to the Mission Hospital.

9. This man was shot through the chest by Japanese soldiers because he could not understand what they wanted. He is a farmer. There are many such cases in the Mission Hospital.

Film 3

1. This is the corpse of a man who had been taken from the Sericulture building of the University of Nanking, with about seventy others. They were all sprayed with rifle fire and some were bayoneted. Then all the bodies were covered with gasoline and set afire. This man had received two bayonet wounds. In spite of being frightfully burned about the face and head he was able to make his way to the Mission hospital where he died after twenty hours.

2. Here is the picture of a clerk in an enamel-ware shop. A Japanese soldier asked him for some cigarettes, but when the clerk could not produce any, the soldier hit him a terrible blow over the head with a bayo-

net, making a gaping hole in his skull behind the ear. The picture was taken six days after he had entered the Mission hospital. The pulsation of the brain can be clearly seen, and a considerable amount of brain had already oozed out causing a complete paralysis of the right side of his body but not impairing his consciousness. He lived for about ten days after entering the hospital.

3. This stretcher-bearer was taken to the riverbank with about 4000 others (according to his estimate) and there machine-gunned. He, with about twenty others, escaped death. He had received only a wound in the shoulder.

4. This man owned a small sampan on the Yangtse River. He was shot through the jaw by a Japanese soldier, then soaked in gasoline and set afire. The upper and lower parts of his body were horribly burned and quite black. He died after two days in the Mission hospital.

5. This man had been a Chinese soldier but was entirely unarmed when captured by the Japanese. He has two bayonet wounds in the head and one through the trachea. He was left for dead, but he was recovered after treatment in the Mission hospital.

6. This boy was taken by Japanese troops when they came through Changchow, although he himself was a refugee there from Woosung. He is between 13–14 years old, and had been with the troops for about three weeks working for them. On Dec. 16, as he had not had any food for two days, he told the soldiers whom he was serving that he wished to go home. They beat him with an iron bar and bayoneted him in the head. The picture was taken just after he had been brought into the dispensary, covered with blood. He has recovered.

7. This man's home was inside the South Gate. When the soldiers came on Dec. 13th, they killed both his brothers and bayoneted him in the chest. He was not brought to the hospital till December 27. The picture was taken in the Dispensary. He had a rattle in his chest and is probably dead now.

8. This woman was living with her husband, an old father, and their little five-year old child inside the Kwang Hwa Gate. When the Japanese entered the city they came to their house and demanded food. They called to the woman and her husband to come out. When he did so they bayoneted him. She was then afraid to come out, so a soldier went into the room and shot her through the arm, the bullet killing the little child accidentally.

9. Mrs. Wu lives behind the Ch'en Hwang Temple, Nanking, with six members of her family. On Dec. 18, four Japanese soldiers came to her home, killed her father who was more than sixty years old and her

brother's child, between 11 and 12 years old, with a bayonet. They also bayonetted her husband, giving him a horrible wound in his neck, and then tried to rape the woman. She said she was ill so they let her go. These soldiers kept coming every day, and one day stabbed a neighbor in the face, demanding money.

10. Yu, Hai-t'ang, an employee of the Telephone Office in Hsiakwan, was among four thousand men refugees living at the University of Nanking. On Dec. 26, Japanese officers came there to effect registration, a requirement for all grown Chinese in the city. The officer told them that if any of them acknowledged that they had been soldiers their lives would be spared but they would be given work; that if they did not acknowledge it and were found out they would be killed. They were given 20 minutes to think it over. About 200 men then stepped forward. They were marched off, and on the street many more men were picked up, whom the Japanese claimed were soldiers. Yu was one of these taken on the street. He said they led him with a few hundred others to the hills near Ginling College and there the J. soldiers started bayonet practice on them. After being bayonetted in six places 2 in the chest, 2 in the abdomen, and 2 in the legs, he fainted. When he came to, the Japanese had left and somebody helped him to get to the Mission Hospital. The picture was taken while Dr. Wilson was operating, at which time there did not seem to be much hope of the man's recovery; but he did recover.

11. This man is a house-owner in Nanking. Japanese soldiers demanded that he procure some women for them. When he said there were none, they bayonetted him twice in the neck, giving him two long gashes, from which, however, the man will recover.

(Supplementary information for Film 2, Case 7) That of a 7-year-old child who had died of bayonet wounds.

This child's mother was first killed by Japanese soldiers and the child ran to its father who was then also killed. The child was then stabbed five times in the abdomen, one thrust perforating the stomach. The foreign head nurse of the hospital says he was a particularly sweet and brave child, but unfortunately died three days after admission.

12. A policeman from the Refugee Zone. A Japanese soldier forced him to accompany a Chinese woman because he himself did not wish to appear publicly to be forcing her to go with him. By the time they reached Kuo Fu Road it was already dark, so the policeman slipped down a side street. He soon ran into other soldiers, however, who tied his wrists with rope and then bayonetted him from behind, leaving him for dead.

When they had gone, he rolled away from the place, and was finally able to release his hands and to get to a house where he found a bed and spent the night. The next day he was able to get to the hospital though very weak, through the help of a Chinese whom he met on the street. He has 22 bayonet wounds, and the marvel is that he will recover.

Film 4

1. This woman was taken with five others from a refugee center to wash clothes for Japanese officers. She was taken upstairs in a building apparently used as a military hospital. During the day they washed clothes and at night entertained Japanese soldiers. According to her story, the older and plainer women were raped from 10–20 times per night, while a younger and prettier one was raped forty times per night. The woman in the picture was one of the plainer ones. On Jan. 2 two soldiers motioned her to come with them. She followed them to an empty house where they tried unsuccessfully to cut off her head. She was found in a pool of blood and taken to the Mission Hospital where she is recovering. She had four deep lacerations along the back of her neck, severing the muscles to the vertebral column. She also has a slash on her wrist and four on her body. The woman has not the slightest idea why they wanted to kill her, nor does she know the fate of the other women.

2.& 3. The case of a Buddhist nun and a little apprentice nun (between 8–9 years old).

This child was bayonetted in the back, although she ran a fever for weeks after the incident. The adult nun has a compound fracture of the left hip, caused by a bullet wound, from which an extensive infection developed. If she recovers, which is questionable, a very specialized operation will be necessary to enable her to walk. She and some other nuns occupied a building behind a temple in the southern part of the city. When the Japanese entered the city they killed a great many people in this neighborhood. The tailor who brought her to the hospital, estimated that there were about 25 dead there. Among the dead was the "Mother Superior" of this nunnery, 65 years of age, and a littler apprentice nun of between 6–7. They wounded the nun and the little apprentice shown in this picture. They took refuge in a pit where they staid for 5–6 days without food or drink. There were many corpses in this pit, and an old nun of about 68 years of age was either crushed or smothered to death by the weight of the bodies. After 5 days the wounded nun heard a soldier say in Chinese "what a pity!" She thereupon opened her eyes and begged the man to save her life. He dragged her out of the pit, and got some Chinese to carry her to an army dressing station, where an army doctor attended to her. Eventually she was brought to the Mission hospital by a neighbor.

4. On January 11 this boy, between 13–14 years of age, was forced to carry vegetables to the southern part of the city by three Japanese soldiers, who then robbed him of all his money and bayonetted him twice in the back and once in the abdomen. About one foot of the large intestine was protruding when he reached the Mission hospital two days after the assault. He died five days after admission to the hospital. The boy was so ill at the time this picture was taken that the doctor did not dare to remove the dressings to show the wounds.

5. Having heard that his mother had been killed, this man left the Refugee Zone, established by an International Committee, to investigate. He went to the Second District, an area which had been designated as safe by the Japanese and to which they were urging the people to return. He could not find his mother's body, but met two Japanese soldiers who stripped him and a friend of all their clothing except their trousers. (It was an icy cold day, about January 12, 1938) They also tore up their registration cards, which they had received from Japanese officers after the general registration. The soldiers bayonetted them both, throwing them into a dugout. About an hour later, when this man recovered consciousness, he found that his friend had disappeared. He was able to make his way back to the Refugee Zone and eventually to the Mission hospital. He had six bayonet wounds, one of which penetrated his pleura giving rise to a general sub-cutaneous Emphysema. He will recover.

6. This man was one of a group of 200 who had stepped forth from a body of 4,000 men when they were being registered with the Japanese authorities after the capture of Nanking, as they had been promised immunity from death if they acknowledged that they had been in the army, many others were picked up at the same time by the Japanese, even though they has not been soldiers, until there were between 300–500 men in the group. They were marched to a house near Wu Tai Shan where they were divided into groups of ten, their wrists being bound behind their backs with wis [sic], and then led off to execution. He heard they were taken outside the west water gate. Before this man's turn to be led off came, he was able to hide inside the building with three others under a great pile of mats, but they were discovered when one man coughed. They were then dragged outside, stood up with a group of about twenty, and bayonetted. He fainted after the first few thrusts, but later recovered consciousness and was able to roll and crawl

to the building of the American School, where a Chinese freed his wrists of the wire and where he took refuge in a drain. He was finally able to reach the Mission hospital, where it was found he had nine bayonet wounds as well as the cuts on his wrists from the wire. He will recover.

7. On January 10th, this elderly man went from the Refugee Zone to his own house which is situated near the Butterfield & Swire residences on Taikoo Shan. Three Japanese soldiers were in his garden. One of them casually shot him through both legs for no apparent reason. One of the wounds was a very nasty one, but he will probably recover.

8. On January 24th, Japanese soldiers tried to make this man set fire to the Chung Ho Hotel on Shuang Dung Hsiang not far from the University hospital. When he refused they bayoneted him in the head. There were three lacerations none of which, however, proved serious. The man had almost completely recovered when the picture was taken.

9. On December 13, about thirty soldiers came to a Chinese house at #5 Hsing Lu Kao in the southeastern part of Nanking, and demanded entrance. The door was opened by the landlord, a Mohammedan named Ha. They killed him immediately with a revolver and also Mr. Hsia, who knelt before them after Ha's death, begging them not to kill anyone else. Mrs. Ha asked them why they had killed her husband and they shot her dead. Mrs. Hsia was dragged out from under a table in the guest hall where she had tried to hide with her one-year old baby. After being stripped and raped by one or more men, she was bayonetted in the chest, and then had a bottle thrust into her vagina, the baby being killed with a bayonet. Some soldiers then went to the next room where were Mrs. Hsia's parents, age 76 and 74, and her two daughters aged 16 and 14. They were about to rape the girls when the grandmother tried to protect them. The soldiers killed her with a revolver. The grandfather grasped the body of his wife and was killed. The two girls were then stripped, the older being raped by 2–3 men, and the younger by 3. The older girl was stabbed afterwards and a cane was rammed into her vagina. The younger girl was bayonetted also but was spared the horrible treatment that had been meted out to her sister and her mother. The soldiers then bayonetted another sister of between 7–8, who was also in the room. The last murders in the house were of Ha's two children, aged 4 and 2 years respectively. The older was bayonetted and the younger split down through the head with a sword. After being wounded the 8-year-old girl crawled to the next room where lay the body of her mother. Here she staid for 14 days with her 4-year-old sister who had escaped unharmed. The two children lived on puffed rice and the rice crusts that form in the pan when the rice is cooked. It

was from the older of these children that the photographer was able to get part of the story, and verify and correct certain details told him by a neighbor and a relative. The child said the soldiers came every day taking things from the house; but the two children were not discovered as they hid under some old sheets.

All the people in the neighborhood fled to the Refugee Zone when such terrible things began to happen. After 14 days the old woman shown in the picture returned to the neighborhood and found the two children. It was she who led the photographer to an open space where the bodies had been taken afterwards. Through questioning her and Mrs. Hsia's brother and the little girl, a clear knowledge of the terrible tragedy was gained. The picture shows the bodies of the 16 and 14 year old girls, each lying in a group of people slain at the same time. Mrs. Hsia and her baby are shown last.

Film 5

1. Scenes on Shanghai Rd., Nanking, February 15, 1938. An improvised market in the Refugee Zone. When this picture was taken the booths had greatly diminished in number, as the people had already begun to filter back to other parts of the city. At the height of the crush here, it was difficult to make one's way along the road. Note the Japanese blimp in the sky, up for observation as Chinese guerilla troops were reported from time to time, in the outskirts of the city, and artillery fire could be heard occasionally.

2. Wu Chang-teh was a member of the police force in Nanking attached to headquarters. He was caught up on December 26 by Japanese soldiers who claimed that he was a soldier, and taken to a place opposite the Capitol Theatre. He was kept here for several hours while about 1000 men were being collected, and was then marched off with them to the Han Chung Gate where they were ordered to sit down. In groups of 70–80, the men were forced to go outside the city gate where each group was shot down with machine guns. Fortunately for Wu, his group was the last to go. By this time it was dark, and when the machine guns began he fell down feigning death, though uninjured. The Japanese then gathered fuel and began to burn the bodies, some of them using picks to draw the wood into a pile. As a soldier came to Wu, he saw that he was still breathing, and hit him in the back with a pick-axe and then pulled some wood over his body. After lighting the fire, the soldiers left, and Wu was able to get out of the pile before the fire reached him. He had to remain outside the city for ten days, but succeeded on

the third attempt in getting into the city gate disguised as a beggar. The picture was taken on February 15, when the wound had practically healed.

3. This young woman was taken by Japanese soldiers from a small hut in the Safety Zone to the South city and kept for thirty-eight days. During that time she was raped from 7–10 times per day. She contracted the three most common venereal diseases and also developed a huge ulcer in the vagina that made it impossible for the soldiers to use her any longer. She was then released, and came to the Mission Hospital on January 26. The picture was taken there several weeks later. On the same day that she was carried off, her husband, a policeman, was seized and nothing has been heard of him since. There is every reason to believe that he was killed with the thousands that were slaughtered at that time.

4. Country people bringing the wounded to the Emergency Hospital in a country place near Nanking. February 17, 1938.

5. Waiting their turn in the Dispensary.

6. This soldier belonged to one of the crack brigades at Nanking, and gave himself up with 8 others at Purple Mountain on December 13. They were kept for three days without food or drink and then made to walk with 200 civilians and soldiers to a place near the mountain where they were lined up in three long rows and shot down with machine guns. He fell with the others although he had not been hit, and feigned death. The Japanese then poured some sort of acid over the bodies which then burst into flame. As it was then dark, this soldier was able to crawl away unnoticed, although one of his legs was badly burnt. He reached this dispensary on December 18. The wound healed with difficulty, but two months later when the picture was taken, the man had almost recovered.

7. This is a farmer from the village of Ch'ang Li Hsiang, in the outskirts of Nanking. On February 15, two Japanese soldiers came to his home demanding girls. When he said there were none, they shot him through the hand making a most painful wound, which is now being dressed in the Dispensary.

8. This 63-year-old farmer named Chow lives at a village called Wu Lung Hsiang, about 6 miles outside the Hoping Gate, Nanking. When the Japanese first arrived he was out looking for his water buffalo. Some of them shot him. He did not reach the hospital till January 26, and had been there for about three weeks when the picture was taken.

9. This 49-year-old woman and her husband were aroused on the night of February 14 by Chinese bandits at their home in the country about 10

miles from Nanking. When they said they had no money, the bandits battered her head and breast with a wooden stool, and then burned her feet until she disclosed the hiding place of over $4, which they had saved up.

10. Farmer Tsu, 56 years old, lives in the Hsu Hsiang Village near the market town of Tungliu in the outskirts of Nanking. When the Japanese soldiers first came to his home, they ordered the whole family to come out of the house. Thereupon they killed his older son, aged 26, shooting him twice in the head, and the other son, aged 21, with a bayonet; while they shot the father through the back, the bullet coming out through the abdomen. His wife and small grandchildren were left unharmed.

Film 6

1. The mother of this child came to a refugee camp protected by foreigners near Nanking, her husband and three-year old child remaining at home. On February 14, when the father saw Japanese soldiers approaching, he fled. Later the child told a neighbor who rescued it that the soldiers had asked him where his "ma-ma" was. When they found the mother not at home they set fire to the house. A neighbor rescued the child from the flames after it had been badly burned. Its recovery is questionable.

2. A young farmer in the country near Nanking. Several soldiers came, on February 9, demanding money of him. Upon his replying that he had none, they threw kerosene oil on him and set his clothes on fire. Note the burns on the upper part of his body.

3. Chinese soldiers who had been executed and thrown into a pond. It is clear that they were executed as their arms are still tied behind them. This is typical of the treatment meted out to tens of thousands of soldiers and civilians.

4. Two scenes of dead Szechuenese soldiers along a country road near Nanking.

5. This Japanese army car was no doubt carrying a load of officers when it hit a Chinese land mine on a road near Nanking. Blood was spattered about the interior of the car. Probably two men on horseback were killed at the same time as two dead horses were lying near.

6. The body of an old woman in a field near a country road. She was probably of the fairly well-to-do class as she had a grey wig. She had evidently been hobbling along the road on her bound feet and had taken refuge behind the bank where the body lay. Whether she was deliberately murdered or was killed by a stray bullet it is impossible to say. But she is typical of the untold thousands of innocent people who have

met death in this barbarous war. About 25 village headmen said that in the country district east of Nanking at least 700–800 civilians had been killed in an area five by five miles in extent.

7. The burnt home of a well-to-do farmer. The village headmen estimated that about 80% of the houses on the main highway to Lungtan, about 15 miles east of Nanking, had been burned, while 40–50% on the smaller roads have been destroyed. The picture shows a family beginning to rebuild their home, the substantial stone walls of which were still standing. Nobody in this village of several houses had been killed.

8. Scenes in a refugee camp where 10,000 people had been gathered together and protected by foreigners. The people brought their own food and erected grass huts of rice straw. Most of them had food for but one month more when this picture was taken on February 17, 1938. They are afraid to go home because the Japanese soldiers come to demand women, and when these are not produced, burn their houses or inflict some other injury.

Film 7

1. 15-year-old girl standing by Mission Hospital car which has just brought her to the hospital. Her father, Yü, Wen-hua, had a shop in Wuhu when the Japanese arrived there. Some soldiers came to their home and began searching for valuables. They looted shop and home. The older brother, who was helping his father, had been drilling like most young men of his age and had a uniform. The soldiers found this and said that he was a soldier. According to the girl, they tried to force the brother to kneel as they wanted to cut off his head, but he refused, so they killed him. The mother and father were kneeling before the Japanese begging for the lives of their children. The soldiers then tried to rape the dead son's wife who was a trained nurse. When she resisted they killed her, as they did the oldest sister who had also resisted. Then they killed the parents as they knelt. All were killed with a bayonet. Before the parents died they told this young girl to do whatever the soldiers wanted. As she had fainted she was tied up and carried off. She revived in another place where she found herself on the floor, having been raped while unconscious. She discovered that she was on the second floor of a building which was used as barracks for 200–300 soldiers. There were a number of prostitutes in the building who were given their freedom and treated well. There were also a number of respectable girls like herself, some from Nanking, Wuhu and other places; she does not know how many as they were all locked up like herself, and presum-

ably had their clothes taken from them as was the case with this child. She knows of one Wuhu girl taken at the same time with herself who committed suicide, and she heard of others. When they tried to rape her she refused and then had her face slapped. She was raped two or three times per day for a month had a half. When she became too ill they let her alone. She was ill for a month, during which time she often wept. One day a Japanese officer who spoke Chinese came into her room and asked why she was weeping. When she told her story he took her to Nanking in a car and set her free inside the South Gate, first writing on a paper, "Ginling College," the famous American Mission College for women, which at the height of the danger had protected over 10,000 women and girls. The girl was too ill to walk the whole distance to Ginling College the first day so she took refuge in a Chinese house enroute. On the second day she reached Ginling and from there was taken to the Mission Hospital.

2. A few Japanese tanks at Nanking, in a parade of about 60 tanks, on a Japanese holiday.

3. A woman being brought in a hospital car to the Mission Hospital. She was the wife of the caretaker of a Church cemetery about a mile outside the city walls of Nanking. On March 11, a Japanese soldier called to her at a considerable distance. She did not dare to run, but began to move off, when he fired his rifle and hit her. The bullet was removed and the woman will recover.

4. A daily scene outside the headquarters of the International Relief Committee at Nanking. These people, many of them women whose men folk have been carried off and killed by Japanese soldiers, are shown on March 15 presenting petitions asking for help.

5. Mrs. Chü is about 47, her mother 77, and her little daughter 10 years of age. For many years they have lived on a secluded street not far from the South Gate of Nanking. She has been a widow for 9 years, her husband having worked in the Government Mint and, at the time of his death, having left her with a sum of money sufficient to support the family. The inheritance had been invested in the coal business.

   The Japanese soldiers first went to her home on the morning of December 13 and in the course of about twenty visits during the day took all her money from her. On the 14th and 15th they again went from 10–20 times each day, taking 13 golden ornaments and most of the contents of twelve trunks or boxes. During these three days Mrs. Chü was raped 12–13 times, mostly in a fierce and brutal manner. On the afternoon of the 15th, fires having been started in the South City, she started to flee to the northern part of the city with her old mother and small daughter and their bedding. Not far from their home the old mother became separated, and in her grief Mrs. Chu and her small daughter jumped into a well by the side of the road to end their sorrows. Fortunately the well was shallow. They remained in the well from 5–8 o'clock when they were discovered by a passing vender who insisted on helping them out. She refused to be rescued at first but finally consented, and with her daughter spent the night in the home of this poor man who rescued them. They reached the refugee camp at Ginling College on the morning of the 16th. Meanwhile the old mother trudged wearily on in a northerly direction and finally sat down on a bench in front of a little shop. A Japanese soldier came out and calling her "lao Ku-niang" (Old Girl) insisted that she move on. She thought he was taking pity on her and inviting her in to rest; but instead of treating her kindly he raped her. He was drunk and vomited all over her. The next evening another soldier raped her, and on the third day after starting from home she reached the refugee camp at Ginling and was reunited with her daughter and grand-daughter. This old lady had been a widow since the age of 32, her husband having been an official. For two nights she slept by the side of the road, and after reaching the refugee camp was unable to walk.

On December 22, because young women were crowding into the camp, a tremendous effort was made to persuade the older women to return to their home even though it meant danger and suffering. There was the great fear that if no women were left outside the camps the latter would be invaded by the soldiers and women taken off by force thus endangering both young and old. Mrs. Chü returned to her home with her old mother and her daughter. That evening three soldiers raped her, one of them forcing her to remove all her clothes, and still another after compelling her to open her mouth spit or vomited into it. Threatened with a bayonet she could not resist. The old mother was unharmed that night. At daylight, the next morning, they trudged their weary way back to the shelter of the Refugee Camp.

Scenes are in this order:
 a. Standing at a door of their house which leads into a small courtyard.
 b. At the street entrance to the house. The third woman, standing on the left, was weeping when the photographer arrived. She is Mrs. Wang who rents a room in the house of Mrs. Chu. She, her daughter, and her son went into the Safety Zone before the Japanese entered the city. Her husband remained at home. The first day after entrance the soldiers came to the home insisting that he secure for them a

girl. when he said he was unable to do so they stabbed him in the head with a bayonet. The next day, they again demanded a young girl from him. When he said he could not find one, they killed him. Mrs. Wang's eldest son was taken from home in the Safety Zone and has not been heard of since. Mr. Wang was 58 years old, the son 24.

    c. Mrs. Chü standing by the well with her little girl. This is the well in which they attempted to commit suicide.

6. (The scene shown here should be joined to Film 4, Case 9,—the story of a household of eleven persons who were killed as it is the same case.)

    a. Japanese poster on the wall of the very next house to that in which these tragedies occurred. A Japanese soldier is shown carrying a small child and giving a bucket of rice to its mother and sugar and other edibles to its father. The writing on the upper right hand corner says: "Return to your homes! We will give you rice to eat! Believe in the Japanese army! You will be saved and helped!" Such posters were frequently found on houses in or near which tragedies had occurred.

    b. Pictures of two children (mentioned in Film 4, Case 9). The little girl, aged 7–8 and her brother 3–4, are standing at the door leading into a little courtyard off the room where their two older sisters, aged 16 and 14, were raped and killed. They are then shown through the door standing by a table upon which one of these tragedies occurred. Blood was on the table and on the floor here and in other parts of the house. The old grandfather and grandmother were killed in this same room, and the older of these children bayonetted in the back and side. The man shown is the uncle of the children who had left for the Safety Zone with his wife before the tragedies occurred.

    c. The same persons standing at the door of the room where their mother was raped and killed, and where the children had remained for 14 days until rescued. Later, scars of bayonet wounds on girl made 3 months before.

    d. Spot in the courtyard where the Mohammedan Ha was killed, the blood still showing on the stone.

    e. Hsing Lu K'ou street, near the house where this tragedy occurred, in southeastern Nanking, and where between 400–500 people were murdered just after the Japanese entered the city.

Film 8

1. Continuation of Case 6, Film 7, Scene e.
2. Some of the 22,000 applications for help handed in on one day at the office of the International Relief Committee in Nanking. Each case has to be investigated.

3. This is the family of Cook Liu of a Christian school. The eldest boy at the left of the picture, aged 16, was seized by Japanese soldiers while washing rice in preparation for the meal of a group of Christian refugees on the afternoon of December 14, 1937. He was taken with a group of about 100 to a spot near the Shanghai-Nanking R.R. tracks in Hsiakwan, where their hands were tied. According to his story the group included two 13-year-old boys, two boys of his own age, a squad of Nanking police, and several men of the Postal Service in their green uniforms. Fortunately for the boy, he and a 42-year-old shopkeeper living near the Drum Tower, were at the back of a long line and had time to loose the knots on their wrists with their teeth while the Japanese were shooting those in the group, one by one. They hid in a dugout for two nights and then came out when it seemed safe. They met a Japanese soldier with a large jar of wine which he made them carry into the city. Thus they were able to get back to the Safety Zone.

4. Mrs. Yü, 65 years old, lives at Yu Chia Ts'un, five miles outside the South Gate. On the evening of March 14, Chinese bandits came to her home and demanded money. When she said she had none, they poured kerosene over her and set her clothes on fire. She was alone at the time, but the next day her grandson and a neighbor carried her to the Mission Hospital in Nanking. The upper part of her back and parts of her arms and breasts were badly burned. The picture was taken in the Hospital Dispensary shortly after her arrival.

5. This boy Tsu, aged 14, lives with his father (also shown in picture) over 3 miles outside the South Gate of Nanking. Japanese soldiers came to their home on the afternoon of February 27 and demanded girls. When they said they had none, a soldier shot the boy in the leg making a compound fracture of the femur. The doctor thinks he will recover.

6. Wang P'ei-hsiang lives in his own house on Kiukiang Road, Nanking. On the evening of March 9, at 8 o'clock, a Japanese soldier knocked at his door and demanded that Wang go with him to search for women. Upon Wang's refusal, the soldier, who must have been at least a sergeant, drew his sword and lunged at him. Wang parried with his hand sustiaing a cut finger; but this saved his life as the wound would probably have been fatal if it had been three quarters of an inch higher. He fled up the street with the soldier after him, but the latter soon gave up the chase.

7. Mrs. Hsia, aged 24, was living outside the South Gate with her 29-year-old husband who was employed as a watchman. Her mother aged 63, and their two children, aged 3 and 1, lived with them. When the Japanese came to Nanking, four or five soldiers came and called her

husband outside the house. Then they shot him dead. Soldiers then began to set fire to the houses round about, and some of them told Mrs. Hsia and the children to follow them, but would not let her mother go along. She was taken to an empty house where a soldier raped her. She escaped to a Chinese house and then hid in the grass in the rice fields for 20 days, this Chinese feeding her. Up till the latter part of March she had not found her mother and fears she is dead as she was ill when they were separated.

8. This is the widow of Ts'ai P'an-sheng who was 36 years old when he was killed. They were living in the southwestern part of Nanking on Wu Fuh-shou Street. On March 10, Japanese soldiers came to the house. While two men kept watch outside, three entered the house demanding money. The whole family fell on their knees begging for mercy. The soldiers placed a wooden ladder in front of the door and strung Ts'ai up with his hands behind his back, his feet dangling off the floor. Then they began a systematic search of the people in the house, stealing all the money they could find, opening trunks, and taking clothing and other articles. Before leaving, they stabbed Ts'ai's thigh six times and each shoulder twice, at last killing him with a shot in the head. They also stabbed Mrs. Ts'ai several times on the head and back as she knelt before them. An old employee, named Wang, was stabbed in three places on the leg. The picture shows the family with Mrs. Ts'ai's four children—a daughter of 13 and three sons, aged 8, 3, and 1 years. Note the ladder to which Ts'ai was tied and the bayonet marks on Mrs. Ts'ai's back and Wang's legs.

9. While the photographer was in the Ts'ai home, four other women came in whose menfolk had also been killed. (Film 8, Cases 7, 9; Film 9, Cases 1, 2) These are but a few of the thousands of women of Nanking whose husbands were either killed in their presence or who were taken off never to return. Mrs. Yu, Keng-shih, shown here is 32 years old. She has four children, aged 11, 7, 3, and 1, and lives in Ming Yang Street, in southwestern Nanking. Her husband, who was 38 years old, was a weaver of silk. When the Japanese entered Nanking over 10 of them came to their home and called Yu out to a little courtyard where they shot him dead. The Yu's rented rooms in the home of another family, the owner of that house being killed at the same time.

Film 9

1. Mrs. Ts'ai Wen-kiang, whose husband, aged 49, was an assistant in a wineshop in the market town of Tan Ch'iao, 25 miles outside the South

Gate of Nanking. She is 39 and has four children, a girl aged 16, and three boys of 13, 10, and 8. About the middle of December Japanese came to her house before daylight while the family was still abed and broke down the door. The soldiers had flashlights and they struck both the man and the woman with an iron bar which they had brought along, forcing the man to go with them, Mrs. Ts'ai following behind. When they reached a pond they stripped him of his clothing, tied his hands behind his back, and threw him in. They staid there till he was drowned so the woman could not attempt to rescue him. She said that eight other men in that town were drowned and 7–8 shot dead. The people of the town fled to the hills and this woman staid for 50 days in a village in the home of a friend. She came to Nanking on March 16 as she had no food or money. She is shown with one of her children in a street in southwestern Nanking.

2. This is Mrs. Li, Kao-shih, a widow who had fled north of the Yangtse before the Japanese reached Nanking. She returned to Nanking on March 16, 1938 to find her father, aged 71, with whom she had previously lived. It was only then that she learned of his murder. He had been staying in a house at Hung Ch'iao on Hung Wu Road. Soldiers had come demanding money, and when he was loth to give up the little he had they stabbed him twice in the head. In the same house three other men were killed, and three in the street outside.

3. This is a farmer named Ho who lives near Molinkuan, about 15 miles outside the South Gate of Nanking. On February 13, Japanese soldiers came to his home demanding cows, donkeys, and girls. He had none, so they strung him up parallel with the ground and about three feet above it. They then opened up his clothing, and put a fire under him, burning his lower abdomen, genitalia, thighs, chest, and left arm, singing the hair from his face and head. One soldier protested because of his age, and put out the fire and tore off his burning clothing. When they left, his family untied him, and relatives carried him the 17 miles to the Mission Hospital.

4. An 18-year-old girl who was raped by two Japanese soldiers. She is being treated in the Hospital for beri-beri, and also for venereal disease contracted from these soldiers. There are thousands like her all over the country.

5. Scenes taken at the Ginling College Refugee Camp:

   On December 1 Ginling College began to prepare itself to take in women and children refugees. By Dec. 8, the first refugees had come— women and children from the area around the city wall which was then being cleared of houses by the Chinese military so that they might better defend the city. While preparations had been made for a maximum of 2,750 persons, by December 20 more than 10,000 had crowded into the campus, begging for a place out of doors if nothing else was available. At the time these scenes were taken, only three thousand were left in the camp, the older women having returned to such homes as they still found standing and unburned.

a. The College Chapel. Every afternoon about 300 women and girls have the privilege of hearing a talk about Christianity. During the weeks before Easter they are being told about the Life of Christ.

b. Coming out from the afternoon service. Note: They are interested in having their picture taken. To the left are 4 blind girls who have been among the refugees, having come from a municipal blind school. The staff of workers, largely recruited from among the refugees, helps in teaching the many classes that have been formed.

c. New refugees coming in with their bedding. Most of them are from refugee camps now being disbanded or from country districts where life is still unbearable for young girls. They report that houses in the country are now being burned to discover the hiding places of the girls. Many have lived in carefully covered holes in the ground for weeks, coming out only by night or when there was no danger.

d. Buying boiling water. On the campus are two large hot water stoves where women can buy water for a few coppers. The owners of these stoves were glad to move them to the shelter of the campus for it meant protection for themselves as well as a lucrative business.

e. Washing clothes. Each morning the campus is a laundry and every tree and shrub and fence is hung with clothes. With hundreds of babies and young children the women have been kept busy with the daily task of washing necessary clothes.

f. Signing the petition for the return of husbands and sons. There is a ray of hope that some of the thousands of missing husbands and sons may be over in the Model Prison. To secure their release the women are signing a petition which will be presented to the Japanese and Chinese officials concerned. 600 women signed during the first two days. Most of them cannot write their own names for they are mostly from the very humble ranks of farmers and truck gardeners. The Chinese scholar therefore writes the name and the women place a thumb-print beneath. Some of the women who have signed have lost their only son—the support of their old age; some have lost as many as 3–4 sons; and one women lost 5 male members of her family. December 16 was the day of greatest loss. One does not have the heart to tell these heartbroken women that their husbands and sons are probably among those ruthlessly killed and their bodies piled in mounds outside the city gates or in secluded valleys where they remained for months before they were buried by the Red Swatika Society or other organisations and individuals. What is the future for many of these women excepting to beg, and under present conditions where can they beg.

g. Once a gymnasium. For three months it has been filled with hundreds of refugees, many of whom retreated to Nanking before the Chinese army from places as far away as Shanghai, Hanchow, Wusih and other cities and towns along the way.

h. Standing in line to be vaccinated. Almost 2,000 have been vaccinated on the campus by Dr. Brady of the University Christian Hospital.

i. Learning to read. This class meets 5 afternoons each week to learn Chinese characters. 23 classes are now being conducted for the refugees, and more than 1,000 are enrolled.

Film 10

1. This picture shows the keeper of a small shop at 60 Hupeh Road, Nanking, named Ch'en, Ching-ho, aged 42, standing with the 16-year-old boy Liu with whom he had escaped from a firing squad on Dec. 14, 1937. (For the boy's story, see Film 8, Case 3) Ch'en went to the Safety zone with his wife and 6 children on Dec. 11, and staid at #7 Ninghsia Road, he was taken from this house by Japanese soldiers on Dec. 14, at 4 p.m., and made to go with a party of 103 Chinese to Hsiakwan. He noticed several other groups of captives enroute. In his group were three Buddhist priests, seven or eight children, and some men over 60 years old. A group ahead of him had over 30 Nanking police, and 6 men of the Postal service in their green uniforms. Before turning into Jehol Road at Hsiakwan he noticed a group of over 300 Chinese near the Chung Shan Bridge with their arms tied behind them. His group was marched near to the International Export Company and then taken back to the Sze So Ts'un, a settlement for laboring classes, near the Shanghai-Nanking R.R. They were divided into two squads facing in different directions. The first person killed was a tall man quite near him, whose hands had been tied with his own girdle and who was then thrown down and beheaded with a big sword, one edge of which was a sharp blade and the other a saw-edge. When Ch'en saw this man killed, without being seen he slipped to the other squad, the members of which had already had their arms tied; and thus Ch'en escaped having his

tied. He was standing a few rows behind the boy Liu. In the meantime the boy had been gnawing with his teeth at the knots on his wrists and was at last able to pull his hands free. While the men in front of them were being killed by revolver and rifle shots, one by one, these two succeeded in slipping into a small dug-out in the railway embankment. It was now 9 o'clock and a cloudy night, so the moon was not shining very brightly; otherwise they could not have escaped.

They staid here for two nights. On the second night Ch'en had a dream in which his father-in-law appeared to him and told him that he would take him out on the morrow. The next day he saw a bee, a strange sight for this time of year; and said to himself, "If my father-in-law has sent you, I will follow the way you fly." The bee then flew north, and west, and north again. They followed these directions to get out of the place where they had hidden, and were finally able to reach a spot outside the Han Hsi Men. Here they met a Japanese soldier with a large cask of wine who made them carry it for him into the city, thus enabling them to get through the city gate. After carrying the wine to the soldier's quarter behind the Ch'ao T'ien Kung (Facing Heaven Palace) they were set free and made their way to the Safety Zone.

2. Views of the destruction by Japanese soldiers in the southern section of Nanking.

    a. Views from the top of the tower of St. Paul's Church on Taiping Road, showing the charred ruins of houses burned by Japanese soldiers.

    b. Ruins of a large Chinese-style residence, belonging to the American Episcopal Church Mission and used for Mission purposes; burnt by Japanese soldiers late in December and again on January 26.

    c. The Parish House of St. Paul's Church which had been struck by a shell before the fall of the city.

    d. Views from the top of the Christian Disciples' Mission, on Chung Hwa Road near the South Gate.

    e. Two buildings belonging to the Disciples' Mission which had been burnt by the Japanese.

    f. Ruins of the Chinese YMCA building on Chung Hwa Road.

3. a. One of a great many ponds in Nanking where people were killed by Japanese and into which their bodies were cast. About Dec. 26, over forty men were killed here, all having had their arms wired together behind their backs. The Red Swastika Society had buried the bodies in mounds visible in the distance. On the day the picture was taken another body had come to the surface with arms still wired, and is shown in the picture.

b. This is a second pond near to the first. Neighbors are standing on the spot where 96 men, with arms wired behind them, were sprinkled with gasoline and kerosene and then set on fire. The blackened bodies, piled high, were seen by several foreigners. A gasoline tin, one of several used at this time, was fished out of the pond on the day the picture was taken. On the particular spot where the men were burnt, all the roots of the grass had been killed, so there was no green or foliage altho other parts of the bank were covered with grass. Some men had started to run when they were set ablaze and were shot down with machine guns. 2–3 succeeded in reaching the house in the distance which was set afire by their burning bodies, as the family fuel caught fire inside.

c. A closer view of the house mentioned above. The family is standing by the ruined walls. The neighbors all fled when these things took place, but some were near enough to hear the sound of the burning and later the sound of the machine guns. One young man saw the sight at a distance but was not seen himself as it was about 5 p.m. and dark. It was possibly here, or at least in this general neighborhood, that the man was burned whose body was shown in the hospital morgue (Film 3, Case 1) as one of the neighbors had met a man walking on a path at that time the description of whose burned head tallied with that of the corpse in the morgue.

Between January 23, when they started work, and March 19, the Red Swastika Society had buried 32,104 corpses in Nanking and the immediate vicinity (around the city walls). They estimate that they have done just about one half of this work. In addition many bodies were buried by relatives and other groups. It is very probable that many bodies were burned up in the innumerable fires that were started in the city possibly for that very purpose. There are still large numbers of unburied bodies in sections outside the city walls.

Film 11

1. Mrs. Koeh, Yieh-shih, aged 74, lived with a sixteen year old girl at Kwanyin Men, about 5 miles down the river from Nanking. When Japanese soldiers came to her home in December, they stole about $1,000 worth of goods, all that she had of value; and also carried off the girl whom she has not seen or heard of since. When she tried to protect this girl, a soldier knocked her down, dislocating her shoulder. She had to come to the hospital three months later to have it set.

2. Mrs. Ch'en, Chu-shih, is 46 years old, and lives in the country near the

town of Ma Hsün east of Nanking where her husband is a farmhand. When the soldiers came in December, they set fire to her house. She rushed in the front door in an attempt to save a few things, not seeing a Japanese soldier who was at the back of the house and who shot her breaking her leg.

3. Mrs. Wang, who is only 18 years old, lived outside the Hsui Hsi Men, Nanking. When the Japanese came a soldier demanded her money (between $1 and $2) which she refused to give. He then shot her in the leg and took the money. As she was not able to come to the hospital promptly, the leg developed gangrene and had to be amputated below the knee.

4. Tung, Liang-yi lived with his wife on a farm near the town of Ta Sheng Kuan, about 8 miles outside the Hsui Hsi Gate of Nanking. When the Japanese came they said he was a soldier and bayonetted him thru the back several times, whereupon he fainted. They came back four times to see if had actually died and each time he feigned death altho conscious.

The case is interesting from a medical standpoint as both bayonet thrusts went clear thru his body from back to front. One thrust entered slightly to the right of the midline of the back and emerged to the left of the left nipple. The other thrust entered about the midline of the back and emerged at the left side of the chest. The man had practically no treatment for two months and for one month he had only simple dressings in a Chinese dispensary. He was then brought to the Mission hospital where he was operated upon. It was found that he had Empyema (an infection of the sack that includes the lungs) with a bronchical fistula and collapsed lung. He also had Chrosteomyilitis of the 7th rib. He will probably never be strong again.

5. Hu, Ching-pao lives in a village near Nanking. He and his older brother were standing together when three Japanese soldiers came there on February 20. For some unknown reason they shot at them from a distance of about 200 yards. The brother was shot thru the shoulder but recovered quickly. The bone of this man's arm was shattered into many pieces, large and small, and was already badly infected on his admission into the Mission Hospital. Amputation was advised but the man refused, so the doctor is trying to save the arm.

6. Ginling College Refugee Camp. April 18, 1938.

Explanation: From February 27–April 9 there were 23 six-weeks classes centering on the life of Jesus. This project culminated in Holy Week and an Easter Pageant. The closing exercises of the six weeks project were held on Monday morning, April 18, when about 600 members of the various classes were present. Each class had prepared some part of the program showing especially something that had been learned. At the end simple prizes were given to the member of each class who had not missed a single day and had made the most progress. The pictures were taken of the various activities and are as follows:

a. The Procession: At 8:20 all the students met on the main quadrangle and marched into the College chapel in single file. The ages ranged from 9–37 years but the large majority were from 15–21. In educational ability they ranged from illiterates to senior middle school graduates. The classes were divided according to educational ability, most of them being from the 3rd to the 6th grade in ability, altho there were more than 20 of senior middle school ability.

b. All stood in the beginning to sing the opening hymn which was "Rock of Ages." Most of the pupils have memorized this hymn and have learned to love it.

c. Illiterates, 18–19 years of age, had memorized and recited the Beatitudes as their contribution to the closing exercises. Another class of illiterates recited the Ten Commandments.

d. A large class of 3–4th grade ability pupils sang, "God of Love, King of Peace."

e. Another member of this same group went to the platform and told the story of Jesus at the age of twelve.

f. A large class of illiterate girls from the ages of 12–17 demonstrated the characters which they had learned to recognize during the six weeks of class work.

g. Representatives from the classes of married women who had studied in private or elementary schools for a few years recited Psalms 121 and 23.

h. A group of second year pupils taught by one of the refugees recited Psalm 121.

i. Sixth grade pupils gave a one act play illustrating the way of living the abundant life. It was called "The Door to the Abundant Life."

j. Sixth grade pupils sang "Arise, Be Free, Ye Slaves Of Sin" from the new church hymnal.

Film 12

[Note: Outline style is per the original.]

1. Easter Pageant, given by the refugees at Ginling College, April 17, 1938.

   a. The Resurrection morning. (Place: South of the Practice School)

    a. Mary of Magdala tells the other Mary and Salome that Christ is risen from the dead.

    b. As they are talking, John and Peter join them and tell them that they too have seen the Risen Lord.

    c. The common people join the group of followers and all rejoice in the news of the Risen Lord.

    b. From darkness to dawn:

    a. Miss Wangjui-chih, dean of the six weeks' school, and teacher of the class of junior and senior middle grade students who gave the Easter Pageant, explains the meaning of the pageant.

    b. A member of class reads the appropriate passages from the New Testament.

    c. Nicodemus and Joseph of Arimathaea return in great distress from the trial of Jesus, hating themselves for being silent disciples of the Master whom they had learned to love. Nicodemus decides that even though late he must go and let people know that he is really a disciple.

    d. Joseph gives money to a servant who is a believer in Jesus and sends him to do his utmost to save him.

    e. Esther, the wife of Joseph, goes with her maid servant who is a believer to see if they can save the Master from crucifixion.

    f. Two servants come hastily saying that the Master is being taken out to be crucified. Joseph at last is persuaded that he must go and try to save Jesus from crucifixion.

    g. Esther has been in great distress over the death of Jesus. She comes and tells her of the resurrection and they both go to seek the Risen Lord.

2. A Cash-relief Project. Poor women among the Ginling refugees earn money by weeding the college lawns.

3. The Staff of the Ginling Refugee Camp. All but five are refugees themselves, but most of them were invited to come to the campus to be ready for just such an opportunity as has come to us.

4. Mrs. Wang and her daughter Lin-sang. The latter was shut outside the city for almost a month at the time of hostilities and the anxious mother who lived on the campus used every method to ascertain whether she was still alive. She disguised herself as a little boy and thus saved herself from harm.

5. A small group of refugees washing their hair.

6. Mrs. Tsen, who is in charge of distributing cash relief, paying the women for weeding the campus.

7. The Rice Kitchen: Conducted under the Nanking Red Cross. Refugees can obtain soft rice twice daily for the sum of three coppers per bowl if

they can pay, free if they cannot pay. Wheat and beans are now being cooked in the rice to increase the food value. For a time the kitchen was just outside the college campus gate.

8. A group of 13 boys and 3 girls from the Tsingpoo and Shanghai war area who refugeed with the Episcopal Mission in Nanking, and who have been with them since November. After 5 months the relatives of all but one were located in Shanghai through the kind offices of the International Red Cross, causing mutual rejoicing. As soon as arrangements can be completed the group will be repatriated. The picture shows them with the New Testaments presented to them prior to leaving Nanking.

(Back: Please return to Mrs. Forster
990, Jespeed RD.
Shanghai

Notes

1. RG8, B263.
2. This sentence seems unfinished.
3. RG10, B 102.
4. RG10, B4, F62.
5. RG8, B263–7.

James H. McCallum

James Henry McCallum was born November 19, 1893, in Olympia, Washington. He finished his college education at the University of Oregon in 1917 and earned his B.D. from Yale Divinity School in 1921; later he finished a Master's Degree at Chicago Divinity School and did doctoral work at the Union Theological Seminary while on furlough. He married Eva Anderson of Philadelphia in 1921 and the newly wedded couple immediately set off for China. For the next thirty years, McCallum engaged in evangelical and community center work for the United Christian Missionary Society, traveling widely in Anhwei and Kiangsi provinces. From 1946 to 1951, he was in charge of rehabilitation work in Nanking as Secretary of the Mission. He handled missionary finances and evacuation at the end of his service in China.

During the Nanking Massacre, McCallum's wife and two children were in Kuling, Kiangsi, while he remained at Nanking as administrator of the University of Nanking hospital and refugee relief work. His diary/letters to his family from December 19, 1937, to January 15, 1938, served as evidence of the Nanking Massacre at the Tokyo Trial of Japanese war criminals. A copy of McCallum's diary was discovered in Shanghai in 1995 and a Chinese translation was published, but that version did not include the entry for January 15, 1938, which is among those published in this volume.

Account of the Japanese Atrocities at Nanking During the Winter of 1937–38[1]

December 19, 1937

It has been just one week now since the collapse of the Chinese Army in its Nanking defence. Japanese soldiers came marching down Chung Shan Road past the hospital on Monday and Japanese flags began to appear here and there. We all breathed a sigh of relief thinking now order would be restored after the panic and stampede caused by the retreating Chinese army. Airplanes could fly over our heads without causing apprehension or tension. But a week has past and it has been hell on earth.

It is a horrible story to relate; I know not where to begin nor to end. Never have I heard or read such brutality. Rape! Rape! Rape! We estimate at least 1,000 cases a night and many by day. In case of resistance or anything that seems like disapproval there is a bayonet stab or a bullet. We could write up hundreds of cases a day; people are hysterical; they get down on their knees and "Kowtow" any time we foreigners appear; they beg for aid. Those who are suspected of being soldiers as well as others, have been led outside the city and shot down by hundreds, yes, thousands. Three times has the staff of our Hospital been robbed of fountain pens, watches and money. Even the poor refugees in certain centers have been robbed again and again until the last cent, almost the last garment and last piece of bedding only remains and this may go ere long. Women are being carried off every morning, afternoon and evening. The whole Japanese Army seems to be free to go and come anywhere it pleases and to do what it pleases. American flags have frequently been torn down from Ginling and the University and Hillcrest school. At the Seminary, B.T.T.S. [Bible Teachers Training School] University, Ginling, University Middle School, Sericulture buildings, Library and scores of other places, there are cases of rape, robbery, shooting and bayonetting every night. Foreigners, when present, have been able in some cases to prevent this. But fifteen or twenty of us available cannot be in every building all the time.

December 29, 1937

Have been so busy every day and five nights of the week the I've had no time to write. A foreigner must be on duty 24 hours here at the hospital in order to deal with the Japanese visitors. It is snowing and bitterly cold; our hearts ache for the thousands who have poor shelter and who are cooped up in such close quarters. Our hospital is full and the lighter cases fill the University Dormitory building. Some we cannot dismiss for they have no place to go. Have had fifteen or twenty babies within the last week; six on Christmas Day. It is easy to find Miss Hynds; she is always in the nursery mothering the whole crowd of babies.

Thought of you all on Christmas Day and hoped it was a happy time for you. We presumed you were still in Kuling. The rumors are reaching us that Kuling may be evacuated. We have been completely out of touch with the rest of the world. No one can get into Nanking and it seems very difficult to get out. We have talked of sending some one of our group out to carry the news of the terrible things that have been and still are happening here, but know that person would never get back if he once left.

I have been living with Mills, Fitch, Smythe, Sone, Wilson, Bates, and Riggs here in the Buck house. All of us have been doing double duty. We scarcely sit down to our meals without someone coming in every other five minutes or so to call for help. Food is swallowed whole and hurried exits are made to save a truck from being stolen or more often to protect women from soldiers. Seldom do we all sit down to eat at the same time. We dare not go out alone after dark but go in twos or threes.

Every day or two I have gone out for an inspection of our mission property. I have found visitors in our house at Peh Hsia Rd. every time I have gone there. Every foreign house is a sight to behold; untouched until the Japanese army arrived, nothing untouched since. Every lock has been broken; every trunk ransacked. Their search for money and valuables has led them to the flues and inside pianos.

Our phonograph records are all broken; the dishes are a broken mass on the floor along with everything else that was discarded after each looting. The front of the piano was removed and all the hammers struck with something heavy. Our house being outside the Safety Zone, this was not to be unexpected but houses within the Zone have shared a like fate. Two of our boys' school buildings were set fire to, one a complete loss. Nanking presents a dismal appearance. At the time the Japanese Army entered the city little harm had been done to buildings. Since then the stores have been stripped of their wares and most of them burned. Taiping, Chung Hwa and practically every other main business road in the city is a mass of ruins. In south city much of the area back of the main street was also burned. We see new fires every day and wonder when such beastly destruction will cease.

But far worse is what has been happening to the people. They have been in terror and no wonder. Many of them have nothing left now but a single garment around their shoulders. Helpless and unarmed, they have been at the mercy of the soldiers, who have been permitted to roam about at will wherever they pleased. There is no discipline whatever and many of them are drunk. By day they go into the buildings in our Safety Zone centers, looking for desireable women, then at night they return to get them. If they have been hidden away, the responsible men are bayonetted on the spot. Girls of 11 and 12 and women of fifty have not escaped. Resistance is fatal. The worst cases come to the hospital. A women six months pregnant, who resisted, came to us with 16 knife wounds in her face and body, one piercing the abdomen. She lost her baby but her life will be spared. Men who gave themselves up to the mercy of the Japanese when they were promised their lives would be spared—a very few of them returned to the Safety Zone in a sad way. One of them declared they were used for bayonet practice and his body certainly looked it. Another group was taken out near Ku-ling Sz; one who somehow returned, lived long enough to tell the fate of that group. He claimed they threw gasoline over their heads, and then set fire to them. This man bore no other wounds but was burned so terribly around the neck and head that one could scarcely believe he was a human being. The same day another, whose body had been half burned over, came into the hospital. He had also been shot. It is altogether likely that the bunch of them had been machine-gunned, their bodies then piled together and burned. We could not get the details, but he evidently crawled out and managed to get to the hospital for help. Both of these died. And so I could relate such horrible stories that you would have no appetite for days. It is absolutely unbelievable but thousand have been butchered in cold blood—how many it is hard to guess—some believe it would approach the 10,000 mark.

We have met some very pleasant Japanese who have treated us with courtesy and respect. Others have been very fierce and threatened us; striking or slapping some. Mr. Riggs has suffered most at their hands. Occasionally have I seen a Japanese helping some Chinese or pick up a Chinese baby and play with it. More than one Japanese soldier told me he did not like war and wished he were back home. Altho' the Japanese Embassy staff has been cordial and tried to help us out, they have been helpless. But soldiers with a conscience are few and far between.

Now it is time to make the rounds of the hospital. There are a hundred on the staff. When we have water and lights again it will be much easier, for the lamps to look after and water to pump each day increases our labor considerably.

December 30

Glorious weather. It feels so good to get out into the air. It is more peaceful but far from good. A man came into the hospital today shot through the intestines with about four feet of them hanging out. He has a chance in a thousand of recovery. Bob Wilson spent the better part of the morning trying to patch him up. Before dinner a 12 yr. old girl was abducted by two Japanese soldiers who drove up in a yellow taxi. Several men were forcibly carried away from Ginling,

Magee's place as well as other places, accused of being soldiers. The men had friends among the group who could identify them as civilians, but because they had calluses on their hands, they were branded without further investigation as soldiers in spite of the protest voiced. Many ricshaw and san-pan men as well as other laborers have been shot simply because they have the marks of honest toil upon their hands. An old caretaker in a German residence near the Kian An bus station is reported to have been killed yesterday. Soldiers found no young men on the place to conscript for labor and he protested about going himself. And I said this had been fairly peaceful today. Can you imagine what was happening when I did not have time to stop and write.

Been busy getting in supplies of rice for the hospital and those Chinese Christians housed in the Drum Tower Church. Moved 50 big bags—about 65 tons.

The Japanese are beginning to tighten up on the police, on the Chinese and a suggestion of further restrictions for the foreigners. It was suggested by Mr. Oki that we Americans be concentrated in one place under guard. Just how much freedom would be allowed in such a case we do not know, but we are a bit suspicious. The registration is proceeding and those Chinese who do not have a certificate of registration are being restricted for free movement within the Safety Zone and are refused exit from the Zone.

Now I must close. I must take some patients home in the Ambulance. Everyone who leaves the hospital must be accompanied by the foreigner. I am the official body guard for even the police. We are so crowded that we are glad to get some out. So many have no place to go to and no money and no clothing that it is quite a problem. We cannot heal them and then kick them out to die of neglect or starvation, or to be killed or reinjured. Most of them have come in from bayonet or bullet wounds since the city was captured.

December 31

This is the last day of the year. Great preparations are being made to celebrate the New Year. It must be one holiday our Japanese friends like. A three-day holiday has been announced. We dread what may take place with more freedom allowed. There is some indication of things for the better. Today I saw crowds of people flocking across Chung Shan Rd. out of the Zone. They came back later carrying rice which was being distributed by the Japanese from the Examination Yuan.

There were some happy people today. We have so many babies in the hospital and the mothers and babies are always happy to be leaving even tho' they have no decent place to go—only over-crowded concentration camps with hundreds in a room. The grandmother and three other children had to escort the new baby "home" as they called it, so I bundled them all into ambulance and took them over to the University where they are "at home" among the 20,000 refugees there. The brother insisted on holding his little baby brother and they were all smiles over the fine, tho' brief, auto ride. But what do they have to be happy over? Well, I hand it to them, they've succeeded in rising above the circumstances in a noble way. Another servant from the American Embassy came in for his final examination and to have the stitches removed from a bullet wound—and he was all smiles.

Registration is under way at the B.T.T.S. Spent part of the morning trying to get some of our Hospital staff registered, but there was such a jam that we could not get near. Our folks are anxious to get registered fearing the time limit will expire, and death if they do not comply. Our busy bunch can not stand in line day after day waiting when they have so much work to do. The rest of the morning was spent in trying to get something to eat for our family of three hundred. They surely eat up a lot every day and food is hard to get. We went way into the south-west part of the city near the wall and had a hard time getting there as some of the fires had caused so much debris to be scattered into the streets one could hardly get by in spots.

The food problem will soon be a very serious one unless something is done to get some in from the outside.

Another woman with a new baby insists on leaving the hospital tho' she has no place to go to, no money, no friends and no provision for her baby. Her husband was taken away days ago and has never returned and probably never will. She wants to get out to seek him, going around from place to place in her search. She has no strength and how can she possibly do it? I have given her name out to several of the camps trying to trace friends or neighbors all to no avail. MY. What misery we witness.

We expect the new government to be inaugurated in Nanking tomorrow—a celebration due Kulou in the afternoon. The former five-color flag has been revived and they say 60,000 have been made to order that they may be flown along with the Japanese flag.

January 1, 1938

The day and the year started gloriously. Firecrackers going full blast woke me and I opened my eyes to wonder what was going on. It was a perfectly beautiful day with the sun a big red ball of fire in the sky. Later Purple Mountain was a lovely blue like the cascades often are. It was very obviously a holiday. Firecrackers—loads of them had been distributed to the Chinese free—and who would refuse the indulgence of making a good noise to relieve the spirit. We learned that yesterday they gave away several hundreds of thousands of 200 lb. bags of rice. The usual New years' greetings were exchanged.

Night before last we were invited to the home of Herr John Rabe where we found a beautiful Christmas tree lighted with many candles. Everything was perfect except the absence of our wives and children—a big lack. We have been worrying about you. We heard one brief sentence over the radio from Tokyo that all Americans were being evacuated from Kuling. I sometimes wish you were all safe in America.

We had a New Year's dinner with Mrs. Twinem, Mr. McGee, Mr. Forster and Mrs. Cheng of Ginling as guests. We ate our last goose. About the time we finished dinner our day began to be spoiled. Two men came running from Magee's place (he has three places full of refugees) saying that two Japanese soldiers had entered and were after the women. We got a car ready and Fitch took Magee and Forster over. Later he brought in two of the women to the Hospital. One had been raped and the other badly beaten had managed with the aid of her father to break away, but had been injured as she jumped from a window. They were hysterical. Then a nun from a Temple in the southeastern part of the city was brought to us. She had been wounded on the fourteenth of December. Five of them had sought safety in a dugout, but the Japanese soldiers came into the dugout from each and killing three of the five, wounding the other two. These two, the nun and a little apprentice girl of ten later saved their lives by hiding under the dead bodies of their friends. Eighteen days with no medical attention and five days without food! A man in the neighborhood managed to get the badly wounded nun to the hospital. She told us of the little girl who had been stabbed in the back, so I took the ambulance down to get her. Her wound had healed; all she needed was food, a bath, and comfortable surroundings. The people who live in the south-east section of the city are a terrified lot—surrounded by Japanese soldiers. They gathered around us as we waited for the little girl—quite a decently behaved group of soldiers. But as we stood there a drunk soldier came by bullying two old Chinese men. The Chinese men were so frightened that they came up to me and begged for me help. I must confess I am afraid of an armed drunken soldier, but with the aid of a few of the sober soldiers who helped by diverting the attention of the drunk, the old men had an opportunity to escape—and how they took to their heels! The drunken soldier evidently cursed me for one of the other soldiers, angered, took a club to him. As I started back to the ambulance, one of my orderlies I discovered had been taken off by another bunch of soldiers. It was the cook, who urged by curiosity had begged to be allowed to accompany us. His Red Cross sleeve band had been taken off; he was scared and thought sure he was about to be shot. I rescued him and by this time I began to fear our ambulance might have been taken, but we hurried back to find the decent bunch of soldiers still surrounding it so we left them with smiles. The last few days we have had to go into the extreme parts of this city where few people dare to venture but we have come back safely each time with our load of food or patients.

Tried today to estimate the extent of destruction of property. From the hospital to Chung Che and Peh Hsia Rds. about 30 per cent; about half on Peh Hsia Rd; on Chung Hwa Rd. to Chein Kan Rd. about 80 percent—beyond there, less and not a great deal burned out in the extreme southern part. Off from S. Kulou towards the East Wall about 20 or 30 per cent concentrated in certain areas.

Another woman came into the Hospital this afternoon who had been wounded before the fall of Nanking. Her home was in a village south of Nanking. She had left home with her five children—the youngest three months and the oldest twelve. Japanese planes flew overhead spraying machine-gun bullets. One hit her in the eye coming out near the throat. She tried to struggle on with her baby but finally had to give up and lay unconscious most of one night with her children gathered near her. In the morning she realized she could not continue with the weight of her baby so she left it in the deserted house and struggled along until she came to some villagers who helped her into one of the refugee camps. After eighteen days she reached us and medical aid.

Tonight at dusk I counted five good sized fires in different parts of the city—and so the burning and looting and raping continues. In the Safety Zone it is much better altho' the soldiers still come in. However in contrast to those days when we were trying to stop them at several places at once, day and night, it is comparatively peaceful and quiet. At least we have time to write. Succeeded in getting half of the hospital staff registered today.

I must report a good deed done by some Japanese. Recently several very nice Japanese have visited the hospital. We told them of our lack of food supplies for the patients. Today they brought in 100 chin of beans along with some beef. We have had no meat at the hospital for a month and these gifts were mighty welcome. They asked what else we would like to have.

But each day has a long list of bad reports. A man was killed near the relief headquarters yesterday afternoon. In the afternoon a Japanese soldier attempted to rape a woman; her husband interfered and helped her resist. But in the afternoon the soldier returned to shoot the husband.

This morning came another woman in a sad plight and with a horrible story. She was one of five women whom the Japanese soldiers had taken to one of their medical units, to wash their clothes by day, to be raped by night. Two of them were forced to satisfy from 15 to 20 men and the prettiest one as many as 40 each night. This one who came to us had been called off by three soldiers into an isolated place where they attempted to cut her head off. The muscles of the neck had been cut but they failed to sever the spinal cord. She feigned death but dragged herself to the hospital—another of the many to bear witness to the brutality of the soldiers. Dr. Wilson is trying to patch her up and thinks she may have a chance to live. Day after day our group has made its report to the authorities of these terrible conditions. They have tightened up and issued orders; still each day brings its atrocities.

January 4

Up early this morning to see twelve Japanese planes flying overhead. It is still clear but terribly cold for these poor people who have to live out in the open or in tents. I failed to note Monday that we had a real air raid from the Chinese. Had almost forgotten what a raid was like. It gave the Japanese a surprise and they were quite uneasy, unready for it. Finally Japanese planes did raise to the occasion and flew like mad in hot pursuit.

I have no idea how to reach you by mail. Your last letter was dated Nov. 25th. I have pictured you as a happy group in the school with the boys having plenty of fun in the snow. Hope you have all kept well. Our life grows awfully monotonous. We are more than fed up with all this cruelty and suffering which is so senseless and unnecessary. Our whole time in the hospital is spent in try- ing to patch up and save the victims of Japanese guns and bayonets; all inno- cent, simple Chinese for whom the Japanese have come to help. When they made their fine speeches on New Year's Day telling us that the Kuomintang had no regards for the needs of the common people, I could not help but think of our whole hospital full of their victims. There is little doubt, too, but that foreign help and support in Chinese affairs will be spurned.

January 5

A perfect morning and a gorgeous view of the sunrise from my attic room in the Buck house. Fixed up a radio in the X-ray room at the hospital with stray equip- ment picked up here and there and it came in good last night—so communica- tions are again established.

Made a trip to South City in the ambulance to get *pai tsai* [cabbage] for our big family. Saw many large fires burning.

A red letter day. Mr. Fukuyi of the Japanese Embassy informs us that three American Embassy men will arrive in Nanking today. They have been making promises for ten days, but apparently had some difficulty in getting Army per- mission. We tried to send a message thru' the Japanese asking for their return, but they refused to send it. They would like to have had us all out of Nanking but now that we have stayed so long and know so much, we are not allowed to leave—we are virtually prisoners.

My radio does not work so well after all. We have secured a second radio but cannot get the short wave to work. We got English reports from Tokyo, Manila and Shanghai and there is some good music, but I spent some hours at the radio yesterday and from all sources I got the same "Pop-eye the sailor man" record so often that I could sing it for our household.

Have a new job. Been delivering babies. O yes, Trin and Wilson DELIVER them, but I take them home, to some crowded refugee camp. Nearly every other day I take the ambulance out to get pai tsai, rice and other foodstuffs. A foreigner must go along to guarantee delivery. Salvaged three cows recently and Mrs. Chang is making some butter for us. Our bachelor group has gone thru' with about 26 dozen tins of Luchowfu[2] peaches and for the past month we have had them every day. We are eating more rice and there is plenty of pai tsai. I understand the Japanese are selling apples, in limited quantities, at ten cents apiece. A few other things are coming in.

January 6

The biggest news of the day has just come. The American Consular representatives told us that the families of McCallum, Trimmer, Mills and Smythe left Hankow for Hongkong on the 30th. He also delivered some letters of yours written the last of November.

It is the first news or mail we've received for more than a month and how welcome it was! I'm hoping you had a comfortable trip, altho' I feel sure you must have been exposed to a lot of inconveniences and possible dangers. I shall be relieved when I hear where you are and what your next move will be. I have concluded in my own mind that if you are permitted to come to Shanghai that you will do so and place the children in the American school there for the rest of the school year. I'm hoping for that move, for it means I might be able to see you before long, altho' we as yet have no assurance that we would be permitted to leave.

I am glad I stayed. Altho' there were only 20 of us foreigners we have been able to help considerably in the various concentration points in the Safety zone. Had there been a hundred of us to guard against the 60,000 soldiers that much more could have been accomplished. Ginling has housed as high as 12,000, the University buildings about 25,000, the Seminary and B.T.T.S. 2 or 3 thousand each and every house in the vicinity crammed full. Some of the men are engaged now in trucking coal and rice; we do not dare leave a truck or car out of our sight.

There is still a corpse in our compound at Peh Hsia Rd., another on the first floor of our South Gate Women's Building, and one in the Plopper' compound—all having met their fate about the 13th. In the Price's yard is a little baby about six months old. It cried while a soldier was raping its mother. The soldier smothered it by putting his hand over its nose and mouth. Permits to bury have not been obtainable. I have buried more than 38 bodies myself in our hospital dugouts; gathering them off the streets nearby; most of them being soldiers. The loss of life has been appalling. Men, women and children of all ages have paid a terrible price. Why does war have to be so beastly?

Japanese talk of getting the people back to their homes, starting up business again and of bringing in a lot of Japanese goods. The diplomatic group want to set up a city government; the Army will not allow it. They want the people to go back to their homes; the Army continues to terrify them so that they dare not leave the concentration camps. They want business started again; the Army has taken away all stocks and burned the stores. They want them to start trade; but the Army has robbed the people of their money. They want them to produce; but the Army has killed all the chickens and pigs and cows, every living thing. The irony of it.

January 9

Some newspaper men came to the entrance of a concentration camp and distributed cakes, and apples and handed out a few coins to the refugees. And a moving picture was taken of this kind act. At the same time a bunch of soldiers climbed over the back wall of the compound and raped a dozen or so of the women. There were no pictures taken out back.

The constructive group want to restore electricity and water. The day before the final arrangements were made through Rabe to get the workmen back on the job, a military detachment headed by non-commissioned officers went to the British Export Co.'s factory and picking out a group of Electric Light Co. Employees, 43 of them, lined them up and machine-gunned them. The Light Co. was a private corporation. The soldiers without investigation claimed they were government employed. That is the general condition after a month's time and there is little hope of improvement.

Now the Japanese are trying to discredit our efforts in the Safety Zone. They threaten and intimidate the poor Chinese into repudiating what we have said. Some of the Chinese are even ready to prove that the looting, raping and burning was done by the Chinese and not the Japanese. I feel sometimes that we have been dealing with maniacs and idiots and I marvel that all of us foreigners have come through this ordeal alive.

We do not know when we will be permitted to leave Nanking. With so few of us we do not want to leave until some more men are allowed to come in. We have been living fairly normally in our bachelor quarters and it has been a grand bunch to be with. All of us have gotten into many amusing situations as well as serious ones and we have jolly times relating them to each other. We could welcome a change from Luchowfu peaches and Chinese cabbage for a diet. How good butter and eggs would taste! But we have plenty of flour, rice and our gardens are still yielding lettuce and carrots and beets. If it is made available by the military there should be enough rice in the city to feed the 200,000 people through the winter. But the economic outlook is pitiful to contemplate. There is no production; only consumption.

Just heard the family had arrived in Hongkong safely. Praise be! Know where?

January 11

Had the American Embassy men in for dinner two days ago and today had the British Embassy men as well as those from the German Embassy. It has been a real treat. Not having seen anyone from the outside for over a month, and having so much to say ourselves, we had a real talk-feast. We hung onto every word spoken by them and still have many questions we would like to ask.

Hospital affairs have gotten past the emergency state. We now have electricity and therefore radio reception which makes us feel closer to the rest of the world. When we can secure more hospital supplies we will feel close to normal again.

We are not finished with raping and robbing but it has become such an old story that more repetition will add nothing of value. There are threats and bribes now—attempts to undermine the present relief organizations. Others are now engaged in providing fuel and food. The International Committee is selling it for $10 a bag. They buy it from the Japanese for $4 a bag, but it costs the Japanese nothing—spoils of war!

I was offered four more cows today. If I had a place to keep them I'd take them gladly for we could use the milk. Food for the cows we have already salvaged is a problem. One of the choicest bits of information today concerned Tanaka, one of the consular policemen. He has been taking us around as we looked over our looted property. He has been seen on various occasions to pick some little things from this place and that but yesterday Mr. Sperling met him coming out of one of the fine German homes with two rickshaws of lovely curios which he no doubt had very much admired.

January 12

At last we hear you are to arrive in Shanghai today. That answers a lot of questions and I presume you are headed directly for the American School. I hope you will be able to get some letters in to us now. The British, German and American Embassy staffs are very accommodating if you can hear when any of them will be coming thru'. The Japanese newspaper men have brought us in a few missiles, but they were, of course, unsealed. I suppose you were able to bring but little out with you and I'm not very optimistic about what you may have had to leave behind. We need Dr. Brady badly and hope there will be a way to get him in. We need helpers. Minnie is especially in need of single women helpers. But anyone coming through should bring his own supplies, food as well as bedding. Aside from furniture in our homes, nothing can be depended upon.

We have been too busy to look after property. Have gone frequently to the places close to the hospital, but it doesn't do much good. Both Japanese and American Embassy seals were broken and completely ignored by the soldiers the first few days of their entry into the city and each place has been looted time and again. It does no good to try to clean up the mess until there is some way to keep them out. There have been but one or two places where one could move things with any assurance of safety. I have been unable to get workmen to repair wall, doors, locks and windows or to put caretakers on the place. They would not be safe for so far no proclamation or letter from the Japanese Embassy has been respected by the soldiers. Any Chinese whether on foreign property or not is subject to seizure and robbery and a possible thrust from the bayonet. We have in some cases secured a Japanese guard. But they demand a charcoal stove, and food and furniture on the place to keep them warm. The American Embassy staff employed Japanese guards, but fired them the second day.

January 13

Hurrah! Hurrah! A note from you written in Shanghai. Now I can write to you there confident you will receive it if I put it in care of our Embassy folks. And you can do likewise.

It has been a busy day. Went out early this morning to Ho Ping Men to get some cow feed—the place had been burned the day before. Then we went to a place near Lotus Lake; here we secured half a load. At another place we got a load of cotton seed cakes. Our ambulance is doing double duty these days. Will go back again for another load. Then I secured a coffin for John Magee for one of their Episcopal Evangelists from Tan Shan, I believe, who committed suicide as a protest against the present conditions. Then I secured a big cask bean-oil, 380 chin. We now have a three months supply on hand. I would worry about this business of supplies if I had time! Yesterday I picked up 15 bags of rice (100 chin each) from the coolies at B.A.T. [?] Most of this was for our Chinese Christians who are at the Drum Tower Church. Four or five of our faithful South Gate men are sheltered there and they have not been bothered at all. There are no evangelistic workers or other workers employed by our mission in Nanking; only about one or two of the city pastors here.

I decided to accept the four other cows; that makes eight cows and two calves. These four cows had been shut up for a month in a single shed, the conditions of which were terrible, so I rounded them out along with two calves, a goat and a kid and led the procession back to the hospital. There was plenty of bawling and some of them went under protest, but we marched them along and parked them in the front garage. That means an additional supply of meat for our patients. And we needed it for we cannot get bean milk which we ordinarily would use.

I go out and get pai tsai by the ambulance loads. The people cannot bring it to us, so someone has to go after it. We found another good nurse today, a graduate of the Wuhu Hospital. About ten of our 50 nurses are real ones.

Had the American Embassy men over for dinner this evening and Trimmer as he had not met them. The Embassy men are not having such a glorious time of it. They have not been able to get heat, light or water and it is difficult setting up housekeeping and getting supplies. And of course they do not have the interest and activities the rest of us do and with no newspapers or outside activities of any sort whatsoever with only problems to handle life seems a bit dull for them. One is shut in and I must admit the atmosphere is extremely gloomy and dull.

We are all anxious to get to Shanghai to see our families now.

January 15

One of the British Embassy men is going to Shanghai tonight and has promised to take any letters we might want to send. I am sending you the letters I have written, but could not mail—quite a stack by now.

Conditions have improved but horrible things still go on. Ten days ago I went into the dispensary and saw a fifteen year old boy on the table there with part of his stomach and some of his intestines protruding. The wound was two days old. He lives out near the Wu Ting Meng Gate. The soldiers had taken him as a laborer to carry vegetables. When he had finished his work they went thru' his clothing and robbed him of the sixty cents which they found, then stuck him several times with bayonets.

Our British Embassy friends have had a difficult time hearing our stories. They are too raw for them to take so we have had to tone them down considerably. But they have been bumping into some pretty terrible things on their own and getting it first hand. They went on a tour of inspection of the British property and near the A.P.C. [?] at Ho Ping Men they found the body of a woman who had had a golf club forced up, internally; a part of it was protruding. Now you know why the people are still in the refugee camps and why they are still terrified. We have been able to protect them on American property when we have been present, but what we have been able to do has been a mere drop in the bucket.

Spent a good share of the day getting hay and cotton seed cakes to feed our dairy cows. Next week I shall have to rustle rice and coal. I was out with one ambulance today; Grace Bauer took the other one to get some Pai Tsai. She went away out Tung Si Meng for her load and got back safely. It is wonderful the limits to which we foreigners can go without mishap. Some of the diplomatic people who have recently arrived wonder that we have not all been lined up and shot for we have gotten by with a lot.

I am glad you are in Shanghai and the boys in school. You seem so much nearer and I hope we can be together before too long. Don't blame me too much for leaving the family responsibilities upon your shoulders alone. I really expected to get out before the bitter end because I felt I owed it to my family. When my mission work was finished and I could have slipped out, the hospital was in such dire need for a business manager and so short handed that it seemed I couldn't refuse when they asked me if I could help. Once in, I was caught in such a whirl pool of work that I couldn't get out had I wanted to. My thoughts and prayers went out to you many, many times. I do not criticize any one who left. I thought it was the thing to do and I have been thankful I urged all our Chinese friends and workers to leave. But I am glad I stayed, hard as it was, and had a small share in helping these poor folk.

If you see a copy of a Sporting News in one of the Bookstores, do send it along with an eagerly waited for letter from each member of the family.

Notes

1. RG8, B119, F24.
2. A brand of canned peaches.

W. Plumer Mills

Wilson Plumer Mills was born in Winnsboro, South Carolina, on December 1, 1883. He received his B.A. from Davidson College in 1903, a B.A. from Oxford University in 1910, and a B.D. from Columbia Theological Seminary in 1912. Mills served under the YMCA in China from 1912 to 1931, and then under the Presbyterian Foreign Mission Board in Nanking from 1933 to 1949. Mills was appointed vice chairman of the International Committee for the Nanking Safety Zone when it was founded on November 22, 1937; he became chairman after John H.D. Rabe left Nanking on February 23, 1938. The Nanking Safety Zone had a population of about 250,000, of which about 70,000 people were dependent upon the Zone Committee for food and fuel. By the end of May 1938, the Committee would have exhausted its cash and supplies of rice and flour.

Just prior to the Japanese occupation of Nanking, Mills played an important role in efforts to bring about a truce that would allow the Chinese army to withdraw from Nanking and the Japanese army to enter the city without fighting. With approval from General Tang Sheng-chih, Mills and M. Searle Bates went to see U.S. Consul J. Hall Paxton on board the U.S.S. Panay *to transmit the truce-negotiating messages. This visit is described in the January 24, 1938, letter from Mills to his wife included in this volume.*

Letter to Japanese Embassy[1]

3 Ping Tsang Hsiang

Nanking, December 22, 1937
To the Officers
Of the Japanese Embassy,
Nanking.

Gentlemen:
As requested by you yesterday the members of the American community in
Nanking have reconsidered the matter of sending a telegram through you
to the American Consulate General in Shanghai. We feel, however, that the
questions which have arisen are so important and so urgent that we cannot
but ask you again to arrange for the transmission of a message on our
behalf.

As we have already reported to you, nearly every American residence in
Nanking has been entered by Japanese soldiers and articles stolen therefrom.
Further, the Ambassador's residence itself was entered, and repeated efforts
have been made to steal cars from the Embassy garage or compound, an Embassy policeman being wounded by a Japanese soldier on one of these occasions. Moreover, as recently as last night one car was actually stolen from the
Embassy garage. Again much American property in the city has been damaged
by Japanese soldiers and some of it burned by them. Finally there have been at
least eight instances where the American flag has either been removed or torn
down by Japanese soldiers themselves, or where servants have been intimi-
dated by them into lowering the flag, or threatened with violence if they raised
it again.

Were similar treatment accorded to your own nationals, your own Embassy,
or your own flag, you yourselves would be rightly moved to make immediate
protest and to ask through proper diplomatic channels that an adjustment of
these matters be made as speedily as possible. We therefore are likewise compelled to make such a protest at this time, and in order that an adjustment of
these matters may be promptly made, to express again our desire for the immediate return of American diplomatic representatives to Nanking. We would therefore respectfully renew our request that the accompanying message be
transmitted through the courtesy of your naval radio services to the American
authorities in Shanghai. Your cooperation in this matter will be greatly appreciated by us.

Sincerely yours,
(signed) W. P. Mills
For the American Community in Nanking

***

Letter to Wife[2]

3 Ping Tsang Hsiang
Nanking
January 24, 1938

Dear Nina:

Memories crowd in on one, as one sits down to write. The last three months have certainly been full. The latter part of November and the first part of December saw the planning of the Safety Zone and the setting up of the machinery for its administration, then came the tense days of the fighting around Nanking and our unsuccessful though strenuous attempts to arrange a truce, and finally since the 13th of December our long continued struggle with the Japanese to establish and maintain order. Then too there have been especially since the first of December, really big problems to deal with constantly in regard to the housing and provisioning of the refugees. I shall try in this letter to speak of these things in consecutive order to enable you, if I can, the better to understand what has happened.

With regard to the Safety Zone, we got our inspiration of course from the success of Father Jacquinot's zone in Shanghai. I have called it his zone, just because his name was so prominently associated with it. Our first task locally was to clear the idea of such a zone with Chinese and foreign friends, then to discuss it with the Chinese officials to make sure that we had their support, and finally to take it up with the Japanese. We had to make as sure as we could of a good location, to get the Chinese to agree to move their troops and military equipment out of the area, and then to get a promise from the Japanese to respect it. These were all difficult things to do. As a matter of fact the last two were never fully accomplished, but we did get both sides sufficiently committed to justify us in going ahead to put the zone into operation. The Chinese promised to move their troops out of the area, but never fully did so until just about the time of their retreat. On the other hand, the Japanese at first made no reply to our proposal, and then only after repeated efforts on our part, finally gave a sort of back-handed recognition to it by saying that while they were not in a position to give an undertaking that the area would not be either bombed or bombarded, it could nevertheless be taken for granted that the Japanese forces had no intention of attacking places not used by the Chinese troops for military purposes. We were never able formally to declare to both sides that the zone was in operation, because by the time the Chinese troops had moved out sufficiently to enable us to make such an announcement honestly, the foreign gunboats had all moved up the river, and we had no way to send any messages out, as all other means of communication had long since ceased to function. What we did do was this. We announced, before all lines of communication were cut, that the International Committee for the Safety Zone, relying on the good faith of both sides in regard to the assurances given, was going ahead with its plans for the operation of the Zone, was inviting the people to come into it, and making provision as far as it could for food, fuel, and housing. In other words, our Nanking Safety Zone was carried through on sheer nerve; or if you refer, on faith; or on a certain sort of boldness that did not know when it was licked. More than once our chances of success seemed slight, but something always happened, or was made to happen, that gave us a new start, until now, ten weeks after its inception, the Zone is still going strong. Of course we all thought and expected that the Zone would have gone out of operation long ago, but as I wrote you on the 22nd, the Zone has proven far more useful after the occupation than it was before. It did give some protection during the fighting, because it proved a haven of refuge especially to the people in the southern and southeastern sections of the city and in the suburbs, where the heaviest fighting took place. But the chief usefulness of the Zone has been in the measure of protection it has afforded to the people since the occupation. I wish you could have seen the way the people flocked into the Zone during the early days of December, and I wish you could see Shanghai Road and Ninghai Road now. These two are now the principal business streets of Nanking. Formerly these used to be Tai Ping Lu and Chung Hua Lu, the old Fund Dung Giai, but those streets are now largely burned out, and instead the formerly more or less little used Shanghai Road up past Hillcrest and the American Embassy, and Ninghai Road in the new residential district, also formerly little used, are now the principal streets. Shanghai Road is now so crowded that one can hardly get through it in a motor car. This change is all a matter of the last few weeks. The reason is simply that the people are here in the Zone, and because by now some sort of order has been established, so that there is no longer the universal plundering and robbing that there used to be, the people now have more confidence than they had before and have begun to come out again on the streets. They have set up scores of temporary shops by the side of the road and business is brisk in these—all of course on a small scale and all within the Zone. Outside of the Zone there is no business at all.

We could never have put the Zone into operation had it not been for the splendid assistance given us in the beginning by the Chinese civil officials, the members of the Diplomatic Corps, the foreign newspaper men, and the foreign business men. They were all for the scheme and aided it in every way they could. Our troubles were solely with the military, Chinese and Japanese. With the Chinese the difficulty was due to the fact that they were so dilatory about moving out of the area. With the Japanese our difficulty lay in getting them to make any reply at all, and even then we got only an indirect recognition of the

Zone, but it proved enough for our purposes. The Committee held steadily to its determination to establish the Zone, and finally succeeded, though it was an uphill task. Almost at the last the Chinese military tried to make us alter the southwest line, claiming that they had not clearly understood just what the civil officials had agreed to, although we had previously been solemnly assured that it had all been thoroughly checked with them. If I ever felt in danger these months in Nanking, it was on the afternoon when Searle Bates, Mr. Rabe, Mr. Sperling and I finally went over that line again with the military, and settled that the line should run as originally agreed upon. While we were out on the hills back of Hillcrest and the Seminary, two Japanese planes appeared overhead, and the anti-aircraft guns close by us began to roar. We were out directly among the soldiers, so we were a fair target so to speak. We lay down on the ground and watched the planes go by, while the guns blazed. For the first time I saw the silver gleam of some of the smaller shells or tracer bullets as they sped after the planes. Fortunately the planes were after other prey that day and we escaped, but as Mr. Rabe said afterwards, "I expected to be bombed that day." I did not exactly expect to be bombed, but both planes and guns were too close for comfort. Searle went back with Mr. Sperling the next day to put up the Zone flags—a red cross within a circle—thus finally marking the line, and he said their experience then was much worse than the day before when I was with him.

All this is only part of the story of the Zone, but I must pass on to other things. Perhaps this is the logical place to tell you a bit about our efforts to get a truce established that would permit the Chinese to withdraw from the city and the Japanese to enter it without further fighting. It was perfectly clear from a variety of reasons that the Chinese could not hold the city, though not so clear that they might not be able to make it somewhat costly for the Japanese. A truce proposal therefore seemed in order. The scheme was all talked through with General Tang, who was in command of the city, one of his secretaries acting as go-between, and had his hearty approval. Officially of course he could not accept the plans without the approval of General Chiang, who had by then left Nanking. It was necessary therefore to send a wire to [him] and one to Tokyo at the same time. The messages were drafted and Searle and I took them out to the *Panay*, which was then lying a little upstream off Hsiakwan. We went out with General Tang's secretary on a special pass through the city gates. Hsiakwan was already ablaze, having been set on fire by the Chinese troops with the idea of leaving no cover for the enemy in their attack on the city. It was weird driving through the streets with the fires blazing on both sides of you. Archie Tsen's house was burning fiercely as we came back towards the city gate. I shall never forget the sadness of that night's drive. The destruction seemed so futile and stupid.

General Tang had assured us that he was confident that Gen. Chiang would accept the truce proposal, so we were surprised to receive a wire from Hankow the next day to the effect that he would not. Naturally this word necessitated further messages and Tang's headquarters were insistent that we communicate with Hankow again. So Searle and I took another trip out to the *Panay* the next night. This was the evening of December 10th, and the hour was much later than our previous trip. It made one feel creepy to drive through the still and deserted streets, and there was a sense of impending catastrophe in the air. Also one had the feeling that there might easily come at any time a burst of rifle or machine gun fire from somewhere in the dark. It not tend to make me feel any better when we got on the boat to have Paxton tell us that some time before we came there had been such firing on shore. But we got the messages off and returned safely around midnight. That was another experience one would rather not repeat. The next day the *Panay* started upstream to her new anchorage and her untimely end. All communications being thus cut off, we could do nothing further to effect a truce. But the story does not end here, though the telling of the rest of it will have to wait next week's letter.

With all my love, Plumer (W.P. Mills)

***

Letter to American Embassy

3 Ping Tsang Hsiang
Nanking
January 15, 1938

Mr. J. M. Allison
American Embassy
Nanking

Dear Mr. Allison:
Under date of January 8th, Dr. Lewis Smythe wrote you giving a record of the number of times that Japanese soldiers entered the property of the American Presbyterian Mission at Shuang Tang, during the afternoon of January 6th and the morning of January 7th. This record was entitled *One Day at Shuang Tang*. I wish now to carry this record a bit further for your information.

The above record will serve to show you how, in spite of flags and proclamations by both the American and Japanese Embassies, our properties are still constantly entered. The soldiers, as you will see by this record, do not always

One Day at Shuang Tang

January 6th

1:50 P.M.	Three Japanese soldiers took away a woman and raped her.
2:10 P.M.	One Japanese soldier took three men away to work.
2:30 P.M.	Four Japanese soldiers came and looked around for twenty minutes and then went away.
3:25 P.M.	Three Japanese soldiers took away ten men to work.
4:10 P.M.	Three Japanese soldiers took a woman away into a small house outside the gate (of the compound) and raped her.
4:40 P.M.	Two Japanese soldiers came and spent fifteen minutes looking around for pretty girls and then went away.
5:05 P.M.	Three Japanese soldiers came in, made a disturbance (turned things upside down) for about twenty minutes, and then went away.
6:35 P.M.	Two Japanese soldiers asked two of the refugees to get girls for them, and when the refugees refused, beat them.
11:00 P.M.	Three Japanese soldiers climbed over the wall and took away two women.

January 7th

10:00 A.M.	One Japanese soldier came and looked around for ten minutes and then went away.
10:15 A.M.	One Japanese soldier armed came in looking for pretty girls but did not take any one away.
10:30 A.M.	Three Japanese soldiers came and asked for girls but did not take any one away. However, they took away the gateman's winter shoes and left their old shoes instead.
10:50 A.M.	One Japanese soldier came in and made a disturbance for about ten minutes.

Jan. 8th	5:10 A.M.	Two Japanese came.
Jan. 8th	11:25 A.M.	Two Japanese came.
Jan. 8th	3:25 P.M.	Two Japanese came and took one man for work.
Jan. 8th	3:30 P.M.	Two Japanese came belonging to the Chung Dao Bu Tui and the Chen Fah Tui came and tore down proclamations from the doors.
Jan. 9th	2:00 P.M.	Three Japanese came and searched people in the camp for money. Also looked for women. After an hour took away a married woman named Pan. Took twenty cents away from a refugee named Liu, and also took from another named Kwang his arm band and badge.
Jan. 10th	9:00 A.M.	One Japanese came.
Jan. 10th	2:00 P. M.	Three Japanese came.
Jan. 10th	3:00 P. M.	One Japanese came.
Jan. 10th	3:10 P. M.	Two Japanese came and took away a married woman named Chen.
Jan. 10th	3:12 P. M.	Two Japanese came and took away a girl named Chen.
Jan. 11th	1:30 P. M.	Three Japanese came and took away two married women by name Chin and Fan.
Jan. 11th	4:30 P. M.	Three Japanese came and took away one married woman named Fan.

harm the people when they come in, but they frequently do. In any case such entries are improper and annoying. I earnestly hope that your representations to the Japanese Embassy on this whole subject of the continual entering of foreign property by Japanese soldiers will be effective in putting a stop to it.

Sincerely yours,
(signed) W.P. Mills

Or rather Mr. Fukuda.
Shuang Tang is one course outside the Safety Zone, but there have been 1,200—1,500 refugees there all along.

W.P.M.

Notes

1. RG8, B103.
2. RG8, B103.

Lewis S.C. Smythe

Lewis S.C. Smythe received his Ph.D. in sociology from the University of Chicago and was appointed to teach at the University of Nanking by the United Christian Missionary Society in 1934. In September 1937, Smythe's wife took their two children to Kuiling for the American school, while he remained in Nanking to teach. When the fall of Nanking was imminent, he refused to leave and devoted himself to establishing the Safety Zone for refugees. As secretary of the International Committee for the Nanking Safety Zone, Smythe wrote sixty-nine letters to the Japanese embassy from December 14, 1937, to February 19, 1938, protesting atrocities committed by the Japanese Army; some of the letters were signed by the chairman of the committee, John H.D. Rabe, but most were by Smythe.[1]

In the spring of 1938, under the auspices of the International Relief Committee, Smythe led a team of about twenty students in making a survey of damages and losses at Nanking and its surrounding counties. This was published as War Damage in the Nanking Area, December 1937 to March 1938. *Smythe and his family left Nanking for Chengtu, Szechwan, in September 1938, where he resumed his teaching at the University of Nanking's relocated campus.*

Included in this volume are excerpts of a letter sent by Smythe and his wife to friends in America, describing what had happened in Japanese-occupied Nanking up to the middle of March 1938. Also published here is a report by Smythe titled "Notes on the Present Situation, Nanking, March 21, 1938." This report describes eleven cases of atrocities, numbered from 460 to 470 with number

469 dated March 20; these eleven cases are not available in either Hsu's book or Timperley's work and therefore are reprinted here.

Smythe Letter[2]

Nanking, December 20th, 1937

Dearest Mardie, Chicks, and Folks:
I will regret to the end of time that I did not get to write up each day's events and each day's reactions to them for the last ten days. They may not have shaken the world, but they have shaken us! . . . But I have been either too busy to write or else too tired and discouraged to write or too bewildered to even think connectedly [in the] evening or else had my typewriter left at the office ......

I had better go back to Saturday morning, Dec. 11th. My last written press release was on the night of the 10th in which I gave the telegrams sent on the night of the 9th asking both sides to agree to a three day truce for the turnover of the city. That Saturday was a day of heavy gunfire and at noon we were all worrying about Bob with his many wounded cases at the Hospital. Small shells landed in front of Foochong Hotel (slightly wounding Mr. Sperling's hand) but one landing back of Foochong Hotel killed and wounded about 20 people. That forenoon 9 shells landed from there west to the alleyway by Plopper's house. So that had been a hot afternoon. That was in the southern border of our Zone and the first day artillery had reached us, so we were anxious to see how well the Japanese gunners would live up to their telegram! Well Bob came in late and remarked, "It looks like the Fourth of July! Never saw so many American flags in my life around here!" Charlie replied, "And it sounds like it too!" That afternoon we had no more shells land and the press conference was an informal affair. We had worked hard all day to get T'ang's men to get soldiers out of the zone, especially around Wutaishan. Eh Hsien ping[?] to clear the Zone promised the day before did not materialize. So we did not have much to say at the press conference. But we had an informal chat with the press men and stated that we thought of the Zone as a place of relative safety rather than a place that had been formally declared in effect. T'ang's men asked that day if we had heard about the truce from the Japanese. That night the gunfire was much heavier. Shells were landing in around Taiping Lu. Sone counted the seconds between the flashes and the report and it was 6 or 7 seconds. So we went to bed feeling that the shells were landing about a mile and a half away. Mills slept in the basement, but we went to our regular beds! The barrage did not come closer so we slept fairly well.

Sunday Morning, Dec. 12th, gunfire was still heavy though there was a lull towards morning. We went to headquarters at 5 Ninghai Road and a little later

Col. Lung and Mr. Chow came from Gen. T'ang's office and asked if we would take over the wounded soldiers. We replied that we could not give any safety to anyone unless the Chinese soldiers were gotten out of the area. If they would do that, we would do what we could about the wounded soldiers. So while they went to convey that message, we talked over and decided we would have to organize an International Red Cross, which Magee had been working on for three weeks, pronto. To our surprise they came back between 11 and 12 and said that Gen. T'ang wanted us to send a man out between the fighting lines to propose the three-day truce to the Japanese directly! We worked around on that with details of how it should be done: Sperling was to go out with a white flag and white sign saying "Please stop firing, we have a message for you." Also we were to telegraph the Ambassador in Hankow and the Japanese in Shanghai. We worked out the message carefully and got their agreement. It was nearly 3 before it was all fixed up,—guess they left about two, though. Mills got some bed sheets from the house and we had the message painted on one of them. We worked in the greatest secrecy, because after the word had been sent to T'ang, we decided we might be involved in treason, because they were not anxious for us to send word to Chiang Kai-shek. But we worked up the message to Johnson afterwards and decided to insist on his being told to notify both the Chinese and the Japanese authorities that this was proceeding. Well, they did not come back. Nor did we get any lunch. Most of the fighting that afternoon was off to the south, and we at headquarters heard very little of it until some Chinese big guns west of us opened up. But in our concentration on these internal (inside the office problems) we did not notice it. So when we went down to the press conference, yes, on the night of the 12th, we remarked that it had been quieter! McDaniel snorted. We found that he and other press men had found the Japanese laying down a regular barrage right along Chung Shan Tung Lu and Kuo Fu Lu (so they said). But by that time we knew the jigs were about up, because at 4:30 there was a dash out in front, and a preaching squad led by Dean Tang we had sent out the day before also to explain to the soldiers in hopes of getting them away from Wutai Shan (so as not to involve anti-foreign feeling on the Zone) came in with word that retreating Chinese troops had tried to commandeer their car. The retreating straggling troops were going right through the Zone. There was great excitement. We had feared the retreat of the troops as the worst of all events we had to face. I insisted on sitting down before staff conference at 5:00 and jotting down what we would do. One was to let the troops go thru the Zone if they would disarm! We had a brief staff conference and then a brief press conference, and decided to let people get home early. On the way home, we found whole regiments of Chinese troops marching through Shanghai and Ninghai Roads, so we kidded George about his announcement at the Press Conference that we would disarm them! They were in full equipment.

Searle remarked when we got home that when that night was over we would probably be past the worst. I was glad the Chinese troops were on their way out in good season because we knew the plan to keep them here to fight in the walled city was like keeping them in a rat-trap. Shell fire continued through the night and machine gun fire. But we slept in our regular beds still. During the night about 3, machine-gun fire sounded close, but there was nothing I could do about it. However I was conscience stricken that we were not out on the perimeter to stop the Japanese from fighting into the Zone. About 6:00 I thought the machine-gun fire was at Shanghai Road, so I decided to get up and investigate. I went down Ping Tsang Hsiang and met a policeman moving his stuff in. He had come from beyond Sing Kai Ko and said there were no Japanese there yet.

(Pardon me, I squeezed over into the 13th. But there were no shells that landed in our Zone on the 12th, so my spot map for that day was clear. That was one reason we slept so peacefully with shellfire going on all night! We trusted the Japanese gunners implicitly not to shell the Zone.)

Monday morning, Dec. 13th As I went down the road on the morning of the 13th, I saw people with their bedding headed out of the zone. So I told them they could find places in the Supreme Court farther north. They looked at me in amazement that the *lao peh sing** could live in the Supreme Court! We had not given out a final announcement of public buildings because the papers stopped—Central News went out the night of the ninth and we had been releasing through them. Our "Safety Measures" warning people to take cover got out Saturday morning, but did not get in print for distribution as handbills. I found people on the road looking for food, so I went over to Wutaishan to see if the soup kitchen was ready to open there. They had not opened the day before because so many Chinese soldiers were stationed there and would eat their rice. Officers had up to about that time held them up on construction because they said they were in a fortified area. I found a number of banners in the wrong place down there and was full of gusto in getting them down, explaining to the crowds that gathered where the boundaries were and it would confuse the Japanese when they came if they were inside the Zone. I went on down to the corner of Han Chung Lu and Shanghai Road. On the way only saw a very few straggling Chinese soldiers in retreat, and they were peaceably buying things from venders along the way. There had been no apparent disorder in the Zone during the night, but retreating troops had discarded various forms of equipment. I came back and went along Kwangchow Lu to see if any soldiers were still there. Found the encampment at the foot of Wutaishan cleared out and a fairly good Nash left.

---

laobaixing: the common people

We had been getting in all the things we could, so determined to send Hatz down to salvage that car. Went over to Ninghai Road by Ginling and found our flags out of place and told people about it. Found several discarded uniforms in the road, so told people and police to carry them out of the Zone. Then back up through Tao Ku Tsuen home. I did not realize it was 8:15! The gang were thru breakfast, but I ate. They were glad to know it was so peaceful out. After eating George took me over much the same road to see some things and we checked up on the Nash, then to Ginling to consult Minnie. She asked me why I looked so weary, but I told her I was enjoying it!

At the office we learned that Col. Lung had left Mr. Rabe $30,000 for the Red Cross and I was terribly anxious to get that committee organized before ten o'clock. Well we got hold of John Magee and Forster and I practically dictated a committee and its chairman, sec., etc. He was for going right out to pick up the wounded first. Then I suggested that he as chairman and Forster as secretary go the three places designated and see if the staff there would cooperate: Waichiaopu, T'ehtaopu and Chuinchengpu. I set to work with Mills and others to get out instructions to be lithographed pronto to the people as to what to do at the "critical moment." Rabe thought the Japanese would machine-gun the streets, so we told the people to take cover. Word was to go out through our housing organization and later by handbill. Well on our way home at one we found that the Japanese had reached Kwangchow Road. We drove down there and met a small detachment of about six Japanese soldiers, our first—but far from our last! (At the corner of Shanghai Road and Kwangchow Road, they were searching a bus, but not harming the people.)

So at lunch we tried to spot the Japanese flags over the city. Even thought the five on Drum Tower, top and each corner, were Japanese flags, but later learned they were still Zone flags. No Japanese flag on the Japanese Embassy yet. As we started back to the office in the car with Fitch, he wanted to also see the Japanese, so we turned down Shanghai Road. As we did so, we saw a small detachment of Chinese soldiers, about 20, marching southwards. Hatz came sizzling down the road and told them the Japanese were just over the hill. So they marched northward again, led by their brave young officer. That reminds me, we did see them before lunch. Two men came to our office, Chinese lower officers, and asked for protection. One they were able to give citizen's clothes, but the other left. He was the young officer leading this detachment. We drove down, saw the Japanese, and came back to warn them to disarm and get away. But they despairingly said they had no "*pien ih*" [?]. At the office we decided Rabe and I must contact the Japanese at once. So we got Cola, who could speak some Japanese, and started out to explain three things to them—as high an officer as we could find: The Zone, the new Red Cross Committee, and the fact there were some disarmed soldiers that had entered the Zone. Magee and Forster had found only a staff at the Chuinchengpu, and staffs at both other places gone. But they were willing to help. So he was keen to organize and decided to set up first at the Waichiaopu and get that going. Fighting was going on further north, so did not know how much he could do. We went down Shanghai Road and found no Japanese soldiers on Kwangchow Road. Near the Seminary we found a number of dead civilians, about 20, whom we later learned had been killed by the Japanese because they ran. That was the terrible tale that day, any one who ran was shot, and either killed or wounded. Our instructions were off, but had not reached the people! But along that street we found a Japanese soldier, riding nonchalantly along on a bicycle with rifle strapped over his back. We hailed him, and he told us we would find an officer on Han Chung Lu near Sing Kao Ko. Sure enough we found a detachment of about 100 men sitting on the south side of the road, and a large group of Chinese civilians on the opposite side looking at them. We tried to explain to the officer the Zone and drew it on his map of Nanking, *note it was not on his map.* He said the Hospital would be all right if there was no one in there that shot at the Japanese. About the disarmed soldiers he could not say. So we took what we thought was the cheerful news to the Waichiaopu and found they had already disarmed the extra men there. Then we took John and were going to T'ehchiaopu and Chuinchengpu to disarm all there. Mills advised against it because of fighting in north city where some Chinese soldiers still held on. Chung Shan Road was strewn with stuff thrown away by retreating soldiers. As we approached Shansi Road Circle, a sight startled us; a crowd of men in motley attire crowded around an auto were coming around the corner. We soon found it was Charlie in a car leading a group of disarmed soldiers to the Law College. They hugged that car! At the circle we met a detachment of soldiers in arms. We told them to disarm and some of them did. Yates McDaniel was there to help in the process and had been helping Charlie. Then a man came down Shansi Road riding on a horse and shooting his rifle in the air. We jumped in our car because we thought it was a Japanese and there would be a fight right there! But it turned out to be a Chinese and Hatz took his rifle away from him! At headquarters, nearly 4:00, Mills decided against going on, but John went to disarm the Tehtaopu and Chuinchengpu with Cola's assistance. At headquarters we found a mob of men outside that Sperling and others had been disarming. The place was becoming an arsenal! They were marched into the police headquarters near us. About 1300 in all, and some still in soldiers clothes. (Written Dec. 22, '37) We argued the Japanese would not shoot disarmed men. That disarmed soldier problem was our most serious one for the first three days, but it was soon solved, because the Japanese shot all of them—at least we will not believe otherwise until more of them turn up again. They marched out all of them finally and finished them. We all put up a terrific fight—in words only—to save those 1,300 Wednesday afternoon, and the officer promised to leave them till the next day if we would divide them up then. So we went to staff conference quite relieved. In half an hour we were called that they had come back for them. Sure enough there they were with 200 soldiers and were roping them up. We, Rabe and I, sped to Fukuda, or anyone, and got him. He politely assured us they would not shoot them, but not firmly enough for us to believe it. Riggs and Kroger stayed to watch, but the soldiers drove them away. We got back in time to see the last of them march out to their fate.

(In spite of my intention to make this a temporal sequence, it is falling into topics. Thursday noon (Dec. 16th) Charlie came home crying. "They have taken them all out and shot them." He struggled all morning at the Ministry of Justice (ironically enough) to keep the officer from taking a group of civilians along with the soldiers. The office insisted on taking all of them and the police stationed there, 50. Forty police from another place were taken on the same charge of harboring soldiers. To date (12/22/37) about half of the police have returned.

Monday night, 13th Minnie came to report that soldiers had camped on their rice for the soup kitchen, so it could not open the next morning. We went to Rabe's to have one of his men draw up a letter in Japanese to present to the guard the next morning. On the way home we ran on a detachment of soldiers at the corner of Hankow Road and Ping Tsang Hsiang. They were very gruff and told us to "Hurry home." When we got there we found Charlie, Gee and Ku. When they came out of Illick's house after supper, Gee went down to the Univ. gate to see what was going on. He called back excitedly to Charlie, so Charlie went down—first tossing a pistol he had saved from the disarming into the hedge. Found the soldiers had shot a civilian passing by, and were examining Gee very suspiciously because of his University badge. After many attempts, Charlie got them to believe Gee and Ku were his personal servants, so they let them come home with him. They all slept here that night and until we opened the University to protect women about Thursday or Friday.

Tuesday morning, the 14th We all got up and felt the fighting was over. There had been a lot of shooting during the night, but we put that down as caused by the fact the Japanese soldiers were "jittery" their first night in town. Now the Japanese were here; would set up an orderly regime and things would be rosy. I typed out a letter to explain our Zone to the Japanese High Command before breakfast and we got Rabe's man to translate it into Japanese. So Rabe, Forster to represent our Red Cross Committee, and I started out to find them with a Japanese interpreter from the Red Swastika. We ran on to Fukuda at Sing Kai Ko. He is Attaché to the Japanese Embassy. He had left here on August 16th.

Almost his second sentence was: "The Army wants to make it hard for Nanking, but we are going to try to moderate them." (When we discovered the Army systematically burning the city night before last (written Dec. 22nd) we at last believed his words!) He sent us to the Chung Yang Fang Tien to see an officer. We went up through broken glass and sand to a bedroom and this officer received us in half dress and a bad beard and a face of iron. He merely replied that the High officer had not come. They had made many sacrifices getting to Nanking and the Chinese had shot the people. That was that! As some one said later, "Holy smoke, these Japanese believe their own propaganda!"

Forster wanted to see the ACM [American Church Mission] property, so we went down Taiping Lu. As on Chung Shan Tung Lu, soldiers in 2's and 3's were going from shop to shop breaking in doors or plate glass windows and taking whatever they wanted, chiefly liquor then. The ACM parish house had one shell hole in it. The church was intact. Then to Peh Hsia Lu and found Mc's house had been gone through. I picked up three photo albums in the yard. We found two soldiers in the next house at the time. Kiesseling and Bader's had been broken into that morning and also Hempel's Hotel. Hempel today (Dec. 22) swore that there was no looting there by Chinese soldiers before they left. A few Chinese hotels opened up to let people drink of their liquor, but soldiers kept people from robbing ordinary shops. And all the shell fire had done comparatively little damage in South City.

As we came back, we found 50 men being led off roped on Hankow Road just above our home. We argued with the soldiers. Finally Forster stayed with them. I went back to get Rabe and started to Chung Yang Fang Tien. When we got there the officer was too busy to see us; then to Sing Kai Ko and the officers there had no interest. Back up—oh, I forgot one important sentence from the man at Nanking Hotel: "We fight the Chinese soldiers; but we love the common people."—We wanted to throw his words back in his mouth!—Back up Chung Shan Lu and found the men had reached the corner of Kwangchow Road, across from S.C.&S. Bank. We argued some more and an officer came by in a car and stopped. He took us to Sing Kai Ko again to see another officer who had just arrived. But he said: "Wait till tomorrow when the head man arrives." We showed all these men our letter in Japanese in which we explained the Zone, the disarmed soldiers and the Red Cross. All they saw was the disarmed soldiers! That was our letter of Dec. 14th, which along with the other, you may see some day. So all we wrote on the 15th was a simple letter further pleading for the welfare of the disarmed soldiers.

Wednesday morning, Dec. 15th, armed with that new appeal for the disarmed soldiers on the basis of humanity and recognizing the laws of war (both ways!) we were going to see the high man when he came. But before the letter was finished, Fukuda called at our Headquarter to find out what the Zone was! We gave him copies of all the documents and answered his questions about population, food supply, etc. Then Mr. K. Sekiguchi came with cards from the Captain and Officers of H.I.J.M.S. Seta. He was glad to cooperate and would help in starting the power plant. He had had a sailor shot by a sniper, so warned us they had to be careful to get all the soldiers cleaned out. But he was much more dapper than the army men and more congenial. Offered any of us a trip to Shanghai and told us about the *Panay* and how sorry they were about it all. Meanwhile, Swen, our interpreter from the Red Swastika, a 60 year old former secretary in the Japanese Embassy here, had arranged for us to meet the head of the Special Service Corps who was to arrived that day, at noon. So we dashed down there, and Fukuda was with him to translate. (Written Dec. 24th, '37) Back to the interview Wed. noon, Dec. 15th)—The Chief of the Special Service Corps told us they must search the city for Chinese soldiers; would post guards at entrances to Zone; people should return home as soon as possible; trust humanitarian attitude of Japanese Army to care for the disarmed Chinese soldiers; police might patrol within the Zone if armed only with batons; 10,000 *tan* of rice we had stored in the Zone could be used by us for refugees; telephone, telegraph, and water must be repaired, so he would go with Rabe to inspect; asked us to assist in getting 100–200 workers for the next day—will pay; will inspect rice locations and guard . . . The only things actually carried out were to put the disarmed soldiers out of their misery; allow police; call on us daily for help in starting electricity, water and telephone, but at the same time shoot the electricity workers; and so far not interfere with our use of the rice we had stored excepting that soldiers took bags and workers from rice shops, so they all closed for nearly a week. Yesterday they were opening in the garage of this house. The way the situation looks now, most of our rice will go out for soup kitchens, for practically free distribution. We had hoped to sell a large part of it and use the proceeds to buy more, so as to use it as a rotating fund for feeding the refugees through the winter. If we do not sell much, we hope later private traders will start getting rice in—if the Japanese Military will ever wake up to the fact that normal economic life on even a restored scale must get started if people are not to starve. At present we are pretty much in the commandeering stage similar to the early days of the Soviet Revolution in Russia—and yet the Japanese Army is fighting Communism!

When we got back from that interview, we ran into the officer taking off the 1,300 men in the police headquarters, which I have already told you about. We were all much depressed that evening about the shooting of disarmed soldiers and the increasing amount of looting and raping by Japanese soldiers. The thing many had feared, either looting by retreating Chinese soldiers or disorders amongst the civilian population, did not occur at all! The one thing we did not expect: raping, robbery, and killing by Japanese soldiers did occur and continues through with decreasing intensity since Sunday.

Dec. 16th—As a result of the terrible situation we are facing, the next morning, *Thursday,* before breakfast I drew up a letter which was criticized at the breakfast table and added to. Besides presenting a list of 15 cases of disorder, (the beginning of our file of cases which now reaches 147), we asked for searching to be done by squads under a responsible officer, guards at the entrances to the Zone at night to keep stray soldiers out, and passes for windshields of cars and trucks—our trucks were at a standstill. So that morning foreigners started trucking. Zial [Cola's mechanic] did this well for a few days, but then was seized in a car by Japanese soldiers and lost his nerve, and would not go on the road. So I think it was Friday or Saturday that Plummer began conveying a truck and coolies! It was that noon, Thursday, that Charlie came home crying. He had been hit twice by an officer. That night Minnie asked for foreign men to come over. We thought it was to stand watch, so three of us went to take turns, Searle, Charlie, and I. I slept in the little house near the gate where Mr. Chen stays. The other two up at the new faculty house, empty though. Nothing happened but a soldier brought in a half *tan* of rice late in the evening!

Friday—Dec. 17th we got out our letter of the 17th, copy of which is at the Embassy, having duplicates made by typists there. That letter was presented to Mr. Fukui about 3:00 and since they could not get regular patrols as asked for, he agreed to our verbal suggestion that guards be stationed that night at eight places where there were mostly women. To our surprise at 5:30 he came to our Headquarters with the head of military police and asked us to show them the eight places, with a truck-load of gendarmes. Only 17 in the city! We took him to Ginling, etc.—We thought action had begun. But after supper we decided to go to Ginling anyway, and Searle to the U.N. because, he said, "I will believe the Military Police are coming when I see them." So Fitch drove Searle to the University of Nanking, and Riggs home and one man to the Univ. Hospital [U.H.]. Then came back for us. Mills was going, but I decided to go along, so as to see what the situation was, and to be with George on the way back. At nights then we traveled at least two together and in a car with American flag. We drove up to Ginling gate and blithely called, "Kai men" [Open up]. The gate opened and Japanese soldiers with bayonets shoved Mills and me into the roadway inside, another poked Fitch out of the car, and took the keys. They lined us up on the East side of the road and Minnie, Mrs. Chan and Mrs. Twinem with a number of stooping servants were on the west side in front of the little gate house. Good thing Minnie at once told us to be careful as they were very rough. The sergeant gruffly made us take off our hats and searched us for pistols. It turned out he spoke French and one of his soldiers a little English and Chinese. George tried to revive his French but it was hesitating enough to create suspicion. We were there for over an hour. We showed our passports. George had none, but had a card. They started to let us to go twice then called us back, at first insisting the women all go with us. Finally they let us go at 9:15. We hated to leave the women but our presence seemed to cause trouble. They declared they must search the place that night for soldiers. We tried to get them to wait until morning. Later we learned that they kept the women at the gate until after 10:00 and then after the patrol had left the women did not dare to move. The soldiers took Mr. Chen, business manager, with them. They saw forms moving out the back gate, so knew soldiers were probably taking women. In the dormitories they found Blanch Wu and she said they had taken women. They went to the Practice School where Minnie lives and found Mr. Chen back drinking tea. Soldiers had released him at Kangchow Road. They took twelve girls in all while the searching party was at the gate. So it is thought to have been a put up job. Our sudden arrival disturbed proceedings! Well, that took away my gumption for chasing Japanese soldiers! (Oh, Consul General Okazaki called at the office P.M. 17th—or was his visit on the 16th?—see letters 17th and 18th—and said could not recognize us, but would treat us as though had.)

Saturday, Dec. 18th We drew up our famous and most comprehensive letter asking for the restoration of order by all military means possible, assuring them there were no large groups of soldiers left and would searching be more careful, including that they take over our police in a regular police system. 3rd point: return 90 police and 45 volunteer police taken. We emphasized we wanted no political power. We got that over to Tanaka in the afternoon, and he calmly said he would take it up with the military. Well, during the day the situation got much worse. The place was alive with Japanese soldiers robbing and raping. So Rabe and I decided to go as representatives to the German and American communities and demand action. We did so at 5:30, and found only Okazaki in, so had to talk to him. Rabe went the limit on the fact he was a German Nazi and a recipient of the highest award in Germany, the badge of a political leader. I emphasized that we were merely interested in the humanitarian welfare of the people. Okazaki said he had sent Mr. Fukuda that afternoon to consult the military. Outside we met Tanaka who had just come back from the Military, and said they would place guards at the Univ. and Ginling. We asked what about the rest—oh, I believed it was the 8 places, but we had increased that request to 18 refugee centers. He said that was all they could do. Luckily Tanaka had been at our office and taken out on a number of cases that afternoon, as had Fukuda. An officer from the special service corps came down to see Rabe about starting the Electric Plant, was called to chase soldiers out of Rabe's place, learned of robbing his sub-manager, Mr. Han, and also a case of rape near by, where the officer caught the man in the act and cuffed him, and then told Rabe he was convinced what he had been saying was right. It was this actual seeing of the cases that convinced the Embassy people. That night we took Mills to Ginling with trepidation and got there just as the military police were stationing a guard and a Consul policeman there. One Consular police also came to UN and was very good. After that Minnie said she did not need anyone to come to Ginling until last night (written Dec. 26th) when they yesterday removed the guard. However, a Consular police was there again last night too.

That night we took Mills over there to sleep, lest guard would not arrive. After the night before Mills was shaky about it. I decided to go along again as escort. But we found the Military and Consular police there stationing a guard so all was happy. But Mills stayed.

Dec. 19th. On the morning of the 19th, the night had been so bad that Bates, Wilson, Fitch and I went to the J. Embassy right after breakfast. Wilson reported the attempted raping in the Nurses Dorm. During the night, Bates at the Univ., and George the difficulty of carrying on our work. From there we went to take Searle to Univ. MS [middle school?]. and found they had had trouble during the night, three women raped. On the way out we met Miss Pearl Wu coming in with soldiers following her. We took her in the car over the objections of the soldiers and went back to the J. Embassy to ask where she would be safe in the city? Started to take her to Ginling, but saw many soldiers at the gate, so brought her on to here. Here she wrote out summaries of cases for me till two. (Sorry job for a Phi Beta Kappa girl from the U.S.!) And then to our house for dinner, and for UH to help Miss Hynds. Not much help there, but safer for her. She had been living by herself on Wutaishan and excepting for being forced into a porcelain shop one day by J. soldiers whom she said were anything but nice, had gotten by.

Dec. 20th, 1937—8:15 P.M.

Dearest Mardie and Chicks:
Well, it is quite evident now that I am not going to get to spend Christmas with you. Nor is anyone else here going to get home for Christmas. And I fear it is going to be the most dismal Christmas we ever saw in this city or any other. But we hope to be doing most for a large number of people that we ever were in our lives. In the tremendous human problem we are facing here these days, we cannot think about our own wishes. But nevertheless, I wish I could be with you all for a happy Christmas in Kuling.

Ten days ago tonight I wrote to you that I hoped the Chinese would not fire

South City before they left. This evening after 5:00 George Fitch and I drove through South City and found the Japanese systematically burning it! We went down Pao Tai Chieh and saw a soldier entering George's back door, in spite of Japanese Embassy proclamation on it. (Place has already been looted badly by the Japanese soldiers, as has nearly every foreign house in the city since they came. And most of them we had checked up that they were O.K. when the Chinese left.) The last two days Mr. Tanaka of the J. Embassy has been anxious to get Japanese proclamations up on foreign property. With tonight's burning, we are more in a mood to accept the statement the writer made to Gee's man when he was making the proclamations at the University: They are to prevent the soldiers burning foreign property when they burn the city! Also the statement to Gee yesterday by the Embassy man, "Another day may be too late."

When we did not find Tanaka at the Embassy, George suggested that we drive around. It was just after five and getting dark, the first we have gotten away from the office before dark. We left our letter filing cases of disorder, 71–96, and went down Pao Tai Chieh and south over to Taiping Lu. When we crossed the creek on that back road, we ran on to a fire in poor Chinese shops. On Taiping Lu large sections were already burned out, probably the big fires we saw last night. We went south of Peh Hsia Lu and found fires on both sides of the road. Groups of 15 or 20 soldiers were cleaning out such things as looters had left and then building fires in the middle of the shops. We had to turn back because the road farther south was jammed from curb to curb with J. motor trucks and cars getting some stuff out. No fires further south then.

We went over on Peh Hsia Lu to Chung Hwa Road and there found the Y.M.C.A. had just gotten under way, with northern half in a sheet of flames from the inside. No fire on either side of it, so it was an inside job. Fires on both sides of the road south of us, so we turned back. Kuo Fu Lu was nearly all burned out last night. So far as we could see, there had been no firing west of Chung Hwa Lu, or west of Chung Shan Lu, as we came farther north. On Tai Ping Road we found a few civilians getting out with their bedding. It was a very depressing sight to see all this distruction, and what it means we are in for here this winter, but I was glad I went. A week ago tomorrow, Dec 14th, forenoon, I was through that same area with Rabe and Forster and the area was intact, excepting for damage done by shell fire. So I can swear before the world that the Chinese did not burn it out, and now the Japanese are burning it out!

There is probably little we can do about it, but we will work out some form of protest tomorrow. T . . . [?] The first outside news we have had in all that time, or rather since Sunday night, Dec. 12th, because we had electricity at headquarters up till that time. Telephones worked till the morning of the 13th! . . . Well for the news today. A Mr. Sindberg, a young man who is watching the Kiangnan Cement Works at Tsi Tsaishan came into the office today. He had walked in the twenty miles today. He got into the city by catching a J. motor lorry. No foreigners are supposed to be allowed to enter—or even reenter the city now. But he has his own Delco radio out there and has been getting the news. He says the *Panay* incident is much more than we had heard. We got that through the Japanese Naval people, who arrived in Hsiakwan on the morning of Dec. 15th, last Wed. And Amer. is making quite a fuss about it, asking the Emperor himself to apologize. Things are also hot around Hongkong, and British ships were involved, — he even said the *Cricket* had been hit by bombs. The *Panay* was also machine gunned and boarded, etc. It was enlightening to know something was happening outside of Nanking.

Dec. 21, 1937—8:30 p.m. Today Rabe answered a note from Dr. Rosen on the *Bee* and gave a list of all 22 foreigners here and said we were all well. Luckily we are! But how much longer it is going to be healthy for us we do not know! But we have plenty of food with all the "loot" each fellow has brought in from his house, and the fact people who are killing their pigs to keep the Japanese soldiers from stealing them know we pay for our meat. The cook has not been on the street since the Japanese got here a week ago yesterday! . . .

Rabe's reply to Rosen was the highlight of the day. We went to the Embassy to present an appeal to the Japanese authorities in the name of the total foreign community, 22 signatures asking that the burning of the city be stopped, disorder amongst their troops be stopped now that it had gone on a full week, and that ordinary civilian life be restored so food could come in: housing, security and food. When we got there, they handed Rabe a note from Rosen asking if we were all well, and if German property was all right! Rabe was spokesman, and after Tanaka read the petition and replied they would do the best they could in a few days, Rabe told him about Rosen's letter and said that he would have to reply that all German houses but two had been damaged by the Japanese! This petition idea was one we had had in mind for several days but held it in reserve. When they started systematically burning the city the last two nights, we decided it was time to use it. At least I so decided during the night and drew up the letter this morning before breakfast—our meal times are our most well represented committee meetings—8 of us with Charlie who is eating here now: Bob, Searle, Charlie, Mc, Plummer, Sone, Fitch and I. In these hard times it is certainly a life-saver to be in a gang. While we get terribly discouraged, we at least can cheer one another up and even make fun over the tragedies. It is the most difficult situation I have ever had to face and last week and through Sunday we were about sunk. But conditions are improving a wee bit now, excepting for the burning of the city. But order is somewhat better. Whether that is because of Military orders or because we have the women and children largely concentrated in big refugee camps, 25 in public and institutional buildings, with a total of 68,000 people. Ginling College had nearly 8,000 today! The place is covered with women and their bedding! But the moving in from other places practically stopped today. Ginling jumped 2,000 yesterday! But this concentration cuts down on the percentage of women raped: 2 or 3 out of 4 to 8,000, instead of 2 in one family household of 30 to 40 people. With guards at some places, that helps. If things clear up soon enough, our reserve of rice will carry us through along with the private supplies any one with any means brought into the Zone. With all the looting by Japanese soldiers, it is surprising how much has survived!

I did not finish Rabe's letter! He used very flowery German to tell Rosen that he was delighted to say that two German houses in the city positively had not been damaged, that Rosen's car, along with many other German cars, was rendering excellent service for the Japanese Military, and that he hoped he would be here for Christmas Eve because by then we hoped to have water, electricity and telephone going! Then added list of foreigners and said all were well. That was a masterpiece! The note had to go open for courtesy's sake through the Japanese Embassy. And when they had turned down the telegram we Americans tried to send yesterday asking our Embassy people to get a diplomatic representative here as quickly as possible, Rabe knew he had to be careful to get anything through. He was much more tactful than we were! We got up with blood in our eyes yesterday morning and had to write the telegram 6 times before we could get it toned down enough at breakfast table to dare send it. Then they turned it down because we said "Situation daily more urgent." Because they claimed it was getting better. There had been enough threatening us by Japanese soldiers that we chased away from women they were about to rape in gatehouses and basements and bedrooms to make us feel feeling was rising against Americans in particular. The flag had been torn down in four places and property was all looted excepting Claude's and this place. (Charlie says our house at 25 has escaped looting at least in any bad way so far, because the wall is hard to get over and there are so many people in it!) However in most of the American houses they have only looked for little things and have not taken a great deal in most places. With us the things they want are in Kuling: bedding, clothes, food and money. I just have enough cash to pay my two weeks' board bill. But Bob is in no hurry to get that! He wants to keep money scattered. But if I need money, there is some mission money Searle has I can draw on.

When Bates talked to Fukuda this morning, he said the situation was better, and for us to let them know of any cases today. So I stayed at the office till six getting out copies of cases reported up to 4:30 this afternoon. That is the sorriest job I ever had in my life! Finished typing up case 113, and most of those are compound cases, and that is not a drop in the bucket of what has been going on. At the peak of the disorder Saturday and Sunday we estimated there must have been over 1,000 women raped every night and on those two days, probably as many by day, in the Safety Zone! Any young women and a few old women were susceptible if caught. Pastors wives, univ. instructor's wives, any one with no distinction of person, only that the prettier ones were preferred. The highest record is that one woman was raped by 17 soldiers in order at the Seminary! In America people used to mention "rape" in a whisper. It is our daily bread here almost! Stories pour in so rapidly and so hard to keep up with, that I began taking them down in short-hand at the table. If I waited till I could persuade people to write them out, they were too old for the Embassy, which wanted reports on the daily situation. So now I take them in shorthand wherever I am.

The thing about the whole situation that startles us all, and we wonder how long the miracle is going to last, is how we unarmed handful of foreigners can go around here and chase the Japanese soldiers out of rooms in school buildings, rooms in foreign houses, out of gate-houses and rooms in Chinese homes, and still no one gets hurt. The soldiers often actually run away. Part of it is pure bluff. If we batted an eye, we would be done for. Sperling is regular policeman over at headquarters and is on call all day for that service in almost any home in the area. The Japanese soldiers now run when they see him coming. The soldiers are all armed. This is especially a miracle when they bayonet or shoot any Chinese that dares to say a word or even runs for help. Saturday and Sunday I expected the charm to break at any moment, and the few threatening ones showed us that we may have to let up on chasing them out of Chinese homes, but pressure from the Military seems to be weakening the nerve of the soldiers too, so they are not so "li hai" [tough]. Although one of three, that four of us (I was detailed for that job and picked up Fitch, Bob and Mc on the way, I am glad to say) chased out of a gate-house, where they were stripping two girls there at the turn of the road on Ping Tsang Hsiang, was hard enough boiled and mean enough to make us realize that it would not take much to make him shoot! But we stood around and said nothing till he finally walked off. I have gotten in for much less of this than others. Searle was driven wild on Sunday with it at the Univ. Charlie had been on it several days too, but yesterday got to trucking rice and coal, and he feels much better because he can see something accomplished by night. It is taking some trucking to keep up with the rice and fuel needs of those big refugee camps! And no Chinese dares go on the street with a truck. Even Plummer was trucking rice and coal on Friday and Saturday, while Charlie was busy chasing out Japanese soldiers. They not only have to ride the trucks, but they have to go to a house at Kulou where Red Swastika coolies are living, escort them to the Univ., watch them and the truck while it is loaded, ride the truck on its rounds making deliveries to keep Japanese soldiers from grabbing it, bring the truck back, and then escort the coolies home! Even then it is a fight to keep Japanese soldiers from taking the coolies or truck.

Today Charlie showed a ray of light to a Japanese officer, He came to the

Univ. to demand 15 workers. Charlie said he could get all he wanted for him if he would give them an arm-band that would protect them and promise them regular pay and food. He said he could do that. So Charlie said he could get him a thousand. The officer had thought only of commandeering them! We offered a week ago tomorrow to open an employment bureau for the Japanese where we could control the terms of employment and give the men some protection, but they did not take us up on it. We may suggest it again. . . .

The Japanese are calling in such business men as there are in town tomorrow for a conference. That is one sign of an attempt by them to return to normal. But the burning of the city is certainly a contradiction of it. So Searle in his letter this afternoon reporting cases—He has a thought for the day just as I do—said "Let us know whether you intend to restore normal conditions or merely want to destroy the city. Then we can act accordingly but please don't kid us!"

Well, if we last long enough, we may wear the Japanese out first! We have gotten away with telling them much more than we thought we could a week ago, and the Embassy people are awake to the problem, but the Military either will not, or are too inefficient.

Dec. 22, '37. Well, it gets closer to Christmas, and I have found no way of communicating with you. Bates and Mills took over a letter this afternoon asking the Japanese Embassy to ask the Army to forward our telegram, but leave out two words "daily more" in the sentence "Situation daily more urgent." This was Mills thought for the day at breakfast this morning. He drew up the letter for explaining why we had a right to have a diplomatic representative here, But I fear our approach has not been as happy as that by Rabe in his humorous letter. Of course, he had a better opening than we did. Well, they were not very happy about it, and will let us know what the Army says. So that queers somewhat our asking them to send a personal message. Sone gave them a long one about his family at Mokanshan asking someone in Shanghai to get them out of there. And that had not been sent yet. We do think that if we can contact the Navy directly, they will send a personal message without question. But then Plummer's move is the only strategical move we made today. The special service corps of the Military Police were up to see Rabe this morning, to say they were going to register all the population. He thought it also included a committee they have for the Safety Zone. So we had some hopes it might mean the beginning of their assuming some administrative responsibility for the city. But so far only orders for registration of "peaceful citizens" and thereafter you can only continue to live in Nanking if you have your registration card! The good old Japanese system!

The new development on the bad side is that now the Chinese who are becoming cronies of the Japanese soldiers are appearing. Last night a Chinese came the second time to the Univ. for girls for a certain detachment of soldiers. "Pimps." Searle had to judge his case. The police wanted to strangle him, but Searle persuade them to put him in safe keeping. This afternoon we found one leading soldiers to girls opposite headquarters. The Chinese were about to tear him up, for Fitch persuaded them to put him in safe-keeping in the basement over night. What then? At the Univ. the police feared to let the man go, for fear he would bring back the soldiers who would clean out the bunch. So these scalliwags who are developing forbode no good!

The other thing is that the systematic burning of the city continued today and tonight. They have burned most of the east side of Chung Shan Lu up as far as Huang Li Kan. The house back of Marx's went this afternoon. And there are indications they are now starting on houses now that they have finished the main shops, big and small, along the main streets. So far no burning that we know of on this side of Chung Shan Lu so we hope they may spare most of the Safety Zone. But it looks as though outside of that, excepting foreign property is marked for destruction.

Poor Rabe has been very anxious to get the electric plant started as a demonstration of willingness to cooperate. But today when they went down to get the workers, they found that of the 54, only 11 could be found. The Japanese had shot the other 43 several days ago! They were at Hogee. And when the Japanese asked there, all the people in the compound were Hogee workers. The care-taker said there were 54 electric plant workers. They said, "Well, that is a govt. institution, so they will have to be shot." The care-taker then said that 11 were men that had helped at fixing the Hogee electric equipment, so they spared them. The others were led out to the river bank, and machine-gunned. What a pitiless and senseless brutality! And now it proves to have been cutting off their nose to spite the face! Bodies are beginning to rise in ponds around town now. And individuals are coming back that have miraculously escaped from groups of 30 to 100 or more who were lined up and shot. Nuff said!

Today robbery and rape continued almost as bad as ever. Yesterday most of the large concentrations reported almost no cases, but last night and today the raids on them began again. The Univ. last night was favored with a raid in autos! High class now! But the Consular policeman sleeping at the gate-house was finally able to talk them out of taking girls. Today near headquarters Kroger and Hatz were trying to save a house from rape and robbery by a drunken soldier. The man turned on Kroger and was going to tie him up and lead him off to shoot him! A Chinese boy ran to Headquarters to get Fitch, who took Rabe with him and dashed to the rescue. By a miracle, Tanaka and a general were touring the Zone and passed the place and somewhat heard the trouble and went in. The General first asked the soldier, who said Kroger had attacked him! Then the General asked Kroger, who told him he merely politely asked him to leave—luckily it was one time Hatz had not biffed the man on the chin! So the General cuffed and kicked the man severely, but let him go! A cuff or a requirement of salute is all they do to stop rape, robbery and shooting! And none of the soldiers have any identification mark on them, so there is no way of recording it against them. This man was actually threatening Kroger with a bayonet too. We are glad it was a German! But I agree with Rabe that we have got to stop trying to get them out of Chinese houses. They only admit our right to do it on foreign property. As Mills said yesterday, they are firmly and sincerely convinced that it is all right to do anything to a Chinese, from the top down! Well, not quite that bad. Bates drove Fukuda in a corner on the burning yesterday afternoon and showed he knew it was intentional. Fukuda said that he wished he were out of this mess and back in Tokyo. We think the Embassy people do not like it, but the army does.

As Mills asked tonight, what do we do next? We have about shot our bolts. We have protected up to the point where the Embassy people admit they can hardly go to the Military about protests any more. So I think we will have to follow Rabe's tactics of laying off for a day or two. Nearly every day since the 14th we have had an ingenious new protest to add to the complaint from the Univ. with all its ramifications from Bates, and a file of cases of disorders by soldiers, with a little covering letter with a jab or two in it! Besides that, Minnie calls on them every day and some of us are over there two or three times. That is a great load. And it is not doing much good.

So we can only go ahead with our pudding: trucking rice and coal to refugee camps, filing cases of disorders, etc. If there does not develop something more serious to protest about tomorrow, as usually does, we may politely ask for a reply to our petition yesterday.

Another miracle—Sindberg got in from Tsitsachi today again in the car Rabe loaned him. Picked up a soldier on the way who talked him in at the gate! Brought us two pigs and three bags of sweet potatoes. And Ginling gave us 2 geese today. So Christmas looks better. . . .

Dec. 23, '37. There was some improvement today. Whether it is because of more guards in various places, or because it began to drizzle today, I can't tell. At least there are less soldiers on the streets and much fewer calls for help. However Sone on his trucking has had trouble. Some Japanese soldiers were pulling down the American flag at Stanley Smith's house. That is the ninth case. It was the special investigation squad for the Zone! They were putting up the banner. After a hard time when they pushed him out in the street, he signed a statement loaning them the house for two weeks, but they put up the flag and put the banner on the gate. Bates says it should be reported to the Embassy in the morning. . . .

The J. took 200 men out of the camp at the RLTS[3] and shot them. Some of them were probably soldiers, but people there say over half of them were civilians. We were in hopes the fury of the Japanese Army had been vented and we would have no more shooting. One man came back to tell the tale. He was wounded and partly burned. We have not been able to clear up whether that was the same as another report or not. But another man came in today with his face all burned and probably his eyes burned out. His report was that 140 of them had been bunched together and then gasoline thrown on them and then set on fire! Horrible! Whether they are the same group or not we do not know. The group that were shot were reported to have been covered with gasoline and the bodies burned. The man that escaped was down underneath and later got away . . .

We have invited Rabe, Sperling and Kroger to supper tomorrow night for Christmas Eve. And are having Minnie, Mrs. Twinem, Blanch Wu and Pearl Wu-Bromley over to dinner Christmas. . . .

Fukuda is going to Shanghai by plane tomorrow and has offered to take any personal message. So, since they are subject to his inspection (!) we will send you a brief telegram to this effect: "Merry Christmas. We are all well and hope you are the same." Hope the American Consulate-General in Shanghai gets it through all right. Mc, Mills, Trim and I will join on it.

Sindberg got back in the city today. . . . He has offered to try to get word to the H.M.S. *Bee* laying off Hsiakwan if it becomes urgent enough.

Bob has those two burned men at the hospital but doubts whether they will live. The one with his eyes gone, it is a question whether it would be a benefit to him if he did live. But how he survived to walk to our headquarters is more than I can tell. A man was kind enough to guide him there. But the report Bates got is that it was only 70 that were taken from RLTS, but that is enough for such business. Kao Ping-san was at the Headquarters first thing today about it. Some relative of one of the weavers was taken. So they all wanted our arm-bands. Arm-bands are more popular here now than Easter hats! Ours spread all over the place in no time and still have considerable popularity. Those with the rising sun have about displaced us though. Now today, we foreigners were all issued arm-bands by the J. Embassy that gives us freedom of the city—inside! . . . Charlie arranged to put the weavers on at the Red Swastika soup kitchen at the Univ., as their arm-bands seem to have the most magic w[ith] the Japanese.

We have a ray of hope. The new soldiers that are replacing those that have given us so much trouble are to arrive in a day or two. They will be instructed that any one caught in any misconduct will be shot. We say we will believe it when they have all been shot! The refugees are much more worried over the registration of the whole population that is to start tomorrow, supposedly. A card index of the population. Then if you lose your card, out you go. That will be a new threat soldiers can hold over their heads. Little shops along the sides of the road were more in evidence yesterday and this morning. So things are somewhat better. As Searle says, it will probably just gradually get better.

This morning Rabe came in with word that the Consular Police wanted a list of all the foreign houses in the city that had been looted by 2:00 today. So that was about all we got done. But of course we gave only very general indications to degree of looting and reserved right to file claims (indirectly) later through American Embassy. Germans have had 38 out of 47 houses they know of looted; Americans 158 out of 174 known houses. However, the loot this time which the Germans put down as "completely looted" is nothing like 1927. Then they took the very doors out. In this case it means the house has been completely ramsacked, and any locked doors or chests broken into the stuff dumped out. The soldiers are after small personal articles or valuables, not furniture. They destroy more than they take. The city has the appearance of destruction now. I have not been down to see the burned sections again—it is on this side of Chung Shan Lu tonight at Kanhoyen. Where it will stop no one knows. If it rains hard for a week, that may stop it! Each bunch of shops has to be set, so it is pretty consistent deliberate work. But rain would be hard on the refugees. Mills and Riggs this afternoon tried to move some from Sericulture that were sleeping out of doors to Hwei Wen, but something fell through on it. We thought moving in to Hwei Wen, Chung Hwa and Ming Deh would relieve the pressure in crowded places and start the trek back into areas outside the zone.

Dec. 24th. Bob Wilson helped out some of our house last night. He got home early, about 5:00 for the first time in two weeks, so he went to the Univ. Gardens and bought six big poinsettias and put them around our living room. Then he dug out some red cut-outs and pasted them around the living and dining room. So we look like Christmas anyway. No, we will not have any tree. No one has had time or chance to buy any Christmas presents, and as there are no children in the house, probably no Santa will come. But today Mr. Rabe gave us all a diary book for next year. Siemens. It is in German, but very pretty and very useful with cash book and address sections, besides a lot of useful information. He is coming to our house tonight for a Christmas dinner on Christmas Eve. Isn't that funny! The Germans think more of Christmas Eve than we do, so we invited three of them for that time. Aunt Minnie and probably Aunt Grace are coming to Christmas dinner tomorrow. So you see we are having two Christmas dinners. . . . Providence has certainly given Nanking the proper weather: rain and clouds during air-raiding time, sunshine and warm weather for this time of year during all the "Safety Zone" time until the light rain yesterday and last night. More soldiers moving in today, but Bob says not as many as previous days. Less soldiers around. Searle had a quiet night at the Univ. and less trouble all around today. But soldiers came and ran off with the police man and I think

12 other men at the UN early this morning. That is hard on morale which had begun to build up. I am going to offer to go over tonight to give Searle a break.

The only trouble last night was on the American front. I told you about Sone's case, and so far it is not straightened up yet. This morning the same outfit took over Hillcrest, but when Mills went there and explained, the soldiers decamped. The worst case was the looting of the Amer. Embassy, both the east and west compounds and taking away several cars and trucks from there. Tanaka was much concerned about that, and will station a guard there. Mills is filing those cases, so I do not have more than a page for today's! The shooting cases we cannot report yet, because so far we have conflicting evidence, and there is no use exposing the soldiers (supposed to be) that escaped. The man with his eyes burned out mercifully died this morning at the hospital. But another came in with a machine-gun wound in his right shoulder. He claims he was one of a group of about 4,000 that were shot on the bank of the Yangtze on the 16th. About 30 survived. Ominously this afternoon as we came by the Embassy to talk over problems with Tanaka, he told Fitch a former Chinese Army officer had reported to them he knew of many former Chinese soldiers in the Zone, many of whom were armed with pistols still. We don't know of any such! It looks like a dastardly deed on the Chinese officer's part to help himself, but at the cost of terrible danger to many civilians. If they find one man in a place with a pistol, they will probably shoot 200! Up until yesterday we hoped we had passed the stage of shooting disarmed soldiers. If there are any left, they're scattered individuals and will give no trouble. There has been no sniping in the Zone even on the 13th or since. However, Tanaka remarked, "You will have less refugees in your camps in a few days." Whether he meant because of soldiers that would be shot, or that young men are to be pressed into labor squads, or they are going to order the people to move to their own homes, some of which are now burned!

Today the registration process is on. The one station we have seen here on Shansi Road has soldiers with bayonets driving or leading people from houses and camps to register! Everything at the point of the bayonet! This afternoon while I was waiting for Fitch outside at the J. Embassy, a Consular police came in, driving a horse-carriage and three or four servants (with arm-bands, just like we have, only we have lower numbers!) hauling charcoal. If they would work on a commercial basis, they could have the coal delivered without troubling to send a Consular policeman after it! But everything is on the commandeering basis. Consequently, no merchant is interested in stocking up, if he could, and everyone is getting rid of everything they can. So there will be a famine, especially of meat before long. As we pointed in our petition from the foreign community, the situation is leading automatically and rapidly towards a serious famine. Bob says we can have guests tonight and tomorrow, but after that no more! Our canned goods won't last forever. If we are looted like most places, it won't be that long. We have miraculously escaped so far, and so has Claude's place. About the registration, some of the Chinese claim they are loading all those between 20 and 35 into trucks and taking them away, I mean the men. But we did not see that. Only in a few places has it been noticed.

Hwei Wen move last night was not so successful because Embassy and soldiers got their wires crossed. Embassy said not many women; soldiers said no men! So it took Charlie and Mills two hours to straighten it out and finally they let the 100 people in. But meanwhile the guard had burned all the firewood the gateman had and started on his furniture until Mills stopped them. So that move is now held over until tomorrow. Will need to make cooking arrangements there, etc.

This morning the coal man on Hankow Road from whom we have bought all his coal for the soup kitchens came to say the soldiers had commandeered it. We appealed to Tanaka when he was here and he said he could do nothing. But at noon when Fitch and I came home, we found Riggs loading coal out of the yard next to 26! He had talked them out of it and all they wanted was charcoal! Fuel is our chief weakness.

This morning Fukuda was going to Shanghai by air and offered to take any messages. So we gave him our group telegram and I wrote a hasty one page letter to you. . . . Searle sent a cable for Rees to send his family. Charlie sent a Christmas card to Grace. Others sent letters to families. Plumer wrote his twice so you may learn more from it. . . .

Sindberg was in again this noon, probably has not been home yet. Says he can take a message to the *Bee* if we will guarantee him the salary he gets for staying at the Cement Works, in case he is detained either by *Bee* or Japanese. Bates thinks it would be a dangerous thing to attempt and probably would not get there. Better wait until he can get word to some passing foreign boat at Tsitsashan.

Today at the J. Embassy Cola told us that Zial, who is repairing Embassy cars there, may be sent to Shanghai to get necessary parts. They burned out the bearings on one of their beautiful cars—the soldiers especially ruin every car they get inside two or three days, so the streets are lined with broken-down cars and trucks, and dead bodies still on the streets. No one hand lifted to clean things up and make it look like a town. Well, if Zial goes, Cola thought we could send some letters by him. So I may get further word off to you.

Mr. Hsu, Housing Commissioner, was just in. The Red Swastika group are working with the Japanese to try to get houses of prostitution started so as to satisfy the Japanese soldiers and officers without endangering private homes! Well, Searle suggested that last Saturday in all seriousness and Charlie gasped! Mr. Hsu says they plan two quarters, one north of Kuleo R R Station for the common soldiers and one south of Sing Kai Kou for officers. And it will be on a commercial basis. He further says that Mr. Wang, whom we took on as business manager, formerly auctioneer on Pao Tai Chieh, has many connections with the underworld in Nanking! He has been one of our most active men. What a group we got into this ad hoc organization! The Germans we have found are sterling men. Since the Japanese came, Rabe has been our veritable salvation. He can push his black swastika out and demand attention! I took the opportunity to explain to Mr. Shu our policy regarding rice. He told Fitch day before yesterday that Fukuda in a confidential moment said, "Why do these foreigners sell their rice instead of giving it to the poor people!" I explained that we were giving at the soup kitchens or I believe for most people a few coppers as has been the custom in Nanking and to some we sell in hopes of getting funds from those who can afford to buy, with which to buy future supplies of rice. Thereby we can rotate our resources and maybe carry the very poor through the winter. If we give to all now, it would last less than two weeks. He understood and said he had told the Japanese the same. I also said that we must get normal business activity going because the Japanese Army's commandeering system is so inefficient that they will, even if unintentionally, starve the population. Any line of business we can get going will help, but more particularly rice and fuel. He is also trying to get them to have the Shanghai and the Wuhu RR running. Then we can get rice from Wuhu. And he says there are a number of fairly good business men in hiding, and they will come out as soon as there is any security at all. The boys laugh: Searle advocating houses of prostitution: I advocating capitalism!

Sunday, Dec. 26, 1937—10:00 A.M. at office. Christmas has come and passed and I did not get home to be with you, I am very sorry to say. . . . We are sewed up in this situation so much now that it is hard to see any chance of leaving for several weeks. We may have to see this refugee population through the winter.

Friday night, Christmas Eve, Kroger and Sperling came for dinner along with Trim. Mr. Rabe felt he had to stay at home to protect his house and 600 refugees in his yard. But after dinner Mills went to stay at Rabe's house while Mr. Rabe came over for a while. Mr. Rabe gave us all good diary books for 1938 Siemens Co. Bob opened one of his bottles of wine given him by the members of the German Embassy for his German guests! Before Bob went to the hospital for the night, he played some Christmas carols and we sat around and sang rather glumly. Kroger has quite an interest in music. Searle again insisted on going to the University.

Yesterday morning the 4 weavers we have left, 3 old-timers and 1 new student, came to the house to see me for Christmas greetings and to ask for special work. Charlie had arranged for them to help at the Red Swastika soup kitchen at the University, but Kao failed to carry through on it, two days previously. But they were content with that. I should have had dollar bills ready for them or just handed to them. Rabe did not come to the office because of protecting his place, so about 11:00 I went by there to talk over a coolie hire shop, exchange she [?] (found from Kroger that small change is piling up from the soup-kitchens, so we want to get it back in circulation as fast as possible) and about methods for encouraging private merchants to bring in rice, because it is evident the Japanese are not going to assign the I. C. any rice. Rabe thought the coolie hire shops should be started by the Tz Chih Hwei which has been meeting with the Japanese for nearly a week. (Autonomous Governing Society). It is composed of a number of small business men, but headed by the fine old man at the head of the Red Swastika. Dr. Hsu, our Housing Commissioner and a fine man with a Ph.D. is on it, and also our Mr. Wang, who has extensive connections with the underworld. (Really a group of business men, who first met on Dec. 22nd to formally organize Jan. 1st.) On the way home I stopped at 25 for the first time in over two weeks, first since the refugees moved in, and gave Chu Sao-Tze a dollar and each of the children a silver dime from the $5.00 worth of dimes I got from Kroger the first small change excepting two dimes I have had since three weeks ago! When I see the weavers, I will give them each a dollar, too. Was going to get some things from my study, but Riggs could not lock it, so he took out the knob! Not broken into so far, though the Japanese soldiers have been through the house several times, Chu Sao-tze and the children were well, and we had no serious bad treatment by the Japanese soldiers, and have rice for either another month, or the remainder of this. She did not want any more money yet.

At noon we had Minnie, Blanch Wu, Grace, and Pearl Wu to dinner for goose that Blanch Wu had given us. With all our canned goods, we were able to put up quite a dinner, but with the cook not going on the street, our canned goods are going fast. But with the daily danger of looting, it is hard to get Bob to hold up on the cook. So later we may be down to rice! Our women guests suggested that we invite the other half of our staff at Ginling and the Hospital for New Years: Mrs. Twinem, Mrs. Chen and Miss Hynds. We will. Dinner was interrupted as usual with calls to get soldiers out of Sericulture, stop them taking trucks at the University, etc. After dinner when I went out to go to the office, there was a young man with a baby in his arms. He said he was a relative of old Lao Sze. I did not recognize him. He wanted me to "sian fa tze"[4] to help him pass the Japanese registration, because he had no relatives here. I could think of no plan then, so told him to return in the evening when I thought Riggs could work out a scheme. He is living in a straw hut near Ginling. At the office I arranged to give him a letter saying he was the son of my gardener, but last night he did not show up and had not this morning. How often an opportunity for service is let slip in our confounded rush. Gee listed all the servants in UN houses yesterday afternoon, and all the refugees, over 10,000! Bates said that if we got him in first thing this morning we could put him at 25. But if he does not come in time, he will have to take his chances at his hut. I told him to try to pass as a member of the family who gave him the baby to carry. I left the letter and a letter for Gee with our cook this morning, in case he comes this forenoon. But today is the day for registering the University staff and refugees, so he may be too late, or rather, I was too late in thinking of what to do. I did not recognize him at first, but he is the boy that used to live at our place with Lao Sze. I hope it works out all right. I may later go up and walk around the Ginling area and see if he comes to me.

During the afternoon there was not a great deal to do at the office. Trucks were interfered with because coolies could not work until registered and I suppose the same will be true today. But after people once pass the bugbear of registeration they feel much relieved. So far reports of any large numbers being taken off as soldiers, about 20 from the Middle School [MS]. Fitch was told yesterday that even soldiers would be pardoned if they had families here to guarantee them and those who had not, would be taken for work corps, not shot. But the officer that took the 20 from the MS said they were to be shot. We certainly hope that will be kept to a minimum.

During the afternoon Fitch and I talked with Mr. Lowe of Metropolitan about business revival. He thinks we are past the worst. But has no assurances that business men will start yet. We are anxious to get rice moving as soon as possible. Our food people estimate that private stores, with what we have on hand, will carry the population a month. But we do not have fuel for more than 10 days.

Fitch and I left here about 5:00 and drove to British Embassy to see how the men there were getting along. Some sections of North Chung Shan Lu have been cleared of the mass of stuff left by the retreating Chinese soldiers on the night of the 12th. But many blocks still remain, as do the many cars and trucks in front of the burned Ministry of Communications. Ministry of Railways is intact and evidently used by Japanese Military officers. 11 cars have been taken from the British Embassy—so the gang cheered for this equality. Buildings not entered tho. We came back the old carriage road and found the road still a mess. Small groups of soldier[s] billeted in houses along the way and using furniture, etc., for firewood for camp fires. Many small shops had been burned out, and we found some burning, one set right in front of British Embassy. But in general the burning has stopped. They seem to have burned the shops they have looted! But only a few private residences not connected with shops have been burned.

Mr. Lowe yesterday said a Japanese officer who is a friend of this, says the

9th Division which has been here and given us so much trouble, leaves this morning, the last 3,000 were to start for Changhsu this morning at 9:00. The 16th that is replacing them is better equipped—we hope so, because the 9th destroyed all the cars and trucks they got their hands on and we hope the 16th will not do the same with what few remain—and while not so good fighters are better men. We hope so. And the Military Police are putting up the appearance of trying to take drastic action with the soldier who raped an office girl at the Hankow road Primary School on the afternoon of the 23rd. They took her to the Bank of Communications and have kept her there till now "to identify the soldier when they catch him." But they say he has gone to Wuhu! Mills has been trying to work an informal habeas corpus to get her out, but failed yesterday. They said today "At 10 or 2:00." They claim they will shoot the soldier if they catch him. But 3 other cases of raping occurred at the same place the same afternoon! So I am thinking, especially since a group of 7 soldiers seem to be returning on raping parties to BTTS[5] each night, that we will put in a special request again for military police at these two places and try to catch this gang. On the whole, though, conditions are much better and we hope will continue to improve. Our rice shop here at 5 Ninghai Road had a good day yesterday, and was after more rice this morning. And Yesterday and this morning we found about as many people on the streets as were there on the 11th and 12th. If we can only get rice and coal to moving into the city soon, we will be out of the worst of it.

Searle went back to the University last night and Mills slept at Ginling. Both reported a quiet night. I definitely arranged with Searle, though, this morning, that I will go to the Univ. tonight. He said he would go with me and introduce me around. He has a cot set up in the Treasurer's office, and has a regular guard system worked out for all night. Gee sleeps in the basement of the same building and is chief of the guard. The consular police has not come the last two nights. I will have to take a lesson in Japanese from Searle too! After this I plan to take alternate nights with Searle. Should have done that from the first, but he was much better at working out the organization with the men there, as they had such great confidence in him.

I must not forget to add that Riggs was hit and slapped by an Inspection Officer in front of Marx's old place yesterday forenoon when he was escorting a woman home he had rescued from Japanese soldiers. We entered formal protest on that. Also on the looting of the American Embassy on the night of the 23rd. Wish those Embassy people would come back to do their own work!

Dec. 27th, 1937—3:50 P.M., Ninghai Road. Well, after two weeks of Japanese occupation, this sorry mess still continues. It is discouraging to the best of spirits. We had begun to hope a better day was arriving. But 3 women were raped at the U. of N. And one carried off last night, 27 were raped at the B.T.T.S., a man taken from duty at the UH to carry things for an officer, flag taken down at RLTS, and today they wanted to carry off our iron-roofed wool building. Rabe this noon got to Sing Kai K'o just in time to see them setting fire to the Mutual Co., that good store east of the Circle, found the new Market in ruins and the State Theatre also burned. Now they are clearing out the stores on the West side of the street north of Sing Kai K'o preparatory to burning them. During the registration process at UN yesterday, they had over 200 men volunteer that they had either been soldiers or military laborers (term used not clearly distinguished for forced civilian labor) on the promise that if they volunteered they would be allowed to work, instead of being shot as they would if they did not confess. This morning a man came to the University with five bayonet wounds and said the group of them were marched out to Ku Ling Sze and there used for bayonet practice by 130 Japanese soldiers. He fainted from his wounds, and when he awoke the Japanese had left, so he made his way back. Wilson thinks one wound is so serious he will not live. That was our diet for lunch this noon when we all reported! Some we had already had for breakfast!

On one hand they talk of restoring order, and on the other they destroy and intimidate the people so that nearly nothing can be done. Rabe is sitting at home to protect his property most of the time, as well as his 600 refugees; Kroger is protecting his property; Magee is protecting his household of refugees as is Forster. Minnie and Mrs. Twinem do not dare leave Ginling together, and one foreigner has to be on duty at the UH all the time night and day. The same is practically true of the UN, where they call Bates during the day if he is away. So he spends his days chasing here and there to run off Japanese soldiers. Riggs and Sone are the only ones that have any feeling of accomplishment these days: they are trucking. By escorting coolies around and watching their truck alertly, they get rice and coal moved and so people are fed, but they are barely able to keep up from day to day with the needs. Trucks and cars are gradually disappearing, and yet the Japanese Embassy has the nerve to ask us to loan them cars, and send them mechanics to fix their cars!

No I did not go the UN last night as planned. At supper Searle said he had better stay with it until the registration was finished. They did the men yesterday; first by volunteer process above, then herding them around and asking if anyone would guarantee this man, and all passed but one. Then Searle and Sone guaranteed him. Today were registering the women more rapidly, and tomorrow will get to private houses. Lao Sze's boy has not shown up, and I have not been able to see him any time I go to Ginling.

My thought for the day was: to get a definite request to the J. embassy for rice, flour, and coal. When we turned in cases last night, I made an appointment with Fukui for Mr. Rabe at 11 today. Then this morning went by Rabe's house, and talked it out, and he came down here. I drafted a letter and he signed it, and we went over. Fukui responded very well, but how much he can do with the Military we do not know. Our gang at the house decided we should just assume we had a right to the remainder of the 30,000 *tan* of rice, and 10,000 bags of flour, given us by the city govt. That means to get 20,000 *tan* of rice and 9,000 bags of flour (Now Mr. Han tells me that the 1,000 bags of flour we got are not from that order at all.) We were not given coal, but we asked the Japanese for opportunity to get coal, because we are shorter of that, only enough to run our kitchens a week now. We may have to buy it, but can do that. Mr. Fukui was very favorable as I said. That is a start, and we hope by a week's negotiations, etc., we may work out a way to get these supplies before dire need sets in. This afternoon Charlie is out looking up coal yards that have not been sealed by the military, to reply to Fukui's request if we knew of places we could get coal. To play safe we are reporting half of them, and trying to go ahead on our own, to buy coal at the other half of the 6 we have heard about!

It was nice and sunny this morning, but has clouded up today, so fear it may snow. Hope not though! Last fall we prayed for rain; now we pray for fair and mild weather. People are anxious to return to their homes after the registration, but unless order improves, we fear they may have a hard time. However, we are encouraging them to try it cautiously. But with shops burned and burning continually, and girls grabbed on the way, it is discouraging to them. However, we hope some will find a way and gradually eke out a way of living in places that have not been burned, etc. The number of girls at Ginling has declined rapidly in the last three days, fell from 10,000 to 8,000, as some order reappeared in the Zone. They went to their families living at other places in the Zone. We hope to get moving pictures of these camps before they break up. Ginling has now cleared their run-ways, which were filled with women's beds a few days ago.

Our request for guards at BTTS last night was not acted on quickly enough. Today Fukui said they were placing guards at these places and UN as well. If I go there tonight, I hope they do have a guard, so I don't have to face the soldiers alone! They have now placed guards at all the Embassies—after the horse was stolen and as Bates says "That is kindergarten work, those guards should have been placed there the afternoon of the 13th!" this afternoon the Consular police were here, and wanted to go to German property to investigate, and are going to inspect and place guard[s] at all foreign property! We can only get them interested in foreign property, but not in lives and honor of women! Rabe says that is because they will have to pay for this.

Dec. 29th, 1937, **5 Ninghai Road**—**4:30 P.M.** Gradually things get better. We were just over to see Fukui about a number of matters, but mainly coal and rice, and he told us that now orders have been issued that soldiers should not enter the Zone and sentries are posted at the main entries. That is what we intimated we wanted on Dec. 14th and specified more in detail in our letter of Dec. 17th. I am going to begin checking off the things we have asked them to do that they have done! That on the 17th or 18th would have stopped all the trouble at once, but that division evidently had been given the right to do as they please. And it was only when the new division took their place and were put to work cleaning up the city that the authorities were able to make even an appearance of controlling the soldiers.

I did not get to write yesterday. Got home early, too, but was tired from two hours talk with a Japanese Military man—and lay down. Riggs came in five minutes and soon after Searle, and so we had a good old-fashioned chin in which Searle pumped Charlie about his serious sicknesses, etc. So I did not get anything done before supper and afterwards—was too tired! Once you start to loaf, you have no pep for anything. Searle went to the Univ. I had a quiet night there the night before, and he did last night. I will go tonight. It seems funny to be undressing in Elsie's office!

The Military man was a Colonel Okay, just arrived from Shanghai with the idea that he must protect foreigners in Nanking, so he wanted all Germans concentrated in one place and all Americans in another. Then he would post a guard. I was glad Rabe was along and we headed it off. Rabe rose to the occasion when I was dragged into a rebuttal argument about there being no more Chinese soldiers in the Zone—Okay said our only danger was fighting in case Chinese soldiers fired on Japanese soldiers! Rabe said: "When I assumed chairmanship of the International Committee, I told the world I would protect these Chinese civilians as well as I could. I am not going to leave them or retire into a protected place." Later, Okay asked him to sign that he absolved them of all responsibility for protecting him. Rabe rose again: "I will sign that I will feel safe when you have protected the Chinese." The German authorities in Shanghai had evidently brought pressure to bear for protection of German lives and property. Not so clear, but probably also the American. Another good news is that Fukui told us an American representative is coming soon.

Day before yesterday, 27th, we presented a letter asking for the right to get the remainder of the rice and flour assigned to us. We also stated our urgent need for more coal, which we were willing to buy from Chinese coal yards if the Japanese Army would let us. We had gone back yesterday afternoon to see if there was an answer. Fukui did not have an answer from the military yet, in fact, had not seen them. Okay ran in on us. Today we were back again and he said the high commander here, General Sarati, was investigating the coal yards we had listed as available—Charlie dug them up definitely the afternoon of the 27th because Fukui asked if we knew the places. So we have some hopes of getting coal, if they do not take it themselves! Rice they prefer to handle through the new Autonomous Committee. But we have now decided to press that on the commercial basis, to be sold to Chinese merchants, and then we reserve our rice for relief work only.

Dec. 31, 1937, **New Year's Eve—6:15 P.M., 3 Ping Tsang Hsiang** . . . Rabe had a bright idea this week. He had been wondering what to do for the Japanese for New Years. So he had some of his practically idle workers make up new year cards with the symbol of the Safety Zone on the front, and on the back leaf made places for all 22 westerners to autograph. He had enough copies made to give Mr. Fukui and the staff of the Japanese Embassy, and the Major General Sasaki in charge of Nanking one, each with a good porcelain pot of flowers. He debated about doing it tomorrow, for fear it would appear we were assuming diplomatic status! So he solved that by going around personally today with it. We have had to do a lot of complaining about the actions of the Japanese Army here, but these Embassy men have been excellent sports about it. They could have told us it was none of our business. And they have made some impression on the military. The army seems now to be really making an effort to clean up the situation, as well as an effort to white-wash it too! So we have nothing but good-will for the men now involved.

Rabe and I went back day before yesterday in the afternoon to see what result Fukui had on coal and rice. He was very friendly with us, and we had a good hour's conversation. He said the Army preferred to handle the rice through the Autonomous Committee, and we agreed, just so it is quick enough. He offered to help on coal, and had had the Consular Police investigate that morning, and expected a reply from the high command. We asked about disarming soldiers for their free time at New Years so as to prevent trouble, and he said they had the day before issued orders that the soldiers were to stay out of the Zone, and had put sentries at the entrances to keep them out. There are now a number of military police in the area either as guards at places or on patrol. So this afternoon there were very few soldiers roaming in the Zone. Rabe said this noon they put up a fence across Kwangchow Road at his place, and would not let him on to Chung Shan Road. So they are making a real effort to keep soldiers out. At the same time we reported trouble with the guard at BTTS and last night they were changed. We had eight at the UN and Searle suggested one was enough. So that was all there was this afternoon. Ginling got rid of their eight guards and gets along now with a Consular police sleeping near the gate nights. As we see it, everything hangs now on getting commercial rice and coal moving into the area. In fact, we need coal for soup-kitchens before a couple of days are over. Charlie was going to try to get some at certain yards out of the Zone this afternoon without military permission, where we knew the owners. Have not yet heard his results. Hope he succeeded. Rice is not so urgent. But private stocks are running out, and people are anxious to buy. So our shop at 5 Ninghai Road, the only place the man considers safe, is doing a rushing business with a rice line morning and afternoon. Besides that, some is sold at the large camps to those who can buy, and we make some private deliveries. This latter has increased so much in the last few days, that this morning we decided to charge $1.00 per bag for delivery (1.25 *tan*) and as we are still selling for $9.00 per *tan*, that leaves it less than $10.00 per *tan*. We will charge $.50 per bag of flour for delivery, selling at $5.00 per bag now. This we hope will check calls for delivery from us and will help check hording. We only allow one tao to be purchased at a time at the regular shop. If we get the Japanese army to allow Chinese rice merchants to buy some of the 100,000 *tan* of rice they took from the Chinese Army, we will be over the rice crisis. We are asking them to reserve 20,000 bags for such purposes, and 10,000 for later relief work in case we need it. Likewise 10,000 and 5,000 bags of flour. As soon as we can get commercial rice moving in, we will stop selling and reserve our supplies for relief. Red Swastika was fortunate enough through a Japanese monk to get 3,000 bags stored south of Han Chung Lu assigned to them, and they are now trucking it in for soup-kitchens. That brings our rice stores about back to where started! Not bad.

The most serious aspect of the situation, and one for which we can see no adequate solution quickly, is that there is no economic basis of life for this community of 200,000. If they go buying rice from the Japanese Army, then the money in the community will be drained out, and no return. The only return service is the food which most of the coolies that go out to work for Japanese Army men, not in great numbers yet, the very few that get any pay, and the few men now employed at the Water and Electric Light Works.* The only other income will be what farmers can raise from the ground. Or what people can find or loot from other areas in the city! As Charlie puts it, we will have a bunch of grubbers for several months! But as Sone says, the Chinese have a wonderful comeback, and if left alone they will find a way to maintain themselves. So as we have insisted since the 16th, order is the first requisite of any form of normal life. I used to laugh at the British respect for "Law and Order" but now I realize how fundamental it is to normal living. Nothing moves in a state of disorder. If they will only let the farmers alone in the city and outside the city, there will be a comeback at least of the means of existence. But now the farmers are in the process of killing all their livestock, and either eating it themselves or selling it. So we have the commandeering period which is very similar to the early days of the Russian Revolution and the Five Year Plan. Every commercial enterprise

---

*Sentence unclear in original.

we can get started will help to change that situation, to one of trade instead of commandeering. You gain a healthy respect for the various ramifications of organized life when you see how hard under these conditions it is to operate such a simple thing as an exchange shop, and a rice shop! However, it is remarkable how well the little street venders along the road keep at it. Little to risk, all to gain, so they daily ply their trade. And what a variety of stuff. We now suspect some of it is looted from areas outside of the Zone where burning has been going on, but anything the people can get in now is all to the good! As one man here remarked, Mills, "I think now Chung Shan Lu is no longer the main street: Shanghai and Ninghai Roads are the main streets!" They are thronged with people now with the return of order, and both sides of each lined with little street venders. Hankow Road down here (above our place) is a vegetable market as crowded every morning as Peh Men Chiao used to be. the rest of the city is practically deserted by civilians except south of [?]. [The Zone?] . . .

Well, I was quite the cock of the walk at supper with my hair-cut! All the fellows wanted to know where I got it. Mills arranged for the man, our "rolly-polly" to come at eight tomorrow morning, so the gang are laying for him. He left his outfit here, and will be glad to get the business, as he has had practically none! His place is so full of people; he does not have room to cut hair. Even he was smart enough to note that with so many buildings and supplies burned or looted, that it was going to be very hard for the people to make a living. We had two, rather three miracle stories at supper.

Bates went to the EMB this afternoon and found Takatama (Consular Police that is going around investigating foreign property) and Fukuda there in Attcheson's [sic] office with Tung. Fukuda told Searle the Army had instructed them to pay all claims promptly! Later Searle went back and found they had settled all claims with the Chinese staff in full excepting bicycles which they will replace with new ones, and a car of his friend that they had some question about. Number 2: Mc investigated the stream of people pouring down Peh Men Chiao today, bringing back rice, and found that some Japanese soldiers had opened up a rice supply, and were just letting the people help themselves. Well, that helps the *lao peh sing*[6] that much, but probably it is merely an irregular procedure and will not continue! Number 3: Our chief looter No.1 went to the Central Univ. Agric. School this afternoon and hauled away 3 tons of coal. A Red Cross coolie at the Ginling soup-kitchen went there to see about getting some more kettles and found the pile of coal, so told Charlie. On this trip the coolie got some clothes left there, and while they were loading the coal, some Japanese soldiers came in, and Charlie thought the game was up. But it turned out they were looking for evergreen trees for New Years! So either honor among looters, or specialization helps. Well, these New Year Eve stories are better than what we had for Christmas Eve!

Rabe is having open house this evening so we may go down for awhile. Bob and I will have to get on to our sleeping-places before nine preferably. But bridge is started downstairs, so I do not think we will get to Rabe's in time. The others can go later. Mrs. Twinem delivered our two geese from Blanch Wu today. We had some of her geese for Christmas, two more this week, and now two for tomorrow. The first were gifts, the others we have bought. Tonight was the first night we have not had meat for supper. I think it is part of the economy program we put into effect this morning. We have been having meat noon and night and canned fruit three times a day. Bob's cook believes in using up what he has! Bob claims we have fruit enough though to last us through. But we cut it to once a day and canned fruit juice one time, and pastry the third, as tonight. Bob told us the bad news tonight, board bill was $3.10 per day for Dec. on account of coal, and $5.00 tip to all the servants. So mine was $96.10 from which I deducted $9.00 for 18 jars of fruit I put in last Oct., since others have charged in theirs at economical rates. I drew $100.00 from Mc on account so as to pay that. Have about $40.00 on hand. Thought I had better not get caught with no cash on hand.

On top of this extravagance, Sone brought in a pot in which he had cooked a day's ration of free raw rice. The bottom of a cereal double cooker about 2/3 full, though there was not enough water. Our ration is 250 persons per *tan* This was 284 to the bag . . .

Jan. 1, 1938—**8:45 P.M. New Year's Day** Well, today has been the noisiest unhappy New Year I ever saw. Firecrackers began early this morning. But the barber was an hour late for his eight o'clock appointment and apologized by saying that he had to go out to fire firecrackers for the Japanese! Well, anyway the children had a grand time firing the crackers given out by the Japanese! At 1:00 the ceremony was held at Kuleo for inaugurating the new "Tze Chih Wei Yuan Hwei" (note new name, no. 3). Wang, our officer manager, was to raise the flag. He is the famous "Jimmy." So Charlie remarked, "That is very fitting for a second-hand government." At 2:00 when we looked over there, sure enough, the five-bar flag was flying over Kuleo. Gee said that while the Japanese were talking to them about cooperation, two new fires went up in the city. One was the Soviet Embassy. Later we went up to the University tower and saw the ruins of the Soviet Embassy. Searle had seen it intact on the 13th with the flag flying. Today its flag was down from its big pole in the yard and the fine building smoldering ruins. Later in the afternoon other fires east of here sent clouds of smoke to the heavens. Love for the Chinese by clouds of smoke by day and pillars of fire by night! However Mc's estimate on a tour of South City today and our view from the tower agreed that only about 10% of the buildings of the city have been burned, Luckily! But most of the business fronts on the main streets have been burned out. Like 1932 in Shanghai, it seems to be mainly a war on Chinese business (Our old wool cloth at Hansen's either went up in smoke a week ago, or went away in a Japanese army looting truck.)

Last evening at 8:30 I went with the fellows in George's car to Rabe's, and had a pleasant visit with him. He lighted the Christmas tree for us, the only one in Nanking (except a small one up stairs at Ginling, that none of us saw.) Tell the Chicks they had a model of the [s]table with the shepherds outside, and then sheep and cattle in the yard, around the base of the tree. We chatted there until ten, then they took me to the University gate and waited until I called "All right." After getting past the military police who were getting ready for bed in the gate-house. Had a fair sleep till 5:30, but no trouble. Gee gave us a New Year's gift today of a real bed instead of the camp-cot. So that will help a lot.

I went to the office this forenoon, but there was not much to do but catch up on making additional copies of documents for my triplicate files. (My old game!) Sone and Charlie had caught up, or rather gained a day on rice and coal, so did not haul today. We all took the afternoon off. That is my first since we started. We opened the office there the afternoon of Dec. 1st. So I can say "thirty-one days at Ninghai Road," because I have not missed a day, Sunday or holiday since, until this afternoon. Charlie spent the forenoon helping check up on a serious case I neglected to mention the other day.

Thursday after lunch, the 30th, word came there was trouble with Japanese soldiers at the Sericulture Bldg. So Searle and Charlie dashed over. Later they came to the office to report that the military police had come to take the housing head there, who admitted he had been a former military officer in the Chinese Army here! But they took four men with him, two Univ. servants, and two refugees, because they had helped bury some arms back of the W.C. So Searle and Charlie drafted a summary of findings pointing out that the chief man involved was not a University employee, but that they would guarantee the two servants and others would guarantee the refugees, one of whom turned out to be a nephew of a contact Charlie dealt with. We took that to the Embassy and they thought we were objecting to the search, but we said we did not. Yesterday morning I got Dr. Hsu, our Housing Commissioner, to investigate the matter to see how we got the man, and at a conference yesterday afternoon with Searle, it developed the chief man was only a Police Inspector! But we do not have definite evidence to prove it. Since Hsu is advisor also to the Tze Chih Wei Yuan Hwei, we had him go directly to the Japanese Embassy about the matter. Then this morning he and Charlie got out the requisite affidavits for the four men, and one was released because his guarantor went for him. So they are to take the guarantors of the others tomorrow morning. It is encouraging to find that now they keep some of these men alive over a day or two while they investigate the case!

After our tower expedition and noting the way the refugees were enjoying the warm sunny day, boys turning cartwheels on the Univ. campus, etc., Searle and I took a walk back of Ginling to see if we could find any of the heaps of bodies of men shot this week. We went over by that temple "Kuling Sze," . . . down through the valleys to the south, searched every pond, but did not find any bodies except the charred ones back of Ginling that Searle found a few days ago—after the burning incident. We found the garden plots over there less than half used up, but every farm house was deserted. Only a few were back loading up pei Tsai[7] to carry over and sell. Not a house outside of the Zone was occupied, not even on the west side of Sikang Road. Then we went on south by Tsing Lian Shan and on to the new gate at Hansimen. Between Tsing Lian Shan and the new gate we only saw three civilians! And that section used to be crowded. A few Japanese soldiers were wandering about, but not even many of them. Every farm house and every house we passed had been broken into and a few burned. A shop at Kwangchow Road had been broken into and was deserted, but the incense sticks had not been taken! Maybe because the nearby temple is deserted, as was Ku Ling Sze. At the gate, we found a young boy coming in from outside the city. He seemed glad to join up with us after successfully passing the guard. (We noted the piles of *kangs* there with only a few broken!) He had been outside Shuisimen, to his old home. His father and mother had tried to stay there but the Japanese soldiers were too rough: beating up the men, shooting others and raping the women and robbing the people, so he brought them into the Nan Min Chu—which he told us about as something we had not heard about! It was the only place a person dared to live, he said! At Shanghai Road we rescued 6 Red Swastika coolies who were bringing in pei tsai from Moh Tsou Lu and had been stopped by the guard on the corner. They could not make the Chinese understand the Japanese word for "hu chao" and when the coolies produced them, they let them pass. On the way up Shanghai Road we noted three houses that might have been the scene of the burning incident, but did not explore that late in the afternoon. The net result of our tour was that the situation regarding piles of bodies is less serious and therefore a more favorable result. As far as opportunities for people to go to their homes outside of the Zone, the outlook is still very dark. (Half of the houses were burned outside Hansimen.) We went up on the wall there and looked down on the ruins. That done by the Chinese before the Japanese entered the city.

A little good news, some more bad, and then I must turn in because I am sleepy after my first walk in over a month, or maybe because of my bath this noon! Sperling failed to find the man about rice at the Nanking Hotel this morning. But he reported to us that the city water was turned on today. However, not much pressure until they can check and repair the leaks, etc. So no water here from that. Charlie however reported that the Japanese are going to assign what was 550 tons of coal at Han Chung Lu to the Tze Chih Wei Yuan Hwei, then they can give 50 tons to us and 500 tons to the soup kitchens. Which means it all goes for the work of relief we are doing. Since the military are still trucking from the pile, we may only get 300 tons, but that will carry us through January. Charlie is going to get two or three trucks on the job tomorrow morning. Dr. Hsu and his friend who is head of the Red Swastika and chairman of the new government (Tze Chih —), Mr. T'ao, arranged this. Rather the Japanese said they preferred to do it this way to giving it to the International Committee. We must decrease, they must increase. But so long as the work gets done, we should worry! One knotty problem is that this is confiscated coal! We may arrange to pay the dealer on the side. But the coal is a big relief to me! Then Charlie fessed up that he knew of 150 tons at the German Club all the time, rather the Inspection Committee discovered it this morning. Charlie had been keeping that under his hat because it is on German property! So we have that for a last ditch emergency!

I did not get it in last night, but many cases of diarrhea have appeared at the Univ. and the old Ministry of Communications. But Trim could not find definite cases today, so we are not sure it is dysentery yet. We think it is not. But that is the opposite effect to a shi fan[8] diet. But some of the people are so poor they are really living on shi fang. With no city water they have been dependent on the well, and some of them are too lazy to pump, so they go to a nearby dirty pond where toilet buckets, etc. are washed. It is only cold weather that has saved us from more disease. With no baths and crowding in as close together as they can lie down in most rooms for sleeping, it is only the lack of communications that probably keeps us clear of typhus. With only two doctors, if we get an epidemic we are finished! We hope that city water and the gradual de-concentration of the big camps may help on this matter.

We had Mrs. Twinem, Mrs. Chen, Magee and Forster here for New Year's dinner at noon. It was only by strong urging the last minute that George got John to come. Then just as we got up from the table, two Chinese came from his house to say 2 or 3 Japanese soldiers had come and were demanding women. George dashed them back in the car, but one woman had been raped before they got there, and another severely beaten because she resisted. John will never forgive us, because they have not left their Christians from Hsiakwan and others in their two or three houses alone a single minute since the 16th! That is, without some foreigner there. The beaten-up woman was taken to the Univ. Hospital and a Japanese "inspector" came to pay a New Year's call, so Miss Hynds showed them this girl and told them about the raping. He was indignant and said to report to Army Headquarters and they would have the man shot! But the men have no identification marks on them (like Chinese soldiers do) so there is no way of catching the man unless a military police happens by. One or two women were also raped this afternoon in Wang Po-chih's house and one at Tzing Teh. So we are in for some more trouble for a few days probably. . . .

January 2, Sunday 3:40 P.M., 3 Ping Tsang Hsiang

Dearest Mardie and chicks:
Sunday afternoon at home! What a luxury! But at that I had to write up some cases, two letters, and then take them to the Japanese Embassy. Just got back. Church service is at 4:30 so I will get some written before dark. Candle or lamp light is not so good. And I have to go to the University tonight.

This will be the first church service since Dec. 5th. I believe. The last one I had a chance to attend was on Nov. 20th. Mc has been ready for three weeks, but could get no congregation. So we promised him half the crowd today! Charlie is racing with the Japanese Military on hauling coal from Han Chung Lu and did not come home for lunch, so probably will not be here for church. I hope nothing has happened to him. Fitch went back to the office for a short while this afternoon.

Well, we get it going and coming! This morning at 5:00 and again about 2:00 this afternoon, Chinese planes came and bombed. This noon they were fired at by a number of anti-aircraft guns, but not so many as the Chinese used to have in operation here.

In my write-up last night I forgot one or two things. The new government for the city was celebrated yesterday by delegates from our 25 refugee camps. That is the first time I have heard of a government founded on such representation! And last Sunday I neglected to tell you that the latter part of the forenoon was taken with hauling in $282.00 worth of coppers from Ginling College—Mills, Fitch and I. Mills, from his experience in Hankow flood relief work, knew they weighed two ton to the $1,000! Well, our exchange shop got going this week, and is putting them out now. Kroger has a great time handling the coppers put up in packs of 100 each.

We verified it today that the Soviet Embassy was fired just the time the celebration at Kuleo took place. We wonder what it means: is it an insult to the Soviet that will lead to complications, or does it mean that Soviet Russia has already declared war on Japan?

Our trip to the Japanese Embassy just now was to report four rape cases yesterday afternoon and to urge them to make stronger efforts to keep soldiers out of the Zone. Fukuda received us in the hall because the new government group were there—they are there most of the time now, but they say listening to the Japanese—and told us that Gen. Sasaki himself was inspecting the Zone to see that order was kept and the gendarmerie had been strengthened. So we hope it will not get worse. But the remainder of the city is full of soldiers and many of them have to leave today.

Bates was surprised this week to have Gee ask that a Bible class be started at the University today, and Chen Yung started one this morning at 9:00. Searle was to go with Takatama to see University property at 8:30 but for the third time he postponed it when Searle got there! Gee also told Searle yesterday that the crowd was searched before the meeting began and kept well distributed! 120 refugees went from the University and about 50 from Rabe's place.

Jan. 5, 1938, 9:20 PM, **3 Ping Tsang Hsiang** Well it is fun to get a letter off to you yesterday by Mr. Tanaka and via air mail from Hongkong to Hankow. I know the chances of that air mail still operating are slim, but it is worth the chance. All our letters sent by Japanese Embassy have to be "open letters"— Searle asked the gang here if they would take Stanley Jones' open letter—and I thought I had a letter that would not be censored. Plumer had to take one of his letters over after I had taken the bunch yesterday noon; he found Fukuda, Tanaka and Fukui busy reading our letters! They ran on to a statement in mine that they said they would have to prevent my sending. So Plumer suggested they cut it out and he brought the slip home. It was a very casual reference to an insignificant air raid here! But it was "military information"! Anyway we found out the sort of thing they are censoring.

In the excitement over actually getting a letter off to you, I have neglected these diary letters since the first. But I guess I can cover the four days easily. Bob showed in one of his letters that what he was sending was not all by marking it "Page 50."

Sunday, the 2nd, we worked about as much as ever until noon. But we decided that it was time to have church again and give Mc a chance to preach the sermon he had prepared four weeks before. I stayed home that afternoon but worked on getting documents straightened out up until nearly church time. Word came in just before church that the military police had thrown a cordon around the 6th housing office but Searle said we had better not interfere down at 55 Ying Yang Ying. Charlie had not shown up for lunch and since he was out trying to get coal from south of Han Chung Lu we feared foul play. So Plumer said he knew the location of the yard and he started off with George but met Charlie at the gate. He had lunch at the Red Swastika. So with bobing around church got under way with Mrs. Twinem at the piano, Mc leading, Grace, Searle, Plumer, George, Sone, Trimmer and I. He preached on "Hope." He said four weeks ago "hope" was what had pulled the Safety Zone through. Now I begin to think it was ignorance—ignorance of all that was in store for us. But none of us would have had us turn back on it as we look back now. Just as church broke up in came Dr. C Y Hsu and Mr. Chen of the I C office. Japanese soldiers had entered a house back of our headquarters and killed a man and others were moving into a house back of our place, so the women staying in the yard would be in danger of soldiers coming over the wall to rape them. Since the man was dead we felt there was little we could do there so we concentrated in getting a foreigner to stay at headquarters that night. As it was better to be a German and partly arranged [?] we went to see Rabe about getting Sperling. Rabe agreed. So I went back to go tell Sperling with George and met Charlie at the gate. Magee had come with full details of the murder. So Magee and Rabe went to the Japanese Embassy to present the case which was weakened by the fact the man killed had slapped the soldier, while George and I drove to Sperling's to get him to cover 5 Ninghai Road that night. I found him eating supper upstairs with Chinese women all over the place—since learned many of them are actors—but he said he would be over in 10 minutes. We found Ninghai Road all quiet so went on home for supper. I had a quiet night at the University but was glad to have George take us in a car and Searle go with me to see the lay of the land.

Plumer came in his bathrobe just now to tell me that the caller that Lao Kua had come up to announce was no other than Fukui! Bob said when the dogs raised a howl that it was probably a Jap soldier! And best of all Fukui came to tell us that Allison of the American consulate was due tomorrow morning at ten. He was formerly at Tsinan where Mills knew him quite well, and here a while and was in Tokyo so knows the Japanese. He is a very good man. They do not know who the others are. Rosen of the German Embassy will be here the 10th and by that time a Secretary of the British Embassy will be here and their military observer, Lovett-Fraser, will come. We had had some expectation of the Americans getting here today but when I went over at noon to inquire Fukui told me they would not be here for a few days. So we thought they were stalling. So we had decided that since we had taken care of ourselves through the worst of it, we could do so now. But representatives of all three countries getting in here will open a new stage in this situation. As Plumer says, the Japanese will have to behave themselves. And increasing the foreign community, especially as this will probably open the way for other missionaries and for business people to return, will add to the "neutral observers" and will also relieve us of the necessity of protesting. As I told Plumer we can go to work with the Tze Chih Wei Yuan Hwei. I am glad that some of the consular and diplomatic representatives are those who were here up till December 10th because they will remember the good condition the city was in then and a superficial drive around the city now will show them the difference. And our little paper on the burning of the city drawn up and signed by a host of us Dec. 21st will be very strategic. Rabe said today that we had better reserve a bed in the hospital for Rosen, he will be so shocked! And these representatives will open up our means of communication with the outside world so I may get some word to and from you, though we will have to be circumspect in what we report out, or we will have to get out! Although now the pressure is to keep us here—to all intents and purpose we have been prisoners with freedom of the inside of the city.

Well, now after that account of the quietest Sunday we have had in four weeks, no six weeks, I will move on to Monday. Sunday Rabe was so panicky about the Japanese having the Tse Chih Wei Yuan Kwei take over the I C and all its resources, that Monday morning I told Searle I thought I had better work out a brief of our position vis-a-vis the Tze Chih Wei Yuan Hwei, i.e. that we were a private relief organization and expected to continue as such. Rabe came back in higher spirits Monday and agreed. Monday Charlie succeeded in hauling coal all night from Han Chung Lu. But Tuesday more trouble developed. On Monday when the consular policeman that was travelling with the truck as guard asked the head man at the Red Swastika soup kitchen on Wutaishan who was sending them coal and the man replied, the Kuo Tsi Wei Yuan Hwei, the consular policeman slapped his face and said, "No, it is the Tze Chih Wei Yuan Hwei!" The same scene was repeated with the man at the University soup kitchen Tuesday. And since there was some question about the coal going to the I C, we decided to let the Tze Chih man who was working on the truck supervise the trucking and Charlie confine his work to organizing the trucks. Then a foreigner would not be so obvious and we asked the chairman of the Tze Chih to give the driver a written order to deliver coal to these places. Talked this all out with Dr. Hsu yesterday. He is very good. Also approached him about rice, saying "What I say unto you I say unto all, RICE." He said the Tze Chih had been asked by the Japanese to organize a committee to handle that matter.

Last night Charlie told us the Tze Chih had appointed a food commissioner after the pattern of our organization. He had asked the Japanese for 2,000 *tan* of rice a day. A good estimate for 200,000 people. He would handle this both commercially and free distribution and let our stores stand as a reserve. But he would like to have our food commissioner and associate, Mr. Han and Sone, work with him and for us to help in the trucking. Who was he? Jimmy! They all snorted and Searle said, "Well, rice must be going to be the most paying proposition." But I remarked, "Well he is the one man in the outfit that may get some rice moving before March first." So they all agreed and that we should cooperate in every ways we could.

But since the Japanese army supply man had offered to sell rice and flour to Sperling, I suggested he try again to see him. Kroger also knew the man so he volunteered to go. So they both went this morning and met the man but he was busy and told them to come back tomorrow morning at the same time, 8:00 at the Nanking Hotel. I hope we can either act as an introducer for Wang or arrange to buy directly enough rice to replace what we have sold with the money we have collected. Right now we would rather hold rice than money. Besides these developments, I have put in considerable of my time getting my triplicate files worked out and classified. Will have a set ready for the American representatives when they get here. They will probably be astounded at the directness and forcefulness of our protests to the Japanese Embassy, but we were in a situation that made us feel much more strongly than we wrote. The documents are merely historical now, but they will show clearly the stand the I C has taken in the whole matter. Oh, it was Monday afternoon that we took over the account of the 6 girls taken to what appeared to be a Japanese military hospital where they washed clothes by day and were raped by night, 10 to 40 times according to their beauty. Finally one girl was taken out and her head nearly cut off with bayonets. She got to the UH and Bob patched up her neck and thinks she will live but have a stiff neck. Rabe and I went with a brief letter asking them to follow it up and try to rescue the other 5 girls. When they read of the case, Fukuda and Tanaka had nothing to say, except, Fukuda's remark: "The Army is very mad because they say it is the first time in history that an army has had to conquer a place with neutral observers on hand." Quite a false view but we felt it was no time to argue so did not. But it made us all feel more thankful than ever that we had been here.

Out of six appointments, Takatama of the consular police has kept one of them with Searle to see the University property in the last six days. Today Searle found trouble at the Middle School and went down to learn that a staff man there, Su, and a refugee who speaks Japanese had been put under great pressure by the consular police to join them in their work. The first assignment for the refugee was to point out the amah of the Soviet Embassy. What for, no one knows yet. And Takatama was the man who searched Su's house last night—no wonder he had "insomnia" today. What is more Takatama showed up at the Middle School while Searle was talking the case out with the man in charge who has done a remarkable job of caring for 12,000 to 15,000 refugees down there, Chiang, and Su and the refugee! He took his surprise out in lecturing Su that he should not drink so much and accepting a verbal guarantee from Searle that Su had been connected with our staff, so was not a police detective as charged. The plot thickens! But just one piece in the jigsaw puzzle that is shaping up into a feudal society; men seeking protection under military conquerors.

I should add that Monday noon the 3rd, we got radio news, but as usual not so much news. Bob got more at the hospital last night. Juice was off at 5 Ninghai Road yesterday and today—well it came on last evening and we got London at 6:00 and Kroger got the other places later in the evening. Today I let Bob take my set to the hospital but still they could not get the short wave stations. But a little news of the outside world gave us a new orientation after four weeks completely cut off.

This noon Plumer struck off a spark that we have all been feeling: that we are being driven to work through the Tze Chih instead of directly with the Japanese Embassy on a number of questions. The Japanese are anxious for the I C to decline rapidly and turn over its responsibilities to the Tze Chih. So Plumer suggested we work on that basis definitely and put things up to the Tze Chih and strengthen their courage to demand things from the Japanese. Two items for a starter: restoration of order in other parts of the city so people could return and stop the burning of the city. (There are a number of fires in different parts of the city every day, though not as many as the first few days after the 19th.) So when I got back to the office I started working out a brief for these two points. Then had Rabe, Kroger, Mills and Bates criticise it so it is growing into a pretty fair statement. I got the idea of doing it section by section. That way we can have a better chance of a good restoration of order before the people return to the areas in question and we can observe its operation better. And it is an indirect way of crowding the soldiers out of large sections of the city, which could not be done at one stroke for the whole city! It simply applies the method that has worked partly successfully in the Zone to the rest of the city piece by piece, probably starting with the corner, the southwest corner, which has been least destroyed and has some people living there.

January 9, 1938, Sunday, 8:15 PM, **3 Ping Tsang Hsiang** When the American representatives got here on the 6th we felt like a burden had been lifted off us. Not that they themselves can do so much or can do anything directly for the Zone, etc., but their very presence we felt would be a deterrent on the Japanese army and it is already having that effect. They are making some effort to straighten up the town—the man in charge has been recalled to Tokyo. And now today the British and German representatives landed so we feel quite reinforced—like a besieged party when relief comes. True we had about made up our minds that we could take care of ourselves because the representatives were so long coming and the Japanese kept saying "a few days more," and we had gotten along fairly well. But now we realize there are a lot of things that can be done with them here that could not before. And one thing they take off our hands the burden of protesting about American property. Reports of damages to business properties in Hsiakwan were beginning to come into us and as much for the protection of the caretakers in charge as anything, we had to do something about it, without the liberty to go to Hsiakwan to check up. We had no intention originally making much effort to defend American property, but when the Japanese Embassy people got here we soon learned that they were only interested in doing something—woefully little at that—in protecting foreign property but not interested in doing a thing for the Chinese as such. So we worked that game to the limit because we had a large proportion of the concentrations of refugees in American institutional property. Especially when the raping season was on—open season—we threw open Ginling and the University to women who were streaming the streets mornings panic stricken to find any place that was safer than where they were the night before. And by getting guards—gradually—at some of those places we were able to give them some protection. But the very mass, 12,000 at Ginling, 15,000 at the Middle School, over 10,000 at the University proper (nearer 12,000) cut down the percentage raped. And we also found that it was only the magic of the westerner with some courage that could stand up to the individual Japanese soldier. We had to use that magic to the limit to the point where we feared they would turn on us. So we felt we had to stand on every effort through the Japanese Embassy to secure respect for us as Americans that we were entitled to. Somehow the miracle continued to work and we 22 Westerners policed the Japanese army that had captured the city while the Japanese only had 17 military police there and they very ineffective at first. The situation did not clear up a great deal until about Dec. 29th when they issued orders that the soldiers were not to enter the Zone and stationed guards at the entrances to keep them out and military police to patrol the Zone. That has not kept all of them out but on the 18th and 19th they were all over the place hopping walls, busting in gates, crawling in cellars, reminding you of some pictures of brownies all over a town. Robbing, raping, looting right down the street night and day. Whew! And that after the high command had arrived on the 15th and a Japanese general toured the Zone with us.

Well, that is a nightmare that is past now. As we told the British representatives when we visited them this afternoon: in reply to their statement, "You must have had a bad time," we said, "No we did not have a bad time and have kept fairly comfortable, but it hurts us so to see the Chinese population suffering so." Prideaux-Brune and Col. Lovett–Fraser also had a tale to tell in connection with the bombing and shelling of British boats on the 12th, the same day the *Panay* was sunk.

Well, the other letters will tell all the story and an epilogue can better be written later. Magee came very close to summarizing the spiritual experience this afternoon in church service here in reading from Psalms 124, 125, 126:

> If it had not been the Lord who was on our side,
> When men rose up against us:
> Then they had swallowed us up alive,
> When their wrath was kindled against us:
> Then the waters had overwhelmed us,
> The proud waters had gone over our soul
> Blessed by the Lord,
> Who hath not given us as a prey to their teeth.

And the concluding hymn: "A mighty fortress is our God." His sermon was on the contrast between Jesus and Pilate (with the whole Roman Empire behind him). As Searle said one day when one of the fellows kidded him, "Are you still a pacifist, Bates?" quick came the reply, "Yes, and I'm getting to be more of one every day." Never in my life have I had such a demonstration of the value of moral courage and what could be done by just purely being on the right side, standing for what was decent and right, without lifting a single hand to use force. It was only that way we could chase out armed Japanese soldiers. One appeal to force or arms, and we would have been finished and our work left undone.

Well, to bring the story up to date. As soon as the policing job let up a little, I decided we must begin to work to get food moving into the Zone for the civilian population. We were trucking our rice to refugee camps and to our rice shop at an ever increasing rate and as private stores ran out that demand would increase, as it has. So the morning of the 27th I began a campaign to get rice from the Japanese. Our shop was then selling 10 bags a day, now it is selling 150 bags a day, with a "rice line" of 700–800 people every day. And we only allow each person to purchase a *tou*. Besides that we are using up 100 bags a day in free distribution and soup kitchens besides about 40–50 bags that the Red Swastika are using from stores they got from the Japanese, 3,000 bags through a Japanese priest. We appealed to the Japanese Embassy but they said the Army preferred to do it through the Tze Chih Wei Yuan Hwei but they would get us coal, our urgent need. We were promised 500 tons through the Tze Chih Wei Yuan Hwei but it dwindled to 100 tons by army hauling, but it has carried us to date and since it was Tze Chih Charlie was able to get consular police to convoy the trucks and get passes for the coolies. While we were pressing the Embassy about rice, Sperling was talking to the Army supply head and he said he could sell us any amount of rice and flour. So I set Sperling on his trail but he did not contact him again until this week, with the help of Kroger. Now we have an order in for 3,000 bags of rice at $13.00 per bag of 1.25 *tan* and 5,000 bags of flour at $3.00. But no definite word as to full acceptance but terms included delivery to University "warehouse" by the army. ("Warehouse"—chapel)

Meanwhile "Jimmy" Wang was appointed food commissioner under the Tze Chih at the suggestion of the Japanese because we were pressing them on the rice question. He asked for 100,000 *tan* free and 100,000 purchased. The Army turned that down. Friday he reported the case was hopeless so we closed our order at a higher price than we cared to pay for rice, though, not too high from the market price point of view, but since the community is entirely on a consuming basis we want to husband their resources, both in supplies and cash. Yesterday he said they would give him 5,000 bags for free distribution *outside* of the Zone. To bribe the people to go home to their destroyed homes. And sell him 100,000 at a cheap price. Today it was 1,250 for free distribution and 10,000 to sell to him at $4–5 which he was to sell for *less than* the International Committee was selling. That tickled us. So he is to buy at about $5 per bag and sell for $8 per *tan*. We are to do the trucking for them! But they will pay us for rice hauled for sale and we will haul the rice for free distribution free. Charlie spent today organizing the trucks after getting them in running condition yesterday. The Japanese refused today, this morning, to use coolies wearing I C insignias. So Charlie had to sign up coolies that would be willing to work under the Tze Chih insignia and they demanded Rabe's consent because they were Siemen's coolies. Then the chauffeurs, who are in the hire of the private owners of the trucks, said they would not drive unless it was their own coolies, so this afternoon Charlie had to repeat the process and get coolies from the *lao pan*[9] of each truck. By night he had it all talked out, six coolies accompany each truck and we pay the *lao pan* $2.00 per trip. The Tze Chih will pay that on all hauls and will pay us for gas and oil for the commercial rice. So Charlie is promoted from truck convoy to chief dispatcher of 5 trucks. One step in advance is the Tze Chih is putting one of their police, which they are now taking over 160 from our police saved from the city police, to accompany the trucks along with the Japanese consular police. Two police for 5 trucks. Tomorrow morning Kroger is to see the supply man. If he agrees to deliver our rice, we will take it in spite of the high price as an insurance against a break down on this scheme.

"Jimmy" came in this forenoon to tell me the arrangements. So we threshed it all over together with Fitch, Rabe and Kroger. He said the Japanese wanted to close our shop by force. So I told him that we were anxious to close our shop. Yesterday morning I got up with the idea of forcibly closing it ourselves Monday morning to see if, it would push the Japanese and the Tze Chih into getting commercial rice going. Our supplies at the present rate of consumption of 250 bags a day would only last two weeks, 4,000 bags. Whereas for free rice only, 100 bags a day, it would last 40 days. So I told Jimmy that since we had one store open today and rice would be moving this afternoon or tomorrow, we would close tomorrow morning. And he could go back and tell the Japanese that he had gotten the I C to close its rice shop on his order! So tomorrow we are out of the rice business but the merchant who was handling it on a small commission refuses to work under the Tze Chih, and just closes up. Small sales will continue at the refugee camps a day or two until more stores can be opened, and then we will stop that and make them go out to buy rice. We started this when things were so bad people did not dare go out to buy rice and in fact no rice shop was open. Our only shop at headquarters—no other place had enough protection, was at the northern end of the Zone. Well, after two weeks of wiggling and haggling and dreaming nights, we have gotten a trickle of commercial rice started. Since it only has to be hauled from Kuo Fu Road it will move in 500–600 bags a day. But coal supply is temporarily stopped, but negotiations are proceeding along the same two lines for more, Tze Chih and the supply master.

Yesterday morning, realizing that if we were to pay out $50,000 for rice and flour we should replace those resources against trouble later. So as Fong Sec had wired Fitch for needs, I started a telegram asking for $50,000 and for him to arrange to ship beans, peanuts or oil, green vegetables or substitutes from Shanghai. We can't keep the people on shui[10] all winter. We are now feeding 50,000 per day on free rice, many of them can still get pei tsai, etc. but that is going fast and no more in sight till spring. Our own diet is settling down to rice, sometimes with tomato juice, pei tsai and Luchowfu peaches. But we have bread, a butter the hospital makes from the scum off boiled milk, and plenty of jam. Carrots occasionally. But today after Church Espy told us that rice was $20 per *tan* a while in Shanghai and was now down to $17. Other supplies are also difficult to get. So we may not be able to get much. But we hope to get by on local rice here as the Chinese army has such big stores and the Japanese are importing their own now.

Allison and Espy are going to help us get supplies up from Shanghai on whatever boat comes up. So we are getting up an order tonight to go down on this boat for hams, (no meat to be had here—not even for our British friends whom we invited to lunch today, accepted for tomorrow since they did not land till 2:00) dried fruits, coffee, sugar, etc. Will combine with them for Kuleo Co-operative Buying Club. Will try to get part of our shipment of powdered milk.

Yes, we have been food tropic for two weeks. But we have visions of other things. In our telegram to Fong Sec we asked for two foreign doctors and two foreign nurses. We want to start more public health work and a travelling clinic to the camps. Minnie wants to start a home for widows and orphans at Ginling. We have organized a rehabilitation committee to help people get back home. We want to push things on to work relief as soon as order permits.

Boy, this house is popping tonight. I went down to get the Hymnal to look up those Psalms and the living room was dark. Every man in his room pounding a typewriter. Poor Searle and Mc drew tonight to sleep at the University and Hospital respectively. Espy told us after church that this tug boat instead of going down river the 12th might go tomorrow.

If you see the Turners, tell them Searle and I checked up on their house this morning and found it just as they had left it with dresses, etc., hanging in the closets. It has not been touched. So they were much luckier than Elmien which has been turned topsy-turvy time and again. I think I have said that looting by the Japs is nothing like by the *law peh sing*. It is only petty looting in most case but they turned everything upside down. Daniels rugs were taken though and some beds, I believe from Elmiaen, to make some officer comfortable in a city they have destroyed. Did I tell you that Ishida, the supply man, when he had Kroger out to lunch the other day remarked, "Nanking is the capital of China. Why don't they have any nice comfortable places to go and eat and visit?" Kroger was taken back, but had to reply, "There were plenty until your army destroyed and burned the city." Plumer and I went down to the Shuang Tang Church this afternoon to take them their rice—1,500 people refugeed there instead of in the Zone—and a lumber merchant refugeeing from Shanghai has taken charge of the camp and handled it excellently. A woman there with a baby in arms had just been raped before we arrived by three Japanese soldiers. The shops are all burned out and the Chiang Tang Kai church is a burned ruin. In South Gate two older school buildings in the west compound were also burned. Other buildings intact ex looting.

Will have to stop soon for the 10:10 broadcast from Shanghai. But must tell how we got the lights. The electricity came on a week ago tomorrow for the first time, I believe. But the Japns went around and cut off all the houses at the poles excepting those for Japanese offices and the hospital. Rabe got light by sending a fitter up a pole to connect it. Kroger got it by talking a local Japanese officer into doing it then tipping the fitters $5.00. Fitch today talked to the Chinese engineer we supplied—tonight we have lights. All a part of living in a feudalistic society that is growing up around us. And after we had spent part of the day digging up scattered cans of kerosene to keep our—some looted—lamps going.

We laughed today after being told by Prideaux—Brune, as Allison had told us about some earlier, that most of the people who were here until Dec. 10th have gone to various places for a vacation after the strain. So someday we may be due a brief vacation. But not until we see this population out of this hole. That is some regular food supply in sight, at least.

But you need not worry about me here. The worst is probably over now. Having direct and immediate contact with the outside world by radio is a big help, I mean naval wireless. And with some boat contact we will be able to get adequate supplies. With a continuance of good weather, water supply and possibly some supplementary foods and more doctors we hope we should be over by the first of March, but you never can tell. We thought the worst was over the morning of December 14th. Instead it was just ahead of us.

For the Folks, I will add what I said in the former letter, all the University and Ginling buildings are intact. In fact no mission property has been destroyed excepting the buildings above mentioned having been burned. A shell hit the ACM parish building, one hit Drum Tower church, one a University dormitory, and one unexploded hit Steward's basement, the last three on the afternoon of the 13th when we thought the fighting was over. Excepting the first, none did serious damage and no one injured. In fact one Chinese girl was hiding in the tower of the ACM church at Taiping Road when that shell must have passed it by inches. We had one library worker at our refugee camp at the new library building bayoneted in the neck one night for not helping Japanese soldiers get women, but not seriously. No others have been injured. But a number of wives of staff men here and women in their families were raped.

Where is wool? Buried. Our cloth did not get off, along with 400 University boxes. Kao had 7 rolls of undyed uniform cloth at the wool place and so far no looting of it. Many refugees in that compound and women more attractive to Japs than wool. Though they took all Searle's wool cloth and bedding at his house.

***

University of Nanking
Nanking, China
March 8th, 1938[11]

DO NOT PUBLISH!

Dear Friends in God's Country,
Your answers to my Christmas letter mailed from here on December 4th are beginning to come through thanks to the Chinese Post Office in Shanghai. They are sorting out mail for us and sending it up on the British and American gunboats. I told you they would get it through some way! The latest, dated January 18th, arrived March 4th. Here's hoping more come because it makes me feel as though I had some ties across the water again! We have been buried here so this winter, both in lack of connections with the outside world and with the immediate task, that we have come to feel quite isolated.

I could make this whole letter a rebuttal or supplementation of press despatches that have filtered back to us one way or another about Nanking. But the error that took the cake was the one put out about the time I wrote you in December in which it said that all Americans had gone on board the *Panay* but the Embassy staff. It would have been more nearly true to say *only* the Embassy staff went on board. A letter from Mardie in Kuling dated December 15th (received here the last of January) said they would not believe that we were all at the bottom of the Yangtze. I had written in my last letter that got through December 4th, that we had just signed our death warrants to stay in Nanking through any "expected eventualities." Mardie remarked, "Thank God for that!" Well, while we have not had exactly a gay time here in Nanking this winter, we feel thankful that we did stay. We do not want to toot our horns any because it was merely doing our duty, but we do believe that we have reduced the amount of suffering for about 250,000 Chinese civilians who were caught here in the city. We have not done a perfect job by far and many Chinese were killed and many others suffered in spite of all we could do. But we raised a storm of protest so strong that finally General Matsui himself came to Nanking to tell his soldiers to behave themselves—but six weeks too late! If he had said that and made it effective on December 17th when he was here before, there would be a different tale to tell.

What most people feared for us was dangers from air raids and the battle. We worked right through the air raids those last days when the alarm sounded in the morning and did not sound any "all clear" all day. We slept in our regular beds through the battle trusting to wake up if the barrage came any closer than the southern part of the city—and foolishly trusting in Japanese instructions to their artillery to respect the Safety Zone. Our hair nearly stood on end when on the afternoon of December 13th we contacted their advance guard in the center of the city and they did not have the Safety Zone marked on their maps! (Although we had notified them we were moving the civilian population into that area.) The Zone proved to be safe (except for 11 shells that landed along the southern border [at] four or five the afternoon of the 13th in the University area) for the simple reason that we followed the advice of foreign military observers here and chose a part of the city that had the least military value. Because we disarmed all Chinese soldiers coming into the Zone on the afternoon of December 13th (trapped in the city) we had no sniping in the Zone at all. But that did not prevent orders from the high command of the Japanese Army from having every disarmed soldier found in the Zone and many civilians along with them tied up and marched out to be shot. We pled and protested but no avail. When we consulted foreign military observers afterwards they told us that no matter what we might have done as long as the Japanese army worked on that basis nothing we could have done would have saved them and if we had tried to scatter them amongest the civilians we would have just lost more civilians. But the case that still irks us most was that on December 26th, when they started registering the population in the camps, over two hundred men were marched off and some machine-gunned and others used for bayonet practice and others half dead finished with buring gasoline. How do we know? Several escaped after dark and found their way, one who had his eyes and face burned to a crisp with the help of a friend, to the University Hospital. And after these men had been told for twenty minutes on the University campus that if they voluntarily confessed to having ever been a soldier or part of a military labor corps they would be given work, but if they did not confess and were caught they would be shot. Now with inadequate organization, reimbursement, and protection of civilian labor in this area, some Chinese soldiers are being brought back from the front for labor but at the time Nanking was captured there was no such foresight.

This gruesome tale has its own irony. The very day the Japanese Embassy, Navy, and Army came to the Headquarters of the "unrecognized Safety Zone" to ask us to help find the men who could start the electricity works, other Japanese soldiers were busy shooting 43 of the best workers of the electric plant! As one British official remarked, "I know the Japanese did not intend to bomb the *Panay*. It was just a part of their complete lack of co-ordination." Germans here remarked that they had learned how weak an ally they had in Japan. If their Army were up against any well-equipped modern Army it would go to pieces. The Allison incident was only the end of a long series of slapping incidents in Nanking beginning with a Major slapping a soldier he caught in the very act of rape and then letting the soldier go! After two weeks of this, it soon became evident that either the Army did not want to stop it or could not—or some of both! Now the latest is from the Japanese paper that they have found eleven Chinese armed robbers who were to blame for it all! Well, if they each raped from 100 to 200 women per night and day for two weeks and got away with the reported ?50,000 they were pretty powerful Chinese when the Japanese Army had pre-empted all those rights in the city! Even looting by Chinese common people did not begin until after nearly three weeks of destruction and then they started to pick up the pieces in the ruins of burned and looted shops. Cases of armed robbery by Chinese did not begin until a few weeks ago—after ammunition had been left lying about the streets along with dead bodies for weeks after Japanese entry. Even the main road along which General Matsui himself rode on December 17th was not cleaned up until it was known the American Embassy people were due back in a few days! Just two weeks ago the Red Swastika Society reported there were still 30,000 bodies to be buried, nearly three months after the Japanese took the city, and the Army not lifting a hand in the process!

Well, now we are thankful that nightmare is past. The Japanese have moved out their troops and trucks to attack our Chinese friends farther north and west. But the sad part of it is that every indication is that the same is true of all the occupied territory in the Yangtze valley and the claim that it is "too dangerous for foreigners" is that they might be horrified. There is no danger from the Chinese snipers for us! The only danger we have faced is that from Japanese soldiers. How we all escaped when we were almost "insolently" policing the Japanese Army—they claimed their 17 military police in the city were inadequate (as they were) but 22 foreigners made a good attempt at it—is more than any one of us can ever explain. One night when things were at their worst—two days after Matsui's triumphal march through the city—the fellows at our house remarked at supper, "The first fellow that gets killed we are going to carry his body over and put it in the Japanese Embassy." Several piped up, "Well, I am willing to either be so carried or do the carrying!" Each night the doctor acting as "Mama" of the household would look around the eight of us and wonder who would be missing the next night. He said, "We just can't *all* get through this alive." Well, we did. The worst was a bayonet scratch in the neck that McCallum got the day after the Allison incident. The greatest paradox of it all is two pacifist missionaries throwing out through a hole in the wall a Japanese soldier they caught in bed with a Chinese girl near their home, and then laughing at his trying to run up the street and hold his pants up because he had left his belt behind him in his hurried exit! A German comrade has a New Year's story that out does that but it can only be printed in the German Embassy's official report, not here! Well, we wondered if we could keep our minds. But we had enough who could laugh at some feature of the worst of it and we came out nearly sane! Japanese action and statements were absurd enough to provide absurdities to give us release in laughter! All the folks who left before December 10th had to have a vacation because of the strain they had been through. Well, we had to take our vacation right here.

In the midst of all that excitement we had to feed 69,000 people who had crowded into the public and institutional buildings we held till the last minute as reservoirs for those who could not make private arrangements for a house in the Zone. Originally we estimated by crowding, we could put only 35,000 in these buildings! The panic of women in private houses every morning during the first week swelled the total by 20,000 because they were relatively more safe in the crowded camps, especially at Ginling College and the University of Nanking. With all this disorder about as, with every truck or auto taken by stray Japanese soldiers if there were not a foreigner sitting right in it, we had a desperate time getting food to them. The first two nights we had to take rice in private cars to some of those camps to keep people from going more than two days without food. Then we faced the daily fear our rice would not hold out because if the whole population were dependent upon what we had hauled in so desparately during the defence of Nanking, it would only last the 250,000 people one week. But we were soon to learn that our two chief assets were the ingenuity and endurance of the Chinese population and good weather. The Chinese are more accustomed to disaster than we so every family that had anything had brought all the rice they could possibly store before we started hauling—all rice shops were closed by them. And that individual foresight has saved the population because the Japanese have not released for sale enough rice for two weeks' total consumption in the three months they have been here. And they confiscated enough from the Chinese army, private stocks, and from our stocks, to feed the population more than three months.

With the Japanese order in the midst of the "Great Cold" for all the people to go home in less than seven days, people did begin to move out and now our camps are down to one-third, 23,000. By hook or crook we have held on to and secured enough rice to carry that many another three weeks yet. As soon as that movement home started the first of February we began to shift as much as possible to cash relief because the people could buy rice outside of the Zone, though irregularly and with difficulty. So now we are putting out more relief in cash than in rice—about $1,000 per day or $3.85 per family in Chinese currency (i.e. US$1.14). To date we have helped over 6,000 families in this way.

March 9th. Well, if reading about December is as disturbing to you as writing about it was to me last night, you won't sleep after reading this. It brought back the sinking feeling in the pit of my stomach that I had up until about two weeks ago. The trouble was we were foreseeing what the future had in store for this population. On the 20th of December when Mr. Fitch and I drove around the southern part of the city in the gathering dusk and found the Japanese Army systematically taking the remaining goods out of stores and loading it in Army trucks, then setting fire to the buildings we realized that it was deliberate destruction rather than accidental. The Y.M.C.A. building had just been fired when we got there. We fully recognized that this deliberate destruction of the city would mean the finish of the local economic resources with which the population had some chance of staging a comeback. In the month following they burned over three-fourths of the stores in town (all the large ones, only some small ones remaining), and all of them were completely looted. Now they are hauling all the loot and wrecked cars etc., out on the railway to Japan. Reminds one of the Punic wars!

When we talked about how badly the Japanese Army was treating Nanking, some of them came back with the remark that it was just like all armies did and instanced Belgium. Our good German comrades did not like that! One of them had seen service in Belgium and while he admitted acts by individual soldiers said this was much greater in extent, and there soldiers caught in such actions were shot. One of our number who had been with the British army in Mesopotamia said the only case of rape they found there was of a Kurdish woman and the soldier was shot before the whole brigade of 5,000 men. Since a lull in our policing job, we have been reading up on Belgium and have about decided that the Japanese killed more civilians and burned more buildings here in one city than the Germans did in all Belguim! When they objected to the German representative here calling it disorder, he quickly asked, "Do you mean to tell me that this was all ordered by Japanese officers?"

I know some of my pacifist and neutrality friends will wonder what stand we took on American rights. When the Zone was started we all definitely decided that it should not concern foreign property or rights. We stayed at our own risk and did not expect any succor. But when the Japanese got here they would not listen to any humanitarian appeal at all. They credited us with only the most narrowly selfish interests for looking out for ourselves as foreigners and our property. The first spark of interest we got from them on the welfare of the refugees was when we finally told them that their soldiers were mistreating refugees on American property. They got excited at once and did nothing! But gradually guards were established at those places (containing nearly two-thirds of the refugees in camps) and we went through a "guarded stage." (But not of our private residences though we had to argue one whole afternoon to prevent that! Our German chairman told them when the Chinese were safe we would be safe.) After the American representatives got here they took a stronger attitude on the illegal entrance of American property than we had thought of, although they based their attitude on a large body of precedent in China. It was merely an attempt to carry through the request that the Japanese ask for permission to search American property that led to the Allison incident. From the very first night the Japanese were here, we had not objected to any legal search. But what gave the trouble was stray groups of three to seven soldiers who would come around and when caught would claim they were looking for Chinese soldiers! Lest I misrepresent the facts, I must insert that after December 27th, the Japanese finally came to do what we had asked for on December 14th—to station guards at the entrances to the Zone and order all soldiers to stay out. That improved the situation but because ineffectively carried out did not clear it up.

Some will think the above is an incitement for America to declare war on Japan. Far from it. When things were at their hottest, one of our group kidded a pacifist. "Well, are you still a pacifist?" He came back. "Yes and becoming more so every day." While it does not excuse the Japanese and they seem to have set a world's record for a modern (?) army, it is true that the background of all this is WAR. It brings out the worst in men. (Yes, even the Japanese as soon as they got to Nanking told us, "This is war," though their propaganda at home and abroad calls it an "incident." They seem to want the advantages of calling it a "war" without assuming the responsibilities of doing so!) Even our own thoughts have been coarsened by it—we discussed rape at a dinner where ladies were present on Christmas day. No, for the United States to go to war with Japanese would just spread this mess around the world. Nor will an isolation policy of "save our own skins" really help solve the problem. We are beginning to have to pay for that now. The decade of hope for some form of collective security has passed and with British capitulation from that formula the die is quite definitely set toward an armament race in which each nation looks out for itself and the devil take the hindmost. Under present conditions it is either collective armament on an economical basis or else individual armament on a competitive and expensive basis. We have chosen the latter course and now we will have to foot the bill. As I tried to point out last fall (but the *Christian Century* would not publish it!) the purely negative solution of the Neutrality

Act would be unsatisfactory and it would probably be swept aside by a tide of belligerency. If we did not want to go the full way of collective armament, there was the form of guarantee of world security for all by the use of international economic sanctions against aggression. But we so feared that would lead to war that our fears have put us in the way that leads to war! And we are so hamstrung by the new-found conscience over our past imperialism that we can do nothing to stop the spread of aggressive imperialism by others. Just because we have engaged in "punitive expeditions" and now realize that such things are not best for world welfare, it is not enough for us to fold our hands any say "we cannot object, because we committed the same sin." Rather we must ask all the nations of the world to live up to the most recent revelation of moral insight. Well, Stanley Jones is stating the moral issue much more clearly than I can! Either the nations of the world must cooperate for a better international order or else all will live in the mess of an anarchical world.

We are having to slow up our relief work because it is reported that the American Red Cross campaign is not progressing favorably. From all indications we are only at the beginning of the relief problem in China, both behind the Chinese lines where the chief problems are care of the wounded soldiers and refugees from the war areas, and behind the Japanese lines where the chief problem is the care of civilians in a war-torn area. We have found the latter problem more difficult than the relief problem created by the Yangtze River Flood of 1931. With an "act of God," such as a flood, relief work can proceed with full force immediately; with an "act of man," the deviltry seems to have only begun and relief work is hampered on every side by the men who committed the act. In 1931 shiploads of wheat were shipped immediately; now we, an international relief committee, are prohibited from shipping anything on either foreign boats or Japanese boats. (Compare this though with Belgium where the American Relief Commission shipped in food supplies long after German occupation.) In 1931 people could return to their farms as soon as the waters had receded; now farmers do not dare return to their fields three and four months after the fighting has ceased. If the winter wheat crop is harvested in June by then the worst may be over; if depredations against farmers by both Japanese soldiers and Chinese bandits continue, we will face serious famine conditions in the fertile Yangtze Valley by late summer and fall. So leading relief workers in Shanghai are telling us to cut our cloth so that it can be spread over at least a year. That includes what is expected from the American Red Cross campaign. If that campaign fails, the suffering here will be much worse. With all the hindrances on our work, with actual cash resources we can find a way. Without the resources, we can do nothing.

(About Chinese banditry, I should explain that the situation is worse now than it was for any time during the last ten years. Japanese destruction of constituted authorities in this area, and assuming no responsibility for a new one, coupled with destruction of the very bases of economic life, is driving the counditry to banditry.)

We have been so worn down by the Japanese period of the Safety Zone that we have nearly forgotten the "Chinese period." The foresight of the Chinese Mayor of Nanking in giving our Committee over 2,400 tons of rice and 500 tons of flour and $80,000 Chinese currency for our work has been the chief salvation of this population through this winter. Now other funds have been made available in Shanghai. If we had the 1,400 tons of rice and 500 tons of flour the Japanese confiscated from the above amounts, we would not have to worry about food for the people on relief for the next few months. The Chinese agreed readily to withdraw all military establishments from the Zone but there was a difference of opinion on the question of time. We urged speed. They said that the Japanese would not be here for two weeks. So we did not get the Chinese military out until it was too late to send any final notification to the Japanese via the ill-fated *Panay*. But the morning of December 13th I checked up on the southern boundary of the Zone myself and there were no Chinese soldiers there. At noon when we went back twenty bodies lay in the road—they had run when the Japanese forces reached the boundary!

In my studies of Sociology I have heard a lot about the terrors of the "interregnum." We passed through the siege of Nanking, the retreat of the Chinese soldiers on the night of December 12th, the period of no authority from the time the Chinese general left Sunday afternoon until the Japanese high command arrived on Wednesday without a single disorder by civilians! The only disorders were by the Japanese soldiers beginning from the night of the 13th. It sounds like a fairy tale and very different from what we expected. It may be that the fact we had the Zone organized, that the heroic Chinese workers kept the light, water, and telephone going until the evening of December 12th which preserved such perfect order in a sea of disorganization. But only a clerk remained of the former City Government and even the head of the police had fled! The burning referred to in news despatches was outside of the city wall, not inside. In other words, we had here a set-up perfectly arranged for the Japanese to take control of the civilian population peaceably and to have had the essential services going in a day or two. They missed that opportunity by being too blind to see it!

But since the occupation by the troops of the Rising Sun, I have come to fully appreciate the value of organized society. In the deluge of vandalism that broke upon this city not a shop dared remain open—our specially organized rice shop had to close because its workers were taken away and the rice stolen by soldiers. Not a ricksha or bicycle dared show itself on the road, much less a car. The streets were deserted excepting for a brief time for curb marketing early in the morning. Then the agony of getting a rice shop started, a simple exchange shop run by college graduates, rice delivered by one of the leading missionaries of Nanking and later for six weeks by an American Professor of the Old Testament, coal hauled by our professor of Agricultural Engineering after he could be released from the "policing job." Then he organized a trucking service for hauling all food supplies for the whole city and still supervises it. To do this he had to piece together trucks damaged by the Japanese while hundreds of Japanese Army trucks stood idle about the streets of the city! What about the much talked of "cooperation"! All these services were taken for granted in Nanking under the Chinese. And the telephone service has not been restored yet, nor the mail, nor the banks, nor the movies, nor. . . . ! The first function of the "Self-government Committee" when called together by the Japanese on December 22nd, was to organize three houses of prostitution for the Japanese Army—and many were those who blessed the event! But it was then we learned with whom we were working. Representatives of our office manager went to the campuses of Ginling College and the University of Nanking and from the midst of the 10,000 refugees at each with a snap of a finger called forth 28 prostitutes! So we laughed and said the International Committee was carrying out its work with American missionaries, Chinese Christian workers, German Nazi business men, Chinese Red Cross, Chinese Red Swastika, and the underworld! But we all surged with the feeling of common humanity in that crucial hour. The five barred flag of the new city government was raised over Drum Tower on January first by a former second hand merchant—for a second hand government!—now Food Commissioner and head of the Department of Labor and Commerce for the city. He told us about "self-government": "When the Japanese say 'Yes,' we do it"!

We have come to understand the Japanese much better than we did. A week before their entry I preached to our retreating University group and gently blamed them for leaving and urged them to have faith in the goodness and humanity of the Japanese. The Chinese that remained are still laughing at us for our innocence! We soon learned that the Japanese sincerely believed from the common private up through the highest men here that while it was necessary to show some regard for foreigners they could do anything to a Chinese. While part of our success in meeting them was possibly due to our looking them straight in the eye and a certain feeling of moral rightness in our position, we realized that our nationality probably protected us from death. But Chinese who went about relief work risked death itself and some met it in faithful service. One refugee young man at the University Middle School had been a big help in keeping Japanese soldiers from molesting women there because he could speak a little Japanese. But when he refused to become a henchman for the consular police, he was arrested—escaped machine-gunning once, then taken from the residence of a missionary who had given him refuge, and shot. When about New Year's some of us were invited to the Japanese Embassy for dinner, this missionary remarked, "Am I to go and eat with the murderers of Liu Wen-pin?" And yet we felt we had to be friendly in a personal way in order to try to get to some working arrangement for the sake of the 250,000 civilians depending on us for their lives, honor, and food.

We also better understand Japanese propaganda! In the midst of such great suffering in January, Japanese news squads went around staging pictures of Japanese soldiers giving candy to a child or an Army doctor examining 20 children. But these acts were not repeated when no camera was around! Whereas in propaganda for the United States, Japan represents herself as defending foreign rights in China and preventing communism, in China the Japanese Army published statements in Chinese recounting her efforts to drive the white race out of Asia. In face she is rapidly "communizing China" in the old sense of creating economic distress which gives rise to banditry, as well as forcing China to turn more and more to Soviet Russia. After what we have seen here the following always gets a laugh: "In former times Khublai Khan's great armies rolled up the continent of Europe like a mat. So why should we oriental peoples, creators of the spiritual culture, sweetly submit to the western peoples' greed and arrogance?" (Press Release by Japanese Army in local Chinese paper, Nanking, March 10th, 1938.)

Some American friends had their houses pretty well looted by Japanese soldiers—oh yes, we caught them in the attics going through boxes and chased them out of basements where refugee women were hiding—but the fact that most of our houses were crammed full of refugees covered up much of our stuff! My house crowded to the attic with refugee families miraculously escaped looting though my refugee guests suffered both looting and rape. Two men stayed at home and protected the refugees in their houses but others of us felt to create such islands in the midst of so much suffering was useless. So we struggled to improve conditions in general and filed two protests with the Japanese Embassy daily for a month and did get the Japanese soldiers excluded from the Zone after two weeks. However, this was only partially effective. The house here where eight of us were staying and none of us could stay during the day to protect escaped. The Japanese soldiers only happened to come when someone was at home or at night. Several of us traded off sleeping at two of our camps and the University Hospital until into February to protect the women there.

What are the prospects of the University re-opening here? About zero for a year at least. I criticized our students and staff for leaving. Now I am glad they did as probably most of the students would have been shot with the Japanese in the mood they were when they took this city. Even the return of one or two

Chinese Seminary professors from the countryside where they hid out has been a subject of much questioning. So if we ever get through with the refugee job here, we will probably filter out to Szechuen where the intelligentsia of China are now gathered. The Japanese only took the physical structure of Nanking and the poorest part of its population, not the "Capital" as we knew it.

On the other hand evangelistic work here has a big opening. In our refugee work we have almost leaned over backwards to make sure that none of it was made conditional upon a man's being a Christian or to give Christians any favoritism out of funds given for the general welfare. (We have helped Christians out of special funds though.) And while we were laboring Sunday like any other day to keep the population fed and protected, the few Chinese pastors left in the city found the people very responsive to the Christian message. As one intelligent pastor expressed it: "Now they believe beyond all belief!" We are struggling now to get some more mission workers back so they can help in the continuing relief work for widows and others who have no home or family to go back to.

I came here last September against the express instructions of the American Embassy "just for three days" and stayed through until now when the American Government is proclaiming that Americans have a right to live and move about in China. The world do move! After all the effort last fall to get missionaries out and some of the thoughtless words that were said about it, I can only say that we were treated in the finest manner by our American representatives here and when they left some of them said they wished they could stay and help us. Since their return in January they have been a help as men as well as representatives of our Government. And without endorsing the policy of foreign gunboats (including Japanese!) on the Yangtze, we can express our appreciation of the fine way the gunboats of both the American and British navies have carried relief supplies and sent urgent radio messages for us.

Our personal plans are unknown! Mardie and the children stayed in Kuling until the American School there broke up on December 26th. Then she travelled as far as Hongkong with the school but stayed there on Cheung Chau Island while the others went on to Shanghai. The children are enjoying a winter in that southern clime although the oldest, Margaret Ann, had dysentery after getting there—but got over it satisfactorily. Joan is thriving. They had hoped I could join them there but since we have been virtually prisoners here and now only go out under danger of not being allowed to come back—as well as the fact the work goes on needing us—keeps me from even having any hopes of getting to Hongkong this spring. Where Mardie will go for the summer (that is, May 1st there) remains to be seen. Baguio in the Philippines is most convenient for her and I certainly do not want to go to Japan! Would like to get where I couldn't see a Japanese for three months. (Oh yes, there are many fine Japanese

I would like to see!) Still others say they have been sweetened on Japan after being inside the country. We are kind of at the back door here. If I go to Chengtu, Mardie says she wants to go with me. That partly depends upon the vigor of the Japanese southern campaign! Well, we might go around by Burma! (Until further word you had better address us here in Nanking—but remember the mail will be censored in Shanghai. This letter will go by hand until it is safely on a foreign steamer out of Shanghai.)

Do I hate the Japanese? No, I dislike very much their policy and I dislike very much the way they are treating the common people of China. And I believe the truth will out and I did not want to stand in its way! But if I am ever given the opportunity of doing the same for Japanese as we have done here for 250,000 Chinese men, women, and children, I would do the same right over again. This experience has also convinced me that there is really no other way for the world but that of Christian love.

Let us hear from you. Thereby you may save our souls!

Your friends in China,
Lewis and Margaret Smythe
Revised, March 14th, 1938.

Cases of Disorder by Japanese Soldiers in the Safety Zone[12]

Filed, December 16th, 1937.

Note: These are only sample cases we have had time to check up on more carefully. Many more have been reported to our workers.

1. Six street sweepers of the second division of the Sanitary Commission of the Safety Zone were killed in the house they occupied at Kuleo and one seriously injured with a bayonet by Japanese soldiers on Dec. 15th. No apparent reason whatever. These men were our employees. The soldiers entered the house.
2. A carriage loaded with rice was taken on Dec. 15th at 4:00 P.M. near the gate of Ginling College by Japanese soldiers.
3. Several residents in our second sub-division were driven from their homes on the night of December 14th and robbed of everything. The chief of the sub-division was himself robbed twice by Japanese soldiers.
4. On the night of December 15th, last night, seven Japanese soldiers entered the University of Nanking library building and took seven Chinese women refugees, three of whom were raped on the spot. (Full

details of this case will be filed by Dr. M. S. Bates Chairman of the University of Nanking Emergency Committee.)

5. On the night of December 14th, there were many cases of Japanese soldiers entering Chinese houses and raping women or taking them away. This created a panic in the area and hundreds of women moved into the Ginling College campus yesterday. Consequently, three American men spent the night at Ginling College last night to protect the 3,000 women and children in the compound.

6. About 30 Japanese soldiers with no apparent leader, on December 14th, searched the University Hospital and the nurses' dormitory. The staff of the Hospital were systematically looted, the objects taken were: 6 fountain pens, $180.00, 4 watches, 2 hospital badges, 2 flashlights, 2 pairs of gloves, 1 sweater.

7. Yesterday, December 15th, every one of our large refugee camps in public and institutional buildings reported that the Japanese soldiers had been there and robbed the refugees several times.

8. On December 15th, the American Ambassador's residence was broken into and searched and some small personal articles taken.

9. On December 15th, the faculty house of Ginling College was entered by Japanese soldiers who climbed over the back fence and smashed in a door. Since every movable thing had been taken out of the building since December 13th, nothing could be stolen!

10. At noon, December 14th, on Chien Ying Hsian, Japanese soldiers entered a house and took four girls, raped them, and let them return in two hours.

11. Our Ninghai Road rice shop was visited on December 15th in the afternoon by Japanese soldiers who bought 3 bags of rice (3.75 *tan* or piculs) and only paid $5.00. The regular price of rice is $9.00 per *tan,* so the Imperial Japanese Army owes the International Committee $28.75 for this.

12. At 10:00 P.M. on the night of December 14th a Chinese home on Chien Ying Hsiang was entered by 11 Japanese soldiers who raped 4 Chinese somen [*sic*].

13. On December 14th, Japanese soldiers entered the home of Miss Grace Bauer, an American missionary, and took a pair of fur-lined gloves, drank up all the milk on the table, and scooped up sugar with their hands.

14. On December 15th, Japanese soldiers entered the garage of Dr. R.F. Brady (American) at Shuan Lung Hsiang, smashed a window in his Ford V8, later came back with a mechanic and tried to start the car.

15. Last night, December 15th, Japanese soldiers entered a Chinese house

on Hankow Road and raped a young wife and took away three women. When two husbands ran, the soldiers shot both of them.

The above cases have been checked up on by foreign members of our Committee or Staff.

Respectfully submitted,

Lewis S.C. Smythe, Secretary.
International Committee For Nanking Safety Zone

Letter to Japanese Embassy

5 Ninghai Road
December 16th, 1937
Mr. Tokuyasu Fukuda,
Attache to the Japanese Embassy,
Nanking.

My dear Sir:
As pointed out by the Major we interviewed with you at the Bank of Communications yesterday noon, it is advisable to have the city return to normal life as soon as possible. But yesterday the continued disorders committed by Japanese soldiers in the Safety Zone increased the state of panic among the refugees. Refugees in large buildings are afraid to even go to nearby soup kitchens to secure the cooked rice. Consequently, we are having to deliver rice to these compounds directly, thereby complicating our problem. We could not even get coolies out to load rice and coal to take to our soup kitchens and therefore this morning thousands of people had to go without their breakfast. Foreign members of the International Committee are this morning making desperate efforts to get trucks through Japanese patrols so these civilians can be fed. Yesterday foreign members of our Committee had several attempts made to take their personal cars away from them by Japanese soldiers. (A list of cases of disorder is appended.)

Until this state of panic is allayed, it is going to be impossible to get any normal activity started in the city, such as: telephone workers, electric plant workers, probably the water plant workers, shops of all kinds, or even street cleaning.

In order to quickly improve this situation, the International Committee respectfully suggests that the Imperial Japanese Army take the following steps at once:

1. Have all searching done by regularly organized squads of soldiers under a responsible officer. (Most of the trouble has come from wandering groups of 3 to 7 soldiers without an officer.)
2. At night, and if possible also in the daytime, have the guards at the entrances of the Safety Zone (proposed by the Major yesterday) prevent any stray Japanese soldiers from entering the Safety Zone.
3. Today, give us passes to paste on the windshields of our private cars and trucks to prevent Japanese soldiers from commandeering them. (Even under the stress of defence of the city the Chinese Army Headquarters supplied us with such passes and the cars that were taken before we got the passes were returned to the Committee within 24 hours after our reporting the cases. Furthermore, even in that difficult situation, the Chinese Army assigned to us three trucks to use for hauling rice for feeding civilians. Certainly, the Imperial Japanese Army in full control of the city, with no fighting going on, and with much greater amount of equipment, cannot do less for the Chinese civilians that have to come under their care and protection.)

We refrained from protesting yesterday because we thought when the High Command arrived order in the city would be restored, but last night was even worse than the night before, so we decided these matters should be called to the attention of the Imperial Japanese Army, which we are sure does not approve such actions by its soldiers.

Most respectfully yours,
Lewis S.C. Smythe

John H.D. Rabe, Chairman.

Notes on the Present Situation[14]

Nanking, March 21, 1938

1. *Order* is becoming a problem again. Robbery and rape are recurring, at least in cases that are closer to our observations. This includes the rape of a young girl on the afternoon of the 19th at one of our refugee camps on American property. A Japanese soldier was found there by an American and he was able, although threatened with a bayonet, to persuade the fellow to leave. But he demanded a woman of the American! And the real damages had already been done.

Western Nationals in Nanking, December 16, 1937[13]

Name	Nationality	Organization
1. Mr. John H.D. Rabe	German	Siemens Co.
2. Mr. Christian Kroger	German	Carlowitz and Co.
3. Mr. Eduard Sperling	German	Shanghai Insurance
4. Mr. A. Zautig	German	Kiesseling and Bader
5. Mr. R. Hempel	German	North Hotel
6. Mr. R.R. Hatz	Austrian	Mechanic for Safety Zone
7. Mr. Cola Podshivoloff	White Russian	Sandgren's Electrical Shop
8. Mr. A. Zial	White Russian	Mechanic for Safety Zone
9. Mr. Charles H. Riggs	American	University of Nanking
10. Dr. M.S. Bates	American	University of Nanking
11. Dr. Lewis S.C. Smythe	American	University of Nanking
12. Dr. C.S. Trimmer	American	University Hospital
13. Dr. Robert O. Wilson	American	University Hospital
14. Miss Grace Bauer	American	University Hospital
15. Miss Iva Hynds	American	University Hospital
16. Rev. James McCallum	American	United Christian Missionary Society, now at University Hospital
17. Miss Minnie Vautrin	American	Ginling College
18. Rev. W.P. Mills	American	North Presbyterian Mission
19. Rev. Hubert L. Sone	American	Nanking Theological Seminary
20. Mr. Geroge Fitch	American	Y. M. C. A.
21. Rev. Ernest H. Forster	American	American Church Mission
22. Rev. John Magee	American	American Church Mission

2. *Food.* The food situation is somewhat relieved now that commercial rice is allowed to come into the city more freely and the Self-Government Committee has received 3,000 bags of rice by boat from Wuhu. But how much there is available and how long it will be free to come no one can say. The price is fixed at $9.00 per *tan* or $11.25 per bag. With rice selling for $4.50 to $6.00 per *tan* in Wuhu, it is hoped the price will fall here somewhat. However, a tax by the Self-Government Committee (with approval of the Special Service Organ) of $0.60 per *tan* will partly prevent a fall in prices. The Committee hopes to be able to buy rice in the open market for its relief work.

3. *Economic conditions.* The serious question for the future is the fact that only a few of the 10,000 gardeners inside the city wall have dared return to their homes and begin spring planting. We are trying to organize their return so as to give them some greater degree of security. Most of them have lost not only their household things, but also their implements and seed. Another phase of the same question is that people are coming in from the countryside hoping to find greater safety here.

Over 300 came one afternoon asking for a camp to take them in. Intelligent observers returning from north of the river say in some areas the winter wheat crop will be less than 30 percent of normal because of late planting due to fighting and that 80 percent of the farmers have no reserve food supplies. In Chuyung *hsien*[15] winter crops are better, probably 70 percent of normal, but 90 percent of the farmers have no reserve food supplies and less than 10 percent have started spring work. North of the river also, country people have gone to the towns for protection. If the countryside depends on the city, what can the city depend on? When farming is the only form of basic production that can be done in this area, it is very important that farming be carried on.

4. *Relief situation.* Because of country people coming into the city and because our "semi-permanent" camps are full with 15,000 refugees, we have had to slow up on closing other camps. But all eight camps in government buildings have been closed excepting one reserved for refugees from other towns. In general, we are trying to get all men to move out, only allowing women between 13 and 40 years of age to stay, but permitting children to stay with their mothers. An inspection of the southern part of the city reveals that many streets are now populated which were deserted a month ago. This extends even to the southeastern section of the city. But very few young women have returned—after the terrible experience of the first week in February the people have learned to leave their young women either in camps or in houses in the Safety Zone. There was even one rice shop open on Moh Tsou Road!

Putting together information from organizations interested in burying the dead and other observations, it is estimated that 10,000 persons were killed inside the walls of Nanking and about 30,000 outside the walls—this latter figure depends upon not going too far along the river bank! These people estimated that of this total about 30 percent were civilians.

5. *Cases*

460. Feb. 27th, about 4 p.m. Ts'ai Djih-lan and his father were standing near a house at a place called Sa Chou Wei Kao Chiao, about ten *li* from Nanking outside of Shuisimen. There were some women in the house near which they were standing. Japanese soldiers were seen approaching and the women ran away. When soldiers came up, they asked where the women were and wanted the boy and his father to lead them to them. They refused, whereupon a soldier shot the boy in the leg, injuring him very badly. He is now undergoing treatment at the University.

461. March 4th, a farmer aged 54 at Molinkwan was asked by Japanese soldiers on February 13th for some cows, donkeys and girls. The neighbors all ran away. The soldiers tied the farmer and spread him out three feet from the ground. Then they built a fire under him and burned him badly around the lower abdomen, genitalia, and chest, and singed the hair of his face and head. One soldier protested because of his age and put out the fire, tearing off the farmer's burning clothes. The soldiers went away and after about an hour his family returned and released him.

462. March 9th, 8 p.m. Japanese soldiers came to Mr. Hwang's house on Chukiang Road and asked him to lead them to women. He did not agree to do so. So one of the soldiers stuck him with a bayonet through the left groin, piercing his flesh one-half inch. The man jumped back and at the same time pushed the bayonet aside with his right hand but cut his hand in so doing. He ran and the soldiers followed but he made good his escape. Bayonet just missed a large artery. (Because of fear the soldiers would return, two families related to him including 12 people, moved into the University Middle School.)

463. March 10th, about 8, p.m. five Japanese soldiers wearing blue and yellow uniforms came to the Ts'ai house in Men-si. While two soldiers kept watch outside, the other three entered the house asking for money. The whole family fell down on their knees begging for mercy. The three soldiers placed a wooden ladder in front of the room door. With a rope they tied the two hands of the husband to the ladder and left him hanging there. They began to search the family and took away: one five-dollar note, one *ten-sen* Japanese coin, three Chinese double dimes, one paper money and copper, after turning over wardrobes and trunks, they took away a fur robe, one woman's winter clothes, one phonograph. On leaving, they stabbed Ts'ai's thigh six time, two on each shoulder, and at last they shot him in his head and killed him instantly. They also stabbed several times the head of Ts'ai Lih Shih who was on her knees, and stabbed Wang's thigh twice. After this they went away.

464. March 11th, a woman was raped by two soldiers in a hut next door.

465. March 15th, a man named Chung, aged 47, living at Hansimen, while walking near Chu So Hsiang at 7 a.m. was hit by a stray bullet at his head. He was sent to the hospital for treatment, where he died shortly after arriving.

466. March 17th, at 10 p.m. six Japanese soldiers went into the house of a 40 year old farmer named Kao who lived at Hou Tsaimen. They demanded that he get some women for them. He replied he didn't have any woman and could not find any women. So they jabbed him many times in the body and in the neck and cut his head with their bayonets. He ran but by the time he reached the door of the house he fell down bleeding very profusely. He died without being able to get up again. The soldiers saw they had killed him so they left quickly.

467. March 19th, between 3:30 and 4:00 p.m. a Japanese soldier committed rape upon a refugee, a nineteen year old girl, in the Language School Refugee camp at the University of Nanking. Dr. Bates arrived there about 4:05 and as he approached the soldier, the soldier brandished his bayonet and insolently said, "want girl." But Dr. Bates persuaded him to leave. The soldier showed no sign of being drunk.

468. March 19th, night, a man and a woman were caught crawling over the wall of the Middle School Refugee Camps. When told they could not come in, they said the woman had been raped twice that evening and they could not go back.

469. March 20th, 9:30 p.m. five poor families near our house were robbed of $283.30 by Japanese soldiers.

470. March 19th, an uncle of one of our staff was marched off by Japanese soldiers because he wore khaki pants. Sperling rescued him.

Notes

1. These letters of protest, with attached reports of atrocity cases, were reprinted in Shuhsi Hsu (ed.), *Documents of the Nanking Safety Zone* (Shanghai: Kelly & Walsh, 1939); an incomplete list of the same is given in Appendixes D and E of Timperley's book *Japanese Terror in China* (New York: Modern Age Books, June 1938).

2. RG8, B103.

3. Rural Leader Training School.

4. Chinese for "think out a way."

5. Bible Teachers Training School.

6. See footnote, p. 254.

7. Chinese cabbage.

8. Chinese pinyin, means porridge.

9. Chinese for "boss."

10. Water.

11. RG10, B4, F64; also RG8, B103.

12. RG10, B102, F863.

13. RG10, B102, F863.

14. Contained in the Miner Searle Bates Papers, Record Group No. 10, Box 102.

15. County.

Albert N. Steward

Albert Newton Steward was born in California in 1897. He married Celia Belle Speak in 1918. Then he got a B.S. from Oregon Agricultural College. From 1921 to 1926, the Stewards were stationed in Nanking as educational missionaries under the Methodist Board of Missions. There he taught botany at the University of Nanking. In 1930 Steward received his Ph.D. in Biology from Harvard. From 1930 to 1937, Steward and his family were stationed in Nanking again. They were evacuated from China in August 1937. In September of the following year Steward returned to China. He was interned at Chapei Camp, Shanghai, in 1943, and then was released in 1945. Later he remained in China to look after the affairs of the University of Nanking until March 1946, in which year he returned to the United States Steward became curator of the Herbarium and a professor at Oregon State College. He died in June 1959.

More detailed information is available in Series IV (particularly box 12, Folder 252, and Box 13, Folder 261) and in autobiographical talks by ANS and CSS located in Series II.

Excerpts of Diary[1]

December 10th, 1938

The first few miles of the trip were through an area of destruction and desolation. Occasionally one might see an old man or woman moving among the ruins, and here and there a Japanese flag floated proudly as a boast of the army's handiwork. Then we began to see patches of land under cultivation, and found a few people working the land or stirring about the villages, but it was long after we had passed into the area of nearly complete cultivation before we saw any farm animals. Later on we saw a number of buffalo and some cattle, but chickens, ducks and pigs seem to have vanished from the landscape. I was sorry to see the people cutting many trees. There are two reasons for this, the price of wood is unusually high on account of the shortage of fuel and lumber from outside, while a good deal of rebuilding is being done; and the Japanese have ordered on account of military necessity the cutting of all trees within a mile on either side of the railway.

The train made good time, reaching Nanking in about 6 1/2 hrs. I was glad for the lunch Mrs. Fuller had prepared for me, since very little was available along the way. I noted with interest a Japanese lunch wrapped in what appeared to be wood shavings about four inches wide, used much as the Chinese might use bamboo sheaths. The rails and ties have both been removed from the railway spur at Yaohuamen which connected with the Wuhu line outside South Gate. Upon arrival at Hsiakwan we were lined up like a row of soldiers for passport inspection. Outside the station we found cars very few and the prices high, so we took a carriage and drove into the city much as in 1921, except that military trucks and cars whizzed by continually. Much of Hsiakwan has been leveled flat, and there is not much activity there. The Episcopal Mission is as beautiful as ever, and is as a spring of water in a dry and thirsty land. We were stopped for inspection only at the city gate. I took the Sommerfreunds to stop with Mr. Gale, and then returned to the University Hospital where I found that Dr. Trimmer had just gone to Shanghai to bring his family up for Christmas; so I am stopping for a while with Mr. Riggs and Dr. Robert Wilson in Riggs' house.

December 11th. This being Sunday, I went to Chiang T'ang Chieh, on foot (3 miles). This part of the city is not so much changed, but the people are few. Pastor Wang was there and made one of his unusually fine prayers. The service was held in the basement, with an attendance about twice what we used to have upstairs before the war. The singing was the best I have ever heard there, and there was almost no inattention during the service. I heard no expression of bitterness or discouragement. The Sones, Miss Brethorst, Mrs. Wang and Yieh Sze Mu and Mr. Yuan asked about Celia and the family.

The anniversary of the entrance of the Japanese Army into Nanking is near, and I have heard many accounts of incidents which occurred about a year ago. A high up Chinese officer who was wounded and cared for in the Hospital gave a good deal of information. It is reported that a certain Hupeh division failed to get into position, somewhere between T'ang Shan and the railway, so leaving a wide open gap through which the Japanese poured in large numbers up to the very city wall, almost before they were known to be there. Then the chief commander of the forces here, who had begged for permission to defend the city when General Chiang first ordered its evacuation, took flight and left the army without any unifying authority the day before the debacle. The officers then turned their men loose to fly, every man for himself, and all through the night they streamed through the streets which were found in the morning to be littered for miles with uniforms, guns and other military equipment, in an effort to escape to the River and up to Central China.

The Japanese had attacked the city on three sides, but apparently had left the side next to the River at Hsiakwan open. When the Chinese soldiers poured out that gate to the bank of the River 40,000 or so of them were mowed down with machine guns as they entered the trap. On the occasion of his first trip outside the city after the occupation Mr. Fitch rode over human bodies packed to a depth of 6 ft. or more. Then the Japanese began searching the city, even inside the neutral zone, for soldiers in disguise, and any man was liable to be taken as such. In most instances such men were taken to the bank of the River in companies of 100 and shot with machine guns, after which their bodies were dumped into the River. In at least two or three cases such groups of men, tied together, were doused with kerosene and burned alive. Altogether, it is estimated that 60–70,000 people lost their lives when the city fell into the hands of the Japanese.

The English service is now held in the Ginling faculty house at 4:00 p.m. Mr. Mills is the acting pastor. Many friends were there, and a few new faces. . . .

December 12th. The household goods and furniture in our house and the Slocums' seemed to be O.K., but a check with the lists showed that several articles are missing from our house, though the store rooms seem to have been unmolested. I estimate the loss at about $150—local currency. A big shell came in the east window near the fire place, doing but slight damage. I got my trunks from the station today and had to open one of them for inspection at the city gate, the only piece I have been asked to open since I got to Vancouver.

Miss Vautrin showed me some very interesting practical work being carried on among the refugees at Ginling, such as weaving and sewing. She finds that it is very difficult to get yarn for the weaving and suggested that we at the University should set up means of getting it made locally from the raw cotton. Mr. Riggs was studying up on the difficult problem of spinning when he ran into the term "osculatory curve" which has an unexpected meaning. We are now waiting for a good chance to tell Miss Vautrin what she got us in to.

Some fifty people passed down river today from Kuling on a Japanese transport. Dr. Gale stopped here to join her husband. They have been separated over a year.

Mr. Y. Chen told me about the four different classes of instruction which are being carried on at the University. There is a primary school at the Rural Leaders Training School, a Farmers School at the Sericulture Building, a tutoring school offering classes in Chinese, English, Japanese and Mathematics in Severance Hall, and a school for older people who want to learn to read at the Kuleo Church. Airmail letters arrived from Chengtu today, having been three weeks on the way.

We keep hearing stories about the terrible days of a year ago. Accompanying the mass murders there was wholesale rape of many thousands of women in the city. Detailed accounts of a number of particular cases have been recorded, but here are two I had not heard before. The bodies of two women were found, one with a golf stick and the other with a beer bottle thrust up into their abdomens so that they died where they lay. During recent months many of the unfortunate women have come to the University Hospital for help, and Dr. — has relieved a number of them of their unwelcome burdens, though there has been some division of opinion among the doctors as to whether or not it was right to do so. I understand that abortion is usually regarded as legal in cases of rape. Dr. — calls himself the No. 1 Jap destroyer of Nanking.

December 13th. I have arranged with Lu Sou Tze (Esther's servant) to clean up the south suite at our house so I can live there after a while. Dr. Daniels eats Chinese lunch with us at noon.

A year ago today Mr. Riggs picked up a couple of pistols on the street and in the evening was trying to give them to Mr. Kuh, a nice young fellow in our business office who had never possessed such equipment but was sorely tempted. Mr. Gee was trying to persuade him not to accept, and I think he did not do so. Within an hour at least two of the three of them had a very narrow escape. Gee and Riggs and just separated on the street to go to their respective houses when Japanese soldiers held Gee up and he called to Riggs. Gee heard Riggs throw his gun over the wall before he came to see what was the trouble. Both were held by the soldiers until McDaniel came along with a press pass and got them free.

14th. The members of the International Relief Committee have been ordered by the Reformed Government to leave the city and six of the Chinese staff who were working for the Committee have been arrested. The problem is complicated, including personal jealousies among the Chinese and resentment of the Japanese against Bates' recent article on narcotics in Nanking as well as the supposed political aspirations of the Committee, as well as the fact that there was an attempt at assassination of the newly appointed mayor of the Reformed Government.

A Japanese pastor who is from their National Y.M.C.A. has been helpful in making contacts through which the Relief Committee problem may be settled. The willingness of the Committee to add a Japanese and a Chinese member, if suitable non-political civilians can be found may go far to clear the air. The present members are all American, British or German.

Today's story is a statement from Riggs to the effect that the cost of the Japanese airplanes shot down in and near Nanking was three times the amount of the damage done by all the air raids.

15th. Mr. Y. Chen told me today that $10,000 worth of cotton was destroyed at the University Farm.

The new puppet government is called the Reformed Government. Mr. Riggs separates the Chinese who are working in it into four classes as follows: (1) Men who are opposed to or have been excluded by the Kuomintang and who have come to tolerate the Japanese regime. Some of them are men of ability. (2) A large number of mediocre crooks who are willing to make what they can out of any situation. (3) Men of modest ability who have served the National Government, but who did not get away before the Japanese came, and who have been given the choice of "serve or die," and are afraid not to serve. (4) A few honest men who feel that they can do good for China by keeping the control of the Reformed Government out of the hands of the crooks, and who secretly hope for an opportunity to return it sometime to National control.

21st. This afternoon I took a depressing bicycle ride down almost to south gate and back by way of T'ai P'ing Lu. The destruction which has been wrought is beyond calculation. The people are still few, and in most places houses of business are still scattered. It is estimated that if both sides had cooperated in giving such protection to civilian life and property as would not have interfered with military operations, not over one or two percent of the actual losses need to have occurred. (See "War Damage in the Nanking Area" by Lewis S. C. Smythe, published by the Nanking International Famine Relief Committee, June 1938).

I learn that disposal of the bodies of the scores of thousands of people who were murdered in Nanking last winter was not carried out by the army which did the killing. It was done over a period of 5–6 months by workers of a Buddhist organization, the Red Swastika Society. Their efforts are held in very high regard locally, far above those of the Chinese Red Cross, I should say. They are supposed to have buried about 40,000 bodies from the streets of Nanking during the first half of 1938. Much of the work was done after the bodies had reached such a state of decay that they could not be handled directly, but were rolled onto straw mats in which they were wrapped and piled on trucks three or four deep. The stench was such that it was very difficult to get men to work on the trucks. It is reported to have been a common sight during those months to have the dogs scatter from some partly consumed carcass as people passed along the streets.

January 15th, 1939. This morning I enjoyed pancakes instead of waffles with the Gales and Miss Simpson because the electric current failed and they could not use their electric waffle irons. Miss Simpson told of four things which she has heard returning Chinese remark on as a surprise in the present conditions: (1) The use by the new government (with Japanese approval) of the 5–bar flag, which is the original flag of the Chinese Republic, given to the people by Dr. Sun Yat Sen. (2) The preservation from destruction of historic buildings. (3) The continuance of effective service in the Chinese Post Office. (4) The name of the country has not been changed.

Mr. Gale told me of an incident which happened recently in the house of Mr. Wang, Dr. Handel Lee's secretary. This house was newly built, and Mrs. Wang came one afternoon to tell Mr. Gale that the Japanese soldiers were tearing it down. Since it is not American property, a protest would have been useless and Mr. Gale was not able to do anything about it. After tearing out such lumber and other material as they wishes [*sic*] to load onto their truck the fourteen soldiers of the crowd caught a Chinese woman who was passing by on the street and took her inside the house where they all raped her before they got on the truck and drove away. This happened near the Nanking Theological Seminary, and not very long ago.

27th. Mr. Shao Teh-hsing, our Farm Manager, has discovered that manure from the horses of the Japanese Army is suitable to fertilize our cotton fields, as well as that secured from the horses of the Chinese Army in past years. And the price is much less this year than it has been in normal times. For the sum of $20. local currency, he has contracted for all he can get hauled during the next month or two.

At Taipingmen where the passes are inspected for those who pass through the gate, the two Japanese soldiers whose job it is to inspect the passes were sitting in easy chairs up on the porch of the police station, leaning on their guns while the Chinese policeman looked at the passes. He did not ask for my pass, but saluted me instead. McCallum says he must be one of the original police force they had organized to keep order in the Safety Zone before the Japanese came into the city. They had 300, and the Japanese took off and shot 100 of them in a single day. I told my Chinese friends that when such well fed indifference and laziness became typical of the Japanese soldiers they would have little to fear from that Army.

Outside Taipingmen we visited in the home of one of Mr. Shao's farmer friends who have come back and built a new house to replace the old one which was burned down. They carry on diversified farming, one line being the production of silk. They have mulberry trees, the leaves from which feed their silk worms. The women of the household are skilled in the spinning of the thread from which light weight silk cloth for summer gowns is made. Their looms were burned and have not yet been rebuilt, but the women were spinning thread, so it looks as though they expected to have the weaving carried on again too.

It is a sad thing to see the cutting of so many of the trees about the city which have been planted during the past 20 or 30 years. At the gate one sees military trucks bringing in great loads of young tree stems to be used for fuel, and hundreds of farmers are also carrying all kinds of fuel into the city. Many trees along the roads have been cut, and our own caretakers have cut the trees on outlying parts of our own property, following the custom of the local farmers, so that the thieves who roam about in the night will not get them first. The thieves are mostly Chinese, for Japanese are afraid to go out at night unless in considerable numbers. The coal supply is limited and the price is very high.

We are looking forward to the organization of a Vocational Committee in Nanking to aid in the discussion and coordination of the various efforts here for rehabilitation of the people in such lines as will enable them to make a suitable living. Miss Vautrin feels that we may be able to secure outside support for such work if we have a desirable program.

Mr. Cheo Ming–i's house outside Shentsemen was stripped of everything, even the windows, but the shell still stands and Mr. Shao has a family living in it to try to care for it. For a while a Japanese family chose to live there, but they have moved. Mr. Shao's Japanese friends wrote a notice which is posted there asking Japanese to please care for his friend's property.

Miss Vautrin is responsive to Dean Milam's interest in China, and is hoping to arrange for her to give training for a few weeks or months to a qualified group of Chinese women, by working with them to make the necessary investigations and set up a model Chinese rural home near Ginling.

Feb. 18th. This afternoon I heard from Mr. Mills something about the work of the International Relief Committee here in Nanking. They handle several hundred applications each a day, and each application is investigated. On the average about one application in four is rejected. All this takes a considerable staff. Sage Chapel is piled high with bags of rice and of beans. They give out mostly food and clothing, very little money. The value of the relief they have handled in the past year or so is well over half a million dollars. Six members of the Chinese staff who work for this Committee were taken by the police just before I reached Nanking in December, and are still held, although no charges have been proved against them. They are reported to be well treated. Inter-Chinese jealousies seem to play an important part in this case.

Mar. 18th. I left at 7:00 this morning, without breakfast since the time was too early for the household where I eat, with our man Kuo to look over the fruit orchards outside Taipingmen. We saw two groups weeding the wheat on the University Farm, one of 17 and the other of 16, mostly women. The apricots are in full flower, as are the cherries. On the weeding job it is figured that 10 people will cover about 6 *mow* in one day. Five *mow* are about one acre.

I heard today a new story from Mr. Mills, of the time when there were 10,000 refugees on the University Campus. This was shortly after the Japanese Army had entered the City. It was rumored that the Chinese were coming back; in fact it was rumored that they were actually back in the city, and a good many people among our 10,000 refugees thought it might be so. Our back fence adjoins the Japanese Consulate and it was easy for some of our women to see some people coming out the back gate of the Japanese consulate with large packages which they assumed to be loot. The word was passed quickly that the Japanese Consulate was being looted by Chinese, and plenty of our 10,000 refugees were quite ready to go in and get their share. In fact some of the women were actually over the fence before our Mr. Gee and the police who were helping us keep order could restrain them. Only with great difficulty were they persuaded that the procession they had seen was only some women taking out clothes to be washed for the Japanese who live in the Consulate. I wonder what would have happened if those women had really stormed the Japanese Consulate in search of loot.

Apr. 21st. My Chinese teacher told me two stories today. The first is to the effect that coffins are being opened at the city gates for inspection, which is a great offence to the Chinese, even though the families have gone to the trouble to have them inspected and get the required certificate before they are taken from the home. The second is of an incident which is reported to have occurred at Suei Hsi Men about two weeks ago. A young Chinese woman was passing the guard of Japanese soldiers at the city gate with a cigarette in her mouth. They claimed this to be an insult, stripped off her clothing and tied her hands behind her back with her belt and sent her down the street. After reaching home she committed suicide.

We learn that it has been promised that Mr. P'an will be released. The accusation against him are three: (1) In 1936 he wrote a thesis as a student at the Nanking Theological Seminary in which he said that Japan is a military nation, and this is not true; (2) Last February he made a talk at Ginling College in which he encouraged friends of China not to worry, for China was gradually winning the war, and this is not true; (3) At the University Hospital he carried on conversations in which he praised the terrorist groups in Shanghai who have carried out many assassinations there among Chinese who are cooperating with

---

*mu in pinyin.

Japan, and said that we ought to have groups like that in Nanking, and that we could easily do so here under the protection of the American flag. We think the first point is probably true, though we do not know what would have happened to Mr. P'an if he had said that Japanese was weak in military power. The second point we doubt, and the third we feel very sure is entirely without foundation.

June 14th. Mr. Sone, our Southern Methodist missionary from the Seminary, who is Director of the Nanking International Relief Committee work does not often talk about the things that happened in Nanking a couple of years ago or less, but he overflowed with a little local color today, concerning one particular family. The story is something like this. The family lived at Shan Ch'ing Ho south of the City. The Japanese came. The father of the family was strung up by his hands and his throat cut. The married daughter was demanded for rape. The mother tried to protect her and was bayoneted to death on the spot. The daughter still refused, so her body was cut open with a sword. The remaining members of the family fled to the City and were refugees in the Bible Teachers Training School compound. A group of girls were taken away from this compound for raping, and some of them later returned, but the girl belonging to this family did not return. A 16–year old boy has been the only support for the remaining members of this family, and the only work he could get was on a Japanese truck. He fell from the truck and suffered an eye injury which incapacitates him for that work, so now the family has no means of support.

22nd. I had a talk with Dr. Brady this evening. We were both guests at the Embassy where a farewell party was being held in honor of Mr. & Mrs. Mills who are soon to leave on furlough. So far as their experience at the Hospital is an indication, the proportion of venereal disease has jumped from about 15% to about 80% in Nanking since the Japanese Army came in. The demand of the Army for prostitutes is so great that there is a continuous business of stealing girls in the country around and sending them to the city for this use. And because they are not resistant to the new strains of the venereal diseases which have come in they are soon infected so seriously as to ruin their usefulness in this profession, and so there is a constant demand for new material.

23rd. This evening Searle Bates told a story of the war that I had not heard before. The Chinese had a good anti-aircraft gun on Wu T'ai Shan, near the American School. He was out with some coolies marking out the boundary of the Safety Zone not so far from there when the Japanese planes came over. They took shelter in a ditch near a mat shed at the foot of Wu T'ai Shan, and the gun nearly deafened them with its activity. After the plane had gone a group of soldiers came hastening down the hill to the mat shed, and he discovered that it was their ammunition storage, in the shelter of which he had been hiding. We got letters today giving details of the Chengtu bombing. One of my former students who was a member of the Plant Pathology Division, Mr. Chang I-cheng, was killed in Chengtu City. A bomb fell about 40 ft. from President Chen's house, wrecking it and injuring several members of his family, but not killing anyone. The effectiveness of the bombs may be judged from the fact that a bomb falling 150 yards away blew in two doors and over 40 windows in the Slocum house. Miss Mary Chen, the President's sister, was badly hurt, but will recover. Our group is fortunate to get off so lightly. About 500 people were killed in the City. Leaflets were dropped saying that Chengtu was not really being bombed this time, but if the Government moved there they would come back and really do a job of it. Our school is carrying on classes again, and they are trying to move staff homes out of the City where the danger of fire is very great. But I have not heard that they plan to move to another place. A girl student in West China Union University was killed also. The damage would have been much worse had all the bombs exploded. About half those dropped on the Campus were duds.

July 5th. Today Dr. Wilson told of a man who was admitted to the hospital within the last day or two. He had been employed in a Japanese-owned store for one day. He was arrested that night and taken to a place on T'ai P'ing Lu where he was accused of the theft of some goods which were missing from the store. He was beaten and tortured with some very severe electric shocking apparatus which broke down his nervous system. The next day they told him it was a mistake, for the goods had been found. So they sent him to the hospital to die, since his nerve centers were irreparably damaged by the electric shocks he received.

24th. Today Mr. Sone told me of a report from Shwen Hua Chen, southeast of Nanking, about three miles from Ch'ing Lung Shan. There was a gathering of farmers at the home of one of their number who was celebrating his birthday, at a small village about five *li* from the town. This gathering is believed to have been reported to the Japanese soldiers in the town by a seller of trinkets who was a spy. Before evening most of the guests had gone home, but a few had remained for a meal together. The place was surrounded by Japanese soldiers, and a couple of men were killed on the spot. The rest of the men found there were then questioned one by one as to whether or not they were guerillas. If they said no they were beaten until they admitted that they were. Then all, about thirty in number, were taken to Shwen Hua Chen where the local official of the new (puppet) government was required to have a large grave prepared. These men were then executed and buried in this common grave. Some of them were badly mutilated with swords and bayonets, and several are believed to have been still alive when they were buried. Yet, one of the leaflets recently distributed in the city, being translated, says, "Japanese soldiers have come to enable you to cultivate the land in peace."

August 6th. Esther Slocum sent me a note from my colleague, Dr. C.Y. Chiao in Chengtu, expressing appreciation for the box of prepared microscopic slides I packed and sent in by the Slocums. He especially mentioned how happy they were to have the paper in which I had wrapped the small boxes as they were packed in the wooden case, for wrapping paper is a rare article in Chengtu.

Miss Wang En-sze, the daughter of our pastor Wang at Chiang T'ang Chieh Church, who has been taking graduate nurses' training in America during the past two years has just returned to China. Just before the Canadian ship on which she was traveling reached the Japanese ports there were rumors that the Japanese might search the personal effects of passengers, so she threw overboard her diary of two years in America. As it happened, they were not searched, but this indicates the psychology of the situation.

9th. Bob Wilson told me today that he had an interesting problem in surgical mechanics to solve when he had to remove a 15 lb. scrotum from a man infected with filari(?) The patient is doing well and plans to go back to his home at Luho and bring in a friend who needs a similar operation.

I have just finished reading Timperley's "What War Means" (Gollancz, 1938). It gives most of the material we saw in letters from our friends who remained in Nanking at the time of the Japanese occupation, and much more that I had not seen. Bates regards it as the best statement of what happened, and I value his opinion most highly. About half the book of 288 pages is filled with copies of the authenticating documents.

March 23rd, 1940. I was saddened today by a trip over Purple Mountain and through Spirit Valley to see the destruction of so many places in the beautiful secluded spots on the south slope of the mountain. It was the scene of a fierce battle before the occupation of the city in 1937. Even the beautiful new pagoda, built at a cost of more than a million dollars is defaced, and many of the ornamental images on the roof have been broken off. I would like to ask some psychologist why men of the West as well as those of the East desire to carve or write their names on the walls and tablets of beautiful buildings, or break and destroy for no apparent purpose beautiful objects of art and architecture.

Note

1. RG20, B11, F243.

Minnie Vautrin

Wilhelmina Vautrin was born in Secor, Illinois, on September 27, 1886. She worked her way through the University of Illinois with a major in education, graduating with high honors in 1912. Vautrin was commissioned by the United Christian Missionary Society as a missionary to China, where she first served as a high school principal for a few years and then became chairman of the education department of Ginling College when it was founded in 1916. She served as acting president of Ginling College when President Matilda Thurston returned to America for fund-raising. With the Japanese army pressing on Nanking [in 1937], Vautrin again was called on to take charge of the college campus, as most of the faculty left Nanking for either Shanghai or Chengtu, Szechwan.

Minnie Vautrin's writings provide a detailed account of the situation in Nanking under Japanese occupation. In addition to several lengthy printed reports and articles, she kept a 526-page diary covering the period 1937 to 1941; about one-fourth of her diary (pp. 90–240) documents the period of the Nanking Massacre from December 1937 to March 1938. Vautrin's reports to the Ginling College administration, entitled "A Review of the First Month: December 13, 1937–January 13, 1938," is published in this volume, as well as excerpts from her diary, including one that documents the fact that atrocities were continuing well into May 1938.

In the last entry of her diary, April 14, 1940, Minnie Vautrin wrote: "I'm about at the end of my energy. Can no longer forge ahead and make plans for the work, for on every hand there seems to be obstacles of some kind. I wish I could go on furlough at once but who will do the thinking for the Exp. Course?"

Two weeks later, she suffered a nervous breakdown and returned to America. A year to the day after she left Nanking, Vautrin ended her own life.

An Informal Report to the Board of Founders, Board of Directors, President Wu, Mrs. Thurston and Members of the Staff of Ginling College.[1]

Confidential. Please do not publish.
A Review of the First Month: December 13, 1937–January 13, 1938

Explanation: My hope for days has been to write a very carefully worded report, but that hope has been given up due to the many interruptions that come each day. Each time I put aside a morning for this work it is finally used for other matters which seem at the moment more important. Have decided that if I am to get any report to you at all it will have to be a very informal and probably disconnected one. Please forgive lack of unity and coherence. M.V.

Background: December 1, 1937–December 13, 1937.

Our President departed from the College on the morning of December 1, although I think that her boat did not finally sail from Hsia Gwan until December 3. It was difficult for her to leave and even more difficult for us to see her go, but we at that time felt it was for the best and certainly conditions since have proved that it was a very wise decision. For the twelve days following her departure we worked at top speed for there were many important things waiting to be done. Before our President left she had appointed an Emergency Committee consisting of Mrs. S. F. Tsen, Mr. Francis Chen and myself, and this small committee has carried the responsibility through these difficult days. It was fortunate that the committee was small for we could make decisions quickly— and we had to do that many times. Meal time—for we all eat at the same table— was often used for meetings and trying to think out the next step. Below I will give some of the many tasks that we performed during those twelve busy days, and something of the conditions in the city during that time.

Putting up flags and proclamations: All day of December 1 we gave to selecting strategic places for the American flags which Gwoh, the tailor had made for us, deciding where the proclamations furnished us by the Defence Commander of the Municipality of Nanking and also those that had been furnished us by the American Embassy should be posted. In the end we had 8 flag poles put up on the outskirts of the campus, and the posters were posted at the gate and on all the outlying buildings such as the South Hill Residence, the laundry, the faculty houses for Chinese men and even up on the little house on the west hill. The large thirty foot American flag was still used in the main Quadrangle to let the aeroplanes know that the property was American owned. Previously Mr. Chen and I had finally found the old college sign boards used in the old Ginling and had them repainted—those boards that said "Great American Ginling College." One of these we hung at the gate and one is in front of the Central Building. These we did not actually use until the Japanese entered the city, but used their reverse sides which merely said "Ginling College."

Putting buildings in condition for refugees: For days and days our faithful staff of servants worked hard carrying all furniture to the attics or storing it in one or two rooms on the first floor. It was a tremendous job but later proved a very wise preparation. Altogether eight buildings were prepared, including the Practice School and the 400 dormitory. These latter two were never occupied because by the time the first six buildings were filled we had probably ten thousand refugees on the campus and did not have strength enough to manage more than that. Our ideals were very high in the beginning for we got out in poster form a carefully planned set of regulations that would help to make for healthful living, we trained a group of young people to act as scouts or ushers, we made a plan of the buildings and according to regulations furnished us we had room for 2,700 refugees in the eight buildings. On December 8 we received our first group—people who had previously evacuated from Wusih and Shanghai and other places along the battle front and also those who were living just inside and outside of the Nanking city wall, as they were forced to leave by the Chinese military for military purposes and later many of their houses were burned. We could well have used a few more days in getting the buildings in order for after the deluge came we had no time to do any moving of furniture, or to plan regulations for living.

Burning of papers and hiding of valuables: The college vault gave us many anxious moments for if there was a long siege of the city there would surely be thorough looting of valuables and any soldier would know that an institution like Ginling would have a vault. We therefore decided to clear out the vault and leave the doors of both the vault and inner safe open. Many of the things we hid—I shall not tell you where for we may want to use the place again. Our money we divided, keeping part of it on the campus and packing the larger part in a case and sending it with some other valuables over to the American Embassy. We knew later that when the American officials at the Embassy would leave these things would be taken down to the U.S.S. *Panay.* Our Emergency Committee decided that Mrs. Thurston's wedding silver should be placed in this same case although we knew that Mrs. Thurston would not want her things protected by a gunboat. You can imagine our consternation later when we heard that the *Panay* was in the bottom of the Yangtze. Everything has been recovered by Russian divers since so we can smile about the matter now but we did not smile then. Of the new Terrace House Building file I made two copies and hid them in different places.

The college incinerator was kept busy during those days of preparation. Mrs. Tsen spent about two days in the President's office clearing out papers that might be misunderstood, and she also spent many hours burning the receipts of the organization of which Dr. Wu had been the treasurer, lest that also be misunderstood. The Municipal New Life Organization which had rented our Neighborhood House for a few months in the autumn left us a rather big piece of work to do for they evacuated quickly and left all their teaching materials for us to destroy. Gwoh, the tailor who lives in our neighborhood also rented room to them this past autumn and when they left they stored a large number of boxes in his little shop. They looked innocent at the time but as the Japanese army came nearer to the city the tailor became more and more afraid of what might happen to him if these things could not be explained. Just two days before the army entered he came over to see if I would go to his house and look into the boxes. This I did and later I called in Mr. Fitch, who was executive secretary or director of the International Committee for the Safety Zone. The two of us decided that it would be better if he destroyed all of the things. I shall never forget that picture of Gwoh and his good wife on December 13th. All day the two of them and all their relatives carried load after load of books and pamphlets over to our incinerator and there burned them. It was not until late in the night that they finished their task—but he was spared from possible misunderstanding and the thrust of an angry bayonet. On the night of December 15th we buried late at night what we considered burying before—the garments that had been made by women in the city for wounded soldiers. We had been loathe [*sic*] to burn them because we felt that the poor of the city would need them during the winter—but on that night that need did not seem so great to us as the need to get rid of them.

Conditions in the City during this period: For weeks and weeks people of the city had been evacuating. The movement began with the wealthy and during that period every truck and car was used and tens of thousands moved up river to Hankow or on further to the westward. Then the middle class began to evacuate and finally the poor and for days and days you could see rickshas going past loaded with boxes and rolls of bedding and people. All who could possibly do so got out of the city, the poor going into the country, especially taking the sons and daughters of the family, leaving the old to take care of the homes. I have often wondered what has happened to these people who evacuated into the country districts for from the reports that we hear these days, the suffering and destruction in the country is even worse than it has been in Nanking if that is possible.

During these twelve days there were constant air raids, and as the Japanese army came closer to Nanking there were no warnings—the planes just came and dropped their bombs—sometimes the whole rack at a time. During the last few days before the entry the shelling of the city was also terrific, in the southern part of the city especially. From my room in the Practice school it seemed to me that there was a fierce pounding on the city gates and the city wall—so fierce that it did not seem possible for the age old wall to resist the onslaught of modern military machinery. It was also during these days that burning began—again for military purposes. I often wondered if this method prevented the Japanese army from entering by a mere twenty four hours if it was worth the while and the terrible suffering that it caused, not to speak of the loss especially to the poor. Each night the sky was red with flames as these houses skirting the city wall were burned and it was during that time that our first refugees came. Within the city—it was Sunday, December 12, I believe that the Ministry of Communications was burned—they did that rather than to let the Japanese occupy that beautiful building. There was some looting by the Chinese soldiers, mostly of money from the stores. None of these calamities reached us in our peaceful little valley and we continued our preparations for the refugees.

On November 23, Dr. Wu took me to the reception which saw the formation of the daily Press Conference which took place until Sunday December 12. At these meetings which took place in the headquarters of the Chinese-British Cultural Association on Peiping Road, there were of course western representatives of the various news agencies and papers; representatives of the police department, the defence commissioners office and of the mayor's office. The mayor himself came to many of the meetings. I started going to these very interesting meetings on Sunday evening, November 28, and each night after that found Mrs. Tsen and me present for through the meetings we could keep in touch with events in the city and also have conferences with people whom we wished to see. I should have mentioned that a goodly number of the missionaries of the city also attended and also a fair number from the business community and the various embassies. It seems to me now as I look back over those meetings that most of them were spent in making announcements either by the military or the chairman, director and secretary of the International Committee for the Safety Zone. The latter committee members kept pushing the Chinese military to get all military organizations out of the Zone as quickly as possible so that the Safety Zone flags could be put in place and cables be sent to Japan and to the world that preparations for such a zone had been completed.

You will have learned from other sources of the formation of the International Committee which in turn proposed, carried out all the plans for the formation of, and later maintained the Safety Zone in Nanking. To this group of men—business men and missionaries, the large group of Chinese in the Safety Zone owe a great debt of gratitude—for what measure of safety and protection they have had during these weeks of terrible strain and stress have been due to them. And I find that the thoughtful Chinese are not unmindful of this great benefit and are deeply grateful for it. Mr. John Rabe, a German business man, has been chairman of the committee and has been fearless and untiring, and Dr. Lewis Smythe of the United Christian Missionary Society and a member of the faculty of the University of Nanking has been the secretary. I cannot go on to mention all the other members of the committee and their splendid work which has been carried on day and night since early in December.

The First Ten Days of Japanese Occupation. December 13–23

When the first group of Japanese soldiers entered the walled city, we do not yet know exactly. We have heard that as early as December 10 a small group entered the old Tung Dzi Gate, now known as the Gwang Hwa Gate. There was very severe fighting in that section of the city for days and we are told that the Japanese troops entered the city and were repulsed a number of times and that the loss on both sides was very high. A young Japanese official told me that the army actually entered at four o'clock in the morning of December 13. All during the night of the 12th retreating Chinese soldiers passed our gate, some begging for civilian clothes, others casting off their uniforms and firearms into our campus. From the ominous silence we knew that something had happened. About two o'clock in the afternoon of December 13 the servant in charge of our South Hill Faculty Residence came running down the hill to tell me that the J. soldiers could be seen on our west hill—the one outside of our main campus at about the same time another servant came running to tell me that a soldier had found the Poultry Experiment and was demanding two chickens. By means of sign language I tried to make clear that the chickens were not for sale and the man left. From the back of the campus I could see a number of men back of our campus. They were asking the people in the little huts back there to cook vegetables and chickens for them. No one on the campus slept that night and in my imagination I could easily interpret the sounds of the firearms and the machine guns as the killing of the retreating Chinese soldiers. How many thousands were mown down by guns or bayoneted we shall probably never know for in many cases oil was thrown over their bodies and they were burned—charred bones tell the tale of some of these tragedies. The events of the following ten days are growing dim, but there are certain of them that a life time will not erase from my memory and the memories of those who have been in Nanking through this period. Some of the most vivid of these scenes I will try to reconstruct for you.

For fully ten days if not more from ten to twenty groups of soldiers came into our campus daily; a few coming through the front gate but most of them breaking open side or back gates or jumping over our fence. Some of them were fierce and unreasonable and most of them had their bayonets out ready for use and on not a few of them I could see fresh blood stains. Our loyal staff of servants were on the job and as soon as a group came in they would run for me. My days were spent in running from the gate to the south hill or the back hill or to the poultry experiment or to one of the dormitories. Although an American flag or an American Embassy proclamation did not seem to deter them, yet the presence of a foreigner was of great help and many were the groups that I escorted out of a dormitory filled with refugee women and children or from the south hill residence. It finally took so much energy that we decided that I should use my strength to save lives and not try to save things. During these days they often tried to take our servants saying that they were soldiers, but in every such case I was able to get the men from them excepting the keeper of Mr. Miao's home—the son of the Kjang Szi-fu who works in the Biology Department. I was not there when he was taken for I could not leave the campus during those days.

The night of December 17 none of us shall ever forget for it is burned into our memories by suffering. Between four and six o'clock, since Mary Twinem had come over to see us, it was possible for me to escort two groups of young women and children over to the main campus of the University of Nanking where they were opening their dormitories for them. We were so crowded [at Ginling College] and so taxed in strength that it did not seem right for us to take in any more at that time. During my absence, two soldiers came in on bicycles, angrily tore the big American flag from its stakes in the main Quadrangle, and started to carry it off. Finding it too heavy they threw it on the ground in front of the Science Building. Mary was called and as soon as they saw her they ran and hid in the Power House from which place she sent them off the campus very much flushed and embarrassed. When we were just finishing our supper—we had persuaded Mary to stay for the night since it was late—the servant from the Central Building came running to the dining room and said that there were two soldiers at the front door trying to get in. Mr. Li and I went to that door and found the men pulling at the door and demanding that we turn over the soldiers "enemies of Japan." They refused to believe me when I said there were no soldiers, only women and children and they insisted on searching. I did not know but later learned that other groups were searching in other buildings at the same time. Finally by a very clever trick they succeeded in the getting almost all of the servants and those of us who were responsible for the refugees out to the front gate and there they carried on what we realized later was a mock trial. They made us feel that they were searching for soldiers, but as a matter of fact they were looking for young women and girls. Fitch, Smythe and Mills appeared unexpectedly on the scene, the latter expecting to spend the night on the campus, and they greatly complicated the mock trial but did not defeat it. A little later they sent off these three men and proceeded in their search for soldiers. Between nine and ten o'clock through a side gate they took off twelve women and girls and the officer at the gate with us took off Mr. Chen. It was not until they were gone that we realized that the trick was to take off girls. I did not expect to see Mr. Chen again for I was sure that he would be shot or bayoneted. That closing scene I shall never, never forget. Mary, Mrs. Tsen and I standing near the gate, the servants kneeling just back of us, Mr. Chen being led out by the officer and a few soldiers. The rusting of the fallen leaves, the shadows passing out the side gate in the distance—of whom we did not know, the low cries of those passing out. Mr. Chen was released at the intersection of Shanghai and Canton Roads, and six of the girls came back at five the next morning unharmed—both of these we believe were wrought by prayer. I think now I might have saved those girls but at the time it did not seem possible. Those of us at the front gate stayed there in silence until almost eleven for we did not know but what there were guards outside ready to shoot if any moved, and then we left for the back part of the campus. Almost every building on the campus had been entered and there was some looting beside the taking off of the twelve. That night I stayed down at the front gate house and you can imagine that there was no sleep for any of us the rest of that night. When I reached the Practice School before going to the gate house, I found Mr. Chen there and also Miss Lo. Soon the other helpers came in for they with Mrs. Tsen's daughter-in-law and grandchildren had been hiding among the refugees. Never will I forget the little prayer meeting we had that night in that room at the practice School. From that time on Mary has stayed with us and helped to carry the responsibility—especially of sending off soldiers. In addition to the twelve girls taken that night, 3 others have been raped on the campus and nine others have been prevented from the same fate by the appearance of a foreigner at the psychological time. I would that we could have prevented all such tragedies but compared with the fate in most refugee campus and private houses this is an exceedingly good record.

Another vivid memory was the military inspection on December 15 by an officer and perhaps one hundred men. They too were looking for soldiers and inspected us thoroughly. A machine gun was placed on the main road leading to the quadrangle, and had any soldiers been in hiding and tried to escape you can imagine what would have happened to the women and children on the campus. We were told later that there were a number of machine guns and men on the roads surrounding the campus. We had been exceedingly careful not to let any men come on the campus excepting those of a few families whom we know and they are living down in East Court, and therefore we had no difficulty in passing this inspection. It is true that they tried to take several of our servants who had close cropped hair something like a soldier's, but in the end after identification they were released. The officer in charge of this inspection left us a letter signed and sealed with his stamp and this was of great use until it was torn in shreds and thrown on the ground by the petty officer who came on the night of the 17th and carried out the tragedy that I described above, this destroyed letter was soon replaced by another which was furnished me by a military attache in the Japanese Embassy and this has been invaluable in getting soldiers out of the buildings and off the campus. If I go off the campus I leave this letter in Mary's possession and if she goes I have it.

Another phase of these ten days and the days that have followed has been the visits of the many civil and military officials. Invariably the former have tried to help us to the extent of their power and at times they have sent us Embassy police to help protect the thousands of refugees and ourselves by night; for two different periods the latter have sent us a guard of soldiers, and these have not always been a safe guard although they have helped. Our first guard consisted of 25 soldiers whom we placed down in the row of rooms occupied by Mr. Chan the assistant registrar—who had long since vacated them for a safer place. After the period of the Embassy police we had a guard of 4 soldiers each day. Each day when the new group came Mr. Wang and I and sometimes Mary would go down to get acquainted, to get the name of the petty officer in charge and to try to make it clear that if they would guard on the outside of the campus, on the big roads, we would be responsible for the inside of the campus. The method worked very well and only on one night did we have any trouble. During this period, the J. Embassy also furnished us with 30 proclamations in Japanese and these we posted on all of our property and at the gate. These have helped a good deal but have not completely prevented soldiers entering buildings on which they were posted. In fact the many groups who used to love to go into the south hill faculty residence had to go past two American flags, two American Embassy proclamations, three Japanese proclamations in order to get inside. We have kept one night watchman and our two former police now in civilian clothes on duty each night to report in case anything is amiss.

The Period of Registration: The registration of the people living in Nanking began at the University of Nanking on December 26 and lasted through the 27. All the men and women who were refugees on the main campus of the University registered during those days. Our registration started on December 28 and by inference we thought it was to be of the women living on our campus. That was not our fate, however. It lasted for nine long days and men and women came from all sections of the Safety Zone and even from the country. Tens of thousands came in four abreast, listened first to the lecture on good citizenship and then got the preliminary slip which enabled them to go to one of Mr. Chen Chung-fang's residences for the final step at which they were given a stamped and numbered registration blank with their name upon it. For the first few days it was limited to men. They formed in line out on Hankow Road and Ninghai Road as early as two o'clock in the morning and all day long they marched through the campus. It had snowed and you can imagine the amount of mud that these tramping feet brought in. This registration at first took place under the military officers. Two guards of soldiers came each time and each group had to have a blazing bonfire and for the officers we furnished two coal ball fires. At first I thought that it would be better to protest this registration of men on our campus for this meant flinging our front gates wide open, and for the sake of the women we had been so careful to exclude stray men from coming in. However at the end of the first day it seemed best to endure the process for when men were selected out of marching lines and accused of being soldiers, their women folk were usually present and could plead for them and thus many innocent men were saved. Although in the announcement the men were clearly told that if they would confess to having served as soldiers they would be pardoned and given remunerative work to do, we are not sure that the promise was kept but we rather suspect that their bodies are in the large mounds of unburied bodies outside of Han Chung Gate which we know were brought there about that time. Finally only 28 men were taken from the tens of thousands that registered at Ginling. I shall never forget how anxiously the women watched this process of registration and how bravely they would plead for their husbands and sons. Although the registration of women began on Monday, January 3 yet it did not take place solely for them until Wednesday of that week and closed on Friday. How they feared the rough treatment of the soldiers, and how they cringed as they passed them to get the preliminary blank. A number of women were suspected of being prostitutes—and it was at that time that they were trying to start up the licensed houses in the city for the Japanese soldiers—but each time when the women could be identified they were released. During the last two days of registration of women it was put under the civil officials and was carried on in a decent and orderly way. All the writing was done by Chinese men and the entire process was carried on in our main quadrangle. I was given permission to bring our group of workers, both staff members and amahs, out in a group and the registration was quickly finished—and thus an ordeal which they had been dreading was passed. Women have found since to their sorrow that the registration blank does not mean protection to them and men have found that it does not prevent them from being seized. Ginling has never had such a large registration in its history.

Ginling College as a Refugee Camp for Women and Children: As I mentioned before we began to take in our first refugees on December 8 and they were of two types, those who had come to Nanking from cities like Wusih, Soochow along the line of the advancing Japanese army and those who had to evacuate their homes due to the orders of the Chinese military. By Saturday,

December 11 we had 850 living in the Central Building and one of the dormitories and we thought that our estimate of 2,700 was far too large. Up to that time the people had brought in their food with them and the rice kitchen which we had hoped to have was not yet functioning. By Thursday, December 16 we had more than four thousand and we felt that we were as crowded as we could be— we did not have the staff to look after more and we felt that it would be better for the University to open dormitories and take in our over-flow, and it was on the following day that I took about 1000 over to the University campus. But we did not stop at 4000, for we began to realize the terrible danger to women if they remained in their own homes, for soldiers were wild in their search for young girls, and so we flung our gates open and in they streamed. For the next few days as conditions for them grew worse and worse, they streamed in from daylight on. Never shall I forget the faces of the young girls as they streamed in—most of them parting from their fathers or husbands at the gate. They had disguised themselves in every possible way—many had cut their hair, most of them had blackened their faces, many were wearing men or boy's clothes or those of old women. Mr. Wang, Mr. Hsia, Mary and I spent our days at the gate trying to keep idlers out and let the women come in. At our peak load we must have had ten thousand on the campus. The big attics in the Science and Arts Buildings which we had cleared were favorite places for the younger women. Stairs and halls were so crowded that it was impossible to get through and even the covered ways were packed as well as all of the verandahs. People did not ask for a place inside but were content to sleep outside if only we would let them come in to the campus. We realized that young girls of twelve and that older women of fifty and even sixty were not free from mistreatment. I shall never forget the faces of the fathers and husbands as they watched their women folk enter the campus. Often times the tears were streaming down their cheeks as they begged us to "just give them a place to sleep outside." Women were faced by a terrible dilemma in those days—it might mean that in saving themselves from being raped they were risking the lives of their husbands and sons, who might be taken away and killed. Even during this period of danger we tried to persuade the older women to remain at home with their husbands and sons, even if it meant mistreatment, and let the younger women come to us for protection. This fearful and beastly treatment of women is still going on and even in the Safety Zone. Two days ago a young girl came running to me just as I was going out of the gate and plead [sic] with me to go to her home as there were three soldiers there at the time she ran away and they were looking for girls. Fortunately the girls were good runners and knew a short cut to our campus so by the time I arrived at the home the soldiers had left without having found the girls.

I suspect you wonder how we fed this vast multitude. The Red Cross on the day that the city was turned over started a Rice Kitchen just north of our campus and that is still furnishing two meals of soft rice each day to our large family. For a number of weeks they brought the steaming rice in to the campus where it was served in two different places on the main quadrangle. We had serving frames made and tried to teach the women not to crowd but to learn to take their turn but it was a difficult lesson for them to learn. Recently the method has been to serve it out at the kitchen and that is a much more satisfactory method as it gives the women and girls exercise twice each day and it enables them to get the rice hot at any time they wish it. If they can afford it they pay three coppers a bowl for it; if they really have no money their case is investigated and they are given a red tag which means free rice. Many of the refugee camps have not been as fortunate as we in having a well managed rice kitchen so near at hand. As for hot water, very early we were able to get two men with big hot water stoves to move into our campus—they were [glad] to do so for it mean personal protection—so our women have had hot water at all times of the day. The cost is low so they can afford it. For those who were without bedding, fortunately we had a supply of comforters on hand, and these have been given to those who are in greatest need. Sanitation has been our biggest problem, especially when we had our peak load. We were non-plussed by this problem for a time for it seemed insurmountable but we are gradually working it out so that the campus does not look as it did in those early days—especially in the mornings. If only we had some time it would help. Dr. Reeves will be sorry to hear that the fish in the pond back of the Central Building have had a hard time surviving for that is the place where the women wash their toilet buckets. As for laundry, every morning and most of the day you can see the women washing out clothes especially for the children. Every bush and tree and every fence is covered with the washing during most of the day. Many would not recognize the campus if they came at this time.

Meetings for Women and Children: Religion has become a reality to many of us during these days of terror and destruction. Jesus becomes a friend who walks by your side as you go forward to meet a group of fierce men whose shining bayonets are marked with fresh stains of blood. From August on to the present time, every Wednesday evening and Sunday evening we have had a service for the campus and building servants. How they have loved to sing "O save my Country, Lord" and "We love our native land." During the peak of our refugee load and during the time of greatest danger to refugees and to men we did not hold these meetings but soon they were started again. They are now held in the South Studio for the Science Lecture Hall was occupied by women and children for a good many weeks. It was also in August that we started our Wednesday and Saturday morning prayer group for staff members. These meetings have now become daily meetings excepting for Sunday morning. Words cannot express the value these meetings have had in strengthening and binding us together and giving us power to meet the difficult problems of each day. How real and vital prayer has become. About twelve are now attending the staff meetings. Our regular Sunday afternoon and Thursday afternoon meetings for women have been continued by Miss Lo. This week with the help of speakers from the American Church Mission we have started regular afternoon meetings for women. Each afternoon at two o'clock sees a group of about 170 women— mostly young—gathered in the South Studio. Only those over fifteen are admitted and no babies in arms are brought in. We take the refugee buildings by turn and admission is by ticket which we distribute the previous evening. Never have I attended more earnest meetings. At the same hour we also have a children's meeting over in the Science Lecture Hall which we have now cleared of refugees, by distributing to other buildings. The day school teacher conducts these meetings.

At Christmas although we were in a period of great danger and we did not know what each day would bring forth, we had a number of special Christmas services—one for Mrs. Tsen's grandchildren whom we have learned to love and who have helped to keep us normal; one for the adults who have been helping carry the burdens of the work and we included their families; one for all the college servants; one for the neighborhood women and still one other for the young people who acted as scouts in those early days. Mary decorated a north facing room on the second floor of the practice School and made it so beautiful that some say they will never forget it. There was an altar with a Cross, a little Christmas tree with colored lights, a great bouquet of Heavenly bamboo with bright red berries, several large pots of poinsettias, the red Christmas cut-cuts and the Christmas scrolls. Fortunately I had a heavy green curtain for the one window, and by putting a thick cloth over the transom we could not be seen either within or without the building. It was not always easy to keep our voices low when we sang the much loved Christmas carols but we were not disturbed in any of our meetings. Later we were loathe [*sic*] to take down the decorations. The staff member in charge of each of the above groups planned the meeting so that no one person carried all the responsibility. We also had light refreshments for the children and young people although such things are not to be purchased these days and there are no stores open in the entire city and all our regular stores have been looted clean and many of them have been burned.

Without the work of a fairly large group of loyal helpers the work that we have been able to do would not have been possible. Mrs. Tsen has not only had charge of the food and general management of dormitory servants but she has been our nurse for the large groups of refugees, has distributed the bedding to the poorest, and has been a wise counsellor in meeting intricate and difficult situations; Mr. Francis Chen has had trying experiences because of his youth— in a situation where youth was a handicap—but he has always been willing to do all that he could to help; Mr. Li, his assistant has been willing to help in any way that he can—from supervising the sale of rice tickets to being general sanitary manager of the compound. He too had to remain in the background during the most dangerous days when young men were being taken out of the city. Mr. Wang, my personal teacher, has really acted as my secretary and has been invaluable in going with me to the Japanese Embassy on many trying visits and also in talking to the guards who have been sent to us from time to time. He also helps when high officials come for inspection or to visit. Just now he is giving most of each morning to writing data given to us by women who have lost either their husbands or sons. To date we have prepared 592 of these slips. You will be interested to know that 432 of these men were taken on December 16. Whether or not the handing in of these requests will be of any avail we do not know, but we can only do our part for these heart broken women. Miss Wang, the only member of the student body of the Seminary who remains in the city, has been an invaluable help in many ways. She has been responsible for investigating the cases of those asking for free rice. Miss Hsueh, the Homecraft School teacher, closed our little school just a few days before the entrance of the J. troops and since that time she too has been a great help in all the investigation work and with the meetings. Miss Lo, the evangelistic worker who used to live west of the campus is now living here and giving all her time and strength to helping and the fact that she knows the neighborhood women so well has been of great assistance. Mary Twinem, whom I mentioned coming on December 17, has been here ever since that time. One of us is always on the campus with the special letter given us by Mr. Fukuda. If in the night we have to go to the front gate she is with me. She and the three women just mentioned live with me down at the practice School and the little sitting room there with the comfort of the stove is a place of relaxation and retreat. Blanche Wu lived in the Science Building until the noise from the refugees became too much for her and then she too moved down so that makes six of us together. Besides being busy with her poultry project she also helps with refugee work when it is possible. Mr. Hsia who lives at the front gate is very good in talking to the soldiers and he often escorts a party around. Mr. Djao, Eva's teacher, who lives with his large family at East Court is very willing to help whenever we need him. Mr. Chan now lives at East Court and does writing for us when needed, but the sight of a soldier is almost too much for him. These are the members of the staff of workers. In addition there are the servants, who have been working hard through all the time of danger—what we would have done without them I do not know. They have willingly taken on the extra work—and no one not living on the campus can realize how heavy the work has been for them and how trying. We hope to give them an extra month's pay when it is over—if it is ever over. In addition we have had to take on extra servants so that we have two in each dormitory—many of these have been willing to work for their board because they felt they were safe here, but we hope to give them a tip. I might add that Tung Lao-ban the carpenter has also lived on the place as a refugee and has worked freely for us whenever we needed him.

The staff members have eaten together in the dining room of 400 and that has been a source of strengthening too—I mean all those who do not have families here. We have been in a quandary as to food. Before the fall of the city we did not put in too much food for fear everything would be looted and now we wish that we had put in more stores. For a number of days, at least two meals a day consisted of two kinds of beans and green vegetable. At no time have we been hungry although I shall be glad when we can get nourishing food to add to the diet for all the workers. The Poultry Project has furnished us with a goodly number of geese and a few chickens which have helped out a good deal, and we have killed Dr. Yuen's goat and three others that were entrusted to us by Mr. Riggs. One of our Practice School Ponds furnished us fish for the whole staff once, which was a treat.

Destruction of College and Private Property: There was no looting by Chinese soldiers before they left the city, and so far there has been no looting by the "lao beh sing," the common people. The J. soldiers entered the South Hill Residence from ten to twenty times and found great joy in the four chests of drawers stored in the large dining room. Again and yet again we have found them there looting and have escorted them out. Dr. Wu, Dr. Chen, Dr. Chang and Alice Morris were the unfortunate owners of the property looted, however I do not think the loss was great as they had packed their best things to take with them. Although they went to the third floor of that house a number of times, yet they did not see [the] attic doors which had been covered by wardrobes. We are hoping that the things stored there will not be touched. Mr. Miao's house was looted and also Chen Er-chang's but how much the loss I have no way of knowing. Those houses are now occupied by refugees. Mrs. Tsen lost some things— her favorite fountain pen among them and some of the rest of us lost pens and gloves. Mr. Li had $55.00 taken from him while he was on the campus and also Mr. Chan's trunks and Mrs. Tung's trunk were searched and some things taken. Those are about all the personal losses—and compared with the loss of many in the city they are very light. The total college loss due to looting by the Japanese soldiers is perhaps less than $200.00 and consists mostly of smashed doors and windows. Our greatest loss is due to the occupation of the refugees. Ten thousand cannot crowd into six buildings without injury to these houses. Walls will have to be refinished, wood work repainted, screens replaced, locks and fasteners replaced or repaired. Trees and shrubs and lawns have all been injured largely by the daily display of washing placed upon them. Our foreign friends have often laughed when they entered the campus and compared it with its former neatness. However the mothers with little children have had to do this washing and we have not wanted to prohibit it. Fortunately in this part of China, nature heals such scars very quickly and in a few years we shall not miss the shrubs that have been trampled or broken, although I have felt sad when a shrub that we have nursed carefully for more than ten years has been badly broken. We have also had some loss due to the nine days of registration which took place on the campus. Some chairs were broken and tables injured and shrubs trampled down. I would estimate this loss at about $100.00 but have not yet found the time to figure it accurately.

Wei Szi-fu, our college messenger boy was taken on December 14, and did not return until December 28. His bicycle was also taken at the same time as he was on his way to the University Hospital with a message to one of the doctors there. At the time he was wearing an arm band furnished for our servants by the American Embassy. We greatly rejoiced when he returned safely. The son of Djang, the head servant of the Biology Department was taken on December 16, and he has never returned although we have made repeated requests for him. He too was wearing one of the arm bands at the time and was in the house which was clearly marked by an American Embassy poster and flying an American flag. The father has been broken hearted for in addition to this loss he does not know where his wife and four other children are as they were down near Wusih. I am fearful that the young man will never return as there were a good many men killed at that time, especially young men.

Surely we have much to be grateful for as we look back over the past months. The fact that we did not open college in Nanking was a great blessing. During these days I have said again and again I was glad that there were no students on the campus and that Dr. Wu had been persuaded to leave the city when she did. I am grateful too that Ginling has been able to shelter and serve the women and children of this great city as she has during these days of intense danger and terror. What the future holds we do not know, but I am confident that if we seek to know God's will for the College, he will guide us into still greater fields of usefulness in the bringing in of his Kingdom.

Respectfully submitted,
Minnie Vautrin

Informal Report: Confidential. Not for publication or broadcasting.

As a Refugee Camp. The period from January 14—March 31, 1938.

A. Conditions in the City and Countryside:
The Self-Government Association which was inaugurated on January 1st in the

shadow of the old five-colored flag to take its place beside that of Japan, has now been followed by the formation of a second government. It was scheduled for March 15, but was finally consummated on March 28. Tang Shao-I is reported to be the head of the new government, but he was not present at the inauguration. Just what the relation of the new government is to that which has been established in Peiping we are not certain. Some have said it is to supersede that government and be the future central government of China, others tell us that it is to be under the northern government, and still others say that the two governments are to be independent of each other. Dr. Macklin and Dr. Bowen would know the members of the new government far better than we do as many of them date back to the previous generation and are men who have not been active in the New China.

The International Safety Zone was formally abolished some time ago and the committee which controlled it has been changed into an international relief committee the members of which keep exceedingly busy.[2] It has taken on a large staff of Chinese workers which is busy distributing relief to the neediest families in the city. An effort is also being made by some of the members of the committee to encourage the farmers to go back to their farms and the gardeners to go back to their gardens and to get spring crops in and thus prevent a possible famine later on. Even the most uneducated country women have a favorable attitude toward it, and if a project is sponsored by this committee they at once have confidence in it. On Thursday, March 17, there was a very simple reception down at the headquarters when after some very sincere speeches, banners expressing appreciation were presented to the members of the committee. Rev. Hubert Sone has taken Mr. Rabe's place as the chairman of the committee.[3] The former left Nanking about February 24th, after numerous receptions and teas and tiffin parties. All were genuinely sorry to have him leave for he had been a tower of strength during the trying months since November and he had greatly endeared himself to his co-workers both westerners and Chinese. The twenty-five refugee camps were gradually reduced to four, and in these remaining ones are mostly the young women who still feel that it is impossible to go back to their homes and also those who have been left without homes. Milk and cod liver oil is distributed in these camps regularly and an effort is being made to provide bedding for those who still come in having been robbed of every possession.

We no longer feel that we live in "the heart of a drum." As you remember, our first contact with the outside world was firmly established when three members of the staff returned to the American Embassy. Their coming made it possible for us to send radiograms to our families and to our organizations and also the send and receive letters by means of the gunboats. Soon followed the return of members to the British and German Embassies. At this time of writing, we are connected by train, bus and merchant boat with Shanghai and it is said that 600 Japanese civilians including women and children are now here. However no American, excepting Dr. Brady, has been permitted to come to Nanking to reside and to carry on business and missionary work, the reason given is that it is not yet safe for them to do so. A very real and persistent effort has been made to secure permission for the return of doctors and nurses, but so far this effort has not been successful. Within the last few days permission has been granted for the return of Mr. Gale from Wuhu. There is great need for the return of the regular evangelistic workers and for the heads of the various missions and it is hoped that by repeated requests permission may be granted. The post office was supposed to be formally opened on March 25th and within a few days after that time it began to function. I understand that there are seven branch offices now open in various parts of the city. I received my first letter from America on Saturday March 26, it having left there on February 28. Newspapers have just started coming through by train—we have not had them regularly since November 12, if I remember correctly. On February 21, I had my first ride in a richsha, which was in the fourth richsha which I had seem on the streets since about December 12th. There are a few carriages left in the city but many were demolished. Trucks and cars are at a great premium, the Embassies and the International Refugee Committee possessing the only ones excepting those used for military purposes. Two days ago I saw one of our former buses. Where all the others have disappeared we do not know. Mary Twinem still has hope that she will be able to secure the return of her little Austin, but I fear it is a vain hope. Recently some have seem a little Austin painted a khaki color and rather suspect that it may be her car.

Police service which has been at a minimum has been gradually increased but it is not yet sufficient or courageous enough to prevent much lawlessness in the city. Looting by the military still continues but in a different form somewhat. The poorer people are still being deprived of bedding and money, even coppers being taken now, and houses of the former well-to-do people, which were fairly safe in the Safety Zone, are now being deprived of rugs and radios and furniture. We do not see the wholesale burning of houses which took place from about December 17th to January 17th—it was on that date that I saw the last fire. The most distressing thing that now exists is the continued looting by the "lao beh sing," the common people. With no law and order in the city the poor and the lawless felt perfectly free to go into any house and take from it anything they wished. Outside of the former Safety Zone, many houses have been robbed of everything, even including doors and windows and floors. Within the last few days I have seen very good doors and windows for sale and that means that the demolishing process is still going on. Naturally our Chinese friends are distressed by this but there is nothing they can do about it. From the middle of January to the middle of February, Shanghai Road underwent an evolution. It developed rapidly into a busy mart and literally scores and scores of little make-shift shops were hastily constructed along both sides of it. There were not only shops which sold every kind of loot, but also tea houses and restaurants. I remember passing one called "The Happy People" tea house. The street became so busy and crowded that one had difficulty in getting through it when walking. Then the order came that these shops must be taken down at once or they would be torn down, and just as quickly as the street had flourished, so it receded into its former state. This development extended down into our neighborhood too. How I wish that I had some pictures of that mushroom development for you to see. During these days and weeks of free looting we longed to go to the homes of friends and salvage some of their possessions for them, but alas we had no truck or car, even if we had had the time and strength.

During this period of lawlessness in the city our campus has been fairly peaceful. At no time have "the people" come to loot or steal. Our soldier guard left us on January 14 and never returned. For many days we were fearful lest something should happen, but nothing beyond our control did happen to us. Three times soldiers came on mischief bent but were persuaded to go on their way. My calendar shows that military callers ranking from high official to soldiers numbered seventeen groups. Most of them came to see the campus and the camp. We usually show them one or two buildings occupied by refugees first and then take them to the Administration-Library Building which now looks quite normal and is open for inspection. They are always pleased to see it and we are glad to show them a clean building.

February 4 was set as the date when all refugees must leave the Safety Zone and go back to their homes. This proclamation was issued by the local autonomous government and was posted quite widely in the city. It brought consternation to the hearts of the young women on our campus and during the week preceding the date I could not go out on the campus without being besieged by a large group asking if we were going to send them away at that time. Invariably we would answer that it was not our order and that our camp was open as long as their homes were unsafe for them. One day Mr. Mills called and his car was so surrounded by kneeling, weeping young women that he finally had to walk to his home and let his driver follow when he could extricate the car. Several weeks later this terrible fear and anxiety had not left the younger women, for when we gave a tea party for Mr. Rabe down at the Practice School, some of them heard about his presence and his plan to go home and they asked Mrs. Tsen to arrange for them to see him just before he got into his car. None of us expected what really did happen. Literally hundreds and hundreds surrounded him in front of the Science building and implored him not to leave the city but to remain on in charge of the International Committee. His assurance reached only a few ears and the crowd grew instead of decreasing. Mary Twinem took him out the back way and I tried to get the crowd of weeping women to go in another direction so that we could also extricate Dr. Rosen and Mr. Ritchie, who were also guests at the same tea. It took more than an hour to bring conditions back to normal and in the meantime all three men had to walk to their homes and their cars followed later—much later. On February 4th no force was used to expel people from the Zone or the camps and the day of tension and terror passed uneventfully.

China New Year came on Monday, January 31. Even the long weeks of terror and sadness did not prevent a certain amount of celebration and feasting. Some people were bold enough to use firecrackers in their celebration, although it had not been many weeks since the sound of a big cracker would have made us start with fear and say "another civilian killed." In the afternoon Lao Shao, the old gardener, and I went out to look for some "lah mei," twelfth month plum. We wanted to go to the little farm house west of the Guling temple where we bought such lovely branches last year, but when we reached the street just east of the temple and saw that the hills and valleys beyond were a veritable "No Man's Land" we were not courageous enough to make the journey. We had passed five unburied bodies on our journey thus far and we knew that at the temple there would be many more. I also knew but did not tell Lao Shao that over in the little valley to the south of the temple beside two ponds were 143 bodies of civilians and unarmed soldiers—men who more than a month before had been cruelly burned and shot there. We came back home without the "lah mei" glad to get back in a crowd again. Few of us used freely the old greetings that are an innate part of the New Year celebration, somehow those happy carefree greetings would not come to our lips this year. The following evening, Mrs. Tsen prepared a "big meal" for us out of the wonderful basket which our friends and coworkers had sent us from Shanghai. How good it was to have pork once more and the other good dishes of food that accompanied it. I for one was glad to leave our steady diet of beans even for one meal.

On February 2nd I made my first visit into the southern part of the city. Mr. McCallum and Mr. Forster took me down to see the property of the Christian Mission first and then over to see the Episcopal compounds. The city was still lifeless save for the groups of soldiers that could be seen on many of the streets. Such terrible destruction had been meted out on our busy city! I cannot give the exact number, but of the best shops it seemed to me that almost 80% had been looted and then burned. More of the little shops were standing, but all had been looted clean of all goods. At our property, two of our school buildings had been burned and at the Episcopal compound the parish house had been destroyed. We passed a group of army trucks hauling loot, evidently from the northern part of the city for there was nothing left to loot in the section through which we passed. Just two days ago when I was again down in this part of the city older members of the community had returned and some of them were rebuilding little shops out of the remains of the big stores. The development that had taken place on Shanghai Road in January and February had been transferred to the "Street of No Sorrows," excepting that not so many temporary shops had been built—the displays were on tables and on the sides of the street. Patiently people are beginning to rebuild. Loot is still being bought and sold—it is the only way that people have of making a living for nothing is being created in the city as far as I know.

Conditions in the surrounding country are not as peaceful as in the city. Beginning late in January women began to steal their way in from the country villages, disguised in every possible way. To get past the soldier guard at the city gates was the dreaded ordeal. Older women came in first, having heard of the refugee camps, they came in first to find out if they were really existing. They begged us to accept their daughters and daughters-in-law if they could get them into the city saying that for weeks and weeks they had been hiding them in carefully concealed holes in the ground or between double walls in their homes, but even in these places they were not always safe. During the past two weeks we have received more than five hundred into our camp from the country places and the University has received an equal number. In addition to the scourge of soldiers there has been the scourge of bandits, and often when people try to come in they are robbed of everything they possess—money first, then bedding and even part of their clothing. Some of our Chinese friends who evacuated to the country places last autumn are now returning. The men come first to make sure that they can get in, they register with the local government, and then go back to bring in their families. During the last two weeks, Mr. Handel Lee, Mr. Shao Deh-hsing and others have come. Just yesterday Wang Bao-ling's brother came from Sanho south of Luchowfu. They all look as if the past months have been months of strain and deep anxiety for themselves, and we realize that most of it has been worry for the women folk in their families.

B. Conditions in the G.C. [Ginling College] Refugee Camp:
Our camp was one of the four selected to continue its existence by the NIRC [Nanking International Relief Committee]. According to the recommendation of the Committee, we have organized into four departments or sections, namely, business, supervision, education and health. Having been granted a small allowance by the Committee for 2 assistants, and 4 servants for each one thousand refugees, we have felt justified in taking on extra staff. These have been mostly from our "invited" refugees such as Miss Rachel Wang, Mr. Wang and Mr. Djao, personal teachers of members of the regular faculty, Mr. Chan, the assistant registrar, and a Mr. Swen, who is a neighbor who has been living

down at East Court. A new office has been started in the former guest room in the Arts Building and it is a busy place from morning to night. Mrs. Tsen has also invited three refugee women to assist her in distributing milk and cod liver oil. Keeping statistics up to date in a shifting refugee camp is no light task. During the first week in February we had a formal registration of all our refugees when the head of each family group was given a white cloth tag bearing her name and the number in her family group. These tags were sewed on by our workers with a special color of thread so that they could not be transferred to others when they wished to leave. According to that registration we numbered 3,200. By the middle of March our new staff felt that it was necessary to re-register all, and they prepared a lavender cloth tag which has been given to each member of the refugee group excepting babies in arms. According to this registration our number now is 3,310. Mr. Chen, who is head of the business department, is now with his staff working on the very difficult problem of the free rice group. Naturally may people want free rice who can afford to pay for it, and to separate this group from those who have absolutely nothing with which to pay is a most difficult task. The free rice group were first given red tags; a month later they were rechecked and given yellow tags, and now a third system is being worked out and will be put into operation this coming week. If people were always sincere, our work would be infinitely lighter and incidentally our dispositions would be better.

After our refugees had been with us about three months we decided that we simply must work out some system whereby they could have baths. We had been playing with the idea before but were not able to get coal. We made our plan and presented it to the International Refugee Committee and they agreed to furnish us with coal and the funds for one fireman and two women to look after each house. For two weeks now, under Mrs. Tsen's supervision we have been operating two bath houses where 168 women and children can take baths each day. The price is four coppers for adults, two for babies and children, and nothing for those who are too poor to afford even this small amount. In addition to the joy this privilege gives to the women, it also gives a livelihood to five persons.

Our Camp has also been granted a fund for cash relief and another to loan to individuals. Women who are very poor, whose homes have been burned and whose husbands have been taken are given a sum in cash when they are ready to go back to their homes. This helps them to start again and has been deeply appreciated by all who have received it. The loan fund has given loans to a number of women whose husbands are in other parts of China and are earning a salary. A good many women of this type have been left stranded in Nanking and as yet have had no means of getting funds from their husbands.

Mrs. Tsen who is head of the Health Department of our Camp has carried on very successfully the distribution of milk and cod liver oil for babies and children. Children who are undernourished are given this extra food each day, the three women who have been taken on as assistants in this department distribute the milk and also attend to the mixing of it. Both of these foods are furnished us by the International Relief Committee. Mrs. Twinem and Mrs. Tsen have also been responsible for the distribution in the other refugee camps and have spent many mornings visiting these other camps and getting the distribution organized. Under our Health Department we also have had three vaccination clinics when almost two thousand were vaccinated by Dr. Brady of the Christmas Hospital staff. During these long weeks of simple living we have had more than 30 deaths and 40 births on our campus. The disposal of the night soil is still one of our major problems, but we are gradually getting the problem solved. Fortunately we have a large campus so that we have room for the huge trenches which we have dug for this purpose. Dai, the regular college bell ringer, sounds a gong about eight in the morning and again at five in the afternoon and this is the time for the women to empty the toilet buckets and clean them.

C. A Project in Religious Education:
For the six weeks from January 17 to February 26 we limited our religious work to two meetings each day, one for the adults and one for the children. As I reported in my previous letter, five pastors from the American Church Mission very generously and faithfully came each afternoon during the week, excepting Saturday, and spoke. In addition the women learned some simple songs. On February 27 we started another project, this time in the life of Christ, which is to culminate in an early service on Easter morning and in a pageant that afternoon or evening, also in special services being held throughout Holy Week. Miss Rachel Wang is dean of our Educational Department and as such she has organized 23 classes according to educational ability all of those studying the life of Christ in one form or another. You will be interested in the classes so I will give you the details ———

2 classes or sections of Junior–Senior Middle School ability
2 of 6th grade elementary school ability
2 of 5th grade elementary school ability
4 of 3rd and 4th grade elementary school ability
6 sections of those who have studied in private school a few years. These are divided according to age, some are children, some adults.
3 sections of adults who have never studied. They are being taught a Gospel Primer.
2 sections of illiterates from 18 to 19 years of age.
2 sections of illiterates from 12 to 27 years of age.

These last two sections meet five times each week and are taught by Mr. Wang and Mr. Djao. Our enrollment is something over a thousand and our attendance each week is perhaps between seven and eight hundred. The older women try to attend regularly but if a baby is ill they have to miss, and often they have to go back to their homes during the day or on some other errand. All the classes but the two I mentioned meet three times each week. In addition to lessons in the life of Christ all are learning certain selected Psalms and hymns and other passages from the Bible. Miss Wang has selected the 23rd Psalm, the 121st, the Beatitudes, the Lord's Prayer. How they love to sing "What a Friend We Have in Jesus" and "Jesus Lover of My Soul." Just now they are learning Easter hymns, the one for this week being "The Day of Resurrection." The teachers have wanted to share with their students those hymns and scripture passages that have been of greatest comfort to them during these days of suffering. All of our teachers, excepting Miss Hsueh, the day school teacher and myself, are refugees, some of them were invited to come, to be sure, and yet they know what it means to be refugees. Our afternoon preaching service continues, but now it is held in the big chapel. The attendance varies from 150 to almost 400 and is usually largest on Sundays. The topics for these meetings have been carefully selected by the five men who come to us from the Episcopal Church and they all are centering on the life of Christ also. You should hear a group of three hundred refugee women sing "What a Friend We Have in Jesus." They love it and how they do sing. We take turns in leading the singing and also in inviting people to the meetings so that the work does not fall too heavily on any one person. One of the difficulties connected with the class work was our lack of classrooms for as you may realize, every room in the Arts Building where our classrooms are, is occupied by refugees. We have converted the North Studio into a very good classroom, the Grecian statues in that room which were stored there by Central University when they moved last fall, being gracefully draped with a big curtain. The stage of the big auditorium is also used as a classroom and makes a very good one indeed with space for more than forty chairs. Another class meets in the chemistry laboratory, which we never used for refugees and many classes meet in the science lecture hall. After Easter we shall have a week's holiday and then begin work again. At that time we shall hope to add different types of classes such as poultry raising; personal, home and community hygiene; child training; and perhaps Japanese. We shall also try to teach some industrial work, but that will need more of a staff than we have available now. Yesterday several of us went on an expedition to the South city to see if we could find some looms and stocking knitting machines. To our disappointment we found that they all had been looted. But where there is a will there is a way.

D. Another Project:

Early in January we became conscious that many of our refugee women—especially wives and mothers were in deep distress because their husbands or sons who had been taken soon after the entry on December 13, have not returned. Many of these women were left with little children and often one or two old people and they had literally no means of support—nothing they could do but beg and even that is impossible now in a community so poor as ours. Again and again they would come to us asking if there was anything that could be done to secure the return of these men—all of them civilians as far as we were able to ascertain. We finally went to the Japanese Embassy and talked it over with one of the more thoughtful officials there and he suggested that we furnish him with the facts and he would see if he could do anything with the military about it. From January 24 to February 8 we were able to secure 738 civilian records. These we handed in not only to the official with whom we had the first conference but also to a higher official who had come up from Shanghai. As far as we know, nothing has happened for we have not heard of any men returning. In the meantime rumors began to reach us that there was a large group of civilian men imprisoned in the Model Prison over near the Central University. A trip over in that direction confirmed the rumor. The exact number of men we could not determine but we learned that men were there and in a pitiful condition. Soon the older women began to come to our campus saying that they had gone to the front of the prison and had seen the men being taken out each morning in trucks to work. A number of the women have told us that they have actually seen their husbands or sons and some of them have been permitted to talk to them. Again the pleas began to come to aid them in securing the release of these men. Chinese men in local government administration suggested that we have our women prepare a petition to be handed in not only to the head of the local government but also to the Japanese military. From March 18 to 22nd 1,245 women came in to sign this petition—most of them were very poor women and could only make a finger print underneath the name which was written in their behalf. Such a pitiful group of women I have never seen before. Most of them were poor—farmers, gardeners, coolies, little merchants; and most of them had had their only means of support taken from them. One woman had lost four of her sons; another had had five members of her family taken; another had lost three sons. There were a goodly number of young women who had been left with three or four little children and they could not possibly make a living for the children. It seems that the petition has born some fruit for now the women are asked to make another giving more data with regard to the time the men were taken, their occupations, etc. Tonight Mr. Wang is making the announcement in the dormitories and tomorrow six people will begin work on this new petition. It will take from three to five days to complete it as the women will come from miles out in the country. Such news spreads like wild-fire and the poor women come trudging in even if there is but a very faint hope. One of the greatest problems facing the people interested in rehabilitation work for this district, is that of the women who have been left with no support and whose husbands will never return. I long for Ginling to help in the solution of this perhaps more than anything else.

E. Ginling losses:
Since the last report sent to you, we have had time to secure facts with regard to the college and faculty losses. The loss to the college property from the looting of Chinese soldiers was nil; from the looting of Japanese soldiers does not exceed $300.00. About fourteen faculty and two servants lost a certain amount through the looting of the Japanese soldiers and this we estimate at about $1,200.00. By far the greatest loss has come from the use of the academic buildings as a refugee camp, for the housing of 10,000 women and children even for a short time means much wear and tear on woodwork and floors. The best estimate that we have been able to secure sets the loss at about seven to eight thousand dollars, and it will probably be higher than that if our refugees continue with us through the coming months. I feel sure that somehow we can raise the money needed to put the buildings back in good repair, but even if we cannot raise the funds it is better for us to face the future with marred and soiled walls than not to have done this humanitarian service for the women and children who have come to us. We could not have closed our doors against them.

This letter is brought to a close with greetings to you from the members of the staff. You must not feel sorry for us thinking that we lack food or social life. We can get the kind of foods now that we need to keep us well. Some of us have even been to two feasts during the past months, one at the Japanese Embassy and another at the Hwei Wen Girl's School. To-morrow, Mrs. Tsen, Mrs. Twinem, Blanche Wu and myself are giving a simple Chinese meal to a group of friends whom we are inviting to the South Hill Faculty Residence. This afternoon we went up and folded up the garments scattered in the living room—since the looting we had never taken the time to do that. The big dining room we shall not disturb, but keep it for the enjoyment and amusement of our friends. Conditions in the city are such that more and more we are able to leave the campus and not feel that our three thousand three hundred will be in danger when we are away. This past week I have had my bicycle brought down from the attic and oiled and I have ridden it when going on an errand down to the South Gate. Mary and I are planning to ride out to the National Park very soon for the thought of the blossoms there is enticing us and it is difficult to resist. We have had some illness among our staff members but all are well now. Blanche was ill with a very severe case of bronchitis and was in the hospital for three weeks. The day she returned Mary went over with the same malady and was also there for three weeks. Mrs. Tsen has had several very severe colds and has been confined to her bed for a number of days at a time. I have had a few days off but otherwise have been feeling very well.

Puh, the shrub man is busy at his work and the campus is beginning to look neat and clean once more. The Practice School campus is at its loveliest now and is a constant delight to those of us who live here. The little children who live at East Court and Mrs. Tsen's grandchildren are having great fun tending to the student flower garden at the Practice School. Every day they spend many hours there watering the flowers. Life would be so lovely if this terrible war and destruction would cease, and if families could be re-united, and the nation go forward on its plan of reconstruction which has been so bravely started. The scores of heavy bombers which fly over us to the northwest each morning make us realize that the end is not yet near and that destruction and terror and suffering continue.

Not many letters have come through from friends, but those that have come have been deeply appreciated. If when you write you prefer to send my mail to our Shanghai office at Room 512A, 133 Yuen Ming Yuen Road, I will receive it in good time. I fear that this general report must be accepted in lieu of more personal letters.

Very sincerely yours,
Minnie Vautrin

Excerpts from Diary (December 12, 1937—May 13, 1938)[4]

Sunday, December 12. As I write these notes at 8:30 this evening there is heavy artillery fire pounding away in the southwest sections of the city. The window panes are shaking, and I have taken the precaution of getting away from the window. All day there has been heavy bombardment. Some say the Japanese army has entered the city but we have not had the report confirmed. One soldier told our gateman that at Gwang Hwa Gate the Japanese troops entered four or five times and were driven back. Have also heard that the 88th Division are being replaced by the 87th. Sad to say troops have been going through the Safety Zone all day. At Press Conference tonight heard that Tang, the Defence Commander, does not have much control over his troops, and in most places in the city—save in the Zone—there has been looting. (From the sound of that terrific bombardment I'm afraid there is not much left of our fine old city wall.) Aeroplanes come freely now, and release their whole rack of bombs, and there is no interference from antiaircraft guns or Chinese planes. I certainly think it was a terrible mistake to burn all the houses outside of the city wall, and many within, if the sacrifice has been of so little value. Who suffers by the destruction but the poor of China? Why not have turned the city over undestroyed?

This morning at 10:30 went to Drum Tower Church. There were about sixty present. One member of the Church Emergency Committee preached a good sermon. There are many refugees living in the Church compound.

(The guns are practically quiet now. I wonder if it means that a breach has been made in wall and Japanese are entering.)

Refugees continue to come in. We now have three buildings filled and are now beginning on the Arts Building. Unfortunately the rice kitchen to be managed by Red Cross has not yet opened up, so it has been most difficult for the people who brought no food with them. After repeated urgings we think we can get it open by nine in the morning—but if the city is turned over in the night even that may not be possible.

Funny things do happen in all this distress and terror. Gwah, the tailor opposite our east gate, foolishly permitted the New Life Movement to store some of their things in a room of his house before they left the city. He has begun to worry about them as the Japanese have drawn nearer. Today I called Mr. Fitch in, and the two of us took responsibility for asking him to destroy all literature. All afternoon he and his wife and all their relatives have been carrying load after load to our incinerator, and there burning it. Drops of perspiration stood out on his forehead as he trudged along. They got rid of it just in time. (From the sound of that shooting I would say the Japanese are in the city.)

Lin, the very efficient janitor in the Central Building is hoarse tonight from his efforts to get the refugee women and children to be clean on his good floors. He was telling the gatemen this afternoon how difficult it was to keep children from wetting on his floors. The gateman said, "Why don't you tell them not to?" "*Tell* them *not* to," said Lin, disgustedly, in his hoarse vice, "I *do* tell them but as soon as I turn my back they do it."

This afternoon at 5 p.m., as I went over to the English service, I saw a great ribbon of fire on Purple Mountain extending along the upper third of the mountain. How the fire started I have not heard, but it means that many pines are burned.

Between 9 and 10 tonight Mr. Chen and I made a tour of the campus. Hu, the laundry man, and Tsu, his farmer neighbor, were both up. They are fearful of retreating soldiers tonight, for they have young girls in their families. Few people will sleep in the city tonight. From the South Hill Residence we could see the South City still burning, and also Hsia Gwan.

Think I shall sleep with my clothes on tonight so I can get up if I am needed. Wish the night were over.

Just a year ago today General Chang was taken prisoner at Sian.

Monday, December 13. (Have heard that Japanese entered Gwang Hwa Gate at 4 a.m.)

All night long the heavy artillery was pounding against the city gates. They say the south, but it sounded to me like the west. There was a good deal of shooting inside the city. I did not really go off soundly to sleep and in my half conscious state I thought the Japanese were chasing Chinese troops out of the city, and firing at them as they retreated. None of us took off our clothes for fear something might happen. Sometime after five I got up and went to the front gate. All was quiet there, but the gateman said retreating soldiers had been passing in large groups and some had been begging for ordinary civilian clothes. This morning many military garments were found inside our compound. Our neighbors have been wanting to come in but we have tried to help them to see that if they are in the Safety Zone they are as safe as we are and that all parts of the Safety Zone should be equally safe.

The soup or rice kitchen at our front gate served rice for the first time this morning. We fed the dormitories in order of their coming on campus. By 10:30 the meal had been finished. They are to have the second meal this afternoon.

Searle Bates came over about eleven and reported that the Ministry of Communications Building has been destroyed (yesterday) according to Chinese orders, and that the next building was to be the Ministry of Railways. I am heart sick about it for I feel it is useless and wrong, and injures the Chinese far more than the Japanese. He also reported that $50,000 has been given to International Red Cross for use for the Military Hospitals. The first one will be established in the Ministry of Foreign Affairs. A committee of seventeen has been organized.

4 p.m. The report came to me that there were Japanese soldiers on the hill west of us. I went up to South Hill Residence to see, and sure enough our West Hill had a number on it. Soon I was called by another servant, who said that one had entered our Poultry Experiment Station and wanted chickens and geese. Immediately I went down and he soon left, after my efforts at sign language telling him the chickens were not for sale. He happened to be polite.

The city is strangely silent—after all the bombing and shelling. Three dangers are past—that of looting soldiers, bombing from aeroplanes and shelling from big guns, but the fourth is still before us—our fate at the hands of a victorious army. People are very anxious tonight and do not know what to expect. Plumer Mills reported this evening that their contacts so far have been pleasant but, to be sure, they have been few.

7:30 p.m. The men managing the rice kitchen report that Japanese soldiers are occupying the house opposite our gate in which the rice is stored. Francis Chen and I tried to make contact with the head man of the group but got no where. The guard at the gate was as fierce as I care to meet. Later I went over to see the Director of Safety Zone about it and they will try to solve the problem tomorrow, but all agree it must be handled circumspectly.

Tonight Nanking has no lights, no water, no telephone, no telegraph, no city paper, no radio. We are indeed separated from all of you by an impenetrable zone. Tomorrow I shall try to get a radiogram through the U.S.S. *Panay* to Dr. Wu and also to N.Y. So far Ginling, people and buildings, has come through safely—but we are not sure of the coming days. We are all fearfully tired. On almost any occasion we give forth deep groans of weariness—a tiredness that permeates through and through. (There are many disarmed soldiers in the safety zone tonight. I have not heard if there were any trapped in the city.)

Friday, December 17. Went to gate at 7:30 to get message to Mr. Sone who slept down in house with F. Chen. Red Cross kitchen must have coal and rice. A stream of weary wild-eyed women were coming in. Said their night had been one of horror; that again and again their homes had been visited by soldiers. (Twelve-year old girls up to sixty-year old women raped. Husbands forced to leave bedroom and pregnant wife at point of bayonet. If only the thoughtful people of Japan knew facts of these days of horror.) Wish some one were here who had time to write the sad story of each person—especially that of the younger girls who had blackened their faces and cut their hair. The gateman said they had been coming in since daylight at 6:30.

The morning spent either at gate or running from South Hill to one of the dormitories or front gate wherever a group of Japanese was reported to be. One or two such trips were made both during breakfast and dinner today. No meal for days without a servant coming "Miss Vautrin, three soldiers now in Science Building" or . . .

The afternoon spent at gate—no easy task to control the traffic, to prevent fathers and brothers from coming in, or others from coming in with food or other conveniences. There are more than 4000 on campus and when 4000 more bring in food the task becomes complicated, especially when we have to be very careful about those who come in.

The crowd coming in all day we simply cannot take care of—if we had room we do not have strength enough to manage. Have arranged with University to open one of their dormitories and they will have a foreign man on duty all night. Between four and six I took over two large groups of women and children. What a heartbreaking sight! Weary women, frightened girls, trudging with children and bedding and small packages of clothes. Was glad I went along for all along the way we met groups of Japanese soldiers going from house to house, carrying all kinds of loot. Fortunately, Mary T. was on the campus, so I felt I could leave. When I returned she said that at 5 p.m. two soldiers came in, and seeing the big American flag in center of Quadrangle they tore it from the stakes and started off with it. It was too heavy and cumbersome to take on bicycles, so they threw it in a heap in front of Science Building. Mary was called from front gate and when the soldiers saw her they ran and hid. She found them out in a room at the Power House and when she spoke to them they flushed, for they knew they were wrong.

As we finished eating supper, the boy from Central Building came and said there were many soldiers on campus going to dormitories. I found two in front of Central Building pulling on door and insisting on its being opened. I said I had no key. One said—"soldiers here. Enemy of Japan." I said—"No Chinese soldiers." Mr. Li, who was with me, said the same. He then slapped me on the face and slapped Mr. Li very severely, and insisted on opening of door. I pointed to side door and took them in. They went through both downstairs and up presumably looking for Chinese soldiers. When we came out two more soldiers came leading three of our servants, whom they had bound. They said, "Chinese soldiers," but I said, "No soldier. Coolie, gardener,"—for that is what they were. They took them to the front and I accompanied them. When I got to the front gate I found a large group of Chinese kneeling there beside the road—Mr. F. Chen, Mr. Hsia and a number of our servants. The sergeant of the group was there, and some of his men, and soon we were joined by Mrs. Tsen and Mary Twinem, also being escorted by soldiers. They asked who was master of the institution, and I said I was. Then they made me identify each person. Unfortunately there were some new people, taken on as extra help during these days, and one of them looked like a soldier. He was taken roughly over to right of road and carefully examined. Unfortunately when I was identifying the servants Mr. Chen spoke up and tried to help me; and for that he was slapped severely, and roughly taken to right side of road and made to kneel.

In the midst of this procedure, during which we prayed most earnestly for help, a car drove up in which was G. Fitch, L. Smythe and P. Mills—the latter to stay all night with us. They made all three of them come in, stand in a line, and remove hats, and examined them for pistols. Fortunately Fitch could speak some French with the sergeant. There were several conferences among the sergeant and his men again and again, and at one time they insisted that all foreigners, Mrs. Tsen and Mary must leave. They finally changed their minds when I insisted this was my home and I could not leave. They then made foreign men get into car and leave. As the rest of us were standing or kneeling there we heard screams and cries and saw people going out at the side gate. I thought they were taking off large group of men helpers. We later realized their trick—to keep responsible people at front gate with three or four of their soldiers carrying on this mock trial and search for Chinese soldiers while the rest of the men were in the buildings selecting women. We learned later they selected twelve and took them out at side gate. When that was complete they went out front gate with F.

Chen—and we were sure we would see him no more. When they went out we were not sure they had left but thought they might be on guard outside, ready to shoot any who moved. Never shall I forget that scene—the people kneeling at side of road, Mary, Mrs. Tsen and I standing, the dried leaves rattling, the moaning of the wind, the cry of women being led out. While we were there in silence, "Big" Wang came, and said two women had been taken from East Court. We urged him to go back. We prayed most earnestly for Mr. Chen's release and for those who were carried off—those who had never prayed before I am sure prayed that night.

For what seemed an eternity we dared not move for fear of being shot; but by a quarter to eleven we decided we would leave. Du, the gatemen looked stealthily out of the front gate—there was no one. He stole to the side gate—it seemed to be closed, and so we all got up and left. Mr. Tsen, Mary, and I went to the Southeast dormitory. No one was there. Mrs. Tsen's daughter-in-law and all the grandchildren were gone—I was horrified, but Mrs. Tsen said calmly she was sure they were hiding with the refugees. In her room we found everything in confusion and realized that it had been looted. We then went to Central Building and there found Mrs. Tsen's family, Miss Hsueh, Miss Wang and Blanche Wu. Then Mary and I went down to the Practice School. To my surprise there we found Mr. Chen and Miss Lo sitting silently in my sitting room. When Mr. Chen told us his story, I realized that surely his life had been saved by a miracle. We had a little meeting of thanksgiving. Never have I heard such prayers. Later, I went down to the gate and stayed in Mr. Chen's home all night—in room next to gate house. It must have been long after midnight when we went to bed—and I venture none of us slept.

Sunday, December 19. Again this morning wild-eyed women and girls came streaming in at the gate—the night had been one of horror. Many kneeled and implored to be taken in—and we let them in but we do not know where they will sleep tonight.

At 8 o'clock a Japanese came in with Mr. Teso from the Embassy. Having been told we had not enough rice for the refugees, I asked him to take me over to headquarters of Safety Zone; this he did, and from there a German car took me over to see Mr. Sone, who has charge of rice distribution. He promised to get us rice by nine o'clock. Later I had to go back with the car to Ninghai Road, the presence of a foreigner is now the only protection for a car. Walking back to college, again and again mothers and fathers and brothers implored me to take their daughters back to Ginling. One mother whose daughter was a Chung Hwa student, said her home had been looted repeatedly the day before and she could no longer protect her daughter.

Later the morning was spent going from one end of the campus to the other trying to get one group of soldiers after another out. Went up to South Hill three times I think, then to the back campus and then was frantically called to the old Faculty House where I was told two soldiers had gone upstairs. There, in room 538, I found one standing at the door, and one inside already raping a poor girl. My letter from the Embassy and my presence sent them running out in a hurry—in my heart I wished I had the power to smite them in their dastardly work. How ashamed the women of Japan would be if they knew these tales of horror.

Then I was called to the northwest dormitory and found two in a room eating cookies—they too went out in a hurry.

Late in the afternoon two separate groups of Japanese officers have come and again I have had the chance to tell of the Friday night experience and this morning's doings.

Tonight we have four gendarmes on our campus and tomorrow we hope to have one. Great fires are burning in at least three sections of the city tonight.

Tuesday, December 21. The days seem interminable and each morning you wonder how you can live through the day, twelve hours.

After breakfast we collected facts about the harm done by our guard of 25 last night (two women raped). But we realize that those facts must be handled with care and tact, or we will incur the hared of soldiers and that may be worse for us than the trouble we have at present.

Mary and Mrs. Tsen are trying to teach the women to stand in line for rice, and perhaps they will teach them in time, if they are patient. We never have enough rice for them and some people take more than they need.

At 11 Mr. Wang and I went over to the Embassy to make arrangements for a car to take us to Japanese Embassy in the afternoon.

At 1:30 I went with Mr. Atcheson's cook in Embassy car over to street west of us. He had heard that his old father of 75 was killed and was anxious to see. We found the old man lying in middle of the road. They took his body over to the bamboo grove and there covered it with matting. The old man had refused to go to the Embassy for protection, saying he was sure nothing would harm him.

When we went to Japanese Embassy at 2 p.m. the Consul was not in, so we arranged to call again at 4 p.m. Fortunately, as we were going out of gate, we met the Consul's car and went back for interview. We told him we were very sorry we could not furnish charcoal, tea, and "dien sin" (cakes) for such a large group, and wondered if we might have just *two* military police for night duty, and *one* for day. He was wise enough to understand that all was not well on our campus last night with 25 guards.

All foreigners in city this afternoon sent in a petition pleading that peace be restored in Nanking—for sake of the 200,000 Chinese here, as well as for the

Japanese army's good. I did not go with the group, having just been there.

After leaving Japanese Embassy, again went without Embassy servant to the home of Mr. Jenkin at San Pai Lou. Although his house had been protected by an American flag, Japanese proclamation and special telegram to Tokyo, it was thoroughly looted. On the garage, found his trusted servant dead—having been shot. He had refused to leave his master's house for the shelter of the Embassy.

Those of you who have lived in Nanking can never imagine how the streets look—the saddest sight I ever hope to see. Buses and cars upset in street, dead bodies here and there, with faces already black, discarded soldiers' clothing everywhere, every house and shop looted and smashed if not burned. In the Safety Zone the streets are crowded—outside you seldom see anyone but Japanese.

Because it is not safe for any car with any flag to go on the streets without a foreigner inside, I took the Embassy car back to the Embassy. Walking home with Mr. Wang and Lao Shao—I would hesitate to go out alone—a man came up to us in great distress asking us if we could do anything for him. His wife of 27 had just gone home from Ginling—only to have her home entered by three soldiers. Her husband was forced to leave and she was left in the hands of those three soldiers.

Tonight we must have 6 or 7000 (9 or 10,000?) refugees on our campus. The handful of us who are managing are worn out—how long we can stand the strain we do not know.

Great fires are now lighting the sky to the northeast, east and southeast, each night these fires light the sky and by day clouds of smoke make us know that the work of looting and destruction still continues. The fruits of war are death and desolation.

We have absolutely no contact with the outside world—know nothing of what is happening and can send out no messages. While watching at the gate tonight, the gateman said that each day seemed like a year, and life had lost all meaning—which is true. And the sad thing is we see no future. The once energetic, hopeful capital is now almost an empty shell—pitiful, heartrending.

Have not yet been able to send out radiogram that I worded days ago.

Wednesday, December 22. There is a great deal of machine gun and rifle firing this morning. Is it merely practice or are more innocent people being shot?

My strength has suddenly come to an end and I feel utterly exhausted from the terrific strain and sadness of these days. Save for an interview this morning with a Japanese Embassy police official, and this afternoon with Mr. Fukuda, military attaché, and this evening with the head of our guard for the night, I've done nothing. Have tried to get as much rest as possible during the day. It is such a blessing to have Mary T. here to help and Big Wang. Mrs. Tsen is very wise in all her advice and is invaluable. She, too, is terribly tired.

Today we are not serving rice to the refugees simply because it has become unmanageable. We are taking time to reorganize our system, sewing on each person too poor to buy, a red tag—and they will be served first, hereafter. Also have prepared tickets for those who do not get rice each day—it always runs out before we get around—so that they will come first on the next serving. I dare not estimate how many we have on the campus—some think about 10,000. The Science building, which has only two rooms, the hall and attic open, has about 1000 in it—so the Arts Building must have 2000. They say the attic alone of that building has almost 1000. On the covered ways at night there must be 1000. Mr. Fitch came over tonight and asked us if we would like Hwei Wen opened for our overflow, and we said we certainly would.

Mr. Forster of the American Church Mission came in this afternoon and told this sad story. The Japanese Embassy wanted the electric light plant repaired so that lights could be turned on. Mr. Rabe therefore got fifty employees together and took them down to the plant. This afternoon forty-three were shot by soldiers saying they were the employees of the Chinese government. Mr. Forster also wanted to know if we could have an English Christmas service here on Saturday. Mary and I are inclined to think it is not wise for all foreigners to get together, for fear we might attract too much attention.

A guard of twenty-five soldiers has been furnished us each night. The first night we had them we had several unfortunate incidents, last night all was well, and the night was peaceful. Tonight we tactfully suggested that the same method be used tonight as last night—they guard on the outside, we on the inside.

People say conditions are somewhat better in city—certainly there are fewer fires, although there are still some. We still have no contact with the outside world.

Thursday, December 23. Two day before Christmas! How different from the usual life on our campus at this time of year. Then all is so busy—preparation, anticipation and joy, now all is fear and sadness, not knowing what the next moment may bring forth. Our campus yesterday and today has been more peaceful—yesterday three groups of soldiers strayed in and today but one. The past two nights have also been peaceful. Our guard is changed every day—and with each new group Mr. Wang and I explain by every means possible that if they will guard outside the campus we will guard inside. This afternoon at 2 o'clock a high military adviser came with three other officers. They wanted to inspect the buildings where refugees are living. Again and yet again we said that just as soon as city becomes peaceful we will urge them to go home. They say that things are better in the city and they think they can go home soon.

Our neighbor Swen from Hu Gi Gwan, who is living at East Court, said that last night from sixty to a hundred men, mostly young, were taken in trucks to the little valley south of the Ginling Temple, shot by machine gun fire, later put into a house and the whole set on fire. I have been suspecting that many of the fires we see at night are to cover up either looting or killing. Am fearing more and more that our messenger boy and the son of the biology servant have both been killed.

We have decided that it is not safe to have a Christmas service together for fear of what might happen on our campus while we are absent. Mary and I are also afraid the gathering might create suspicion.

Food is getting more and more scarce. For several days now we have had no meat—it is impossible to buy anything on street now—even eggs and chickens are no longer available.

Lights go off at 8:30 tonight. We have been using only candles in Practice School for days for fear of attracting attention.

As soon as the way opens up, I am anxious for Francis Chen, Mr. Li and Mr. Chen to leave Nanking, for I do not feel that youth is very safe.

Mary Twinem's house was thoroughly looted today. Most residences have been looted unless a foreigner is present in them and that has been impossible when people are so busy.

It is raining today. All people who have been sleeping on verandahs will have to squeeze inside somehow. The good weather of past weeks has been a great blessing.

Friday, December 24. The day before Christmas! About ten o'clock I was called to my office to interview the high military adviser for the — division. Fortunately he had an interpreter with him, an old Chinese interpreter for the Embassy. The request was that they be allowed to pick out the prostitute women from our ten thousand refugees. They said they wanted one hundred. They feel if they can start a regular licensed place for the soldiers then they will not molest innocent and decent women. After promising they would not take any of the latter, we permitted them to begin their search, the adviser sitting in my office during the search. After a long time they finally secured twenty-one. Some, they think, made off when they heard such a search was to be made and some are still hiding. Group after group of girls have asked me if they will select the other seventy-nine from among the decent girls—and all I can answer is that they will not do so if it is in my power to prevent it.

This afternoon Mary has been decorating a Christmas tree and the room for our Christmas services. Have chosen a north facing room upstairs for which I have a heavy green curtain for the one window. The room is lovely now with its heavenly bamboo, its Christmas tree, its red Christmas scrolls.

This evening at 6:30 we had a simple Christmas service there with only ourselves and Mrs. Tsen's daughter-in-law and four children. The little children enjoyed the simple gifts,—it was wrong not to have something for them, although the grandmother did not approve. Tomorrow we shall use the room four times for other groups.

At 4:30 went over to the University to check the report that a number of weeping women brought to me. They were told that a number of men have been selected out from refugees and are to be killed unless they are identified at once.

Many women are faced with a terrible dilemma—to stay with their husbands and be raped by soldiers when their husbands are turned out of house at point of bayonet; to come to Ginling, and leave their husbands—the latter then runs risk of being carried off and killed.

Stray groups of soldiers have almost ceased to come to the campus since we have the guard and patrol at the gate. This lessens the strain for me a great deal.

Great fires still light up the southern and eastern sky. Evidently all shops are being thoroughly looted and then burned. I do not want to see Nanking for I am sure it is desolate waste. People say conditions in city are somewhat better. Still no connection with outside world—I learned this from calling at American Embassy today.

Saturday, December 25. At Christmas dinner today Searle Bates said he had been trying to write an article on "Christmas in Hell." It really has not been that for us here at Ginling; in fact we have had some bits of heaven on our campus—although the day certainly has been different from any Christmas I have ever experienced at Ginling.

The night again was one of peace—with our guard of twenty-five at the gate patrolling both Hankow and Ninghai Roads. For the first time in weeks and weeks I slept soundly through the night.

In the south studio at 7:30 this morning we had a very wonderful prayer meeting led by F. Chen. Every hymn we sing has a meaning to us now and we eagerly accept the comfort and strength it gives. There were nine of us present including Big Wang. No one thinks of preparing a talk for a prayer meeting these days—we pray for the deep longings in our hearts.

Between 8:30 and 9:30 two groups of soldiers came, but they caused no trouble—were interested largely in the power plant.

At 12:30 Blanche and I went over to Buck home for Christmas dinner. Grace Bauer was also a guest. Searle and C. Riggs were called out again and again to go either to University or to a residence to rescue either a truck, a group of men or some women—they spend their days doing such tasks now.

Going over I had an interesting experience. Just as we went out the gate a woman came imploring me to save her daughter who had just been taken from their home. I hurried along in the direction she showed me and went south on Shanghai Road only to be told they had turned north. Just as I started north I saw Mills in a car, halted him, and got in with the mother and Blanche. Soon we saw two soldiers going along with the girl following. As soon as she saw she turned and appealed for help, and then when she saw her mother she rushed into the car. The soldier seeing what had happened was quite insistent that we had mistreated him, sat in Mill's seat and refused to get out. An officer came along who understood some English and he tried, in what seemed to us an unnecessarily gentle way, to get the soldier out and let us go on. It was not until Mills said he was sorry we had taken the girl that he let us go.

At two this afternoon a very successful Christmas was held for campus servants in the little Christmas chapel, Miss Wang in charge. At three Miss Lo had a Christmas service for the Christian neighborhood women and some refugee families on campus. At seven this evening Miss Houch had a Christmas service for the day school pupils and the other children who have helped her in the Service Corp. We could do nothing for the large group of refugees—impossible to handle.

Tonight we have no guard. One police has been sent to us from the Embassy. Soldiers are being moved out of the city. Some of our refugees going home, altho S.M.B. [M.S.B.?] says it has been a bad day at the University so far as taking women is concerned.

Monday, December 27. It's a day off for me. Have not been feeling well for two days so friends insisted on my staying in bed. Mary being here made it possible and I was glad of an excuse.

The night again was peaceful, with one Embassy police at front gate. One of the foreign men also came over to stay with F. Chen. For some reason our Practice School dogs barked a good deal in the night which makes me think there may be prowlers. Do not know how my dogs have escaped bayonets of soldiers. Military police came over during day to check up and see that all is quiet. They really seem like clean, well-disciplined men, and in the main have kind faces.

In the afternoon there were a number of official callers—one a Colonel Oka who will come in the morning to see me.

Destruction is still going on in city, now in direction of Beh men chiao for we can still see clouds of smoke and fire. I suspect all shops from South Gate to Beh men chiao have been looted and burned. Looting is now being done by truck, and big things taken, such as rugs and beds. People say they are being taken to Giyung. Women coming in at gate this morning say that looting is still going on in private homes, and that even small money like coppers are being taken. Mary said a truck came to the college, asking for three girls; when she showed them our official letter they went away.

How Ginling looks as a refugee camp needs greater power of description than I possess.

Needless to say it would not receive any blue ribbon for cleanliness. When we had our first 400 refugees we had ideas of cleanliness and tried to have rooms and halls swept every day and paper picked up every day. Not so now. With 10,000 or more here we can do nothing except to persuade people not to use main campus as a toilet. Harriet's ideal of having grass walked on has been realized so fully that there is practically no grass left, and in many places—especially where they serve the rice, there are mud puddles.

The shrubs and trees have been badly used and some of the former have been trampled until they have disappeared. On every sunny day every tree and shrub and railing and fence is strewn with diapers and pants of all description and colors. When the foreign men come over they laugh and say they have never seen Ginling look thus.

To date we have had fourteen births and four deaths. Mrs. Tsen is the only nurse we have and she is terribly over worked.

Wednesday, December 29. Registration of the men of this district and many from the city in general continues. Long before nine o'clock a long line extends far beyond the gate. Today they were more severe than yesterday. Then they asked for ex-soldiers to confess, promised them work and pay. Today they examined their hands and selected men whom they suspected. Of course many who were selected had never been soldiers. Countless mothers and wives asked me to intercede in their behalf—their sons were tailors, or bakers, or business men. Unfortunately I could do nothing.

Mr. Wang, Mr. Hsia, Mr. Djao (your teacher, Eva, who now lives in East Court), went before seven and by ten had completed registration—the rest will go tomorrow morning at 6:30. They seemed to have no difficulty. It is reported that the registration slip means little to the common soldier and has been torn up by them in several instances.

This afternoon I went over to the American Embassy. No foreigner has as yet returned, and they have no exact word as to when one will return. To date we are still cut off from the outside world and no foreigner from outside has been able to get in—to any Embassy or business firm, and it is more than two weeks since Nanking was entered. They say trains are beginning to run to Shanghai for military supplies.

This morning I went with a group of the men who sell hot water on the campus in order to help them get a cart load of coal—they were afraid to go alone lest they and their cart be taken. As I was standing in front of the coal shop waiting for the loading to be finished, a woman came up and began to talk. She said she was from Hsia lingwei, out near the National Stadium. She says that town has been completely burned, first partially, by Chinese military, and then completely, by Japanese soldiers. Of her family of ten, three are left—she, her husband and one grandson. Her two sons, three daughters-in-law and one grandson are scattered, and she has no idea where they are. This is but one of many such tragedies we hear about every day.

There are fewer soldiers in the city and therefore there is less looting, although some looting and burning still continues. Our refugees are slightly fewer. Rice could only be served once today because of registration. The campus is a field of mud.

Tonight we again have an Embassy police and our three watchmen are on the job.

Friday, December 31. Registration took place this morning—not of 260 college women, but of about 1,000 refugee women between ages of 17 and 30. By 9 o'clock they were lined up in front of Central Building and given a discourse—first by the Japanese military official, and then by Mr. Jan Yung-gwang—both in Chinese. They were told a number of things which I did not hear, but the things I heard were, "You must follow the old custom in marriage, letting your parents make arrangements for you. You must not go to theaters, study English, etc. China and Japan must become one, and then the nation will be strong, etc." After the lecture they marched single file one line to south and one to north through the frames we have made for selling cooked rice. Most of the women and girls got their first tickets, but about twenty were singled out because they looked different—either had curled hair, or dressed too well. Later these were all released because a mother or some other person could vouch for them. Once in awhile I can "Count a blessing." Today the blessing was that we had no college or Middle School students on the campus.

After the women were through the men were again allowed to register. Du, the gateman, said that men began to form in line this morning by 2 o'clock. At 5 I heard them out at Ninghai as far down as the Practice School. Registrations have now ceased until Jan. 3.

This afternoon I did not go to the office—did nothing but wind some yarn and that seems to be about as much mental effort as I am capable of these days.

M.S.B. [Bates] came in this afternoon and brought us a bit of news. Rumor says that people are being asked to evacuate from Kuling; that Chiang has ordered Canton to be turned into "scorched earth" before it is evacuated. Mr. Cola, a young white Russian, has been down Tai Ping Road (Hwa Pai Lou) and reports there is nothing left of it—the big stores, on both sides were evidently thoroughly looted first and then burned.

This evening at 7 in our upper room, we had a service, to end the old year and usher in the new with prayers of forgiveness and of thanksgivings [sic]—

for there have been blessings and miracles in the midst of the suffering and sorrow and these we cannot forget. After service we went down to living room and had some canned pineapple.

This morning a very fine Japanese called, a Mr. Endo, who has his headquarters in what was the Metropolitan Hotel. I liked him very much, also the military police with him. They had kind and understanding faces. Mr. Endo said he was deeply interested in the refugee work and offered to help later. At noon Major — called—he was the one who called at midnight soon after December 13.

What does the New Year hold in store for China, for Nanking and Ginling? We must not lose faith.

Saturday January 1, 1938. New Year's Day! The first day of the year—1938. The words "Happy New Year" die on one's lips and one can only say "May you have peace." There were nine of us at our 7:30 fellowship service—which we try to have daily now. Since we are still so completely cut off from the outside world our prayer for others is becoming imaginary—we know not in what condition our friends are.

The morning was uneventful save for a surprise breakfast Mrs. Tsen gave us—pineapple, a kind of fried cake, and cocoa were added to our regular breakfast, and were a real treat.

At noon Mrs. Tsen and Mary went over to the Buck house for New Year's dinner—it was difficult to get Mrs. Tsen to go, for she is too sad and discouraged to feel like making merry. This afternoon I took my turn at staying in my office, and before four o'clock there were two events. About three, one of the servants came in hastily and said a soldier was taking off one of our girl refugees. I went out hastily and caught him with her in the bamboo grove just north of the library. He beat a hasty retreat when he heard my voice. Later I sent off two more soldiers who had come on campus at same time.

Some of the young girls on the campus are terribly foolish for they will not stay inside the buildings but wander out toward the front gate, in spite of all we can do.

Perhaps a half hour later three military advisers came to call. They were clean-looking men and seemed genuinely interested in, and sorry for, the plight of the refugees, which they blamed on Chiang Kai-shek! After they left I went to call on Mr. Jan Yung-gwang, an interpreter, to see if he can indirectly prevent further registration of men on our campus. We have been very careful about keeping all men—high and low degree—from bringing food in, or coming to see any refugee, but this registration of men has broken down that custom temporarily.

A great fire is burning over toward Beilimen chiao tonight—looting continues. We believe that the raping of women has decreased, although a few days ago twenty-seven women were raped on B. T. T. S. [Bible Teachers Training School] compound. We were told that the military police—who seem distinctly superior—rounded up a number of common soldiers (7) today for grave misdemeanor and, they think, shot them.

There was a great meeting in Drum Tower Park this afternoon at which time the new city officers were installed. Our district was asked to send 1000 representatives. There was a great array of the five colored flag and Japanese flag. I have not heard the details—but I know one of our representatives felt sick at heart about it and would eat no supper. Undoubtedly you will see the pictures of this spontaneous burst of enthusiasm for the new regime.

It is New Year' night and our Embassy police are not yet come—which worries us.

Monday, January 3. Registration continues—supposedly at eight places, but certainly at Ginling we have the crowds. By 8 a.m. the Japanese guards had arrived, and by 8:30 the lecturing had started—first to women, and then to men. The method worked out yesterday by the Chinese of the new "Self Government" organization was completely and rudely discarded by the Japanese official in charge—at least at Ginling. During the morning I went to the University and found that they were registering there and at the Agriculture Building, but crowds are small compared to ours. For us it means cutting down rice to one meal a day which is terribly hard on the children, but I rather think men prefer to register here where some of their women folk can bear witness, in case they are taken for soldiers. We have no trouble from stray soldiers as long as registration is going on on the campus. Wrote a letter or petition for five women today, trying to help them find their husbands.

Tonight Wei, the messenger boy, told me his story in full. On December 14 he was taking letters, first to International Committee and next to the Hospital. Near the Drum Tower he was stopped by two soldiers, one put a bayonet at his stomach, the other a gun back of him. The American Embassy sleeve band which he was wearing was torn from his arm, my letter was taken from him and torn up, and the chit book he was carrying was thrown away—and of course his bicycle was taken. He was forced to go to Hsia Gwan, where for ten days he did nothing but carry loot for them, and load it on trucks. He said he saw hundreds and hundreds of people killed—some soldiers, some civilians, some old, some young. Everywhere there were dead bodies. Very few houses seem to be left standing—he remembered the Yangtze Hotel and Episcopal Church property as still standing. He said the furniture that was not carted off was used as fuel— *not* in stoves, but in bonfires. The next two days he was taken to a house just west of Central University, and again continued to carry loot. At last he was made to carry things to Giyung, starting before dawn and reaching there long after dark—without food or drink for the entire day. After the eighteen men reached there, they were given a statement of dismissal and told they could return to Nanking. Although the journey in the dark was dangerous, they decided to risk it. Again and yet again they were stopped at point of bayonet, but finally reached Nanking. In the end all but two of them were taken to do more carrying. He said that every pond they passed was filled with dead bodies of people and animals—but in spite of it they had to drink to quench thirst. He arrived home on December 28—thin and exhausted. Even now he is still too tired to get about.

Two young women came in to my office this afternoon and wanted me to help find their husbands. Of the three brothers in the family two were taken on December 14. The family kept a duck shop near South Gate.

Women are gradually learning to stand in line to buy rice—and they think it is a much better method than crowding and fighting for it.

Shanghai Road today near us looked like Fu-Dz Miao at China New Year. Some foods can now be bought. We have killed Dr. Yuen's goat for meat for ourselves and servants. No meat can be purchased yet.

Friday, January 7. Registration for women finished about three today. The methods used the last two days have been most satisfactory, and have taken the strain and fear from the women, as the work is all done by Chinese. There is only a small guard of Japanese soldiers off at one side. A few Japanese Embassy police are on hand to cooperate with Chinese police. At noon I passed a small group of women hurrying in, who said they had come from 17 li west of Nanking. They feel that if they have registered then they will be safe.

This morning a group of Japanese officers together with one military police, called. They said they were connected with the postal service. When two of them went out of my office they saw some gospels in Chinese and asked if they might have them.

Blanche is still in bed with a very bad cold but is better today. The weather is considerably colder but still clear and sunshiny. Groups gather to the south of the buildings and get warm in the sunshine.

This morning I wrote the report requested by the three Americans who arrived yesterday at the Embassy. It will help to have them back. It seems they did not wait for permission to come, but just sent word that they were arriving at a certain time. I also took over a letter to Ruth, Florence and Alice, for a ship is going to Shanghai today and will take it. It is difficult to know what to write for one does not know how drastic censorship is in Shanghai.

Today the Red Cross started a new system for serving *lisi-fan* (rice) to people on our campus. Heretofore it has been served at two places in our main quadrangle. From now on it will be sold at the kitchen, which is just north of and across the road from our faculty garden.

For the first time we received scraps of radio news today. It brought us word of what we have been fearing—that with these moonlight nights there are bad air raids in Hankow. In such a crowded city that would be terrible. Hangchow is reported to have become a city of horrors like Nanking. God pity the poor! May they be spared our ten days reign of terror!

I went to 3 Ping Tsang Hsiang at 4:30. Tung Kao-ban, still living down at our carpenter shop, went with me—as I still think it is better not to go out alone lest something should happen. Several of the men are greatly worried about their wives, especially P. Mills and L. Smythe. (They were in Kuling, later in Hankow.)

The men on the Safety Zone Committee have done magnificent work, giving all their time and energy for the good of the large group of Chinese—letting their own homes be looted. The German business men have been great, too, and there has been excellent team work. Rabe, chairman, has been fearless.

Sunday, January 9. Sunshine, but quite cold. One half inch of ice on ponds. No refugees sleeping in covered ways and verandahs, but some still in halls. Many come for the night and go to their homes for the day. Many of the problems of poor Searle at the University, Sericulture Building and middle school we have not yet had—i.e. quarreling among Chinese in charge, and then one side reporting to the Japanese. Also bringing in of loot by refugees and then quarrel over it ensuing. Also the problem of spies within.

Mr. Wang, Mr. Li, Miss Hsueh and I went to Drum Tower to church service. You cannot imagine the dense crowd of people on Shanghai Road, mainly in the section between Ningpo Road (American Embassy) and north to Gin Ying Giai. On both sides of the road are hundreds of venders now starting up small shops. I'm sorry to say that most of the things they are selling are loot from shops. Our servants are beginning to buy it too, for the temptation is great. Church service was good, and about fifty people were out. You see much traffic on Chung Shan Road now, mainly Japanese trucks and cars. Also many soldiers in the section outside the Safety Zone.

Mrs. Twinem helped at 2 o'clock women's meeting. The South Studio was filled. Miss Lo has charge of the meeting. We also have a Thursday meeting for women. Tonight at the servants' meeting the South Studio was packed, probably by many who came out of curiosity.

Fourteen of us attended the English service at 4:30. John Magee led. Mr. Espey of the Embassy attended and for the first time I really learned that the U.S.S. *Panay* was sunk and at the same time two Standard Oil boats. It seemed to be a deliberate act on the part of Japan—why, I cannot understand. In all my contacts with Japanese soldiers and officers they seem friendly to the Americans, but invariably warn me against Russians and English. We are rejoicing over the fact that three British officials arrived today—that now makes six additions to our numbers, which means more stability.

Nice Mrs. Tsen "looted" Eva's house today—which by the way has not been entered once—and having found some extracts she had our old cook Chen Ben-li make a cake, which we had at supper. She intended to give it to No. 3 P.T.H. [Ping Tsang Hsiang?] but when we told her they had a good cook, and often had cake and cookies, she let us have the cake. Mary and I are going to have him make some mince pies before long—for Mary found that they had not taken the mincemeat from her house.

Dr. Trimmer says that a Japanese store has been opened on Chung Shan Road. Mr. Riggs spends all his time delivering coal to the rice kitchens, and Mr. Sone spends his time delivering rice. Had it not been for their toil I suspect many would be starving.

Thursday, January 13. A month ago today the city was entered. Some progress made—Looting and burning less, slightly more sense of security, only a few soldiers—especially in Safety Zone, raping of women practically stopped in the Zone. Outside we only hear talks and do not know acts. Looting going on, not only by soldiers but also by "beh sing."

Spent goodly part of morning trying to work out problem of five young women short course nurses—who came to us for shelter and protection. Did not feel we could take them all—endanger them as well as other refugees. Selected five camps, including our own, and let them draw lots. Later wrote letters of introduction for them and sent a servant with them. Wu, our messenger boy, since his bitter experience, is afraid to go outside our gate.

This afternoon spent almost four hours trying to get rice delivered to the college. Finally succeeded in getting in twelve bags. The International Committee has given over the handling of it to the Autonomous Government and they are having all sorts of difficulties. They have had their sales depot over near Hillcrest but now will be forced to move it out of the Safety Zone—why, we do not know. They are now getting rice from the Japanese—formerly Chinese military rice. Heard Mr. Riggs say that today he went to seven coal shops and there is no coal to be had. Fuel is a growing problem. Houses and furniture will increasingly be used for fuel unless somehow it can be brought in from outside.

Food that will keep people well is also a problem. Practically no green vegetables left anywhere in the country side. With 70,000 soldiers living off the land for a time there are few or no chickens, pigs, or cows left. Donkeys are being killed for meat, and horses also. Some one saw horse meat for sale today. An effort is being made to get beans, peanuts, and green things from Shanghai.

Mary, Mrs. Tsen and Blanche still in bed with colds, and Mr. Chen up, but not out.

Two hundred attended Miss Lo's meeting for women this afternoon—the fact that there was to be a meeting was kept very quiet. Wish there was a good person here who could give whole time to this work.

Monday, January 17. Raining today. The sunshine which has been such a blessing has left us. Mud-bed—you should see building.

For several nights now we have not had a soldier guard at the gate, nor even an Embassy police. Last Saturday I reported this at Japanese Embassy but nothing has been done about it. Not many soldiers seen in Safety Zone. Unfortunately the Chinese police now have little power.

Wasted whole morning. No creative energy left. Have many things to do but cannot seem to get them done.

This afternoon at 2 we began a series of meetings at which the workers from the Episcopal Church are helping us. Five days a week they will come and give the same talks to five different groups. Last night in the Arts Building we distributed 200 tickets to the women who really wanted to come. They are not to bring children, and no girl under 14 is to come. They were so orderly and the ushers had no difficulty with them. They learned to sing the simple hymn very quickly and very well. Tonight we distributed 200 tickets to the women in the Science Building and they will come tomorrow afternoon. They listened most attentively this afternoon. The South Studio was well filled. I am so glad there are enough workers in the city to carry on such meetings. Have sent to Shanghai to N.C.C. for new tracts.

Tonight we have been watching the great clouds of smoke to the south— probably outside the south gate. At times the dark sky is aglow with the flames. Destruction still continues. How much of Nanking will remain depends on how long the looting by soldiers and populace continues. People are being urged to return to their homes but how dare they do so. The older women are gradually going, but the young girls remain.

No soldiers have come to campus today. Mary and Mr. Forster went down to South City and also to the Foreign Cemetery. The latter has sustained no other injury than a hole in the surrounding wall. Of all the streets they visited Tai Ping Road seems to be the most completely and ruthless destroyed.

A month ago tonight the 12 girls were taken from our campus. Will we ever forget the horror of that night?

Thursday, January 20. Snowing today, but not too cold. You can imagine what buildings look like with mud and slush being tracked inside. Am not sure we shall ever be clean again.

Mr. Wang and Mr. Swen continue to write data for those women whose husbands or sons were taken and have not returned. One woman has just told me that her husband of 58 and son of 17 were both taken on December 16 and that only she and her little daughter are left. I doubt if she could have saved them had she stayed at home—those terrible days—but who knows? Mrs. Tsen does not think I should hand these in to Mr. Fukuda—that we must never forget that China is the hated enemy and Japan does not care how much she makes her suffer. In a day or two I will see Mr. Fukuda and tell him about the many women who are employing me to help them and ask if there is anything that can be done.

This morning I spent beginning a report to the Board of Founders. So much has happened that it is difficult to condense into a brief report. In the midst of my writing I was called to my office to confer with a young Japanese officer who was about to leave Nanking and who wanted us to take two young Chinese girls, one of 20 and one of 14, who are now living over near the Wai Giạo Bu. He said it was quite unsafe for them to live there—which I thought interesting, since refugees are bring urged to go home! I explained very clearly how uncomfortable it is here as a refugee and let him see how the women are living. It will be interesting to see if he brings them. I really hope they do not come. My guess is that he has become interested in the older girl and is afraid to leave her in her own home outside the Safety Zone.

A radiogram came from Rebecca today and was delivered to me from the American Embassy. Will send the answer tomorrow. Have been informed that our Embassy has a sending station now.

Meetings this afternoon were splendid. The one for the women was attended by about 170 and that for children by abut 150. Tonight Mary and I distributed tomorrow's tickets in one of the dormitories and some of the women begged for them. We still have too many people on the campus to do anything constructive.

Those of you who remember Shanghai Road as wide would scarcely recognize it now. This afternoon I counted 38 newly constructed shops on the right side of Shanghai Road as I went between Hankow and Ningpo—the latter is just north of the American Embassy. Of course they are rudely made of either matting or wood but they seemed to be doing a thriving business in selling food or looted materials of various kinds. Some were tea shops and others were restaurants. Very few people are brave enough to live outside the Safety Zone as yet.

Mr. G — of Red Cross Society said that when he went out to get rice on January 17 he saw great heaps of bodies of men outside the Han Chüng Road. The people in vicinity said they were brought there about December 26 and killed by machine guns. Probably the men who admitted at time of registration that they had been soldiers at one time and were promised work and pay if they confessed.

Friday, January 21. Today the weather has been almost mild in spite of the snow on the ground. Mud is our problem now. The hundreds who go out to the Rice Kitchen to purchase rice and the other hundreds who bring in food to their relatives here, bring into buildings more mud than we are able to cope with.

Soon after the noon meal, as I was going over to the northwest dormitory to announce the afternoon women's meeting, several refugees came running toward me saying there were soldiers on the back campus. I went toward the back gate just at the right time, for four soldiers saw me and released three girls whom they had taken from the refugee huts that are near Farmer Tsü's house. The soldiers disappeared over the hill. A very short time later a group of military police came on the campus and I was able to report the incident to them. Still later two officers came—said they were stationed out at Nanking.

During the last few days sad, distraught women have reported the disappearance of 568 (?) husbands or sons since December 13. They continue to hope that they have been taken off to work for the Japanese Army but many of us fear that their bodies are with the many charred ones in a pond not far from Gu ling Temple, or among the heap of unburied, half-burned bodies outside the Hau Djung Gate. On December 16 alone 422 were taken—and that is the report of women mainly on our campus. Many young lads of sixteen or seventeen were taken, and one boy of twelve reported as missing. All too often the one taken was the only bread earner in the family.

Our afternoon meetings for women and children continue. We are beginning on plans for a rehabilitation school for women without support.

At five went over to our Embassy and had a most satisfactory talk with Mr. John Allison, senior secretary. He is anxious for us to report any violation of American rights. Cannot convey to you what it means to poor old Nanking to have the official representatives of Germany, England and America back to plead and act in our behalf. Mr. Allison seems very understanding.

In the new newspaper that is being published called "Sin Shun Pao" in the January 8th number there is an article entitled "Japanese Troops Gently Soothe the Refugees. The Harmonious Atmosphere of Nanking City Develops Enjoyably." There are 25 sentences in the article, 4 sentences are true, one about the sun, the Drum Tower, military police and the position of the Japanese flag; one is half true, 19 are false and one is unknown to me. Not a very high score on a true-false test!

Sent a radiogram to Rebecca today.

Last night at En Tiao Hsiang—within the Safety Zone—soldiers went four times to the home of Mr. Wang's relative. They tried to take a young girl, who was able to make her escape, and three other times they did petty looting. You can see why we cannot persuade our women refugees to go home.

Monday, January 24. This morning started typing informal report but did not get far when Mr. Forster came in with a good deal of news. He told us the facts about what happened at the Embassy last Saturday evening.

It seems that Mr. Allison and the others were at dinner, George Fitch and P. Mills being guests, when one of the servants came in and reported that two soldiers were in the #3 garage. Mr. Allison went out and he found them there playing mahjong. He told them to leave, and later, as he returned to the dinner table, he felt he had perhaps been a bit severe, and wondered if he had done the right thing. He had no more than gotten seated when another servant came saying that his daughter had been taken—he and his family living in the #5 garage. Mr. Allison said surely he must be mistaken for he had just ordered the two soldiers to leave the compound. But the servant said it was a third soldiers and that at first he had wanted his youngest daughter but the parents had absolutely refused. Mr. Allison then started out to look for the girl, and met her coming back. It seems that the soldier with the girl had been met by the two soldiers and the latter had said that he must let the girl go as he had taken her from the American Embassy. Although I do not wish to harm anyone, yet I have been glad about the shooting of Sir Kuat Hugeson, the bombing of the *Panay,* with the wounding of the Italian and American officials, and the taking of the girl from the American Embassy. As least such things catch the attention of Japan and Western nations.

Our afternoon meetings continue.

Right after the noon meal I went to our Embassy for a car which took me to the Japanese Embassy. In a conversation with Mr. Fukuda, I told him of the large number of women who had been imploring me to do what I could to get back their men folk some of whom were taken on December 13. He told me to bring him the data and he would do all he could, for he too felt sad about the situation. He will be surprised when I take him 532 data cards tomorrow.

When I was leaving our gate to go to the Embassy a young girl came up telling me that three soldiers had just entered her home and were carrying off young women. I went with her and found that the soldiers had already left, and the girls they had tried to get, being nimble and quick, had succeeded in getting out a back gate and running down to Ginling. As we walked back together the girl told me that when the soldiers first entered the city her father of sixty-seven and her little sister of nine had been bayoneted to death.

A good many aeroplanes—bombers—have gone westward today. Fires in the city are fewer, but they continue—one or two each day.

Tuesday, January 25. We are adapting ourselves to new conditions. For a time we closely curtained all windows and covered all lights with black shades— now we think it wiser to have lights to show that a place is inhabited.

Last night two servants foolishly shut all windows and put a coal ball stove in their room. This morning they were unconscious from carbon monoxide. Mrs. Tsen and I and all the others here worked to arouse them and by this evening they are considerably better.

From 9–12:30 there was a meeting of heads of Refugee Camps held at 5 Ninghai Road. If only there was an experienced social worker at the head of each camp or in each camp to study the needs, so that we could work constructively. It is so difficult to get at the true condition of each family, so easy to make people dependent instead of independent. Each camp is now working on an investigation of the most needy families. Encouraging word has come from Shanghai of funds raised, and of extra medicine like cod liver oil.

Wu Ai-djin, an evangelistic worker of the Presbyterian Church, who is a grateful and happy refugee here, started a phonetic class this morning for twenty girls. She is also helping with the afternoon meetings. If we had more workers and vacant classrooms we would begin some Bible classes.

This afternoon I took 532 blanks over to Mr. Fukuda and reported same at our Embassy. We also went to the secretary of the "Automatic Government"— the name given by Mr. Chen to the Nanking Autonomous Government, to see him about the possibility of excluding from the Safety Zones the shops that sell loot. The fact that hundreds of little shops are starting up along Ninghai and Shanghai roads means that more and more looting is being done each day by the poor. They would not have dared to start it if the Japanese soldiers had not led the way.

How we devour the bit of news that comes to us each day from the foreign men. They very generously write down the broadcasts they hear and send them to us. How we wonder about the friends who evacuated to Hankow, Wuchang, Changsha, and Chungking. It sounds from the broadcasts as if Chungking is having air raids, too. It all seems like a hideous dream—the scattering of friends, the breaking up of schools, the terrible destruction of life, and property. Can it be true?

Rickshas? I haven't seen one on the street since December 12—I believe it was. Many without tires or wheels can be seen hidden away but none are plying the streets. We walk, or go in cars.

Went with Mrs. Tsen over to Grace Chu's home this afternoon—but not to a tea. The house is filled with refugees—and you cannot imagine the condition it is in. Mrs. Tsen brought home some of the things still left—most of her things are gone—radio, dishes, etc., some taken by soldiers and the rest by refugees.

Friday, January 28. Much aeroplane activity all morning. Heavy bombers that are carrying death and destruction pass over our heads in a northwesterly direction. It seems to us here that all of China is being destroyed. I wonder so often what has happened to Lu Chowfu.

Spent all morning working on letters to the outside world. We have an opportunity to get them off on U. S. S. *Oahu* if we get them to the American Embassy by 9:30 tonight. I will leave here by 5:30, for I do not go off campus at night—have not done so for years it seems—as a matter of fact since December 12.

This afternoon there was a meeting of heads of the districts in the Safety Zone called at the headquarters of the Automatic Society—the name used by Mr. Chen and which we think too exact to change. A Japanese officer was present. The plan was announced that all refugees in the Zone must go back to their homes by February 4 and that all the mushroom shops on the streets of the Safety Zone will have to be taken down after that date. Order is to be maintained in the city, and plans have been worked out so that soldiers found misbehaving can be reported and dealt with. Soldiers are to be in a restricted district. We devoutly hope all this may come to pass as announced.

Three philanthropic societies in the city are planning to distribute 1000 bags of rice and $2,000 in money to the most needy. We were granted—upon our request—$200 for vegetables and oil for our "free-rice" or red-tag group, now numbering about 1000 including children.

This morning about 10, a large envelope of mail was delivered at our gate, brought from Shanghai by one of the foreign ships. How famished we are for news of our friends! This evening after supper we had quite a party in Mrs. Tsen's sitting room reading the letters addressed to the group and such others as are of interest to all. So far we have had no foreign mail.

Among our refugees are four blind girls who are now living in a room in Mrs. Tsen's dormitory. They are such happy, eager girls and wait so eagerly for us to come to see them. They know our footsteps now. Took them to the service on Sunday afternoon and ever since they have been asking what certain phrases in the Lord's Prayer mean. Sometime I hope we can send them to Shanghai to Blind School.

Lights go out at 8:30 since we received our refugee family, so much of the evening I write by candle or lantern light. City electricity is restored in certain sections of the Zone. City water also on again, at least in Zone. No telephone service yet.

Lt. Col. Oka called this evening for a friendly visit. He took my first letter through to Ruth in Shanghai.

Sunday, January 30. No aeroplane activity today.

Occasional fire crackers heralding the China New Year give us a start—too near the time when guns and bayonets held away.

Church service this morning not so well attended. Can it be that people are staying home to prepare for China New Year? The streets between here and the University were dense with the crowd that packed them.

Afternoon service was by ticket, and only for women and girls who are either Christians or have attended Christian schools. Every seat in S.S. filled. Miss Lo gave a good talk on "Preparing for the New Year"—not in homes but in hearts. At the same time there was a Sunday School for the Children. Four lovely bouquets of poinsettias and pussy willows gave a festive look to the room.

Mary's turn to go to English service at #3 Ping Tsang Hsiang. She learned that George Fitch went to Shanghai yesterday by same boat that took our mail—a British gunboat. He is the second person allowed out. In imagination we followed him to the service at the Community Church. How eagerly those women with husbands there, pressed him for news. He received promise that he would be allowed back. I wonder? The men at No. 3 have provisions from Shanghai—milk, butter, baking powder, canned goods. How their cook must be rejoicing after these lean weeks for the larder! Cakes or cookies were an impossibility for a good many weeks.

The service for servants this evening was in the form of a New Year's Eve service—forgiveness for the past, strength for the new and its unknown road. There is a fine spirit among the servants. They have been loyal, and they have had heavy work.

The International Committee sent two gifts of money—which we are using as tips for the extra servants who have had only their food, and for extra food for all. Pork is 70 cents a pound today. Extra vegetables and oil for the free rice group were served.

Monday, January 31. If fire crackers have the power to drive away evil spirits and usher in a New Year of prosperity, then surely the coming year will be one of great happiness and bounty. Early, long before it was light, the fire crackers began to go off; not singly, but in boisterous confusion; and they continued more or less through the morning. It is a dismal, muddy day for which I am sorry, as it seems that China New Year ought to be one of sunshine. While you do not feel like using the old set phrases of "Congratulations, may the New Year be as you like it," "May you grow rich," I found I could say with deep meaning "May the New Year be one of peace!"

After the women and children's meetings this afternoon, the old gardener and I started out to see if we could purchase some sprays of "lah mei" or "twelfth month plum" from the farmer from whom I got such glorious branches last year. We went north on the road west of our campus. On our way there we passed two unburied bodies—one has been there since the middle of December. The country to the west of the road is a veritable no-man's land, with no sign of life. Every little house has windows boarded and doors barred. When we reached the temple district it looked too deserted for us to venture past it to the farm house, at some distance beyond, even for a spray of "lah mei," and so we turned back. When we came almost to our campus we turned up the hill, and there were still the bodies of the three men whom I heard shot about December 16, and who looked to me like civilians. At the gardener's home he insisted on serving me a steaming bowl of chicken soup and poached egg. He, too, should be a character in a Book of Earth, for he is so typical of the industrious farmer of China, so close to the soil.

When I arrived on the campus several large groups of young girls crowded around me begging to be allowed to stay after the 4th of February, the day set by the "Automatic" Society for the return of refugees to their homes. What a dilemma they are facing.

Tuesday, February 1. Day fairly clear and mild. Again there is aeroplane activity, heavy planes to northwest. The blimp is also up today—over near Pukow. Why so near we do not know.

At nine this morning in the six refugee buildings we began our own registration of refugees for we want to find out more details about each family before they go home. There are two of our helpers in each building doing this work. It will take two days to complete the work. Mr. Wang and Francis Chen went to the meeting of heads of Refugee camps. It seemed best for Mr. Wang to go in my place since they are discussing the important problem of the return of refugees to their homes. The greater part of meeting was filled with reports of outrages on men and women who have tried to go to their homes. How the young women can go to their homes is more than I can imagine—and why the heads of the military want them to do so also passes my comprehension, for the stories of mistreatment and outrages will be greatly multiplied. The people at the meeting felt that since a high military official is coming that it might be possible to get the date postponed.

Just before noon a woman of thirty-nine came to talk over her troubles. This morning she persuaded a man, who worked in the family where she worked, to go back to their home to get things that might still be there. The woman was seized and raped by 5 soldiers, and the man was slapped and relieved of $9.00. The woman's husband was taken on December 27 and has not returned. Just after this woman left my office, another of fifty-seven came in. She and her husband had gone home on Sunday. Her husband had been forced out of the home and two soldiers had mistreated her. Women do not willingly tell me these tales for they feel the disgrace of it too deeply. How can young girls be asked to go home. Again today, every time I went across the campus a group would gather and implore me to make it possible for them to stay. How my heart aches for them!

This morning, thanks to John Magee for loan of his car, Mary and Mrs. Tsen took two old men down to Christiana Tsai's home to see if they can protect what remained of that fine old residence. It has already been badly looted, but some of the heavier mahogany furniture was still there. Blanche Wu and I at 1:30 went over to the National Research Institute in the eastern part of city. What a sickening sight it was! Houses and shops everywhere are burned or looted clean. We saw practically no one about but soldiers. In the Institute, three of the five major buildings were burned and we could see the charred remains of the great herbarium—the work of years. The biology building had been looted but not burned. We went to Dr. Ping's office and tried to collect what seemed to be the remains of his research data. We shall try to get some old and reliable men to go over there to be caretakers and preserve what is left. After we returned Mrs. Tsen and Mary went out again—this time to Mary Chen's home. What a sight it was—everything looted and mutilated. What will be left of old Nanking by spring?

Tonight we had a special meal for our staff, and at the end we each had half of a honey orange and some chocolate.

Thursday, February 3. Snowing steadily. Quite cold. Finished our local registration in all but the two academic buildings where there are perhaps more than 900 per buildings. Lewis Symthe called this morning and again this afternoon, to discuss methods of distributing cod liver oil and powdered milk to the babies and sick children. He also says that the Safety Zone Committee want all of us in charge of Camps to remain at our posts tomorrow—the date set for refugees to go home.

What a fearful decision is before the people—to go to their homes, where they are still in very grave danger of being robbed or stabbed, and the women of being raped. Part of our strength today was used in urging older women to go home—in spite of risk and danger—and thus make it safer for the young girls to remain here.

Mrs. Li—former matron of women's dormitory at Seminary was sent over by young women in Seminary Camp. When that camp is disbanded they want to come over here. They have heard a fantastic tale that we are going to take all the young girls to Shanghai on a boat.

Mr. Forster called and brought radio news which he and John Magee have kindly written out for us. Also told us that a Mr. Bishopric of the International Export Company, who has been in the city for a number of days, is going to Shanghai tomorrow morning by car, and will take mail which will probably be placed in an Embassy sealed envelope. This is another opportunity to get letters off—if we have time to write them.

I have a sore, inflamed eye tonight which Mrs. Tsen has treated and bandaged. I now have more sympathy for the four blind refugee girls. How can they be so cheerful.

Friday, February 4. This is the day of terror for the poor women and girls—the day when they should go to their homes. What the day will bring forth we do not know. We are not expecting to force people to go home—they must take the responsibility.

During morning five girls came over from B. T. T. S. saying that camp was disbanded yesterday, that they had gone to their homes, that soldiers had come in the night, that they had scaled the wall of their home and run back to B.T.T.S. They want to come here. We are fearful about taking them lest we have a deluge which will bring added danger to the 4000 or more that we still have. Later in the day we decided to let them come. If in the next few days girls who have gone home from other camps find they cannot remain at home, we will have to receive them and take the consequences.

At ten and at 12:30 two military police called and inspected some of the buildings. Said they had come to see if we were all right—although they may have had an additional purpose. We explained that many had gone home—we had ten thousand, but now only about 4000. We also tried to make it clear that some of our refugees are from Shanghai and Wusih and other places and cannot go home until communications open up; that others have had their sons or husbands taken, the breadwinners of the family, and have no means of support; that still others have had their houses burned and have no homes to which to return.

At 3 p.m. two Embassy Police and a Chinese came and asked us to get all the refugees together so they could explain to them the plan of returning to their homes. We suggested that we get those in the Science Building into the big lecture room and they begin with that group and thus take building by building. This plan they approved—but stopped with the first building. It is no easy thing to make a group of refugee women understand. The three points were—

1. All must go home. Military police, ordinary police and special district organizations will protect them. (There are four special districts in city.)
2. If husbands have been taken or homes burned, or if they are very poor, they should report to the Special District Organization.
3. Hereafter there will be no protection for Safety Zone—only the four districts will be protected. You must not bring property back into Safety Zone.

The Chinese man lingered long enough to let us know in a whisper that he felt young women were not safe and that they should remain with us.

At 5:30 p.m. Plumer came to talk over plans for Relief, also reported no forcible eviction in any camp. At 5 p.m. about 200 young women came to Kowtow and beg to remain. We have had no thought of forcing them to go. Later when Plumer went they had quite a demonstration in front of his car, weeping and kowtowing. Poor youngsters.

Saturday, February 5. Spring started yesterday according to Chinese calendar. Today the sunshine is quite warm—snow has all melted.

Because of inflamed eyes and a touch of tonsillitis, I have been in my room all day. Mr. Wang has been in my office all day—to receive guests, and to classify the missing men according to professions. If possible I want to see Mr. Hidarka about the matter. Rest of staff have been working on classifying the data which they have spent three days of this week in securing. Relief from the International Committee will depend upon our recommendations. How inadequate the staff of trained workers in Nanking is to cope with this huge problem! Five of us spent three hours this afternoon making the recommendations for our group.

Four of the women who went home yesterday came back this morning. One of these, a woman of 40, in going out of city gate yesterday was relieved of $3.00 by the guard, and a little farther on in her journey led off by another soldier to a dugout. When her captor saw a woman of twenty coming across the field, he released her. It is not strange that even the old women prefer to starve on our campus than to venture back to their home—or the remnants of homes. Some prophesy that within a week all will be back in the Safety Zone. Poor, poor women—what a dilemma to be in!

A good many young women have slipped in without even the gateman being aware of it. They are from disbanded refugee camps. Yesterday we tried to prevent a rush from other camps to ours.

Today we think we have about 4000 refugees still on the campus—the large majority being young women. To date we have had 37 births and 27 deaths, five of the latter were adults. Today we are trying to send girls from lower hall of Arts Building to rooms upstairs—and this will enable us to clean the hall-way—which it certainly needs. There are girls still occupying the glass enclosures under the stairway—people living in glass houses.

This afternoon the warning siren sounded quite distinctly—and what memories it recalled! Chinese planes were probably going to Giyung.

Monday, February 7. This morning there was a meeting of our women workers to reconsider our plans. We have assigned one person to each refugee building—her purpose for the week being to get better acquainted, to comfort, to work out best means of giving direct aid, and to talk informally about starting a class in home making and hand work—we are calling it a "class" and not a "school."

Mr. Wang came down this morning to report on cases of mistreatment . . . [of] older refugees who have gone home. The head of one of the disbanded camps brought his two daughters over today. He and his wife are trying to live down at Hugigiai (?) said that yesterday soldiers drove up in a truck and took all the good bedding from his neighbors—fortunately his was not new or very clean so his was spared. It seems that in several homes out near West Flower Gate the soldiers, failing to find young girls, are using teen-age boys.

So far the classified summary of the men reported missing by our refugees are, Business men, 390; Gardeners, farmers, coolies, 123; Artisans, tailors, carpenters, Masons, cooks, weavers, etc. 193; Policemen, 7; Firemen, 1; young boys (14–20 years) 9; total 723. The large majority of these were taken on December 16 and have not yet returned.

Typewritten radio news was brought to us this afternoon by John Magee. It looks as if Hofei is being endangered. How I wonder what conditions are up in the country!

Sunday, February 13. Raining heavily this morning. At last no sound of heavy bombers. Because of cough and sore throat am staying in today.

It has been reported to us that last night about midnight four to six soldiers went to Farmer Tsu's near our laundry, and pounded loudly on his door, demanded "hwa guniang." The door was not opened and they finally went away. I suspect those girls will be moving back to the college tonight.

About 3 p.m. two officers, a soldier and about four Chinese from the "Automatic Society" came on the campus and asked if we could find four washer women for them. Want women between 30 and 40. Will pay them in rice. They will come back tomorrow morning for them. In the meantime we shall do what we can to find some. I have also told our laundry man, who is quite willing to go if he can come home at night. Strange to say before I got back to the Practice School one woman came and applied for the work. I happened to know she has been raped by three soldiers. She certainly has courage.

George Fitch is back and has a promise of $200,000 for refugee relief. The question in my mind is how we can distribute that amount wisely.

More letters came in today and more packages from Shanghai. Our friends are too good to us. If we ask them to make purchases for us they make gifts instead. Quite a post office system is being started. Think I must have sent 20 letters for refugees yesterday—mostly to relatives in Shanghai asking for money.

A good letter from W.Y.F. today which was sent from Chengtu on January 27 and another from Catherine in Wuchang dated Jan. 28.

Tuesday, February 15. Spring birds are here. "Welcome the Spring" is opening in my living room.

This morning we have a group of refugees moving newspapers and magazines back to the attic of library—all that work of clearing the attic happily was in vain. Reason for moving is that we need to get at the bookcases which have been covered. Later Mr. Li and I spent about an hour back of Central Building trying to work out a better method of getting rid of night soil. We have trench after trench filled with it—and it is everywhere. It has become an everlasting problem which haunts us—and people say our camp has solved the problem more successfully than others! If we do not get lime soon, we shall all be in our graves from disease before the end of summer.

Yesterday I invested one dollar in pork which we had for dinner this noon. My, it tasted good!

One would like to know just how many Chinese soldiers were sacrificed in the attempt to hold Nanking. This morning a report came to me that the Swastika Society estimate about 30,000 killed around Hsia Gwan, and this afternoon I heard another report that "tens of thousands" were trapped at "Swallow Cliff"— Yen Dz Gi—there were no boats to get them across the river. Poor fellows!

A few weeks ago I told you how the many shops, tea houses and restaurants went up along the sides of Shanghai Road almost in a day, like mushrooms after rain. Today they are disappearing in the same manner, for the order has gone out that if they are not down by night they will be torn down. Good naturedly people are taking them down and carrying them away. I saw "The Happy People Tea House" disappear. Most of the things sold in them was loot, which some of us thought should never have been allowed in the Zone. I would like to be the head of the Sanitation of the city for a month or two and have a good corps of coolies under me in order to clean up the roads.

We hear that Mr. Ritchey, former Directorate of Posts for Nanking, is back in the city, and is to try to revive the postal service. Our only connection with the outside world is by way of gunboats.

Mary and I are planning to have a farewell tea for Mr. Rabe on Thursday. My living room will hold only 8 people, so we can have but five guests and for any refreshments we would like to serve we find we lack the most essential ingredients.

Thursday, February 17. Spring today. Much aerial activity. Anti-aircraft gun practice. Anniversary of that terrible December 17.

Again I am making the rounds with Mr. Li to try to get back campus cleaned up. Fearful condition back of Central Building at southwest corner—but Sone says we are clean compared to many. Room 304 had a real house cleaning. Women took out all their bedding and cleaned windows and floors. Hope this will become contagious.

Two officers and a soldier with interpreter called early this afternoon presumably to look around. How easy it is for us to suspect that every caller has a deep and sinister motive.

Spent about two hours working on accounts this morning. Have neglected them badly since December 1st. Fortunately there have not been many things to buy, so items are not many.

This afternoon Mary and I had our farewell tea party for Mr. Rabe, no easy thing to manage under present conditions. Guests were Mr. Rabe, Dr. Rosen, Mr. Allison, George Fitch, Mr. Ritchey and Searle. Mrs. Tsen helped us. We served a salad, opened our first box of chocolates, had oranges. The cake was not bad—kind of fruit cake made with Esther's mince meat, taking the place of fruit. Not a Chinese store open in Nanking yet, so one's menu must be adjusted to the foods in one's own depleted larder, or that of her best friends.

Mr. Allison was escorted by a Japanese guard, so we suggested he leave first, because Mrs. Tsen had heard that our women refugees wanted to see Mr. Rabe and implore him to stay. We were not prepared for the sight that met our gaze when we arrived in front of Science Building. Between 2 and 3 thousand women were there and as Mr. Rabe approached them they all knelt and began to weep and implore. He spoke a few words and then Mary got him away by a back path. I tried to get them away so that Dr. Rosen and Mr. Ritchey could leave but it was a difficult job—Mary again got them out while I tried to divert the attention and lead them to the other side of the quadrangle. After a long time we were able to get the car out—but not until the men must have been well on their way home.

Mr. Ritchey goes by car to Shanghai tomorrow. He reports that the post office will probably open soon under Chinese management.

Wednesday, February 23. Mr. Rabe left this morning. Took one servant with him. As far as I know this is the third Chinese who has been permitted to leave Nanking.

A mother brought in three young girls this afternoon and begged us to receive them. One is her daughter who went to the country in early December, the other two were country girls. They say it has been terrible in the country. Girls had to be hidden in covered holes in the earth. Soldiers would try to discover these hiding places by stamping on the earth to see if there were hollow places below. They said they had spent most of their days since December 12th in these holes.

This afternoon between five and six Francis Chen and I went around our campus by way of Hankow, Hugigwan and Canton Roads. We met a number of old men going back to the Zone for the night. They say that during the day the stealing of money continues. I put Mr. Chen's money in my pocket for fear we might meet the same fate. On Hugigwan I saw only four old people who were living there at night. Most houses are still boarded up. Truly it looks deserted and sad. Not a young person in sight and no normal activities going on.

At nine this morning two young girls came running to the campus from the street between the University and Ginling saying that soldiers were in their home and they had escaped. It chanced that Lewis was on our campus in a car so we both went over to the house. The soldiers had left, but one had relieved a poor man of $7.00 before going.

The planes continue to go over us to the northwest.

Tree planting and cleaning still continue on our campus. We have made a huge trench in the back hill and are about to begin one on the hill north of the library.

Mrs. Tsen, Francis Chen and I are trying to estimate the cost of refugees to Ginling, aside from injury to the buildings. The latter will be well over $2,000, I am sure. Our camp has been fortunate in many ways, but largely because we had only women and children, and because our people did not have to do cooking in their rooms.

Monday, February 28. Beautiful weather continues. Refugees love to wander out in sunshine. Gathering "greens" everywhere. Gardener taking out broken and trampled shrubs and replacing with better ones. Roof of Arts Building being repaired.

Tung Lao-ban has spent the day estimating losses due to refugee occupation. They amount to $6,800, roughly, for the six buildings. All woodwork will need repainting and all floors. Most walls need refinishing. Hardware such as window fasteners has been treated badly when they could not make it work.

Spent most of the day preparing a statement to send to New York which I sent over to the Embassy at five o'clock; also preparing a statement of losses due to Japanese military. Would that other people's losses were as light as ours!

Mary went to the hospital this morning with a miserable cold and deep cough; Blanche Wu returned from an eighteen-day stay there. She insists on living in Science Hall, and I am helpless to argue against it.

An officer and two soldiers called at 1:30 p.m. to see how conditions are on the campus. They also asked about number of refugees. I had a good opportunity to talk to them about the husbands and sons who have not returned. The officer reported that there are more than 1,000 captives in the Model Prison and they are soldiers and officers—no civilians according to his report.

About 3 p.m. four soldiers came on a sight-seeing trip. They were friendly and showed much interest in the Library. The brightest one had a map in his hand—he was evidently planning to see the sights of Nanking.

One of the men in the Swastika Society who has had charge of burying the bodies of soldiers and civilians, reported that bodies are now coming up from the Yangtze where they were thrown. He promised to give me a report of numbers.

Tuesday, March 15. Warmer today and glorious sunshine. Much aeroplane activity. We are told that there are new troops in the city—and that does not add to our peace.

At 9 o'clock went over to former Bank of Communications for a renewal of permit to transfer materials belonging to National Science Research Institute. We may be able to secure the use of a truck today, and would like to complete the moving process. If possible, we want also to bring over two pianos—of friends. Now I wish we had brought in such things before. Received a permit for a period of 5 days. Saw two Chinese there to whom I made my plea for release of civilians from Model Prison. I rather think they will try to do something about it.

Met my class at 10:30. It now has almost fifty enrolled in it. I wish I could really speak and write good Chinese.

At 11:30 went with J.M. to south city to take pictures of one of our tragedies —the woman of 48 who was raped 18 or 19 times and her mother of 76 who was raped twice. The story is vastly beyond heartless belief. Some of the south gate streets are still pretty much deserted, and even where there are people one sees few women excepting old ones. The whole of Mo Tson Road is a busy market place. There is much buying and selling—some one said the eight out of ten are in the business for there is nothing else to do. I suppose one reason people crowd together on the streets is because they feel safer that way. Danger to women is certainly less, but robbing is still going on. The pity is that Chinese often lead the soldiers to the home of a merchant where there is a bit of money, and a gun or bayonet makes it unwise not to hand it over.

The re-registration of our refugees has just taken place. There are now 3310. Fourteen new refugees have just been received—women and girls who evacuated to the country late last fall. Their money has all been used up, and the bandits are active; so they chose to face the perils of the return journey and Nanking. They probably have heard of the Safety Zone or of some Refugee Camp.

This morning in south city saw many soldiers, cavalry and common soldiers. How everything within me rebels to see them strutting down the street as if they owned it! Most of the shops we passed on the main street are either burned completely, looted completely, or boarded up. The former Chocolate Shop has been opened by the Japanese, but I did not notice the nature of the business.

Visit from two groups of soldiers today.

As I finish this page, I hear several bombers on their way back to Gi Yung from the north west. It is a clear moonlight night and nothing to hinder their flight.

Friday, May 13. Spent morning—or what was left of it in trying to work out a curriculum for J.—S. middle grade work for this autumn.

Here are two typical cases that came to my office this morning–
Giang Lao Tai and daughter called. Her story–

Has son of 53 who has had T.B. for years.

He has a wife and son.

Has another son of 33 who was earning $40 per month running a machine in a rice hulling shop. This son has a wife and four children from 3–10 years of age.

All nine were dependent on this one son of 33. Eight of the family evacuated north of river last fall and used up everything they had. The son of 33 was killed by the Japanese soldiers.

Then came a person telling me the story of Liu Lao Tai—a woman of almost 50 living down near San Pai Lou. She has three sons and two daughters-in-law. Four nights ago two soldiers came to her door about ten p.m., unable to push the door in they forced their way in through a window and found themselves in Liu Lao Tai's room. They demanded her daughters-in-law and when she refused and started to go for a military police, they cut two gashes in her face and one in her heart. She died from the wounds.

These two tragedies were told me today. Almost every day I hear others as heart-breaking. One cannot wonder that people ask you most pitifully, "How long will this terrible situation last? How can we bear it?"

Mr. Li and I went out between 5 and 7 this evening and accomplished several worthwhile errands. First we went to the Science Research Institute to see how the two old men were getting along. We tried to encourage the neighbors at the back to cooperate with the old men in protecting what little is left. Thence we went to see the old mother of Dr. Hwang Meng-yu, who has evacuated to Hankow. The old mother is trying to protect three large empty foreign buildings which were formerly used as a hospital. Instead of giving her an American flag as she had hoped we said we would send her two or three reliable refugees to live in her home and help her protect the place and thus she could assist some homeless people and they can assist her.

Huli, my good young watchdog is very ill tonight and I fear I will lose him.

Notes

1. RG8, B102. President Wu, refers to Wu Yifang, graduated from Ginling College in 1919, acted as the president of Ginling from 1928 to 1951. Mrs. Thurston, the first president of Ginling College.

2. The International Safety Zone changed its name Feb. 18, 1938.

3. It is Mills who takes the place of Rabe, Robert Sone acts as administrative director.

4. RG11, B134, F2698.

Robert O. Wilson

Robert O. Wilson was born in Nanking on October 5, 1906, son of Methodist missionaries William F. and Mary Rowley Wilson. Wilson graduated from Princeton University and received his M.D. from Harvard Medical school in 1929. He was appointed to the staff of the University of Nanking Hospital in 1935, arriving in 1936. Wilson continued working in the hospital throughout the Japanese occupation while most Chinese doctors had left Nanking well before the city was captured. Wilson's diary/letters to his family published in this volume describe the incredibly heavy load of medical work carried by Wilson with the help of his colleague C.S. Trimmer, and a few nurses, one of whom was the 67-year-old American Iva Hynds. Not until April 1938, when Dr. Lee of the St. Andrew's hospital at Wuhsi came to the university hospital with another doctor (apparently R.F. Brady) and two nurses, did Wilson and his staff get some relief. In early June 1938, Wilson was able to leave Nanking for a furlough in Shanghai.

Letters to Family (December 15, 1937–January 9, 1938)[1]

University of Nanking Hospital
Nanking, China
December 15, 1937

Dear Family:

You will have to pardon the unceremonious ending of the last installment. When I got home this noon I found that Smith and Steele were leaving for Shanghai on a Japanese destroyer. I had just time to rush upstairs and jamb the pages into an envelope which I addressed while they were starting the car. Page 35 is the carbon copy because I couldn't find the original. I didn't even have time to sign my name.

It would be interesting to see what are in the headlines of your papers. We received confirmation today of the sinking of the U.S.S. *Panay* on which all of us were supposed to be, by Japanese bombing. You undoubtedly have fuller information than we have. Our story says that an Italian newspaper correspondent and an American captain of one of the Socony river steamers were killed and a number wounded including Hall Paxton. The group were taken directly to Shanghai by the U.S.S. *Oahu* so that we have not seen any of them.

The hospital gets busier every day. We are about up to our normal capacity as far as patients go. There were about thirty admissions today and no discharges. We can't discharge any patients because they have no place to go. About ten of the hundred and fifty cases are medical and obstetrical and the rest are surgical. Neither of our Chinese doctors has the ability to care for them except under careful supervision so that keeps me humping.[2] Yesterday I wrote that I had eleven operations. Today I had ten operations in addition to seeing the patients on the ward. I got up early and made ward rounds on one ward before coming home to breakfast. After breakfast I spent the morning seeing the other wards and then started operating after lunch.

The first case was a policeman who had had a bomb injury to his forearm shattering the radius and severing about three-fourths of the muscles. He had had a tourniquet on for about seven hours and any attempt to stop the hemorrhage would have completely shut off the remainder of the circulation to the hand. There was nothing to do but amputation. The next case was a poor fellow who had a large piece of metal enter his cheek and break off a portion of the lower jaw. The metal was extracted as well as several teeth imbedded in the broken off portion of the jaw. Then came a series of cases under the fluoroscope with Trim's assistance. One fellow had a piece of shrapnel in his parotid gland, it having severed his facial nerve. Another had a bullet in his side. It had entered his epigastrium and gone straight through his stomach. He vomited a large quantity of blood and then felt better. His condition is excellent and I don't believe I will have to do a laparotomy on him at all. I got the bullet out of the side without difficulty. Another case had his foot blown off four days ago. He was very toxic and I did an open flap amputation of his lower leg. Another case was that of a barber bayoneted by Japanese soldiers. The bayonet had cut the back of his neck severing all the muscles right down to the spinal canal, through the interspinous ligaments. He was in shock and will probably die. He is the only survivor [of] the eight in the shop, the rest having all been killed.

The slaughter of civilians is appalling. I could go on for pages telling of cases of rape and brutality almost beyond belief. Two bayoneted cases are the only survivors of seven street cleaners who were sitting in their headquarters when Japanese soldiers came in and without warning or reason killed five or six of their number and wounded the two that found their way to the hospital. I wonder when it will stop and we will be able to catch up with ourselves again.

Saturday, December 18, 1937

(Two nights ago I was here in the same spot writing a page of this epistle and when I came to put it with the rest I couldn't find it. I hope the Japanese haven't located.) Today marks the sixth day of the modern Dante's Inferno, written in huge letters with blood and rape. Murder by the wholesale and rape by the thousands of cases. There seems to be no stop to the ferocity, lust and atavism of the brutes. At first I tried to be pleasant to them to avoid arousing their fire but the smile has gradually worn off and my stare is fully as cool and fishy as theirs.

Tonight as I came back from supper to stay here for the night I found three soldiers had ransacked the place. Miss Hynds had accompanied them to the back gate. Two of them arrived and the other had disappeared. He must be hiding somewhere around the place. I motioned the others outside stating in no uncertain terms that this was a Beikoku Byoyen [?]. How do you like that? The two that were there allowed themselves to be led out. They had taken Miss Hynds' watch and several other watches and fountain pens as well.

Let me recount some instances occurring in the last two days. Last night the house of one of the Chinese staff members of the university was broken into and two of the women, his relatives, were raped. Two girls, about 16, were raped to death in one of the refugee camps. In the University Middle School where there are 8,000 people the Japs came in ten times last night, over the wall, stole food, clothing, and raped until they were satisfied. They bayoneted one little boy, killing him, and I spent an hour and a half this morning patching up another little boy of eight who have [sic] five bayonet wounds including one that penetrated his stomach, a portion of oment [?] was outside the abdomen. I think he will live.

I just took time out because the third soldier had been found. He was on the fourth floor of the nurses' dormitory where there were fifteen nurses. They were scared within an inch of their lives. I don't know how much he had done before I arrived, but he didn't do anything afterwards. He had a watch or two and was starting off with one of the girl's cameras. I motioned for him to give it back to her and to my surprise he obeyed. I then accompanied him to front door and bade him a fond farewell. Unfortunately he didn't get the swift kick that I mentally aimed at him. One of the earlier ones was toying around with a rather formidable looking pistol which I'm thankful he didn't use.

One man I treated today had three bullet holes. He is the sole survivor of a group of eighty including an eleven year old boy who were led out of two buildings within the so-called Safety Zone and taken into the hills west of Tibet Road and there slaughtered. He came to after they had left and found the other seventy-nine dead about him. His three bullet wounds are not serious. To do the Japanese justice there were in the eighty a few ex-soldiers.

One girl I have is a half-wit with some sort of birth injury, I believe. She didn't have any more sense than to claw at a Japanese soldier who was taking away her only bedding. Her reward was a bayonet thrust that cut half the muscles of one side of her neck.

Another girl of seventeen has a terrific gash in the neck and is the only survivor of her family the rest of whom were finished off. She was employed by the International Export Company.

As I left the hospital for supper after finishing my rounds on the 150 cases now under my care the full moon was rising over Purple Mountain and was indescribably beautiful and yet it looked down on a Nanking that was more desolate than it has been since the Tai Ping Rebellion. Nine-tenths of the city are totally deserted by Chinese and contain only roving bands of plundering Japanese. The remaining tenth contains almost two hundred thousand terrified Citizens.

Last night Mills, Smythe, and Fitch went over in Fitch's car to escort Mills to Ginling. Minnie Vautrin holds the fort there with several thousand women. When they got to the front gate they were held up by a patrol of Japanese soldiers under the command of a pugnacious, impudent lieutenant. He lined the men on one side and Miss Vautrin, Mrs. Chen and Mrs. Twinem on the other side. He snatched the hats off the men and ordered everyone off the place including the women. Fitch told him he didn't have a place for them to stay but he insisted. They just got into the car when he ordered them back again and again harangued them for some minutes finally sending the men back where they came from. Later we learned that while this was going on some Japanese soldiers had climbed over the wall and helped themselves to sixteen women.

The population faces famine in the near future and there is no provision for winter's fuel. It is not a pleasant winter that we look forward to. It is too bad that the newspaper reporters left on the day they did instead of two days or so later when they could have been more detailed in their reports of the Reign of Terror.

Another interruption to usher two Japanese soldiers off the premises.

As I probably won't get much sleep tonight I had better turn in, dressed, to get what I can.

December 19. I guess it's Sunday

After writing last night's installment the night passed peacefully. I came home this morning to listen to a dozen more tales of plunder and rape. After writing an account of last night's visitation to the hospital I went with Bates, Smythe and Fitch to the Japanese Embassy. (They still call it that), and we talked with Mr. Tanaka, one of secretaries of the Embassy, who was formerly here in Nanking. He read over the account and listened to many other tales. He himself is sympathetic but has no control over the military and can only make representations like we do. There seems to be a very small glimmer of light but it is very faint and today was one of the worst days so far.

Practically every American house in the city was broken into. I dropped in at Daniels' on my way home. Three Japanese soldiers were in there when I got there. As I have said, my smiles have ceased and I ordered them out in no uncertain terms. They had broken into our locked room in the attic and everything in our big trunk was strewn all over the floor. Somewhat to my surprise, they actually ran down the stairs and out of doors. Probably they came back when I had gone but I can't stay there all day. The second floor is sacked clean. ... How thankful I am that Marjorie³ managed to get as much stuff away as she did, and that most of my useful clothing is over here.

Just as I came home to supper the Brady's cook and Mr. Chu who live where we were last summer had come in to get someone to go over there and interfere with the raping of all their women. Bates, Smythe and Fitch went over, caught three soldiers at it in the basement of the house and Bates sent them packing. Again, they will probably return as soon as all is clear. The Japanese are swarming all over the place and I fully believed that the hospital is the only building in town except the one we are in where someone has not been raped and I'm not sure that there wasn't some done at the hospital before I located the fellow on the fourth floor. A later account of that states that the fellow had undressed and gotten into bed with three nurses, each time the nurse yelled so that he hastily dressed and went out to see if anyone was coming. It was after the third that I arrived so think that I probably got there in time.

Another stunt today seems to be a big burning tear. Yesterday there were a number of fires but today several large blocks near Tai Ping Road were ablaze about supper time and one house about two hundred yards from us here was burned. From the hospital it looked as if this house was going up in flames and I didn't feel comfortable about it until I had finished my rounds and come home to find it still intact.

I made rounds on two wards this morning starting late because of the visit to the Embassy. This afternoon I took out the third eye I have operated on lately and did five other smaller operations, adding two pieces to my museum. Another day has passed without an amputation. At least four American flags have been torn down lately. Today at Hillcrest the flags were taken down and a woman raped and then bayoneted in the basement. A pool of blood was on the floor when Mills took a consular policeman from the Japanese there this evening. The woman apparently is still alive and has been taken to the hospital where Trim will see her as he is on call tonight. I will see her in the morning.

All the food is being stolen from the poor people and they are in a state of terror-stricken, hysterical panic. When will it stop!

December 21

This is the shortest day in the year but it still contained twenty-four hours of this hell on earth. We heard yesterday that the Japanese news agency, Domei, reported the Nanking population returning to their homes, business going on as usual and population welcoming their Japanese visitors, or words to that effect. If that is all the news going out of Nanking it is due for a big shake up when the real news breaks.

Huge fires are set in every business section. Our bunch has actually seen them set the fires in several instances. Yesterday before going home to supper I counted twelve fires. Tonight at the same time I counted eight. Several of them include whole blocks of buildings. Most of the shops in our vicinity have been burned. The populace is crowding into the refugee camps even from the private residences within the Zone as the degree of safety is slightly greater though there is no guarantee anywhere. If it were not for the way the International Committee had gathered rice beforehand and done what they could to protect the population there would be a first class famine already and the slaughter would have been considerably greater than it has.

Several more stories of the slaughter keep coming in. One man came to John Magee today with the tale of what happened to one thousand men led away from a place of supposed safety within the Zone. The bunch contained perhaps one hundred ex-soldiers that had given up their arms and donned civilian clothes. The thousand were marched to the banks of the Yangtze, lined up two deep and then machine-gunned. He was in the back row, fell with the others and played dead until, several hours later, the Japs had gone and he sneaked back to the city.

As we have seen a good many similar round-ups in this part of the city with no returns. We presume the same has happened to all of them.

Yesterday a seventeen-year-old girl came to the hospital in the morning with her baby. She had been raped by two Japanese soldiers the night before at seven thirty, the labor pains had begun at nine o'clock, and the baby, her first, was born at twelve. Naturally at night she dared not come out to the hospital so she came in the morning with the baby who miraculously seemed to be safe and healthy.

This afternoon I put a cast on a lovely little girl of 13. When the Japanese came to the city on the 13th she and her father and mother were standing at the entrance to their dugout watching them approach. A soldier stepped up, bayoneted the father, shot the mother and slashed open the elbow of the little girl, giving her a compound fracture. She has no relatives and was not brought to the hospital for a week. She is already wondering what to do when she has to leave. Both the father and mother were killed.

Day before yesterday at Hillcrest a young girl of nineteen who was six and a half months pregnant [tried] to resist rape by two Japanese soldiers. She received eighteen cuts about the face, several on the legs and a deep gash of the abdomen. This morning at the Hospital I could not hear the fetal heart and she will probably have an abortion. (Next morning: She aborted last night at midnight. Technically a miscarriage.)

Yesterday at lunch time some Chinese mechanics who live a few doors away from us asked what they could do with two young women at their place who were in danger. We suggested taking them to the University where they have finally established military police at night, and said that we would pick them up and take them ourselves. George Fitch and I started for them after lunch and had not got out of the door before the mechanics rushed up to say that the Japs were already there. He went to the place, Lewis, Smythe and MacCallum coming along. On arrival, the terrified Chinese round about pointed to the gate house of which the door was shut. We yelled and pushed the poor open to find three soldiers fully armed but only partially clothed at the time and the two women also disheveled but fortunately intact. One of the soldiers was extremely angry and did some threatening but it didn't come to anything and we took the girls to the University. The mechanics were afraid to stay there any longer when we left and so slept in our garage last night.

Yesterday the soldiers again made themselves at home at 5 Hankow Road. They were there for three hours in spite of a proclamation on the gate in Japanese by their own military, telling them to keep out. When the people in the place protested that they had no women (there were some in the cellar) they went out, picked up the first one they saw and spent three hours with her upstairs. There were three soldiers. When they came out, the girl was wearing one of Imogene Ward's best winter coats and most of her other valuable property went with them. What little we had left had been thoroughly sacked before. My microscope went yesterday.

This noon I went over with the cook, whose things were thoroughly looted yesterday. We picked up a few odds and ends, such as my cornet and the two or three pieces left of our silver. That in the hospital is intact. The little cups given us by Mr. Nyi had only half disappeared. How thankful I am for every kori [?] full of stuff that we got out in September.

The Americans composed a telegram yesterday asking for the immediate return of an American diplomatic representative. The Japanese military refused to send it in spite of the fact that they had said before that they would send messages. Today the entire American community and several Germans went to the Japanese embassy to put in protests. I was too busy to go.

We have every bed filled. There are only about —— [?] nurses out of our staff of twenty or so that have ever had any training, as far as I can gather. We have three male nurses on one of my wards and I'm sure that they are nurses only because they say so and think that is about the safest profession there is at present. I have a very sick case there with through and through wound of the chest wall. The chart naively told me that his temperature was 99, his pulse 80, and his respiration 24. Realizing that all was not well I retook them myself and found a pulse of 120, temperature 102.6 and respiration of 48. The little discrepancy is typical of the nursing on the floor.

This noon I came as near to being shot as I ever hope to be. On my way home the police in front of the girls' dormitory at the University told me that a Japanese soldier was inside and begged me to see to it. As that is getting to be an old story now I barged in and ordered him out in no uncertain terms. He was having them pump up one of their own bicycles for him to ride but I put a stop to that and kept urging him out. He also wanted to take a ricksha and bicycle pump along and I roughly objected to that but that is where I overplayed my hand as he had brought the ricksha along himself with the poor coolie in tow. We were now no longer friends and he proceeded calmly to load his rifle and play around with it a little. The Chinese then told me that he had brought the ricksha and pump so I told him to take them and get along which he did. He then went outside and as I passed loaded several more bullets in his rifle. I fully expected to be shot in the back as I went beyond him towards our house. He must have lost his nerve.

Christmas Eve

This seems like anything but Christmas Eve. It is sort of tough to sit in a small X-ray room to keep Japanese soldiers from looting a hospital in the center of what was a few weeks ago a great city while the rest of the family is scattered all over the globe. My baby will be six months old in four days and I have only seen her for seven weeks of that time.

The burning seems almost over. Only a half a dozen fires were started today to finish up the job of wiping out the shops on both sides of all the main streets. The looting continues. They carried off the Daniels' rugs today, one of them requiring four men to take. The poor people who stay in the house can of course do nothing about it and can only tell about it later. J. Loesing Buck has no idea how extremely lucky he is to date. His house, by virtue of the fact that there are eight Americans in it has so far been spared the ravages of looters. Thompson's[4] house next door has also been left untouched. The remaining houses are mere shells.

This morning Trim and I went over and rescued some eatables from the Gales' house. There were some preserves and canned fruit which are most welcome. Our larder is getting low with no prospect of replenishing. We also looked in at the Bishop's. Both houses have been pretty thoroughly sacked. I took the opportunity of dropping in at the Masonic Temple where I rescued my Chinese dress suit along with a half a dozen others. They had been through and broken most of the doors and windows and taken off a few things.

Tonight we invited Trim and three of the five Germans in town to Christmas Eve dinner. Mr. Rabe, head of the International Committee, didn't feel he could come and leave the 600 refugees that are crowding every corner of his house and yard. Every time he leaves them they are looted. He is well up in Nazi circles and after coming into such close contact with him as we have for the past few weeks and discovering what a splendid man he is and what a tremendous heart he has, it is hard to reconcile his personality with his adulation of Der Fuhrer. He has labored incessantly for the thousands of poor people that have crowded into the Zone. The other two Germans, Kruger and Sperling, have given themselves wholeheartedly to the work of the committee and its attempt to save some of these poor people. No one will ever know how many have been ruthlessly slaughtered.

One man who just got in today says he was a stretcher bearer and was one of four thousand marched to the banks of the Yangtze and machine-gunned. He has a bullet wound through his shoulder and dares not talk above a whisper and then only after carefully peering about to see if he is going to be overheard. One of the two burned wretches died this morning but the other is still hanging on for a while. Searle Bates went over this afternoon to the place described as the scene of the burning and found the charred bodies of the poor devils. And now they tell us that there are twenty thousand soldiers still in the Zone (Where they get their figures no one knows), and that they are going to hunt them out and shoot them all. That will mean every able-bodied male between the ages of 18 and 50 that is now in the city. How can they ever look anybody in the face again?

Simburg was back in the city today with some more horror tales. He says that the big trenches that the Chinese built for tank traps along the way were filled with the bodies of dead and wounded soldiers and when there weren't enough bodies to fill the trench so that the tanks could pass they shot the people living around there indiscriminately to fill up the trenches. He borrowed a camera to go back and take some pictures to bear out his statement.

Good night and Merry Christmas!

December 26, Sunday

Since writing on Christmas Eve I have been primarily an obstetrician. After finishing the installment I went to bed only to be called at eleven and again at three thirty to preside at the inauguration ceremonies of two little Chinese. It was like being back on the obstetrics service at the medical school with the slight difference that no matter what happened I was still the ultimate medical authority.

Yesterday I managed to make complete rounds on all wards before dinner and went home to a Christmas dinner with the eight members of our immediate family and four guests. This time we had Grace Bauer, Minnie Vautrin and two Chinese girls, Blanche and Pearl Wu (no relation). Miss Hynds refused our most urgent entreaties. Miss Blanche Wu had supplied the two Christmas geese from Ginling and in addition made us a present of a dozen fresh eggs, our first in several weeks.

I had postponed any operations possible that afternoon and took the afternoon off catching up a little on some sleep and reading a rather engaging book written by an adventuresome rascal named Negley Farson, an autobiography entitled, "The Way of a Transgressor."

This morning we found Trim struggling with a temperature of 102 and feeling pretty miserable. We put him to bed at Grace Bauer's where he would get a little better food than at the hospital and he is feeling some better tonight but will probably be out of things for a couple of days.

My rounds this morning were broken up by two birthday parties, one at ten-thirty and another at eleven thirty. Earlier in the morning Miss Hynds, Miss Ngo and I were betting on which one would crash through first. After a run of girls one of these turned out to be a boy. As a matter of fact one of the ones the other night was a boy but before that we had had five girls in succession.

This afternoon I started off with another amputation and had a few minor cases. The amputation was that of a leg I had been trying to save for a couple of weeks. The patient was going downhill steadily and it seemed to be a choice between his leg and his life. The outcome is not by any means settled yet, as he may well lose both. After finishing the operations there were still seventy patients yet to see on two wards as yet unvisited.

Shortly after seven the day's work seemed to be done and I went over to Grace Bauer's for supper and to pay Trim another visit. We had a semiofficial visit from some Japanese officers this morning who looked over the place very carefully. They are now engaged in registering in the most inefficient manner possible all the residents of the city, all of whom are now cooped up in the Safety Zone. They have given us all arm bands which are a sort of a pass within the city and told us to be sure and wear them.

Charlie Riggs was held up by one of the officers of the registration group yesterday and slapped about a good deal. I don't know what my reaction would be to that sort of treatment but the temptation to give him a vicious uppercut to the jaw would be all but insurmountable. I hope that if that time comes I will be able to keep my hands in my pockets as he did.

Except for the rather sketchy news from Simburg we have had no news for two weeks and we are sure that no real news from Nanking has escaped during that time. When it does get out, feeling will probably have simmered down so that it will come as a sort of anticlimax. We would all like to see some light ahead but as yet there doesn't [seem] to be even a glimmer.

December 28, Tuesday

Elizabeth[5] is six months old today. How I wish I could be with her and Marjorie to celebrate it! Just to think that that she is probably cutting teeth now and doing all sorts or things that I have not seen her do. We managed to spend seven weeks of those six months together and there seems to be no immediate indication that matters will settle down here for some time.

Trim is feeling much better and was around to see the medical cases today. Last night I had one obstetrics case at nine thirty and had one more today at noon. The latter was a twenty year old primipara and her littler son refused to start breathing for about ten minutes. It was some relief to see him start. Including the babies, I have had one hundred and seventy five cases while Trim has been sick. He will relieve me of about twenty of them.

It is almost a day's work just to make rounds on them all. Yesterday we had one case which will have to go down in the black book if his story is true. He was a worker in the Hsia Kwan telephone buildings, refugeeing at the University. He had gone on the street to find a friend, was seized by some Japanese soldiers and led to a place where there were several hundred other men. These turned out to be also from the University. When they had registered them, they first made some pretty speeches, stating that they were frankly looking for ex-soldiers. If, they said, anyone would come forward and admit that had been soldiers, their lives would be spared and they would be formed into a military labor corps. This was repeated several times in the presence of everyone including Mr. Sone, Mr. Bates, and Mr. Riggs. Two hundred men stepped forward and admitted that they had been soldiers.

According to our case's story these several hundred men were led into the hills in the west of the city and used for bayonet practice. He has no idea of how many survived. He had five bayonet wounds himself including one that perforated his peritoneum. I operated with the impression that his intestines had been pierced but found only a lot of dark blood in the peritoneal cavity. The bayonet had struck him almost in the midline but had gone in at such a slant that it had pierced the peritoneum in the right lower quadrant injuring some blood vessels but not entering the intestine. He will probably recover unless the peritonitis is too severe.

The Japanese are apparently sincerely trying to cut down the lawlessness. There are quite a few gendarmes and when they are present the looting stops. After they have passed there is still some going on. Only one or two big fires a day now remind us that there are still a few unburned buildings. Groups of soldiers and coolies are now busy cleaning up the street which were littered with every kind of rubbish. They are making a lot of bonfires also in the streets, using the contents of stores as material. Near Sing Chai Ko the Nanking Music Shop had all its music and musical instruments piled up in the middle of the street and set afire. It seems so senseless. I suppose the idea is to destroy everything and then load up on cheap Japanese goods. The people are so completely robbed now that they won't even be able to buy the cheap Japanese wares.

Trim was at the hospital this afternoon and we did some fluoroscopies. One man had a through and through bullet wound from sacrum to right lower quadrant and apparently had developed a traumatic arteriovenous aneurysm of the right common iliac artery and vein. I'm afraid he is doomed as operation and attempting a repair now in the face of his present infection is out of the question and just tying it off would mean gangrene of the entire right leg. After we finished the fluoroscopies we turned on his little radio in time to get some outside news. We heard of the fall of Tsinan and that the *Panay* incident was declared closed and that diplomatic representatives were expected back in Nanking soon. We will be glad to see them.

Thursday, December 30

The year is fast drawing to a close. It would be pleasant to close the year with some sort of a brighter outlook for the next but we seem to be closing on a note of deepest gloom without a glimmer of light ahead. The only consolation is that it can't be worse. They can't kill as many people as there aren't any more to kill. I can't get any farther away from my family even if I tried. The hospital can't possibly get back on a self-supporting basis as none of the patients have any more money.

The gendarmerie are busy, all right. Tonight coming home from the hospital, Mac and I were challenged by fixed bayonets on two occasions. Night before last the sentry at the Bible Teachers' Training School asked for a woman among the refugees. None was forthcoming so last night he raped one without permission. Today some poor fool who was annoyed at the man in charge of one of the refugee camps in the University sericulture building brought some Japanese soldiers around and showed them where a half a dozen rifles had been buried on the grounds. There was an unholy row and four men were taken away one being charged with the heinous crime of being a colonel in the Chinese army. We don't have to wonder whether he is still alive.

This morning a fairly well dressed Chinese business man ventured outside the Safety Zone to inspect the remains of his home and business. He was walking past Kuilan Church with three companions when some Japanese soldiers fired on them for a reason as yet undiscovered. One man was killed and they brought our subject to the hospital with four feet of small intestine hanging out of a gaping wound in his abdomen. The bullet had entered in the left side of the abdomen and emerged through the right. It was still in his trousers and has been added to my collection.

On opening him up I found the small intestine completely severed in six places and bruised and punctured in as many more. I resected all the lacerated portion and put in an enterostomy tube but figure his chances at considerably less than one in a thousand. The case I reported last time is doing very well and has a very good chance of patient recovery. Another case today was one of our chest cases who had developed empyoma and I resected a rib. We must have ten cases shot through the chest. The man with a fair portion of his brain gone finally died after a week in the hospital. I am trying to save the leg of a ten year old boy who has a frightful compound fracture of the lower third of the tibia and fibula. He is steadily losing ground and I'm afraid I'll have to amputate to save his life.

Trim is back on full time again and has taken over my obstetrics cases. One little boy I delivered was discovered to have a minute little extra thumb attached by a small pedicle to his normal one. It wasn't noticed at the time of delivery. I snipped it off today. The little seventeen year old girl who was raped at seven thirty one evening before starting her labor pains at nine, has now developed a rip-roaring case of acute gonorrhea. She runs a temperature of 105 part of the time and the outlook is not too bright. We are giving her baby temporarily to the girl who lost hers prematurely when she was stuck in the abdomen with a bayonet in the basement of Hillcrest. She has plenty of milk.

We listened to the radio tonight at the same time and learned to our disgust that the only station broadcasting news at that time, when we have our little machine running, was Tokyo. They mentioned that all Americans were being evacuated from Kuling but we don't know whether to believe it or not. [The following manuscript is not clear.] The only paper in tower now is a Japanese one printed in Chinese. When I earned it the first few lines that they had destroyed as Chinese.

January 1, 1938

The world must be in [?] to think it strange that no direct word has come from Nanking for over two weeks. The diplomatic representatives have not yet been allowed to return and no newspaper correspondents have come back although they hoped when they left on the 15th to be back in 48 hours. The Japanese Domei and other reporters are of course hopelessly inaccurate.

The Japanese put over a typical ceremony today when they had representatives from the refugee camps came to Kulou where they raised the old five bar flag and had a few speeches, supposedly inaugurating an autonomous government. One of the chief men has been working in a rather subordinate capacity under the International Committee and has a long record of connections with the Nanking underworld and other undesirable characteristics. He is by business an auctioneer. The other been working for the Committee. It certainly is a second-hand crowd but then there aren't any first classes in town.

A three day holiday was declared though no one knew just what to do about it. There aren't any shops to close. They apparently imported or resurrected countless firecrackers that have been popping off all day. The soldiers feel that it is the time to get drunk and go on rampages. After several days of comparative guist [sic] the raping broke out afresh. In the house of Mr. Wang, religious director of the University, three soldiers broke in, one standing on guard outside and the others enjoying a helpless girl inside.

We had a New Year's dinner this noon with four guests, Mrs. Twinem, Mrs. Chen of Ginling, Mr. Magee and his roommate, Mr. Forster. It was the first time the latter two had left their place together since the trouble started. They have about 250 refugees in their place. We had just finished dinner when someone arrived to call them away and they arrived just too late to prevent the raping of one girl and the beating up of another because she resisted too strenuously.

A nun was brought in this afternoon with a compound fracture of the femur of two weeks duration. She had been in [a] dugout with three others when the Japanese had entered the city. They came to the dugout and one soldier opened fire from each end of the dugout. The other three were killed. Her wound is badly infected and her prognosis grave.

Another pathetic case came in this afternoon. A woman of 29 who has had six children of whom the oldest was 13, lived in a small village south of the city. The Chinese soldiers burned the village in their retreat and she took her five children (one died earlier) and headed for Nanking. Before evening an airplane dove around spraying machine gun bullets, one of which went through her right eye and came out her neck. She was unconscious until the next morning when she came to and found her five children crying and cold beside her. The youngest was three months old and, of course, breast fed. She was in a pool of blood and very weak. She was too weak to carry the baby and had to leave it behind in an empty house. With the remaining four she somehow struggled to the city and into the refugee Zone where she finally got them settled and found her way to the hospital.

With this sort of thing as a steady diet it is hard to go around and wish people a Happy New Year. This is my turn at the hospital and so this is written on the typewriter of the treasurer's office. Next night our whole crowd went down and spent an hour or so with Mr. Rabe in his house as a New Year's Eve celebration. He had some good records and we got the current situation pretty well discussed before we left. None of us stayed up to see the new year in.

January 3, 1938

You will undoubtedly get page 50 long before you get many pages before and after it. I hope the paging will imply that as there was no chance to write anything we did not mean for Japanese consumption.

Day before yesterday I contrived to drop a four pound iron weight on my big toe and so have been limping around the hospital for a couple of days. Yesterday being Sunday I made a complete set of rounds in the morning and then rested in the afternoon with the result that the toe is almost well by now.

Three rather interesting cases turned up today. One boy of seventeen comes with the tale of about ten thousand Chinese men between the ages of 15 and 30 who were led out of the city on the 14th to the river bank near the ferry wharf. There the Japanese opened up on them with field guns, hand grenades and machine guns. Most of them were then pushed into the river, some were burned in huge piles, and three managed to escape. Of the ten thousand the boy figured there were about six thousand ex-soldiers and four thousand civilians. He has a bullet wound in the chest which is not serious.

A women of forty or so came in with the tale of having been taken from one of the refugee camps on December 31, ostensibly for the purpose of washing clothes for some officers. Six women were taken. During the days they washed clothes and during the nights they were raped. Five of them had from ten to twenty visits a night but the sixth was young and good looking so she had about forty. On the third day two soldiers took our patient away from the place where they all were and went to some isolated spot where they tried to cut off her head. One tried to do so with four blows but only succeeded in cutting all the muscles of the back of the neck down to the vertebral column. She also had six other bayonet thrusts in her back, face and arms. She will probably recover.

While she was lying in this condition, another Japanese (!) soldier found her and had her brought to a place of safety.

The third case was a young girl of fourteen who wasn't yet built [?] for rape and will have to have considerable surgical repair.

I have had five operations this afternoon, including the extraction of two more bullets, which are in my collection. I wrote last time that the young mother of six had a bullet pass through her eye socket and come out her neck, but the bullet hadn't yet come out and I extracted it this afternoon. I am getting discouraged over the cases of compound, comminuted fractures of the upper end of the femur. They just don't do well at all. One of my cases of that kind died today after six weeks in the hospital. The infection had been steadily travelling upwards and a few days ago he started to bleed from his wound. It was too high for a tourniquet and incising into it only revealed a tremendous foul abscess cavity that you could put both fists into and which extended clear to the midline and partway up the back. The femur was completely shattered in its whole upper portion. I tried to get the leg off in a hurry but was too late. I don't believe it would have helped much to try earlier but perhaps it might.

One Japanese officer who has spent four years in America is very solicitous about our welfare and comes every day to inquire what we need. Today he brought us a whole sack of beans and some fresh meat. I wish there were more like him.

Yesterday we had a church service at our house, and Trim, Mrs. Twinem, and Grace Bauer were here in addition to our family. Mac led the service with the sermon, which he prepared for the service four weeks ago and which had been postponed week by week. He had to revise it a bit.

Thursday, January 6

Three more busy days have passed with some new developments but beyond the gradual quieting down of the troops there is little to report. This morning three members of the American diplomatic service returned. Mr. Allison, who formerly was in Tsinan and has been a guest here since we took up residence in the Buck house, is now the American consul. He has with him two younger men, Bary and Mactadyen. We had them here for lunch today and tonight they are the guests of the Japanese Embassy.

They brought some mail, mostly from the families in Kuling. It will probably be quite some time before any regular mail comes though from the States. They also brought news that the Americans in Kuling had evacuated on December 30 to Hong Kong, via Hankow. So it seems that we did the right thing in the first place, as there wasn't very likely much baggage on this trip.

The Japanese are leading north on the Tientsin-Pukow Railway and are intending to take Hsuchow, the junction of that line and the Lunghai Railway. They have already taken Tsinan and Tsian, and are heading for Hsuchow also from the north. The main Chinese forces are preparing themselves. From what we have seen here it is difficult to imagine what the Chinese are using for troops.

We occasionally get evidence that the Chinese air force is not yet defunct, but so far they have confined their efforts to the air fields around the city, which is as it should be.

At the hospital our out-patient department is picking up again and keep our Chinese doctors busy most of the day. We are again going on regular schedule for surgical and medical clinics, starting next Monday. Yesterday I spent most of the afternoon operating on a strangulated hernia that had been strangulated for five days and was gangrenous, necessitating a resection of about eight inches of small intestine. Today I got back into the old December schedule and took off two legs that I had been trying to save for about a month. One was on a little boy whose leg had been badly shattered. I did my best to save it, but the foot has been gradually becoming gangrenous from lack of circulation and the infection was spreading instead of getting under control so it had to come off to save his life.

The Japanese have not yet allowed the British or German diplomats to return but are going to let them in on the tenth. We don't know when they will allow reporters.

This afternoon Mac drove—with the patched up unpainted ambulance that Charlie Riggs had fixed up for us—to south city for some vegetables. When he got there they had a flat tire and were without the necessary equipment to fix it. The chauffeur chased all the way back to the hospital, terror-stricken lest he be seized by the Japs on the way. I had just finished the most important of the operations and so went to his rescue in the beautiful new Studebaker ambulance given to us by the Red Swastika Society. It is painted white, has four rolling stretchers in it, and has only been driven 1,000 miles. It is just about the last word in ambulances and much superior to anything I saw in New York. They gave it to us to prevent its being stolen by the Japanese. It was getting dark when we arrived and we found that the nuts on the spare tire were fastened in such a way that with the instruments we took we couldn't get sufficient leverage to loosen them. All we could do was to take off the offending tire and bring it back to be repaired. Travelling at night is not very healthy, yet we decided to leave it there and get it first thing in the morning, if it is still there. It is in the extreme southwestern portion of the city, only a few hundred yards from the wall. There are no Jap soldiers in the immediate vicinity so we think our chances of recovering it are fair. Mac is staying at the hospital for his turn tonight and will drive down for it before he comes back to breakfast.

Saturday, January 8, 1938

When I got home this noon I found a message from the Embassy marked. "Important, Urgent." It turned out to be the Christmas and anniversary greetings from Marjorie sent through Cousin Helen and Brigadier-General Beaumont. Allison had forgotten all about having it when he was here for lunch the other day and had brought letters to everyone else. It was certainly a great and glorious feeling to get it. Where they are and what they are doing and when we will get together again are three questions that are continually on my mind. Elizabeth's first teeth must be in by now and she is trying them out on various things.

With the hospital electricity now going for most of the time we have been able again to be in touch with the world by radio, and it is good to have daily news. The news, however, doesn't particularly add to our peace of mind. Both countries are apparently settling down to a protracted struggle. The Japanese do not seem to have advanced much since they captured Nanking.

The city is continually filled with wild rumors, which we are able to check by our radio connections. Today an amusing incident occurred. The Chinese had rumors that Chinese troops were at the gates of the city and that it was about to be recaptured. Some women who had been at the Japanese embassy washing clothes came home with large bundles in their arms. As they approached the University, the news spread like wildfire that the Japanese had left the embassy and that these women were coming away with loot. Immediately a crowd of women clambered over the barbed wire fence around the embassy to get in their share of looting. They were hustled out by the Chinese servants in the rear of the buildings before any serious break occurred.

Also today the gendarmes bound and took a young lad who has been living in the middle school and who speaks Japanese. He has been acting as interpreter there, much against his will. Searle Bates went to their headquarters to see what he could do and was roughly pushed out with no satisfaction. The people are rightly afraid to go back to their homes in spite of the apparent wish of the Japanese authorities for them to do so. As soon as they get out of the Safety Zone, and even to a lesser extent within it, they are subject to all kinds of indignities, the men being led off as carriers and the women being raped.

Another Chinese air raid came this morning, and they apparently made a direct hit on an ammunition store in the eastern portion of the city. A huge fire raged all morning with continual popping of ammunition. The fires continue every day to the sum of ten or more. Last night coming home from the hospital for supper I didn't see one, and that was the first night I could say that for three weeks. However, the record was kept up, as when I went back to sleep at the hospital there were several fires going. When I got there the Chinese police at the gates were all excited and said that a bunch of Japanese soldiers had pounded on the gate and tried to get in, but they kept them out by pretending not to hear. It turned out today that they were some officers who were sent to tell us not to have so many lights burning. They came today to tell us, and then apparently emphasized their request by the simple method of turning off all the lights at about six thirty just as two obstetrics cases were in labor. It is Trim's night on so he will attend to them. There were none during my night last night.

Tomorrow the British and German embassy representatives are expected, a day earlier than previously reported. We hope to have the three British here to lunch but do not know whether they will arrive in time. Some words from Nanking is now escaping through the U.S. embassy, so you will have news.

Sunday, January 9, 1938

At last there seems to be an opportunity to get out some mail with a fair chance of escaping Japanese censorship. It is to be sent down on the American tugboat that has been up river salvaging the *Panay.* They are to put it in the hands of Mr. Walline of the Presbyterian mission who is to get it aboard an American boat so that it will not reach regular mails until it reaches America. You can do anything you like with it, Marjorie. I wish I could have made several copies of most of it, for I would like the family to see it and Kulia and Franklin, and then some of it could be used for such publicity as might be suggested by Frank Price's office or Mr. Garside. He would doubtless be very much interested in it.

Taken together with the first portion written before you left it makes quite a tale. I hope you got the pages sent by Steele and Smith without having them censored. I have one copy here as a safeguard. Lewis Smythe has been doing most of the official recording and has compiled a long series of tales as I have told in this of my own experiences are in his list.

Today was Sunday and after having breakfast a little later than usual, I made most of my rounds and then found John Magee and his movie camera ready to finish up some pictures that he hadn't taken on his previous trip. This morning we took pictures of an elderly man with two long gashes in his neck. He had been asked to procure women for some soldiers and his crime was in not being able to produce them. The next one we took was the policeman who had eighteen (no it was twenty-two) bayonet wounds of the back, chest and arms. There were no accusations against him. The third was the woman I wrote of the other day, who was taken with five others and made to wash clothes in the day time and to entertain at night. Her neck is gradually healing and she has avoided the pneumonia which I though she was getting.

Notes

1. RG11, B229, F2875.
2. Because these Chinese doctors are [not full] physicians.
3. Marjorie was Wilson's wife.
4. Buck was a famous agricultural economist, a professor of the University of Nanking. Thomson is a professor of the Chemistry Department; his wife taught in the English Department, Professor Zhang Kaiyuan was one of her students.
5. Elizabeth was Wilson's daughter.

Appendix A

Chronology

November 5, 1937
Japanese land at Hangchow.

November 11
Military Commission of Nanking government prepared to defend the city.

November 19
Chiang Kai-Chek orders Tang Sheng-Chih to be the general in charge of the defense of the city.

November 20
The National government issues a proclamation moving the capital to Chongqing.

Chiang Kai-chek deploys the forces at Guangde and Si'an near Nanking.

November 22
Japanese airplanes assault Nanking.

The International Committee for the Nanking Safety Zone is established.

November 30
Guangde falls. Japanese army marches toward Nanking from three routes.

December 1
Japanese commander-in-chief Iwane Matsui leads the army and, together with the Japanese navy, attacks Nanking.

December 6
The city of Nanking proclaimed under martial law. The refugee zone is designated from Sing Kai Ko to the west of Chung Shan Road between Han Chung Road and Shansi Road.

December 7
At 5:45 A.M., Chiang Kai-chek leaves Nanking by airplane.

The international government announces that Nanking has become a belligerent area.

December 8
Japanese launch a frontal attack on Nanking by three forces.

December 9
Iwane Matsui sends a letter to Tang Sheng-chih, urging him to hand over the city of Nanking before the 10th.

December 10
Tang turns Matsui's proposal down. The two armies are on the offensive again.

December 12
Japanese capture most of Nanking's city gates: Zhonghua Gate, Zhongshan Gate, Shuixi Gate, Ande Gate, and Guanghua Gate.

December 13
The fall of Nanking. Japanese wholesale atrocities and vandalism begin.

200,000 to 250,000 refugees throng into the Safety Zone.

December 16
About 10 A.M., Japanese soldiers force their way into Ginling College in search of former Chinese soldiers.

December 26
Registration of refugees starts at the University of Nanking.

December 30
Japanese announce that those who did not register with the government before 2:00 A.M. on December 31 will be shot. (Later it proves to be only an empty threat.)

January 2, 1938
Tze Chih Wei Yuan Hwei, the puppet government manipulated by the Japanese, is established in Kulow.

February 18
The International Committee for the Nanking Safety Zone changes its name to the International Relief Committee.

IRC does a great deal of relief work with the refugees and farmers.

May 21
Close of the last of the refugee camps.

Appendix B

Report of the Nanking International Relief Committee

Report of the Nanking International Relief Committee
November, 1937 to April, 1939
Nanking International Relief Committee Report of Activities
November 22, 1937–April 15, 1938*

The International Committee for the Nanking Safety Zone was organized on November 22, 1937. The first problem was the establishment of the Zone itself. This meant the selection of a favorable site and the securing of recognition for the Zone by the Chinese and Japanese authorities. After careful inquiry and much discussion, that part of the city lying roughly west of Chung Shan Road between Han Chung Road and Shansi Road, and east of Sikang Road and a line from the southern end of that road to the intersection of Han Chung Road and Shanghai Road, was chosen.** The Chinese authorities readily agreed to the idea of the Zone, though the military were naturally reluctant to move out of the area before the very last minute. The Japanese authorities never formally recognized the Zone, but did say that they would not attack an area which was not occupied by Chinese troops. On this narrow margin of agreement, the Chinese promise to evacuate the area and the Japanese statement that they would not intentionally attack an unoccupied place, the Safety Zone was finally put through.

The co-operation of the local Chinese authorities with the Committee was all that could be desired. Twenty thousand bags of rice and ten thousand bags of flour were assigned to us, and $80,000 in cash was given us. Of the rice, owing to difficulties of transportation, only 9,067 bags were finally brought into our godown (the University of Nanking Chapel!) before outbreak of hostilities around the city. None of the flour allotted to us by the City Government was secured, though one thousand bags were obtained from the Ta Tung Flour Mills. The city also gave us 350 bags of salt.

The people coming into the Zone were urged to bring with them what food

---

*From the Miner Searle Bates Paper, Record Group No. 10, Box 102.
**See map, p. xxviii.

supplies they could and it was well they did so, as these private stocks were what carried most of the population during the six weeks following the Japanese entry, when little in the way of food could be brought into the city.

It is estimated that about 250,000 people entered the Zone. Only a relatively small number, probably not more than ten thousand in all, remained outside. Of these refugees approximately 70,000 were cared for in twenty-five large concentration centers or "camps," in whose management the International Committee co-operated, either by giving food or fuel, or providing supervision, or both. The work for the refugees was carried on at first by three commissions, Food, Housing, and Sanitation. These commissions were under the direction of Mr. H.L. Han, Dr. C.Y. Hsu, and the Rev. Y.S. Shen respectively. Later a fourth Commission, the Rehabilitation Commission, under the chairmanship of Mr. Walter Lowe, was added to the other three. Dr. T.M. Tang has had charge of the secretarial and translation work of the General Office, and Mr. Wang Chen Dien and later Mr. Chen Wen-shu have conducted the Business Office. To all these gentlemen, and to their many colleagues and associates, the International Committee would like to express its appreciation of the way they have carried on their work under many and often insuperable difficulties, and sometimes even at the risk of life itself.

When the Safety Zone was first organized the International Committee hoped that its task would soon be over, and that once the actual fighting around the city was ended the people might speedily go back to their homes. However, these hopes were doomed to disappointment. Nearly four months passed before conditions became normal enough for the majority of the refugees to return to their homes. But encouragement was steadily given to all who felt they could return to do so, and by the end of May it became possible to close down all of the refugee camps conducted by the Committee. At that time also the Committee moved its headquarters from No. 5 Ninghai Road, which had been kindly loaned to it by the German Embassy, to No. 4 Tientsin Road, a building on the campus of the University of Nanking. From that time forward the latter building has served as the headquarters of the Committee.

Summer and Autumn Program, 1938. During this period work was maintained on a less extensive scale than before. This was due partly to the closing of the camps, partly to the improvement of conditions and revival of trade, and partly also to the fact that summer is an easier time for people to get along than the winter. Even so, however, this period was marked by the distribution of considerable supplies of rice and wheat under the joint management of the local Red Swastika and the Committee, save the salaries of the representatives of the Red Swastika upon the joint Committee which supervised that piece of work.

The International Committee continued small-scale effort in work relief, cash relief, and small loans for productive business.

A second noteworthy activity of this summer and autumn of 1938 was the completion of two surveys which had been authorized by the Committee. The first was a survey of war damage in the Nanking area, and the second was an investigation of agricultural conditions in the several *hsien* immediately contiguous to Nanking. The surveys were designed jointly to show the condition of the people, their material loss and their prospects of economic recovery. The results of the two studies were most informing to the general public and were also of great assistance to the Committee in enabling it to determine along sound lines its program of relief for the following winter and spring.

Winter-spring Relief Work, 1938–39. Hardly had plans been made and the winter's work gotten under way, when it was interrupted in early December by the sudden arrest of six persons connected with the International Committee staff, and one other person, not at the time connected with the Committee, but who had formerly been on its staff. One of the first six mentioned, who happened to be our Assistant Treasurer, was promptly set free, but all the others were confined for more than four months, in spite of constant efforts to secure their release. Naturally the sudden arrest of these men at the beginning of our winter's program of work, caused considerable uneasiness among the others of our staff, with the result that for a period of one month the administration of relief was interrupted and thereby the entire winter program was injured and delayed, at the expense of the city's poorest families. Measures against the members of the Committee itself were broached, but were restrained by wiser counsels.

When it became clear in early January that no other members of the staff were in immediate danger of arrest, and that no further interference with the Committee was contemplated, work was resumed and carried on steadily until the program was completed at the end of April. In order to make the work of the Committee more readily understood by the Chinese and Japanese authorities in Nanking, the Committee added to its membership, which had hitherto been composed entirely of neutrals, one Chinese and one Japanese member. These new members of the committee were chosen by the Committee itself without suggestion from other quarters and were persons in civil life, not in official positions. In this way the non-official and purely philanthropic character of the Committee was maintained.

The work of the Committee during the winter and spring consisted chiefly of food distribution, but a great deal of bedding and clothing were given out, and a certain amount of cash relief, work relief, and aid through small loans was provided. The scale and nature of these enterprises are shown in the following sections.

I. Housing and Camps

Procedure in the Zone

The problem of housing in the original Safety Zone was approached on this principle: that every possible private arrangement should be made, reserving institutional and public property for an expected remainder of the poorest of the population plus some others who might rush in at a late moment of danger when all houses were full. The Zone was about one-eighth of the area within the wall, and was densely built only in a small part of that, hardly built at all in considerable portions. It comprised the "New Residential District." There were spacious houses already evacuated by their previous occupants of the official class and other houses of a modern type left vacant by intelligentsia and other middle-class people who had withdrawn to the west to keep free of the approaching army. In some cases servants or relatives remained upon these private properties or were in charge of them. The actual residents of the Zone at the time the Committee was organized in late November 1937, were perhaps a few more than 10,000.

Many thousands streamed into the Zone as friends and relatives of residents, or by rental arrangement with owners and others in actual control of private houses. Then the Mayor gave public approval for the use of unoccupied houses under the combined direction of the International Committee and the Police, which direction carried to the sealing of movables in one or two rooms, in order that the rest of the house might be assigned to refugees coming in from other parts of the city.

The Committee formed a strong Housing Commission, which placed an office in each of eight small districts into which the Safety Zone was divided for that purpose, and carefully surveyed the available space and the process of utilizing it to the full. Good humor, persuasion and authority, in varying mixture, assisted the pressure of the human throngs to find a fairly efficient and fairly equitable use of every habitable structure that was or had been under private control.

Meanwhile the Housing Commission had thoroughly examined the possibilities in private institutions (one of the many reasons for choosing this particular area as a Safety Zone was the comparative wealth of institutional buildings under foreign ownership, which could therefore be handled almost at will so long as there was decent order in the city), and also in public buildings which were rapidly being evacuated at that period. When private houses were reaching apparent saturation, as measured by a narrow calculation of flow space, the larger buildings were gradually opened up under supervision, which attempted to pack one building before another could be entered, and to check any combination of persons that attempted to secure disproportionate space or advantage for their own group. At this time the Committee had the active and friendly co-operation of the units of police that had not yet left the city, and 400 patrolmen under its own direction. It should be noted in passing that there were scarcely a half-dozen arrests in the Zone for any cause, for the people were remarkably decent in their conduct.

The last desperate rush during the assault on the wall at the southeast, and the pitiful flight of those who survived their efforts to stay in the other portions of the city after the fall filled the stairways of buildings, the very dugouts, and numberless primitive lean-tos and other shelters hastily erected with what men had carried on their backs from their former dwellings. Very nearly 250,000 people were packed into the Safety Zone.

Organization of Camps

From the taking of the city on the 12–13th December, the need for the work of the Housing Commission among private dwellings was slight, and the general position of the International Committee was sharply altered toward relief and away from supervision. On the other hand, the need for care and management of the refugees in the large buildings became greater and far more prolonged than any one had anticipated. This task was to absorb a big part of the total effort of the Committee for several months.

The Housing Commission appointed managers, and in some cases assistants as well, to conduct refugee camps in institutional buildings suitable for that purpose and made available by those in charge. Usually a group of buildings were under one management. The situations and personnel of these camps were extremely varied. In the University of Nanking, Ginling College, and the Nanking Theological Seminary, the institutional personnel were asked by the Committee to open their buildings to refugees under their own management, accepting appointment and assistance from the Housing Commission. In other institutional properties management was provided from among persons not originally belonging there, but temporarily resident with the approval of those in charge.

In some cases the Housing Commission made its own appointments from its own acquaintance among persons remaining in the city; in others it actively searched among refugees upon the property for promising material; in still others it more or less willingly recognized persons who came to the top of their own groups, either because their new neighbors observed their qualities or be-cause they had the ambition and the aggressiveness to do something—for motives good, bad, or mixed. As might be expected, some of these arrangements of personnel were stable, and some were not; some resulted in excellent conduct of the camps; some in inefficiency; some in petty extortion.

All in all, however, a great deal of faithful effort by superior people accomplished much in itself and much by example and direction to others. Scarcely less credit is due to the large number of humble workers who kept at their tasks of cooking and cleaning and carrying water; and to the many half-clerical, half-supervisory workers who kept track of the scores of refugees for whom each was individually responsible, settling disputes, protecting the weak and the sick, guarding against fire and the worst of filth in incredibly crowded and difficult conditions. Speaking generally, during all the months of their existence, the camps had no electricity, no public water supply, no mechanism of any kind for sewage disposal, no telephones, no friendly or adequate police that could be called upon. The refugees included the poorest, the invalid, the least energetic, of a great city that had largely removed itself. Collective life under such conditions was an achievement which led foreigners frequently to comment in one form or another: "Only the Chinese could stand this. Only the Chinese could get along with as little serious trouble among themselves."

The average camp population, below the maximum in each case, was 70,750 for the last fifteen days of December; 62,500 for January; 36,800 for February; 26,700 for March; 21, 750 for April; 12, 150 for May. As is explained more fully under the discussion of Food, a considerable part of the camp population provided its own food throughout; but the burden of general care was very heavy.

Varied Types of Camps

Space and time do not permit a description of each of the 25 "permanent" camps. But a number will be mentioned as indicating the variety of situations which they presented. Ginling College maintained a camp for women and their children, numbering some 10,000 in the worst days of December, declining gradually in January, and remaining around 3,000 for the remainder of the period. This camp's history was closely connected with the problem of security, though poverty was always a factor. On the various properties of the University of Nanking were conducted six camps, of which the University staff undertook complete management of two. The average for the six in late December was 28,000 refugees, of whom 11,000 were in the Middle School property alone. The use of the main buildings at the Drum Tower was limited almost entirely to women.

Another type of camp was a group of refugees independently organized but seeking help, along with inspection: of this sort was the body of several hundred on the Quaker Mission property; a similar number in the Wei Ch'ing Li, a large apartment house; and the one considerable group of persons who managed to survive outside the Safety Zone; the thousand-odd at the Shuang Tang

Presbyterian Church in the southwest corner of the city (fortunately apart from the main movements of soldiers, though suffering cruelly for weeks). Then there were three camps in the buildings of municipal primary schools, caring for some 1,500 persons each in the first month or two.

Most unhappy were the abortive camps in the sadly named Ministry of Justice and the Supreme Court Building; they were practically wiped out by the military, and remnants were driven out by the 17th of December. Among the most difficult to manage were the 10,000 who crowded at the last minute into the recently abandoned Ping Kung Shu (Army Stores; formerly Ministry of Communications); they were in general the poorest elements of the city, and by that time good personnel had been absorbed in organization elsewhere; the 2,500 at the Chemical Research Shops were a similar problem, and the 3,200 in old Army Staff College also. Such public properties suffered more from the soldiery than did institutions obviously private, under a foreign flag, and visited more frequently by foreigners. The position of the camp leaders was dangerous and difficult in the extreme.

The International Committee was organized with the expectation of performing an emergency service during a period of military operations which would last at most a few weeks. Despite the fact that military operations were quickly passed (indeed, the city was under real attack only parts of four days), the resultant disorder and dislocation of all ordinary life and destruction of economic resources and opportunities were so great as to impel the gradual transformation of the Committee into a continuing relief organization. However, it felt required to reduce its functions in time and scope, partly because of frequent difficulties with the authorities, such as an order forbidding the Committee to purchase grain, and also because of the strong desire to avoid the promotion of dependence in any form. Obviously the semi-administrative work of the Safety Zone should have been and was quickly dropped upon the establishment in the city of the new military authority (though unfounded suspicions of the Committee in this respect continued to trouble its work for fully a year's time).

Program of Reduction and Closing

From the close of December, 1937, the main work and the main problems for five months centered on the provision and care for the refugee camps and the question of their diminution. The Committee was always conscious of the needs of homeless persons who had lost everything, including employment and sometimes the possibility of employment. On the other hand, the more people there were in the camps over a lengthening period, the faster melted away the Committee's resources, and the greater the danger that some would become habituated to the camp life, making less than their best efforts to re-establish themselves with home and work. The experience of Shanghai and of some other cities has shown the perils of that tendency, combined with the growth of a vested interest of relief workers in their job, which prejudices any attempt at fundamental improvement. In Nanking there was also the powerful influence of insecurity throughout the city and its environs, which checked many who wished to strike out for themselves, and at times pressed deeply upon the Committee's policy.

But there were also forces working toward dispersal in one way or another. The military authorities considered at the existence of the camps as a reflection upon the condition of the city, and regarded them with hostility as places where a considerable number of Chinese remained under what they believed to be hostile foreign influence; they felt less free to apply drastic police measures upon foreign property or where they would be reported by foreigners (though the term, "less free" is highly relative). Official instructions were given out for the disbandment of the camps by or on February 4th, by armed force if necessary. Fortunately a calmer view met the representations made by the Committee through the German and other Embassies, and the instructions were disavowed. Meanwhile the new terror drove out many thousands of persons into parts of the city where they suffered so severely that many women and some men returned shortly to the camps. But the net result was a distinct push away from the camps, however cruelly accomplished.

Again, people whose houses had not been burned or completely looted, wished as soon as at all possible to have at least part of the family living there in order to protect the remainder from the civilian search for fuel and salable articles that had now developed. Moreover, the slow opening up of communications to the coast and to a few nearby districts enabled some people to leave Nanking in order to rejoin families or to seek aid from relatives elsewhere (soon to be more than balanced by incoming streams from the burned and pillaged areas all about).

The Committee's work was thenceforward continually to be affected by the departure of persons of some initiative and education who had been willing to help while caught here in Nanking, but who desired as soon as they could to seek places of greater opportunity, often driven by the needs of families resident elsewhere. It must be remembered that the Committee's work was all organized on a voluntary basis, that for several weeks its helpers received at most their rice alone, that even in later times it has never promised continuing employment, and that in the spring of 1938 its low maintenance allowances were accompanied by the continual reduction and announced dismissal of camp staffs.

In fine, the Committee encouraged prompt return to homes and economic effort outside the camps as early as possible, and soon began to bring some pressure to eliminate those persons and those camps which least required maintenance. The process was painful in certain cases, and resulted in a few instances of hardship not desired by the Committee; but in general the results were more than worth the sacrifices involved. Nearly the maximum in independent effort was achieved; and the Committee's resources were conserved for a greater total service in later relief than could possibly have been rendered if the camps had been kept up for a longer time. Actually, 6 of the 25 camps in service for the period of December to February had been closed in that month or in early March; 13 more were closed in March and April, leaving only 6 to carry through the month of May. In certain cases the closing of a camp involved the transfer to other camps of some scores or even hundreds of refugees who could not well be turned out so long as any such provision was available.

Aside from the incomplete but valuable mitigation of war risks provided by the Safety Zone enterprise the Committee had aided several tens of thousands of persons to secure space in privately owned buildings and had provided shelter under organized management for over 70,000 persons through periods up to six months.

Other aspects of the work in and for the camps are discussed in relation to "Food," "Cash Relief," "Health Services," "Personal Aid," and "Administration."

II. Food

Period I

During the period December 17–31, the International Committee made regular deliveries of rice averaging 84.5 bags per day among 2 camps, plus 28.5 bags to kitchens, plus 3 to police and sanitary workers, plus 20 among special grants including the Red Swastika Society. Of the regular kitchens there were two in camps conducted by the Committee, two conducted by the Red Swastika Society largely serving persons from the camps, and one by the Red Cross Society entirely serving persons in the camps. The remainder of the rice to the camps was given out dry. Of the camp population averaging 70,750 during this period, 20,150 were fed inside the camps, 8,200 in kitchens adjoining camps. About 5,000 were fed by the special grants. Thus some 38,350 [sic] persons were receiving their basic food, some of them their only food, from the Committee. Some groups had private supplies of rice with which they could provide for themselves wholly or in part, and some were able to get supplements of vegetables, oils, or peanuts. Meat was seldom seen in the camps, and supplies of green vegetables or of beans were small and costly. The total number of bags of rice given out free or at the nominal charge made by the kitchens for those able to pay it, was 2,035.

All figures for the December half-month and for the following months are on the basis of the full time specified. Actually a larger number of people were fed, but some of them for less than the time specified. It was expected that one bag of rice would feed 300 persons for one day in the form of thick gruel made in a collective kitchen. Where rice was given out dry, the calculation was 250 person-days per bag. In many instances the rice was spread even more thinly, since some people were served from the kitchens only once a day, or received relatively small allotments of dry rice. A bag of rice of the lower middle grade which constituted the bulk of the Committee's supplies weighed on the average 212.25 pounds, or nearly 77.5 kilograms; it represented 1.25 *shih tan* by measure.

For January the average of the camp population was 62,500, of whom 25,250 were fed inside the camps by a distribution of 79 bags daily among the 25 camps; there were also given out 4.5 bags daily among police and sanitary workers and other staff not covered in the camps, and 4.5 bags in grants to the Red Cross Hospital and other special interests. Thus about 27,125 persons were largely or wholly maintained by the free rice. In this period the kitchens conducted by the Red Swastika Society did not need to draw considerably upon the International Committee for rice, and that under the Red Cross was moved inside a camp. The total number of bags used by the Committee was 2,721.

In February the camp population was sharply reduced to an average of 36,800, which included, however, many of the poorest people whose private resources were early exhausted; 20,800 were fed in the camps by a daily distribution of 69 bags. The Committee's workers now received a maintenance allowance in cash, and all other special grants were stopped. Total 1,935 bags.

For March the average total population of 22 camps was 26,700, of whom 17,300 were fed by the Committee on a daily allowance of 59 bags, totaling 1,821.

In April the number of camps was reduced to 16, with a total population averaging 21,750, of whom the Committee fed 11,300 with a daily distribution of 31 bags of rice and 12 of wheat, 5.5 bags of wheat were also supplied as aid to the kitchens conducted by the Red Swastika Society. Nearly 18 bags of wheat per day were used in work relief and special grants. Altogether the Committee distributed 930 bags of rice and 1,059 of wheat feeding some 16,000 persons.

In May, 7 camps with an average of 12,150 persons contained 7,250 dependent on the Committee for grain, which was supplied with 4 bags of rice and 10.5 bags of wheat daily. In addition, 4 bags of wheat were provided for the Red Swastika kitchen, and almost 18 bags were used in work relief and special grants. Altogether, 474 bags of rice and 969 bags of wheat were used, feeding 11,650.

For the entire period Dec. 17 to May 31, 1937–38, 9,916 bags of rice worth $109,700.96, and 2,208 bags of wheat worth $7,098.00 were distributed free. Because of the grants to other organizations and the element of shifting in and out of camps, it is impossible to give an exact figure for the number of persons who received some portion of their maintenance from this distribution. We estimate it conservatively at 55,000, of whom some 20,000 benefited greatly over a period of two months or more, and some 10,000 through four months or more.

Upon medical advice an effort was made to introduce necessary food elements into the rice gruel which tended to be the exclusive food of the poorest persons, by providing the Chinese *ts'an ton* (broad bean). With great difficulty 87 tons of beans were secured from Shanghai after weeks of negotiations, and were distributed in 1,077 bags of 161.55 pounds per bag. It is estimated that in March and April 17,500 of the poorest persons in the camps received an average of 11.25 pounds per person. From April onward through the summer the problem of food content was partly solved by the use of a large element of whole wheat in the grain distribution.

In the general period, besides the 1,077 bags of beans, 75 bags of flour and 22 bags of salt were also given out free: a total value of $9,334.94. Thus the grand total of food distribution was $126,133.90, with the wheat priced at an exceptionally low figure.

In an effort to assist people who had the means and will to buy, but for whom supplies were not available in the conditions of the winter of 1937–38, the Committee sold rice, flour and salt at approximately standard prices, from the stocks of commodities given to it before the military crisis. The Committee had the further purpose of encouraging private trade by example, particularly in the insecure periods of December and January when no regular shops survived in Nanking; and desired to give any reasonable assistance to persons outside the camps in lodgings of their own arranging. The total sales were not large, but in the conditions of the time were very useful. There were sold 1,886 bags of rice, 804 bags of flour, and 243 bags of salt, valued in gross at $26,574.00 (less $1,592.65 in discounts for agents and in shortages). This represented a month's supply of cereals for well over 15,000 persons.

The Committee supplied its own and associated kitchens with fuel, some 658 tons of coal and supplementary wood, amounting to $10,192.00 at prices that now seem incredibly low.

Period II

During the summer of 1938, a large part of the distribution of food from the resources of the International Committee was carried out through the mechanism of the Joint Project, directed by a Committee combining representation of the Red Swastika Society with that of our own organization. This arrangement was made in order to implement a request from the Nanking International Relief Association (Shanghai) that $22,000 be set aside from funds contributed by them, to be used in such an enterprise. In order to complete the program that was attempted, the International Committee added $4,339.22 in cash, making $26,339.22; and 1255.5 bags of wheat valued at $4,394.25 making a total of $30,743.47 used in the Joint Project. Of this amount staff allowances and incidentals amounting to $644.67 were charged against the project, and the remainder was used entirely for grain.

Full maintenance allowance of cereal was calculated 37.32 *ho* per week (one-half for children eight years of age and under), given half in rice and half in wheat. (This would be equivalent to 188 person-days per bag, an allowance made a little more liberal than that of the preceding winter, partly because it was half in wheat which is lighter per unit of measure than rice and less effectively used by Chinese of this region). On the average, each of the 56,726 adults and 11,940 young children who received grain was given a supply for 2.7 weeks or 19 days, though some of the poorer ones were given enough for 4 or even for 6 weeks.

Thus 13,865 families were given a real boost for the months, June to September, with the heaviest distribution in August. They represented nearly 20 percent of the total population within the walled city. The International Committee indirectly subsidized the Joint Project further by supplying the purchased wheat and part of the rice from its own supplies at cost, and by carrying the responsibilities of purchase, storage, and general overhead. Altogether 2,535 bags of rice and 2,511 bags of wheat were given out.

Outside the Joint Project, but within the sub-period June to November 1938, the International Committee gave out 690 bags of rice worth $6,909.50; 2,022 bags of wheat worth $7,077.00; and small lots of beans, flour, maize and salt worth $874.74. Two hundred eight bags of flour were sold for $525.00 net. The rice and wheat supplied 20 day's cereals to about 24,500 persons. Part of the wheat was used in payment for work.

In the course of the Winter-Spring Program from December 1938 through April 1939, the Committee gave out 10,847 bags of rice worth $116,609.70; 592 bags of beans worth $5,624; and 21.5 bags of salt worth $426.56. The rice was distributed on the basis of 5 *ho* per day for an adult and 3 *ho* for a child of 8 years or under. The 105,075 adults and 23,065 young children (128,140 persons) thus aided were enabled to receive on the average nearly 23 days' full supply of cereal. The poorer ones drew for 4 weeks, even 6 or 8 weeks. Thus 36,090 families were given a fair fraction of their food for a bad period of the year. During the late winter and spring the price of rice was rapidly rising, with consequent burden and misery for the poor. The Committee attempted to supplement the fundamental cereal in the most needy cases by giving to 26,250 of the poorest persons 28 *ho* of red beans, equivalent to a good ratio of beans to cereal for 4 weeks diet.

The methods employed in the distribution of food are discussed under the topics of Administration; the costs and relative importance of this primary work of relief are shown in the presentation of Financial Statements and in consecutive detail among the items of the audited Income and Expenditure Accounts (Appendix C).

Here it is sufficient to recall in conclusion that the International Committee expended $364,000 directly in its enterprises of food distribution. Well over 55,000 received food during Period I; over 78,000 in the summer and autumn of 1938; 128,000 in the winter spring program of 1938–39. During Period I the grants of food were largely within the camp population and often continued for a time measured in months. Some three weeks' supply was the average in Period II, with few receiving more than 6 weeks' supply of cereal in one program.

It should be remembered that during the course of the Committee's work under review, the population within the walled city increased by fully 100,000 persons, most of them returning to ruined homes after losing or exhausting what they had taken with them in earlier flight to the country. The Committee therefore faced an enormous number of impoverished people, and felt that the major part of its work should be the supplementing of their meager food with such grants as could be made from resources available. Throughout Period II persons approved by the processes described under "administration," came to the Committee's distributing costs were kept to the minimum consistent with careful selection of recipients.* This food policy is not fully satisfactory to the Committee, but in the actual situation it seemed on balanced consideration to be the way of maximum relief.

III. Cash Relief

Period I

In March to May 1938 small cash grants were made to 17,609 poor families selected among some 56,000 who were investigated after they applied for aid of one sort or another. The cash grants gave some help to the bottom groups outside the camps, and aided the return to homes and independent effort outside the Refugee Zone, besides stimulating a much-needed private trade in rice from the few country places that could then provide supplies for Nanking. Thus $54,588.20 was given out at the rate of $3.10 per family.

---

*Sentence unclear in original.

Period II

Cash grants were used more sparingly, to care for needs other than those which could be met by dry cereal alone. The plight of persons arriving from the country with no other possession or resource than scanty clothing, or of families already subjects for relief who were burned out in the frequent fires among crowded straw huts, is suggestive of the problems confronting the investigator and administrators who depended mainly upon grants of rice. In this period a sum of $10,671 was so given out, at the rate of $3.29 to each of 3,240 families.

Summary Total

20,849 families received $65,529.71 in cash, or $3.13 per family. Expenses for staff and minor items amounted to $3,$80 [?].

IV. Work Relief

Period I

Appropriations were made in the form of cash plus some wheat, for wages of workers on approved projects. The direct expenditure on work relief in money was $7,622 of which only $158 was used for field staff and servants, and less than 3 per cent for materials. Several of the larger projects were in the form of subsidies to other organizations or institutions, with which they provided the supervision and materials, subject to the International Committee's approval of detailed budgets and its inspection at will. For example, $2,540 was used to complete the necessary burial enterprises undertaken by the Red Swastika Society, which covered over 40,000 bodies otherwise uncared for. During some 40 working days, this employed nearly 170 men. On this and a number of other work relief jobs, forty cents per day of actual work was taken as the standard wage. Other important projects included over $1,500 in sanitary and street cleaning work under the Committee's own management of casual labor; $1,430 in grading undertaken by the University of Nanking; some hundreds each in dyke work labor on farms otherwise uncultivated, road repair, and the transport and cleaning of the Committee's large purchase and distribution of wheat.

Over 18,000 wage-days were paid for in cash, representing approximately the employment of 720 men for a month. The Committee would have been willing to expend more in work relief if it had been able to secure the time and any of sufficiently competent managers, within or without its own organization.* However, it must be recognized that in a situation of general distress for

---

*Sentence unclear in original.

an emergency period, work relief is relatively costly and gives direct benefit to a small number of people unless vast public resources are available.

Period II

In this period the major enterprise of work relief was interrelated with the provision of winter clothing and bedding in the general program of direct relief. Here the labor undertaking began with the cleaning and beating of the cotton, a specialized task more difficult than it seems. But the major sums were put out for the cutting and sewing of clothes and quilts, done in Christian schools and churches by women and girls. For administrative convenience, the initial part of this work was undertaken as a department of work relief, with an outlay of just over $2,000. (This was only a small part of the making of clothing and bedding which is reported under that heading hereafter.)

Just over $1,500 was used in drainage and grading work; almost $1,000 in farm labor; $600 in road repair; $250 in sanitary work; $250 in clerical work to improve the Committee's records of relief cases; and the remaining part of $5,850 in smaller enterprises. Field staff and assistance cost $920, as the cotton and clothing work was very complicated. It is impossible to give an accurate figure of the number of work-days, since the labor of the women and girls was partly paid for in piece work. But for all types of labor concerned, fully 15,500 wage days were provided, equivalent to over 600 persons for one month.

V. Clothing and Bedding

The report under this heading is incomplete and inadequate, for the triple reason that the International Committee acted somewhat casually as receiver for certain stocks and gifts of clothing and bedding which were passed on to responsible heads of refugee camps or to church organizations for distribution, that the Committee only for one brief time had a separate unit and set of records concerned with this matter alone, and finally that the brief time referred to was brought to a disastrous conclusion by the arrest and indefinitely continuing detention of the man in charge. Nevertheless, the financial records are clear, and the enterprises undertaken by the Committee itself can be reported, plus a considerable part of the transmitting service above referred to.

Period I

In the confusion at the fall of Nanking, individual friends made available supplies of clothing and bedding that had been prepared by benevolent organizations for the care of the wounded, but eventually were abandoned. The Committee also paid refugee women for completing and remaking some articles. Some 1,100 pieces of bedding, 1,600 pieces of clothing, and 540 towels were given out, aside from minor transfers made personally rather than through the Committee's organization. $498.52 was spent for sewing and materials, a small supplement to the considerable value of the cotton-filled quilts and the padded winter garments, which was probably $7,000.

Period II

The Committee received in gifts 4,003 pieces of unused winter clothing, and 3,696 pieces of used summer clothing. It made 6,141 pieces of winter clothing at an average cost of $1.80, or $11,092.01. The summer clothing, valued conservatively at $0.50 per piece, was distributed through church organizations to 880 families, representing just over 4 pieces per family and a total value of $1,848. 6,129 winter garments were given out, and 4,015 are prepared for distribution in the late autumn. The winter garments given out represent a value of $11,071.01; those on hand at the close of the period, $7,347.45.

The Committee received in gifts 154 pieces of good-grade winter bedding, and made 939 more at $6.19 per piece, totaling $5,809.12. Five hundred straw mattresses without covers were made for $92.44, 1,043 pieces of winter bedding, representing $6,445.74 in value, were distributed, along with all the straw mattresses; 50 pieces of winter bedding are ready for the coming season.

Because some parts of the clothing and bedding distribution were carried out through subordinate or co-operating units, figures as to the number of families aided are not complete. They can, however, be given in fairly close estimates based on the Committee's own records and reports from some of the other units. We reckon that 1,800 families received aid in winter clothing and bedding during Period I, and 3,950 during Period II, aside from the straw mattresses. Usually one family would receive only one suit or one long garment, but sometimes help for a second member, and bedding. The making of the clothing and bedding in Period II was managed so as to become an extensive work relief project.

The beating and preparation of the cotton was carried out locally; part of the cloth was made by local weavers who were aided in securing yarn to start the process; and all of the cutting and sewing was done by poor women and girls in church and school enterprises, paid for, with few exceptions, by the funds of the International Committee.

Summary Total

7,729 pieces of unused winter clothing, 2,143 pieces of unused good-grade winter bedding, 3,696 pieces of used summer clothing, 540 towels, and 500 straw mattresses were given out: a total value of $27,063.71, from which 5,750 families received considerable benefit directly and over 600 workers indirectly (to say nothing of the 880 families who got summer clothing and the 500 who had straw mattresses). There is a percentage of overlapping in these records of families helped; but it is insignificant within each period, and is unknown for the entire undertaking. Because of the considerable aid from gifts of clothing and bedding, the Committee was able to do this work with a direct expenditure of $17,400.25, and still have ready for the coming season $7,737.45 in winter garments with a little bedding.

VI. Small Loans

In the course of Period II, the International Committee gave considerable attention to the granting of small loans as a measure of rehabilitation. Preference was given to men with small beginnings or apparently sound projects for productive business rather than for a mere increase in the desperate competition of petty traders. The limit for each loan was set at $50, with an agreement calling for repayments in 6 or 10 months, with interest at 1 per cent per month.

About one-fourth of the loans were granted for enterprises in each of three groups; the making of clothing and shoes; weaving; the processing of food. Smaller aid went to the making of furniture and household utensils, to printing, to metal work, to setting up barbers, and to work in bamboo and matting. Eighty-five percent of those who received loans were re-entering former trades from which they were dislodged by pillage, burning, or other war disturbance.

Moderate interest, a fraction of the current usurious rates which many would be glad to pay if they could find some one able and willing to lend, was planned in order to make the obligation realistic to the borrower, and to reduce the temptation to let a relief loan run indefinitely or even to sub-loan. It must be observed that during the entire time under consideration, Nanking has had no commercial bank, no exchange shops or pawn shops able to provide credit in the familiar ways, and (to the best of our knowledge) none of the mutual saving or credit societies which in the past have given a boost to many a humble enterprise. The Municipal Government has done some work with small loans, but not enough to touch the general problem. Therefore what little the International Committee could do has been warmly welcomed.

Each applicant for a small loan was required to show that he needed aid and was capable of using it successfully, with the specific guarantee of two responsible men satisfactory to the Committee. The guarantors were largely men with shops in the food, clothing and metal trade, with capital ranging from $100 to $1,000. Every case was investigated on the spot, and the applicant who was approved by the specialized investigator had still to be approved by the subcommittee on small loans.

One hundred forty-seven individual loans were issued with an average amount of $42 and also one group loan of 16 families of satin weavers of totaling $660; and one to 13 families of weavers and spinners combined, totaling $850. In the case of the group loans, each family represents about 30 workers, many of them hired. The complete total let out was $7,675. Repayments including interest were $2,356.71 within the period. Very little difficulty was met, saving the one important exception of the detention of the experienced man responsible for such work, from December on far into the spring. When the general work of the International Committee was suspended for some five weeks, that had a bad effect on struggling beginners in business. Only gradually did the Committee provide a substitute for the detained man, and he naturally gave more attention to new applications than to outstanding loans connected with another person whose release was continually expected. It is hoped that recent follow up will result in clearing most of the old loans, for experience before December and in late spring was favorable.

VII. Aid to Farmers

Wartime difficulties of communication and politics have greatly restricted aid to farmers. It should also be said, however, that the International Relief Committee through its own studies and the advice of such expert counsel as could be secured, decided that in the main its resources should be used in the city. For the farmer did not lose his basic capital, and on the average suffered a smaller shock than did his cousin in Nanking, devastating as the war has been for thousand of villages in this area.

Aside from a fairly important enterprise in the making of farm tools, to which the Committee contributed significant but indirect aid in the form of indispensable personnel, its help to farmers has been limited to two sorts: loans to cooperative societies and the grant of seeds to market gardeners.

Near the close of period I, $1,840 was lent to a group of 13 societies with a membership of 302 families. This was promptly followed in Period II by the lending of $2,460 to three groups totaling 9 societies with a membership of 295 families, 90 per cent of the loans were granted for the provision of implements, 8 per cent for seeds, and 2 per cent for animals. All but $180 of these funds was repaid within Period II, or immediately after its close, with the customary interest of 1/2 per cent monthly. The loans to one group were returned under military and political pressure, which fortunately has lessened in recent months. Indeed, for a time lending and borrowing was a unique and venturesome business in the economy of this region, and the mere transfer of cash through the city gates to and from the country required the efforts of one of the bolder members of the Committee.

The societies to which loans were made were all village groups of long standing, which had good records before the war in handling loans made by the University of Nanking or by banks under its arrangements. Because it had in any case to depend upon University personnel for this work, and because it has its own hands more than full with direct relief work that is supposedly temporary in character, the International Committee at the close of Period II asked the College of Agriculture and Forestry of the University of Nanking to take over the whole enterprise of aid to farmers. In cash and loans receivable a fund of practically $10,000 was entrusted to the College for farm relief, preferably in the form of loans. The sum should be sufficient, with close management, to pay from interest of the charges of routine administration, though not of course for responsible supervision. (In May, 1939, two-thirds of the sum was let out to 21 societies comprising 495 member-families, under a program which provides for expert counsel and service including the supply of improved seeds.)

Grants of vegetable seeds to market gardeners within and near the city were a quiet but very useful piece of work. In this area the farmers' own supply of seeds suffered severely from burning and indiscriminate pillaging, and the ordinary commercial means of supply had practically disappeared. In the spring of 1938 seeds of a dozen kinds of vegetables recommended by local experts were supplied from Shanghai firms by the Nanking International Relief Association at a cost of $966.98. These were carefully distributed among some 185 families of gardeners whose circumstances and specific needs had been sought out in house-to-house visits. Since in that period and indeed continuously thereafter, military and political factors have made the price of vegetables abnormally high, the general population as well as these particular families have benefitted from the increase in production of necessaries.

In Period II the needs for particular seeds continued if not so acutely. Again the Nanking International Relief Association assisted with the purchase of $283.50 worth of varieties not obtainable in Nanking; while the University of Nanking supplied at half-price $253 worth and there were other purchases of $187.85. A glimpse into the conditions under which such work has had to be done is afforded by the fact that most of the seeds purchased in Shanghai were stolen by a sentry who took the larger part of the load of a messenger. Nevertheless, 217 gardening families, comprising 702 workers, received seeds of varieties especially needed. Also, $74.31 was put out in wheat of the finest quality for a special project.

All told, $10,000 has been provided in farm loan funds of which half is doing its second turn of service; and $1,639 was paid out in seeds to market gardeners. Some 900 families received direct aid in production of food, most of them in two successive seasons.

VIII. Health Service and Personal Aid

Direct activities of the International Committee in relation to health were largely centered in the camp life and the crowded streets of the Safety Zone area during the period when the welfare functions of government had largely disappeared from Nanking. The Sanitation Commission for a few weeks commanded the services of about 400 men, who were used in street cleaning, the construction and care of latrines in crowded places, and the removal of refuse from camps and certain other centers of accumulation. Persons accustomed to Chinese life can scarcely imagine a concentration of 250,000 persons with very few dogs and pigs, and with none of the usual economic process of collecting, storing and distributing night soil to market gardens. Yet Nanking was many months in returning to a fair degree of "normalcy" in such matters.

Five of the street-cleaning coolies were killed in the general slaughter of mid-December, and for a considerable time little work could be done away from camps or secluded houses. Later, however, street cleaning and the removal of refuse were undertaken as small work relief projects where supervision could be provided.

Fortunately for the people of the city, the University (Drum Tower) Hospital continued its work throughout all difficulties; and the Nanking International Red Cross Committee, after completing certain emergency services for wounded soldiers, was able to turn its efforts to the development of clinic work for the sick among the poor, while assisting in the payment of fees for a part of the patients carried by the University Hospital. Thus the type of service in which the International Relief Committee would naturally be interested as a necessary complement of its own work, was being maintained as well as could be expected under all the circumstances. The Relief Committee has therefore looked upon the medical field as one for cooperation, not for direct participation. It has solicited and aided in securing staff, funds, and supplies for the Hospital and the Red Cross Committee.

The International Relief Committee has arranged for the transfer of needy cases to the Hospital, particularly in the period of the camps, and sometimes made contributions to medical service in the form of cash relief or payment of fees. In certain camps the Committee assisted in the maintenance of groups of nurses who did simple clinical work and cared for maternity cases; one of these groups included a doctor from the Red Swastika Society. Although the general death rate among the refugees was high, particularly among children, there was never a critical run of illness. Beri beri, measles, and scarlet fever gave anxiety; but considering the circumstances, deaths were few.

A squad from the University Hospital, partly supported by Red Cross funds, was given facilities and assistance in a preventive campaign among the camps, which vaccinated in the late spring of 1938 a total of 16,265 persons, and inocculated more than 12,000 against typhoid and cholera. The Committee secured large supplies of cod liver oil for the University Hospital, and acted as agent for distributing considerable quantities (with great difficulty) among the children of the camps. Continuously from March of 1938, the Committee has maintained a supply of powdered milk for the use of the Hospital among refugee babies; and also gave it out to some scores in the camps.

Aside from lack of money, the acute difficulties of transportation and official passes hindered many refugees from leaving Nanking to rejoin their families elsewhere. Where such a venture seemed to promise a solution of a family problem or to give some hope of economic betterment, the Committee's workers found ways to assist by means of friendly contact with the local authorities; and supplied money when needed, which is listed in the amounts for cash relief. Similarly there were important needs for counsel and assistance in initiating communication with relatives elsewhere, or in arranging for the transfer of small personal funds to and from Nanking. A limited postal service was restored only from April of 1938, and not for some time longer was there a considerable money order system. Altogether several hundred persons were aided with problems of the types just described. A few tens were found work directly, and of course many others were aided indirectly or by relief measures described under other headings. A job is the universal need, and in many ways the hardest to meet in the gloomy economics of wartime Nanking.

It is impossible to list the many types of personal service rendered directly, or through institutions which were rendering personal service, by the Committee's trucks and cars, supplies of needed commodities, facilities for communication and light transport from Shanghai (by foreign gunboats for necessities), and means of securing and providing practical information for those who had little access to it. More than once in this report it had been convenient to use the brief and general term, "special grant." Usually the term covers aid to an existing institution or organization for useful work which it could not finance or supply. A large instance is the subsidy of more than $1,600 given to the Ginling College camp and school for some 600 young refugee women, maintained through the summer of 1938. This was a continuation of the camp principle, considering protection, relief for extreme poverty, and some elementary training. Another example was the partial support of five blind girls left helpless in camps, concluded by payments of over $500 for their entry into an excellent school for the blind in Shanghai.

IX. Surveys

Beginning with March, 1938, as soon as such efforts were physically possible, the Nanking International Relief Committee has undertaken systematic studies of the condition of the people and of important economic and social factors in their problems. Where the results have been of apparent value to those elsewhere who are interested in relief either as contributors or as workers, they have been published. These studies also have a modest place in the analysis of war and social disorganization. The first important undertaking was completed in July, 1938, under the title, "War Damage in the Nanking Area" (Smythe). For several weeks 30 men carried out careful sampling inquiries among families of the city and of five counties round about. Some of the workers were well qualified for their tasks, and there were available both experienced direction and competent statistical service. The investigation was twofold in purpose: to learn what was the fundamental injury to economic life and to understand the immediate situation of the people a few months after the major catastrophe. The report was not printed commercially, but was supplied in fair quantities to relief committees abroad.

The war damage survey revealed a distressing picture of the slaughter of civilians and the unnecessary destruction of basic property by useless burning before the crisis and by extensive plundering and burning thereafter. On the farms, one resident in every seven families was killed; in the city, one resident in every five families was killed, injured, or taken away, which works out to about the same degree of murder and misery. Forty percent of all farm buildings were burned. Farm losses (domestic property not considered) for a surveyed population of 1,078,000 were $41 millions ($220 per family). The 221,000 persons surveyed in Nanking lost $838 per family, $40 millions in total. Buildings and contents for the entire city showed losses of $246 millions, or $1,262 per family of the pre-war population. Only 9 percent of the Nanking population were employed in late March, 1938. Family earnings averaged $0.14 per day, as compared with $1.23 reported for the same families in former times. The losses to life and property caused by actual warfare were one to two per cent of the total losses.

A simpler study followed in the summer and autumn of 1938, published as "Crop Investigations in the Nanking Area, and Sundry Economic Data" (Bates). Six investigators were sent into a like number of surrounding counties to secure systematic information as to planted area, condition of crops, and injury from flood. Results were limited by several critical experiences, but they proved sufficient to give an accurate estimate of grain production. The Nanking markets for fuel, cotton, clothing, and bedding were carefully analyzed as a basis for judging those elements in public need and in a relief program. There was added a composite report from 30 general observers of business, employment, and conditions of need.

These studies found a most remarkable demonstration of the recuperative and staying powers of the Chinese peasant, 96 of the farm families were at work in the areas covered, and those at work had planted 99 per cent of their arable land in summer crops. However, losses of buildings, animals, tools, and seed, plus some slow returns of workers from wartime dislodgment, took their toll from quality of cultivation. Local floods caused serious injury. The yield of rice was estimated at 45 per cent of "normal" (a "normal" crop is practically a perfect one), or at 58 per cent of "most frequent yield." Rice supplies were sufficient for the Nanking area, but quantities were shipped out by privileged interests. Markets in general were manipulated by political and military controls of transportation. Supplies of fuel, clothing, and bedding were scanty in relation to needs, but abundant in relation to effective demand. Many shopkeepers reported: "The people have no means to buy." Thirty workers in churches and schools reported 44 percent of their communities to be destitute.

A third study covered for the winter of 1938–39. "The Nanking Population: Employment, Earnings and Expenditure." Family conditions were by that time relatively stabilized in the new conditions, so that information as to size of family and groupings by age and sex would be of continuing value. Conditions of employment and earnings by occupational groups, by sex, and in totals, were discovered and compared with the former conditions reported by the persons investigated and with those of the previous year's survey. Analyses of expenditures were revealing as to the supreme importance of grain among all payments of an impoverished community and also as to the sad state of housing.

As of the past winter, there are in Nanking only 94 men of vigorous age (15 to 19 years) to 100 families; whereas before the war there were 130. The percent of all families which have no male head is now 16, double the pre-war 8. There are today within the walled city 14,100 of such families. The existing employment rate is 27 per cent of the total population, or about two thirds of normal. Almost half of all employed persons make less than $10 monthly; only 4 per cent of them $30. Present average earnings of this remnant population are about 40 per cent of their reported former earnings. Military and economic policy severely limits the possibilities for improvement. The living standard of the whole Chinese population of Nanking is very close to that of the poorer groups selected in various Chinese cities for surveys by social workers before the war. The events of the last two years have reduced the native population to that level, which means of course that many are on the margin of survival. 20,000 women are now working, at an average wage of $0.18 per day; of these, only 1,800 worked before the war. Even the unfavorable selection of men remaining in Nanking show a fearful descent from productive and middle-class occupations into casual labor and peddling.

At the close of Period II, the Committee appropriated funds for a thorough study of the 30,000 families relieved in the winter-spring program of 1938–39, on the basis of the investigation blanks already in hand, including an analysis of the relief actually given, and a comparative view of the families investigated but refused relief. This effort will throw some light on the validity of the investigations and judgments that have been practiced. More significantly, perhaps, it will give more extensive and presumably more accurate averages of the distribution of age and sex and the size of family, among families applying for and getting relief than have previously been available. The study introduces a new attempt to classify all families as "with earning capacity," "without earning capacity," or "with inadequate earning capacity." These classifications will run through all the data mentioned above; they are based upon reports of age, sex, and physical condition. Blanks are sorted in that manner, and thus the least capable of self-maintenance can be sought out in future relief work if that seems desirable. For reasons of administrative convenience, this work was turned over to the University of Nanking for supervision on behalf of the Committee.

X. Administration

General

In Appendix D are found annotated lists of the membership and officers of the International Committee, which in themselves convey some idea of the size, nature and working basis of the policy forming and directing body. Since this report is concerned with the work of relief as such, it is not necessary for the Committee to say more about itself. In relation to the whole enterprise, however, it might be well to point out that the members of the Committee and other westerners who assisted in relief work have contributed their services, whether individually or through the consent of their organizations. No member of the Committee is a professional relief worker, and with the single exception of one man for a period of eight months, all have had to carry other duties and interests, some of them heavy and even exacting. However, there are few committees of as long a history in which so large a fraction of the membership has given so much time to the work in hand and has been ready to rise to rather extended emergencies.

In order to centralize responsibility in current administration, a Director is in immediate supervision of the staff and signs all orders for payments within the budgets and instructions of the Committee. Month in and month out, the Director's duties have been the heaviest in the organization. The work previously reviewed gives an idea of the complex body of payments and of commodity transactions for which the Treasurer has had to be responsible. Expecting a very brief period of duty, the Committee began with a simple cash book in the hands of the Chairman, but quickly was required to develop complete books and a considerable mechanism for handling and checking thousands of financial items. For each of the main periods of the Committee's work, its accounts were audited by the well known firm of Thomson and Co., Shanghai. Their arrangement of our Income and Expenditure account is printed in the two sections of Appendix C of this Report. The auditors declared themselves well pleased with the books and vouchers, and in several days of work found nothing to disapprove save minor points of classification.

Transport, storage, and distribution of commodities constituted a large part of the mechanical work of the International Committee's enterprises throughout the entire seventeen months under review. Much of the grain and coal and all of the flour received as contributions in the three weeks before the city fell, were stored outside the city in relatively dangerous places. The securing, repairing, and manning of trucks was a tremendous task. Laborers had to be taken to the job and brought back; sometimes they had to carry a long distance to the truck because of defective bridges, and so on. Air raids became almost continuous, and the transport men had some terrific experiences; it was extremely fortunate that the loss of one eye was the only important injury suffered. In the time of best success, twelve trucks were on the road, and some supplementary means were employed. It is best not to discuss here the difficulties of retaining and operating motor transports in the first weeks after the capture. The camps received the necessary minimum of supplies only through remarkable effort and that by narrow margins.

The major storage was that of grain, for which Sage Hall, the auditorium and large chapel of the University of Nanking, proved to be excellently suited under the conditions of the time. Several hundred tons of rice is no small responsibility either for a custodian in time of disorder, or for the floor of a building. Gasoline and motor oil, clothing and cod liver oil, cash in tens of thousands of dollars, each presented its own peculiar problems of preservation and of handling. Once again it may be said, that the Committee was extremely fortunate in suffering no significant loss, with much thanks to the prevailing exertion and honesty within the organization.

A word more must be said about the bearing of actual conditions upon the work that had to be done. For weeks Nanking had scarcely a vehicle in civilian hands, and it was months before even a fraction of public transport was restored. Yet workers of the Committee had to get over considerable areas as soon as it was safe for the people to scatter somewhat. In particular, investigators in homes could be speeded up in their long tasks if they could be taken and fetched, perhaps in groups, to the parts of the city in which they were to work for a day. An enormous amount of work was done on foot, but sometimes that was downright wasteful. Again, the disappearance of banking from Nanking—even of small exchange shops—for a long time, placed many extra burdens upon the Committee's own tasks and added to its duties in aiding others. No telephone service has been available; for long months there has been no regular transportation from Shanghai or other points outside Nanking. Most of the enormous amount of detailed and supervisory work has been carried on under primitive conditions not yet fully remedied.

Staff

In the era of the camps, the sanitary squads, and the committee's policemen—running say to the end of January, 1938—almost 1,500 persons were listed as on the Committee's staff. All were on a volunteer basis, expecting short service. The policemen passed out of the picture, some squads too literally so. The sanitary squads were soon cut down. But the large number of workers in the camps, as described under that topic, had to be maintained. When they needed it, staff members could receive rice like other refugees, which indeed they were, with few exceptions.

By February it was necessary to arrange maintenance allowances for workers who were retained. The voluntary system could not be long continued among poor people, most of whom had been thoroughly looted and many of whom had lost their homes entirely. Moreover, the Committee's workers included a good many, particularly in the more responsible positions, who were formerly clerks, teachers, and small shopkeepers. They were prepared neither to enter the ranks of coolies employed largely by the military, nor to join the crowds of nocturnal roughs who completed the pulling to pieces of thousands of buildings; and they had little to hope for in the way of other opportunity, except in the gradual and fractional recovery of petty business. From then right through to the present, allowances to staff have largely been in the nature of work relief, part of it to laborers and servants, part to men of the long-gown class. The general scale has run like this: $25 to $35 per month for investigators and the more important of the supervisory and clerical workers; around $20 for clerks and general second-rank men; $10 in the camps for laborers and servants, later rising to $15 for semi-permanent workers. Even the higher allowances have hardly kept large families in a bare living condition, and small families have not lived in luxury on what is something like a mill-worker's pay.

March of 1938 represents a midpoint in the work of Period I, when the large staff of the original enterprise had been reduced and the camps were being cut down. Then there were 15 Chinese volunteers directly attached to the work of the Committee (besides many Chinese on the staffs of Christian organizations who gave part or full time to work in the camps); and 503 workers receiving allowances, of whom 55 were classed as investigators and distributors or supervisors, 299 as office and clerical (most of whom were really petty supervisors of a group of refugees in a certain section of a camp), and 149 as servants and watchmen. The total paid in allowances was $4,725, or about $9.50 per man on the average. This very low average is due to two facts: some were let go with less than the full month's allowance, and many in the camps arranged to share the original allotment for ten men among fifteen, or the like.

By the summer the camps had been closed out, and work was on the basis of outdoor relief, with the Joint Project of food distribution as the largest single enterprise. In August for example, there were 8 Chinese volunteers, and 45 paid workers, of whom 12 were investigators and distributors, 15 were office and clerical men, and 18 were watchmen, servants, and laborers. The total of allowances was $968, or about $21.50 per man. After a still lighter autumn, a heavier program was inaugurated from December, of which February, 1939, is a representative month. Then there were 8 Chinese volunteers, and 70 who required allowances, of whom 28 were investigators and distributors, 21 office and clerical men, and 21 watchmen, servants, and laborers. Allowances totaled $1,700, or about $24.50 per man. April was the final and heaviest month of this program, running 82 paid workers at $2,$ [?]. Then the maintained staff was cut to two men.

One or two words of explanation are in order. In the later Period, servants were necessary chiefly to care for grain in the godown, to carry it from the godown to the distribution office across the street, and then to measure it out against tickets, while helping the distributors and watchmen to handle the crowds. The importance and function of the investigators and office men will appear in a description of the process by which relief has been administered during the major efforts of Period II, and which was partly developed during Period I, as in portions of the work done by the Rehabilitation Commission.

How It's Done

Family requests for aid were received through personal delivery or by mail (which some refugees imagined to be more effective and which certainly was more convenient), usually in the form of scraps of paper scrawled with one or more names, an address, the number of mouths in the family, and occasionally with other information or a petition. Committee workers pasted these scraps upon a serially numbered application-information blank with spaces for the names, ages, indications of sex, physical condition, education, former occupation, present occupation, and current income of each member of the family; plus details of the place and type of work of the head. The blank also had spaces for the judgment of the investigator and of a possible second investigator and for a recommended grant in indicated units of rice, beans, garments, pieces of bedding, cash, cod liver oil, and milk powder (of which usually only one or two would be employed); or suggested transfer to the hospital, work relief, or small loan. Finally for the decision of the responsible head, approving or modifying the investigator's proposals.

The blanks were sorted by streets and checked against an accumulating file for possible duplications. Streets proved better index guides than the common Chinese surnames; and an address was less likely to be met with twice in a confusing manner than the frequent duplicates among Chinese personal names. At this stage each new blank was checked against an accumulating file of previous blanks, to avoid duplications; and at all later stages of the whole process workers were continually watching for duplications, sometimes presented in the name of a second member of the same family, who perhaps had a different surname. One to three days' stint was given out to each investigator, say 30 to 50 blanks per day of applicants living in the same locality.

The work of the investigator was of primary importance to the whole enterprise. He first checked the address and names and number of family members, calling for police registration slips and using the answers of children and neighbors when desirable. He could also call upon the officers of the local tithing system if there was a question of changed location or recent alteration in the resident membership of the family; and if his total efforts still left him in doubt about some part of the inquiry, he could request a second investigation later. An able investigator soon learned to detect misrepresentation, for which the ordinary penalty was immediate dropping of the whole matter. Many obvious drug addicts were also dropped forthwith. The actual economic condition of the family he examined by methods that a westerner would consider inquisitorial, sometimes opening the boxes in which their clothing and other small possessions might be concealed.

The investigator's blanks with recommendations were returned to the desk of the superintendent of distribution, who indicated any point of doubt, and endorsed or modified or suspended the recommendations. The blanks were then passed to the men in charge of the distribution of different types of relief, most of them going to the food department, of course; some to the clothing and bedding department; and others to the group of less frequently used types of relief. These men checked again the blank and particularly the recommendation, raising any question that they wished. All blanks then passed under the inspection of the Director who affixed his seal.

Next came notification by messenger to each family approved for a particular grant of relief, naming a day and hour for distribution. When a member of the family appeared, he exchanged his notification slip for a distribution ticket. He (often she) could actually get the allotted relief only after telling the name of the family head, the address, and the number of mouths, in exact tally with the report in the Committee's hands.

Grain was measured out in the presence of the recipient. This was ordinarily the end of the Committee's effort for that case, apart from the filing of the investigator's blank with the distribution tickets used for that family. It should be added that certain names were recommended or referred to the Committee's office by individuals known to it; with few exceptions, they were investigated and handled much as others. At times the Committee was able to secure the help of some Christian workers for undertaking or checking investigations in particular localities. Finally, the administration from time to time sent out men to go over samples of the work of each investigator, to be sure that his reports were properly accurate and dependable.

A large part of the Chinese who could naturally be called upon to undertake tasks of public welfare great or humble, having long since left the city, generally speaking, the available human material is not such as to arouse enthusiasm. Yet from the very beginning the Committee was remarkably fortunate to secure the active aid, often voluntary, of a number of men who usefully carried heavy burdens over a long period of time. Scores of others did their lesser duties well, and many more gave no reason for serious complaint. The record is not perfect for efficiency or for honesty. Yet a very small percentage of the Committee's resources went to others than the very poor for whom they were intended. Given the whole situation, there is reason to be grateful for the work of the staff and for the fact that no critical trouble occurred within the organization.

XI. Summarized Financial Report

This report is taken from the audited Income and Expenditure Accounts, as certified by Thomson and Co. for the two periods December 1, 1937 to May 31, 1938, and June 1, 1938, to April 30, 1939. The accounts as audited are found in full in Appendix C. Here the main headings only are presented, in figures rounded to the nearest thousand.

XII. Contributors and Cooperation

A list of contributors who gave $1,000 or more in cash or in commodities will include all but $7,000 of the Committee's income from gifts. In several cases, notably those of the Nanking International Relief Association (Shanghai), these are compound contributions, made up of a large number of individual gifts.

Gifts in service and transportation by business and municipal organizations and by private individuals in Nanking, particularly in the period of preparation of the Safety Zone were very useful. Possibly the greatest collective gift of all was that of the use of buildings for refugees; in the case of one institution alone this meant some $30,000 in minimum repairs for six months of hard usage. The contribution of personnel, full time or part time, western and Chinese, by mis-

Table B-1

Financial Report

	Period I	Period II	Total
Income			
1. Contributions	$428,000	$84,000	$512,000
2. Sales	26,000	7,000	33,000
3. Profit on Exchange	—	5,000	5,000
Total Income	$454,000	$96,000	$550,000
Brought forward	—	182,000	—
Available for use	$454,000	$278,000	$550,000
Expenditure: Relief			
4. Food and Fuel	$178,000	$164,000	$342,000
5. Joint Project	—	22,000	22,000
6. Housing	11,000	2,000	13,000
7. Health and Sanitation	3,000	—	3,000
8. Cash Relief	57,000	12,000	69,000
9. Work Relief	8,000	7,000	15,000
10. Special Projects	2,000	22,000	24,000
11. Agricultural Loans	2,000	8,000	10,000
12. Miscellaneous	—	1,000	1,000
13. Small Loans	—	1,000	1,000
Total for Relief	$261,000	$239,000	$500,000
Expenditure: Overhead			
14. Staff	$3,000	$2,000	$5,000
15. General Expenses	8,000	6,000	14,000
Total Expenditures	$272,000	$247,000	$519,000
Surplus at close of period	182,000	31,000	31,000
Available for use	$454,000	$278,000	$550,000

Explanatory notes, numbered to correspond with entries above:

2. Sales receipts were from certain commodities received as contributions, and from the fees collected from persons able to pay for rice-gruel in the kitchens operated during Period I.

3. Profit on exchange was realized from gifts in foreign currencies received and reported in Period I, but not actually exchanged therein.

5. Spent almost entirely for rice and wheat, as reported under Food Distribution. (This figure could therefore be added to Number 4 above.)

6. Staff and labour for 25 refugees camps, plus miscellaneous costs for sanitation, water, light, watchmen, burials.

7. General services, partly in aid of camps. See elsewhere for information about the health services provided by the International Red Cross and other organizations.

10. Bedding and clothing $17,000. Surveys $6,500.

11. The figure of $10,000 represents the total sum made available for loans, parts of which are already being used a second time after repayment, and parts of which were loaned only recently. The sum is here charged to Cost of Relief because it has been entrusted to the University of Nanking as an Agricultural Welfare Fund (to be administered preferably on a loan basis).

13. The sum listed is for staff. One hundred forty-nine loans have been granted, for a total sum of $7,695. of which $5,340 was outstanding at the close of the period. In the auditor's statement (Appendix C) this sum is recorded under "Surplus Available" and is part of $31,000 reported above.

Table B-2

Contributions

From and through the Nanking Municipal Government (1937)	$189,890.00
Nanking International Relief Association	
(in addition to services and smaller gifts)	92,436.09
National Relief Commission	100,000.00
American Advisory Committee for Civilian Relief in China	72,378.40
American Advisory Committee, American Red Cross	15,000.00
British Fund for Relief in China	10,000.00
Mrs. George A. Fitch (for various American groups)	5,760.57
Golden Rule Foundation	5,949.14
Ta Tung Flour Mill	5,000.00
China Club of Seattle	2,521.01
Anonymous	2,255.00
China Club of Southern California	2,000.00
Rotary International	1,039.31
Mr. Ching Sheng Tang	1,000.00
Total gifts received in units of more than $1,000	$505,229.52

sions, institutions, business firms, and churches, was indispensable. The auditors gave their services in two successive years, and the British and American navies made many a troublesome exertion in transport of supplies and transfer of persons and radiograms.

Special mention should be made of the Nanking International Relief Association (Shanghai), an organization made up largely of former residents of Nanking who not only made repeated and generous contributions of their own, but through their committees and officers solicited other gifts and performed a multitude of agency services in the months when communication and transport required unusual effort.

The uncomfortable position of neutrals who try to do active service in the midst of war, is such as to preclude full and frank thanks to governments. But it is possible to say in regard to the Chinese and to the Japanese authorities, that the opportunity to aid common people in distress has been highly valued; and that assistance in various forms, both before and after the crisis, has been gratefully received. Of the German, British, and American diplomatic and consular services, it is difficult to restrain the Committee's appreciation for generous assistance given with personal grace and interest in humanitarian work.

In the practice of relief, the Nanking International Committee has worked in cooperation with other bodies and institutions serving in Nanking, as mentioned frequently in preceding sections of this report: notably, the Nanking International Red Cross, the (International) Red Swastika Society, and the Local Chinese Red Cross Society; the University Hospital; Christian schools and churches.

With the larger of these groups there have been links in personnel and in program that have maintained continual touch. As members of the International Relief Committee or as important men on its staff there have worked together Protestant and Catholic Christians, Mohammedans, and an officer of the (Buddhist) Red Swastika Society; and men of several nationalities—German, American, British, Chinese, Japanese, Danish. The staff developed their own short name for the organization, simply "International" (Committee). No barrier has been found in race or nationality or religion among men who desired to aid the poor in time of need.

XIII. Outlook

The International Relief Committee has from the beginning hoped that its duties might be required for only a brief time. As each new unfolding of distress has come, a seasonal program continuing at longest for a few months has been adopted, after which expenditures and staff have been sharply cut down and the situation re-examined. In the course of time, it is natural that fewer members of the Committee are able and ready to give large amounts of time to relief work, usually for adequate reasons. Satisfactory Chinese workers are also fewer, owing to continued withdrawals from Nanking of the more useful type of men, or to their absorption in other tasks which also press upon the shortage of good personnel. The easiest course is to disband, seeking justification in the fact that an emergency organization has already worked a year and half under serious difficulties.

But the needs of the people make such a course impossible. The Committee's own experience and studies, as presented in this report, are crowded by a desperate poverty grossly abnormal for this region. No general economic improvement is in sight, while factors of a military and governmental nature continue to worsen the currency situation and potentially to endanger much else. It is not for us to assess the program of the Japanese authorities or the attentions of the Chinese; we are here merely observing the actual influences at work upon the people's livelihood, some of which originate on one military side and some on the other. Prosperity and security seem pitifully remote from the local people.

Even the picture drawn by the past twelve months is recently made more grim. Until February of this year, rice was sold at around $8.00 per *shih tan*, not much above the common price of previous times. But from May until early August, when this report is completed, the price has been $17.00 and above. Increases in several supplementary foods have been similar. There has been no improvement in employment or change in wages from the hard figures shown in the Committee's survey of employment, earnings, and expenditure. Indeed, many shops have fallen into new distress. The result is semi-starvation for very large numbers of persons. Crop reports are fairly good. But political and military lines are now drawn in such a manner that a narrowly constricted area is all that can supply grain to the cities of the lower Yangtze Valley. There is no transport free to bring grain from a distance even if it could be financed. The autumn harvest may be expected to bring a brief improvement, succeeded by several months of higher prices and greater scarcity than this past year.

Under such conditions, the International Relief Committee feels that it must do what it can for those who suffer most acutely. Studies and discussions are in progress and in prospect, which will result in a plan of moderate proportions, suiting method and scale as well as possible to the "given" factors of local circumstances as they appear in early autumn, and to such resources of funds and personnel as are within reasonable expectation. The Committee ended Period I with resources of $182,000; but as of May 1, 1939, at the close of period II, it had a surplus of only $31,000 on its books. Of this amount, some is out on loan, and the Committee has aided some small welfare undertakings in the early summer. Considerable gifts will be needed in the autumn and continuing through the winter, if appropriate service is to be rendered to the large community of Nanking.

The Nanking Committee welcomes information and counsel from relief organizations in other parts of China, and from friends in other countries. The problem of methods is always with us, ever presenting itself in new forms. Philanthropic persons all over the world will appreciate the Chinese saying, born of multiple experience: "To open the door of benevolence is a difficult matter."

Appendix C

Copies of Auditors' Statements

Table C-1

Nanking International Relief Committee
Income and Expenditure Account
For the Period 1st December, 1937 to 31st May, 1938

Income
Contributions
Cash and Commodities $427,993.22
Sale of Commodities   22,126.71
Kitchen Receipts   4,530.98
                                                  $454,650.91
Less: Loss on Exchange   280.47 $454,370.44

Expenditure
Relief
Food and Fuel
Commodities $160,616.62
Fuel   10,192.30
Transportation   5,698.86
Food Commission Expenses   287.31
Kitchen Expenses   384.82
Field Staff   410.60
Labour   756.70 $178,347.21

Housing
Refugee Camp Expenses $2,615.75
Field Staff   4,983.06
Labour   3,312.42   10,812.23

Health and Sanitation
Milk and Cod Liver Oil $283.70
General Expenses   414.46
Field Staff   583.80
Labour   2,213.02   3,494.98

Cash Relief
Cash Payments $54,588.20
Field Staff   1,995.00
Servants   69.00   56,652.20

Work Relief
Disbursements $7,464.18
Field Staff   150.00
Servants   8.00   7,622.18

Special Projects		
Surveys	$1,503.90	
Seeds for Gardeners	78.50	
Bedding and Clothing	498.52	2,080.92
Agricultural Loans		
Loans	$1,840.00	
Field Administration	57.08	1,897.08
Relief		
Overhead Expenses		
Staff		
Office	$2,100.04	
Police and Servants	895.60	
General Expenses		
Transportation	6,856.32	
Office Expenses	715.11	
Zone Inspection and Flags	663.30	
Rehabilitation Expenses	271.25	11,501.62
Total Expenditure for Period		$272,408.42

Surplus Available at 31st May, 1938			
Cash			
National City Bank of New York,			
Shanghai	$105,792.81		
-do- U.S. $1,760.10	5,949.14		
American Embassy Deposit, Nanking	27,100.00		
Cash held in Nanking	4,996.83		
Cash held in Shanghai	10,000.00		
Cash in transit	169.70		
	$154,008.48		
Commodities	30,361.03		
Advances	1,155.00		
Accounts Receivable	380.18		
	$185,904.69		
Less: Accounts Payable	3,942.67	181,962.02	
		$454,370.44	$454,370.44

We have prepared the above account from the books and vouchers of the Committee and the information and explanations given to us, and certify it to be correct in accordance therewith.

Thomson and Company
Chartered Accountants,
Honorary Auditors.
Shanghai, 4th August, 1938

Table C-2

Nanking International Relief Committee
Income and Expenditure Account
For the Period 1st June, 1938 to 30th April, 1939

Surplus Available at 1st June, 1938		$181,962.02
Income		
Contributions		83,66.87
Sale of Commodities		1,384.46
Sale of Truck		1,500.00
Sale of Fuel		4,405.03
Kitchen receipts		27.96
Profit on Exchange		4,908.58
		$277,854.92
Expenditure		
Relief		
Food and Fuel		
Commodities	$150,497.88	
Milk Powder	474.50	
Fuel	2,869.00	
Transportation	442.30	
Food Commission Expenses	1,027.88	
Field Staff and Labour	8,294.73	$163,606.29
Housing		
Refugee Camp Expenses	$982.81	
Field Staff and Labour	738.41	1,721.22
Cash Relief		
Cash Payments	$10,671.51	
Field Staff and Labour	1,032.80	11,704.31
Work Relief		
Disbursements	$5,856.69	
Field Staff and Labour	952.00	6,808.69
Special Projects		
Surveys	$4,910.37	
Seeds for Gardeners	388.66	
Bedding and Clothing	16,901.73	22,200.76
Joint Project		21,198.87
Agricultural Loans		
Loans	$8,080.55	
Field Administration	147.47	8,228.02
Miscellaneous Expenses		1,488.98

Small Loans		
Staff Expenses		1,076.00
Relief		
Overhead Expenses		
Staff		
Office, Police, Servants	$2,363.50	
General Expenses		
Transportation	$2,442.86	
Office Expenses	2,586.60	
Rehabilitation Expenses	247.14	7,640.10
		246,673.15
Supplies Available at 30th April, 1939		
Cash		
National City Bank of New York,		
Shanghai	$8,457.74	
-do- U.S. $2,273.85	13,643.10	
Cash held in Nanking	1,428.29	
	$23,529.13	
Small Loans	5,338.29	
Commodities	2,314.35	31,181.77
	$277,854.92	$277,854.92

We have prepared the above account from the books and vouchers of the Committee and the information and explanations given to us, and certify it to be correct in accordance therewith.

Thomson & Company
Chartered Accountants,
Honorary Auditors,
Shanghai, 15th May, 1939

Appendix D

Personnel of the International Committee

Table D-1

Membership November 22, 1937, to June, 1938

* John H.D. Rabe	German	Siemens Company
† J.M. Hansen	Danish	Texas Oil Company
† P.H. Munroe-Faure	British	Asiatic Petroleum Company
W.P. Mills	American	Northern Presbyterian Mission
Lewis S.C. Smythe	American	University of Nanking
M.S. Bates	American	University of Nanking
† G. Schultze-Pantin	German	Hsinmin Trading Company
† Ivor Mackay	British	Butterfield & Swire
Charles H. Riggs	American	University of Nanking
Eduard Sperling	German	Shanghai Insurance Company
† D.J. Lean	British	Asiatic Petroleum Company
† P.R. Shields	British	International Export Company
C.S. Trimmer	American	University Hospital
† J.V. Pickering	American	Standard Vacuum Oil Company
John Magee	American	American Church Mission

*Withdrawn from Nanking by order of his company, February 1938.

†Withdrawn from Nanking by order of their respective companies by early December 1937. These men were therefore able to participate only in the organizing work of the International Committee, leaving a small group for the succeeding months. (It should be noted, however, that several other persons participated actively in service for refugees, and were so closely related with the Committee that there was little distinction.)

Table D-2

Membership from June, 1938, and Continuing

	W.P. Mills	American	Northern Presbyterian Mission
	M.S. Bates	American	University of Nanking
*	Charles H. Riggs	American	University of Nanking
	Eduard Sperling	German	Shanghai Insurance Company
†	D. J. Lean	British	Asiatic Petroleum Company
	P.R. Shields	British	International Export Company
	C.S. Trimmer	American	University Hospital
	J. V. Pickering	American	Standard Vacuum Oil Company
‡	John Magee	American	American Church Mission
	Hubert L. Sone	American	Nanking Theological Seminary
†	Ernest H. Forster	American	American Church Mission
†	James H. MaCallum	American	United Christian Missionary Society
	F.C. Gale	American	Methodist Mission
	James F. Kearney	American	Society of Jesus
§	C.Y. Hsu	Chinese	University Hospital
§	S. Yasumura	Japanese	Japan Baptist Church
#	Albert N. Steward	American	University of Nanking

*Withdrawn from Nanking for furlough and transfer, February 1939.
†Withdrawn from Nanking for furlough, June and July 1939.
‡Returned from furlough, May 1939.
§Elected December, 1938. Mr. Yasumura withdrew from Nanking, February 1939.
#Elected April 1939.
(June 1938 is only a representative date for the changes connected with the names of Messrs. Smythe, Lean, Shields, and Pickering).

Table D-3

Officers of the Committee

Chairman:
John H.D. Rabe	November, 1937 to February, 1938
W.P. Mills[1]	February, 1938 to May, 1939
M.S. Bates	From May, 1939

Secretary:
Lewis S.C. Smythe	November, 1937 to July, 1938
Ernest H. Forster	July, 1938 to April, 1939
James H. Kearney	From May, 1939

Treasurer:
Christian Kroeger[2]	December, 1937 to February, 1938
Lewis S.C. Smythe	February to July, 1938
James H. McCallum	July, 1938 to April, 1939
Albert N. Steward	From May, 1939

Administrative Director:
George Fitch	December, 1937 to February, 1938
Hubert L. Sone	From February, 1938

Notes

1. Mr. Mills was elected Vice-Chairman shortly before Mr. Rabe's withdrawal in February 1938, and for a time thereafter was considered as Acting Chairman, with Mr. Rabe retaining his original title. However, in practice Mr. Mills was Chairman and soon was recognized as such. Mr. Lean was Vice-Chairman May to July 1939.

2. Mr. Kroeger, German, of Carlowitz and Company, was not a member of the Committee, but served in various capacities at the request of the Chairman. Mr. Fitch, American, Young Men's Christian Association, was also not a member of the Committee. The original working basis was that the Director could refer problems of policy to the Committee, and received its backing or instructions in matters of difficulty. However, the Committee as a whole was a working body throughout the bad months of 1937–38, and several of its members have continually given much time to detailed tasks.

Index

Zhang Kaiyuan, a native of Wuxing County, Zhejiang Province, was born in July 1926. He studied under M. Searle Bates in the history department of the University of Nanking. In May 1992, Augustana College conferred upon him the honorary degree of LL.D. He served as president of Central China Normal University from 1984 to 1992.

From 1990 to date, Professor Zhang has been lecturing and conducting research in several celebrated institutions of higher learning in the United States. He was a visiting researcher in the history department of Princeton University, Luce Fellow in History at Yale University, and visiting professor at the University of California at San Diego. He also served as visiting professor at Chengchi University, Taiwan. In 1995, he was the Siu Lien Ling Wong Visiting Fellow at Chung Chi College, Chinese University of Hong Kong, where he gave public lectures and conducted academic research programs.

As a world-renowned scholar specializing in modern Chinese history, Zhang has won his reputation as an expert in the study of the 1911 Revolution, the modern Chinese bourgeoisie, and modernization in present-day China. Since the 1980s, he has devoted himself to the work of promoting historical research on Christian colleges in China, especially the missionary group represented by his teacher M. Searle Bates.

Donald MacInnis spent his first year in China, 1940–41, teaching English in a boys' high school in its wartime location, a village in the interior of Fujian Province. He spent a second year there in the military service as a coast watcher for the O.S.S., and returned with his wife for two more years of teaching at Fujian Christian University, leaving in May 1949 as the civil war threatened their city. Dr. MacInnis is the author of four books, including *Religion in China Today: Policy and Practice* (1989), and a fifth that will be ready for publication in 2001.